Lecture Notes in Computer Science   14406

Founding Editors

Gerhard Goos
Juris Hartmanis

Editorial Board Members

The series Lecture Notes in Computer Science (LNCS), including its subseries Lecture Notes in Artificial Intelligence (LNAI) and Lecture Notes in Bioinformatics (LNBI), has established itself as a medium for the publication of new developments in computer science and information technology research, teaching, and education.

LNCS enjoys close cooperation with the computer science R & D community, the series counts many renowned academics among its volume editors and paper authors, and collaborates with prestigious societies. Its mission is to serve this international community by providing an invaluable service, mainly focused on the publication of conference and workshop proceedings and postproceedings. LNCS commenced publication in 1973.

Huimin Lu · Michael Blumenstein ·
Sung-Bae Cho · Cheng-Lin Liu · Yasushi Yagi ·
Tohru Kamiya

Editors

Pattern Recognition

7th Asian Conference, ACPR 2023
Kitakyushu, Japan, November 5–8, 2023
Proceedings, Part I

Springer

Editors
Huimin Lu
Kyushu Institute of Technology
Kitakyushu, Fukuoka, Japan

Michael Blumenstein
The University of Sydney
Sydney, NSW, Australia

Sung-Bae Cho ⓘ
Yonsei University
Seoul, Korea (Republic of)

Cheng-Lin Liu
Chinese Academy of Sciences
Beijing, China

Yasushi Yagi
Osaka University
Osaka, Ibaraki, Japan

Tohru Kamiya
Kyushu Institute of Technology
Kitakyushu, Japan

ISSN 0302-9743   ISSN 1611-3349 (electronic)
Lecture Notes in Computer Science
ISBN 978-3-031-47633-4   ISBN 978-3-031-47634-1 (eBook)
https://doi.org/10.1007/978-3-031-47634-1

This Springer imprint is published by the registered company Springer Nature Switzerland AG
The registered company address is: Gewerbestrasse 11, 6330 Cham, Switzerland

Paper in this product is recyclable.

Preface for ACPR 2023 Proceedings

Pattern recognition stands at the core of artificial intelligence and has been evolving significantly in recent years. These proceedings include high-quality original research papers presented at the 7th Asian Conference on Pattern Recognition (ACPR 2023), which was successfully held in Kitakyushu, Japan from November 5th to November 8th, 2023. The conference welcomed participants from all over the world to meet physically in beautiful Kitakyushu to exchange ideas, as we did in our past ACPR series of conferences. The conference was operated in a hybrid format allowing for both on-site and virtual participation. With all your participation and contributions, we believe ACPR 2023 was a special and memorable conference in history!

ACPR 2023 was the 7th conference of its series since it was launched in 2011 in Beijing, followed by ACPR 2013 in Okinawa, Japan, ACPR 2015 in Kuala Lumpur, Malaysia, ACPR 2017 in Nanjing, China, ACPR 2019 in Auckland, New Zealand, and ACPR 2021 in Jeju Island, South Korea. As we know, ACPR was initiated to promote pattern recognition theory, technologies and applications in the Asia-Pacific region. Over the years, it has actually welcomed authors from all over the world.

ACPR 2023 focused on four important areas of pattern recognition: pattern recognition and machine learning, computer vision and robot vision, signal processing, and media processing and interaction, covering various technical aspects.

ACPR 2023 received 164 submissions from 21 countries. The program chairs invited 141 program committee members and additional reviewers. Each paper was single blindly reviewed by at least two reviewers, and most papers received three reviews each. Finally, 93 papers were accepted for presentation in the program, resulting in an acceptance rate of 56.7%.

The technical program of ACPR was scheduled over four days (5–8 November 2023), including two workshops, four keynote speeches, and nine oral sessions.

The keynote speeches were presented by internationally renowned researchers. Tatsuya Harada, from University of Tokyo, Japan, gave a speech titled "Learning to reconstruct deformable 3D objects". Longin Jan Latecki, from Temple University, USA, gave a speech titled "Image retrieval by training different query views to retrieve the same database images". Jingyi Yu, Shanghai Tech University, China, gave a speech titled "Bridging recognition and reconstruction: Generative techniques on digital human, animal, and beyond". Mark Nixon, from University of Southampton, UK, gave a speech titled "Gait Biometrics – from then to now and the deep revolution".

Organizing a large event is a challenging task, requiring intensive teamwork. We would like to thank all members of the organizing committee for their hard work, with guidance from the steering committee. The program chairs, publication chairs, publicity chairs, workshop chairs, tutorial chairs, exhibition/demo chairs, sponsorship chairs, finance chairs, local organizing chairs, and webmaster all led their respective committees and worked together closely to make ACPR 2023 successful. Our special thanks go to the many reviewers, whom we cannot name one by one, for constructive comments to improve the papers. We thank all the authors who submitted their papers, which is the most important part of a scientific conference. Finally, we would like to acknowledge the student volunteers from our local organizers.

We hope this proceedings could be a valuable resource for the researchers and practitioners in the field of pattern recognition.

November 2023

Cheng-Lin Liu
Yasushi Yagi
Tohru Kamiya
Michael Blumenstein
Huimin Lu
Wankou Yang
Sung-Bae Cho

Organization

Steering Committee

Seong-Whan Lee	Korea University, South Korea
Cheng-Lin Liu	Chinese Academy of Sciences, China
Umapada Pal	Indian Statistical Institute, India
Tieniu Tan	Nanjing University, China
Yasushi Yagi	Osaka University, Japan

General Chairs

Cheng-Lin Liu	Chinese Academy of Sciences, China
Yasushi Yagi	Osaka University, Japan
Tohru Kamiya	Kyushu Institute of Technology, Japan

Program Chairs

Michael Blumenstein	University of Sydney, Australia
Huimin Lu	Kyushu Institute of Technology, Japan
Wankou Yang	Southeast University, China
Sung-Bae Cho	Yonsei University, South Korea

Publication Chairs

Yujie Li	Kyushu Institute of Technology, Japan
Xizhao Wang	Shenzhen University, China
Manu Malek	Stevens Institute of Technology, USA

Publicity Chairs

Jihua Zhu	Xi'an Jiaotong University, China
Limei Peng	Kyungpook National University, South Korea
Shinya Takahashi	Fukuoka University, Japan

Workshop Chairs

JooKooi Tan   Kyushu Institute of Technology, Japan
Weihua Ou   Guizhou Normal University, China
Jinjia Zhou   Hosei University, Japan

Tutorial Chairs

Shenglin Mu   Ehime University, Japan
Xing Xu   University of Electronic Science and Technology
                            of China, China
Tohlu Matsushima   Kyushu Institute of Technology, Japan

Exhibition/Demo Chairs

Zongyuan Ge   Monash University, Australia
Yuya Nishida   Kyushu Institute of Technology, Japan
Wendy Flores-Fuentes   Universidad Autónoma de Baja California,
                            Mexico

Sponsorship Chairs

Rushi Lan   Guilin University of Electronic Technology, China
Keiichiro Yonezawa   Kyushu Institute of Technology, Japan
Jože Guna   University of Ljubljana, Slovenia

Finance Chairs

Quan Zhou   Nanjing University of Posts and
                            Telecommunications, China
Ainul Akmar Mokhtar   Universiti Teknologi Petronas, Malaysia
Shota Nakashima   Yamaguchi University, Japan

Local Organizing Chairs

Nobuo Sakai   Kyushu Institute of Technology, Japan
Naoyuki Tsuruta   Fukuoka University, Japan
Xiaoqing Wen   Kyushu Institute of Technology, Japan

Webmaster

Jintong Cai   Southeast University, China

Program Committee Members

Alireza Alaei	Shinya Takahashi
Noriko Takemura	Xing Xu
Yuchao Zheng	Weifeng Liu
Michael Cree	Kaushik Roy
Jingyi Wang	Quan Zhou
Cairong Zhao	Daisuke Miyazaki
Minh Nguyen	Byoungchul Ko
Huimin Lu	Sung-Bae Cho
Jinshi Cui	Yoshito Mekada
Renlong Hang	Kar-Ann Toh
Takayoshi Yamashita	Martin Stommel
Hirotake Yamazoe	Tohru Kamiya
Weiqi Yan	Xiaoqing Wen
Weihua Ou	Xiaoyi Jiang
Umapada Pal	Jihua Zhu
Wankou Yang	Michael Blumenstein
Shuo Yang	Andrew Tzer-Yeu Chen
Koichi Ito	Shohei Nobuhara
Qiguang Miao	Yoshihiko Mochizuki
Yirui Wu	Yasutomo Kawanishi
Jaesik Choi	Jinjia Zhou
Nobuo Sakai	Yusuyuki Sugaya
Songcan Chen	Ikuhisa Mitsugami
Sukalpa Chanda	Yubao Sun
Xin Jin	Dong-Gyu Lee
Masayuki Tanaka	Yuzuko Utsumi
Fumihiko Sakaue	Saumik Bhattacharya
Jaehwa Park	Masaaki Iiyama
Hiroaki Kawashima	Shang-Hong Lai
Hiroshi Tanaka	Shivakumara Palaiahnakote
Wendy Flores-Fuentes	Limei Peng
Yasushi Makihara	Jookooi Tan
Jože Guna	Shenglin Mu
Yanwu Xu	Zongyuan Ge
Guangwei Gao	Ainul Mokhtar
Rushi Lan	Shota Nakashima
Kazuhiro Hotta	Naoyuki Tsuruta

Contents – Part I

Contents – Part II

Contents – Part III

Towards Explainable Computer Vision Methods via Uncertainty Activation Map

Seungyoun Shin[1], Wonho Bae[2], Junhyug Noh[3], and Sungjoon Choi[1(✉)]

[1] Korea University, 13 Jongam-ro, Seongbuk-gu, Seoul 02841, Republic of Korea
{2022021568,sungjoon-choi}@korea.ac.kr
[2] University of British Columbia, 2329 West Mall, Vancouver, BC V6T 1Z4, Canada
whbae@cs.ubc.ca
[3] Ewha Womans University, 52 Ewhayeodae-gil, Seodaemun-gu, Seoul 03760,
Republic of Korea
junhyug@ewha.ac.kr

Abstract. This paper focuses on the problem of highlighting the input image regions that result in increasing predictive uncertainty. In particular, we focus on two types of uncertainty, *epistemic* and *aleatoric*, and present an uncertainty activation mapping method that can incorporate both types of uncertainty. To this end, we first utilize a mixture-of-experts model combined with class-activation mapping (CAM). The proposed method is extensively evaluated in two different scenarios: multi-label and artificial noise injection scenarios, where we show that our proposed method can effectively capture uncertain regions.

Keywords: Visual explanation · Uncertainty estimation · Explainable machine learning

1 Introduction

Artificial intelligence is permeating every aspect of our lives. For example, the recent success of autonomous driving would not be made without the recent progress in computer vision. At the same time, however, this often gives rise to catastrophic accidents caused by such systems' malfunction. To mitigate these issues, researchers have focused on achieving explainability in the inference phase and uncertainty acquisition in data-driven methods.

Class Activation Mapping (CAM) [24] is a popular technique used in computer vision to provide interpretability for deep neural network predictions. In particular, Grad-CAM [20] employs gradients to generate a heatmap that highlights regions of the input image that contribute to a specific class prediction. However, CAM-based methods are not well-suited for explaining predictive uncertainty, which is an important aspect of deep learning models. Several methods have been developed to estimate prediction uncertainty [8,16,21].

Although understanding predictive uncertainty in deep learning is crucial, most methods only estimate uncertainty without indicating which input image regions contribute to it. This interpretability gap can hinder some applications.

H. Lu et al. (Eds.): ACPR 2023, LNCS 14406, pp. 1–14, 2023.
https://doi.org/10.1007/978-3-031-47634-1_1

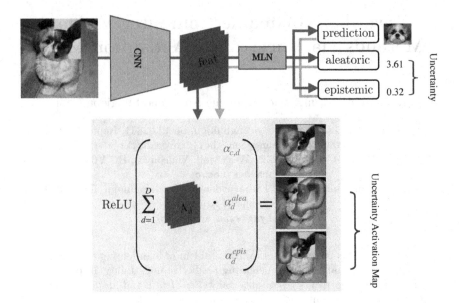

Fig. 1. Proposed architecture for generating uncertainty activation maps: aleatoric activation map (M_a) and epistemic activation map (M_e). Our method enables the identification of regions within the image where uncertainty emerges, providing clear insight into the source of uncertainty.

Recent studies have delved into uncertainty estimation in computer vision [13], but primarily address predictive uncertainty without pinpointing the specific image regions causing it.

This paper aims to achieve the best of both worlds by highlighting the region of input images that causes the predictive uncertainty. Specifically, we incorporate two different types of uncertainty, *aleatoric* and *epistemic* uncertainty, and highlight the regions that contribute to each type. To this end, we first utilize a mixture-of-experts model to estimate the predictive uncertainty without the necessity of sampling processes. Hence, it is not only computationally efficient in the inference phase but also enables to use of the gradient-based CAM method [20]. Figure 1 depicts the proposed method and how the uncertainty activation map is computed.

The proposed method is evaluated in two different scenarios. First, we show that the proposed method can successfully capture the input image region with artificial noise injected. Then, we further illustrate that it can be helpful in a natural setting of a single-label classification task where the input image contains multiple objects [23]. Our contributions in this work are summarized as follows:

1. We propose two types of uncertainty activation mapping methods: Aleatoric Activation Mapping (AAM) and Epistemic Activation Mapping (EAM). These methods utilize gradient-based CAM during uncertainty acquisition - hence sample-free and efficient.

2. We present an effective evaluation protocol of the proposed UAM on two different settings: artificial noise injection and multi-label scenarios.

This paper is organized as follows. Section 2 introduces the uncertainty estimation methods and visual explanation methods. Proposed uncertainty activation mapping is illustrated in Sect. 3. Section 4 proposes two different evaluation protocols that can assess the quality of the uncertainty activation. Finally, related work and conclusion are presented in Sects. 5 and 6, respectively.

2   Preliminaries: Uncertainty and Visual Explanation

This section briefly recaps how uncertainty has been measured in machine learning literature. As an independent field of study, we also describe some visual explanation methods used in computer vision. Then in the following Sect. 2, we will propose a novel algorithm that can describe both uncertainty and visual explanation.

Notations. Suppose $\mathcal{D} = \{(x^{(i)}, y^{(i)})\}_{i=1}^{N}$, where $x^{(i)} \in \mathbb{R}^{3 \times H \times W}$ are images and $y^{(i)} \in \{0, 1\}^{C}$ are image labels, with C the number of classes. We drop the superscript (i) for simplicity unless it is necessary in a context. Also, we define $softmax(\cdot)$ as a softmax function over an arbitrary vector, and $[K] = \{1, 2, \dots, K\}$.

Uncertainty Estimation. Bayesian neural networks [9] have emerged as a popular approach for estimating predictive uncertainty in deep learning. The primary objective of Bayesian neural networks is to estimate the posterior distribution of the network's parameters, which is often computationally challenging. To tackle this problem, variational methods [10,12] are used to approximate the posterior distribution. However, even with this approximation, inference remains challenging, requiring sample-based techniques to estimate predictive mean and variance. In addition to Bayesian methods, non-Bayesian approaches such as Deep Ensemble [15] have also been extensively explored for uncertainty estimation. These methods offer the advantage of surpassing existing results and enabling the calculation of uncertainty in a single forward pass. For instance, in the case of DDU [17], aleatoric uncertainty is defined using Softmax Entropy, while Epistemic Uncertainty is estimated using the likelihood of a Gaussian Mixture Model (GMM) in the feature space.

Visual Explanation. Interpreting the behavior of a neural network can be highly challenging, often rendering it as a black box. To enhance the interpretability of neural networks, various methods have been proposed. In particular, visualizing the regions of an input image that a neural network focuses on for making predictions has gained significant attention. One notable framework for visual explanation is class activation mapping (CAM) [24]. CAM is designed to be applicable to neural networks with a fully connected layer as the final layer. Building upon this framework, Grad-CAM [20] expands its applicability to any general neural network architecture by replacing weights with gradients. Suppose an output of a neural network f up to an arbitrary layer is $A \in \mathcal{R}^{D \times H' \times W'}$ where D, H' and W' denote the size of output channels, height, and width, respectively. With the output logit of the neural network at class c denoted by f_c, a class activation map is computed as,

$$M_{\text{G-CAM}}^c = ReLU(\sum_{d=1}^{D} \alpha_{c,d} A_d) \tag{1}$$

where $\alpha_{c,d}$ denote importance weights with a normalizing constant $Z_c = \sum_{d=1}^{D} \alpha_{c,d}$

$$\alpha_{c,d} = \frac{1}{Z_c} \sum_{h=1}^{H'} \sum_{w=1}^{W'} \frac{\partial f_c}{\partial A_{d,h,w}} \tag{2}$$

In this work, we build our proposed uncertainty visualization mapping based on the Grad-CAM method.

3   Measuring Uncertainty Using Mixtures

In this section, we first introduce Mixture Logit Networks (MLN) as a means of measuring both aleatoric and epistemic uncertainties for image classification tasks. MLN can estimate two different types of uncertainty using a single forward path. Then, we present uncertainty activation mapping (UAM) by combining MLN with Grad-CAM.

3.1   Mixture Logit Networks

Choi *et al.* [5] propose that uncertainty estimation can be done with a single forward propagation without Monte Carlo sampling. Similarly, we propose Mixture Logit Networks (MLN). As "mixutre" in the name implies, a MLN takes input images and outputs predicted probability distributions for each of K mixture models denoted by $\mu \in \mathbb{R}^{K \times C}$, and weights for each mixture $\pi \in \mathbb{R}^K$; hence, $\sum_{c=1}^{C} \mu_{k,c} = 1, \forall k \in [K]$ and $\sum_{k=1}^{K} \pi_k = 1$. A MLN consists of a backbone structure such as ResNet50 [11] followed by a MLN head. The backbone denoted by f takes an input x and outputs a feature $h(\cdot) \in \mathbb{R}^D$. The following MLN head consists of two linear models: one parameterized by $W^\mu \in \mathbb{R}^{K \times C \times D}$ outputs $\mu_k = softmax(W_k^\mu \cdot h)$, and the other parameterized by $W^\pi \in \mathbb{R}^{K \times D}$ outputs $\pi = softmax(W^\pi \cdot h)$. Then, the classification loss of the MLN is computed as,

$$\mathcal{L}_{MLN} = \frac{1}{N} \sum_{i=1}^{N} \mathcal{L}_{MLN}^{(i)} \tag{3}$$

where on i-th input image,

$$\mathcal{L}_{MLN}^{(i)} = -\sum_{k=1}^{K} \pi_k \left(\sum_{c=1}^{C} y_c \log \mu_{k,c} + (1 - y_c) \log (1 - \mu_{k,c}) \right). \tag{4}$$

If the MLN is trained only using Eq. (3), however, it tends to exploit only a few mixtures (leading to having negligible weights π_k for most of the mixtures). To fully utilize all the mixtures, we add a regularization term to Eq. (3). We will introduce the regularization term after describing aleatoric and epistemic uncertainty estimates of MLN in the following section.

At inference time, we select the predictions of the mixture with the highest weight as the final predictions. We measure the performance of classification based on these final predictions. Formally, our final predictions are defined as,

$$\mu^* := \mu_{\mathrm{argmax}_{k \in [K]} \pi_k}. \tag{5}$$

3.2 Uncertainty Estimation with Mixtures

One of the important benefits of the MLN is that we can measure both aleatoric and epistemic uncertainties without running Monte Carlo sampling. We define aleatoric uncertainty (σ_a) on an input image x, as follows,

$$\sigma_a := \mathbb{H}[y|x; f, W^\mu, W^\pi] \approx -\sum_{k=1}^{K} \pi_k \sum_{c=1}^{C} \mu_{k,c} \log \mu_{k,c}. \tag{6}$$

Also, we define epistemic uncertainty as

$$\sigma_e^2 := \sum_{k=1}^{K} \pi_k \|\mu_k - \sum_{j=1}^{K} \pi_j \mu_j\|^2. \tag{7}$$

As aforementioned, training only $\mathcal{L}_{MLN}$ leads the MLN to use only a few mixtures. Hence, we add the negation of epistemic uncertainty as a regularization as it encourages the mixtures to have different "opinions". Finally, the total loss for the MLN $(\mathcal{L})$ is defined as,

$$\mathcal{L} = \mathcal{L}_{MLN} - \lambda \sigma_e \tag{8}$$

where λ is a hyperparamter that controls the regularization term.

One interesting and practically important phenomenon reported by Yun *et al.* [23] is that the performance of classification goes down when there is more than one object in an image. We conjecture it happens as it is confusing to determine which object to focus on in the perspective of a model; it leads to an increase in the uncertainty of the model's predictions. Since this uncertainty originates from the annotation process, we expect our aleatoric uncertainty will capture this irreducible noise. We demonstrate that it is indeed the case through thorough experiments in Sect. 4.

3.3 Explaining Uncertainty with Mixtures

In this section, we introduce how two different uncertainty activation maps (*i.e.*, *aleatoric* and *epistemic* uncertainty) are generated using the MLN architecture. But first, let us explain how the predictive class activation map for MLN is produced.

Grad CAM of MLN. The importance weight $(\alpha_{c,d})$ of MLN can be calculated as follows:

$$\alpha_{c,d} = \frac{1}{Z_c} \sum_h \sum_w \frac{\partial (\sum_{k=1}^{K} \pi_k \mu_k)^c}{\partial A_{d,h,w}}. \tag{9}$$

Here, c and d denote the class and channel indices, respectively. $\pi_k \in \mathbb{R}$ represents the weight of the mixture, while $\mu_k \in \mathbb{R}^C$ represents the softmax output of the k-th mixture. Subsequently, the Grad-CAM $(M_{\text{G-CAM}}^c)$ is obtained according to Eq. (1). In essence, we compute the Grad-CAM by considering the average prediction of mixtures. The proposed aleatoric and epistemic uncertainty activation maps are computed in a similar manner.

Aleatoric Activation Map (AAM). The predictive aleatoric uncertainty of MLN can be computed using a single forward pass, as shown in Eq. (6). This allows us to utilize Grad-CAM to highlight the input regions that contribute to aleatoric uncertainty. Specifically, the importance weight of aleatoric uncertainty of d-th channel (α_d^{alea}) is computed as follows:

$$\alpha_d^{\text{alea}} = \frac{1}{Z_c} \sum_h \sum_w \frac{\partial \sigma_a^2}{\partial A_{d,h,w}}. \tag{10}$$

Intuitively, α_d^{alea} determines the contribution of the d-th feature map to the increase in aleatoric uncertainty. The importance weight is multiplied by the corresponding convolutional feature map and then channel-wise addition is performed to generate the final aleatoric activation map $(M_a = ReLU(\sum_{d=1}^{D} \alpha_d^{\text{alea}} A_d))$.

Epistemic Activation Map (EAM). The computation of the epistemic uncertainty map follows a similar procedure. The importance weight of the epistemic uncertainty (α_d^{epis}) is defined as follows:

$$\alpha_d^{\text{epis}} = \frac{1}{Z_c} \sum_h \sum_w \frac{\partial \sigma_e^2}{\partial A_{d,h,w}}. \tag{11}$$

And the final epistemic uncertainty map is computed by multiplying α_d^{epis} to the corresponding convolutional feature map and channel-wise addition $(M_e = ReLU(\sum_{d=1}^{D} \alpha_d^{\text{epis}} A_d))$.

4   Experiments

In this section, we evaluate the performance of the proposed uncertainty activation map (UAM) via two different scenarios. First, we show that the UAM can effectively handle the multi-label scenario. In often cases, in particular, the given image to classify may contain multiple objects, and it often leads to unstable

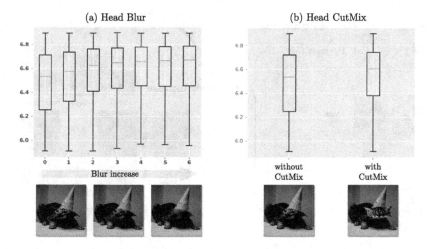

Fig. 2. Aleatoric uncertainty on two different artificial noise injection scenarios (*i.e.*, *blur* and *CutMix*). The increase in uncertainty is evident as noise is introduced into the image.

classification results. Hence, we show that our proposed method can distinguish the main object to classify with other objects and background using different types of UAMs, which may be helpful for the data annotation process. Furthermore, our proposed method can not only estimate the predictive uncertainty but also can localize where the uncertainty stems from. To evaluate the property, we inject different types of artificial noises to the foreground object and show that the epistemic activation map can effectively capture such an area.

4.1 Artificial Noise Injection Scenario

Uncertainty tends to rise when noise is present within an object. Figure 2 shows that uncertainty increases when noise is added to the image. We utilize following two datasets for both training and evaluation purposes:

1. ImageNet [6]: Our model is trained to predict uncertainty using the ImageNet1K dataset, which comprises 1,000 object classes and 1,281,167 training images.
2. PASCAL-Part [3]: To introduce noise into specific object parts and assess the focus of each uncertainty activation map, we require data with labels for individual object parts, in addition to labels for entire objects. The PASCAL-Part dataset, based on PASCAL VOC 2010 annotations, provides such part-level labels. For instance, in the case of a dog, labels are assigned to the head, body, and feet.

Figure 3 illustrates our 3×3 matrix setup to identify sources of uncertainty. Rows represent Grad-CAM, AAM, and EAM. Columns show images with artificial noise, images without noise in object areas, and a background. We employed

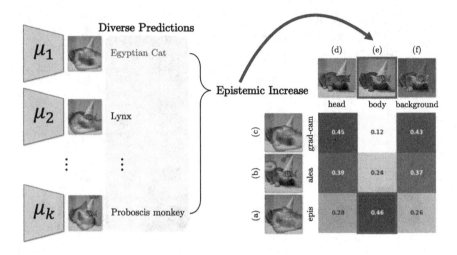

Fig. 3. Artificial noise injection scenario. The figure on the left illustrates that MLN produces different results due to artificial noise. (a) Grad-CAM of MLN, (b) Aleatoric Activation Map, (c) Epistemic Activation Map, (d) head mask, (e) body mask, (f) background. The 3×3 matrix provides a representation of normalized IoA scores.

CutMix [22] for noise addition, inserting random, non-overlapping heads from the dataset as the head is key for classification. When the original image is altered using CutMix to produce unfamiliar data, the model perceives it as Out of Distribution. This unfamiliarity causes varied predictions, elevating epistemic uncertainty. Thus, the model, focusing on the head, increases uncertainty in the torso. Qualitative results for this noise scenario are in Fig. 4.

4.2   Multi-label Scenario

In classification tasks, images usually receive labels describing their content. Yet, many datasets include images with multiple objects, leading to multi-label scenarios and uncertainty. In these instances, the Uncertainty Activation Map (UAM) often highlights objects beyond the foreground, highlighting on uncertainty sources.

To conduct our experiments, we utilize distinct training and test sets from two different datasets: (1) ImageNet [6] and (2) Pascal VOC [7]. Pascal VOC consists of images that contain multiple objects, and it provides pixel-level annotations for 20 different object categories, including people, animals, household appliances, and vehicles. It is important to note that the labels present in the Pascal VOC are also covered by the labels provided in ImageNet.

To evaluate the focus of the Uncertainty Activation Map (UAM), we utilize a 3×3 matrix that includes a row representing the foreground, objects, and background, and a column containing Grad-CAM, Aleatoric Activation Map, and Epistemic Activation Map. The separation of foreground and objects is described

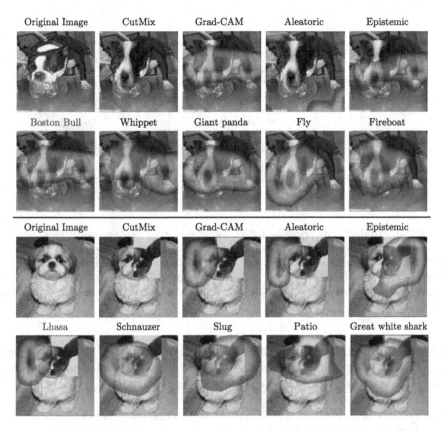

Fig. 4. Qualitative results for artificial noise injection scenario. (Row 1 and 3) Original images and CutMix images. The last three are Grad-CAM and Uncertainty CAMs. (Row 2 and 4) Grad-CAM results of top 5 mixtures.

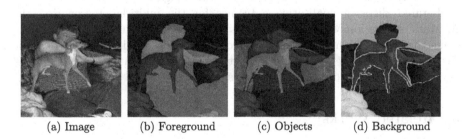

Fig. 5. Foreground, object, and background. (Blue) foreground; labels that most relevant to prediction. (Red) objects; segmentation labels other than foreground. (Yellow) background. (Color figure online)

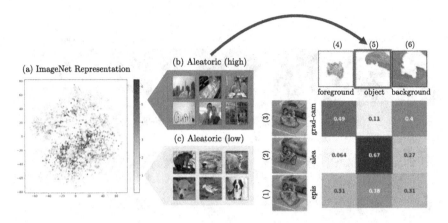

Fig. 6. Multi-label scenario. (a) T-SNE plot illustrating aleatoric uncertainty values for Imagenet samples. Darker regions indicate higher aleatoric uncertainty. (b) Samples with high aleatoric uncertainty. (c) Samples with low aleatoric uncertainty. (1) to (3) represent Grad-CAM, Aleatoric Activation Map, and Epistemic Activation Map, respectively. (4) Foreground, (5) Objects $\in$ (Image \ (Foreground $\cup$ Background)), (6) Background.

in Fig. 5. The localization ability of the UAM is measured using Intersection over Area (IoA). As shown in Fig. 6, our Aleatoric Activation Map effectively captures inherent noise by emphasizing the objects rather than the foreground.

The representation of ImageNet [6] reveals that aleatoric uncertainty increases at the boundaries where more than two classes intersect. Accordingly, we select images with high and low aleatoric uncertainty. Images containing multiple objects tend to exhibit higher aleatoric uncertainty. For instance, if we consider centroids representing cats and dogs, as depicted in Fig. 6, images containing both cats and dogs would be located near the boundary of the two classes. The 3×3 matrix in Fig. 6 illustrates that our Aleatoric Activation Map successfully captures the objects present in the images.

Figure 7 displays qualitative outcomes for the multi-label scenario. The Aleatoric Activation Map emphasizes objects over the foreground. For instance, while Grad-CAM highlights the motorcycle in the first-row image, the Aleatoric Activation Map detects the subway in the background, indicating heightened aleatoric uncertainty due to the subway's presence.

5   Related Works

Our research not only presents visual explanation [2,19,20], but also goes further and suggests the reasons behind the uncertainty [5,8,9,13] of the model (uncertainty explanation).

Input   Label   Grad-CAM   Aleatoric   Epistemic

Fig. 7. Qualitative results for multi-label scenario. Each columns represents input, label, Grad-CAM, Aleatoric Activation Map, and Epistemic Activation Map.

5.1 Uncertainty

Bayesian neural networks [18] are frequently used to quantify uncertainty. However, the posterior distribution of the parameters of Bayesian neural networks is computationally intractable. Approximation methods such as Gal *et al.* [8] show how a Gaussian process can be approximated using their proposed Monte Carlo Dropout method while also capturing model uncertainty. Kendall *et al.* [13] propose to define aleatoric uncertainty as predictive variance and epistemic uncertainty as a variance of predictive posterior estimated using Monte-Carlo samples. However, MC sampling is computationally burdensome. As a result, approaches have been presented for obtaining uncertainty in a single forward pass. Choi *et al.* [5] propose a single-forward pass uncertainty acquisition method with a mixture density network. Liu *et al.* [16] enhances distance-awareness with spectral normalization to obtain predictive uncertainty. Mukhoti *et al.* [17] use a softmax entropy and Gaussian mixture model to estimate each aleatoric and epistemic uncertainty.

5.2 Visual Explanation

Zhou *et al.*[24] introduced Class Activation Mapping (CAM) to visually localize objects using image-level labels. CAM is derived by weighing the features of the final convolutional layer with weights from the last fully connected layer. Grad-CAM [20] enhances CAM by using class-targeted gradient sums as weights, making it compatible with any CNN architecture. Several approaches [1,4,14], however, present limitations of CAM. Choe *et al.* [4] note that CAM often highlights only a small region of an object. For more complete visual explanations, they introduce the Attention-based Dropout Layer (ADL), pushing models to recognize non-discriminative object areas. Addressing the same concern, Bae *et al.* [1] suggests techniques like thresholded average pooling, negative weight clamping, and percentile-based thresholding. Unlike ADL, these methods work with existing feature maps without introducing a new architecture. Meanwhile, CALM [14] posits that integrating CAM calculation within a computational graph yields superior explanations. Chefer *et al.* [2] adapt an explanation method for transformer architectures by defining relevance propagation on self-attention and residual layers, enabling transformer interpretation. U-CAM [19] is the most closely related work to ours. It improves the performance of visual explanation on VQA using uncertainty-aware learning and estimating certainty based on gradients. However, it still cannot capture which part of an image causes uncertainty, unlike our proposed method.

6   Conclusion

In this work, we proposed Uncertainty Activation Mapping (UAM), a localization technique for identifying the regions in an input image that contribute to increased uncertainty. The performance of UAM was evaluated through effective evaluation protocols, including artificial noise injection and multi-label scenarios. The empirical results demonstrated that the epistemic uncertainty activation map predominantly focused on the body part of the CutMix image, whereas the aleatoric uncertainty activation map highlighted objects other than the foreground. These findings highlight the effectiveness of UAM in capturing and visualizing different sources of uncertainty within deep learning models.

Acknowledgement. This work was supported by Institute of Information & communications Technology Planning & Evaluation (IITP) grant funded by the Korea government (MSIT) (No. 2019-0-00079, No. 2022-0-00871, No. 2022-0-00612, No. 2022-0-00480).

References

1. Bae, W., Noh, J., Kim, G.: Rethinking class activation mapping for weakly supervised object localization. In: Vedaldi, A., Bischof, H., Brox, T., Frahm, J.-M. (eds.) ECCV 2020. LNCS, vol. 12360, pp. 618–634. Springer, Cham (2020). https://doi.org/10.1007/978-3-030-58555-6_37
2. Chefer, H., Gur, S., Wolf, L.: Transformer interpretability beyond attention visualization. In: Proceedings of the IEEE/CVF Conference on Computer Vision and Pattern Recognition, pp. 782–791 (2021)
3. Chen, X., Mottaghi, R., Liu, X., Fidler, S., Urtasun, R., Yuille, A.: Detect what you can: detecting and representing objects using holistic models and body parts. In: Proceedings of the IEEE Conference on Computer Vision and Pattern Recognition, pp. 1971–1978 (2014)
4. Choe, J., Shim, H.: Attention-based dropout layer for weakly supervised object localization. In: Proceedings of the IEEE/CVF Conference on Computer Vision and Pattern Recognition, pp. 2219–2228 (2019)
5. Choi, S., Lee, K., Lim, S., Oh, S.: Uncertainty-aware learning from demonstration using mixture density networks with sampling-free variance modeling. In: 2018 IEEE International Conference on Robotics and Automation (ICRA), pp. 6915–6922. IEEE (2018)
6. Deng, J., Dong, W., Socher, R., Li, L.J., Li, K., Fei-Fei, L.: ImageNet: a large-scale hierarchical image database. In: 2009 IEEE Conference on Computer Vision and Pattern Recognition, pp. 248–255. IEEE (2009)
7. Everingham, M., Eslami, S., Van Gool, L., Williams, C.K., Winn, J., Zisserman, A.: The pascal visual object classes challenge: a retrospective. IJCV **111**(1), 98–136 (2015)
8. Gal, Y., Ghahramani, Z.: Dropout as a Bayesian approximation: representing model uncertainty in deep learning. In: ICML, pp. 1050–1059. PMLR (2016)
9. Gal, Y., et al.: Uncertainty in deep learning (2016)
10. Graves, A.: Practical variational inference for neural networks. In: Advances in Neural Information Processing Systems 24 (2011)
11. He, K., Zhang, X., Ren, S., Sun, J.: Deep Residual Learning for Image Recognition. In: CVPR (2016)
12. Hinton, G.E., Van Camp, D.: Keeping the neural networks simple by minimizing the description length of the weights. In: Proceedings of the Sixth Annual Conference on Computational Learning Theory, pp. 5–13 (1993)

13. Kendall, A., Gal, Y.: What uncertainties do we need in Bayesian deep learning for computer vision? arXiv preprint arXiv:1703.04977 (2017)
14. Kim, J.M., Choe, J., Akata, Z., Oh, S.J.: Keep calm and improve visual feature attribution. In: ICCV, pp. 8350–8360 (2021)
15. Lakshminarayanan, B., Pritzel, A., Blundell, C.: Simple and scalable predictive uncertainty estimation using deep ensembles. In: Advances in Neural Information Processing Systems 30 (2017)
16. Liu, J.Z., Lin, Z., Padhy, S., Tran, D., Bedrax-Weiss, T., Lakshminarayanan, B.: Simple and principled uncertainty estimation with deterministic deep learning via distance awareness. arXiv preprint arXiv:2006.10108 (2020)
17. Mukhoti, J., Kirsch, A., van Amersfoort, J., Torr, P.H., Gal, Y.: Deterministic neural networks with appropriate inductive biases capture epistemic and aleatoric uncertainty. arXiv preprint arXiv:2102.11582 (2021)
18. Neal, R.M.: Bayesian learning for neural networks, vol. 118, 1st edn. Springer, New York (2012). https://doi.org/10.1007/978-1-4612-0745-0
19. Patro, B.N., Lunayach, M., Patel, S., Namboodiri, V.P.: U-CAM: visual explanation using uncertainty based class activation maps. In: Proceedings of the IEEE/CVF International Conference on Computer Vision, pp. 7444–7453 (2019)
20. Selvaraju, R.R., Cogswell, M., Das, A., Vedantam, R., Parikh, D., Batra, D.: Grad-CAM: visual explanations from deep networks via gradient-based localization. In: Proceedings of the IEEE International Conference on Computer Vision, pp. 618–626 (2017)
21. Van Amersfoort, J., Smith, L., Teh, Y.W., Gal, Y.: Uncertainty estimation using a single deep deterministic neural network. In: Daumé, III, D., Singh, A. (eds.) Proceedings of the 37th International Conference on Machine Learning. Proceedings of Machine Learning Research, vol. 119, pp. 9690–9700. PMLR (13–18 Jul 2020). http://proceedings.mlr.press/v119/van-amersfoort20a.html
22. Yun, S., Han, D., Oh, S.J., Chun, S., Choe, J., Yoo, Y.: CutMix: regularization strategy to train strong classifiers with localizable features. In: Proceedings of the IEEE/CVF International Conference on Computer Vision, pp. 6023–6032 (2019)
23. Yun, S., Oh, S.J., Heo, B., Han, D., Choe, J., Chun, S.: Re-labeling ImageNet: from single to multi-labels, from global to localized labels. In: Proceedings of the IEEE/CVF Conference on Computer Vision and Pattern Recognition, pp. 2340–2350 (2021)
24. Zhou, B., Khosla, A., Lapedriza, A., Oliva, A., Torralba, A.: Learning deep features for discriminative localization. In: Proceedings of the IEEE Conference on Computer Vision and Pattern Recognition, pp. 2921–2929 (2016)

Robust Detection for Autonomous Elevator Boarding Using a Mobile Manipulator

Seungyoun Shin[1], Joon Hyung Lee[1], Junhyug Noh[2], and Sungjoon Choi[1(✉)]

[1] Korea University, 13 Jongam-ro, Seongbuk-gu, Seoul 02841, Republic of Korea
{2022021568,dlwnsgud8823,sungjoon-choi}@korea.ac.kr
[2] Ewha Womans University, 52 Ewhayeodae-gil, Seodaemun-gu, Seoul 03760, Republic of Korea
junhyug@ewha.ac.kr

Abstract. Indoor robots are becoming increasingly prevalent across a range of sectors, but the challenge of navigating multi-level structures through elevators remains largely uncharted. For a robot to operate successfully, it's pivotal to have an accurate perception of elevator states. This paper presents a robust robotic system, tailored to interact adeptly with elevators by discerning their status, actuating buttons, and boarding seamlessly. Given the inherent issues of class imbalance and limited data, we utilize the YOLOv7 model and adopt specific strategies to counteract the potential decline in object detection performance. Our method effectively confronts the class imbalance and label dependency observed in real-world datasets, Our method effectively confronts the class imbalance and label dependency observed in real-world datasets, offering a promising approach to improve indoor robotic navigation systems.

Keywords: Object detection · Mobile manipulator · Class imbalance in detection methods

1 Introduction

Indoor robots have become a ubiquitous presence in diverse fields, ranging from hospitality and delivery services to cleaning and security. The development of localization techniques and the study of legged robot locomotion on stairs has been the focus of significant research efforts. Nevertheless, navigating multi-level buildings using elevators remains an underexplored topic in the field. A crucial skill that robots require to leverage elevators effectively is perception. This involves accurately determining parameters, such as the current floor and the elevator's location, by processing and interpreting sensory information. Advanced perception capabilities are thus essential for robots to navigate multi-level buildings with accuracy and efficiency. However, equipping robots with additional sensors can be prohibitively expensive and may not be a scalable solution. To address this challenge, we propose a novel method to recognize the state of an elevator using only an image sensor, thereby eliminating the need for additional equipment.

© The Author(s), under exclusive license to Springer Nature Switzerland AG 2023
H. Lu et al. (Eds.): ACPR 2023, LNCS 14406, pp. 15–28, 2023.
https://doi.org/10.1007/978-3-031-47634-1_2

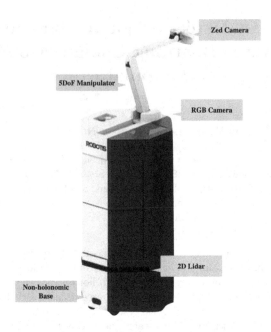

Labels on figure: Zed Camera, 5DoF Manipulator, RGB Camera, ROBOTIS, 2D Lidar, Non-holonomic Base

Fig. 1. GAEMI is a sophisticated mobile manipulator equipped with a 5DoF robotic arm and a ZED camera. Its non-holonomic base features a 2D LiDAR sensor for obstacle detection and localization within a mapped environment. Additionally, GAEMI has a forward-facing RGB camera.

When attempting to perform object detection under elevator conditions, it became evident that real-world datasets present significant challenges that deviate from pre-existing benchmark datasets, such as COCO [10]. Two prominent issues that arose were label dependency and small object detection.

Addressing the challenges of issues requires careful consideration and specialized techniques to mitigate their impact on object detection performance. To this end, we have developed a comprehensive system for indoor robots that focuses on these challenges and enables intelligent interaction with elevators.

In summary, we introduce a **robotic system adept at indoor navigation and intelligent elevator interaction**. It effectively addresses challenges like small object detection and label dependency to ensure accurate elevator state recognition and precise interaction. The primary contributions are:

1. Development of an autonomous robotic system that interacts with elevators using advanced SLAM, kinematics, and perception, ensuring dependable real-world navigation and interaction.
2. Tackling small object detection and label dependency in our dataset, enhancing the robot's perception and performance in real-world tasks.

In Fig. 1, we present GAEMI, the robot employed throughout our experiments, which demonstrates the capabilities of the autonomous system developed in this work.

2   Related Work

Our study tackles the challenge of autonomous elevator operation by emphasizing perception and its translation into robotic actions. Utilizing advances in
object detection and elevator button recognition, we aim to establish a dependable system for indoor robots' inter-floor movement. This section provides a
brief overview of pertinent literature on object detection and prior research on
elevator-interacting robots.

2.1   Object Detection

Object detection has been a crucial area of research within the field of computer
vision, with numerous techniques and models developed to advance its capabilities. In this section, we briefly discuss key approaches, including real-time object
detection and anchor-based and anchor-free methods.

Real-time object detection focuses on achieving high-speed detection while
maintaining acceptable levels of accuracy. This aspect is particularly important
for applications where real-time response is vital, such as autonomous vehicles
and robotic navigation. Several notable models, such as YOLO [14], SSD [11],
and MobileNet [3], have been proposed to address the trade-off between speed
and accuracy.

Anchor-based object detection methods, such as Faster R-CNN [15] and Reti-
naNet [9], use predefined anchor boxes to generate region proposals for detecting
objects. These methods benefit from improved localization accuracy but may suffer from increased computational complexity due to the need to evaluate multiple
anchors per image.

Conversely, anchor-free object detection approaches, such as CornerNet [8]
and CenterNet [20], eliminate the need for predefined anchor boxes by directly
predicting object bounding boxes and class probabilities. These methods have
the potential to simplify the detection pipeline and reduce computational overhead, making them attractive for real-time object detection tasks.

In the following sections, we will delve into the specifics of these object detection techniques and explore their relevance to addressing the challenges associated with real-world vision tasks, such as extreme class imbalance and label
dependency.

2.2   Autonomous Elevator Boarding Using Mobile Manipulators

Recent research advancements in indoor robots have contributed significantly
to understanding indoor environments and the development of robot navigation and interaction capabilities [1,4,13,16,17]. However, limited attention has
been dedicated to the problem of robots autonomously moving between floors
using elevators. Most existing studies have primarily focused on elevator button
recognition, lacking a comprehensive pipeline for autonomous inter-floor movement [5–7]. This underscores the need for further investigation to address the
challenges associated with autonomous elevator operation for indoor robots.

Conventional computer vision algorithms have been employed in some studies for elevator button recognition due to their low data requirements. However, these methods suffer from limited accuracy and necessitate specific postures or environments for the robot's operation. This indicates the need for more advanced techniques for autonomous elevator operation in real-world robotic services. To address the challenges associated with conventional methods in button recognition, Dong *et al.* [2] introduced a deep learning approach to improve elevator button recognition. Nevertheless, button location identification still relied on conventional methods.

Yang *et al.* [19] proposed an end-to-end method for button recognition using the YOLO [14], which enables real-time object detection. Zhu *et al.* [21] introduced a large-scale dataset specifically for button recognition and highlighted the presence of a high-class imbalance in this task.

A related work worth mentioning is an autonomous robotic system that utilizes an eye-in-hand configuration [22]. This system addresses button operation by incorporating a deep neural network for button detection and character recognition along with a button pose estimation algorithm. However, it remains essential to develop a comprehensive pipeline for autonomous inter-floor movement and advanced techniques for autonomous elevator operation in real-world scenarios.

3   Proposed Method

3.1   Perception System

Label Superset and Elevator Status Perception. The primary objective of robotic perception for elevator usage is to ascertain the elevator's status, such as whether the door is open or closed, the current floor of the robot, and the location of the elevator floor. To achieve this level of perception, essential for seamless navigation and interaction with the elevator system, we first design a label superset that clearly defines the problem and covers all possible scenarios to accommodate diverse sites, as shown in Table 1.

With our designed label superset, we can address various elevator statuses vital for robot planning. For a task like "Go to room 406," the robot needs to recognize its floor and the elevator's status. This helps decide whether to press up or down and prepare for boarding based on the elevator's position. The robot must also ascertain the elevator door's movement. Our label superset equips the robot to make decisions and navigate intricate settings effectively.

Object Detection Model. We utilized the YOLOv7 [18] for both object detection and instance segmentation tasks. YOLOv7 is a cutting-edge object detection model that outperforms other detectors in terms of speed and accuracy. We deemed YOLOv7 an appropriate choice for detecting elevator status. To optimize the YOLOv7 object detection and instance segmentation models for our hardware (NVIDIA Orin), we implemented float16 quantization. This optimization led to a single forward path inference time with an FPS ranging between 50 and 80, which is well within the acceptable range for real-time processing.

Table 1. Label superset. White rows represent labels processed by the indicator detection module, while the gray row indicates labels handled by the button detection module. We employ an instance segmentation model for the gray row.

Category	Parameters
Elevator Door	Opened, Moving, Closed
Current Robot Floor	B6, B5, ..., B1, 1, ..., 63
Current Elevator Floor (Outside/Inside)	B6, B5, ..., B1, 1, ..., 63
Current Elevator Direction (Outside/Inside)	Up, Down, None
Elevator Button (Outside/Inside)	Up, Down, B6, B5, ..., B1, 1, ..., 63

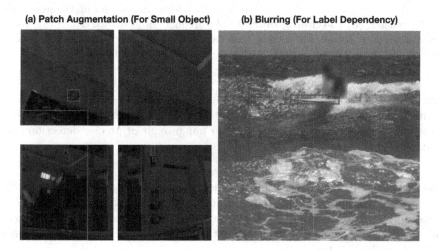

(a) Patch Augmentation (For Small Object)   **(b) Blurring (For Label Dependency)**

Fig. 2. Our two-fold strategy for addressing **label dependency** and **small object detection**. (a) The **patch-augmentation** technique involves cropping high-resolution images, which helps to maintain the resolution of smaller objects when they are resized for input to the model, ultimately enhancing recognition of fine details. (b) The **Gaussian blur** applied to the bounding box region effectively mitigates label dependency and class imbalance by altering the visual features and removing certain labels from the image.

3.2 Addressing Label Dependency and Small Object Detection

In our data collection phase for training elevator indicators, we faced two significant challenges: label dependency and small object detection. Label dependency is an issue where some labels, like those for elevator doors, appear regularly in the images, while others are seen less often. This unequal distribution creates a class imbalance, making it hard to compile a balanced dataset with a variety of labels. Our second challenge was related to the size of the objects in our

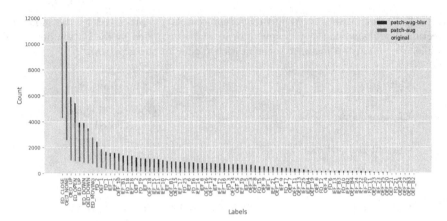

Fig. 3. Augmentation strategy. To tackle challenges like small indicator detection, label dependency, and class imbalance, we employ a two-step augmentation process. (1) Original dataset. (2) Patch-aug: We crop the original dataset for higher-resolution training images. **(3) Patch-aug-blur:** We blur frequent objects such as elevator doors in high-resolution images and remove their labels. This strategy increases the dataset size and effectively mitigates class imbalance and label dependency issues.

images. Most indicators, except for the elevator doors, are quite small, which can make accurate detection by object detection models more difficult. This size discrepancy posed an additional hurdle in our pursuit of precise detection and identification.

Patch Augmentation. In addressing the challenge of detecting small objects, we employed a technique called patch augmentation. We divided high-resolution images into cropped sections, thereby increasing the resolution of smaller objects and enriching the visual features in the dataset. The patch-augmentation process is illustrated in Fig. 2(a).

Label Blurring. To tackle the label dependency issue, we adopted a method that involves duplicating portions of the dataset and applying a Gaussian blur to the bounding box region, effectively eliminating the visual features from the image. In our dataset, certain labels such as Elevator Door Closed (ED_CLOSE) and Current Elevator Direction Outside with None (OED_NONE) appeared more frequently. This was because elevator doors are present in every image, and most sites have a direction indicator. As a consequence, sampling scarce labels would result in an increase in ED_CLOSE and OED_NONE occurrences, leading to an imbalanced dataset. To address this issue, we selectively blurred these two classes. For instance, if an image displayed an elevator door in the closed state and the current floor was 4, we blurred the elevator door to remove the label from the image. This strategy efficiently mitigates the label dependency issue and generates a more compact, balanced dataset. Figure 3 illustrates the resolution

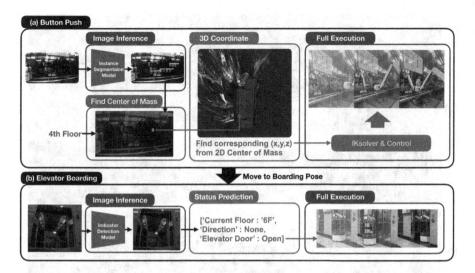

Fig. 4. An overview of the autonomous elevator boarding process. The procedure is divided into two main categories: (a) button-pushing operations and (b) elevator boarding, which encompass tasks such as path planning, object detection, and interaction.

of label dependency and class imbalance, as demonstrated by the dark blue bar. The implementation of blurring is shown in Fig. 2(b).

3.3   GAEMI: Robotic System

Robot Configuration. In this study, we employed a GAEMI robot, produced by ROBOTIS, as our indoor mobile manipulator for self-driving service applications. The GAEMI robot measures $50 \times 50 \times 117$ cm^3 and features a non-holonomic base along with a 5-degree-of-freedom (DoF) manipulator. The base of the robot is equipped with a 2D LiDAR sensor, and a ZED camera is mounted on the manipulator arm's end effector. A comprehensive illustration of the entire robot is available in Fig. 1.

Robot Operation. Our primary objective for the robot operation is to achieve autonomous elevator boarding without relying on additional equipment, such as network connections with the elevator or specialized sensors. We divided the mobile manipulator tasks into two main categories: (1) navigation and (2) interaction. Our complete procedure is depicted in Fig. 4.

Navigation. We employed Cartographer to generate a 2D map. Subsequently, we used the ROS2 Navigation2 package [12] to direct the robot toward the target pose. We utilized the Adaptive Monte Carlo Localization (AMCL) method to determine the robot's current position within the map and the Dynamic Window Approach (DWA) for path following.

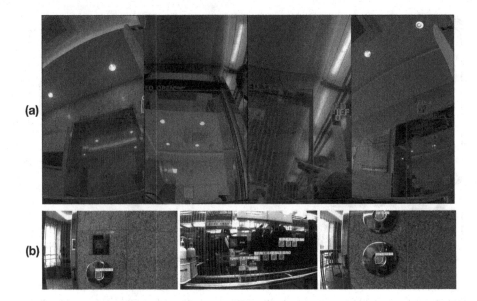

Fig. 5. Dataset overview. (a) Indicator dataset: object detection dataset is tailored to capture the basic status of an elevator. (b) Button dataset: instance segmentation dataset designed to identify points of interaction between the robot and the elevator, facilitating precise and successful task execution.

Interaction. In the elevator boarding task, the primary physical interaction with the environment involves 'button pushing.' To achieve this, we first perform instance segmentation on RGB images to identify relevant objects within the scene. For example, if we intend to push the 'down' button, we locate the corresponding mask that represents the 'down' button in the image.

Next, we calculate the 2D center of mass from the obtained mask image, resulting in a 2D (x, y) point. To determine the corresponding 3D (x, y, z) coordinate, we use the camera's intrinsic parameters to transform the 2D point. This transformation allows us to obtain the relative pose of the button with respect to the camera's position.

Once the relative pose is established, we can solve the inverse kinematics (IK) problem to determine the target joint angles for the robotic manipulator. Finally, we implement a manipulator control system to execute the desired button-pushing operation. This approach enables us to achieve effective and precise interactions with the elevator's button panel.

4   Experiments

4.1   Mitigating Class Imbalance and Label Dependency

We partitioned the perception dataset into two distinct parts to address different aspects of elevator perception. The first part is the Indicator dataset, which focuses on identifying the overall status of the elevator without requiring manipulator interaction. This dataset encompasses categories such as elevator door status, current robot floor, and elevator direction. The second part of the dataset addresses perception skills that necessitate precise interaction points, such as the elevator button. For these cases, instance segmentation is employed to detect flexible and reliable actions once the button is perceived by the robot. This division enables a comprehensive understanding of the elevator environment, ultimately facilitating seamless robot operation. Figure 5 shows some examples of the two datasets, and further details are provided below:

- **Indicator dataset:** In this study, we compiled a dataset consisting of 5,000 images sourced from seven distinct origins. The images were captured using two types of devices: a robot-mounted camera, providing varied viewpoints, and a smartphone camera. The inclusion of images from multiple perspectives aimed to enhance the dataset's robustness. The dataset consists of pairs of (image, bounding boxes).
- **Button dataset:** Additionally, we collected button data to identify interaction points. This dataset differs from the indicator dataset in that it includes pairs of (image, bounding boxes, instance segmentation masks). We hypothesize that incorporating instance segmentation masks can improve interaction capabilities, resulting in more successful robot operations.

Before training the robot perception datasets (Indicator and Button datasets), we first evaluated the effectiveness of our proposed method (Blur elimination of class) on a general dataset. We aimed to assess how different variations in the dataset influenced the performance of our model. The evaluation results are summarized in Table 2, which presents the mean Average Precision (mAP) scores at different Intersection-over-Union (IoU) thresholds (0.5 and 0.95) for various dataset variations. The evaluation was conducted using the COCO-test dataset. We established a baseline using the COCO-mini dataset, which consists of 1,000 images randomly sampled from the COCO-train dataset. The baseline model achieved a mAP@0.5 score of 0.014 and a mAP@0.95 score of 0.007. To create the COCO-blur dataset, as described in Sect. 3, we applied our proposed Gaussian blur elimination technique to the COCO-mini images and replicated them ten times, resulting in a dataset of 10,000 images. The COCO-blur dataset exhibited improved performance, with a mAP@0.5 score of 0.018 and a mAP@0.95 score of 0.009. In contrast, the COCO-cutout dataset, which replaces the blurring process with zero-value regions, demonstrated lower mAP scores compared to both the baseline and COCO-blur datasets. These results highlight the effectiveness of our proposed Blur Elimination Technique in addressing two common challenges in machine learning: class imbalance and label dependency. By employing this technique, we successfully enhanced the performance of our model on more generalized datasets, specifically the COCO-mini dataset.

Our analysis provides strong evidence supporting the effectiveness of the Blur Elimination Technique in improving model performance on a general dataset. Based on these encouraging results, we extended the application of this method to our Indicator dataset.

Table 2. Comparison of mAP scores on COCO-mini variations.

Dataset	mAP@0.5	mAP@0.95
COCO-mini (base)	0.014	0.007
COCO-blur	0.018	0.009
COCO-cutout	0.012	0.006

Our experiments demonstrate that diverse augmentations boost YOLOv7's performance. Without patch and blur augmentations, YOLOv7's accuracy drops. Using patch augmentation alone increased mAP@0.5 by +0.054, due to improved visual features aiding model accuracy.

However, adding blur after patch augmentation showed a trade-off between localization and status accuracy. Even though exact object localization slightly suffered, status accuracy improved. This is expected, as blurring affects localization but adds noise beneficial against class imbalance.

For our mobile robot's needs, status accuracy was prioritized over exact localization since it directly affects the robot's actions. Thus, even with slight localization losses, the model's effectiveness hinges on improved status accuracy, shown in Table 3.

Table 3. Experimental results on Indicator dataset. Different variations of the YOLOv7 model are evaluated based on mAP@0.5 and Status Accuracy. Rows in white represent standard and patched YOLOv7 models, while the gray row denotes the performance of the YOLOv7 model augmented with both a patch and the proposed blur elimination technique.

Method	mAP@0.5	Status Accuracy
YOLOv7	0.730	0.813
YOLOv7 + patch	0.784	0.878
YOLOv7 + patch + blur	0.779	0.879

4.2 Real-World Robot Operation

To evaluate the performance of our proposed method in real-world scenarios, we conducted various tasks in the Woojung Hall of Informatics at Korea University. For this purpose, we constructed an occupancy map of the 6th floor of the building, as shown in Fig. 6. We focused on three essential tasks to assess the effectiveness of our method. The tasks were as follows: (1) navigating to the button position (GOTO_BUTTON_POSE), (2) pressing elevator buttons (BUTTON_PUSHING), and (3) boarding the elevator (ELEVATOR_BOARDING). The success rates for each

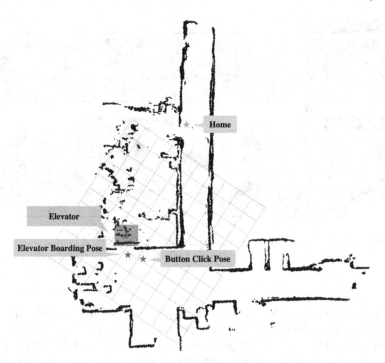

Fig. 6. Occupancy map of Woojung Hall of Informatics. This figure illustrates the constructed occupancy map of the 6th floor of Woojung Hall of Informatics at Korea University, which serves as the operational landscape for all our real-world robot experiments.

Table 4. Real-world experiment results. This table reports the success rates of three distinct tasks executed by the robot. Each success rate corresponds to the proportion of successful trials out of a total of ten attempts.

Task	Success Rate
GOTO_BUTTON_POSE	10/10
BUTTON_PUSHING	9/10
ELEVATOR_BOARDING	3/10

task are presented in Table 4, demonstrating the performance of our method in real-world applications.

In the GOTO_BUTTON_POSE task, the robot successfully achieved optimal positioning for button actuation (the button click pose, as shown in Fig. 6) in all ten trials, resulting in a success rate of 100%. The task was considered successful if the positioning error was within 15cm of the target button click pose. In the BUTTON_PUSHING task, the robot effectively pressed the correct elevator buttons in nine out of ten trials, leading to a success rate of 90%. The evaluation cri-

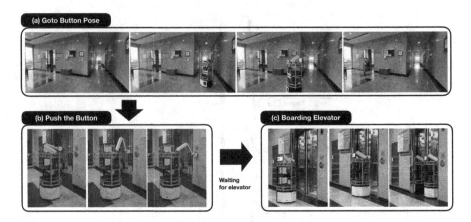

Fig. 7. Demonstration of our integrated robotic system. A comprehensive illustration of the robot successfully performing tasks within a real-world indoor environment.

terion for this task was the successful actuation of the targeted button by the robot. However, in the ELEVATOR_BOARDING task, the success rate was only 30% over ten trials. The suboptimal performance in this task can be attributed to environmental limitations, such as potential obstructions at the elevator door.

The experimental results presented in Table 4 validate the efficacy of our proposed method and the robustness of our integrated robotic system in real-world indoor environments. The high success rates in the GOTO_BUTTON_POSE and BUTTON_PUSHING tasks demonstrate the ability of our method to overcome label dependency and detect small objects effectively. These achievements significantly contribute to enhancing robotic navigation and interaction capabilities in multi-floor buildings.

Figure 7 provides a comprehensive demonstration of the autonomous elevator boarding process.

5   Conclusion

In this work, we introduced a comprehensive robotic system capable of intelligent interaction with elevators in multi-floor environments. We developed a unique solution that successfully addresses the challenges of class imbalance and label dependency in object detection, leading to an enhanced perception system. Our system integrates cutting-edge SLAM, kinematics, and perception technologies, enabling the robot to reliably navigate within its environment and interact effectively with elevator buttons and doors. In real-world scenarios, our system demonstrated high accuracy and reliability, achieving commendable success rates in targeted tasks. The developed approach significantly improves the robot's functionality and effectiveness, paving the way for broader applications of robotics in complex indoor environments.

Acknowledgement. This work was supported by "Research of Elevator Indicator Recognition Technology for Indoor Autonomous Navigation" project funded by ROBO-TIS Co. Ltd. and Institute of Information & communications Technology Planning & Evaluation (IITP) grant funded by the Korea government (MSIT) (No. 2019-0-00079, No. 2022-0-00871, No. 2022-0-00612, No. 2022-0-00480).

References

1. Chaplot, D.S., Gandhi, D.P., Gupta, A., Salakhutdinov, R.R.: Object goal navigation using goal-oriented semantic exploration. Adv. Neural. Inf. Process. Syst. **33**, 4247–4258 (2020)
2. Dong, Z., Zhu, D., Meng, M.Q.H.: An autonomous elevator button recognition system based on convolutional neural networks. In: 2017 IEEE International Conference on Robotics and Biomimetics (ROBIO), pp. 2533–2539. IEEE (2017)
3. Howard, A.G., et al.: MobileNets: efficient convolutional neural networks for mobile vision applications. arXiv preprint arXiv:1704.04861 (2017)
4. Huang, C., Mees, O., Zeng, A., Burgard, W.: Visual language maps for robot navigation. arXiv preprint arXiv:2210.05714 (2022)
5. Kang, J.G., An, S.Y., Choi, W.S., Oh, S.Y.: Recognition and path planning strategy for autonomous navigation in the elevator environment. Int. J. Control Autom. Syst. **8**, 808–821 (2010)
6. Kim, H.H., Kim, D.J., Park, K.H.: Robust elevator button recognition in the presence of partial occlusion and clutter by specular reflections. IEEE Trans. Industr. Electron. **59**(3), 1597–1611 (2011)
7. Klingbeil, E., Carpenter, B., Russakovsky, O., Ng, A.Y.: Autonomous operation of novel elevators for robot navigation. In: 2010 IEEE International Conference on Robotics and Automation, pp. 751–758. IEEE (2010)
8. Law, H., Deng, J.: CornerNet: detecting objects as paired keypoints. Int. J. Comput. Vision **128**(3), 642–656 (2019). https://doi.org/10.1007/s11263-019-01204-1
9. Lin, T.Y., Goyal, P., Girshick, R., He, K., Dollár, P.: Focal loss for dense object detection. In: Proceedings of the IEEE International Conference on Computer Vision, pp. 2980–2988 (2017)
10. Lin, T.-Y., et al.: Microsoft COCO: common objects in context. In: Fleet, D., Pajdla, T., Schiele, B., Tuytelaars, T. (eds.) ECCV 2014. LNCS, vol. 8693, pp. 740–755. Springer, Cham (2014). https://doi.org/10.1007/978-3-319-10602-1_48
11. Liu, W., et al.: SSD: single shot multibox detector. In: Leibe, B., Matas, J., Sebe, N., Welling, M. (eds.) ECCV 2016. LNCS, vol. 9905, pp. 21–37. Springer, Cham (2016). https://doi.org/10.1007/978-3-319-46448-0_2
12. Macenski, S., Martín, F., White, R., Clavero, J.G.: The marathon 2: a navigation system. In: 2020 IEEE/RSJ International Conference on Intelligent Robots and Systems (IROS), pp. 2718–2725. IEEE (2020)
13. Menini, D., Kumar, S., Oswald, M.R., Sandström, E., Sminchisescu, C., Van Gool, L.: A real-time online learning framework for joint 3D reconstruction and semantic segmentation of indoor scenes. IEEE Robot. Autom. Lett. **7**(2), 1332–1339 (2021)
14. Redmon, J., Divvala, S., Girshick, R., Farhadi, A.: You only look once: unified, real-time object detection. In: Proceedings of the IEEE Conference on Computer Vision and Pattern Recognition, pp. 779–788 (2016)
15. Ren, S., He, K., Girshick, R., Sun, J.: Faster R-CNN: towards real-time object detection with region proposal networks. In: Advances in Neural Information Processing Systems 28 (2015)

16. Song, J., Patel, M., Ghaffari, M.: Fusing convolutional neural network and geometric constraint for image-based indoor localization. IEEE Robot. Autom. Lett. **7**(2), 1674–1681 (2022)
17. Vidanapathirana, K., Ramezani, M., Moghadam, P., Sridharan, S., Fookes, C.: LoGG3D-Net: locally guided global descriptor learning for 3d place recognition. In: 2022 International Conference on Robotics and Automation (ICRA), pp. 2215–2221. IEEE (2022)
18. Wang, C.Y., Bochkovskiy, A., Liao, H.Y.M.: YOLOv7: trainable bag-of-freebies sets new state-of-the-art for real-time object detectors. arXiv preprint arXiv:2207.02696 (2022)
19. Yang, P.Y., Chang, T.H., Chang, Y.H., Wu, B.F.: Intelligent mobile robot controller design for hotel room service with deep learning arm-based elevator manipulator. In: 2018 International Conference on System Science and Engineering (ICSSE), pp. 1–6. IEEE (2018)
20. Zhou, X., Wang, D., Krähenbühl, P.: Objects as points. arXiv preprint arXiv:1904.07850 (2019)
21. Zhu, D., Li, T., Ho, D., Zhou, T., Meng, M.Q.: A novel OCR-RCNN for elevator button recognition. In: 2018 IEEE/RSJ International Conference on Intelligent Robots and Systems (IROS), pp. 3626–3631. IEEE (2018)
22. Zhu, D., Min, Z., Zhou, T., Li, T., Meng, M.Q.H.: An autonomous eye-in-hand robotic system for elevator button operation based on deep recognition network. IEEE Trans. Instrum. Meas. **70**, 1–13 (2020)

A Novel Convolutional Neural Network with Large Kernel for Classification of Crash Test Photos

Jiajing Liu[1], Qin Xiao[1], Jiacheng Liu[1], Ziyi Huang[1], Tianhua Wang[3], and Guangxu Li[1,2(✉)] (ID)

[1] School of Electronic and Information Engineering,
Tiangong University, Tianjin 300387, China
liguangxu@tiangong.edu.cn

[2] Tianjin Key Laboratory of Optoelectronic Detection Technology and System, Tianjin 300387, China

[3] CATARC (Tianjin) Automotive Engineering Research Institute Co.,Ltd, Tianjin 300300, China

Abstract. Since variation of car's types, direction classification of crash test photos for multiple type of vehicles is a big challenge to office automation. Moreover, because of the similarity of images before and after crash test, semantic identification of these two classes is also difficult. Inspired by recent advances in large kernel CNNs, in this paper, we introduce a 31×31 extra-large convolutional kernel to gain more effective receptive field and makes the model more powerful for semantic segmentation. To meet the requirement to generate testing report, totally 14 classes were applied in our experiment. The accuracy of 97.1% was obtained on a self-build photo dataset.

Keywords: Image Classification · Convolutional Neural Networks · Crash Test

1 Introduction

1.1 Background

The NCAP (New Car Assessment Program) has become a compulsory means to test the safety of a new vehicle. In 2006, the China Automotive Technology and Research Center proposed the C-NCAP to make the car crash test as the compulsory contents [1] https://www.c-ncap.org.cn/guicheng/. A crucial process in the formation of a C-NCAP report is the intricate car crash evaluation, which requires evaluators to have comprehensive experience and skills in handling crash test photos. In general, nearly thousands of photos are required for crash tests once time, caused by which, filtering and classifying the tested pictures cost most of the time for forming the final inspection report.

Office automation based on artificial intelligent technology enables to recognition of objects in an image clip rapidly and accurately, which can increase the efficiency of crash tests. Generally, in disciplines of C-NCAP the car crash test photos are mainly composed of 14 categories as Fig. 1 illuminates.

H. Lu et al. (Eds.): ACPR 2023, LNCS 14406, pp. 29–40, 2023.
https://doi.org/10.1007/978-3-031-47634-1_3

Fig. 1. Crash test photos. The photos before the crash test are listed in the top block, while the bottom block includes the photos after the crash test. For each block, the first row arranges the external view of the car. The second row arranges the view of the driver dummy, driver's knees, and view of the passenger Collision dummy separately from left to right. The third row shows the view facing the windshield.

Compared to the task of recognition of car parts, the issue of automated assessment of damaged parts of a car represents the foremost challenge in the car crash test. This similar study has been applied in the areas of accidental damage evaluation [2]. Since the crashed car can take any form containing scratches, major dents, and even parts missing, recognition of these categories is a big challenge. Moreover, the recognition of crash dummies is the crucial stage in the evaluation of the quality of airbags. Because statements of the dummy vary largely, photo classification involving these parts, like the second row in Fig. 1, is also difficult.

Machine learning (ML) technology has been broadly applied in many vehicle industries to reduce the cost of manual endeavors in recent years. Detecting the crashed parts of the appearance of cars has received great attention [3, 8, 11]. However, because of some issues such as variable outer surface in different kinds of vehicles, light reflection, deformation of parts damages, etc. al., applying frameworks using ML strategies is a very challenging task.

Amirfakhrian et al. [2] suggested a clustering approach based on the fuzzy similarity criteria using the color spectrum to identify the damaged parts of a car. He et al. [4] introduced the Bag of Features algorithm to recognize and classify the parts of car models by extracting their outlines. Parhizkar et al. [5] proposed a cascade convolutional neural network to recognize the damaged parts even in the complex conditions of illumination. Moreover, the local binary pattern (LBP) and local directional number pattern (LDN) are used to produce some edge maps for creating an encoded image.

Wang et al. [3] used a multi-layer neural network based on Caffe's deep learning framework to recognize car models. He achieved the recognition of car model images by setting up the convolutional neural network and processing different car model images. Shirode et al. [2] recognize the damaged parts of a car using two VGG16 models. The first one completes the identification of the damaged parts and their severities. Consequently, the precise damaged regions are masked out in the second model. Pasupa et al. [6] recognize the car-damaged parts using a convolutional neural network (CNN) framework, which classifies all pixels inside the image into the background, damaged parts, and normal parts. Moreover, the image patches are further divided into normal and damaged parts of the car.

Inspired by recent advances in transformer techniques, in this paper, a large convolutional kernel (31×31) is used instead of a stack of 3×3 kernels, which are commonly used. We practice whether the re-parameterized large depth-wise convolutions could achieve comparable results for the task of recognition of car parts.

1.2 Related Works

CNNs is a deep learning model or a multilayer perceptron similar to artificial neural networks. CNNs perform the construction of neuron-like mechanisms of action by mimicking the interaction of neurons in biology. The purpose of CNNs is to extract features from things in a certain model, and later classify, identify, predict, or make decisions about that thing based on the features. The most important step is feature extraction, i.e., how to extract the features that can distinguish things to the maximum extent, and implementing this model requires iterative training of the CNNs.

Convolutional neural networks have excellent performance in modern computer vision fields, such as image recognition and image classification. The development of Object Detection was accelerated by the Region-CNN(R-CNN) [5] proposed in 2014. The RCNN first generates several region proposals for the target image, and then deflates the region proposals to different degrees. At the same time, R-CNN uses the pre-trained network model to perform feature extractors and finally uses SVM to classify them. In 2015, Girshick et al. proposed Fast R-CNN [7], implementing Multi-task Learning, which accelerated the training speed and detection speed. In the same year, Girshick et al. proposed the regression-based target detection algorithm YOLO (You Only Look Once) [8], which greatly improved the detection speed by dropping the region proposal generation module.

In our previous study, we have tried three training models, VGG, Mobile Net V2, and Inception V3. These three training models can achieve good results in car collision image classification, but they still cannot achieve the accuracy of manual classification. Therefore, we have made some changes to these training models to build a model more suitable for this project research.

The large convolutional kernels [9] used in the work are highly facilitative for downstream tasks, and the large kernel design greatly increases the effective sensory field and introduces more shape bias to the network. Human recognition of objects is mainly based on shape cues rather than texture, and the model used in this project has good performance in classifying car crash images based on the difficulty of recognizing some of the images in car crash experiments with the human naked eye. The CNNs with large kernels show promising scalability on large data. Moreover, the large kernel has a larger effective receptive field and higher shape bias rather than texture bias than the small kernel.

2 Method

2.1 Network Framework

For a small model, it is typical practice to scale it for better performance, so the scaling strategy plays a crucial role in the final accuracy-efficiency trade-off. For CNNs, existing scaling methods typically focus on model depth, width, input resolution, bottleneck ratio, and cluster width [10, 11]. However, kernel size is often ignored. Instead, we discovered that a design paradigm using a small number of large kernels is significantly better than today's dominant paradigm of stacking a large number of small kernels. For example, depth-wise large convolution with structural re-parameterization is used to design efficient and powerful CNNs with large convolutional kernels. Using shortcut or structural re-parameterization with small kernels is more effective in improving model performance (Fig. 2).

The structure of the network model used in this project is shown in the figure, which mainly consists of stems, stages, and transition blocks.

Stem. We want to capture more details by several conv layers at the beginning of the starting layer (stem). After the first 2x down sampling(3×3), we arrange a DW (3×3) layer to capture the low-level patterns, a ConV(1×1), and another DW(3×3) layer to down-sampling. Due to these structures, we achieve high performance in the downstream intensive prediction task.

Stage. The first to fourth Stages contain several blocks each with a shortcut and DW with large kernels. Identity shortcut is very important, especially for networks with very large kernels. We use MobileNet V2 for the benchmark test. It makes heavy use of DW layers and has two published variants (with and without shortcuts). For the large kernel, we simply replaced all DW(3×3) layers with DW(13×13) layers. All models were trained on ImageNet using the same training configuration for 100 epochs. Table 1 shows that the large kernel improves the accuracy of MobileNetV2 by 0.77% with the shortcut [8]. However, without the shortcut, the large kernel reduces the accuracy to only 53.98%.

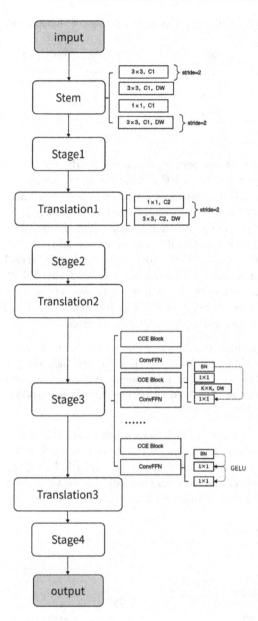

Fig. 2. The structure of CLKNet.

The large convolutional kernels are also applies to ViT (Vision Transformer) [12], which approvals that without the use of shortcuts, attention is lost exponentially with depth, leading to over-smoothing problems. While large kernel CNNs may degrade by a different mechanism than ViT, we also observed that without a shortcut, the network has difficulty capturing local details. From a perspective similar to this, the shortcut makes the

Table 1. Different kernel sizes in the last stage of MobileNet V2.

Kernel size	Accuracy(%)	Cityscapes mIoU(%)
3 × 3	71.76	72.31
7 × 7	72.00	74.30
13 × 13	72.31	74.62

model an implicit integration of numerous models with different receptive fields (RFs) that benefits from a larger maximum RF without losing the ability to capture a small range of patterns [3]. In addition, we use ConV(1 × 1) before and after the DW conv, and each DW large convolution is re-parameterized using kernels (5 × 5). In addition to the large conv layer providing sufficient sensory field and the ability to aggregate spatial information, the representational power of the model is also closely related to the depth. To provide more nonlinear and cross-channel information exchange, we want to use layers to increase the depth. We use a block called ConvFFN Block, which is a CNN-like style block consisting of shortcut, BN, two layers (1 × 1), and GELU. The advantage of BN over classical FFNs that use layer normalization before fully connected layers is that it can be fused into conv for efficient inference.

Transition Blocks.   The transition blocks are placed in the middle of each stage, first increasing the channel dimension by conv (1 × 1), and then bursting the row 2 × down-sampling with DW 3 × 3 conv. In summary, each stage has three architectural hyperparameters: the number of CCE BlocksB, the channel dimension C, and the kernel size.

The whole network consists of Stem, Stages, and Transitions. Except for the deep-wise (DW) kernel, all components include DW 3 × 3, dense 1 × 1 conv, and batch normalization [2] (BN). Note that each conv layer has a following BN, which is not described here. These convent-bn sequences use ReLU as the activation function, except for sequences before shortcut addition (as a common practice [8, 13]) and sequences before GELU [7].

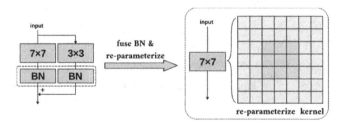

Fig. 3. An example of re-parameterizing a small kernel into a large one.

2.2 Optimization

Dropout Layer. Dropout is mainly to optimize the deep neural network, the specific measures are in the training process, the part of the weight or output of the implicit layers to zero randomly, the importance level between the nodes of the same layer can effectively maintain a balance, to avoid after all the large weight completely control the output and reduce the correlation and dependence between the neurons of the situation. Thus, it can achieve the regularization of the network, reduce the loss of the model, optimize the network structure, and prevent the problem of network over-fitting and gradient disappearance.

Batch Normalization. Batch Normalization (BN) is the most commonly used method of Normalization to make the output of the activation functions satisfy the Gaussian distribution as much as possible. The purpose is to speed up the Convergence speed of the neural network model, thus reducing the influence of the initial values on the training process and improving the generalization ability and the accuracy of the model. Connected Layer.

Loss Function and Model Training. The loss function is used to estimate the degree of inconsistency between the predicted value of your model f(x) and the true value of Y. It is a non-negative real-valued function, usually denoted by L(Y, f(x)), where L represents the loss function, and the smaller the loss function, the better the robustness of the model. The difference between the predicted value and the true value is the loss value. After obtaining the loss value, the model updates each parameter value by backpropagation to reduce the loss between the predicted value and the true value, so that the predicted value generated by the model keeps converging to the true value, thus achieving the purpose of learning. In this project, the principles of some loss functions involved are shown below:

1. Mean-square error (MSE) is the most commonly used error in the regression loss function and is the sum of the squares of the differences between the predicted and target values. The formulae are shown below.

$$MSE = \frac{\sum_{i=1}^{n} (y_i - y_i^p)^2}{n} \tag{1}$$

2. Mean absolute error (MAE) is another commonly used regression loss function, which is the sum of the absolute values of the differences between the target and predicted values and represents the average magnitude of the error in the predicted values, rather than considering the direction of the error. The formulae are shown below.

$$MAE = \frac{\sum_{i=1}^{n} |y_i - y_i^p|}{n} \tag{2}$$

3 Experiments

In this paper, feature collection and image classification are performed on two projects for CLKNet and ResNet34, respectively, and we obtained the performances of those models. on two projects for CLKNet and ResNet34, respectively, and we obtained the performances of those models.

As for CLKNet, we fine-tuned the existing CNN code in the integrated development environment of the pytorch framework and expanded the kernel to 31×31. We used Pycharm software to load the code, set the model parameters, process the image dataset, summarize the experimental results, and analyze them. We modified the shortcut and corrected the model parameters several times to continuously improve the accuracy of the experimental results to 97.1%.

3.1 Dataset

The datasets for this project were all provided by the China Automotive Technology Research Centre, and the specific global parameters we used for the training process on this dataset are shown in Table 2. In setting the global parameters, we first created the folder where the model was saved and then determined whether a GPU was present in the environment and used Automatic Mixed Precision (AMP). In this paper, the data is read by pytorch by default (Table 3).

Table 2. Parameters of CLKNet.

Parameters	Value
Batch size	16
Drop path	0.1
LR	1×10^{-4}
Warmup epoch	10
Epoch number	60

Table 3. Comparison of prediction results using CLKNet and ResNet50.

Model	Param(M)	Train Time(min)	Acc(%)
CLKNet	112	722.5	97.1
ResNet50	86	237.3	91.3

3.2 Network Configuration

Before the model training, we need to pre-process the data. Here we added the image cropping class data enhancement method Cutout, resized and normalized the image, set the image size to (224, 224), the mean value to 0.37, 0.35, 0.31, and the standard deviation to 0.22, 0.21, 0.21, respectively. In our experiment, training loss function, validation loss function, and model were set experimentally. And then the pre-trained model was loaded with 12 classes set. If the resume is True, the model is loaded and then trained last time. The optimizer is set to adamW [14], the learning rate adjustment strategy is chosen to cosine annealing, and mixed precision training is turned on.

The main steps of the model training are:

1. Determine whether the iterated data is odd or not. Since mixup_fn can only accept even numbers, if it is not even then one digit is subtracted to make it even. But it is possible that the last iteration has only one piece of data and it becomes zero after subtracting it, so you also have to judge that it cannot be less than 2. If it is less than 2, the loop will be interrupted directly.
2. Input the data to generate mix-up data, and then input it into the model to calculate the loss.
3. Calculate gradient and makes the derivative of loss concerning weight 0.4.
4. Calculate lose to back-propagate the gradient if using mixed accuracy, otherwise, back-propagate the gradient directly. Then gradient clipping is performed to prevent gradient explosion.
5. Update the parameters.
6. Obtain the learning rate, get the loss, and calculate the accuracy of this Batch.

Before conducting the test, we need to adjust the image size to (224, 224) to meet the image size requirement of our trained model, since the size of the captured image is affected by factors such as distance from the car and the shooting orientation. Since the images are initially represented as arrays, in the model we use, we first convert the array form to tensor form and normalize it to (0, 1). After that, we normalized the model by channel, and the mean values of the three channels were 0.5, 0.5, and 0.5, and the standard deviations of each channel were 0.22, 0.21, and 0.21. We trained a total of 14 sets of data, and the accuracy rate has reached about 95%, to better test the accuracy of the model, we grayed out the captured images, extracted a part of the images, and so on. To better test the accuracy of the model, we grayed out the captured images, extracted a part of the images, etc. The accuracy of the test was slightly reduced during the test but the test results were within our expectations.

4   Results and Discussion

The training results are shown in Fig. The training results show the best accuracy of 95.56%. The red curves in Fig. 3 and Fig. 4 represent Train Acc/Loss, and the blue curves represent Val Acc/Loss. Figure 5 and Fig. 6 represent the accuracy and loss of ResNet34 respectively. From these figures, it can be seen that the combined performance of ResNet in Automotive The maximum accuracy of the two models is 97.1% and 91.3% respectively.

First of all, due to the characteristics of the CLKNet network model structure, the model can obtain a larger Effective Receptive Field (ERF) than the model using many small kernels. ERF is positively correlated with kernel size and negatively correlated

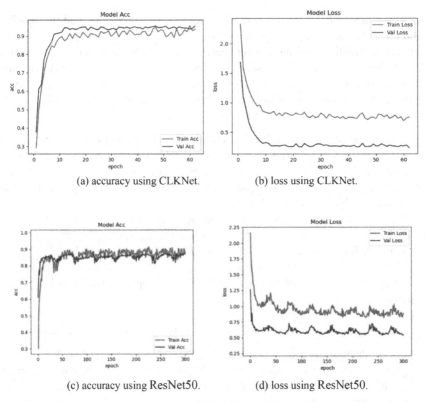

(a) accuracy using CLKNet.   (b) loss using CLKNet.

(c) accuracy using ResNet50.   (d) loss using ResNet50.

Fig. 4. Comparison results of accuracy using the CLKNet and ResNet50 respectively.

with depth. He et al. [2] proposed a ResNet approach with a shortcut structure that seems to solve this problem, but some studies suggest that ResNet may not be as deep as it seems [13]. In conclusion, the large kernel avoids the degradation problem caused by inception depth while obtaining larger ERFs.

Fig. 5. A part of misclassified images.

The images above show some misclassified images, with the left being the images captured before the collision test, and the right being the images captured after the collision test. The common characteristic of these images is that the changes before and after the test are very subtle. We initially expected these images to be classified as pre-test, taken from the passenger side, but they were incorrectly classified as post-test, taken from the passenger side. We believe that the cause of this error is the minimal changes in these images before and after the test, combined with the small number of images, which resulted in the model not being adequately trained. In our upcoming research, we plan to incorporate attention mechanisms in the large kernel convolutions and optimize the model framework to improve accuracy without compromising computational speed.

5 Conclusion

In this paper, we proposed a computer vision and deep learning-based method to solve the problem of cumbersome classification of car collision images in related companies, and to predict vehicle safety characteristics using images of vehicles after collisions. Estimating feature points from images, producing datasets, etc. is a challenging problem, and to the best of our knowledge, we are the early group to apply a deep learning approach to the problem of classifying images in automotive crash tests. In this work, we evaluate the performance of various deep convolutional neural networks and their integration for car collision image classification, using deep learning methods to predict the post-collision grayscale images of these objects. We have shown that metrics such as frontal collisions in photographic templates can be accurately distinguished in systems with large convolutional kernels.

More specifically, our approach is a breakthrough in processing image data in large batches in the context of existing collision test photo methods that are traditional and relatively outdated. We demonstrate the effectiveness of using large convolutional networks for highly accurate and efficient model training. In frontal crash test image classification, our method achieves 98.0% accuracy on the validation set and 97.92% accuracy on unseen test students. Future work will continue to explore optimizing the accuracy in terms of optimizing the way of taking pictures and adjusting the convolution size and depth.

References

1. https://www.c-ncap.org.cn/guicheng/
2. Ioffe, S., Szegedy, C.: Batch normalization: Accelerating deep network training by reducing internal covariate shift. In: International Conference on Machine Learning, pp. 448–456 (2015)
3. Veit, A., Wilber, M.J., Belongie, S.: Residual networks behave like ensembles of relatively shallow networks. In: Advances in Neural Information Processing Systems, pp. 550–558 (2016)
4. Dong, Y., Cordonnier, J.-B., Loukas, A.: Attention is not all you need: Pure attention loses rank doubly exponentially with depth. arXiv preprint arXiv:2103.03404, (2021)
5. Krizhevsky, A., Sutskever, I., Hinton, G.E.: Imagenet classification with deep convolutional neural networks. In: Advances in Neural Information Processing Systems, pp. 1097–1105 (2012)
6. Pasupa, K., Kittiworapanya, P., Hongngern, N., et al.: Evaluation of deep learning algorithms for semantic segmentation of car parts. Complex Intell. Syst. **8**, 3613–3625 (2022)

7. Hendrycks, D., Gimpel, K.: Gaussian error linear units (gelus). arXiv preprint arXiv:1606.08415, (2016)
8. Sandler, M., Howard, A., Zhu, M., Zhmoginov, A., Chen, L.-C.: Mobilenetv2: inverted residuals and linear bottlenecks. In: Proceedings of the IEEE Conference on Computer Vision and Pattern Recognition, pp. 4510–4520 (2018)
9. Ding, X., Zhang, X., Ma, N., Han, J., Ding, G., Sun, J.: Repvgg: making vggstyle convnets great again. In :Proceedings of the IEEE/CVF Conference on Computer Vision and Pattern Recognition, pp. 13733–13742 (2021)
10. Doll´ar, P., Singh, M., Girshick, R.: Fast and accurate model scaling. In: Proceedings of the IEEE/CVF Conference on Computer Vision and Pattern Recognition, pp. 924–932 (2021)
11. Radosavovic, I., Kosaraju, R.P., Girshick, R., He, K., Doll´ar, P.: Designing network design spaces. In: Proceedings of the IEEE/CVF Conference on Computer Vision and Pattern Recognition, pp. 10428–10436 (2020)
12. Dong, Y., Cordonnier, J.-P., Loukas, A.: Attention is not all you need: Pure attention loses rank doubly exponentially with depth. arXiv preprint arXiv:2103.03404, (2021)
13. He, K., Zhang, X., Ren, S., Sun, J.: Deep residual learning for image recognition. In: Proceedings of the IEEE Conference on Computer Vision and Pattern Recognition, pp. 770–778 (2016)
14. https://www.fast.ai/posts/2018-07-02-adam-weight-decay.html

Underwater Image Restoration Based on Light Attenuation Prior and Scene Depth Fusion Model

Xu Zhu[1], Yujie Li[1(✉)], and Huimin Lu[2]

[1] Yangzhou University, Jiangsu, China
yzyjli@gmail.com
[2] Kyushu University of Technology, Kyushu, Japan

Abstract. Underwater images often suffer from blurry details, color distortion, and low contrast due to light absorption and scattering in water. Existing restoration technologies use a fixed attenuation coefficient value, which fails to account for the uncertainty of the water body and leads to suboptimal restoration results. To address these issues, we propose a scene depth fusion model that considers underwater light attenuation to obtain a more accurate attenuation coefficient for image restoration. Our method employs the quadtree decom-position method and a depth map to estimate the background light. We then fuse and refine the depth map, compute the attenuation coefficient of the water medium for a more precise transmission map, and apply a reversed underwater imaging model to restore the image. Experiments demonstrate that our method effectively enhances the details and colors of underwater images while improving the contrast. Moreover, our method outperforms several state-of-the-art methods in terms of both accuracy and quality, showing its superior performance.

Keywords: Attenuation coefficient · Depth map · Background light · Transmission map

1 Introduction

Underwater images are essential for exploring the ocean and discovering its secrets. They are widely used in marine mineral resource extraction, marine ecological environment monitoring, and military applications [1]. However, due to the absorption and scattering of light in water, underwater images often exhibit color casts, blurred details, and low contrast. These problems impair the visual quality and information content of underwater images, which hinders the effective observation and analysis of the ocean. Therefore, developing effective underwater imaging methods is of great importance for acquiring ocean information. The attenuation of light in water depends on both the wavelength and the distance of the light. Red light with longer wavelengths attenuates the fastest and is most affected compared to green and blue light, resulting in a blue-green hue in underwater images. Moreover, scattering effects increase with distance, which reduces the contrast and sharpness of underwater images.

© The Author(s), under exclusive license to Springer Nature Switzerland AG 2023
H. Lu et al. (Eds.): ACPR 2023, LNCS 14406, pp. 41–53, 2023.
https://doi.org/10.1007/978-3-031-47634-1_4

In addition to the influence of the water medium itself on the light, suspended particles in the water can also scatter the incident light, which can cause severe image degradation. Due to the large amount of noise introduced by scattering, underwater images have defects such as blurring, fogging, and reduced clarity [2]. To address these challenges, researchers have proposed various methods based on traditional strategies, which can be broadly categorized into two groups: underwater image enhancement and restoration. The former aims to improve the quality of the acquired underwater image by manipulating its pixels. However, these methods do not consider the imaging and degradation processes of underwater images, nor do they account for the scattering properties of different wavelengths and the relationship between the degree of degradation and the depth of the scene. This may lead to local hyperenhancement or hypoenhancement. The latter attempts to recover the true underwater scene by considering the imaging process of underwater images. However, this approach requires information such as the optical parameters of the water body, which need to be estimated through other techniques [11]. Many underwater restoration methods ignore the type of water body parameters, leading to poor performance in some underwater scenes and reduced robustness of the restored image compared to the original. In this paper, we propose a method for restoring a single underwater image and estimating the attenuation coefficients of water through background light and a depth map. Our method is designed to be adaptable to various underwater scenarios. The specific framework of our method is shown in Fig. 1.

Our contributions are as follows:

(1) We propose a simple method for estimating background light using quadtree decomposition.
(2) We propose a depth map fusion model based on light attenuation to estimate the transmission map of the scene more accurately.
(3) We demonstrate that our method outperforms existing methods in restoring underwater images across different scenes through our experimental results. The remainder of this paper is organized as follows. Section 2 reviews related work. Section 3 presents our proposed method. Section 4 provides a qualitative and quantitative comparison of our method with six image restoration methods. Section 5 concludes this paper.

2   Related Work

2.1   Underwater Image Enhancement Method

The category of methods involves direct image processing to enhance image clarity. Several methods have been proposed for this purpose. A multi-feature fusion method is proposed in [3] to improve the cross-color and low contrast of underwater images. [5] uses an underwater image visual quality enhancement method based on multi-feature prior fusion, which is realized by extracting and fusing multiple feature priors of images. Another method, proposed by [6], uses fusion-based image enhancement to avoid halos in the output image during single-scale fusion. [7] proposed a method based on minimum color loss and local adaptive contrast enhancement, and achieved good results.

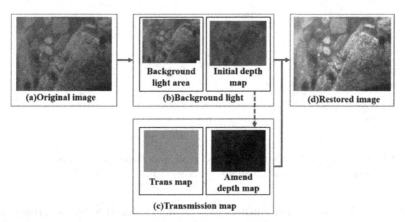

Fig. 1. Flow chart of our method. (a) An original input image; (b) An illustration of our background light estimation method; (c) Obtaining the transmission image by using the amended depth map; (d) The restoration effect of our method.

2.2 Underwater Image Restoration Method

The restoration methods typically rely on imaging models that were originally designed for haze removal. The model parameters need to be estimated using different assumptions or priors. One commonly used method for underwater image restoration is based on the dark channel prior, which was originally proposed for atmospheric haze removal [9]. However, the method based on dark channel prior may produce unreal colors in recovered images due to its assumptions about the scene and easy interference from white objects. To address this issue, some methods use learning-based approaches to estimate the depth map based on the underwater light attenuation prior (NULAP) [19], which can help remove the influence of suspended particles and estimate the accurate background light.

However, they both used a constant water attenuation coefficient in calculating the transmission map, which is wrong. Because the optical properties of natural bodies of water exhibit extreme differences compared to the atmosphere. The different optical water types are classified by Jerlov [4], and the attenuation coefficient versus wavelength for different Jerlov water types is shown in Fig. 2. It is therefore inaccurate and unreasonable to assume the same attenuation coefficient values for all images to be restored.

Overall, existing restoration methods have limitations regarding accuracy and adaptability to different scenarios. More advanced methods are needed to take into account the scattering properties of various wavelengths.

3 Proposed Method

Figure 1 depicts a schematic figure of our proposed method, which comprises three main components: background light estimation, depth map fusion, and transmission map estimation. Firstly, we employ the hierarchical search method based on quadtree

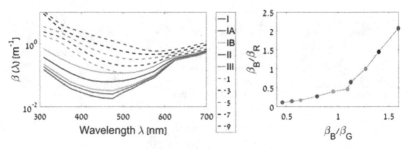

Fig.2. Approximate attenuation coefficients (β) of Jerlov water types. Solid lines mark open ocean water types while dashed lines mark coastal water types [26].

subdivision and the one-dimensional entropy formula to identify the background light estimation region and then estimate the background light by combining it with the initial depth map obtained from the NULAP method. Afterward, fusing the initial depth map with the depth map in [21], and subsequently correcting it based on the initial transmittance obtained by the backscattering removal method. The final output is a high-quality image with a natural appearance.

3.1 Underwater Model

The underwater model [8] can be expressed as:

$$I^c(x) = t^c(x)J^c(x) + (1 - t^c(x))B^c, c \in \{r, g, b\} \tag{1}$$

where $I^c(x)$ is the input image, $J^c(x)$ represents the restored image, B^c represents the background light, and $t^c(x)$ represents the transmission map, which is given by:

$$t^c(x) = e^{-\beta^c d(x)} \tag{2}$$

$$Nrer(c) = e^{-\beta^c} \tag{3}$$

where $d(x)$ is the scene depth at pixel point x, $Nrer(c)$ represents the normalized residual energy ratio, β is the overall wavelength-dependent attenuation coefficient, $\beta^r \in (\frac{1}{8}, \frac{1}{5})$ in [18].

It can be seen from [15] that the relationship between the transmission maps of blue and green channels and those of red channels is as follows:

$$\begin{cases} t^g(x) = [t^r(x)]^{\beta^g/\beta^r} \\ t^b(x) = [t^r(x)]^{\beta^b/\beta^r} \end{cases} \tag{4}$$

Then the mathematical relationship of the water attenuation coefficient β^c is obtained from [17]. It can be expressed as:

$$\frac{B^k}{B^r} = \frac{\beta^r(m\lambda^k + i)}{\beta^k(m\lambda^r + i)}, k \in \{g, b\} \tag{5}$$

where λ^r, λ^g, and λ^b are the wavelengths of the red, green, and blue channels, respectively. According to [14], they are 620 nm, 540 nm, and 450 nm, respectively.

3.2 Background Light Estimation

Our proposed method uses the principle that the higher the one-dimensional entropy value of a local patch, the more information it contains. However, instead of using a simple method to locate the background region, we use a hierarchical search technique and select the region with the lowest entropy value for background light estimation. As shown in Fig. 3(b), we divide the underwater images by quadtree decomposition. We use (3) to compute the entropy values for each local patch. We select the local patch with the lowest entropy value as the estimated region. The preset threshold size is 50×40.

$$H(y) = -\sum_{0}^{255} P_x log_2 P_x \tag{6}$$

where H(y) denotes one-dimensional entropy, P_x is the probability of a pixel with intensity x in the grayscale image of $J^c(x)$, y $\in \{1,2,3,4\}$.

The NULAP method is then used to estimate the initial depth map. The calculation process is given by (7):

$$d_n(x) = w_0 + w_1 \cdot mvgb(x) + w_2 \cdot vr(x) \tag{7}$$

where $d_n(x)$ represents the depth value of the scene at the pixel point x, $mvgb(x)$ represents the maximum value of the G-B intensity, and $vr(x)$ represents the value of the R intensity. w_0, w_1, and w_2 are 0.53214831, 0.51309828, and -0.91066193, respectively.

After the depth map is generated, the most distant point of 0.1% is removed first, which can remove the influence of suspended particles, and then the brightest pixel in the candidate region is selected as the background light.

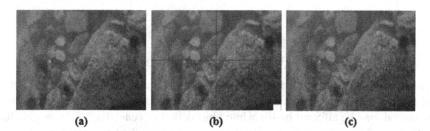

(a)   (b)   (c)

Fig. 3. Background light estimation figure. (a) Input image; (b) Background light estimation region selected using the 1D entropy formula and the quadtree decomposition method; (c) the result of searching for the background light in the refined depth map.

3.3 Depth Map Fusion Estimation

NULAP measures the degree of attenuation of underwater images through deep learning methods to obtain depth maps. However, the methods based on deep learning are not robust. Inspired by the depth map fusion algorithm, this paper compares $d_n(x)$ to the depth map $d_m(x)$ [21] for fusion. An example to illustrate depth map fusion is shown in Fig. 4.

$$d_m(x) = \max_{y\in\Phi(x)} I^r(y) - \max_{y\in\Phi(x)} \{I^g(y), I^b(y)\} \tag{8}$$

where $\Phi(x)$ denotes a non-overlapping local block of size 9×9 centered at x.

$$d_s(x) = \alpha(1 - d_m(x)) + (1 - \alpha)d_n(x) \tag{9}$$

$$d(x) = DK \cdot d_s(x) \tag{10}$$

$$\alpha = \frac{1}{1 + e^{-M \cdot avg(B)}} \tag{11}$$

where $d_m(x)$ is the color attenuation depth map, $d_n(x)$ is the NULAP, and DK is the proportional constant of the relative distance to the actual distance, set to 5. M is the empirical constant, set to 20.

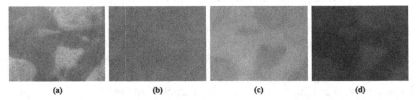

Fig. 4. An example to illustrate depth map fusion. (a) Input image; (b) NULAP; (c) Depth image obtained by the method proposed in [21]; (d) Depth image fusion result.

3.4 Transmission Map Estimation

We use the remove backscattering method [20] to obtain the initial transmission map t_i^r of the red channel. Then we compute t_i^g and t_i^b according to (2) and (5). However, this method may be affected by the white objects in the scene. Therefore, we use the equation in [15] to refine the transmission map and obtain the final transmission map. The calculation procedures are given by (12)–(15):

$$\begin{cases} t^{g-r}(x) = [t_i^r(x)]^{\beta^g/\beta^r} \\ t^{b-r}(x) = [t_i^r(x)]^{\beta^b/\beta^r} \end{cases} \tag{12}$$

$$\begin{cases} t^{r-g}(x) = [t_i^g(x)]^{\beta^r/\beta^g} \\ t^{b-g}(x) = [t_i^g(x)]^{\beta^b/\beta^g} \end{cases} \tag{13}$$

$$\begin{cases} t^{r-b}(x) = [t_i^b(x)]^{\beta^r/\beta^b} \\ t^{g-b}(x) = [t_i^b(x)]^{\beta^g/\beta^b} \end{cases} \tag{14}$$

$$\begin{cases} t^r(x) = (t_i^r(x) + t^{r\text{-}g}(x) + t^{r\text{-}b}(x))/3 \\ t^g(x) = (t_i^g(x) + t^{g\text{-}r}(x) + t^{g\text{-}b}(x))/3 \\ t^b(x) = (t_i^b(x) + t^{b\text{-}g}(x) + t^{b\text{-}r}(x))/3 \end{cases} \qquad (15)$$

where $t_i^r(x)$, $t_i^g(x)$ and $t_i^b(x)$ represent initial transmission maps of the input image.

3.5 Scene Radiance Restoration

When the background light B^c and the transmission maps $t^c(x)$ are acquired, the clear image $J^c(x)$ can be calculated by using (16).

$$J^c(x) = \frac{I^c(x) - B^c}{max\{t^c(x), 0.1\}} + B^c \qquad (16)$$

4 Experiments and Discussions

In this section, we combine our proposed method with the dehazing method (MIP) of [23], the typical image dehazing method (DCP) by [9], the DCP variant (UDCP) proposed by [24], the IBLA [21], ULAP proposed by [10], and the underwater-hl proposed by [26], abbreviated as HL. To demonstrate the outstanding performance of our proposed method, we give some examples of restored images and introduce quantitative evaluation in this section. To demonstrate the outstanding performance of our proposed method, we present qualitative results for three scenes and quantitative results for 15 images. The test set is shown in Fig. 5.

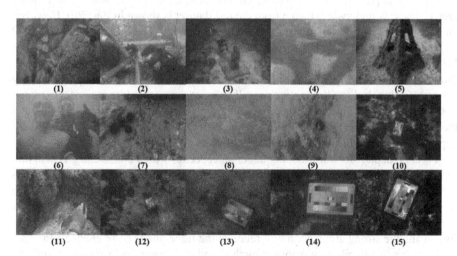

Fig. 5. The test set. The numbers are (1)–(15) from left to right and top to bottom.

4.1 Qualitative Analysis

Figure 6 shows the channel pixel distribution of the input image and the restored image using our proposed method. Figure 7 and 8 show the scene comparison with six restoration methods in different scenarios. As shown in Fig. 7(h) and Fig. 8(h), our method can effectively remove scattering and haze from different underwater images, enhance the details and colors of the input images, and produce natural underwater images. We can clearly see from the two channel pixel histograms in Fig. 6 that the original image is restored using our method, and the pixel values of the three channels are more balanced. The brightness of the restored image is significantly improved. Moreover, the high brightness pixel values of the blue-green channel are greatly reduced, resulting in a background color shift from slightly green to normal.

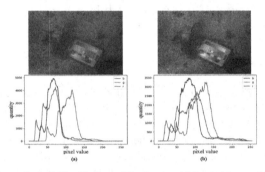

Fig. 6. The channel pixel distribution of the image. (a) Input image; (b) Our method.

Figure 7 depicts a hazy underwater optical scene captured as a downward-looking image. The raw underwater image from the test dataset is shown in Fig. 7(a). However, the restoration results from different methods vary greatly. The image restored by DCP in Fig. 7(b) appears dark, has a color cast problem, and looks sea blue. In Fig. 7(c), MIP improves the local brightness of the image, but the restoration effect is minimal. Similarly, UDCP in Fig. 7(d) estimates the transmission map incorrectly, which may not be effective. In Fig. 7(e)-(f), the overall color of the restored image is deviated due to the wrong estimation of the background light, resulting in color distortion. Although the restored image in Fig. 7(g) effectively restores the scene details, the overall color appears dark, and some image details are not visible.

Figure 8 depicts forward-looking underwater scenes with a bluish and greenish tint. In Fig. 8(b), DCP fails to improve the test image significantly, similar to Fig. 7(b). This shows that applying outdoor image dehazing methods directly to underwater image restoration is not suitable. In Fig. 8(c), the recovered image using MIP not only shows poor restoration but also exhibits overexposure, resulting in worse image quality. Therefore, using the strong attenuation difference of the three image color channels in water to estimate water depth is an incorrect method and may lead to poor image restoration. In Fig. 8(e)-(f), the overall color cast problem in the restored image still exists, caused by incorrect background light estimation. As we can see in Fig. 8(g), HL's method of restoring images by analyzing the attenuation coefficient ratio of different water types may lead to the problem of local missing details.

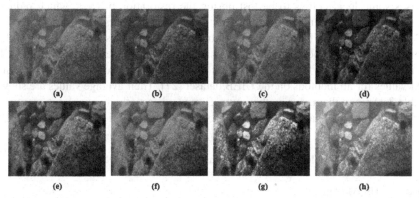

Fig. 7. (a) Original image; (b) DCP; (c) MIP; (d) UDCP; (e) IBLA; (f) ULAP; (g) HL; (h) Our method.

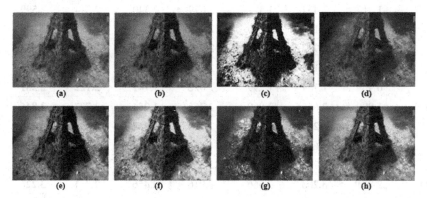

Fig. 8. (a) Original image; (b) DCP; (c) MIP; (d) UDCP; (e) IBLA; (f) ULAP; (g) HL; (h) Our method.

4.2 Quantitative Analysis

We objectively evaluate our method on 15 images from the test dataset. We use two reference-free underwater quality evaluation metrics, UIQM and SSIM, to measure the performance of our method. UIQM is a linear combination of color, sharpness, and contrast, with corresponding weights of 0.2953, 3.5753, and 0.0282, respectively. SSIM is an index used to measure the similarity between two digital images. Compared with traditional image quality metrics, SSIM is more consistent with human perception of image quality. Table 1 and Table 2 show the UIQM and SSIM values of the restored images by different methods. The first two maximum values of each row in the table are marked in bold, indicating the best results among the compared methods. The last row of the table gives the average values of the metrics for 15 test images under seven methods. It can be seen that our method achieves the highest average UIQM and SSIM scores. Although the HL method produces visually pleasing results and high UIQM values, it causes some local details to be lost during the restoration process, which reduces the correlation of adjacent pixels in the digital image and lowers the SSIM value. The DCP method has low UIQM values and moderate SSIM values, which indicates that its restoration effect is poor and does not change the pixel correlation significantly. In addition, to demonstrate the high robustness of our model, we compute the UIQM and SSIM values for all methods on the UIEB dataset [27]. Their average values are shown in Table 3. Among them, our method outperforms other methods by a large margin in both UIQM and SSIM values. In summary, our method is superior to other methods.

Table 1. Qualitative evaluation in terms of UIQM

Image	UIQM/Method						
	DCP	MIP	UDCP	IBLA	ULAP	HL	Our
(1)	2.670	2.937	2.453	**3.071**	2.826	2.879	**3.083**
(2)	1.713	**2.432**	1.522	2.079	2.340	2.314	**2.599**
(3)	1.934	1.185	2.270	**2.977**	2.588	**2.651**	2.646
(4)	2.019	2.787	2.296	**2.969**	2.947	2.163	**2.988**
(5)	2.059	1.173	2.386	2.033	2.339	**2.413**	**2.473**
(6)	0.969	1.754	1.299	2.022	1.747	**2.122**	**2.281**
(7)	1.989	2.666	2.069	2.765	1.954	**2.777**	**2.846**
(8)	0.897	1.206	1.172	1.774	1.437	**2.499**	**2.578**
(9)	1.216	1.617	1.863	1.865	2.134	**2.184**	**2.216**
(10)	2.256	1.720	2.220	**3.357**	1.257	2.812	**3.264**
(11)	2.831	**3.203**	2.666	2.916	2.456	2.331	**3.226**
(12)	2.480	**3.049**	2.290	2.263	1.908	2.368	**3.272**
(13)	2.272	2.959	2.195	**3.071**	2.554	2.678	**3.160**
(14)	2.181	2.164	1.871	**3.012**	2.122	2.772	**3.047**
(15)	1.679	0.886	**2.339**	1.586	0.649	2.303	**3.059**
avg	1.944	2.116	2.061	**2.517**	2.084	2.484	**2.849**

Table 2. Qualitative evaluation in terms of SSIM

Image	SSIM/Method						
	DCP	MIP	UDCP	IBLA	ULAP	HL	Our
(1)	0.859	**0.994**	0.557	0.786	0.894	0.619	**0.931**
(2)	**0.963**	0.927	0.520	0.903	0.882	0.573	**0.978**
(3)	**0.969**	0.331	0.853	0.966	0.934	0.656	**0.972**
(4)	0.909	**0.995**	0.544	0.943	0.931	0.378	**0.972**
(5)	**0.919**	0.558	0.853	0.767	0.830	0.688	**0.940**
(6)	0.970	**0.990**	0.869	0.964	0.920	0.689	**0.976**
(7)	0.943	**0.949**	0.662	0.869	0.922	0.560	**0.964**
(8)	**0.989**	**0.993**	0.967	0.955	0.949	0.667	0.921
(9)	**0.989**	0.942	0.940	0.954	0.948	0.712	**0.973**
(10)	0.836	0.591	0.764	**0.869**	0.421	0.678	**0.965**
(11)	0.755	**0.978**	0.582	0.622	0.780	0.462	**0.955**
(12)	0.904	**0.972**	0.841	0.672	0.696	0.513	**0.961**
(13)	0.906	**0.963**	0.631	0.816	0.808	0.571	**0.967**
(14)	0.901	0.876	0.659	**0.962**	0.731	0.784	**0.966**
(15)	0.658	0.525	**0.892**	0.588	0.304	0.650	**0.912**
avg	**0.898**	0.839	0.742	0.842	0.797	0.613	**0.957**

Table 3. The average value of UIQM and SSIM in UIEB dataset

	DCP	MIP	UDCP	IBLA	ULAP	HL	Our
UIQM	2.004	2.041	2.069	1.881	2.225	**2.261**	**2.380**
SSIM	**0.878**	0.789	0.697	0.741	0.863	**0.708**	**0.928**

5 Conclusion

We propose a scene depth fusion model based on underwater light attenuation prior. This model adopts a depth map fusion method, which improves the contrast and preserves the details of the restored images. We evaluate our model on 15 test images and show that it produces high-quality images and enhances their visual effect. Moreover, we conduct quantitative tests and demonstrate that our method outperforms existing techniques. However, our approach has some limitations. Specifically, when the background color of underwater images is close to pure green or blue, our method may not work well. Furthermore, we acknowledge that our initial transmission map estimation algorithm needs improvement, which will be the direction of our future work.

References

1. Lu, H., Li, Y., Zhang, L., et al.: Contrast enhancement for images in turbid water. JOSA A **32**(5), 886–893 (2016)
2. Serikawa, S., Lu, H.: Underwater image dehazing using joint trilateral filter. Comput. Electr. Eng. **40**(1), 41–50 (2014)
3. Zhou, J., Zhang, D., Zhang, W.: A multifeature fusion method for the color distortion and low contrast of underwater images. In: Multimedia Tools and Applications, pp. 17515–41 (2021)
4. Jerlov, N.G.: Marine Optics, vol. 14. Elsevier, Amsterdam (1976)
5. Zhou, J., Zhang, D., Zhang, W.: Underwater image enhancement method via multi-feature prior fusion. Appli. Intell., 16435–16457 (2022)
6. Ancuti, C.O., Ancuti, C., De Vleeschouwer, C., Bekaert, P.: Color balance and fusion for underwater image enhancement. IEEE Trans. Image Process. **27**(1), 379–393 (2018)
7. Zhang, W., Zhuang, P., Sun, H.H., et al.: Underwater image enhancement via minimal color loss and locally adaptive contrast enhancement. IEEE Trans. Image Process., 3997–4010 (2022)
8. McCartney, E.J.: Optics of the Atmosphere: Scattering by Molecules and Particles. Wiley, New York, USA (1976)
9. He, K., Sun, J., Tang X.: Single image haze removal using dark channel prior. IEEE Trans. Pattern Anal. Mach. Intell., 2341–53 (2010)
10. Song, W., Wang, Y,, Huang, D., Tjondronegoro D.: A rapid scene depth estimation model based on underwater light attenuation prior for underwater image restoration. In: Pacific Rim Conference on Multimedia, pp.678–88. Springer, Cham (2018). https://doi.org/10.1007/978-3-030-00776-8_62
11. Akkaynak, D., Treibitz, T.: A revised underwater image formation model. In: Proceedings of the IEEE Conference on Computer Vision and Pattern Recognition, pp. 6723–6732 (2018)
12. Lu, H., Wang, D., Li, Y., et al.: CONet: a cognitive ocean network. IEEE Wireless Commun **26**(3), 90–96 (2019)
13. Horimachi, R., Lu, H., Zheng, Y., et al.: Underwater image super-resolution using improved SRCNN. In: International Symposium on Artificial Intelligence and Robotics 2022, vol. 12508, pp. 87–102. SPIE (2022)
14. Dai, C., Lin, M., Wu X.: Single underwater image restoration by decomposing curves of attenuating color. Optics Laser Technol. (2020)
15. Zhou, J., Yang, T., Chu, W., et al.: Underwater image restoration via backscatter pixel prior and color compensation. In: Engineering Applications of Artificial Intelligence (2022)
16. Onoyama, T., Lu, H., Soomro, A.A., et al.: Image quality improvement using local adaptive neighborhood-based dark channel prior. In: International Symposium on Artificial Intelligence and Robotics 2021, vol. 11884, pp. 191–195. SPIE (2021)
17. Gould, R.W., Arnone, R.A., Martinolich,. P.M.: Spectral dependence of the scattering coefficient in case 1 and case 2 waters. Appl. Opt., 2377–2383 (1999)
18. Chiang, J.Y., Chen, Y.-C.: Underwater image enhancement by wavelength compensation and dehazing. IEEE Trans. Image Process., 1756–1769 (2012)
19. Liu, K., Liang, Y.: Enhancement of underwater optical images based on background light estimation and improved adaptive transmission fusion. Optics Express **29**(18), 28307–28328 (2021)
20. Chao, L., Wang, M.: Removal of water scattering. In: 2010 2nd International Conference on Computer Engineering and Technology. IEEE (2010)
21. Carlevaris-Bianco, N., Mohan, A., Eustice, R.M.: Initial results in underwater single image dehazing. In: OCEANS 2010 MTS/IEEE SEATTLE, USA, Seattle, WA, pp. 1–8 (2010)

22. Lu, H., Li, Y., Zhang, Y., et al.: Underwater optical image processing: a comprehensive review. Mobile Netw. Appli. **22**, 1204–1211 (2017)
23. Carlevaris-Bianco, N., Mohan, A., Eustice, R.M.: Initial results in underwater single image dehazing. In: Proceedings of IEEE Oceans, pp.1–8 (Sep 2010)
24. Drews Jr., P., do Nascimento, E., Moraes, F., Botelho, S., Campos, M.: Transmission estimation in underwater single images. In: 2013 IEEE International Conference on Computer Vision Workshops, Australia, Sydney, NSW, pp. 825–830 (2013)
25. Li, Y., Lu, H., Li, J., et al. Underwater image de-scattering and classification by deep neural network. Comput. Elect. Eng. **54**, 68–77 (2016)
26. Berman, D., Levy, D., Avidan, S., Treibitz, T.: Underwater single image color restoration using haze-lines and a new quantitative dataset. IEEE Trans. Pattern Anal. Mach. Intell. **43**(8) 2822–2837 (2021)
27. Li, C., Guo, C., Ren, W., et al.: An underwater image enhancement benchmark dataset and beyond. IEEE Trans. Image Process. **29**, 4376–4389 (2019)

Efficient Shapley Values Calculation
for Transformer Explainability

Tianli Sun[1], Haonan Chen[2], Yuping Qiu[1], and Cairong Zhao[1]([✉])

[1] Tongji University, Shanghai, China
zhaocairong@tongji.edu.cn
[2] Alibaba Group, Hangzhou, China

Abstract. Class activation mapping (CAM) methods have achieved great model explainability performance for CNNs. However, these methods do not perform so well for Transformers, whose architectures are fundamentally different from CNNs. Instead, gradient-weighted attention visualization methods, with effective consideration for the self-attention and skip-connection, achieve very promising explainability for Transformers. These methods compute gradients by backpropagation to achieve class-specific and accurate explainability. In this work, to further increase the accuracy and efficiency in Transformer explainability, we propose a novel method which is both class-specific and gradient-free. The token importance is calculated using Shapley value method, which has a solid base on game theory but is conventionally very computational expensive to use in practice. To calculate the Shapley value accurately and efficiently for each token, we decouple the self-attention from the information flow in Transformers and freeze other unrelated values. In this way, we construct a linear version of Transformer so that the Shapley values can be calculated conveniently. Using Shapley values for explainability, our method not only improves the explainability further but also becomes class-specific without using gradients, surpassing other gradient-based methods in both accuracy and efficiency. Furthermore, we show that explainability methods for CNNs and Transformers can be bridged under the 1st-order Taylor expansion of our method, resulting in (1) a significant explainability improvement for a modified GradCAM method in Transformers and (2) new insights into understanding the existing gradient-based attention visualization methods. Extensive experiments show that our method is superior compared to state-of-the-arts methods. Our code will be made available.

Keywords: Transformer · Explainability · Shapley Values

1 Introduction

In the field of explainable AI, in order to understand the decision process of CNNs, explainability methods are used to generate heatmaps which highlight the most influential area of the input image. These methods can be divided into two categories based on their ability to explain different target classes: class-specific and class-agnostic.

H. Lu et al. (Eds.): ACPR 2023, LNCS 14406, pp. 54–67, 2023.
https://doi.org/10.1007/978-3-031-47634-1_5

Most explainability methods for CNNs are class-specific, e.g., class activation mapping (CAM) methods ([4, 9, 15, 20]). If there are multiple objects with different classes in the image, heatmaps can be visualized for each class.

In recent years, with the fast development in Transformers ([7, 8, 13, 17]), the explainability in Transformers is becoming an important topic, which will be helpful to understand, debug and eventually trust the models. Because Transformers are significantly different from CNNs, some CAM methods (e.g. GradCAM shown in [6]) are applicable, but make degraded explainability. Therefore, some explainability methods specifically designed for Transformers are proposed [1, 3, 18]. These early methods focus on the self-attention and computation process to generate the heatmap, but many of them are class-agnostic, which means they can only generate heatmap for the predicted class.

Gradient is helpful for class-specificity, as shown in GradCAM and other gradient-based methods for CNNs. Therefore, it can be used in Transformer for class-specific explainability methods. The attribution method [6] is the first to introduce gradient into rollout. It computes the relevance scores [2] based on the Deep Taylor Decomposition principle [12] and then propagates the relevance scores through the self-attention layers with gradients. Similarly, transition attention mapping (TAM) method [19] regards the computation process in Transformer as a Markov Chain and propagates the attention with integrated gradients [16] for visualization. Using gradients, these methods introduce class-specific information to the relevance score for explanation results. However, the computation of gradients relies on back-propagation, which is computational expensive.

In addition to class-specificity, using gradient also helps to improve the explainability performance by a large margin. This can be seen in the comparison between the methods of GradCAM [15] and CAM [20], as well as between the methods of attribution [6] and rollout [1]. As for GradCAM, [15] proves that using gradient in GradCAM generalizes CAM for a wide range of CNN-based architectures, which partially illustrate the reason for its superior performance. However, the utilization of gradient in attribution [6] is not so clearly investigated.

In order to find a class-specific, accurate and efficient solution for Transformer explainability, we propose a novel method to utilize Shapley values [11] to compute the heatmap. Shapley value method is based on classic equations from cooperative game theory to compute explanations of model predictions, and it is class-specific. For any particular prediction, it assigns an importance value to each feature which represents its effect on the model prediction. According to [11], this method is the only additive feature attribution method that satisfies three desired properties for model explainability: local accuracy, missingness and consistency. This ensures the accuracy of Shapley values for model explanation.

Computational efficiency is the biggest challenge in using Shapley values to generate heatmaps. Directly computing Shapley values for Transformer is impractical because for the Shapley value of a token, it computes the difference between two simple explanation models (linear models) output, one is trained on a subset of all tokens with the target token present, and the other is trained with the token absent. All possible subsets of the input tokens are needed, resulting in $2^{|F|}$ differences to be computed. Therefore, we solve this problem in two steps.

First, to calculate the Shapley values for Transformer tokens, we decouple the self-attention flow and freeze the other unrelated values, to construct a linear version of Transformer. Then we sequentially select each token and mask the attention of all the other tokens to get the logits output, which represents the Shapley values. Specifically, in order to freeze unrelated values, we conduct two inferences sequentially in different models. The first inference takes place in the original Transformer (auxiliary model) to record the values that should be frozen, and the second inference is in the Transformer with masked attention (masked model) to calculate Shapley values.

Second, to further lower the time complexity of our method, we compute the Shapley values of each input token within one batch. The direct calculation of such a big batch (196 for ViT-base/16 [8]) has great time and space complexity. Therefore, we propose a fast batch propagation skill which lowers the computational complexity. Specifically, we manage to calculate the batch propagation using only one pair of attention and value matrices in the self-attention layer by permutation.

To the best of our knowledge, our method is the first class-specific explainability method without using gradients in Transformers, which is highly efficient compared to traditional methods relying on back-propagation to compute gradients. Qualitative and quantitative experiments show that our method outperforms states-of-the-arts in both accuracy and efficiency.

2 Related Work

2.1 Explainability for Transformer

Class activation mapping (CAM) methods aim to generate heatmaps with highlighted regions, which indicate the image parts corresponding to the prediction. In this way, the decision-making of CNNs can be explained. One of the most widely used methods, GradCAM [15], is the first to use gradients for class-specific explainability. It utilizes the gradients back-propagated to linearly combine the feature maps.

GradCAM achieves good performance in CNNs, but it has an inferior performance in Transformers [17], because they use self-attention rather than convolution to process images. Naturally, the attention scores in Transformers can be used for better explainability, as the attention on a token is related to its contribution to the prediction. With consideration for other computations in Transformers, including skip-connection and feed forward, attention scores in different layers are combined to visualize a heatmap.

Rollout method [1] tracks the information propagated through the model following the information flow in Transformers, including self-attention and skip-connection. LRP method [2, 3], as a general method for multilayered model, can be used on Transformers, which back-propagates relevance score from the predicated class to the input image. LRP can also be applied only to the last layer for better performance (Partial LRP [6, 18]). The attribution method [6] computes the relevance scores [2] based on the Deep Taylor Decomposition principle [12] and then propagates the relevance scores through the self-attention layers with gradients. Similarly, transition attention mapping (TAM) method [19] regards the computation process in Transformer as a Markov Chain and propagates the attention with integrated gradients [16] for visualization.

2.2 Shapley Values

As an additive feature attribution method, Shapley value method uses an explanation model (linear model) to explain the original complex model. It satisfies three desirable properties for model explanation, which are local accuracy, missingness and consistency. Local accuracy means that when approximating the original model with an explanation model for a specific input x, the two models should have same outputs at least for this specific input. Missingness constrains the features missing in the original input have no impact on the output. Consistency states that if one feature has a larger contribution to the output in a model f compared to another model g, it also has larger attribution.

The exact computation of Shapley values is challenging because of its complexity. For some subset $z \subseteq x$, the attribution of feature i is computed as $f(z) - f(z \backslash i)$. Then the Shapley value of feature i is computed as a weighted average of all possible subsets [11]. For image tasks, because the number of subsets is numerous, Shapley values are too time-consuming to compute in most cases.

3 Method

3.1 Decoupling Self-attention Flow

We start by defining the notations in Transformers. Suppose there are B self-attention layers in a Transformer. Let $x^{(b)}$, $Q^{(b)}$, $K^{(b)}$, $V^{(b)}$ and $A^{(b)}$ represent the input, query, key, value and attention matrix in the b-th self-attention layer, respectively. $Q^{(b)}$, $K^{(b)}$, $V^{(b)} \in \mathbb{R}^{s \times d_h}$, s is input length and d_h is feature dimension. The calculation within the b-th self-attention module is as follows:

$$A^{(b)} = \text{softmax}(\frac{Q^{(b)} \cdot K^{(b)^T}}{\sqrt{d_h}}) \tag{1}$$

$$x_{attn}^{(b)} = A^{(b)} V^{(b)} + x^{(b)} \tag{2}$$

$x_{attn}^{(b)}$ is propagated to the next self-attention layer through a feed forward network (FFN):

$$x^{(b+1)} = FFN\left(x_{attn}^{(b)}\right) + x_{attn}^{(b)}$$

$$= FFN\left(x_{attn}^{(b)}\right) + A^{(b)} V^{(b)} + x^{(b)} \tag{3}$$

In Eq. 3, it can be seen that the output of a Transformer layer, $x^{(b+1)}$, consists of three terms, which are the results of a feed forward module, a self-attention module and a skip-connection, respectively. Therefore, the information flow in Transformer can be separated into three sub-flows: the feed forward flow, the self-attention flow and the skip-connection flow.

According to the researches on attention visualization in Transformers [1, 5, 6, 19], we can make use of the attention matrix $A^{(b)}$ to get explainable heatmaps on model decisions. In our work, we decouple the self-attention flow, and leverage the idea of Shapley value method [11] to get the explainability of Transformers.

We first reformulate Eq. 3 to a linear function with respect to the binary variable $z \in \{0, 1\}^s$:

$$x^{(b+1)}(z) = \sum_i^s A_i^{(b)} z_i V^{(b)} + V_0^{(b)} \qquad (4)$$

where $V_0^{(b)} = \text{FFN}\left(x_{attn}^{(b)}\right) + x^{(b)}$. $A_i^{(b)} \in \mathbb{R}^{s \times s}$ equals $A^{(b)}$ only for the i-th column and zeros in other columns. $z_i = 1$ indicates the presence of attention on the i-th token, and $z_i = 0$ its absence. If all z_i is 1, $\sum_i^s A_i^{(b)} z_i = \sum_i^s A^{(b)}$.

Equation 4 reveals that, if $\text{FFN}\left(x_{attn}^{(b)}\right)$ (feed forward flow), $x^{(b)}$ (skip-connection flow) and $V^{(b)}$ (values in self-attention module) are constant, the output of a self-attention layer, as well as the logits output of a Transformer, are linearly decided by the presence of attention on each token.

According to [11], the Shapley values in a linear model can be calculated using the logits output and the expectations of the input. To calculate the importance of tokens in Eq. 4, if we consider the expectations of each token to be equal, the Shapley values can be calculated using only the logits output. In the last self-attention layer, the importance of the attention of the i-th token with respect to class c is:

$$\phi_i = \omega_c \left(A_i^{(B)} V^{(B)}\right)^T \qquad (5)$$

where ω_c represents the weights of fully connected layer f_c with respect to class c.

Consider all self-attention layers, we calculate $A_i^{(b)} V^{(b)}$ in each layer, and propagate through the Transformer to get the importance of the attention of the i-th token. Especially, we use two forward propagation processes (Fig. 1). The first forward propagation takes place in the original Transformer (auxiliary model) to record $\text{FFN}\left(x_{attn}^{(b)}\right)$, $V^{(b)}$ and $A^{(b)}$. The second forward propagation is in the masked model, where we replace $\text{FFN}\left(x_{attn}^{(b)}\right)$ (the feed forward flow) and $V^{(b)}$ in the self-attention flow with the values from the auxiliary model. The values $A^{(b)}$ in self-attention flow is changed to $A_i^{(b)}$ in each layer. The skip-connection flow is untouched so that the value change in every layer can be propagated through the whole network.

3.2 Fast Batch Propagation

To compute the importance for all tokens, according to Eq. 5, we have to make a forward propagation for each token, which is very redundant and time-consuming. For example, in ViT-base/16 [8], there will be 196 forward propagations, which is about 100 times slower than normal gradient-based methods. Alternatively, we can do all the calculations within one batch, whose batch size $N = s$. However, the storage consumption is too large, and the time consumption is still high.

Here we introduce a solution to speed up the batch propagation, with low space complexity. In computation of self-attention, we notice that:

$$A_i V = a_i v_i \qquad (6)$$

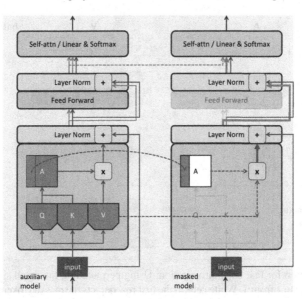

Fig. 1. Overview of our method. Left: auxiliary model which is identical to original model. Right: masked model for importance computation. Information flow from feed forward, self-attention and skip-connection are denoted in orange, green and blue lines, respectively. Dashed lines indicate the values introduced from the auxiliary model.

where $a_i \in \mathbb{R}^{s \times 1}$, $v_i \in \mathbb{R}^{1 \times d_h}$ represent the i-th column of A and the i-th row of V, respectively. Utilizing Eq. 6, we can compute Eq. 5 for all tokens in a single forward propagation with low cost, by permuting dimensions (1, 3) of $A^{(b)}$ and dimensions (1, 2) of $V^{(b)}$ as follows:

$$A^{(b)} \in \mathbb{R}^{1 \times (s \times s)} \rightarrow A^{'(b)} \in \mathbb{R}^{s \times (s \times 1)} \tag{7}$$

$$V^{(b)} \in \mathbb{R}^{1 \times (s \times d_h)} \rightarrow V^{'(b)} \in \mathbb{R}^{s \times (1 \times d_h)} \tag{8}$$

For a better understanding, we illustrate this permutation in Fig. 2.

Thus, without compute Eq. 5 repeatedly for each token, we can virtually compute the self-attentions for all tokens with the same cost for a single token:

$$\Phi = \omega_c \left(A^{'(B)} V^{'(B)} + V_0^{'(B)} \right)^T \tag{9}$$

where $\Phi = \{\phi_1, \phi_2, \cdots, \phi_B\}$. $V_0^{'(B)} \in \mathbb{R}^{s \times (s \times d_h)}$ is $V_0^{(B)}$ copied s times along batch dimension. We show the calculation of our method in Algorithm 1.

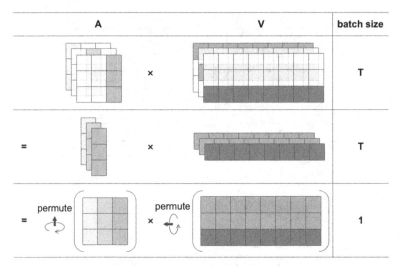

Fig. 2. Permutation for fast batch propagation. Using permutation, the batch size of a forward propagation drops to 1 from T. White cells in the first row depicts the masked tokens, whose values are zero.

Algorithm 1 Decoupling Self Attention.

Require: Auxiliary Model F_a, Masked Model F_m, Input Image x
Auxiliary Model
  calculate $y = F_a(x)$
  return $A^{(b)}$, $V^{(b)}$, FFN$^{(b)}$ for $b = 1, 2, \cdots, B$ (Eq. 3)
  permute $A^{(b)} \in \mathbb{R}^{1 \times (s \times s)} \longrightarrow A'^{(b)} \in \mathbb{R}^{s \times (s \times 1)}$
  permute $V^{(b)} \in \mathbb{R}^{1 \times (s \times d_h)} \longrightarrow V'^{(b)} \in \mathbb{R}^{s \times (1 \times d_h)}$
Masked Model
  calculate $\Phi = F_m\big(x, A'^{(1)}, \cdots, A'^{(B)}, V'^{(1)}, \cdots, V'^{(B)}, \text{FFN}'^{(1)}, \cdots, \text{FFN}'^{(B)}\big)$ (Eq. 9)
  return $\Phi \in \mathbb{R}^{s \times 1}$

3.3   Bridging Methods of GradCAM and Attribution

Apart from the outstanding explainability performance, our method also shows that the methods of GradCAM and attribution [5, 6] share a similar working principle.

For clarity, suppose an input with length $s = 1$, the self-attention matrix becomes a scalar a. Consider the 2nd-order Taylor expansion for Eq. 5, we have:

$$\phi_i(a) = \phi_i(0) + \phi_{i'}(a)a - \frac{1}{2}\phi_i''(a)a^2 \tag{10}$$

Equation 10 shows a way to approximate the Shapley value of a single token. Applying it to a token series, and only taking the 1st-order part of the expansion, we can get the Shapley value of the i-th token in a way that bridges methods of GradCAM and attribution, which involves the inner product of a self-attention matrix and its gradient:

$$\phi_i(A_i) = \nabla\phi_i(A_i)A_i \tag{11}$$

While in CNNs, GradCAM calculates the inner product of the feature and gradient of the last layer, with a global average pooling (GAP), Eq. 11 shows that in Transformers, GradCAM can be used on the self-attention matrix and its gradient of the last layer, without GAP. Our experiments show that GradCAM without a GAP can largely improve the explainability performance.

Furthermore, utilizing the 2nd-order part of Eq. 10, we can optimize GradCAM:

$$\phi_i(A_i) = \nabla \phi_i(A_i)A_i - \frac{1}{2}\nabla^2 \phi_i(A_i)A_i^2 \tag{12}$$

Our experiments show that Eq. 12 further improves the performance of Grad-CAM. However, the improvement is marginal, and the calculation of $\nabla^2 \phi_i$ is too time-consuming.

4 Experiments

4.1 Evaluation Settings

In this section, we conduct experiments to demonstrate that our method can accurately and efficiently explain the prediction of Transformer.

For qualitative evaluation, we compare the explainability heatmaps of our method with others. For quantitative evaluation, we follow [5, 6, 19] and conduct the perturbation and segmentation experiments to show the accuracy of our method.

Perturbation Tests. Perturbation tests [6] consists of positive and negative perturbations on the testing set of ImageNet dataset. In positive perturbation, image patches (tokens) are masked from the highest activations to the lowest in the explainability heatmap, while in the negative version, from the lowest to the highest. In positive perturbation, good explanation results will result in a steep decrease in performance, which indicates that the masked tokens are important to the classification score. In negative perturbation, good explanation results maintain the accuracy of the model, because the removed tokens are not related to the prediction. Therefore, the positive perturbation test with lower AUC means better explainability. In negative test, the higher AUC is better.

Segmentation Tests. Segmentation tests are conducted on ImageNet-Segmentation dataset using the generated heatmaps as soft-segmentation results of the input images. Higher segmentation accuracy represents a better explainability method. We use pixel-accuracy (acc), mean-intersection-over-union (mIoU) and mean-Average-Precision (mAP) as evaluation metrics.

In addition, we also measure the computation speed in segmentation test to show the effectiveness of our method.

4.2 Explainability Results

In this part, we report the performance of our method in visualization, segmentation tests, perturbation tests and computational efficiency. The Transformer we use is ViT-base/16 [8]. CAM-T1 and CAM-T2 are modified GradCAM methods with Eq. 11 and Eq. 12, respectively.

Visualization.   To qualitatively evaluate our method, in Fig. 3, we show the visualization results of different explainability methods with respect to the target class. It can be seen that, (1) our method generates more accurate visualizations comparing to others, and (2) CAM-T1 and CAM-T2 visually outperform GradCAM by a large margin.

Segmentation and Perturbation.   In order to quantitatively evaluate our method, we perform segmentation and perturbation experiments following the evaluation settings in recent papers on Transformer explainability [6, 19].

In segmentation tests, we utilize the mean value of heatmap as the threshold of segmentation on ImageNet-Segmentation dataset [10]. Pixel-accuracy (acc), mean-intersection-over-union (mIoU) and mean-Average-Precision (mAP) are used to evaluate segmentation performance. Table 1. reports the results, in which our method significantly outperforms all others.

Table 1. Segmentation results on the ImageNet-segmentation dataset (percent).

Method	Pixel acc	mAP	mIOU
GradCAM [15]	65.47	71.37	41.06
CAM-T1	75.61	83.92	56.73
CAM-T2	75.64	83.94	56.76
rollout [1]	73.54	84.76	55.42
partial LRP [18]	76.32	84.67	57.95
attribution [6]	78.96	85.93	61.15
TAM [19]	74.55	85.29	56.66
Ours (last)[1]	78.21	84.82	60.25
Ours	80.25	87.6	63.36

In perturbation tests, we sequentially mask out the tokens of input according to their importance, and compute AUC of the top-1 classification accuracy on ImageNet validation set [14]. In positive perturbation, pixels are masked from the highest importance to the lowest, and a lower AUC means better explainability, while in the negative version, higher AUC is better. Table 2 shows the results in which our method achieves the 1st and 2nd in positive and negative tests, respectively.

Efficiency. In traditional gradient-based methods, back-propagation is the most time-consuming computation. In our method, we manage to be class-specific with two forward propagations instead of using gradients. With the fast batch propagation method as we described in Sect. 3.2, the efficiency of our method greatly outperforms attribution method (Fig. 4). Rollout is the fastest, but it is class-agnostic. GradCAM is faster than our method, but the performance in Transformers is inferior. TAM and CAM-T2 are not shown in the experiment because they are too time-consuming.

---

[1] Only computes SHAP values for the last layer.

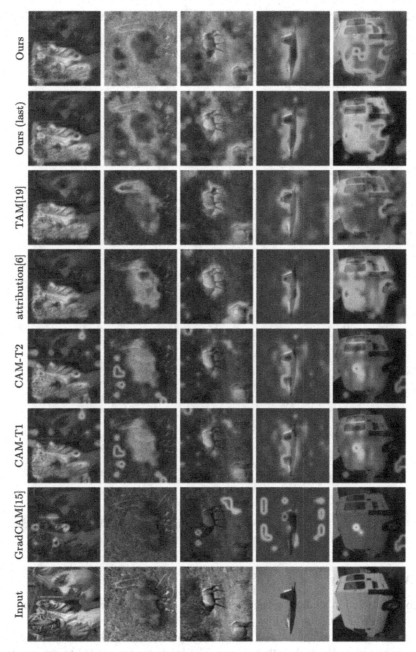

Fig. 3. Visualization results of some SOTA methods. It can be seen that heatmaps from our method are more explainable, and CAM-T1 and CAM-T2 generate better heatmaps than GradCAM.

Table 2. Perturbation AUC results (percent) for the predicted classes on the ImageNet validation set.

Method	positive	negative
GradCAM [15]	34.07	41.52
CAM-T1	19.27	50.85
CAM-T2	19.24	50.87
rollout [1]	20.05	53.11
partial LRP [18]	19.81	50.3
attribution [6]	17.03	54.21
TAM [19]	16.27	55.21
Ours (last)	17.9	52.5
Ours	16.2	55.07

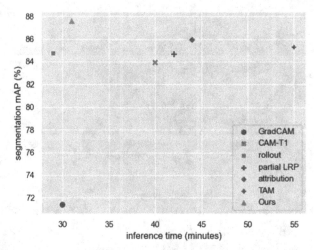

Fig. 4 Speed (minutes) versus mAP (%) in segmentation tests. Rollout is the fastest, but it is class-agnostic. Our method achieves the best accuracy with comparative efficiency.

4.3 Ablation Study

We conduct ablation studies on segmentation and perturbation tests to investigate the influence of different compositions in Transformer's information flow. We start with a naive masking method applied to input. To compute the i-th token's importance, we skip it over and mask all the other tokens. The logits output is used to represent the importance.

Next, we turn to mask attention matrix. We conduct the experiment on masking attention only (method A), masking attention and keeping V constant (method A + V), and finally our complete method, masking attention and keep V and feed forward flow constant (method A + V + FF).

Table 3 and 4 show gradual performance improvement on perturbation and segmentation tests from the naive method to our method, which proves that the decoupled self-attention flow is essential for Transformer explainability.

Table 3. Ablation study on perturbation.

Method	positive	negative
Naive	31.85	35.21
A	25.28	39.79
A + V	16.67	54.31
A + V + FF	16.2	55.07

Table 4. Ablation study on segmentation (percent).

Method	Pixel acc	mAP	mIOU
Naive	51.58	57.34	33.31
A	56.07	61.48	37.18
A + V	77.53	84.56	59.65
A + V + FF	80.25	87.6	63.36

5 Conclusion

In this work, we propose a class-specific yet gradient-free heatmap generation method for Transformer explainability, which has an outstanding performance in both the accuracy and efficiency. The contribution of each token is calculated based on the Shapley value method. To efficiently calculate the Shapley values, we decouple the self-attention information flow from the whole model, and turn the Transformer into a linear model. In addition, we use a permutation method to further speed up the calculation. Experiments show that our gradient-free method has a better accuracy and efficiency than other gradient-based methods. Furthermore, we show that explainability methods for CNNs and Transformers can be bridged under the 1st-order Taylor expansion of our method, resulting a significant accuracy improvement of the explainability using a modified GradCAM in Transformers. This also brings some new insights into understanding the existing gradient-based attention visualization methods.

In the future, we will continue to improve our method, and investigate its application for other models. With the accurate segmentation ability of our method, we will also explore its utility in guiding the training of image classification and object detection models.

References

1. Abnar, S., Zuidema, W.H.: Quantifying attention flow in transformers. In: Proceedings of the 58th Annual Meeting of the Association for Computational Linguistics, ACL 2020, Online, 5–10 July 2020, pp. 4190–4197. Association for Computational Linguistics (2020)

2. Bach, S., Binder, A., Montavon, G., Klauschen, F., Müller, K.R., Samek, W.: On pixel-wise explanations for non-linear classifier decisions by layer-wise relevance propagation. PloS one **10**(7), e0130140 (2015)

3. Binder, A., Montavon, G., Lapuschkin, S.: Layer-wise relevance propagation for neural networks with local renormalization layers. In: Villa, A.E.P., Masulli. P. (eds.) ICANN 2016. LNCS, vol. 9887, pp. 63–71. Springer, Cham (2016). https://doi.org/10.1007/978-3-319-447 81-0_8

4. Chattopadhyay, A., Sarkar, A., Howlader, P., Balasubramanian, V.N.: Grad- cam++: generalized gradient-based visual explanations for deep convolutional networks. In: 2018 IEEE Winter Conference on Applications of Computer Vision, WACV 2018, Lake Tahoe, NV, USA, 12–15 March 2018, pp. 839–847. IEEE Computer Society (2018)

5. Chefer, H., Gur, S., Wolf, L.: Generic attention-model explainability for interpreting bimodal and encoder-decoder transformers. In: 2021 IEEE/CVF International Conference on Computer Vision, ICCV 2021, Montreal, QC, Canada, 10- 17 October 2021, pp. 387–396. IEEE (2021)

6. Chefer, H., Gur, S., Wolf, L.: Transformer interpretability beyond attention visualization. In: Proceedings of the IEEE/CVF Conference on Computer Vision and Pattern Recognition, pp. 782–791 (2021)

7. Devlin, J., Chang, M., Lee, K., Toutanova, K.: BERT: pre-training of deep bidirectional transformers for language understanding. In: Burstein, J., Doran, C., Solorio, T. (eds.) Proceedings of the 2019 Conference of the North American Chapter ofthe Association for Computational Linguistics: Human Language Technologies, NAACL-HLT 2019, Minneapolis, MN, USA, 2–7 June 2019, Volume 1 (Long and Short Papers), pp. 4171–4186. Association for Computational Linguistics (2019)

8. Dosovitskiy, A., et al.: An image is worth 16x16 words: Transformers for image recognition at scale. In: 9th International Conference on Learning Representations, ICLR 2021, Virtual Event, Austria, 3–7 May 2021. OpenReview.net (2021)

9. Fu, R., Hu, Q., Dong, X., Guo, Y., Gao, Y., Li, B.: Axiom-based grad-cam: Towards accurate visualization and explanation of cnns. In: 31st British Machine Vision Conference 2020, BMVC 2020, Virtual Event, UK, 7–10 September 2020. BMVA Press (2020)

10. Guillaumin, M., Küttel, D., Ferrari, V.: Imagenet auto-annotation with segmentation propagation. Int. J. Comput. Vis. **110**(3), 328–348 (2014)

11. Lundberg, S.M., Lee, S.: A unified approach to interpreting model predictions. In: Guyon, I., von Luxburg, U., Bengio, S., Wallach, H.M., Fergus, R., Vishwanathan, S.V.N., Garnett, R. (eds.) Advances in Neural Information Processing Systems 30: Annual Conference on Neural Information Processing Systems 2017, 4–9 December 2017, Long Beach, CA, USA, pp. 4765–4774 (2017)

12. Montavon, G., Lapuschkin, S., Binder, A., Samek, W., Müller, K.R.: Explaining nonlinear classification decisions with deep, taylor, decomposition. Pattern Recogn. **65**, 211–222 (2017)

13. Radford, A., et al.: Learning transferable visual models from natural language supervision. In: Meila, M., Zhang, T. (eds.) Proceedings of the 38th International Conference on Machine Learning, ICML 2021, 18–24 July 2021, Virtual Event. Proceedings of Machine Learning Research, vol. 139, pp. 8748–8763. PMLR (2021)

14. Russakovsky, O., et al.: Imagenet large scale visual recognition challenge. Int. J. Comput. Vis.Comput. Vis. **115**(3), 211–252 (2015)

15. Selvaraju, R.R., Cogswell, M., Das, A., Vedantam, R., Parikh, D., Batra, D.: Grad- cam: Visual explanations from deep networks via gradient-based localization. In: Proceedings of the IEEE International Conference on Computer Vision, pp. 618–626 (2017)
16. Sundararajan, M., Taly, A., Yan, Q.: Axiomatic attribution for deep networks. In: International Conference on Machine Learning, pp. 3319–3328. PMLR (2017)
17. Vaswani, A., Shazeer, N., Parmar, N., Uszkoreit, J., Jones, L., Gomez, A.N., Kaiser, L., Polosukhin, I.: Attention is all you need. In: Advances in Neural Information Processing Systems, pp. 5998–6008 (2017)
18. Voita, E., Talbot, D., Moiseev, F., Sennrich, R., Titov, I.: Analyzing multi-headself-attention: Specialized heads do the heavy lifting, the rest can be pruned. In: Korhonen, A., Traum, D.R., M'arquez, L. (eds.) Proceedings of the 57th Conference of the Association for Computational Linguistics, ACL 2019, Florence, Italy, 28 July- 2 August, 2019, Volume 1: Long Papers, pp. 5797–5808. Association for Computational Linguistics (2019)
19. Yuan, T., Li, X., Xiong, H., Cao, H., Dou, D.: Explaining information flow inside vision trans- formers using markov chain. In: Explainable AI Approaches Fordebugging And Diagnosis (2021)
20. Zhou, B., Khosla, A., Lapedriza, A., Oliva, A., Torralba, A.: Learning deep features for discriminative localization. In: Proceedings of the IEEE Conference on Computer Vision and Pattern Recognition, pp. 2921–2929 (2016)

Detecting Data Drift with KS Test Using Attention Map

Tsunemi Nitta$^{(\boxtimes)}$, Yuzhi Shi, Tsubasa Hirakawa, Takayoshi Yamashita, and Hironobu Fujiyoshi

Chubu University, 1200 Matsumotocho,, Kasugai Aichi, Japan
{ntsunemi0122,shi,hirakawa}@mprg.cs.chubu.ac.jp,
{takayoshi,fujiyoshi}@isc.chubu.ac.jp

Abstract. Data drift is a change in the distribution of data during machine learning model training and during operation. This occurs regardless of the type of data and adversely affects model performance. However, this method can only analyze the drift detection results from the difference in the distribution of the output of a two-sample test, and does not analyze the actual degradation of the prediction performance of the machine learning model due to drift. In addition to class probability, we believe that detecting drift for changes in the local region that the model is actually gazing at will improve accuracy. In this study, we propose a drift detection method based on the Attention Branch Network (ABN), which enables visualization of the basis of judgment in image classification. In our method, drift is detected using the class probabilities output by the attention branch and perception branch, which constitute the ABN, and the attention map. The results show that the detection rate can be improved by introducing an attention map to drift detection in addition to class probability. We also observed that the attention map tended to shrink with drift.

Keywords: Drift detection · KS test · Attention branch network · Attention map · Maximum mean discrepancy

1 Introduction

Data drift is a change over time in the data distribution during model operation from the data distribution during model training. Drift occurs under various conditions, such as noise and loss-of-focus due to the deterioration of the camera lens over time, and misalignment and reversal caused when replacing the camera. When such drift occurs, the data distribution is different from that of the training data, which can degrade the performance of the machine learning model [5]. These factors make it particularly important to monitor changes in data distribution and detect drift during visual inspection and surveillance camera operations.

Drift detection is detected by comparing the data distribution during training with the data distribution during operation by using a two-sample test [8].

H. Lu et al. (Eds.): ACPR 2023, LNCS 14406, pp. 68–80, 2023.
https://doi.org/10.1007/978-3-031-47634-1_6

Rabanser et al. [9] proposed a method of detecting data drift caused by changes in the feature distribution of input data. Both methods detect drift by performing a two-sample test on the class probability distribution output by the trained model. However, these methods can only be used to analyze the drift detection results from the difference in the output distribution of a two-sample test, and do not analyze the actual degradation in the prediction performance of the machine learning model resulting from drift.

In this study, we propose a drift detection method using the Attention Branch Network (ABN) [2] and two-sample test, which enables visualization of the basis for model decisions. In our proposed method, drift is detected by performing a two-sample test on the class probability distributions output by the attention and perception branches that comprise the ABN, and on the attention map that indicates regions that contributed highly to model inference. The ABN is used to obtain an attention map for the drift data and to analyze the detection results.

2 Related Work

This chapter describes conventional drift detection methods and a method for visualizing the gazing region of a model.

2.1 Drift Detection

Three types of drift have been defined by Zhao et al. [12]: concept drift, label drift, and data drift. The concept drift means that the interpretation or concept of data for input data changes between model training and operation. The label drift means that the label distribution during model training changes from the label distribution during operation. It is known that seemingly trivial changes in the distribution of such data can affect the performance of the model's classifier [14], and when model decisions are made under uncertainty, even a change in the distribution of labels can affect the performance of the model [11].

Drift id detected by comparing the data distribution during model training with the data distribution during operation using a two-sample test. The two-sample test is a method to determine if there is a significant difference between two distributions. Typical two-sample tests used for drift detection include the Kolmogorov-Smirnov (KS) test and Maximum Mean Discrepancy (MMD) [3].

Lipton et al. [8] proposed a method for detecting label drift using KS test and MMD on the class probability distribution output by the trained model.

However, in addition to label drift, here is also data drift, which refers to a change in the feature distribution of the input. Examples of data drift include noise due to age-related deterioration of camera lenses and out-of-focus images. Thus, Rabanser et al. [9] conducted a study aimed at detecting both label drift and data drift. In their method of, drift is detected by performing dimensionality reduction on each data set and comparing the distributions with a two-sample test. The results show that the detection method using the KS test is the most accurate for the class probability distribution output by ResNet-18 [4].

2.2 Visualization of Model's Gazing Area

Class activation mapping (CAM) [13] is a method for visualizing the gazing region of a model. CAM can use the response values of the convolutional layer to create a heatmap representation of the areas where the network contributed highly to recognition. This visualized heat map is called the class activation map. CAM uses the average of the feature maps in each channel output by global average pooling (GAP) as weights and generates a class activation map from the weighted sum of each feature map. Thus, CAM requires a GAP to output the class activation map, which limits the model structure. In Gradient-weighted CAM [10], the weight of each channel is calculated from the gradient. Therefore, there are no restrictions on the model structure and the model can be generalized. However, these methods require processing such as replacing the fully connected layer with a convolution layer, which can cause performance degradation in image classification.

The Attention Branch Network (ABN) was proposed as an alternative to CAM. To avoid the performance degradation caused by conventional visual explanation models, the ABN applies the attention map generated from the visual explanation model to the attention mechanism, and simultaneously improves the performance of the visual explanation model and visualizes the gazing area using the attention map. The model is shown in Fig. 1. The attention mechanism is a method to improve the generalization performance of a network by emphasizing features in specific regions. The ABN consists of three modules: the feature extractor, attention branch, and perception branch. The feature extractor outputs a feature map for the input image. The attention branch consists of a convolution layer and a GAP as in CAM, and outputs an attention map. In the perception branch, the inner product of the feature map output from the Feature extractor and the attention map output from the attention branch is taken as the new feature map, and the final probability in each class is output. The feature extractor and the perception branch are constructed by partitioning the baseline network at specific layers, and the training errors output from the attention and perception branches are used for learning.

3   Preliminaries on Data Drift Detection

The KS test determines whether there is a significant difference by using the maximum difference of the cumulative distributions obtained by accumulating the two distributions as the statistical test quantity, as shown in Eq. (1).

$$D = \max |F_X(x) - F_Y(x)| \tag{1}$$

where D is the test statistic and $(F_X(x), F_Y(x))$ means the cumulative distribution function obtained from the sample (X, Y).

MMD estimates the distance between distributions using a kernel function to determine if there is a significant difference between two distributions. A kernel function is a function for computing data similarity. There are various types of

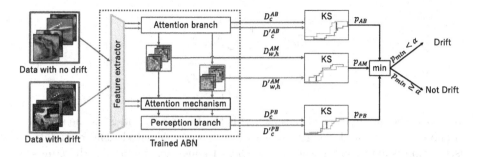

Fig. 1. Flow of drift detection by proposed method.

kernel functions, but the kernel function here is the Gaussian kernel shown in Eq. (2).

$$k(x, x') = e^{\frac{1}{\sigma}\|x - x'\|^2} \tag{2}$$

where σ is a positive constant and (x, x') is the input of the two distributions. The MMD is shown in Eq. (3).

$$\widehat{MMD} = \|\hat{P}_X - \hat{P}_Y\|_H^2 \tag{3}$$

where $\widehat{MMD}$ is the test statistic and $(\hat{P}_X \ \hat{P}_Y)$ is the characteristic distribution transformed from the two distributions (X, Y) by the kernel function. H means the space where $(\hat{P}_X, \hat{P}_Y)$ exists.

4   Proposed Method

In this study, we propose a drift detection method using the ABN. In ABN, the attention map obtained from the attention branch is input to the attention mechanism, and inference is performed by highlighting features in specific regions. Therefore, the change in the attention map due to drift should enhance the features in response to changes in the input image and improves the accuracy of drift detection. The flow of drift detection using the ABN is shown in Fig. 1.

4.1   Drift Detection Using Class Probability Distribution

The proposed method detects drift from three outputs, focusing on the different feature spaces of the layers that make up the ABN. The first is the class probability distribution output from softmax for the GAP of the attention branch, and the second is the class probability distribution output from the perception branch. First, the cumulative distribution used in the KS test is shown in Eq. (4).

$$F_n(x) = \frac{1}{n} \sum_{i=1}^{n} X_i(x) \,,$$

$$X_i(x) = \begin{cases} 1 \ (x_i \le x) \\ 0 \ (x_i > x) \end{cases}$$

(4)

where n is the number of samples, $X_i(x)$ is the frequency, and x_i is the sample. x denotes a class, and the frequencies for x_i are calculated. The cumulative distribution is expressed as the sum of these frequencies divided by the number of samples. Because the class probabilities output by the attention branch and the perception branch exist for C number of classes, the class probability x output per sample is $\{x_1, x_2, ..., x_C\}$. In drift detection using the class probability distribution, the cumulative distribution of class probabilities output by the attention branch, D_c^{AB}, is expressed as in Eq. (5) because a KS test is performed for each class probability in each class, where c is the class number of $1 \sim C$, n is the number of samples, and x_c^i is the class probability of class number c for the ith sample. Similarly, the class probability distribution D_c^{PB} output by the perception branch, the attention branch for the operational data, and the class probability distribution $(D_c'^{AB}, D_c'^{PB})$ output by the perception branch are calculated in the same way as in formula (5).

$$D_c^{AB} = \frac{1}{n} \sum_{i=1}^{n} X_c^i(x) \,,$$

$$X_c^i(x) = \begin{cases} 1 \ (x_c^i \le x) \\ 0 \ (x_c^i > x) \end{cases}$$

(5)

Next, the KS test is performed for the class probability of each class on $(D_c^{AB}, D_c'^{AB})$ calculated by formula (5), as shown in formula (6), and the minimum value of the result is p_{AB}. The p value is the probability that the test statistic obtained from the KS is greater than or equal to that obtained from the KS under the assumption that the populations of the two distributions are the same. To perform multiple testing where the KS test is repeated for the number of classes and the p value is calculated, a Bonferroni correction [1] is performed for the significance level α used to determine the drift. For the class probability distribution output by the perception branch, p_{PB} is also calculated as shown in Eq. (7).

$$p_{AB} = \min_c(\mathrm{KS}(D_c^{AB}, D_c'^{AB}))$$

(6)

$$p_{PB} = \min_c(\mathrm{KS}(D_c^{PB}, D_c'^{PB}))$$

(7)

4.2 Drift Detection Using Attention Maps

In the proposed method, an attention map showing the gazing region of the model is also used for drift detection. By applying the attention map to drift detection, it is possible to capture the characteristics of changes in the actual gazing region of the model, unlike the method [9] of Rabanser et al. Because drift detection using an attention map requires a KS test for each pixel, the feature distribution $D_{w,h}^{AM}$ of the attention map is expressed as in Eq. (8). Where (w, h) denotes the coordinate values of each pixel in the attention map. The feature distribution $D_{w,h}'^{AM}$ of the attention map for the operational data is also calculated in the same way as in formula (8).

$$D_{w,h}^{AM} = \frac{1}{n} \sum_{i=1}^{n} X_{w,h}^i(x) \, ,$$

$$X_{w,h}^i(x) = \begin{cases} 1 \ (x_{w,h}^i \le x) \\ 0 \ (x_{w,h}^i > x) \end{cases} \tag{8}$$

Next, for $(D_{w,h}^{AM}, D_{w,h}'^{AM})$ calculated by the formula (8), KS test is performed for each pixel in the attention map as shown in the formula (9) and the minimum result is p_{AM}. As with drift detection using the class probability distribution, the significance level α is adjusted by the Bonferroni correction depending on the number of times the KS test is performed.

$$p_{AM} = \min_{w,h}(KS(D_{w,h}^{AM}, D_{w,h}'^{AM})) \tag{9}$$

4.3 Flow of Proposed Method

In the proposed method, drift detection is performed by preprocessing the following data set and proceeding with Steps 1 to 3.

Step1. ABN Training
   The ABN learns using training data. Here, the ABN does not simulate drift on the training data but learns to improve the accuracy of image classification on the training data.

Step2. Calculation of class probability distributions and attention maps
   The specified number of samples is obtained from the data without drift and from the operational data and input into the trained ABN. For each data set, the class probability distribution of the attention branch and perception branch is calculated as in Eq. (5). The feature distribution of the attention map is calculated as in formula (8). The calculated distribution is temporarily stored for drift detection.

Step3. Drift detection
   The KS test is performed for each distribution obtained in Step2 and the p value (p_{AB}, p_{AM}, p_{PB}) is calculated for each distribution. Next, the results

are integrated by taking the minimum of each p value, p_{min}, as shown in Eq. (10). The p_{min} obtained is the one determined to have the largest difference between the distribution of the training data and the operational data when the KS test is performed on the three outputs. This enables the three outputs to be used jointly to detect drift.

$$p_{min} = \min(p_{AB}, p_{AM}, p_{PB}) \tag{10}$$

Finally, if $p_{min} < \alpha$, we conclude that drift has occurred, where α is the threshold value equivalent to Rabanser et al.'s method [9], and the Bonferroni correction is made on the basis of to the number of times the KS test is performed. This value is the significance level of 5% commonly used in two-sample tests.

5   Experiment

To investigate the effectiveness of the proposed method, we compare its drift detection accuracy with that of Rabanser et al.'s method [9].

5.1   Datasets

The MNIST [7] and CIFAR-10 [6] datasets are used in this experiment. The MNIST dataset consists of black-and-white images of handwritten 0 to 9 and contains 50,000 training images, 10,000 validation images, and 10,000 test images. The CIFAR-10 dataset, which consists of 10 object color images, contains 40,000 training images, 10,000 validation images, and 10,000 test images.

The training data for each dataset will be used to train the ABN. The validation data is defined as the data during training, since it has the same data distribution as the training data. Test data shall be used as operational data after drift simulation.

5.2   Drift Simulation

The drift simulation method used in this experiment is as follows.

Gaussian Blur. Gaussian blurring is the process of blurring an image using a Gaussian function. In this experiment, three levels of blur intensity are used, and the percentage of simulation applied to the test data for each intensity is set to {10%, 50%, 100%}.

Gaussian Noise. Gaussian noise is a process of adding noise by changing the luminance of each pixel in an image on the basis of a normal distribution. In this experiment, three levels of noise intensity are used, and the percentage of simulation applied to the test data for each intensity is set to {10%, 50%, 100%}.

Geometric Transformation. Geometric transformations combine rotation, horizontal and vertical translation, shear, scaling, and horizontal and vertical flipping on an image. In this experiment, there are three levels of strength for each element of the geometric transformation, and the percentage of simulation applied to the test data for each intensity is set to {10%, 50%, 100%}.

Class Imbalance. Class imbalance involves reducing the number of samples in one particular class. In our experiments, we have three levels of reduction of the number of samples for a particular class: {10%, 50%, 100%}.

5.3   Comparative Method and Evaluation Metrics

We compare the proposed method with that of Rabanser et al. by averaging the detection rate for all drift simulations. To evaluate the number of samples required for drift detection in steps, the number of samples used for drift detection is provided in eight steps. In the experiment, the process involves obtaining a specified number of samples from the training and operational data and inputting them into ABN.

5.4   Comparison of Drift Detection Rates

First, the drift mean detection rates of Rabanser et al.'s method and the proposed method on the MNIST dataset are compared as shown Fig. 2(a). As seen in the figure, the proposed method generally improves the average detection rate compared to the conventional method. Next, a comparison of the drift mean detection rate on the CIFAR-10 dataset is shown in Fig. 2(b), which indicate an improvement in the average detection rate. Moreover, the improvement is greater for detection on the CIFAR-10 dataset compared to detection on the MNIST dataset. These results, demonstrate the effectiveness of the proposed method for in detecting drift.

5.5   Identification of Trends in Changes in the Attention Map

Next, we determine the change in the attention map for the image that simulates the drift. Figure 3 shows the attention map for an image with no simulated drift and the attention map obtained for an input image with Gaussian blurring and Gaussian noise added. As seen in the figure, the gazing area tends to shrink when simulating the drift caused by Gaussian blurring and Gaussian noise. Even in cases where it is difficult to distinguish the change in the input image before and after the addition of Gaussian noise, as shown in Fig. 3(c), it is possible to understand the change from the gazing region of the model by acquiring an attention map. Because the proposed method uses the ABN, which uses an attention map for performing inference, obtaining these changes should improve the accuracy of drift detection.

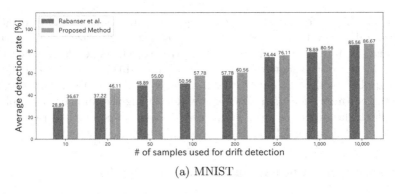

(a) MNIST

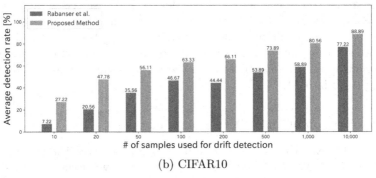

(b) CIFAR10

Fig. 2. Comparison of average detection rate of drift on (a) MNIST and (b) CIFAR-10 datasets.

5.6 Comparison of Detection Rates for Each Drift Simulation Method

Next, to analyze the average detection rate, we compare the detection rate for each drift simulation method for the CIFAR-10 data set, which had a large improvement rate. To facilitate the evaluation of the detection rate, the number of samples used for drift detection is 100 and 1,000. The results of the experiment shown in Table 1 indicate that Gaussian noise is the drift simulation method that contributes the most to improving the average detection rate. The detection rate for 1,000 Gaussian blur images was improved by 26.6pt, which is the next highest improvement rate after Gaussian noise.

5.7 Comparison of P-Value Adoption Rates

Next, to verify the effectiveness of the proposed method against the detection rate in each drift simulation method, we investigate the contribution of each p value, (p_{AB}, p_{AM}, p_{PB}), calculated in the proposed method. The contribution is the ratio of the number of times each p value is selected for successful drift detection, divided by the number of times all p values are selected. The results

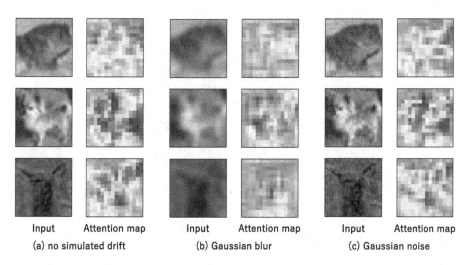

Input   Attention map   Input   Attention map   Input   Attention map

(a) no simulated drift   (b) Gaussian blur   (c) Gaussian noise

Fig. 3. Attention map changes due to drift.

Table 1. Comparison of each drift detection rate (CIFAR-10)

| Drift type | Method | # of samples to detect drift | |
		100	1000
Gaussian blur	Rabanser et al.	53.3%	57.8%
	Proposed	60.0%	84.4%
Gaussian noise	Rabanser et al.	24.4%	26.7%
	Proposed	53.3%	68.9%
Geometric transformation	Rabanser et al.	46.7%	73.3%
	Proposed	66.7%	86.7%
Class imbalance	Rabanser et al.	62.2%	77.8%
	Proposed	73.3%	82.2%

of the experiment shown in Table 2 indicate that the overall contribution of p_{PB} is high. However, in Gaussian blurring, p_{AB} is utilized about 48%, the highest among the three, while p_{AM} is utilized 12.6%. It can be seen that P_{AM} is employed about 9% in the Gaussian noise. This indicates that the method of integrating the three outputs is effective for drift detection. The attention map obtained from the ABN can be used for drift detection, and under certain conditions it is more effective than the method using the model class probabilities, contributing to an improvement in the average detection rate of drift.

5.8   Comparison of Two-Sample Tests for Attention Maps

We then compare the two-sample test methods for the attention map. As investigated by Rabanser et al. [9], the two-sample test used for drift detection includes

Table 2. Contribution of each p value (CIFAR-10)

Drift type	p_{AB}	p_{AM}	p_{PB}
Gaussian blur	47.9%	12.6%	39.5%
Gaussian noise	34.9%	8.9%	56.2%
Geometric transformation	41.6%	2.6%	55.8%
Class imbalance	46.7%	2.2%	51.1%

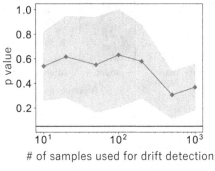

(a) KS test used for attention map.

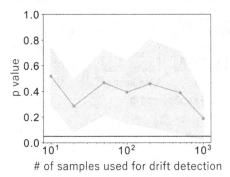

(b) MMD used for attention map

Fig. 4. Comparison of two-sample test methods used for attention map

the KS test as well as MMD [3]. Rabanser et al. showed that the KS test is the optimal test method when performing a two-sample test on the class probabilities output of the model. However, no experiments have been conducted on the attention map. Therefore, the two-sample test for $(D^{AM}_{w,h}, D'^{AM}_{w,h})$ in Fig. 1 is changed from the KS test to MMD for our experiment. The drift simulation method and significance level are not changed, but the number of samples used to detect drift is limited to 1000, when using MMD, as in rabanser et al.'s experiment. As an evaluation index, we use the change in p values relative to the training data that showed a change in the experiment.

Figure 4(a) shows the transition of p values when the KS test is used for the attention map, and Fig. 4(b) shows the transition of p values when the MMD is used for the attention map. The black line on the graph indicates the significance level. Because the experiment visualizes the evolution of p values for data with no simulated drift, a line graph and its surrounding range below the significance level indicates a false positive. As Fig. 4(a) and Fig. 4(a) show, there are no false positives when the KS test is used, whereas in Fig. 4(b), there are false positives when the MMD is used. It can also be seen that the results are less stable when using MMD. These results indicate that the KS test is a viable option when conducting a two-sample test on the attention map.

6 Conclusion

We proposed a data drift detection method based on the ABN and Kolmogorov-Smirnov test. The proposed method detects drift by integrating the class probability distributions output by the attention and perception branches, which construct the ABN, and the results of the KS test using the attention map. Experiments verified that the proposed method improves the average detection rate of drift compared to the conventional method. The drift detection results were analyzed by obtaining an attention map for the drift data. We also investigated the extent to which each output contributes to drift detection and demonstrated the effectiveness of using both the class probability distribution and the attention map to detect drift. Future issues include a detailed analysis of drift detection results, additional drift simulation methods, and the introduction of two-sample tests appropriate for each distribution to increase accuracy.

References

1. Dunn, O.J.: Multiple comparisons among means. J. Am. Stat. Assoc. **56**(293), 52–64 (1961)
2. Fukui, H., Hirakawa, T., Yamashita, T., Fujiyoshi, H.: Attention branch network: Learning of attention mechanism for visual explanation. In: Proceedings of the IEEE/CVF Conference on Computer Vision and Pattern Recognition (CVPR) (2019)
3. Gretton, A., Borgwardt, K.M., Rasch, M.J., Schölkopf, B., Smola, A.: A kernel two-sample test. J. Mach. Learn. Res. **13**(25), 723–773 (2012)
4. He, K., Zhang, X., Ren, S., Sun, J.: Deep residual learning for image recognition. In: Proceedings of the IEEE/CVF Conference on Computer Vision and Pattern Recognition (CVPR) (2016)
5. Hendrycks, D., Dietterich, T.: Benchmarking neural network robustness to common corruptions and perturbations. In: International Conference on Learning Representations (ICLR) (2019)
6. Krizhevsky, A., Hinton, G., et al.: Learning multiple layers of features from tiny images. Tech. reort, University of Toronto (2009)
7. LeCun, Y., Bottou, L., Bengio, Y., Haffner, P.: Gradient-based learning applied to document recognition. Proc. IEEE **86**(11), 2278–2324 (1998)
8. Lipton, Z., Wang, Y.X., Smola, A.: Detecting and correcting for label shift with black box predictors. In: Proceedings of the International Conference on Machine Learning (ICML), pp. 3122–3130 (2018)
9. Rabanser, S., Günnemann, S., Lipton, Z.: Failing loudly: an empirical study of methods for detecting dataset shift. In: Advances in Neural Information Processing Systems, vol. 32 (2019)
10. Selvaraju, R.R., Cogswell, M., Das, A., Vedantam, R., Parikh, D., Batra, D.: Gradcam: visual explanations from deep networks via gradient-based localization. In: Proceedings of the IEEE International Conference on Computer Vision (ICCV) (2017)
11. Zhang, K., Schölkopf, B., Muandet, K., Wang, Z.: Domain adaptation under target and conditional shift. In: Proceedings of the International Conference on Machine Learning (ICML), pp. 819–827 (2013)

12. Zhao, S., et al.: A review of single-source deep unsupervised visual domain adaptation. IEEE Trans. Neural Networks Learn. Syst. **33**(2), 473–493 (2022)
13. Zhou, B., Khosla, A., Lapedriza, A., Oliva, A., Torralba, A.: Learning deep features for discriminative localization. In: Proceedings of the IEEE/CVF Conference on Computer Vision and Pattern Recognition (CVPR) (2016)
14. Zügner, D., Akbarnejad, A., Günnemann, S.: Adversarial attacks on neural networks for graph data. In: Proceedings of the 24th ACM SIGKDD International Conference on Knowledge Discovery & Data Mining (ICKD) (2018)

Frequency Information Matters for Image Matting

Rongsheng Luo[1], Rukai Wei[2], Changxin Gao[1], and Nong Sang[1(✉)]

[1] Key Laboratory of Image Processing and Intelligent Control, School of Artificial Intelligence and Automation, Huazhong University of Science and Technology, Wuhan, China
{rongshengluo,cgao,nsang}@hust.edu.cn
[2] Wuhan National Laboratory For Optoelectronics, Huazhong University of Science and Technology, Wuhan, China
weirukai@hust.edu.cn

Abstract. Image matting aims to estimate the opacity of foreground objects in order to accurately extract them from the background. Existing methods are only concerned with RGB features to obtain alpha mattes, limiting the perception of local tiny details. To address this issue, we introduce frequency information as an auxiliary clue to accurately distinguish foreground boundaries and propose the **Frequency Matting Network (FMN)**. Specifically, we deploy a Frequency Boosting Module (FBM) in addition to the Discrete Cosine Transform (DCT) to extract frequency information from input images. The proposed FBM is a learnable component that empowers the model to adapt to complex scenarios. Furthermore, we design a Domain Aggregation Module (DAM) to effectively fuse frequency features with RGB features. With the assistance of frequency clues, our proposed FMN achieves significant improvements in matting accuracy and visual quality compared with state-of-the-art methods. Extensive experiments on Composition-1k and Distinctions-646 datasets demonstrate the superiority of introducing frequency information for image matting.

Keywords: Image matting · Frequency matting network · Frequency boosting module · Domain aggregation module

1 Introduction

Natural image matting is a crucial task in computer vision which involves extracting a high-quality alpha matte (i.e., the opacity of foreground object at each pixel) from an image, as shown in Fig. 1. This task has numerous applications in modern life, particularly in fields such as virtual reality, film production, and digital image processing. Generally, the input image is represented as a linear combination of foreground and background colors with alpha mattes [22]. This representation can be expressed mathematically as:

$$I_i = \alpha_i F_i + (1 - \alpha_i) B_i, \alpha_i \in [0, 1], \tag{1}$$

H. Lu et al. (Eds.): ACPR 2023, LNCS 14406, pp. 81–94, 2023.
https://doi.org/10.1007/978-3-031-47634-1_7

where α_i refers to the opacity of foreground objects at pixel i, I_i refers to the RGB color at pixel i, and F_i and B_i refer to the RGB colors of the foreground and background at pixel i, respectively. Obviously, the image matting problem is highly ill-posed since there are seven values to be determined, but only three values are known for each pixel of a given image.

Most matting approaches typically require a well-annotated trimap as an auxiliary input [2,9,10,16,18,27,28]. Since they depend excessively on the quality of trimaps to predict alpha mattes, automatic matting algorithms [13,14,20,28,29] have recently garnered significant attention from the academic community due to their ability to eliminate auxiliary guidance.

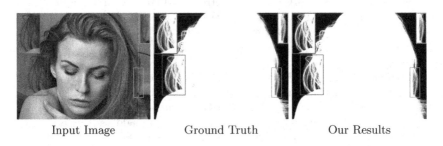

Input Image   Ground Truth   Our Results

Fig. 1. The alpha matte generated by our FMN and the corresponding ground truth on Composition-1k test set.

All these matting methods [13,14,18–20,28] share one common characteristic, i.e., they rely solely on RGB information for feature extraction, which limits the model to perceive local tiny details, e.g., changes of boundaries and illumination in hair. According to the studies of biology and psychology [32], some animals may beat humans in visual recognition since they have more wavebands (e.g., frequency information) than humans. Therefore, in this study, we claim that matting problems should not be limited to replicating the visual perception abilities of humans in the single RGB domain, but rather should incorporate the additional frequency information for superior recognition ability.

To this end, we propose a novel matting method named **Frequency Matting Network** (FMN). We first follow existing methods [13,28,29] to deploy the CNN encoder for RGB feature extraction. Meanwhile, we use Discrete Cosine Transform (DCT) to transform the image into the frequency domain for frequency feature extraction. However, the fixed offline DCT algorithm fails to address real-world images with various foreground objects and complicated backgrounds. This motivates us to design a Frequency Boosting Module (FBM), which consists of band-wise boosting and space-wise boosting modules (See Sect. 3.3). In this way, the model can adapt to complex scenarios for accurate frequency information collection. Furthermore, we propose a Domain Aggregation Module (DAM), achieving effective feature fusion from the two domains (i.e., frequency domain and RGB domain) to generate informative feature maps (See Sect. 3.4). Finally, we adopt the Progressive Refinement Module (PRM) following [29] and define a frequency perception loss to provide additional supervision for further frequency modeling.

Our main contributions can be summarized as:

- Different from previous matting approaches which only extract features in the RGB domain, we claim that matting should go beyond the RGB domain. Therefore, we present a new perspective that matting can be improved by incorporating frequency information with RGB information.
- To leverage information in the frequency domain, we present a novel matting network, i.e., **Frequency Matting Network (FMN)**, which comprises a Frequency Boosting Module (FBM) and a Domain Aggregation Module (DAM). The former assists in enhancing frequency signals and the latter effectively fuses features from RGB domain and frequency domain. Furthermore, we design a frequency perception loss to provide supervision in the frequency domain.
- Comprehensive experiments on two widely-used matting datasets (i.e., Adobe Composition-1k and Distinctions-646) show that the proposed method outperforms state-of-the-art methods by a large margin.

2 Related Work

In this section, we provide a brief overview of the image matting methods, including traditional methods and deep-learning methods as well as knowledge about learning in the frequency domain.

2.1 Image Matting

Traditional Methods. Traditional matting methods typically rely on color model established form the input image. According to the manner additional inputs are utilized, traditional matting approaches are further divided into sampling-based approaches and affinity-based approaches. Sampling-based methods [10,23] mainly calculate alpha mattes by representing each pixel inside transition regions with a pair of known foreground and background color. Affinity-based methods [1,4,11,12] propagate the alpha values from known regions to unknown ones based on the affinities among adjacent pixels, resulting in high computational complexity.

Deep-learning Methods. Deep-learning methods typically provide superior performance than traditional methods and compensate for their shortcomings. Trimap-based learning methods require annotated trimaps as additional inputs. In the pioneering work, [27] proposes an encoder-decoder network that takes an RGB image and its corresponding trimap as inputs to estimate alpha matte. [9] presents a context-aware natural image matting method for simultaneous foreground and alpha mattes estimation. [2] proposes AdaMatting, which disentangles the matting task into trimap adaptation and alpha estimation. To address cross-patch dependency and consistency issues between patches, [28] proposes a patch-based method for high-resolution inputs. [18] proposes a transformer-based architecture with prior-tokens which imply global information of each trimap region as global priors.

In contrast to trimap-based methods, trimap-free methods predict alpha mattes without trimaps. [30] proposes a structure with two decoders to classify foreground and background and fuses them in an extra network. [20] employs spatial and channel attention to integrate appearance cues and pyramidal features. [29] uses a binary mask as additional input and proposes a method to progressively refine the uncertain regions through the decoding process. [13,14] predict trimap parallel to alpha matte of the transition region and then fuse them to obtain the final alpha matte.

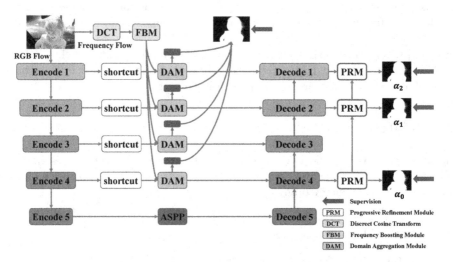

Fig. 2. The overall architecture of the proposed FMN. The frequency features from FBM and the RGB features from CNN encoder are integrated by DAM. Subsequently, the outputs from DAM, on the one hand, are fed to the decoder for alpha matte prediction at multiple resolutions. On the other hand, they are used for frequency perception to achieve more effective guidance for the network in the frequency domain.

2.2   Learning in the Frequency Domain

The frequency-domain compressed representations contain rich patterns for image understanding tasks. [8] conducts image classification task based on features extracted from frequency domain. [26] first converts information to frequency domain for better feature extraction and uses the SE-Block to select the beneficial frequency channels and simultaneously filter meaningless ones. [21] proposes that global average pooling(GAP) operation is dissatisfactory in capturing a range of features since it is equivalent to the lowest frequency elements from perspective of the frequency domain. Our proposed FMN benefits from existing trimap-free methods in terms of the model design. We also innovatively introduce frequency information into the matting task to perceive more local details.

3 Frequency Matting Network

In this section, we present the overall network architecture of our **Frequency Matting Network (FMN)** and provide details on its implementation. Additionally, we discuss the loss functions adopted in this paper.

3.1 Architecture Overview

We adopt ResNet34-UNet [15] with an Atrous Spatial Pyramid Pooling (ASPP) as the matting fundamental framework. As illustrated in Fig. 2, the input image is processed by two data flows, i.e., the RGB flow and the frequency flow. For the RGB flow, we use a CNN encoder to extract RGB features. While for the frequency flow, we utilize FBM after DCT to extract frequency features simultaneously. Then the features from two domains are fed into DAM for feature fusion. On the one hand, the output of DAM is processed by a convolution layer to reduce the dimension. The 1-d feature is used for frequency perception loss, which provides supervision in the frequency domain. On the other hand, the output is sent into decoder at the corresponding layer to reserve information lost in the decoding process. Finally, the outputs from Decoder 1, 2 and 4 are used by the Progressive Refinement Module (PRM) to selectively fuse features at different scales. We use weighted l_1 loss, composition loss and Laplacian loss to calculate loss in the RGB domain. Note that We provide supervision for the network in the both RGB domain and frequency domain. Therefore, we obtain high quality alpha mattes.

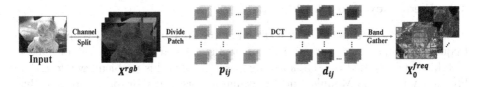

Fig. 3. The pipeline of Discrete Cosine Transform for an image.

3.2 DCT for Image Transformation

DCT utilizes an orthogonal cosine function as the basis function, which brings the energy of the image together and facilitates the extraction of features in the frequency domain. As shown in Fig. 3, the input RGB image x^{rgb} is firstly split into three channels, then we can obtain $\left\{p_{i,j}^c | 1 \le i, j \le \frac{H}{8}\right\}$ by dividing x^{rgb} into a set of 8×8 patches. Specifically, we divide patches densely on slide windows of the image for further frequency processing. Finally, each patch of a certain color channel $p_{i,j}^c \in \mathbb{R}^{8 \times 8}$ is processed by DCT into frequency spectrum $d_{i,j}^c \in \mathbb{R}^{8 \times 8}$.

After operations discussed above, each value corresponds to the intensity of a certain frequency band. To group all components of the same frequency into one channel, we first obtain $d_{i,j} \in \mathbb{R}^{8 \times 8 \times 3}$ by concatenating each channel $d_{i,j}^c$ and then we flatten the frequency spectrum and reshape them to form $x_0^{freq} \in \mathbb{R}^{\frac{H}{8} \times \frac{W}{8} \times 192}$. In this way, we rearrange the signals in zigzag order within one patch and each channel of x_0^{freq} belongs to one band. Therefore, the original RGB input is transformed to the frequency domain.

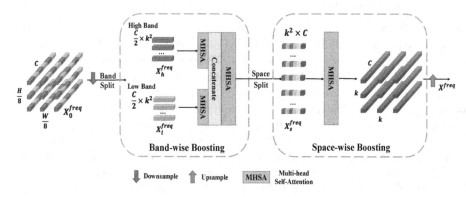

Fig. 4. The illustration of Frequency Boosting Module. It comprises two parts, i.e., band-wise boosting and space-wise boosting for interactions within individual patches and between patches, respectively.

3.3   Frequency Boosting Module

Although DCT is capable of transforming the image from RGB domain into frequency domain, its characteristic of having no learnable parameters makes it difficult to adapted to complex scenarios. To solve this problem, we design a Frequency Boosting Module, and the framework is shown in Fig. 4. Specifically, we boost the signals form two aspects, including within individual patches and between patches. On the one hand, we enhance the coefficients in local frequency bands, i.e., band-wise boosting, and on the other hand, we establish interactions between patches, i.e., space-wise boosting. Firstly, we downsample and partition the signals into two parts, the low x_l^{freq} and high signals $x_h^{freq} \in \mathbb{R}^{96 \times k^2}$, where k means the size. To boost the signals in the corresponding frequency bands, we feed them into two multi-head self-attention (MHSA) separately and concatenate their outputs to recover the original shape. Secondly, we utilize another

MHSA to reconcile all the different frequency bands, whereas the rich correlation information between each channel in the input features is captured. We denote the output of band-wise boosting as x_f^{freq}. However, the above procedures only enable interactions between different frequency spectrums within a single patch. Therefore, we need to establish connections between patches. To this end, we first reshape x_f^{freq} to $x_s^{freq} \in \mathbb{R}^{k^2 \times C}$ and use MHSA to model the relationships among all the patches. Finally, we upsample these features and get the enhanced frequency signals x^{freq}.

3.4 Domain Aggregation Module

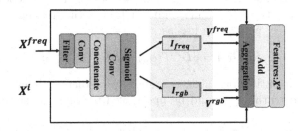

Fig. 5. The illustration of Domain Aggregation Module. It is designed to fuse features from the RGB domain and the frequency domain.

We have already obtained RGB features and frequency features by CNN and FBM, respectively. However, it remains a challenge to aggregate features from two different domains. To this end, we design the Domain Aggregation Module (DAM) to fuse these features, as shown in Fig. 5. The feature aggregation is a mutually reinforcing process, where frequency features are discriminative for local details while RGB features have a larger receptive field to perceive global semantics.

As CNNs are more sensitive to low-frequency channels, we first apply a filter to extract high-frequency channels manually. For an input frequency domain feature x^{freq}, the network can focus on the most important spectrum automatically. Specifically, we use a binary base filter f^{base} that covers the high-frequency bands and a Conv block to adjust the channels of frequency features for concatenation. Then we feed the aggregated features into another Conv block with two output channels and a sigmoid. In this way, we obtain the matrix I_{freq} for the frequency domain and I_{rgb} for the RGB domain, separately. Secondly, we aggregate features from two domains. Multiplied with the matrix and a learned vector $v \in \mathbb{R}^{1 \times C}$ to adjust the intensity of each channel, the aggregated features of each domain can be defined as:

$$X_s^{rgb} = I_{rgb} X^{rgb} \otimes V^{rgb}, \quad X_s^{freq} = I_{freq} X^{freq} \otimes V^{freq}, \qquad (2)$$

Finally, we can obtain the fused features by adding two domain features: $X^s = X_s^{rgb} + X_s^{freq}$. In this way, we can make full use of discriminative frequency information while maintaining semantic information to ensure that both integrity and details of the foreground can be preserved.

3.5   Network Supervision

To further capture the frequency information that differs from human perception, we introduce a novel loss, i.e., frequency perception loss. Besides calculating loss directly in the RGB domain, we also intend to provide supervision for the network in the frequency domain. And we assume that the predictions should be correct not only at each pixel location but also in the coefficients after DCT when they act on the original images. As a result, we design the frequency perception loss to make the network mine more information in the frequency domain. We can define frequency perception loss as:

$$L_f(\alpha_p, \alpha_g) = ||DCT(\alpha_g) - DCT(\alpha_p)||_2^2/q, \qquad (3)$$

where q is the quantization table, α_p refers to predicted alpha matte and α_g refers to ground truth. α_p should be upsampled to the same size as α_g before loss calculation.

As can be seen in Fig. 2, the four predicted alpha mattes under different resolutions are rescaled to the input image size and then supervised by the frequency perception loss L_f in the frequency domain. The overall loss functions in the frequency domain are as follows:

$$L_{freq} = \sum_l w_l L_f(\alpha_p, \alpha_g) \qquad (4)$$

where w_l is the loss weight of different scales. We set $w_{\frac{1}{8}} : w_{\frac{1}{4}} : w_{\frac{1}{2}} : w_1 = 1 : 2 : 2 : 3$ in our experiments.

We also provide supervision in the RGB domain. Previous scale alpha mattes preserve relatively complete profiles while they may suffer from ambiguous details, and current scale alpha mattes retain detail information while they may be subjected to background noises. Therefore, following [29], we adopt Progressive Refinement Module (PRM) to selectively fuse the alpha mattes from different scales with a self-guidance mask. Meanwhile, we employ their loss functions as overall loss functions in the RGB domain:

$$L_{rgb} = \sum_l w_l L(\alpha_p, \alpha_g)$$

$$L(\alpha_p, \alpha_g) = L_{l1}(\alpha_p, \alpha_g) + L_{comp}(\alpha_p, \alpha_g) + L_{lap}(\alpha_p, \alpha_g)$$

$$(5)$$

where w_l is the loss weight of different scales. We set $w_{\frac{1}{8}} : w_{\frac{1}{4}} : w_1 = 1 : 2 : 3$ in our experiments.

The final loss function for the FMN can be expressed as:

$$L_{final} = L_{rgb} + L_{freq} \qquad (6)$$

4   Experiments

In this section, we evaluate the proposed **F**requency **M**atting **N**etwork (FMN) on two datasets: Adobe Composition-1k [27] and Distinctions-646 [20]. We first compare FMN with SOTA methods both quantitatively and qualitatively. Then we perform ablation studies for FMN on Composition-1k and Distinctions-646 to demonstrate the importance of several crucial components.

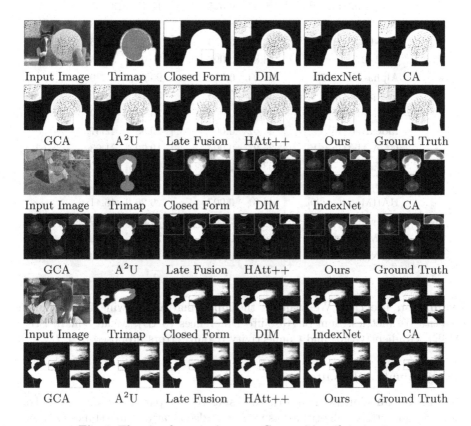

Fig. 6. The visual comparisons on Composition-1k test set.

4.1   Datasets and Evaluation Metrics

Datasets. The first dataset is the public Adobe Composition-1k [27]. It consists of 431 foreground objects for training and 50 foreground objects which are composed with 20 background images chosen from PASCAL VOC [6] for testing. The second one is the Distinctions-646 dataset which improves the diversity of Composition-1k. It comprises 596 foreground objects for training and 50 foreground objects for testing, and then we produce 59, 600 training images and 1000 test images according to the composition rules in [27].

Table 1. The quantitative comparisons on Composition-1k test set. Upper part: trimap-based approaches. Lower part: trimap-free approaches.

Methods	SAD↓	MSE(10^3)↓	Grad↓	Conn↓
Share Matting [7]	125.37	0.029	144.28	123.53
Learning Based [31]	95.04	0.018	76.63	98.92
ClosedForm [12]	124.68	0.025	115.31	106.06
KNN Matting [4]	126.24	0.025	117.17	131.05
DCNN [24]	115.82	0.023	107.36	111.23
Info-Flow [1]	70.36	0.013	42.79	70.66
DIM [27]	48.87	0.008	31.04	50.36
AlphaGAN [17]	90.94	0.018	93.92	95.29
SampleNet [25]	48.03	0.008	35.19	56.55
CA Matting [9]	38.73	0.004	26.13	35.89
IndexNet [16]	44.52	0.005	29.88	42.37
GCA Matting [15]	35.27	0.004	19.72	31.93
A^{2}U [5]	33.78	0.004	18.04	31.00
Late Fusion [30]	58.34	0.011	41.63	59.74
HAttMatting [20]	44.01	0.007	29.26	46.41
HAttMatting++ [19]	43.27	0.006	27.91	44.09
PP-Matting [3]	46.22	0.005	22.69	45.40
FMN(Ours)	**40.01**	**0.004**	**19.97**	**33.59**

Evaluation metrics. We evaluate the alpha mattes following four common quantitative metrics: Sum of Absolute Differences (SAD), Mean Square Error (MSE), Gradient(Grad) and Connectivity (Conn) errors proposed by [27].

4.2 Evaluation Results

Evaluation on Composition-1k test set. We compare the FMN with 6 traditional hand-crafted algorithms as well as 11 deep learning-based methods. For the trimap-based methods, we can generate trimaps by dilating alpha mattes with random kernel size in the range of $[1, 25]$. As the qualitative and quantitative comparisons shown in Fig. 6 and Table 1, respectively, the proposed FMN exhibits significant superiority over traditional trimap-based approaches. With respect to trimap-based learning approaches, FMN still produces much better results than DIM [27], AlphaGAN [17], SampleNet [25], IndexNet [16] in terms of all the four metrics. For example, IndexNet achieves SAD 44.52 and MSE 0.005, while our method obtains a superior performance with SAD 40.01 and MSE 0.004. Moreover, our approach is slightly inferior to Context-aware [9] but a little worse than GCA Matting [15] and A^{2}U [5]. However, our method can achieve equivalent performance without any auxiliary inputs, which is very convenient for novice users. The lower part of Table 1 illustrates that our FMN outperforms

Table 2. The quantitative comparisons on Distinctions-646 test set. Upper part: trimap-based approaches. Lower part: trimap-free approaches.

Methods	SAD↓	MSE(10^3)↓	Grad↓	Conn↓
Share Matting [7]	119.56	0.026	129.61	114.37
Learning Based [31]	105.04	0.021	94.16	110.41
ClosedForm [12]	105.73	0.023	91.76	114.55
KNN Matting [4]	116.68	0.025	103.15	121.45
DCNN [24]	103.81	0.020	82.45	99.96
Info-Flow [1]	78.89	0.016	58.72	80.47
DIM [27]	47.56	0.009	43.29	55.90
HAttMatting [20]	48.98	0.009	41.57	49.93
HAttMatting++ [19]	47.38	0.009	40.09	45.60
PP-Matting [3]	40.69	0.009	43.91	40.56
FMN(Ours)	**34.28**	**0.006**	**19.93**	**27.23**

the SOTA trimap-free approach to a great extent, which decreases SAD and Conn metrics heavily: from 46.22 and 45.40 to 40.01 and 33.59, respectively, indicating the effectiveness of our FMN.

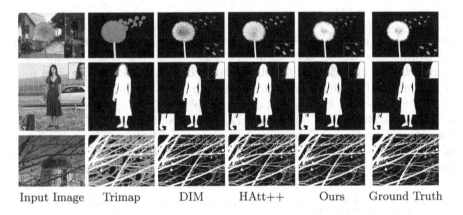

Input Image   Trimap   DIM   HAtt++   Ours   Ground Truth

Fig. 7. The visual comparisons on Distinctions-646 test set.

Evaluation on Distinctions-646 test set. We compare the FMN with 10 recent matting methods. We also use random dilation to generate high-quality trimaps [27] and relevant metrics are computed on the whole image. As qualitative and quantitative comparisons on the Distinctions-646 dataset displayed in Fig. 7 and Table 2, respectively, our FMN shows a clear advantage compared to all the mentioned matting approaches. It is noted that FMN outperforms trimap-free matting approach by a large margin, especially in terms of Grad and Conn metrics. We can see a sharp decrease on Grad and Conn metrics, i.e., from 43.92 and 40.56 to 19.93 and 27.23 for PP-Matting, which indicates that our model can achieve high-quality visual perception.

Table 3. Ablation Study on Composition-1k dataset.

FBM	DAM	L_{freq}	SAD↓	MSE(10^3)↓	Grad↓	Conn↓
			64.33	0.018	42.68	48.42
✓			42.61	0.007	22.16	34.57
✓	✓		40.24	0.004	20.26	34.05
✓	✓	✓	**40.01**	**0.004**	**19.97**	**33.59**

Table 4. Ablation Study on Distinctions-646 dataset.

FBM	DAM	L_{freq}	SAD↓	MSE(10^3)↓	Grad↓	Conn↓
			51.46	0.012	45.68	56.71
✓			35.88	0.009	23.16	36.57
✓	✓		34.38	0.009	22.64	36.77
✓	✓	✓	**34.28**	**0.007**	**19.93**	**27.23**

4.3   Ablation Study

We validate the effectiveness of different components on Composition-1k dataset and Distinctions-646 dataset, separately. The correlated evaluation values are summarized in Table 3 and Table 4. Compared with results in the first row, the utilization of FBM can bring considerable performance improvements on all the four metrics to a great extent. For example, SAD error decreases sharply from 64.33 to 42.61 on Composition-1k dataset and from 51.46 to 35.88 on Distinctions-646 dataset. The main reason is that FBM introduces frequency information into matting assignment and thus provides more precise local tiny details to compensate for RGB features. Moreover, the results also show that DAM plays a vital role in fusing RGB features and frequency features, which provides a slight rise in alpha matte quality compared to simply adding the features from two domains in the second row. In addition, the application of frequency perception loss to constrain frequency features has proven to be valuable, particularly in terms of Grad and Conn metrics. Specifically, we observe a significant improvement in these metrics, with values decreasing from 22.64 and 36.77 to 19.93 and 27.23, respectively.

5   Conclusion

In this paper, we utilize frequency information of an image to help predicting alpha values in the transition areas, i.e., foreground boundaries. To extract the discriminative cues in the frequency domain for complex scenario perception, we design a Frequency Boosting Module (FBM), which comprises band-wise boosting and space-wise boosting, to boost the coefficients in all the frequency bands. Furthermore, we integrate features from the RGB domain and the frequency domain through the Domain Aggregation Module (DAM). Besides, by providing supervision in both RGB domain and frequency domain, we can compensate for RGB information, which may tend to provide a large receptive field with details from frequency features. Experiments demonstrate that our proposed FMN achieves better performance than state-of-the-art matting methods on two commonly-used benchmarks. This work will inspire researchers to explore the utilization of frequency information in computer vision.

References

1. Aksoy, Y., Ozan Aydin, T., Pollefeys, M.: Designing effective inter-pixel information flow for natural image matting. In: Proceedings of the IEEE Conference on Computer Vision and Pattern Recognition, pp. 29–37 (2017)
2. Cai, S., et al.: Disentangled image matting. In: Proceedings of the IEEE/CVF International Conference on Computer Vision, pp. 8819–8828 (2019)
3. Chen, G., et al.: PP-matting: high-accuracy natural image matting. arXiv preprint arXiv:2204.09433 (2022)
4. Chen, Q., Li, D., Tang, C.K.: KNN matting. IEEE Trans. Pattern Anal. Mach. Intell. $35(9)$, 2175–2188 (2013)
5. Dai, Y., Lu, H., Shen, C.: Learning affinity-aware upsampling for deep image matting. In: Proceedings of the IEEE/CVF Conference on Computer Vision and Pattern Recognition, pp. 6841–6850 (2021)
6. Everingham, M., Van Gool, L., Williams, C.K., Winn, J., Zisserman, A.: The pascal visual object classes (VOC) challenge. Int. J. Comput. Vis. 88, 303–308 (2009)
7. Gastal, E.S., Oliveira, M.M.: Shared sampling for real-time alpha matting. In: Computer Graphics Forum, vol. 29, pp. 575–584. Wiley Online Library (2010)
8. Gueguen, L., Sergeev, A., Kadlec, B., Liu, R., Yosinski, J.: Faster neural networks straight from jpeg. In: Advances in Neural Information Processing Systems 31 (2018)
9. Hou, Q., Liu, F.: Context-aware image matting for simultaneous foreground and alpha estimation. In: Proceedings of the IEEE/CVF International Conference on Computer Vision, pp. 4130–4139 (2019)
10. Karacan, L., Erdem, A., Erdem, E.: Image matting with KL-divergence based sparse sampling. In: Proceedings of the IEEE International Con Computer Vision, pp. 424–432 (2015)
11. Lee, P., Wu, Y.: Nonlocal matting. In: CVPR 2011, pp. 2193–2200. IEEE (2011)
12. Levin, A., Lischinski, D., Weiss, Y.: A closed-form solution to natural image matting. IEEE Trans. Pattern Anal. Mach. Intell. $30(2)$, 228–242 (2007)
13. Li, J., Zhang, J., Maybank, S.J., Tao, D.: Bridging composite and real: towards end-to-end deep image matting. Int. J. Comput. Vis. $130(2)$, 246–266 (2022)
14. Li, J., Zhang, J., Tao, D.: Deep automatic natural image matting. arXiv preprint arXiv:2107.07235 (2021)

15. Li, Y., Lu, H.: Natural image matting via guided contextual attention. In: Proceedings of the AAAI Conference on Artificial Intelligence, vol. 34, pp. 11450–11457 (2020)
16. Lu, H., Dai, Y., Shen, C., Xu, S.: Indices Matter: learning to index for deep image matting. In: Proceedings of the IEEE/CVF International Conference on Computer Vision, pp. 3266–3275 (2019)
17. Lutz, S., Amplianitis, K., Smolic, A.: AlphaGAN: generative adversarial networks for natural image matting. arXiv preprint arXiv:1807.10088 (2018)
18. Park, G., Son, S., Yoo, J., Kim, S., Kwak, N.: MatteFormer: transformer-based image matting via prior-tokens. In: Proceedings of the IEEE/CVF Conference on Computer Vision and Pattern Recognition, pp. 11696–11706 (2022)
19. Qiao, Y., et al.: Hierarchical and progressive image matting. ACM Trans. Multimed. Comput. Commun. Appl. **19**(2), 1–23 (2023)
20. Qiao, Y., et al.: Attention-guided hierarchical structure aggregation for image matting. In: Proceedings of the IEEE/CVF Conference on Computer Vision and Pattern Recognition, pp. 13676–13685 (2020)
21. Qin, Z., Zhang, P., Wu, F., Li, X.: FcaNet: frequency channel attention networks. In: Proceedings of the IEEE/CVF International Conference on Computer Vision, pp. 783–792 (2021)
22. Rhemann, C., Rother, C., Wang, J., Gelautz, M., Kohli, P., Rott, P.: A perceptually motivated online benchmark for image matting. In: 2009 IEEE Con Computer Vision and Pattern Recognition, pp. 1826–1833. IEEE (2009)
23. Shahrian, E., Rajan, D., Price, B., Cohen, S.: Improving image matting using comprehensive sampling sets. In: Proceedings of the IEEE Conference on Computer Vision and Pattern Recognition, pp. 636–643 (2013)
24. Shen, X., Tao, X., Gao, H., Zhou, C., Jia, J.: Deep automatic portrait matting. In: Leibe, B., Matas, J., Sebe, N., Welling, M. (eds.) ECCV 2016. LNCS, vol. 9905, pp. 92–107. Springer, Cham (2016). https://doi.org/10.1007/978-3-319-46448-0_6
25. Tang, J., Aksoy, Y., Oztireli, C., Gross, M., Aydin, T.O.: Learning-based sampling for natural image matting. In: Proceedings of the IEEE/CVF Conference on Computer Vision and Pattern Recognition, pp. 3055–3063 (2019)
26. Xu, K., Qin, M., Sun, F., Wang, Y., Chen, Y.K., Ren, F.: Learning in the frequency domain. In: Proceedings of the IEEE/CVF Conference on Computer Vision and Pattern Recognition, pp. 1740–1749 (2020)
27. Xu, N., Price, B., Cohen, S., Huang, T.: Deep image matting. In: Proceedings of the IEEE Conference on Computer Vision and Pattern Recognition, pp. 2970–2979 (2017)
28. Yu, H., Xu, N., Huang, Z., Zhou, Y., Shi, H.: High-resolution deep image matting. In: Proceedings of the AAAI Conference on Artificial Intelligence, vol. 35, pp. 3217–3224 (2021)
29. Yu, Q., et al.: Mask guided matting via progressive refinement network. In: Proceedings of the IEEE/CVF Conference on Computer Vision and Pattern Recognition, pp. 1154–1163 (2021)
30. Zhang, Y., et al.: A late fusion CNN for digital matting. In: Proceedings of the IEEE/CVF conference on computer vision and pattern recognition, pp. 7469–7478 (2019)
31. Zheng, Y., Kambhamettu, C.: Learning based digital matting. In: 2009 IEEE 12th International Con Computer Vision, pp. 889–896. IEEE (2009)
32. Zhong, Y., Li, B., Tang, L., Kuang, S., Wu, S., Ding, S.: Detecting camouflaged object in frequency domain. In: Proceedings of the IEEE/CVF Conference on Computer Vision and Pattern Recognition, pp. 4504–4513 (2022)

Tomato Leaf Disease Classification with Vision Transformer Variants

Waheed Moonwar, Mohammad Rakibul Hasan Mahin$^{(\boxtimes)}$, Yasmin Nadia, Fahmid Bin Kibria, Aurnab Biswas, Fatiha Ishrar Chowdhury, Sifat E. Jahan, and Annajiat Alim Rasel

School of Data and Sciences, Brac University, Dhaka, Bangladesh
{waheed.moonwar,mohammad.rakibul.hasan.mahin,fahmid.bin.kibria,
aurnab.biswas,fatiha.ishrar.chowdhury}@g.bracu.ac.bd,
sifat.jahan@bracu.ac.bd

Abstract. Agriculture has played a significant role for many years. Its growing significance is attributable to the money it has generated. The full advantages of crop cultivation are, however, prevented by several circumstances. Organic plant diseases have a role in this case. For an agriculture dependent country like Bangladesh, extreme weather and heavy pesticide use are accountable for its economic crisis. This work aims to offer farmers visual information to facilitate the implementation of preventive measures beforehand. This work proposes four different transformer models for tomato leaf disease classification, which includes Vision Transformer (ViT), Swin Transformer (SwT) and Compact Convolutional Transformer (CCT). In addition to that, a distinct variation of the ViT algorithm was incorporated into the categorization process. It centers on employing a comparative analysis of various transformer models, which represents a novel contribution to the existing literature. The models have been trained and validated on the PlantVillage dataset which resulted in test accuracy of 95.22%, 82.61%, 82.82%, and 92.78% for ViT, SwT, CCT, ViT with Shifted Patch Tokenization and Locality Self Attention respectively.

Keywords: Plant Disease Classification · Vision Transformer · Tomato Disease

1 Introduction

It is vital to have timely diagnosis of plant diseases as it plays an important role in the production of healthy crops. As plants are a crucial source of food for us humans, it is necessary that there should be a reduction in the negative of plant leaf diseases. However, as the size of the symptoms are comparatively small and the local farmers do not have the knowledge and expertise to identify these diseases, it becomes a difficult task to accurately diagnose diseases in most cases. Artificial Intelligence (AI) has been used to aid with the notable convolutional neural network (CNN), disease recognition and the latest Vision

© The Author(s), under exclusive license to Springer Nature Switzerland AG 2023
H. Lu et al. (Eds.): ACPR 2023, LNCS 14406, pp. 95–107, 2023.
https://doi.org/10.1007/978-3-031-47634-1_8

Transformer (ViT) structure [1]. ViT variations have attention mechanisms that work with patches, and leaf diseases have location-specific spots, an attribute that is essential to identifying the disease. For this reason, ViT variations are a strong potential for identifying plant leaf diseases. Moreover, ViT detects the object based on how a human perceives an image. Generally, a person may concentrate on certain parts of the area of attraction; the ViT structure classifies pictures in the same manner. Both CNN and ViT have been successful in various plant disease identification tasks [2].

While pre-designed models such as ViT and ResNet are widely used in image processing tasks, they consist of a large number of trainable parameters that require a large dataset to generate a suitable output. Usually, models like these are trained on ImageNet and then are refined to implement transfer learning. Pre-designed architectures like these may struggle to obtain a fair result when trained on tiny datasets only if the domain of the second dataset differs from the first dataset. Moreover, pre-designed architectures are compute-intensive as big models might run slow due to lack of powerful machines and can cause issues for real-time applications. Furthermore, it is necessary to decide if transfer learning is always advantageous or whether lighter architectures can provide a decent output.

Considering the popularity and the growth of transformers in vision tasks [3], we use multiple variants of vision transformers in this study. Islam et al. [4] show how different vision transformer variants performs differently in terms of reliability and robustness. We select three transformer architectures experimented in [4] which are ViT, SwT and CCT. We further add one more model for experimental purposes. Summary of our work is given below:

- Four cutting-edge Vision Transformer models, CCT, ViT, ViT with Shifted Patch Tokenization and Local Self Attention, and Swin Transformers, have been implemented. Comparisons are made between their different parameters and results are produced.
- The models were trained and tested on the dataset, and the produced results were compared with each other to find out the most accurate Vision Transformer that gives the best results for tomato leaf disease identification.

2   Related Works

There have been several works on plant disease classification, mostly with convolutional neural network architectures. Li et al. [2] provides an overview of plant leaf disease classification using deep learning. Recently image classification tasks in different fields using vision transformer based models are increasing [5]. In this section, we describe literature related to our work.

The images of the plant have been surveyed to find out about the diseases of the specific plants. The images that make up the dataset are photographed under suitable conditions. For analyzing diseases in wheat rusk in [6], both aerial and non-aerial pictures were captured and labeled for object detection. Using object detection networks to localize the wheat leaf by recognizing the corresponding bounding box, this was the idea put forward by the researcher. Then, to determine the actual class, the cropped box was treated as the classification network's input. For this research, VGG16 [7], ResNet-50 [8], Inception [9], MobileNetV3 [10] and EfcientNet-B0 [11] are 5 Computer vision models developed for categorization. From comparative analysis, the most accurate classification model was the EfficientNet-B0 whilst having less computational complexity and cost.

In [12], various models are utilized, which include the C-DenseNet structure. The dataset in this literature was balanced according to the allocation of pictures in each class. All the images in the dataset were cropped for preprocessing because of which the images did not have a complex background. In addition to this, six class divisions are made for the magnitude of the disease intensity. The C-DenseNet was implemented to address the minute differences in the features of images in some levels. Dense layers were integrated into the convolutional layers, and the convolutional layers, comprising the channel-specific and location-specific attention methods, being applied. From the feature map in the channel attention module, features are retrieved using fully connected layers. Later on, with the help of sigmoid, the section of the input channel that needed better attention was found out. The output of the CBAM is achieved by multiplying the output of both the models (channel and spatial attention) with the input feature map. The main feature finding of the images is more precise, around 97.99% because of implementing the attention mechanism. M-bCNN structure [13], which is a matrix based convolutional neural network, was also used especially for small wheat leaf disease features. This structure could highlight the key characteristics of the images and overpowered the need of AlexNet [14] and VGG-16 [7] networks.

The plant village dataset [15] consists of colored images of numerous leaves and their associated diseases. However, the grayscale and segmented set can also be found. In [16], each version was subjected to individual testing with various multiple training and distinct configurations. The base models were AlexNet [14] and GoogLeNet [17]. The dataset versions were used for training various train-test split ratios, which are 1:4, 2:3, 3:2 and 4:1. The training was held twice, firstly with arbitrary weight parameters and then with transfer learning using pre-trained AlexNet and GoogLeNet on ImageNet. The models with transfer learning demonstrated greater productivity and functionality compared to those trained from zero, as thought of. The researchers in [18] used the tomato leaf images from the Plant village dataset and the tomato leaves were diagnosed with the implementation of a CNN. For their network, LVQ was used as the classifier and resulted in around 86% accuracy rate.

In [19], AlexNet and VGG16 architectures were implemented where segmented version of the tomato leaf images (from the Plant village dataset) were used. The background pixels have a value of zero and this paper resulted in a precision of 97.49%. Although segmented images make it simpler for a neural network to classify objects, they are rarely available in real-world situations. In such situations, either the pictures must be categorized manually, expensing time, or a neural network must be used. A neural network that is capable of segmentation is also capable of classification. Additionally, a classification-designed convolutional neural network can independently process images with non-zero backgrounds. Halil et al. attempted to attain a framework which can be implemented in immediate application using that class from the same dataset (plant village). They attained 95.6% and 94.3% accuracy by training with AlexNet and SqueezeNet [20]. For AlexNet and SqueezeNet [21], 150ms and 50ms respectively, were noted as the prediction time.

In their study, Mondal and Islam et al. [22] propose a method that utilizes a resource-constrained deep convolutional network to effectively identify and classify plant leaf diseases. This method yields superior performance with fewer factors, according to experimental study. Another lightweight convolutional network model [23] with LIME was used to predict plant leaf illness. It uses a lightweight model for low-end device implementation. The model resulted in 99.87%, 99.54%, 99.54% accuracy in training, validation and testing respectively. LIME was used for explainable predictions in order to ensure reliable disease diagnosis. Chy et al. [24] investigated the performance of ensemble learning in corn leaf disease categorization. The ensemble network employed in this research was an unique CNN model with dropout, CNN model with stochastic depth, and DenseNet101. It averages to 98.36% accuracy and outperforms the state-of-the-art models.

The papers [25,26] highlight the use of original variants of ViT (ViT-B16 having 16 and ViT-B32 having 32 attention heads) except modifying the classification in the agriculture sector. In [27], two ViT models are used parallelly for managing pictures having different resolutions. The papers [26,27] addressed a specific plant disease, while [25] is centered on the classification of the plant leaf. With increasing quantities of plants and their diseases, the classification process turns out to be more complex. In addition to that, the speed of forecast, a deciding factor for instantaneous categorization, was not taken into consideration. Implementing a complex framework for unhealthy leaf categorization may be rigorous, and rather simpler structures may suffice in some cases. This paper presents low-parameter frameworks for immediate unhealthy crop categorization using Vision Transformer. These frameworks will be run on 3 different pictorial data, and compared with CNN-based frameworks with similar complexity in terms of accuracy and prediction speed. Additionally, combinations of CNN and ViT were looked into, to improve accuracy, and the impact of image size on the outcomes will be examined.

3   Dataset

Fig. 1. Sample Images of dataset.

Table 1. Image Distribution of Plant Village Dataset.

Name	Number of Images
Bacteria Spot	2127
Early Blight	1000
Healthy	1591
Last Blight	1909
Leaf Mold	1000
Septoria Leaf Spot	1771
Spider Mites	1676
Target Spot	1404
Mosaic Virus	1000
Yellow Leaf Curl	5357
Total	18835

This research project used the publicly available dataset known as Plant Village [16] dataset which contains images of 38 different classes combining both healthy and diseased images. However, only the classes that belong to the tomato leaf were used. In total, there are 9 diseased classes and 1 class containing healthy images as illustrated in Fig. 1. Combining diseased and healthy images, the dataset contains around 18835 images. It was split into 80:10:10 ratio for train, test and validation respectively. In Fig. 1 we can see one image from each class. Moreover, in Table 1 we can see a detailed image distribution of our dataset.

4   Methodology

4.1   Vision Transformer (ViT)

The Vision Transformer, commonly referred to as ViT, is a framework for image classification that employs a Transformer-based architecture across many regions of the image. The given procedure involves partitioning a picture into patches of a predetermined size. These patches are next subjected to linear embedding, followed by the addition of position embeddings. The resulting sequence of vectors is then inputted into a conventional Transformer encoder. Assigning a learnable "classification token" to the sequence is the standard way for categorization.

Fig. 2. Normal and Patched Images.

Figure 2 shows the model overview. The conventional Transformer model is designed to accept a one-dimensional sequence of token embeddings as its input. In order to process 2D images, a common approach is to transform the image into a series of flattened 2D patches. In this context, (H, W) represents the resolution of the original image, C denotes the number of channels, (P, P) indicates the resolution of each image patch, and N is calculated as $N = \frac{HW}{P^2}$, representing the resulting number of patches. Notably, N also serves as the effective input sequence length for the Transformer model. Flattening the patches and mapping to D dimensions with a trainable linear projection is necessary since the Transformer employs constant latent vector size D throughout its layers. The patch embeddings are this projection's output. We prepend a learnable embedding to the series of embedded patches whose state at the Transformer encoder output represents the image, similar to BERT's class token. A classification head is fitted to the encoder during pre-training and fine-tuning. The classification head is an MLP with one hidden layer pre-training and one linear layer fine-tuning. To keep positional information, patch embeddings include position embeddings. Since 2D-aware position embeddings have not improved performance, we use normal learnable 1D position embeddings. The encoder receives the embedding vector sequence.

4.2 ViT with Shifted Patch Tokenization and Locality Self Attention

We have implemented one variant of the Vision Transformer, which is ViT with Shifted Patch Tokenizer and Locality Self Attention. The architecture of the model is illustrated in Fig. 3 and Fig. 4. First, the input image is spatially transformed, and the combination of transformed images are either left-up, right-up, left-down and right-down. Then, concatenation of the transformed images are performed to produce a concatenated feature, which is then forwarded to the patch partition layer to extract the patch features. Afterwards, we generate a 1D flattened patch, which is then propagated to the normalization and projection layers to generate the tokens for visual features.

It is also based on an attention mechanism similar to that of BERT. Initially, a dot product of the query and key is computed which emphasizes the attention score of the token. Then, it is propagated to a softmax activation layer, before being scaled and masked, to introduce non-linearity. Finally, the attention score is generated using dot product of the input value and the scaled score.

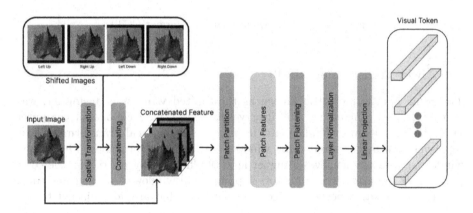

Fig. 3. Vision Transformer(ViT) with Shifted Patch Tokenization.

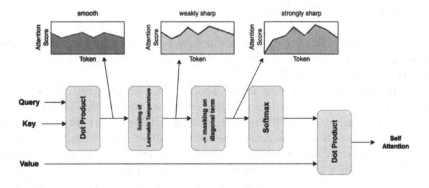

Fig. 4. Vision Transformer(ViT) with Locality Self Attention.

4.3   Compact Convolutional Transformer (CCT)

Compact Convolutional Transform (CCT), which incorporates convolutions into transformer models, is the idea put out by Hassani et al. [28]. The CCT technique improves inductive bias and eliminates the need for positional embeddings by using sequence pooling and patch embedding in place of convolutional embedding. One of the numerous benefits of the CCT is that input parameter flexibility is proliferated along with precision. Figure 5 shows the architectural design of CCT.

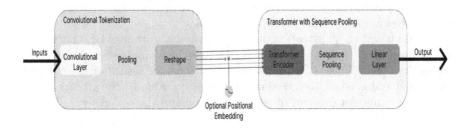

Fig. 5. Compact Convolutional Transformer(CCT).

4.4   Swin Transformer (SwT)

The Swin Transformer, also known as the **S**hifted **win**dow Transformer, was first introduced in reference [29]. It serves as a versatile backbone for computer vision tasks. In its most fundamental form, it is a hierarchical Transformer whose representation is computed using windows with shifting positions. The shifted windowing strategy achieves a higher level of efficiency by restricting the computation of self-attention to non-overlapping local windows. At the same time, the scheme makes it possible to connect windows that are not adjacent to one another.

5   Results and Analysis

To keep experiments fair for comparison between models, the same environment was used for all the models. All models were trained with Intel i5 7500, 24 GB of RAM and RTX 3060 GPU.

All the models were trained for 30 epochs. The learning rate is 0.001 and weight decay is 0.001. Moreover, a batch size of 32 was used. The model was trained with an image size of 100 by 100. Now for patch size we kept image size of 72 and patch size of 6, then to determine number of patches we used the formula $(\frac{image\_size}{patch\_size})^2$. For the loss function, Sparse Categorical Cross entropy was used. Model Checkpoint was used to save the best weights found during our training process. For testing, the best weights were loaded and evaluated the model with the test set.

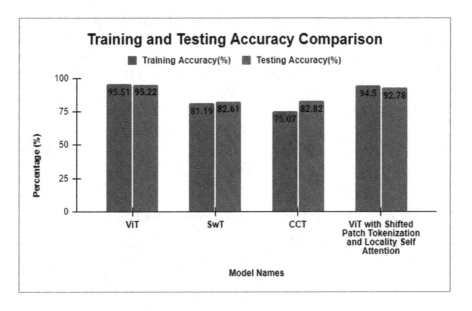

Fig. 6. Accuracy Comparison of 4 Models.

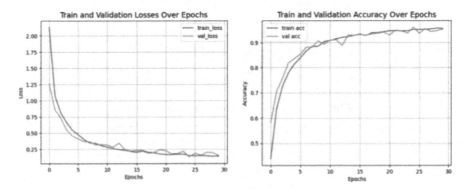

Fig. 7. Accuracy and Loss curves of ViT.

Using the Plant Village dataset, the evaluation of the performance of five different models was made. The dataset consists of 18,835 plant leaf images of 10 classes of tomato leaves affected by various types of diseases. The four models that were implemented here are Vision Transformers (ViT), Swin Transformers (SwT), CCT, ViT with Shifted Patch Tokenization and Locality Self Attention. Figure 6 shows the training and testing accuracy of each model. The Vision Transformer (ViT) shows the highest training and testing accuracy of 95.51% and 95.22% respectively (Fig. 7). Following this, ViT with Shifted Patch Tokenization and Locality Self Attention (Fig. 10) had a training accuracy of 94.50% and a testing accuracy of 92.78%. Afterwards, the Swin Transformer (SwT) had a

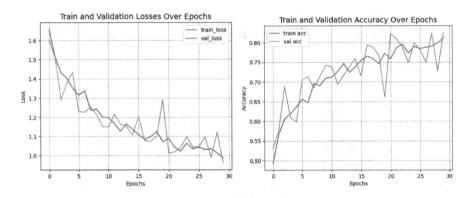

Fig. 8. Accuracy and Loss curves of SwT.

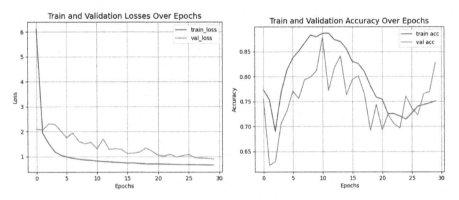

Fig. 9. Accuracy and Loss curves of CCT.

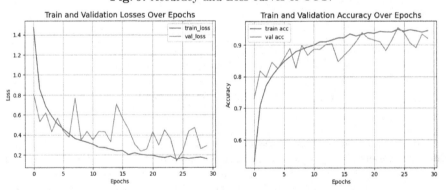

Fig. 10. Accuracy and Loss curves of ViT with Shifted Patch Tokenization and Locality Self Attention.

training and testing accuracy of 81.19% and 82.61% accordingly (Fig. 8). Lastly, from Fig. 9, it is evident that CC is the model with the minimal training accuracy of 75.07% and testing accuracy of 82.82%.

6 Conclusion and Future Works

To improve the accuracy and precision, ensemble learning may be used. The dataset may be extended in the future, which can help to further validate the efficacy of the models. Moreover, web implementation can be done, more ViT model implementations may be added, such as the recently introduced Mobile ViT architecture. Using more ViT Models could lead to more practical and accessible solutions for farmers and plant researchers. Web Implementation would allow more accessibility of the models. The farmers and researchers can be enabled to get access easily and utilize these models for real life applications.

Plants are one of the most important elements of the environment. Saving plants by identifying diseases is one of the most significant responsibilities for everyone right now. In this work, the Vision Transformer (ViT) has been used. For which, the result of this work can be gained quickly and the cost will be reduced. It is also important for farmers to understand the disease of the plant. This research can help to play a huge economic benefit while farmers can recognize the disease through it. By getting visual information through this project, the farmers can have a clear concept about preventions.

References

1. Dosovitskiy, A., et al.: An image is worth 16x16 words: transformers for image recognition at scale (2021)
2. Li, L., Zhang, S., Wang, B.: Plant disease detection and classification by deep learning—a review. IEEE Access **9**, 56683–56698 (2021)
3. Han, K., et al.: A survey on vision transformer. IEEE Trans. Pattern Anal. Mach. Intell. **45**, 87–110 (2023)
4. Islam, M., et al.: How certain are transformers in image classification: uncertainty analysis with Monte Carlo dropout. IN: Fifteenth International Conference On Machine Vision (ICMV 2022), vol. 12701 p. 127010K (2023). https://doi.org/10.1117/12.2679442
5. Khan, S., Naseer, M., Hayat, M., Zamir, S., Khan, F., Shah, M.: Transformers in vision: a survey. ACM Comput. Surv. **54** (2022). https://doi.org/10.1145/3505244
6. Safarijalal, B., Alborzi, Y., Najafi, E.: Automated wheat disease detection using a ROS-based autonomous guided UAV (2022)
7. Simonyan, K., Zisserman, A.: Very deep convolutional networks for large-scale image recognition (2015)
8. He, K., Zhang, X., Ren, S., Sun, J.: Deep residual learning for image recognition. In: 2016 IEEE Conference on Computer Vision and Pattern Recognition (CVPR), pp. 770–778 (2016). https://doi.ieeecomputersociety.org/10.1109/CVPR.2016.90
9. Szegedy, C., Vanhoucke, V., Ioffe, S., Shlens, J., Wojna, Z.: Rethinking the inception architecture for computer vision (2015)

10. Howard, A., et al.: Searching for MobileNetV3 (2019)
11. Tan, M., Le, Q.: EfficientNet: rethinking model scaling for convolutional neural networks (2020)
12. Mi, Z., Zhang, X., Su, J., Han, D., Su, B.: Wheat stripe rust grading by deep learning with attention mechanism and images from mobile devices. Front. Plant Sci. **11** (2020). https://www.frontiersin.org/articles/10.3389/fpls.2020.558126
13. Lin, Z., et al.: A unified matrix-based convolutional neural network for fine-grained image classification of wheat leaf diseases. IEEE Access **7**, 11570–11590 (2019)
14. Krizhevsky, A., Sutskever, I., Hinton, G.: ImageNet classification with deep convolutional neural networks. In: Advances In Neural Information Processing Systems, vol. 25 (2012)
15. Hughes, D., Salathe, M.: An open access repository of images on plant health to enable the development of mobile disease diagnostics (2016)
16. Mohanty, S., Hughes, D., Salathe, M.: Using deep learning for image-based plant disease detection (2016)
17. Szegedy, C., et al.: Going deeper with convolutions (2014)
18. Sardogan, M., Tuncer, A., Ozen, Y.: Plant leaf disease detection and classification based on CNN with LVQ algorithm. In: 2018 3rd International Conference on Computer Science and Engineering (UBMK), pp. 382–385 (2018)
19. Rangarajan, A., Purushothaman, R., Ramesh, A.: Tomato crop disease classification using pre-trained deep learning algorithm. Procedia Comput. Sci. **133**, 1040–1047 (2018). https://www.sciencedirect.com/science/article/pii/S1877050918310159, International Conference on Robotics and Smart Manufacturing (RoSMa2018)
20. Iandola, F., Han, S., Moskewicz, M., Ashraf, K., Dally, W., Keutzer, K.: SqueezeNet: AlexNet-level accuracy with 50x fewer parameters and <0.5MB model size (2016)
21. Durmuş, H., Gunes, E., Kirci, M.: Disease detection on the leaves of the tomato plants by using deep learning (2017)
22. Mondal, J., Islam, M., Zabeen, S., Islam, A., Noor, J.: Note: Plant Leaf Disease Network (PLeaD-Net): Identifying Plant Leaf Diseases through Leveraging Limited-Resource Deep Convolutional Neural Network.. Association for Computing Machinery (2022). https://doi.org/10.1145/3530190.3534844
23. Mahin, M., Moonwar, W., Chy, M., Rafi, F., Shahriar, M., Karim, D., Rasel, A.: Interpretable disease classification in plant leaves using deep convolutional neural networks. In: 2022 25th International Conference on Computer And Information Technology (ICCIT), pp. 645–650 (2022)
24. Chy, M., Mahin, M., Islam, M., Hossain, M., Rasel, A.: Classifying corn leaf diseases using ensemble learning with dropout and stochastic depth based convolutional networks (2023,6)
25. Reedha, R., Dericquebourg, E., Canals, R., Hafiane, A.: Transformer neural network for weed and crop classification of high resolution UAV images. Remote Sens. **14** (2022). https://www.mdpi.com/2072-4292/14/3/592
26. Wu, S., Sun, Y., Huang, H.: Multi-granularity feature extraction based on vision transformer for tomato leaf disease recognition. In: 2021 3rd International Academic Exchange Conference On Science And Technology Innovation (IAECST), pp. 387–390 (2021)
27. Thai, H., Tran-Van, N., Le, K.: Artificial cognition for early leaf disease detection using vision transformers. In: 2021 International Conference On Advanced Technologies For Communications (ATC), pp. 33–38 (2021)

28. Hassani, A., Walton, S., Shah, N., Abuduweili, A., Li, J., Shi, H.: Escaping the big data paradigm with compact transformers (2022)
29. Liu, Z., et al.: Swin transformer: hierarchical vision transformer using shifted windows (2021)

Toward Defensive Letter Design

Rentaro Kataoka[1]([✉]), Akisato Kimura[2], and Seiichi Uchida[1] [iD]

[1] Kyushu University, Fukuoka, Japan
`rentaro.kataoka@human.ait.kyushu-u.ac.jp`
[2] NTT Corporation, Kanagawa, Japan

Abstract. A major approach for defending against adversarial attacks aims at controlling only image classifiers to be more resilient, and it does not care about visual objects, such as pandas and cars, in images. This means that visual objects themselves cannot take any defensive actions, and they are still vulnerable to adversarial attacks. In contrast, letters are artificial symbols, and we can freely control their appearance unless losing their readability. In other words, we can make the letters more defensive to the attacks. This paper poses three research questions related to the adversarial vulnerability of letter images: (1) How defensive are the letters against adversarial attacks? (2) Can we estimate how defensive a given letter image is before attacks? (3) Can we control the letter images to be more defensive against adversarial attacks? For answering the first and second questions, we measure the *defensibility* of letters by employing Iterative Fast Gradient Sign Method (I-FGSM) and then build a deep regression model for estimating the defensibility of each letter image. We also propose a two-step method based on a generative adversarial network (GAN) for generating character images with higher defensibility, which solves the third research question.

Keywords: Adversarial attack · Adversarial defense · Letter image generation

1 Introduction

Adversarial attack, one of the hot topics in recent machine learning research, is a technique to give artificial distortions or deformations to a sample so that a classifier misrecognizes the sample. The main focus of adversarial attack research is to analyze the vulnerability of deep neural network (DNN)-based classifiers. Many attack algorithms have been developed so far [2] and applied to various types of data, such as images, speech signals, and texts. Especially for images, we can find various attack algorithms [1,5,6,8,12]. In a recent survey [6], major image attack algorithms are classified into gradient-based, transfer/score-based, decision-based, and approximation-based algorithms . *Adversarial defense*, also a hot topic, is a technique to make the DNN-classifiers resilient to adversarial attacks by utilizing the results of analyzing adversarial vulnerability. Like the attack algorithms, many defense algorithms have been proposed, and they

H. Lu et al. (Eds.): ACPR 2023, LNCS 14406, pp. 108–122, 2023.
https://doi.org/10.1007/978-3-031-47634-1_9

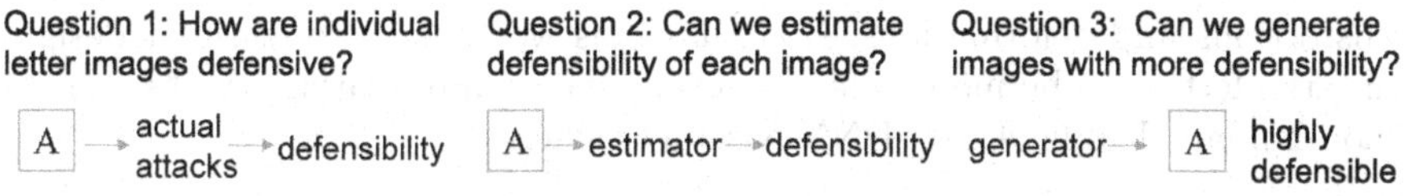

Fig. 1. Three research questions on adversarial attack and defense of letter images.

are classified into gradient masking (including adversarial training and defensive distillation), auxiliary detection models, statistical methods, preprocessing techniques, classifier ensembles, and proximity measurements [6].

Meanwhile, this paper focuses on the *defensibility* of *letter images* (such as 'A'-'Z'); in other words, we focus not on the defensibility (or vulnerability) of classifiers but on the defensibility of classification subjects, i.e., letters. Specifically, we set three research questions on adversarial attacks and defenses of letter images, as summarized in Fig. 1. These questions are specific to letter images because they have unique characteristics as *artificial symbols designed by humans for humans*, whereas general visual objects, such as "pandas" and "cars," do not. In the following, the three questions are detailed with their purposes.

- **Question 1: How defensive are the letters against adversarial attacks?** We, humans, can read letters that are attacked by various distortions and deformations, such as perspective distortions, handwriting fluctuations, partial occlusions, blurs, dot noise, and styles (i.e., typeface designs, such as Romans, Grotesque, and Geometric). Therefore, for "human classifiers," letter images are already robust to these attacks. In other words, the letter images are designed to keep their discriminability (at least for humans) under various attacks. In contrast, we do not know how letter images might have high defensibility against attacks on DNN-based classifiers.
- **Question 2: Can we estimate how defensive a given letter image is before attacks?** Different letter images (i.e., letter appearances) may have different strengths against the attacks. If so, the strength should depend on the appearance of the letter images. In other words, we need to confirm the possibility of estimating the defensibility of each image without actual attacks.
- **Question 3: Can we control the letter images to be more defensive against adversarial attacks?** As noted above, standard approaches for defending against adversarial attacks try to control only image classifiers to be more resilient, and they do not care about visual objects (such as "pandas" and "cars") in images. In other words, visual objects are just left to be attacked without any defensive actions. However, letters are artificial symbols, and we can freely control their appearance unless losing their readability. In other words, we can *design* the letter images to be more defensive against the attacks. Over thousands of years of our history, humans have controlled the letters from cuneiform to the modern Latin alphabet so that they would be defensible (i.e., readable) to human classifiers even under the above

distortions and deformations. Now, it seems worthwhile to consider design-ing the letters to be more defensive even against adversarial attacks against non-human classifiers, i.e., DNN-based classifiers.

Our main contributions are to give possible answers to the above three ques-tions, which are summarized as follows.

- **Measuring Defensibility by attacking**: The first contribution is to mea-sure the actual defensibility of each letter image $\mathbf{x}$ by repetitive attacks. We define the defensibility of a letter image $\mathbf{x}$ as $k(\mathbf{x}) = k$ when $\mathbf{x}$ is first mis-recognized only after k attacks. As an attacking algorithm, we use Iterative Fast Gradient Sign Method (I-FGSM) [4], one of the most popular repeti-tive attacking algorithms. We also observe the differences in the defensibility between letter classes.
- **Estimating defensibility by regression**: The second contribution is to realize a deep regression model that can estimate the defensibility $k(\mathbf{x})$ of each letter image without actual attacks. More formally, we build a nonlinear function $\hat{k} = \hat{k}(\mathbf{x})$ that obtains an estimate $\hat{k}$ of the defensibility of a letter image $\mathbf{x}$. If we can obtain such a regression model $\hat{k}(\cdot)$ accurately, it will experimentally prove a mutual relationship between letter shapes and their defensibility.
- **Generating defensive letter images**: The third contribution is to propose a two-step method for generating letter images with higher defensibility based on a generative adversarial network (GAN). After pre-training the model with a standard GAN framework for generating readable letter images, we further train the generator with a new loss function to increase the defensibility of generated letter images.

To the authors' best knowledge, it is the first attempt to understand the defensibility (or vulnerability) of letter images from the viewpoint of adversarial attack and defense. Although this defensibility is evaluated by a non-human classifier (i.e., a DNN-based classifier), we expect that the results will help our future work to understand the robustness of letters for humans.

2   Adversarial Attacks

As noted in Sect. 1, many algorithms for adversarial attacks and defenses have already been proposed. Since the main focus of this paper is not to propose some new algorithm for adversarial attacks and defenses, we will not go into their details. For readers interested in them, please refer to recent surveys, such as Mechado et al. [6].

In our trial, we use Iterative Fast Gradient Sign Method (I-FGSM) [4]. We employ I-FGSM because of two reasons. First, I-FGSM is a general attack method and gives the basis of state-of-the-art attack methods [10,11]. Second, I-FGSM is a repetitive attack method, and thus suitable for quantitatively mea-suring the defensibility of each sample. Using different attack methods might produce different results than this paper. (In fact, any attempts at adversarial attack and defense cannot escape from the dependency on the attack method.) We expect that choosing I-FGSM makes our results as general as possible.

I-FGSM can be seen as an extension of a classical gradient-based attack called Fast Gradient Sign Method (FGSM) [3]. FGSM uses the gradient $\nabla_\theta J(\theta, \mathbf{x}, y)$ with respect to the target model to be attacked for generating adversarial examples $\mathbf{x}'$, where θ is the parameters of the target model, $\mathbf{x}$ is the input example, y is the ground-truth class label for $\mathbf{x}$, and $J(\theta, \mathbf{x}, y)$ is the loss function for training the model. Specifically, the adversarial example $\mathbf{x}'$ generated from $\mathbf{x}$ by FGSM is expressed as:

$$\mathbf{x}' = \mathbf{x} + \epsilon \cdot \text{sign}\left(\nabla_\theta J(\theta, \mathbf{x}, y)\right), \tag{1}$$

where the second term on the right side is an adversarial perturbation, and ϵ controls the amplitude of the perturbation. The perturbed example $\mathbf{x}'$ is expected to give a larger loss value than $\mathbf{x}$, and thus $\mathbf{x}'$ can behave as an adversarial example.

Roughly speaking, I-FGSM generates adversarial examples by repeating FGSM of Eq. (1). By repetitive attack operations, I-FGSM will generate "more adversarial" examples. In fact, we can repeat Eq. (1) until $\mathbf{x}'$ is misrecognized as a different class from the original class of $\mathbf{x}$. Formally, this repetitive attacking process is described as follows:

$$\mathbf{x}'_{t+1} = \mathbf{x}'_t + \epsilon \cdot \text{sign}\left(\nabla_\theta J(\theta, \mathbf{x}'_t, y)\right), \tag{2}$$

where t is the number of attacking iterations.

As noted in Sect. 1, all letters are designed by humans. In the past, there were typefaces for not only human classifiers but also computer classifiers. For example, OCR and MICR fonts were designed for OCR (optical character reader) systems and MICR (magnetic-ink character reader) systems, respectively. Letter shapes of OCR fonts are designed to have clear discriminability. For example, '0' of an OCR font called "OCR-A" (developed in 1968) looks like '◇' to keep discriminability from '0' (zero). Literature [9] designs characters where computer-readable class information is embedded in a special way for perspective-invariant information retrieval. These classic attempts are pioneering works in which defensive letter designs were made for non-human classifiers against certain types of attacks.

3 Measuring Defensibility by Attacking

3.1 Attacking Letter Images by I-FGSM

To answer Question 1 in Sect. 1 (*"How are the letters defensive against adversarial attacks?"*), we attack letter images by I-FGSM and then measure their actual defensibility. Specifically, we first train a CNN for letter classification using training and validation sets of letter images. Then, we classify the letter images in a test set and discard the misrecognized images. Finally, we run I-FGSM for each non-discarded image $\mathbf{x}$. The number of attacking iterations until misrecognition for $\mathbf{x}$ is determined as the defensibility $k(\mathbf{x})$. Note that $k(\mathbf{x}) > 0$ for any correctly recognized (i.e., non-discarded) image $\mathbf{x}$.

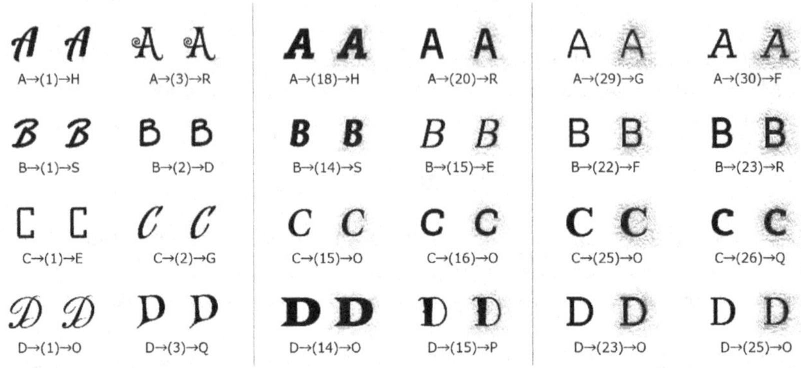

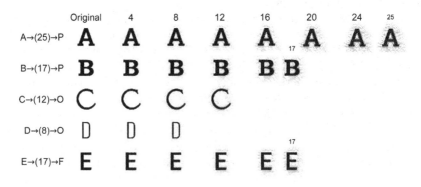

Fig. 2. Examples of attacked letter images. For each example, the original image and the attack result are shown. The notation "A →(1)→ H" means that the original class is 'A,' the number of attacking operations (i.e., defensibility k) is 1, and the misrecognized class is 'H.'

Fig. 3. The attacking process by I-FGSM.

We set the parameter ϵ of the step size in FGSM at 0.02 through a preliminary experiment. Although there is neither a theoretical nor experimental criterion to determine the value of ϵ, it is inappropriate to set it at a large value. This is because most images are misrecognized just by a one-time attack with a large ϵ, and we cannot observe the different defensibility among letter images for this case. Setting ϵ at a very small value is also inappropriate because it requires too many iterations until misrecognition. Considering these points in preliminary experiments, we set $\epsilon = 0.02$ as a reasonable compromise. Under this setting, the defensibility k fell in the range $[1, 32]$ for any image used in the experiment.

3.2   Attack Experiment

Letter Image Dataset. We used Google Fonts to collect the letter images to be attacked. Specifically, we used images of 26 alphabets ('A'-'Z') of 3,124 different fonts from Google Fonts. Each letter image is a 64×64 binary image with ± 1 pixel values. All the images $(26 \times 3,124)$ are split into three font-disjoint datasets, i.e., training, validation, and test sets, and they contain about 30,000, 4,000, and 30,000 images, respectively.

CNN to Be Attacked. A simple CNN C with two convolutional layers and two fully-connected layers is trained for the 26-class classification task. Each convolutional layer is accompanied by ReLU activation and max-pooling. In its training process, the negative log-likelihood loss is used and minimized by AdaDelta. The training process is terminated by the standard early stop criterion, whereby training stops if the validation loss does not decrease over the next 10 epochs. After training, the training, validation, and test accuracies are 98.3%, 95.1%, and 95.7%, respectively.

Attacked Examples. The correctly recognized images in the test set (i.e., about $28,700 \sim 30,000 \times 95.7\%$ images) are attacked by I-FGSM. Figure 2 shows the examples of attacked letter images. Among the three columns (separated by vertical lines), the left, middle, and right columns show low defensive (i.e., fragile), moderate defensive, and highly defensive (i.e., robust) cases, respectively. Below each image, its defensibility k and the misrecognized class (after k attack operations) are shown.

Those examples suggest that the letter images by decorative fonts tend to have smaller defensibility; that is, they are often fragile against adversarial attacks. This is because they are often outliers or located far from the center of the distribution of each letter class and, therefore, nearby the distribution of a neighboring class. Consequently, even with a small number of attack operations, they move into the neighboring class. In fact, in most cases, the misrecognized class resembles the original class, such as 'A' $\leftrightarrow$ {'H,' 'R'} and 'B' $\leftrightarrow$ {'S,' 'D,' 'E'}.

In contrast, the letter images by orthodox fonts have large defensibility k since they are located around the center of the distribution. By many attack operations, those robust letters are often misrecognized as a class with a largely different shape, such as 'A' $\leftrightarrow$ {'G,' 'F'} and 'B' $\leftrightarrow$ 'F.'

Figure 2 also shows that the letter images with more attacks (> 15) seem like a blurred version of their original image. In other words, the attacks appear as gray pixels nearby the original strokes and do not like random salt-and-pepper noise over the entire image region. This result proves that the computer classifier misrecognizes the letter images just by those blurring-like attacks; in other words, more harsh attacks, such as drastic stroke shape deformations, are not mandatory. See Sect. 6.1 for a discussion about the type of attack.

Figure 3 shows the sequence of the attacking operations by I-FGSM. As seen in the case of 'A,' the blurred area around the stroke expands gradually and monotonically along with attacking iterations, k. It is also confirmed that I-FGSM does cause neither abrupt changes nor drastic stroke shape deformations.

Class-Wise Analysis of Defensibility. Figure 4(c) shows a violin plot showing the distribution of the defensibility k for each letter class. The median, minimum, and maximum k values are plotted for each class as short horizontal lines. The test classification accuracy before attacks is also plotted as a red line.

The median defensibility values are around 15 ∼ 25 for most classes. Among 26 classes, 'E' shows the lowest median defensibility, although its classification

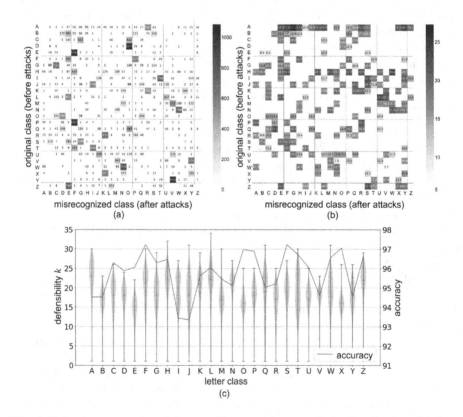

Fig. 4. Pair-wise summaries of the attacking experiment and the distribution of defensibility k of each letter class. (a) shows class confusion matrix, (b) shows average defensibility, and (c) shows the distribution of defensibility k and test classification accuracy. The average defensibility (b) is shown only for the class pairs with more than 10 misrecognized images in (a). The red line graph shows the test classification accuracy of each class before attacks in (c). (Color figure online)

accuracy is not low — like this, this plot indicates no clear class-wise correlation between the classification accuracy and defensibility. It is interesting to observe that the range of frequent k values is narrow for 'N,' 'V,' and 'X' and wide for 'J,' 'Q,' 'T,' and 'W.' Namely, the defensibility of the former classes is less variable by font styles, and that of the latter classes is more.

Class-Pair-Wise Analysis of Defensibility. Figure 4 shows two matrices for class-pair-wise analysis of defensibility. Figure 4(a) shows a class confusion matrix. As expected, character images are misrecognized as their neighboring class by attacks. For example, the similar class pairs, such as 'D'→'O,' 'E'→'F,' 'P'→'F,' and 'Y'→'V,' have more misrecognition pairs. This fact simply confirms that misrecognitions after repetitive attacks occur not randomly but in a similar class.

Although the confusion matrix is roughly symmetric, careful observation reveals many asymmetric cases. For example, 'B'→'E' is frequent (383 images), but 'E'→'B' is rare (10 images). Other examples are 'A'↔'R' (591 and 33), 'H'↔'F' (418 and 20), 'L'↔'U' (337 and 16), and 'T'↔'F' (415 and 25). These asymmetric cases inherit the asymmetric property of the nearest-neighbor relationship; the nearest neighbor class of 'A' will be 'R,' and that of 'R' will not be 'A' but 'K.'

Figure 4(b) shows the average defensibility of each class pair. For example, the average defensibility of the class pair 'A'→'E' is 22.9, which is the average number of attack operations on the 47 samples of 'A' misrecognized as 'E.' Simply speaking, an average of 22.9 attacks is required to misrecognize 'A' as 'E.' Note that the average defensibility is not shown in (b) when the number of misrecognized images is less than 10 for reliable analysis.

Like Fig. 4(a), this matrix (b) has a nonzero value for a similar class pair. In addition, it is roughly symmetric but still includes asymmetric pairs (such as 'E'↔'F' (14.2 and 20.6)), like Fig. 4(a). The class pairs with large shape differences, such as 'A' ↔ {'G,' 'F'} and 'B' ↔ 'F,' tend to have large average defensibility.

Interpretation of the average defensibility values is neither straightforward nor intuitive. For example, a similar class pair 'O'→'Q' needs 17.0 attacks, whereas 'B'→'H' only needs 11.4 attacks. This difficulty in interpretation is thought to be because defensibility varies greatly depending on the position within the intra-class distribution.

As noted above, the average defensibility matrix of Fig. 4(b) is similar to the confusion matrix (a); however, they represent different relationships between each class pair. If the element of $c \rightarrow c'$ is large (say, 800) in the confusion matrix (a), the class c includes many (i.e., 800) images whose nearest neighbor class is c'. On the other hand, if the element of $c \rightarrow c'$ is large in the average defensibility matrix (b), the 800 images in c are far from the class boundary between c and c' on average. In short, the matrix (a) shows a sample count, whereas (b) a distance. These different meanings of the matrices cause inconsistent relationships between class pairs. For example, 'E'→'F'(1042) >'F'→'E'(455) in (a), whereas 'E'→'F'(14.2) < 'F'→'E'(20.6) in (b).

4   Estimating Defensibility by Regression

4.1   Deep Regression Model for Defensibility Estimation

To answer Question 2 in Sect. 1 (*"Can we estimate how defensive a given letter image is before attacks?"*), we try to estimate the defensibility of each original (i.e., non-attacked) letter image by a deep regression model (without actual attacks). If we can develop a regression model with high accuracy, it will indicate a correlation between the letter shape and its defensibility.

A deep regression model is trained for each of the 26 letter classes, and its details are as follows. The model is a simple CNN with the same structure as for letter classification presented in the previous section, except for the number of output units (26 → 1). Then, the CNN model is trained to estimate the defensibility of the input letter image with the standard MSE loss and AdaDelta optimizer. As noted above, the input image is an original (i.e., non-attacked) image. The ground-truth of the defensibility k is determined by the experimental result of the previous section. The same criterion as the previous experiment is used to terminate the training process.

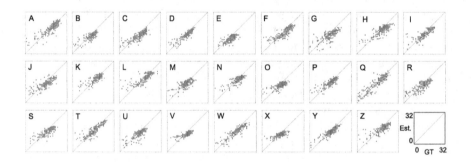

Fig. 5. Defensibility estimation result for each class.

In this experiment, we use about 28,700 images of the test set for Sect. 3. This is because we know their defensibility k through the attack experiment of the previous section. We split them into training, validation, and test sets for the experiment in this section. Consequently, for each model (i.e., for each letter class), these sets contain about 800, 100, and 200 images, respectively.

4.2   Estimation Experiment

Figure 5 shows the estimation result for each letter class as a y-y plot. Its horizontal axis corresponds to the ground-truth, i.e., the defensibility k measured by the attack experiment in Sect. 3, and the vertical axis to the estimated defensibility. From these plots, we found a clear positive correlation between ground-truth and estimation. This fact proves that there are strong correlations between letter shapes and defensibility.

Another observation is that the defensibility of fragile letters is often over-estimated[1]. As noted above, fragile letters are often printed in some decorative fonts and thus show large variations. On the other hand, the number of fragile letters is not large. Consequently, the regression model failed to learn such fragile letters accurately and gave erroneous defensibility estimates.

5   Generating Defensive Letter Images

5.1   Defensive Letter Image Generation by GAN

To answer Question 3 in Sect. 1 (*"Can we control the letter images to be more defensive against adversarial attacks?"*), we try to generate letter images with higher defensibility. For this purpose, we propose a cGAN-based image generation model. Its technical highlight is a two-step training process, as shown in Fig. 6. The first step is a standard GAN training process for generating realistic letter images, where we train a simple cGAN with a pair of a generator and a discriminator, and the discriminator tries to detect fake images by the generator. We adopt the binary cross entropy loss for this step. Specifically, loss functions for the generator G and the discriminator D are as follows:

$$\mathcal{L}_G = \mathbb{E}_{(\mathbf{z},y)\sim p(\mathbf{z},y)}[-\log D(G(\mathbf{z},y),y)], \tag{3}$$

$$\mathcal{L}_D = \mathbb{E}_{(\mathbf{x},y)\sim p(\mathbf{x},y)}[\log D(\mathbf{x},y)] + \mathbb{E}_{(\mathbf{z},y)\sim p(\mathbf{z},y)}[1-\log D(G(\mathbf{z},y),y)], \tag{4}$$

where $\mathbf{x}$ is an input image, y is a class label, $\mathbf{z}$ is a random noise vector, $G(\mathbf{z},y)$ is a generator that outputs an image of class y from noise vector $\mathbf{z}$, and $D(\mathbf{x},y)$ is the probability that the input image $\mathbf{x}$ of class y is real (i.e., non-generated) rather than fake (i.e., generated).

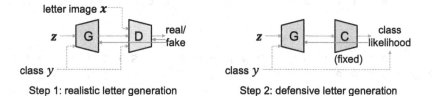

Step 1: realistic letter generation   Step 2: defensive letter generation

Fig. 6. Defensive letter image generation by GAN.

---

[1] Assume a regression problem regarding $y = f(x)$. When y is non-negative, it is well-known that the resulting f tends to show such overestimation ($y > 0$) for the sample x whose $y \sim 0$. (By the non-negativity, y fluctuates only in positive directions and never becomes negative.) However, the y-y plots in Fig. 5 show more significant overestimation around $y \sim 0$.

118   R. Kataoka et al.

Then, in the second and more important step, the discriminator is replaced with a letter image classifier C so that the generator can generate more defensive letter images. Note that we use the CNN C prepared as a classifier to be attacked in Sect. 3.2, and all the parameters of C are frozen during this step. The loss function for this step is the following negative log-likelihood:

$$\mathcal{L}_C = \mathbb{E}_{(\mathbf{z},y)\sim p(\mathbf{z},y)}[-\log C_y(G(\mathbf{z},y))], \tag{5}$$

where $C_y(\mathbf{x})$ is the y-th element of the logit vector obtained from the classifier. The idea behind this loss function Eq.(5) is that we want to train the generator to output the character images that can minimize the classification loss; in other words, the generated letter images will become more easily recognized by C. It is an operation opposite to the attacking operation by Eq. (1), and therefore the generated images will have higher defensibility.

5.2 Generation Experiment

Quantitative Evaluation of Generated Results. Figure 7 shows the defensibility histogram of each letter. Each histogram shows the defensibility distributions of 1,000 original and 1,000 generated images. In addition to those 26 histograms, the total histogram of 26 letters is shown in the lower right corner.

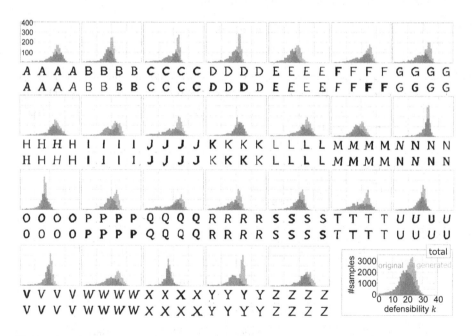

Fig. 7. Generation results of defensive letter images. For each letter, the histogram of defensibility for 1,000 original images (blue) and 1,000 generated images (orange) are shown along with the generated images with the top eight defensibilities. (Color figure online)

The defensibility $k(\mathbf{x})$ of each image $\mathbf{x}$ is counted by actually attacking the original (or generated) image $\mathbf{x}$ by I-FGSM, like the experiment in Sect. 3. In other words, the defensibility here is *not* an estimation $\hat{k}(\mathbf{x})$ by the regression model of Sect. 4.

First, we can see a successful result that the generated images by the GAN-based model of Fig. 6 have more defensible than the original images. The average defensibilities of the original and generated images were 17.8 and 21.7, respectively. This means four more attacks are necessary to misrecognize the generated images on average. Such an increase in defensibility in the generated images can be seen in all classes. In addition, none of the generated images have defensibility of less than 10.

Second, the maximum defensibility of the generated images is not significantly higher than that of the original images (except for 'E,' 'I,' 'J,' and 'W'). This suggests that the current GAN model of Fig. 6 has difficulty generating character images that have never been seen, even though it tries to increase the defensibility.

Qualitative Evaluation of Generated Results. Figure 7 also shows the generated images with the top eight defensibilities for each class. Therefore, these images correspond to the rightmost side of the orange histogram of the generated image. As noted above, these generated images have defensibility equal to or greater than the maximum defensibility of the original images.

Despite their higher defensibility, their style is neutral (except for tiny fluctuations in the stroke contour) and not very decorative. This result coincides with Fig. 2, where less decorative images have higher defensibility. One more observation is that their style is similar to each other; they keep higher defensibility at the cost of variety. In summary, both the discriminative approach (to the first research question) and the generative approach (to the third question) confirmed that standard characters are defensive.

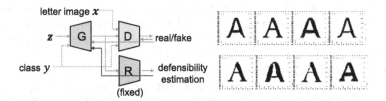

Fig. 8. A GAN-based defensive letter generation model that did *not* work as expected. Eight 'A' images are the generated images by this model and show noisy dots around their image boundary.

6 Discussion

6.1 What Are Reasonable Attacks?

In this paper, we do not assume any constraint on the attacking process by I-FGSM and the attacked images. However, we may introduce some constraints to regulate the attacked images. In fact, a popular attacking method, called Projected Gradient Descent (PGD) [7], projects the attacked image to a prespecified image subspace. For example, we can use the subspace of all binary images so that the adversarial letter images become binary. Although it seems a reasonable constraint, our preliminary trial proves that the resulting images often showed extra black pixels or black connected components in the background region, independently of letter shapes. To suppress them, we needed to introduce another extra constraint besides the binary constraint.

However, it is also true that there are no *reasonable* constraints that everyone can agree on. In other words, tuning the constraint Q would give adversarial images strongly biased by our prejudices towards our own "ideal" attacked letters. Since this paper is the first attempt to know the defensibility of letter images, we try not to optimize such a constraint to be free from our prejudices. In future work, we will design constraints Q that fit a specific application scenario.

6.2 Why Is the Regression Model *Not Used with GAN?*

One might think that the regression model is useful in the GAN-based defensive letter generation. For example, we can consider another GAN-based defensive letter generation model like Fig. 8 instead of Fig. 6. In this model, the regression model prepared in Sect. 4 is added to estimate the defensibility of a generated letter. Then, the model provides a gradient to the generator to generate letters with higher defensibility.

However, in the current setup, this model does not work as expected. As explained in Sect. 4, the regression model is trained with the letter images attacked I-FGSM. In other words, the model does not know the images other than these attacked images. Therefore, for example, if the generator generates strange noisy images like 'A' shown in the right part of Fig. 8, the model might give overestimated defensibility for them. In fact, we measured the true defensibility of these 'A's by I-FGSM and found that their true defensibility is much lower than the estimated one. As this result, unfortunately, the generator continues to generate letter images like these 'A's, which actually have low defensibility. A naive remedy is to update the regression model jointly with the newly generated images and their real defensibility; our preliminary trial, however, found this training strategy is unstable. Consequently, we need to develop a totally new framework other than Fig. 8 as future work.

7   Conclusion and Future Work

Unlike the standard adversarial defense research, where classifiers are the target to be defended, our purpose is to defend classification targets, i.e., letter images. For this purpose, we conducted various experiments and analyses for the three tasks: (1) Measurement of the actual defensibility of letter images. (2) Estimation of the defensibility from letter images. (3) Generation of letter images with higher defensibility. From (1), we confirmed that letters in simpler and more standard fonts tend to have higher defensibility. From (2), we confirmed a close relationship between the letter shape and the defensibility. Finally, from (3), we confirmed that a GAN-based model with a classifier could generate letter images with higher defensibility.

To the best of the authors' knowledge, this is the first attempt to observe the defensibility of letter images, and thus, as discussed in Sect. 6, there are many open questions regarding further analyses of the letter defensibility. The design of adversarial attack algorithms and constraints during the attack is an important future direction because it determines not only the defensibility of each letter image but also the appearance of the generated defensive letter images. In addition to the current bitmap-based generation, we may generate letter contours (in, for example, TrueType format). Also, we are going to realize a generation model that transforms a given letter image to be more defensive.

Throughout this paper, we have seen the defensibility of letter images against adversarial attacks to non-human classifiers (i.e., CNN-based classifiers). On the other hand, as noted in Sect. 1, letter images have high defensibility against various natural attacks, such as perspective distortions, handwriting fluctuations, partial occlusion, and decorations, to human classifiers. If we can tie together these various findings about the defensibility of letter images for computers and humans, we may find clues to understanding why and how letter images (i.e., alphabets) are designed to retain their readability against various distortions (i.e., attacks).

Acknowledgment. This work was supported in part by JSPS KAKENHI Grant Numbers JP22H00540.

References

1. Akhtar, N., Mian, A.: Threat of adversarial attacks on deep learning in computer vision: a survey. IEEE Access **6**, 14410–14430 (2018)
2. Chakraborty, A., Alam, M., Dey, V., Chattopadhyay, A., Mukhopadhyay, D.: Adversarial attacks and defences: a survey. arXiv preprint arXiv:1810.00069 (2018)
3. Goodfellow, I.J., Shlens, J., Szegedy, C.: Explaining and harnessing adversarial examples. In: Proceedings of the 3rd International Conference on Learning Representations (ICLR) (2015)
4. Kurakin, A., Goodfellow, I.J., Bengio, S.: Adversarial examples in the physical world. In: Proceedings of the 5th International Conference on Learning Representations (ICLR) (2017)

5. Long, T., Gao, Q., Xu, L., Zhou, Z.: A survey on adversarial attacks in computer vision: Taxonomy, visualization and future directions. Computers and Security 121 (2022)
6. Machado, G.R., Silva, E., Goldschmidt, R.R.: Adversarial machine learning in image classification: a survey toward the defender's perspective. ACM Comput. Surv. **55**(1), 1–38 (2021)
7. Makelov, A., Schmidt, L., Tsipras, D., Vladu, A., Science, C.: Towards deep learning models resistant to adversarial attacks. In: Proceedings of the 6th International Conference on Learning Representations (ICLR) (2018)
8. Sara, K., Ki, J.H., Insoo, S.: Adversarial attacks and defenses on AI in medical imaging informatics: a survey. Expert Syst. Appl. **198**, 116815 (2022)
9. Uchida, S., Sakai, M., Iwamura, M., Omachi, S., Kise, K.: Extraction of embedded class information from universal character pattern. In: Proceedings of the 9th International Conference on Document Analysis and Recognition (ICDAR), pp. 437–441 (2007)
10. Weibin, W., Yuxin, S., Michael, R.L., Irwin, K.: Improving the transferability of adversarial samples with adversarial transformations. In: Proceedings of the IEEE/CVF Conference on Computer Vision and Pattern Recognition (CVPR), pp. 9024–9033 (2021)
11. Xiaosen, W., Kun, H.: Enhancing the transferability of adversarial attacks through variance tuning. In: Proceedings of the IEEE/CVF Conference on Computer Vision and Pattern Recognition (CVPR), pp. 1924–1933 (2021)
12. Xu, H., Ma, Y., Liu, H.C., Deb, D., Liu, H., Tang, J.L., Jain, A.K.: Adversarial attacks and defenses in images, graphs and text: a review. Int. J. Autom. Comput. (IJAC) **17**(2), 151–178 (2020)

Using Motif-Based Features to Improve Signal Classification with Temporal Neural Networks

Karthikeyan Suresh[1] and Brian Kenji Iwana[2]([✉])(iD)

[1] University of Lorraine, GENIAL, Lorraine, France
[2] Department of Advanced Information Technology, Kyushu University, Fukuoka, Japan
iwana@ait.kyushu-u.ac.jp

Abstract. Time series motifs are repeated subsequences within a time series. Finding motifs is a large field in time series recognition. For example, Matrix Profile is a robust and scalable data structure that helps with motif discovery. In this paper, we demonstrate that motif discovery, namely Matrix Profile, can be used as a feature to increase the accuracy of temporal neural networks. While current temporal neural networks are effective, they lack specific considerations of time series properties, such as periodicity, motifs, and discords, etc. Therefore, we propose using multi-modal fusion networks to classify signals that use both the original features and the motif-based features. We demonstrate the proposed method's effectiveness on all of the signal and device datasets of the 2018 UCR Time Series Classification Archive. The results show that the proposed Matrix Profile-based features are useful for fusion networks and can increase the accuracy of temporal neural networks.

Keywords: Matrix Profile · Fusion Neural Network · Signal Classification · Time Series Motifs

1 Introduction

Recently, many state-of-the-art time series classification methods use Artificial Neural Networks (ANN), such as Recurrent Neural Networks (RNN) [29] and Temporal Convolutional Neural Networks (TCNN) [38]. They have shown to be widely effective for time series and signal classification [3,38]. However, while neural networks might be effective for time series, they do not inherently have considerations for some aspects and elements of signals, such as motifs and discords.

Time series motifs are repeated subsequences within a time series and discords are anomalies in times series. Finding motifs and discords, or the field of *motif discovery*, is essential for finding patterns in time series. Motif discovery has been used for time series analysis in many domains, such as protein sequences [22,41], actions [36], sounds [9], and signals [23,25].

This research was partially supported by MEXT-Japan (Grant No. JP23K16949).

H. Lu et al. (Eds.): ACPR 2023, LNCS 14406, pp. 123–136, 2023.
https://doi.org/10.1007/978-3-031-47634-1_10

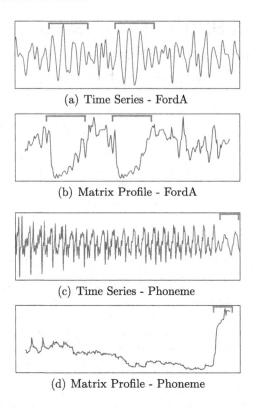

(a) Time Series - FordA

(b) Matrix Profile - FordA

(c) Time Series - Phoneme

(d) Matrix Profile - Phoneme

Fig. 1. Example of time series and the resulting Matrix Profile. The green brackets of (a) and (b) are an example of a motif, and the orange brackets of (c) and (d) are an example of a discord. (Color figure online)

One powerful tool used for motif discovery is Matrix Profile [40]. Matrix Profile is a robust and scalable data structure that helps with motif discovery. Specifically, Matrix Profile is a sequence calculated based on a sliding window of subsequences and the distance to its nearest neighbor subsequence. An example time series and Matrix Profile calculation result is shown in Fig. 1. In the figure, the dips in the Matrix Profile correspond to the locations of the motifs and the peaks are discords. The use of Matrix Profile has shown to be effective at large-scale motif discovery [39, 42].

We propose the inclusion of motif and discord information as supplemental information for signal classification. Namely, Matrix Profile is used to improve the classification ability of temporal neural networks by providing additional motif-based features alongside the original signal features. This is done by considering the Matrix Profile vector as a sequence and combining it with the original time series features in fusion neural networks. These motif-based features can be considered a self-augmented extra modality to represent the signal. Therefore, we are able to use both features in a single multi-modal model. Through this, we demonstrate that the motif-based features can supplement the original time series features and improve classification.

The contribution of this paper is as follows:

- We propose the use of Matrix Profile-based features to supplement time series in classification. This is done using fusion networks to combine the features.
- We demonstrate that the proposed method can improve the accuracy of neural networks in signal classification. To do this, we evaluate the proposed method on 24 datasets taken from the 2018 University of California Riverside (UCR) Time Series Archive [7]. The 24 datasets are all of the sensor and device datasets with at least 100 training patterns from the archive.
- We examine the effect that the window size of Matrix Profile has on the accuracy of the proposed method.
- The code for the proposed method can be found at https://github.com/uchidalab/motif-based-features

2   Related Work

The use of fusion neural networks is a common solution for multi-modal data recognition [11]. They have been used for a wide range of applications. Of them, there are a few works that use fusion neural networks with different features extracted from the same time series. For example, the Long Short-Term Memory Network Fully Convolutional Network (LSTM-FCN) [17] uses a fusion network to combine an LSTM branch and an FCN branch for time series classification. Similarly, Song et al. [34] combine the features from an LSTM and a CNN for time series retrieval. Features can also be derived or learned from the original time series representation. For example, Iwana et al. [16] propose using local distance-based features with the original features in fusion 1D CNNs and Oba et al. [24] combines data augmentation methods in a gated fusion network. Matsuo et al. [20] uses a learned self-augmentation by converting the time series into images and then uses a multi-modal network. Wang et al. [37] uses a fusion network with multi-scale temporal features and distance features.

3   Using Matrix Profile as a Feature Extraction Method

3.1   Motif Discovery

A motif is a repeated pattern in a time series. Specifically, given time series $\mathbf{t} = t_1, \ldots, t_n, \ldots, t_N$ of length N and $t_n \in \mathbb{R}$, a continuous subsequence $\mathbf{t}_{s,M} = t_s, \ldots, t_{s+M-1}$ of length M starting from position s, where $1 \leq s \leq N - M + 1$, is a motif if it shares similar values with any other subsequence $\mathbf{t}_{s',M}$ within $\mathbf{t}$ with a different start position s'. Note, time series element t_n can one dimension (univariate) or multiple dimensions (multivariate).

Motif discovery refers to finding sets of similar short sequences in a large time series dataset. Motifs are essential as these primitive patterns can be used as inputs for algorithms to perform segmentation, classification, anomaly detection, etc. Further, studying motifs can provide insight into the functional properties of the time series [43].

3.2 Matrix Profile

Matrix Profile [40] is a powerful motif discovery algorithm that represents times series based on the distances of subsequences to their nearest neighbors. Specifically, using a sliding window, we can extract all of the subsequences from the time series. We can then compute the pairwise distances between these subsequences and store them in the form of a matrix. This matrix is then stored in a vector that only holds the information on the distances of each subsequence to the nearest neighbor of that subsequence. This vector is called the *Matrix Profile*.

Namely, given time series $\mathbf{t}$, first the *all-subsequences set* is created. The all-subsequences set $\mathcal{A}$ is an ordered set of all possible subsequences of time series $\mathbf{t}$, obtained by a sliding window of length M across $\mathbf{t} = t_1, \ldots, t_{N-M+1}$, where M is a user-defined subsequence length. We use $\mathcal{A}[s]$ to denote the subsequence $\mathbf{t}_{s,M} = t_s, \ldots, t_{s+M-1}$.

Next, a *Distance Profile* $\mathbf{d}_i$ is created for each subsequence in $\mathcal{A}$. The Distance Profile is the ordered vector of distances between each subsequence in all-subsequences set $\mathcal{A}$ and all other subsequences in $\mathcal{A}$. For this distance, traditionally, the Euclidean distance is used. Using each Distance Profile, a *similarity join set* $\mathcal{S}$ is constructed with each subsequence $\mathcal{A}$ with its nearest neighbor,

$$\mathcal{S}_s = \arg\min_{s'} \mathbf{d}_s[s'], \tag{1}$$

for each s-th subsequence of $\mathcal{A}$. Matrix Profile $\mathbf{p}$ is the vector of distances between $\mathcal{A}$ and $\mathcal{S}$, or:

$$\mathbf{p} = ||\mathcal{A}_1 - \mathcal{S}_1||, \ldots, ||\mathcal{A}_s - \mathcal{S}_s||, \ldots, ||\mathcal{A}_{N-M+1} - \mathcal{S}_{N-M+1}||. \tag{2}$$

An example of the result of a Matrix Profile calculation is shown in Fig. 1. Matrix Profile has many advantages over conventional methods of motif discovery and anomaly detection representations. To state a few, it is space efficient, parallelizable, scalable, and can be used efficiently on streams of data [40].

3.3 Matrix Profile as a Motif-Based Feature

As described previously, Matrix Profile is a vector that is used to identify motifs and discords by containing the distance of each subsequence to its nearest neighbor. In other words, the values of the Matrix Profile will be small for repeated subsequences and large for anomalies. The values of the Matrix Profile vector have a nonlinear relationship to the original time series features. Thus, it is possible to exploit Matrix Profile to create a feature vector that contains information that is not inherent to the original time series features.

In order to use the Matrix Profile features, we consider vector $\mathbf{p}$ as a sequence, or:

$$\mathbf{f} = \mathbf{p}^\top = p_1, \ldots, p_s, \ldots, p_{N-M+1}. \tag{3}$$

This gives a sequence $\mathbf{f}$ of length $N - M + 1$, which is similar in size to the original time series features $\mathbf{t}$. The motif feature sequence $\mathbf{f}$ can now be used alongside the original $\mathbf{t}$ in multi-modal classification.

4   Multi-modal Classification with Fusion Neural Networks

The original features **t** and the motif features **f** are different modalities that contain different information about the same signal. Therefore, we combine the two features in one multi-modal model to improve classification. Using the additional motif features can supplement the original time series.

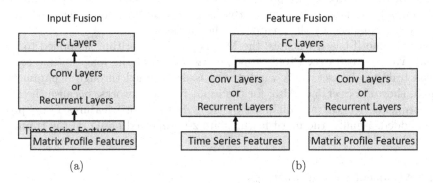

Fig. 2. Different arrangements of combining features in multi-modal fusion networks.

There are various methods of creating a multi-modal classification model. We propose to use a fusion neural network. Specifically, we implement a multi-modal neural network and combine the modalities through model fusion. The modalities can be combined at different points in the neural network. Some common places modality fusion can take place is at the input level or at the feature level, as shown in Fig. 2. Input-level fusion combines the inputs by concatenating them. The combined input is then used with a typical temporal neural network. Feature-level fusion concatenates separate modality branches within a network.

5   Experimental Results

5.1   Data

In order to evaluate the proposed method, we use 24 time series datasets from the UCR Time Series Archive [7]. The datasets are all of the device and sensor type datasets with at least 100 training patterns. There are 8 device datasets, ACSF1, Computers, ElectricDevices, LargeKitchenAppliances, PLAID, RefrigerationDevices, ScreenType, and SmallKitchenAppliances and 16 sensor datasets, AllGestureWiimoteX, AllGestureWiimoteY, AllGestureWIimoteZ, ChlorineConcentration, Earthquakes, FordA, FordB, FreezerRegularTrain, GesturePebbleZ1, GesturePebbleZ2, InsectWingbeatSound, Phoneme, Plane, StarLightCurves, Trace, and Wafer. The sensor and device datasets are used since they are examples of signal data. However, there is no theoretical limitation to the type of time series used. Furthermore, datasets with less than 100 training patterns are not used because very small datasets are not suitable for neural networks.

The datasets used in the experiments have a wide range of lengths. The dataset with the shortest time series is the ElectricDevices dataset with 96 time steps and the longest one is the ACSF1 dataset with 1,460 time steps. Six of the datasets, AllGestureWiimoteX, AllGestureWiimoteY, AllGestureWiimoteZ, GesturePebbleZ1, GesturePebbleZ2, and PLAID have varying number of time steps. For these datasets, we pre-process them by post pattern zero padding. In addition, all the datasets except for the six previously mentioned datasets were already z-normalized by the creators of the datasets.

For the motif-based features, the Matrix Profile algorithm is applied to the signal. We use a Matrix Profile window size of 7% of the longest time series in the training dataset. This window size is determined through a parameter search, shown in Sect. 5.6. Also, for the input-fusion networks, because the feature sequence lengths are different by $M - 1$, the motif features $\mathbf{f}$ are post zero-padded. Finally, the motif features are z-normalized based on the training set.

5.2   Architecture and Settings

Two time series recognition architectures were used as the foundation of the experiments, a 1D Very Deep Convolutional Network (VGG) [33] and a Bidirectional LSTM (BLSTM) [31]. The 1D VGG is a VGG adapted for time series in that it uses 1D convolutions instead of the standard 2D convolutions. It has multiple blocks of convolutional layers followed by max pooling layers. There are two fully-connected layers with 1,024 nodes and dropout with a probability of 0.5. The number of blocks and filters per convolution are determined by the suggestions of Iwana and Uchida [15]. For the BLSTM, there are two layers of 100 cells each. The hyperparameters of the BLSTM are the optimal suggestions by Reimers et al. [28]. In the case of the feature-fusion networks, two streams with the same hyperparameters are used and the concatenation is performed before the first fully-connected layer of each.

For training the 1D VGG, Stochastic Gradient Decent (SGD) with an initial learning rate of 0.01, momentum of 0.9, and weight decay of 5×10^{-4} is used. These settings are suggested by [33]. For the BLSTM, following [28], we use an Nadam [8] optimizer with an initial learning rate of 0.001. For both networks, we use batch size 50 and train for 10,000 iterations. The datasets used have fixed training and test sets that are provided by the dataset authors.

5.3   Comparison Methods

To demonstrate the effectiveness of the proposed method, the following evaluations were performed:

- *Single-Modality Network with Time Series Features (Single, TS)*: The original time series features are used as a baseline.

– *Single-Modality Network with Matrix Profile Features (Single, MP)*: This uses the same networks as TS, but using only the Matrix Profile-based features. Single MP (7%) refers to using a 7% window for matrix profile. Single MP (Best) uses the best window for each dataset.
– *Input-Level Fusion with Time Series and Matrix Profile Features (Input Fusion, TS+MP)*: For the input-level fusion network, the time series features and Matrix Profile features are concatenated in the dimension direction and then fed to the neural network.

The evaluation of all of the comparisons use the same hyperparameters and training scheme, with exception of the feature-level fusion which has two modality streams with their own set of feature extraction layers.

5.4 Results

Training and testing were performed five times, and the average of the five results was recorded as the final value in order to obtain an accurate representation of the accuracy of each method. The results are shown in Table 1. For the applicable comparisons, the window size was set to a fixed percentage of the longest length time series in the training set. For the MP (7% Win.) features, all datasets use a window of 7% of the maximum time series length. For MP (Best Win.), the best accuracy is used for each dataset.

From the table, it can be seen that input fusion with the time series features and the proposed Matrix Profile features had the highest accuracy for most datasets. The results with the best window for each dataset predictably had the highest accuracy. However, a window of 7% of the time series length still performed better than without using the fusion network. This is true for both the 1D VGG and the BLSTM.

We also compare the proposed method to other comparison methods. A Nemenyi test is performed using results reported from literature. Figure 3 compares the proposed BLSTM and VGG using TS+MP (7%) and (Best) to Bag of Patterns (BoP) [18], Bag of Symbolic Fourier Approximation Symbols (BOSS) [30], Collective of Transformation Ensembles (COTE) [2], Complexity Invariant Distance (CID) [4], Derivative DTW (DD_{DTW}) [12], Derivative Transform Distance (DTD_C) [13], Elastic Ensemble (EE) [19], Fast Shapelets (FS) [26], Feature Fusion CNN using Local Distance Features and series features (CNN LDF+TS) [16], Learned Pattern Similarity (LPS) [6], Learned Shapelets (LS) [21], Multilayer Perceptron (MLP) [1], Random Forest (RandF) [1], Residual Network (ResNet) [10], Rotation Forest (RotF) [1], Shapelet Transform (ST) [14], Symbolic Aggregate Approximation - Vector Space Model (SAXVSM) [32], SVM with a linear kernel (SVML) [1], Time Series Bag of Features (TSBF) [5], SVM with a quadratic kernel (SVMQ) [1], 1-NN with Euclidean Distance (1-NN ED) [7], 1-NN with DTW (1-NN DTW) [7], 1-NN with DTW with the best warping window (1-NN DTW (Best)) [27], and 1-NN with Move-Split-Merge (1-NN MSM) [35]. In the figure, BLSTM and VGG refer to the previous models with only time series features. It can be seen that the

Table 1. Average Test Accuracy (%) Trained Five Times

Type: Feature:	Single TS	Single MP (7%)	Single MP (Best)	Input Fusion TS+MP (7%)	Input Fusion TS+MP (Best)
1D VGG Backbone					
ACSF1	34.6	27.6	31.6 (15%)	36.8	**43.0** (13%)
AllGestureWiimoteX	**70.3**	27.1	28.2 (5%)	68.6	69.6 (9%)
AllGestureWiimoteY	**72.2**	25.5	26.3 (5%)	68.9	71.3 (3%)
AllGestureWiimoteZ	**63.9**	29.7	31.0 (13%)	58.9	**63.9** (15%)
ChlorineConcentration	**83.4**	69.0	69.0 (7%)	73.2	74.3 (15%)
Computers	60.7	50.0	55.0 (5%)	62.8	**63.4** (1%)
Earthquakes	68.8	72.9	**74.8** (Multi)	70.2	71.4 (11%)
ElectricDevices	70.4	63.8	63.8 (7%)	**72.3**	72.3 (7%)
FordA	**94.0**	55.0	86.0 (3%)	93.5	**94.0** (13%)
FordB	82.6	55.9	75.7 (1%)	82.3	**83.1** (15%)
FreezerRegularTrain	**99.2**	55.5	88.8 (5%)	94.9	97.8 (15%)
GesturePebbleZ1	16.0	44.8	53.8 (5%)	59.5	**74.4** (3%)
GesturePebbleZ2	15.3	34.7	34.7 (7%)	71.3	**84.4** (1%)
InsectWingbeatSound	59.1	37.2	42.6 (13%)	**59.5**	**59.5** (7%)
LargeKitchenAppliances	79.8	53.7	14.4 (3%)	78.6	**81.8** (1%)
Phoneme	15.9	10.7	14.4 (3%)	15.5	**17.6** (5%)
PLAID	12.2	36.0	**72.9** (5%)	12.2	12.2 (Multi)
Plane	98.7	96.0	**99.0** (13%)	97.1	98.7 (11%)
RefrigerationDevices	47.9	42.0	47.8 (3%)	51.0	**52.2** (9%)
ScreenType	39.9	38.3	43.4 (1%)	40.7	**51.4** (1%)
SmallKitchenAppliances	70.5	54.8	72.4 (3%)	75.5	**78.4** (13%)
StarLightCurves	**96.7**	92.0	93.7 (11%)	96.1	96.6 (15%)
Trace	83.4	78.2	87.0 (5%)	99.6	**100** (5%)
Wafer	99.6	99.6	**100** (3%)	99.6	99.9 (3%)
Total	63.97	52.08	60.44	68.27	**71.38**
BLSTM Backbone					
ACSF1	**73.0**	34.0	34.0 (7%)	61.0	68.5 (5%)
AllGestureWiimoteX	**68.4**	24.6	30.4 (13%)	67.5	67.7 (9%)
AllGestureWiimoteY	65.2	24.5	26.1 (9%)	65.9	**68.7** (9%)
AllGestureWiimoteZ	63.9	31.6	34.1 (15%)	59.8	**66.0** (15%)
ChlorineConcentration	**61.8**	58.4	59.4 (9%)	61.1	61.1 (7%)
Computers	60.0	60.5	61.4 (7%)	59.9	**62.9** (11%)
Earthquakes	73.4	69.4	**74.6** (15%)	73.6	74.1 (15%)
ElectricDevices	69.6	63.0	63.0 (7%)	**73.3**	**73.3** (7%)
FordA	60.2	76.5	80.5 (3%)	**91.1**	**91.1** (7%)
FordB	69.5	66.1	71.1 (3%)	78.0	**82.6** (1%)
FreezerRegularTrain	92.5	83.3	89.5 (15%)	93.4	**95.9** (11%)
GesturePebbleZ1	43.5	51.7	55.2 (11%)	44.6	**67.6** (9%)
GesturePebbleZ2	40.3	43.2	57.0 (13%)	44.5	**70.6** (15%)
InsectWingbeatSound	**55.8**	29.5	35.8 (15%)	51.9	54.5 (11%)
LargeKitchenAppliances	85.5	53.9	58.8 (1%)	84.6	**86.2** (5%)
Phoneme	11.7	**14.8**	**14.8** (7%)	13.0	14.1 (3%)
PLAID	50.5	73.8	75.9 (5%)	**76.0**	**76.0** (7%)
Plane	97.1	92.2	97.0 (15%)	99.0	**99.2** (11%)
RefrigerationDevices	45.3	46.6	49.4 (3%)	48.7	**53.4** (15%)
ScreenType	38.6	39.7	46.5 (3%)	41.3	**49.3** (1%)
SmallKitchenAppliances	68.7	73.0	75.7 (3%)	**80.3**	**80.3** (7%)
StarLightCurves	91.8	87.2	93.4 (15%)	95.8	**95.9** (9%)
Trace	84.0	70.5	**98.0** (15%)	80.0	90.7 (13%)
Wafer	99.1	99.0	99.5 (3%)	99.0	**99.6** (3%)
Total	65.39	56.96	61.70	68.47	**72.99**

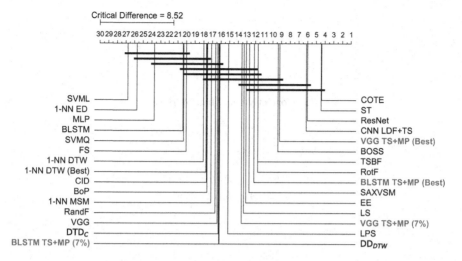

Fig. 3. Critical difference diagram using a Nemenyi test comparing the proposed method to reported methods. Green highlighted methods are the proposed input fusion networks. (Color figure online)

proposed method performed on the upper end of the methods. Using the best window with VGG was ranked higher than most of the models. The methods with better overall scores were a large ensemble of many classifiers (COTE), a classical method, and two other neural networks.

5.5 Qualitative Analysis

Figure 4 is a comparison of test samples classified by a standard VGG using the normal time series features and the proposed Input Fusion network with a VGG backbone using both the time series features and the matrix profile features. Noticeably, the proposed method performed better when the matrix profile features had more discords. In Figs. 4(b) and (c), the matrix profile features were often small with only sparse and narrow peaks. Conversely, when the proposed method excelled, the discord peaks were wider and more frequent. Thus, it can be inferred that the proposed method is better suited to signals with more frequent discords.

5.6 Ablation

An ablation study is performed to demonstrate the usefulness of adding matrix profile-based features. Table 2 compares using a network on a single feature (time series features or matrix profile features) as well as the difference in using an input fusion network versus a feature fusion network. Feature Fusion refers to a network that has branches for both features and concatenates them at the fully connected layer. Also, in order to demonstrate that the improved results

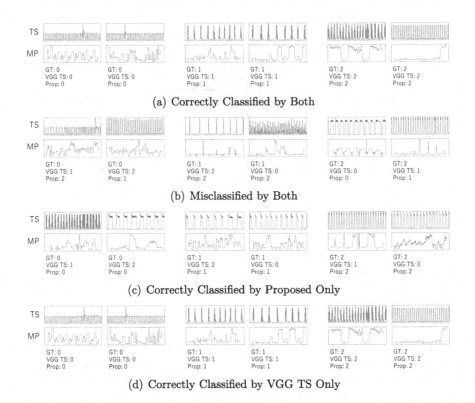

(a) Correctly Classified by Both

(b) Misclassified by Both

(c) Correctly Classified by Proposed Only

(d) Correctly Classified by VGG TS Only

Fig. 4. Examples of test patterns classified by Single VGG TS and the proposed Input Fusion VGG TS+MP (7%) from the RefrigerationDevices dataset. The upper row of each subfigure is the original Time Series feature and the lower row is the Matrix Profile feature. Two examples from each class are shown.

Table 2. Average Test Accuracy (%) of the 24 Datasets Trained Five Times

Network	Feature	Model	
		1D VGG	BLSTM
Single	TS	63.97	65.39
Single	MP (7% Window)	52.08	56.96
Single	MP (Best Window)	60.44	61.70
Input Fusion	TS+TS	63.32	66.47
Feature Fusion	TS+TS	64.07	64.33
Input Fusion	TS+MP (7% Window)	68.27	68.47
Input Fusion	TS+MP (Best Window)	**71.38**	**72.99**
Feature Fusion	TS+MP (7% Window)	66.08	66.95
Feature Fusion	TS+MP (Best Window)	67.91	70.45

of the proposed method are not strictly due to having more parameters, a fair comparison is made using only the time series features for modalities of the fusion networks (TS+TS).

Table 2 shows that using a fusion network with only time series does not have a significant difference with just having a single network. The results between Single TS and Input Fusion/Feature Fusion TS+TS are within a percent of each other. However, the TS+MP trials all have large increases over Single TS. This indicates that the matrix profile-based features provide supplemental information for the network to learn from.

5.7   Effect of Window Size

Matrix Profile has one hyperparameter, the window size. The value of this hyperparameter has an effect on the robustness of the proposed method. Figure 5 shows the average accuracy at different window sizes. As can be seen in the figure, after about a window size 7% of the time series, the accuracy starts to decrease. Furthermore, when using the Matrix Profile features only, the accuracy of the VGG quickly decreases after a small window. Despite this, the Input Fusion and Feature Fusion still increases.

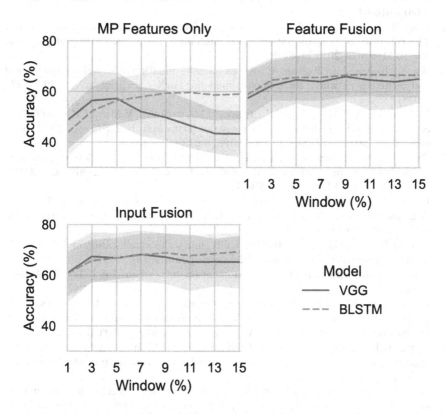

Fig. 5. Effect of the Matrix Profile window size.

6   Conclusion

In this paper, we propose the use of motif-based features to supplement time series in classification. The motif-based features are features that represent motifs and discords in time series. The features are created by using Matrix Profile to generate a second modality of data to represent the time series. Due to the features being similar in length to the original time series, we can use them as a sequence in multi-modal neural networks.

Through the experiments, we demonstrate that using the motif-based features alongside the time series features can be used to increase the accuracy of BLSTMs and Temporal CNNs in fusion networks. We performed an extensive evaluation using all of the signal and device time series patterns from the UCR Time Series Archive, which includes 24 time series datasets.

References

1. Bagnall, A., Lines, J., Bostrom, A., Large, J., Keogh, E.: The great time series classification bake off: a review and experimental evaluation of recent algorithmic advances. Data Min. Knowl. Disc. **31**(3), 606–660 (2016). https://doi.org/10.1007/s10618-016-0483-9

2. Bagnall, A., Lines, J., Hills, J., Bostrom, A.: Time-series classification with COTE: The collective of transformation-based ensembles. In: ICDE (2016). https://doi.org/10.1109/icde.2016.7498418

3. Bai, S., Kolter, J.Z., Koltun, V.: An empirical evaluation of generic convolutional and recurrent networks for sequence modeling. arXiv preprint arXiv:1803.01271 (2018)

4. Batista, G.E.A.P.A., Keogh, E.J., Tataw, O.M., de Souza, V.M.A.: CID: an efficient complexity-invariant distance for time series. Data Min. Knowl. Disc. **28**(3), 634–669 (2013). https://doi.org/10.1007/s10618-013-0312-3

5. Baydogan, M.G., Runger, G., Tuv, E.: A bag-of-features framework to classify time series. IEEE Trans. Pattern Analy. and Mach. Intell. **35**(11), 2796–2802 (2013). https://doi.org/10.1109/tpami.2013.72

6. Baydogan, M.G., Runger, G.: Time series representation and similarity based on local autopatterns. Data Min. Knowl. Disc. **30**(2), 476–509 (2015). https://doi.org/10.1007/s10618-015-0425-y

7. Dau, H.A., et al.: Hexagon-ML: The UCR time series classification archive (2018). https://www.cs.ucr.edu/~eamonn/time_series_data_2018/

8. Dozat, T.: Incorporating nesterov momentum into adam. In: ICLR Workshops (2016)

9. Exadaktylos, V., Silva, M., Ferrari, S., Guarino, M., Taylor, C.J., Aerts, J.M., Berckmans, D.: Time-series analysis for online recognition and localization of sick pig (sus scrofa) cough sounds. J. Acous. Soc. Am. **124**(6), 3803–3809 (2008)

10. Fawaz, H.I., Forestier, G., Weber, J., Idoumghar, L., Muller, P.A.: Data augmentation using synthetic data for time series classification with deep residual networks. arXiv preprint arXiv:1808.02455 (2018)

11. Gao, J., Li, P., Chen, Z., Zhang, J.: A survey on deep learning for multimodal data fusion. Neural Comput. **32**(5), 829–864 (2020). https://doi.org/10.1162/neco_a_01273

12. Górecki, T., Łuczak, M.: Using derivatives in time series classification. Data Mining Knowl. Disc. **26**(2), 310–331 (2012). https://doi.org/10.1007/s10618-012-0251-4
13. Górecki, T., Łuczak, M.: Non-isometric transforms in time series classification using DTW. Knowl.-Based Sys. **61**, 98–108 (2014). https://doi.org/10.1016/j.knosys.2014.02.011
14. Hills, J., Lines, J., Baranauskas, E., Mapp, J., Bagnall, A.: Classification of time series by shapelet transformation. Data Min. Knowl. Disc. **28**(4), 851–881 (2013). https://doi.org/10.1007/s10618-013-0322-1
15. Iwana, B.K., Uchida, S.: An empirical survey of data augmentation for time series classification with neural networks. PLoS ONE (2021). https://doi.org/10.1371/journal.pone.0254841
16. Iwana, B.K., Uchida, S.: Time series classification using local distance-based features in multi-modal fusion networks. Pattern Recogn. **97**, 107024 (2020). https://doi.org/10.1016/j.patcog.2019.107024
17. Karim, F., Majumdar, S., Darabi, H., Chen, S.: LSTM fully convolutional networks for time series classification. IEEE Access **6**, 1662–1669 (2018). https://doi.org/10.1109/access.2017.2779939
18. Lin, J., Khade, R., Li, Y.: Rotation-invariant similarity in time series using bag-of-patterns representation. J. Intell. Info. Sys. **39**(2), 287–315 (2012). https://doi.org/10.1007/s10844-012-0196-5
19. Lines, J., Bagnall, A.: Time series classification with ensembles of elastic distance measures. Data Min. Knowl. Disc. **29**(3), 565–592 (2014). https://doi.org/10.1007/s10618-014-0361-2
20. Matsuo, S., Iwana, B.K., Uchida, S.: Self-augmented multi-modal feature embedding. In: ICASSP (2021). https://doi.org/10.1109/icassp39728.2021.9413974
21. Mitzev, I.S., Younan, N.H.: Time series shapelets: training time improvement based on particle swarm optimization. Int. J. Mach. Learn. and Comput. **5**(4), 283–287 (2015). https://doi.org/10.7763/ijmlc.2015.v5.521
22. Mohamed, S.A.E.H., Elloumi, M., Thompson, J.D.: Motif discovery in protein sequences. Pattern Recogn.-Analy. and App. (2016)
23. Mueen, A.: Time series motif discovery: dimensions and applications. Data Mining Knowl. Disc. **4**(2), 152–159 (2014)
24. Oba, D., Iwana, B.K., Matsuo, S.: Dynamic data augmentation with gating networks for time series recognition. In: ICPR (2022)
25. Patel, P., Keogh, E., Lin, J., Lonardi, S.: Mining motifs in massive time series databases. In: ICDM, pp. 370–377 (2002)
26. Rakthanmanon, T., Keogh, E.: Fast shapelets: A scalable algorithm for discovering time series shapelets. In: SIAM ICDM (2013). https://doi.org/10.1137/1.9781611972832.74
27. Ratanamahatana, C.A., Keogh, E.: Three myths about dynamic time warping data mining. In: SIAM ICDM (2005). https://doi.org/10.1137/1.9781611972757.50
28. Reimers, N., Gurevych, I.: Optimal hyperparameters for deep lstm-networks for sequence labeling tasks. arXiv preprint arXiv:1707.06799 (2017)
29. Rumelhart, D.E., Hinton, G.E., Williams, R.J.: Learning representations by back-propagating errors. Nature **323**(6088), 533–536 (1986). https://doi.org/10.1038/323533a0
30. Schäfer, P.: The BOSS is concerned with time series classification in the presence of noise. Data Min. Knowl. Disc. **29**(6), 1505–1530 (2014). https://doi.org/10.1007/s10618-014-0377-7
31. Schuster, M., Paliwal, K.K.: Bidirectional recurrent neural networks. IEEE Trans. Sig. Proc. **45**(11), 2673–2681 (1997). https://doi.org/10.1109/78.650093

32. Senin, P., Malinchik, S.: SAX-VSM: Interpretable time series classification using SAX and vector space model. In: IEEE ICDM (2013). https://doi.org/10.1109/icdm.2013.52

33. Simonyan, K., Zisserman, A.: Very deep convolutional networks for large-scale image recognition. arXiv preprint arXiv:1409.1556 (2014)

34. Song, D., Xia, N., Cheng, W., Chen, H., Tao, D.: Deep r -th root of rank supervised joint binary embedding for multivariate time series retrieval. In: KDD (2018). https://doi.org/10.1145/3219819.3220108

35. Stefan, A., Athitsos, V., Das, G.: The move-split-merge metric for time series. IEEE Trans. Knowl. Data Engin. **25**(6), 1425–1438 (2013). https://doi.org/10.1109/tkde.2012.88

36. Tanaka, Y., Iwamoto, K., Uehara, K.: Discovery of time-series motif from multi-dimensional data based on mdl principle. Mach. Learn. **58**(2), 269–300 (2005)

37. Wang, T., Liu, Z., Zhang, T., Hussain, S.F., Waqas, M., Li, Y.: Adaptive feature fusion for time series classification. Knowl.-Based Sys. **243**, 108459 (2022)

38. Wang, Z., Yan, W., Oates, T.: Time series classification from scratch with deep neural networks: a strong baseline. In: IJCNN, pp. 1578–1585 (2017). https://doi.org/10.1109/ijcnn.2017.7966039

39. Yeh, C.C.M., Kavantzas, N., Keogh, E.: Matrix profile vi: Meaningful multidimensional motif discovery. In: ICDM, pp. 565–574 (2017)

40. Yeh, C.C.M., et al.: Matrix profile i: All pairs similarity joins for time series: a unifying view that includes motifs, discords and shapelets. In: ICDM (2016). https://doi.org/10.1109/icdm.2016.0179

41. Zambelli, F., Pesole, G., Pavesi, G.: Motif discovery and transcription factor binding sites before and after the next-generation sequencing era. Brief. Bioinform. **14**(2), 225–237 (2013)

42. Zhu, Y., et al.: Matrix profile ii: Exploiting a novel algorithm and gpus to break the one hundred million barrier for time series motifs and joins. In: ICDM, pp. 739–748 (2016)

43. Zimmerman, Z., et al.: Matrix profile xiv: Scaling time series motif discovery with gpus to break a quintillion pairwise comparisons a day and beyond. In: SoCC (2019). https://doi.org/10.1145/3357223.3362721

SimCLR-Inception: An Image Representation Learning and Recognition Model for Robot Vision

Mengyuan Jin[1], Yin Zhang[2], Xiufeng Cheng[3], Li Ma[1], and Fang Hu[1,4(✉)]

[1] College of Information Engineering, Hubei University of Chinese Medicine, Wuhan 430065, People's Republic of China
naomifang@hbtcm.edu.cn
[2] School of Information and Communication Engineering, University of Electronic Science and Technology of China, Chengdu 611731, People's Republic of China
[3] School of Information Management, Central China Normal University, Wuhan 430079, People's Republic of China
[4] Department of Mathematics and Statistics, University of West Florida, Pensacola 32514, USA

Abstract. Effective feature extraction is a key component in image recognition for robot vision. This paper presents an improved contrastive learning-based image feature extraction and classification model, termed SimCLR-Inception, to realize effective and accurate image recognition. By using the SimCLR, this model generates positive and negative image samples from unlabeled data through image augmentation and then minimizes the contrastive loss function to learn the image representations by exploring more underlying structure information. Furthermore, this proposed model uses the Inception V3 model to classify the image representations for improving recognition accuracy. The SimCLR-Inception model is compared with four representative image recognition models, including LeNet, VGG16, Inception V3, and EfficientNet V2 on a real-world Multi-class Weather (MW) data set. We use four representative metrics: accuracy, precision, recall, and F1-Score, to verify the performance of different models for image recognition. We show that the presented SimCLR-Inception model achieves all the successful runs and gives almost the best results. The accuracy is at least 4% improved by the Inception V3 model. It suggests that this model would work better for robot vision.

Keywords: Image Augmentation · Representation Learning · Positive and Negative Sample Generation · SimCLR-Inception Model · Robot Vision

1 Introduction

Accurate image recognition plays a vital role in the research domain of robot vision [3,15,27]. Image recognition approaches mainly refer to two components:

H. Lu et al. (Eds.): ACPR 2023, LNCS 14406, pp. 137–147, 2023.
https://doi.org/10.1007/978-3-031-47634-1_11

feature extraction and classification. Effective image feature extraction is considered the most significant process, which directly determines the performance of image recognition. Recently, Convolutional Neural Network (CNN), one kind of deep learning model, and its variants for image recognition have been considered the master models applied in robot vision [13,16]. Some representative CNN-based models, such as VGG [18], Xception [4], Inception [20], DenseNet [10], provide outstanding performance in image recognition. These models also have good feature extraction performance in labeled images, however, they have poor learning capabilities for unlabeled images. Moreover, these models exceedingly depend on the large volume of images to get satisfactory identification results [12,30]. Therefore, the effectiveness and accuracy of image recognition for unlabeled and small-scale images should be improved further.

An emerging technique, Contrastive Learning (CL), achieved considerable success in the research fields of speech recognition, natural language processing, computer vision, etc. [8,28]. CL was first proposed by Hadsell et al. [9], which has a powerful capability to learn the features from unlabeled data. It trains a model by distinguishing between similar and dissimilar pairs of data points by maximizing similarity within the identical category and minimizing similarity between different categories [6]. The development of CL has led to significant improvements in the performance of image recognition, especially on data sets with limited labeled examples. CL can be better extended to new, unseen images. In addition, CL can be used in combination with other approaches to improve image recognition performance, such as data augmentation, transfer learning, etc. [11]. However, it requires large amounts of data to learn useful representations, and the computational effectiveness should be improved further.

The most challenges of effective and accurate image recognition in robot vision refer to two aspects as follows:

- Recent studies show that most image recognition models have poor learning capabilities for unlabeled image data. Moreover, these models need a huge number of labeled images to learn for obtaining optimal parameters and the computational cost of image annotations is too high [1].
- The existing image recognition models for robot vision are over-reliant on the data labels and the large amounts of data. The effectiveness and accuracy of image feature extraction and recognition still need to be further improved [2].

To address these challenges, this study proposes an image representation learning and recognition model, termed SimCLR-Inception, which combines the superiority of contrastive learning and a convolutional neural network. It has a great learning capability for unlabeled image data and extracts the optimal image features for them. Furthermore, this model realizes the pre-training of the Inception V3 model using the trained image representations acquired from the SimCLR model, a fact that can improve the performance of image recognition. SimCLR-Inception outperforms the representative CNN models in almost all evaluation metrics on a real-world image set. We summarize the contributions of the proposed SimCLR-Inception as follows:

- Based on the contrastive learning theory, the presented SimCLR-Inception model can generate positive and negative samples using an image augmentation mechanism, and it can effectively extract the feature vectors from unlabeled images by minimizing the contrastive loss function.
- The SimCLR-Inception model realizes pre-training for the Inception V3 model using the trained unlabeled image representations, which can improve the effectiveness and accuracy of image recognition even if the image data scale is small. Compared to the representative models, it provides better performance in image recognition for robot vision.

The remainder of the article are presented as follows: Sect. 2 gives the related work. Section 3 elaborately presents the architecture of SimCLR-Inception model and its realization steps. Then, we show the experimental design, data sets, baselines, evaluation metrics, results, and related analysis in Sect. 4. Finally, we give the conclusion and present the future work in Sect. 5.

2   Related Work

In this section, we focus on recent studies of image recognition in robot vision, which refer to the CL-based and CNN-based models.

Researchers have studied a series of image recognition models based on contrastive learning. Zeng et al. investigated a novel positional contrastive learning (PCL) architecture that significantly improves medical image segmentation performance by using the positional information in medical images to generate contrastive data pairs [29]. Xie et al. investigated a simple and effective self-supervised object detection approach, DetCo, which transmits well over downstream instance-level intensive prediction tasks while preserving high image-level classification accuracy [26]. Tan et al. presented an image recognition model combining the contrastive learning-based multi-branch generation network, which makes the CL-based bidirectional content consistency methods to guarantee the generated images' effectiveness [23]. Wang et al. presented a Long-Short Temporal CL (LSTCL) approach that has a self-supervised pre-training strategy to effectively capture the dependencies over extended time spans and achieve superior performance on a large-scale image data set [25].

For the CNN-based models of image recognition, Dong et al. combined a weighted feature fusion CNN with Graph Attention Network (WFCG) for hyperspectral image classification, which provides an image feature extraction mechanism and can effectively improve the performance of image recognition [5]. Wan et al. presented robot a vision model using a faster R-CNN for multi-class fruits detection, which obtained efficient, more accurate, and faster detection [24]. Gao et al. presented a multi-modal data fusion and multi-scale parallel CNN model, which enhances the accuracy and dependability of robot gesture recognition [7]. Singh et al. presented a Multi-level Particle Swarm Optimization (MPSO) algorithm, which can be used in a specified search space to recommend the optimal CNN architecture and its hyperparameters [19].

Although the recent studies of the CL-based and CNN-based models provide good performance in image recognition, these models still have poor learning capabilities for unlabeled images and overly rely on the quality and quantity of image data for accurate recognition. Hence, it needs to be developed further an accurate and effective image representation learning and recognition model.

Therefore, a novel robot vision model is investigated to solve the problems that image recognition overly relies on the annotated data and has low effectiveness and accuracy. In the SimCLR-Inception framework, we utilize the SimCLR to achieve effective feature extraction of unlabeled data and then leverage Inception V3 with a pre-training mechanism to improve the accuracy of image recognition.

3   Image Representation Learning and Recognition Model

3.1   Architecture Design

The architecture of the proposed image representation learning and recognition model for robot vision, SimCLR-Inception, is illustrated in Fig. 1.

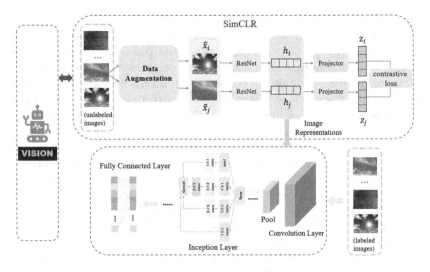

Fig. 1. Image Representations Learning and Recognition Model for Robot Vision.

This architecture mainly consists of two components: image feature extraction and classification. The specific steps of SimCLR-Inception are shown as follows:

3.2   Algorithm Steps

1) Image Feature Extraction

Step 1: Construct the SimCLR model, input 3-channel unlabeled image data, expressed as $\mathbf{X} = \{\mathbf{x}_1, \mathbf{x}_2, \cdots, \mathbf{x}_i, \cdots, \mathbf{x}_N\}$, where the number of samples is N.

Step 2: The input images are augmented and divided into positive and negative samples. Then, the Encoder layer and Projector layer are constructed successively. The Encoder layer is denoted as follows:

$$h_i = f(\tilde{\mathbf{x}}_i) = ResNet(\tilde{\mathbf{x}}_i) \tag{1}$$

where f is ResNet network and $\tilde{\mathbf{x}}_i$ denotes the augmented $\mathbf{x}_i$. Then, SimCLR takes the multilayer perceptron (MLP) as the Projector layer, which is denoted as follows:

$$z_i = g(h_i) = W_{(2)}\sigma\left(W_{(1)}h_i\right) \tag{2}$$

where g is the projection head, which maps the encoded representation h_i to the latent space where the contrastive loss is applied. h_i is the output of the Encoder, of which the dimension is $2,048$. $W_{(1)}$ and $W_{(2)}$ represent the weight matrices. σ denotes the activation function: ReLU.

Step 3: Minimize the contrastive loss function, which is denoted as follows:

$$l_{i,j} = -\log \frac{exp\left(sim\left(z_i, z_j\right)/\tau\right)}{\sum_{k=1}^{2N} \mathbb{I}_{[k\neq i]} exp\left(sim\left(z_i, z_k\right)/\tau\right)} \tag{3}$$

where $sim(u,v) = \frac{u^T v}{\|u\|\|v\|}$ is the sample similarity, u and v are positive and negative sample representation vectors, respectively. $\mathbb{I}_{[k\neq i]} \in \{0,1\}$ denotes an indicator function that equals 1 when $k \neq i$. τ represents the temperature variable. N is the number of samples.

Step 4: Finally, the weight matrix W is extracted from the last Encoder layer as the image representations.

2) Image Feature Classification

Step 5: Construct an Inception V3 model with 5 convolutional layers, 2 pooling layers, 11 Inception module, and a fully connected layer. The 2 pooling layers follow the 3 and 2 convolutional layers, respectively. Each convolutional layer and Inception module is followed by a batch normalization (BN) layer to speed up training and avoid overfitting. $\mathbf{y}_i$ is the output of a BN layer.

$$\mathbf{y}_i = \omega \left(\frac{\mathbf{x}_i - \mu_b}{\sqrt{\sigma_b^2 + \varepsilon}} \right) + \theta \tag{4}$$

where the ith input of a BN layer is $\mathbf{x}_i$; μ_b represents the mean of a batch input samples; σ_b denotes the standard deviation of a batch input samples; ε is a very small constant; ω and θ denotes the parameters to be optimized.

Some hyperparameters are set as follows: epoch = 24, batch size = 32 for each epoch, and learning rate = 0.00001. Take the cross entropy function as the loss function and the Adam as the optimizer.

Step 6: Split the labeled image data into the training and test sets $\mathbf{X}_{train}$ and $\mathbf{Y}_{train}$. Realize the pre-training of Inception V3 model using the extracted weight matrix W from the last Encoder layer of Sim-CLR. Train Inception V3 model by $\mathbf{X}_{train}$ to get the optimal model parameters. Finally, use the trained model to predict $\mathbf{X}_{test}$ and output the image recognition result $\hat{\mathbf{Y}}$.

4   Experiments

To verify the presented SimCLR-Inception model, we conduct a variety of experiments and give the comparison analyses.

4.1   Experiment Design

Based on a 16 GB RAM 3.6 GHz Intel (R) Core (TM) CPU, we designed the contrast experiments with four representative models on four evaluation metrics: accuracy, precision, recall, and F1-Score, to test the performance of the SimCLR-Inception for robot vision on the Multi-class Weather (MW) data set.

4.2   Data Set

Multi-class Weather (MW)[1], a real-world data set of outdoor weather images, consists of 215 rainy images, 357 sunrise images, 253 sunny images, and 300 cloudy images [17]. This study divides it into 900 training set and 225 test set.

4.3   Baselines

We compare the performance of SimCLR-Inception to four typical CNN models for image recognition: LeNet [14], VGG16 [18], Inception V3 [21], and Efficient-Net V2 [22].

---

[1] https://data.mendeley.com/datasets/4drtyfjtfy/1.

(a) LeNet: it consists of 7 layers, with two convolutional layers, two 2×2 pooling layers, and 3 fully connected layers, excluding the input layer, all of which contain the parameters (weights) to be trained.

(b) VGG16: it is one of the convolution networks. VGG16 is a VGG network with 16 weight layers, which contains 5 convolutional layers and the maximum pooling layer, and the kernel size of convolution is set to be 3×3 and 3 fully connected layers. For the constructed convolutional and fully connected layers, ReLU is selected as the activation function.

(c) Inception V3: it has a network depth of 42 hidden layers. In this model, one of the most important improvements is decomposition, which decomposes the 7×7 convolutions into two one-dimensional convolutions 7×1.

(d) EfficientNet V2: it is an improved version of EfficientNet. It uses the MBConv module and also introduces the Fused-MBConv structure, which composed of a 3×3 convolutional layer, multiple Fused-MBConv and MBConv layers.

4.4 Evaluation Metrics

Four representative evaluation metrics: Accuracy, Precision, Recall, and F1-Score are taken to verify the proposed SimCLR-Inception model' performance. TP (True Positive) denotes that a sample is a positive one, and the model correctly predicts it as a positive example. TN (True Negative) is represents that a sample is a negative one, and the model gives a correct predict, the negative sample. FP (False Positive) where a sample is predicted to be positive but its label is negative. FN (False Negative) denotes that a sample is a positive one, but the model predicts it as a negative example. The definitions of these metrics are as follows.

1) Accuracy

$$Accuracy = \frac{TP + TN}{TP + TN + FP + FN} \tag{5}$$

2) Precision

$$Precision = \frac{TP}{TP + FP} \tag{6}$$

3) Recall

$$Recall = \frac{TP}{TP + FN} \tag{7}$$

3) F1-Score

$$F1 - Score = \frac{2 * Precision * Recall}{Precision + Recall} \tag{8}$$

4.5 Experimental Results and Analysis

A series of comparison experiments are conducted on LeNet, VGG16, Inception V3, EfficientNet V2, and the presented SimCLR-Inception models. Then, We show the experimental results regarding four evaluation metrics: Accuracy, Precision, Recall, and F1-Score, in Fig. 2 and Table 1. We also give the related analysis and summarize the superiority of our SimCLR-Inception model.

Figure 2 and Table 1 show the experimental results of accuracy, precision, recall, and F1-Score comparing the SimCLR-Inception to four representative models on the MW data set. The SimCLR-Inception achieves the best performance and it almost obtains the highest evaluation results compared to the other models. The accuracy values of SimCLR-Inception, LeNet, VGG16, Inception V3, and EfficientNet V2 are 0.8929, 0.8356, 0.8889, 0.8489, and 0.8756. The Precision values of SimCLR-Inception, LeNet, VGG16, Inception V3, and EfficientNet V2 are 0.9021, 0.8534, 0.8857, 0.8409, and 0.8806. The recall values of SimCLR-Inception, LeNet, VGG16, Inception V3, and EfficientNet V2

Table 1. Experimental results of four evaluation metrics on different models.

Models	Accuracy	Precision	Recall	F1-Score
LeNet	0.8356	0.8534	0.8093	0.8136
VGG16	0.8889	0.8857	**0.8780**	0.8804
Inception V3	0.8489	0.8409	0.8531	0.8418
EfficientNet V2	0.8756	0.8806	0.8564	0.8595
SimCLR-Inception	**0.8929**	**0.9021**	0.8771	**0.8837**

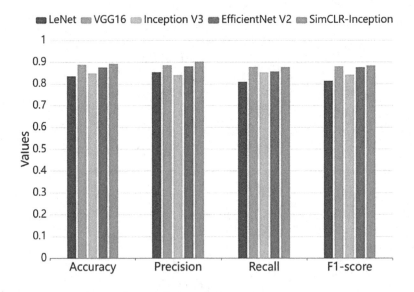

Fig. 2. Comparison on Different Models using Four Evaluation Metrics.

are 0.8771, 0.8093, 0.8780, 0.8531, and 0.8564. The F1-Score values of SimCLR-Inception, LeNet, VGG16, Inception V3, and EfficientNet V2 are 0.8837, 0.8136, 0.8804, 0.8418, and 0.8595, respectively. Compared to the other representative models, the presented SimCLR-Inception improves the accuracy values by around 6%, 0.4%, 4%, and 2%, the Precision values by around 5%, 2%, 6%, and 2%, and the F1-Score values by around 7%, 0.3%, 4%, and 2%. However, the recall value of SimCLR-Inception is slightly lower than VGG16, compared to LeNet, Inception V3, and EfficientNet V2, it also promotes by around 7%, 2%, and 2%.

The results also show that the integration of SimCLR and Inception models can achieve superior image recognition compared to the existing representative models. By the effective image representation generation mechanism using the SimCLR model, more appropriate features can be acquired for the subsequent image classification task. This model also combines with the advantages of Inception V3 referring to the effective dimensional reduction and feature extraction methods, the overfitting avoidance techniques, etc. Therefore, accuracy and effectiveness of the presented SimCLR-Inception model can be greatly promoted.

5 Conclusion

In this study, an image representation learning and recognition model, SimCLR-Inception, for robot vision is designed, which aims to achieve effective image feature extraction and accurate image recognition. We focused on the performance improvement and verified it on a real-world MW data set. The implementation of a contrastive learning model, SimCLR, can realize the image augmentation of unlabeled data, generate more positive and negative sample pairs, and obtain the most appropriate image feature information. After acquiring effective image representations, the Inception V3 model is used for the further classification task. Moreover, four representative image classification models, including LeNet, VGG16, Inception V3, and EfficientNet V2 are used for comparison. The experimental results demonstrate that the proposed SimCLR-Inception can almost get the best performance on four evaluation metrics, including accuracy, precision, recall, and F1-Score.

Nonetheless, the SimCLR-Inception model cannot overcome the problem of the high computational costs that existed in the SimCLR and Inception models. We just used one data set to verify the SimCLR-Inception model' performance and the model's generalization was not considered. In the future, we are going to further improve the generalization of the presented model using various image data sets in different real-world scenarios. Moreover, we will dive into an improved contrastive learning model for more accurate image recognition in robot vision with lower computational costs compared to the existing models.

Acknowledgement. We acknowledge the funding support from the National Natural Science Foundation of China (71974069).

References

1. Albelwi, S.: Survey on self-supervised learning: auxiliary pretext tasks and contrastive learning methods in imaging. Entropy **24**(4), 551 (2022)
2. Bae, H., et al.: IROS 2019 lifelong robotic vision: object recognition challenge [competitions]. IEEE Robot. Autom. Mag. **27**(2), 11–16 (2020)
3. Cao, M.: Face recognition robot system based on intelligent machine vision image recognition. Int. J. Syst. Assur. Eng. Manage. **14**(2), 708–717 (2023)
4. Chollet, F.: Xception: deep learning with depthwise separable convolutions. In: Proceedings of the IEEE Conference on Computer Vision and Pattern Recognition, pp. 1251–1258 (2017)
5. Dong, Y., Liu, Q., Du, B., Zhang, L.: Weighted feature fusion of convolutional neural network and graph attention network for hyperspectral image classification. IEEE Trans. Image Process. **31**, 1559–1572 (2022)
6. Falcon, W., Cho, K.: A framework for contrastive self-supervised learning and designing a new approach. arXiv preprint arXiv:2009.00104 (2020)
7. Gao, Q., Liu, J., Ju, Z.: Hand gesture recognition using multimodal data fusion and multiscale parallel convolutional neural network for human-robot interaction. Expert Syst. **38**(5), e12490 (2021)
8. Grill, J.B., et al.: Bootstrap your own latent-a new approach to self-supervised learning. In: Advances in Neural Information Processing Systems, vol. 33 (2020)
9. Hadsell, R., Chopra, S., LeCun, Y.: Dimensionality reduction by learning an invariant mapping. In: 2006 IEEE Computer Society Conference on Computer Vision and Pattern Recognition (CVPR 2006). IEEE (2006)
10. Huang, G., Liu, Z., Van Der Maaten, L., Weinberger, K.Q.: Densely connected convolutional networks. In: Proceedings of the IEEE Conference on Computer Vision and Pattern Recognition (2017)
11. Kim, H.E., Cosa-Linan, A., Santhanam, N., Jannesari, M., Maros, M.E., Ganslandt, T.: Transfer learning for medical image classification: a literature review. BMC Med. Imaging **22**(1), 69 (2022)
12. Lai, X., et al.: Semi-supervised semantic segmentation with directional context-aware consistency. In: Proceedings of the IEEE/CVF Conference on Computer Vision and Pattern Recognition (2021)
13. Lan, R., Sun, L., Liu, Z., Lu, H., Pang, C., Luo, X.: MADNet: a fast and lightweight network for single-image super resolution. IEEE Trans. Cybern. **51**(3), 1443–1453 (2020)
14. LeCun, Y., Bottou, L., Bengio, Y., Haffner, P.: Gradient-based learning applied to document recognition. Proc. IEEE **86**(11), 2278–2324 (1998)
15. Li, S., et al.: An indoor autonomous inspection and firefighting robot based on slam and flame image recognition. Fire **6**(3), 93 (2023)
16. Li, Y., Yang, S., Zheng, Y., Lu, H.: Improved point-voxel region convolutional neural network: 3D object detectors for autonomous driving. IEEE Trans. Intell. Transp. Syst. **23**(7), 9311–9317 (2021)
17. Oluwafemi, A.G., Zenghui, W.: Multi-class weather classification from still image using said ensemble method. In: 2019 Southern African Universities Power Engineering Conference/Robotics and Mechatronics/Pattern Recognition Association of South Africa (SAUPEC/RobMech/PRASA). IEEE (2019)
18. Simonyan, K., Zisserman, A.: Very deep convolutional networks for large-scale image recognition. arXiv preprint arXiv:1409.1556 (2014)

19. Singh, P., Chaudhury, S., Panigrahi, B.K.: Hybrid MPSO-CNN: multi-level particle swarm optimized hyperparameters of convolutional neural network. Swarm Evol. Comput. **63**, 100863 (2021)
20. Szegedy, C., et al.: Going deeper with convolutions. In: Proceedings of the IEEE Conference on Computer Vision and Pattern Recognition (2015)
21. Szegedy, C., Vanhoucke, V., Ioffe, S., Shlens, J., Wojna, Z.: Rethinking the inception architecture for computer vision. In: Proceedings of the IEEE Conference on Computer Vision and Pattern Recognition (2016)
22. Tan, M., Le, Q.: EfficientNetV2: smaller models and faster training. In: International Conference on Machine Learning (2021)
23. Tan, Z., Teng, Z.: Improving generalization of image recognition with multi-branch generation network and contrastive learning. Multimedia Tools Appl. **82**(18), 1–21 (2023)
24. Wan, S., Goudos, S.: Faster R-CNN for multi-class fruit detection using a robotic vision system. Comput. Networks **168**, 107036 (2020)
25. Wang, J., Bertasius, G., Tran, D., Torresani, L.: Long-short temporal contrastive learning of video transformers. In: Proceedings of the IEEE/CVF Conference on Computer Vision and Pattern Recognition (2022)
26. Xie, E., Ding, J., Wang, W., Zhan, X., Xu, H., Sun, P., Li, Z., Luo, P.: Detco: Unsupervised contrastive learning for object detection. In: Proceedings of the IEEE/CVF International Conference on Computer Vision (2021)
27. Xu, F., Xu, F., Xie, J., Pun, C.M., Lu, H., Gao, H.: Action recognition framework in traffic scene for autonomous driving system. IEEE Trans. Intell. Transp. Syst. **23**(11), 22301–22311 (2021)
28. Yang, J., et al.: Unified contrastive learning in image-text-label space. In: Proceedings of the IEEE/CVF Conference on Computer Vision and Pattern Recognition (2022)
29. Zeng, D., et al.: Positional contrastive learning for volumetric medical image segmentation. In: de Bruijne, M., et al. (eds.) MICCAI 2021. LNCS, vol. 12902, pp. 221–230. Springer, Cham (2021). https://doi.org/10.1007/978-3-030-87196-3_21
30. Zhou, W., Wang, H., Wan, Z.: Ore image classification based on improved CNN. Comput. Electr. Eng. **99**, 107819 (2022)

Anime Sketch Colourization Using Enhanced Pix2pix GAN

Nikhil Prashant Mudhalwadkar[1], Hamam Mokayed[1(✉)], Lama Alkhaled[1],
Palaiahnakote Shivakumara[2], and Yan Chai Hum[3]

[1] Lulea Tekniska Universitet, Lulea, Sweden
`nikmud-1@student.ltu.se`, {`hamam.mokayed,lama.alkhaled`}`@ltu.se`
[2] Centre of Image and Signal Processing, Faculty of Computer Science and
Information Technology, University of Malaya, 50603 Kuala Lumpur, Malaysia
`shiva@um.edu.my`
[3] Department of Mechatronics and Biomedical Engineering, Lee Kong Chian Faculty
of Engineering and Science, Universiti Tunku Abdul Rahman, Petaling Jaya, Malaysia
`humyc@utar.edu.my`

Abstract. Coloring manga sketches is challenging due to the wide gap
between the meaning of color and sketches. Unlike Western comics,
Japanese manga sketch does not provide color, rather they are in binary
form using a screening technique. These styles differ in how regions
are filled, but converting between them is a difficult task that is typically done manually. This paper aims to develop a method for coloring
Japanese manga composed of sketches and dialogue. Coloring is considered a challenging and time-consuming task for creators. The proposed
method proposes using a pix2pix GAN (Generative Adversarial Network)
to color a manga sketch when given as input. Additionally, an alternative approach is suggested, which involves modifying the generator
loss function to improve the performance. This paper aims to automate
the process of coloring a single sketch, with the potential to extend the
research in the future to apply the colors consistently across multiple
manga strips.

Keywords: pix2pix · Conditional Generative Adversarial Network ·
manga · colorization

1 Introduction

Day by day demand for Japanese manga is increasing because the story presented
in comic books, graphics, and novels attracts readers at all levels, irrespective of
age and gender. It is evident from the following statement [1].

*Manga is an umbrella term for a wide variety of comic books and graphic
novels originally produced and published in Japan.*

H. Lu et al. (Eds.): ACPR 2023, LNCS 14406, pp. 148–164, 2023.
https://doi.org/10.1007/978-3-031-47634-1_12

The Japanese Manga cap is valued at 4 billion USD in 2020 [2]. The North American Manga market is valued at 250 million in 2020 [3]. It is noted that American manga focuses more on aesthetic properties while Japanese manga focuses more on stories. Therefore, American Mangas are colorful, but Japanese manga is binary without any color. There are several methods proposed for coloring Japanese manga to make it attractive and enhance the details [4]. However, those models work well for manga but not different types of manga, such as gray manga sketches and binary manga sketches. In addition, there is a big gap between the color and the meaning of the sketches. Thus, coloring Japanese manga is still considered an open challenge. For example, Sample gray and binary Japanese manga are shown in Fig. 1, where one can see gray manga is more informative than the binary manga. Different machine learning methods and deep learning models are widely implemented in different sectors such as document analysis [5], medical investigation [6], traffic monitoring [7,8], and many others. Hence the aim of the proposed work is to color binary manga sketches to make them informative and attractive. An exploration of the proper model to address such challenges is the main objective of this study. We propose a new Pix2Pix Generative Adversarial Network (GAN). This is because the GAN could generate relevant samples and more discriminative power to choose the colors according to the meaning of the content in the images. Further, the proposed method introduces a new loss called cosine similarity loss to improve the colorization of sketches.

Fig. 1. Grey-scale and skitch image example (Color figure online)

The main contributions are as follows. (i) Developing a model for coloring both gray and binary sketches is new compared to the state-of-the-art methods. (ii) Exploring Pixel2Pixel GAN for coloring is new and (iii) Proposing cosine similarity loss for reducing the gap between the ground truth and input image is also new compared to the existing GAN-based models. The rest of the paper is organized as follows. Section 2 reviews different existing methods of coloring sketches. The Pix2Pix GAN has been presented and illustrated for coloring sketches in Sect. 3. Experimental setup and discussion on the results to validate the proposed model are presented in Sect. 4. Furthermore, Sect. 5 summarizes the findings and discussion.

2   Literature Review

Several models have been developed in the past for coloring gray and binary Japanese manga sketches [4]. The methods explored different types of models with human intervention, semi-automatic and automatic to address the challenges of coloring. We review the same models to justify the gap between the coloring and the meaning of sketches.

Sýkoray et al. present LazyBrush tool [9] for coloring sketches. However, this tool requires careful user strokes made with a color brush. Although the proposed tool is good, it has the following limitations. The success of the method depends on human intervention, and it is computationally expensive. To reduce the number of computations, Fourey et al [10] proposed a model for colorization based on a geometric analysis using spline curves. However, the results are not satisfactory. Another early attempt at colorization of manga sketches was proposed by Qu et al. [11] which also depends on user interaction to draw scribbles on input images. To reduce the effect of human intervention or interaction, the models [12,13] used a semi-automatic tool.

After the recent progress in the successful implementation of deep neural networks, especially conditional generative adversarial networks (cGAN) [14], deep learning-based methods for colorizing black and white images have been presented by various researchers since 2017. As a very first approach Liu et al. [15] presented a method based on a cGAN. They called their method Autopainter in which the user can determine the color of the resulted colorized image by adding color strokes as color hints to the sketch image which is derived from Sangkloy et al. [16]. There is also a web application [17] which colorizes sketches using a UNet [18] pretty well. It is available for general users and the main source code is available via GitHub [19]. The application is very user-friendly and allows the user to change the color of different parts of the output image by drawing scribbles on the input sketch image. Moreover, the user can choose between three colorizing styles. Zhang et al. [20] present a two-stage sketch colorization method: 1) Drafting stage, 2) Refinement stage. They use two GANs for each stage. In the first stage, different colors are splashed over the input sketch image and in the second stage wrong colors are removed. In this two-stage method, the user can improve the quality of the result by putting hint points. Ci et al. [21] propose a new cGAN structure (combined with a local features network) to improve color shading in a scribble colors-based colorization method. They also use WGAN-GP [22] with perceptual loss [23] as a criterion to train their network. Apart from the methods that utilize color hints via color strokes or scribbles Xian et al. [24] introduce a new method called TextureGAN that utilizes textures as color hints which require the user to specify different texture images for different parts of the sketch image.

Using a style image as a reference to deep colorization of another sketch image is also done in a method presented by Zhang et al. [25] that utilizes an auxiliary classifier generative adversarial network (AC-GAN) [26]. Sun et al. [27] propose a dual conditional GAN to colorize icon images. The proposed network gets a contour icon and a colorized reference icon as inputs and generates a colorized icon that has the same contour as the first input and the same color style as the reference icon. To minimize the effort of providing color hints Kim et al. [28] present a tag-based method which in addition to the input sketch image requires color variant tags to be fed to a GAN structure they called Tag2Pix.

When you are dealing with a sequence of sketch images to colorize an animation, you have to face another challenge, and that is maintaining color consistency between successive frames. Thasarathan et al. [29] present an automatic method based on cGAN to reduce flicker in colorizing video sequences. They achieve this goal by adding an extra condition to the generator and discriminator networks. However, their method suffers from wrong color accumulation. To address this issue Shi et al. [30] propose a deep architecture that consists of a color transform network and a temporal refinement network. They consider some colored frames as reference frames for colorizing other sketch frames. The wrong color accumulation is avoided by using distance attention layers to determine the regional correspondence between the sketch and reference frames.

A well-suited deep neural network for image colorization is an image-to-image conditional generative adversarial network. Indeed image to image GAN has a much wider application than just colorizing images [25]. One can train this network to learn almost all kinds of image-to-image transformation including style transfer [31], image restoration tasks such as increasing image resolution [32], image in-painting which aims to repaint portions of an image which have lost data [33], image de-raining [34] (removing rain effect in images). One of the first successful implementations of such a network is called Pix2Pix GAN [14]. Its structure contains a U-Net generator network and a discriminator network called PatchGAN and can be used to solve various image-to-image transformation tasks.

Liu et al. [35] uses Pix2Pix GAN to generate synthetic paintings from sketches with different art styles (post-impressionism, expressionism, ...) and artist styles (Van Gogh, Claude Monet, ...) styles. Wang et al. [36] proposed a Pix2Pix GAN called Perceptual Adversarial Network (PAN) which can be used in de-raining images, generating a real image from a segmented (labeled) image, creating a street map from top view real images, image in-painting and creating real colorful images from sketch images. Albahar et al. [37] present a guided image-to-image network structure that concatenates the guide image with the hidden layers of a bi-directional feature transformation network. They demonstrate the superiority of their method in pose transfer, texture transfer, and up-sampling image-to-image transformation tasks.

In summary, the advanced models have been used for coloring sketches which include different versions of GAN. However, it is noted that none of the methods obtains satisfactory results for coloring gray and binary sketches. In addition, the GAN has been used for coloring sketches, but Pix2Pix GAN has not been explored for coloring sketches. Furthermore, none of the methods fill the gap between the color and the meaning of the sketches. Therefore, this work aims at adapting Pix2Pix GAN for coloring sketches.

3   Proposed Work

3.1   Data Source

Historically manga is handcrafted by the creator [38] by either sketch or digitally altered. It is also noted that manga is not coloured [39]. Hence, the challenge is to create or find a dataset that has manga and its colored counterpart or a suitable alternative. Also, in order to train a Pix2pix [40] network the dataset must have a sketch(not a colored image) and a reference colored image.

A dataset that satisfies the criteria was identified [41]. This dataset is a true sketch-colored pair relationship. Hence, the trained model can learn a one-on-one relationship. Here is an example of a sketch-colored image pair:

Fig. 2. Sketch-Coloured image pair example

3.2 Background

This subsection establishes context. This paper builds atop the pix2pix network. The model training process is the exact same as described in the original paper [40]. For this context, the model training would look like Fig. 3.

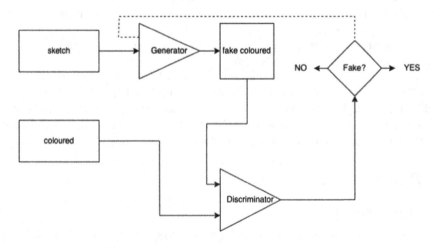

Fig. 3. Model Training

The blocks can be described as follows:

1. sketch: This is the sketch from input images.
2. Generator: This is the unet256 [42] described further in Sect. 4.2.
3. fake coloured: This is the sketch coloured by the generator.
4. coloured: This is the coloured counterpart of the sketch images.
5. Discriminator: This is the patchgan model [40].

The basic mechanism of the architecture remains intact. The major experiments pertain to patchgan discriminator and data. The generator is unchanged in all experiments barring the changes to batch size and data input size.

3.3 Method

The main objective of this paper is to conduct a comparative analysis among 4 main experiments as summarised in the Table 1:

Table 1. List of experiments

	Experiment Name	Details	train batch size	validation batch size
1	Baseline	Simple pix2pix model	16	1
2	Higher batch size	Increasing the train and validation batch size	64	16
3	Custom PatchGAN	Flatten the output of 16*16 patches in patchGAN to a 1*1 output	64	16
4	Adding cosine similarity to GAN loss	Using a resnet 50 model create embeddings to calculate the cosine similarity between real and fake coloured images	32	16

Experiments 1 and 2. These are basic pix2pix GANs. The only difference is the batch size for training and validation. These can be considered baseline experiments.

Experiment 3: Remove Patchgan. Experiment 3 (depicted in Fig. 4) is effectively neutering the patchGAN [40] mechanism. The patchGAN layer outputs a 16*16 layer. Two more additional layers are placed after it:

1. Flatten the output of the pix2pix layer to 256*1
2. Create a fully connected layer network that is a single node to output the probability.

The patchGAN mechanism evaluates individual N*N patches of the output image. This mechanism worked reasonably well with real-world objects. The objective behind this experimentation was that since anime/manga are not real objects but rather artistic interpretations, it could be interesting to remove the patchGAN mechanism and evaluate the output image as an entire entity.

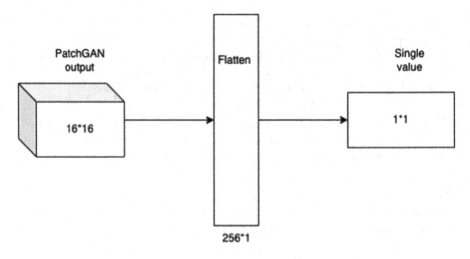

Fig. 4. Discriminator network

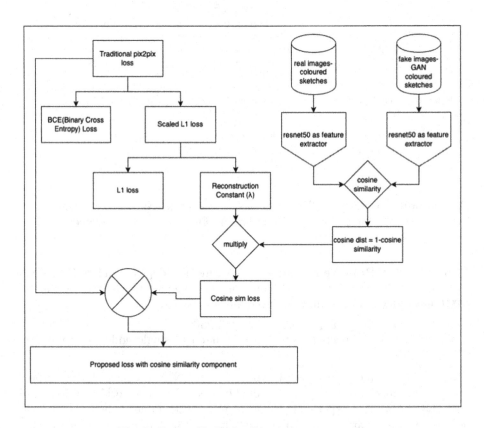

Fig. 5. Cosine Similarity Discriminator network

Experiment 4: Cosine Similarity Component. In this experiment, cosine similarity was added as a third loss component. This is depicted by Fig. 5. The steps are as follows:

1. Use a pre-trained resnet50 model [43] as a feature extractor.
2. On generator
   (a) Create feature embedding from real images
   (b) Create feature embedding from fake colored images
   (c) Use cosine similarity [44] to calculate the similarity between fake colored images and real images.
3. Add this new loss function to the original loss function.
4. Use 1-cosine similarity to calculate cosine distance.

As a result, the GAN loss can be expressed as:

$$G* = arg \overset{min}{G} \overset{max}{D} L_{cGAN}(G, D) + \lambda(L_{L1}(G) + CosineSim(G)) \qquad (1)$$

4 Experimental Setup

4.1 Data

The data used in this paper is the anime-sketch-colorization-pair from kaggle [41]. The dataset is already divided into train and validation sets. This data contains 14200 pairs of sketch and colored anime in the train data. There are 3545 pairs of sketch and colored anime in the validation set. All the images are (.png) files. The size of this data is 6.5 GB.

Each image will be sized 1024×512 containing 2 images (colored and sketch)2. The colored image will take half of the size of the full image and the sketch image will take the other half. Hence, the resultant image will be a (512×512) color image and a (512×512) sketch image.

4.2 Model Architecture

All experiments are based on the pix2pix architecture [40]. A UNET256 [45] is used as the generator. The patchgan [40] is used as a discriminator. Both these implementations were taken from the pytorch-lightning-bolts [46] library and were used in the experimentations.

4.3 Data Augmentations

The albumentations [47] library was used to implement data augmentation. The image size of (512*512) was resized to (256*256) for faster model training and less memory consumption. A random horizontal flip with a probability of 0.5 was added to the images to introduce variability.

For the sketches, a random color-jitter with a probability of 0.1 was added to add variability to the quality of input images.

4.4   Training and Hosting

The experimentation has been done with the pytorch lightning framework [48]. All experiments[1] were run on the kaggle [49] platform for 100 max epochs using free community GPUs. As the focus was to establish feasibility of the architectures, no parameter tuning was conducted. All experiments are hosted on huggingface [50].

5   Results

5.1   Training Metrics

There were four main experiments carried out as stated in Table 1. Table 2, contains a summary of the metrics across all experiments. Please note, the cosine similarity generator loss is different than the other experiments from equation (1). Hence, it cannot be compared to the other three experiments directly.

The first two rows of the table show the batch size used during training and validation for each configuration. It can be seen that the "Higher Batch Size" configuration uses a larger batch size of 64 during both training and validation, while the "Baseline" configuration uses a batch size of 16. The "PatchGAN" configuration uses the same batch size as the "Higher Batch Size" configuration. The third row of the table shows the number of training epochs used for each configuration. All configurations were trained for 100 epochs except the cosine similarity experiment.

The next four rows of the table show the loss values for the generator and discriminator networks during training and validation. It can be observed that the "Higher Batch Size" configuration performed better than the "Baseline" configuration in terms of generator loss during training (26.86 vs 34.56). However, this configuration did not perform as well on validation, resulting in a higher generator loss (41.17 vs 43.42). It can also be seen that the "PatchGAN" configuration did not perform as well as the other two configurations in terms of generator and discriminator loss during both training and validation.

The results of this experiment show that using a larger batch size during training on this dataset improves the performance of a GAN in terms of generator loss. However, this improvement may not be reflected in validation performance. Additionally, the use of a PatchGAN architecture did not result in improved performance in this experiment.

---

[1] Experiment's link: https://huggingface.co/spaces/nmud19/Sketch2ColourDemo.

Table 2. Experiment Results

Property	Baseline	Higer Batch Size	PatchGAN	cosine Similarity
train batch size	16	64	64	32
val batch size	1	32	32	16
n epochs	100	100	100	84
train gen loss	34.56	26.86	34.7	54.05
train disc loss	0.015	0.12	0.015	0.02
val gen loss	43.42	41.17	39.12	84.66
val disc loss	1.33	0.91	1.64	1.4

5.2 Evaluation

A popular metric to evaluate GANs is the FID score [51]. This paper uses two
FID score reference datasets- the original colored images, viz, the validation
dataset [41] and the cifar10 data [52]. To generate statistics for the cifar10 data,
a self authored kaggle notebook was utilized [53].

The FID score can be interpreted as, the lower the better. Table 3 compares
the results of the 4 experiments in Table 1 and the original coloured and sketch
images from the validation dataset [41] to the original coloured images and the
cifar10 [52] data respectively. The best-performing experiment is the cosine similarity component experiment in 3.3. The ideal score is the data compared with
itself, i.e., the original colored validation data [41].

Table 3. FID scores with original colored images and cifar10 dataset.

Input Dataset	Original coloured images	Cifar10
original coloured images	$-1.14E-13$	257.677
original sketch images	182.844	343.333
cosine sim	100.608	280.573
modified summarized	134.822	285.916
train16 val1	118.520	284.289
train64 val16	112.099	288.142

5.3 Visualizations

The figures below are examples of the output across all models. The figure is
a (2*3) image where the first 4 images(left to right) are the outputs of models.
The next two are the raw images.

Fig. 6. Example 1- Image with textures

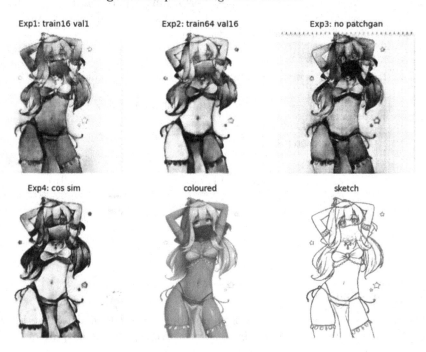

Fig. 7. Example 2- Full body anime

5.4   Observations

Table 4 does a comparative analysis of the experiments specified in Table 1
    The experiments have established an interesting insight into training the pix2pix model.

1. There are multiple parameters in the experiment that could be tuned better. The first two experiments demonstrate this potential.
2. From the third experiment in Table [1], it is observed that for this problem a patchgan is better as compared to a simple discriminator.
3. The final experiment in Table [1] establishes an improvement over the existing loss function to stabilize training and ascertain the problem objectively.

Table 4. Experiments and observations for the 4 experiments

Property	Baseline	Higher Batch size	Custom PatchGAN	Cosine Similarity
GAN loss observations	Generator loss is unstable and decreasing	Generator loss stable and decreasing	Stable loss as compared to baseline but loss not decreasing with same velocity	Most stable and decreasing loss
PatchGAN loss observations	High variability	Less variablitiy as compared to baseline but more than exp 4	High variability	Lowest variability out of all experiments
Sample Image Grid observations	Loss was unstable due to low train sample in batch and high variablity in batches	Stable loss produces better colours	Output images have a grainy top. PatchGAN of 16*16 is better than 1*1	Output images are better quality as compared to rest.

5.5   Limitations and Future Work

1. Data Quality for Model training: All the current implementations use a unet256 [42] model. The next step could be to use the images with their highest quality, viz, (512*512) instead of resizing it to (256*256) as stated in 4.3.
2. Model Training: All experiments were done on the kaggle platform (Sect. 4.4) with the gpu free tier that had limitations on the runtime of the notebooks [49]. Using better hardware would improve the runtime of the experiments, i.e., experiments could be run for more epochs.
3. Model tuning: Due to hardware constraints, none of the experiments had hyperparameters tuned. All existing parameters had vanilla values. This could drastically improve the model's performance.
4. Data Diversity: The data contains anime characters that are humanoid. However, if a non-humanoid cartoon character is used the models will not work well. This can be demonstrated in the Fig. 8. To combat this, the dataset can be extended to include cartoon characters if needed.

Fig. 8. Example 3- Anime on cartoons

5. Post Processing: To improve the output quality and consistency some post-processing methods can be applied. The existing thesis creates a single-shot image colouring mechanism. This architecture can be improved further by taking inspiration from [54]. Human intervention to fix the colour palette could be included as an aid to the manga creator. There can be multiple pipelines based on the genre of manga [54].

5.6   Implications of Results

Comparing all the experiments side by side in Figs. 6 and 7, the results seem encouraging to the naked eye. In both cases, the model is able to distinguish between various contours of the image. The models assign a different color tone to the skin as opposed to the clothing. Inferring the evaluation of the experiments in Table 3, there could be significant improvements made to the model considering the best FID score vs the actual FID score(in the best experiment too). These potential improvements are discussed in the previous section, Sect. 5.5. To conclude, these models could be used as baseline models; the main takeaway being the comparison of different experiments.

6   Conclusion

This paper attempts to formulate a problem for the colouring sketches. Firstly, various datasets are explored along with the feasibility of certain problem statement formulations. Secondly, an extensive literature survey is undertaken to isolate and compare the most appropriate GAN architectures. Thirdly, various experiments are conducted using the pix2pix architecture. Finally, results are computed and the model is hosted using huggingface spaces.

While implementing this, a conscious decision was taken to forgo cross-domain learning and focus on image translation. However, this architecture can be useful to establish the characters with the same palette over and over again.

References

1. Amanda, P.: A Beginner's Guide to Manga (2018). https://www.nypl.org/blog/2018/12/27/beginners-guide-manga
2. Crystalyn, H.: Manga Market in Japan Hits Record 612.6 Billion Yen (2020). https://www.animenewsnetwork.com/news/2021-02-26/manga-market-in-japan-hits-record-612.6-billion-yen-in-2020/.169987
3. Milton, G.: Manga Sales in North America Hit All-time High (2020). https://icv2.com/articles/markets/view/48728/manga-sales-north-america-hit-all-time-high-2020
4. Zhao, Y., Ren, D., Chen, Y., Jia, W., Wang, R., Liu, X.: Cartoon image processing: a survey. Int. J. Comput. Vision **130**(11), 2733–2769 (2022)
5. Shrinidhi, K., Alain, P., Hamam, M., Marcus, L., Didier, S., Muhammad, Z.A.: EmmDocClassifier: efficient multimodal document image classifier for scarce data. Appl. Sci. **12**(3), 1457 (2022)
6. Wingates, V., et al.: Performance analysis of seven convolutional neural networks (CNNs) with transfer learning for invasive ductal carcinoma (IDC) grading in breast histopathological images. Sci. Rep. **12**(1), 19200 (2022)
7. Muhammad Ahmed, U.K., et al.: A comprehensive survey of depth completion approaches. Sensors **22**(18), 6969 (2022)
8. Hamam, M., Mohamed, A.: A robust thresholding technique for generic structured document classifier using ordinal structure fuzzy logic. Int. J. Innovative Comput. Inf. Control **10**(4), 1543–1554 (2014)
9. Daniel, S., John, D., Steven, C.: LazyBrush: flexible painting tool for hand-drawn cartoons. In: Computer Graphics Forum, vol. 28, no. 2, pp. 599–608. Wiley (2009)
10. Sébastien, F., David, T., David, R.: A fast and efficient semi-guided algorithm for flat coloring line-arts. In: International Symposium on Vision, Modeling and Visualization (2018)
11. Qu, Y., Wong, T.-T., Pheng-Ann, P.-A.: Manga colorization. ACM Trans. Graph. **25**(3), 1214–1220 (2006)
12. Sato, K., Matsui, Y., Yamasaki, T., Aizawa, K.: Reference-based manga colorization by graph correspondence using quadratic programming. In: SIGGRAPH Asia 2014 Technical Briefs, SA 2014, pp. 1–4. Association for Computing Machinery (2014). https://doi.org/10.1145/2669024.2669037 ISBN 978-1-4503-2895-1
13. Chen, S.-Y., et al.: Active colorization for cartoon line drawings. IEEE Trans. Vis. Comput. Graph. **28**(2), 1198–1208 (2022). https://doi.org/10.1109/TVCG.2020.3009949

14. Isola, P., Zhu, J.-Y., Zhou, T., Efros, A.A.: Image-to-image translation with conditional adversarial networks. In: Proceedings of the IEEE Conference on Computer Vision and Pattern Recognition, pp. 1125–1134 (2017)
15. Liu, Y., Qin, Z., Luo, Z., Wang, H.: Auto-painter: cartoon image generation from sketch by using conditional generative adversarial networks. arXiv:1705.01908 (2017)
16. Sangkloy, P., Lu, J., Fang, C., Yu, F., Hays, J.: Scribbler: controlling deep image synthesis with sketch and color. In: Proceedings of the IEEE Conference on Computer Vision and Pattern Recognition, pp. 5400–5409 (2017)
17. Petalica paint (2022). https://petalica.com/index_en.html
18. Ronneberger, O., Fischer, P., Brox, T.: U-Net: convolutional networks for biomedical image segmentation. arXiv:1505.04597 (2015)
19. Yonetsuji, T.: Paintschainer (2017). https://github.com/pfnet/PaintsChainer
20. Zhang, L., Li, C., Wong, T.-T., Ji, Y., Liu, C.: Two-stage sketch colorization. ACM Trans. Graph. 37(6), 1–14 (2018)
21. Ci, Y., Ma, X., Wang, Z., Li, H., Luo, Z.: User-guided deep anime line art colorization with conditional adversarial networks. In: Proceedings of the 26th ACM international conference on Multimedia, MM 2018, pp. 1536–1544. Association for Computing Machinery (2018). https://doi.org/10.1145/3240508.3240661 ISBN 978-1-4503-5665-7
22. Gulrajani, I., Ahmed, F., Arjovsky, M., Dumoulin, V., Courville, A.C.: Improved training of Wasserstein GANs. arXiv:1704.00028 (2017)
23. Johnson, J., Alahi, A., Fei-Fei, L.: Perceptual losses for real-time style transfer and super-resolution. In: Leibe, B., Matas, J., Sebe, N., Welling, M. (eds.) Computer Vision – ECCV 2016. ECCV 2016. Lecture Notes in Computer Science, vol. 9906, pp. 694–711. Springer, Cham (2016). https://doi.org/10.1007/978-3-319-46475-6_43
24. Xian, W., et al.: TextureGAN: controlling deep image synthesis with texture patches. In: Proceedings of the IEEE Conference on Computer Vision and Pattern Recognition, pp. 8456–8465
25. Zhang, L., Ji, Y., Lin, X., Liu, C.: Style transfer for anime sketches with enhanced residual U-Net and auxiliary classifier GAN. In: 2017 4th IAPR Asian Conference on Pattern Recognition (ACPR), pp. 506–511 (2017). https://doi.org/10.1109/ACPR.2017.61 ISSN: 2327-0985
26. Odena, A., Olah, C., Shlens, J.: Conditional image synthesis with auxiliary classifier GANs. In: International Conference on Machine Learning, pp. 2642–2651. PMLR (2017)
27. Sun, T.-H., Lai, C.-H., Wong, S.-K., Wang, Y.-S.: Adversarial colorization of icons based on contour and color conditions. In: Proceedings of the 27th ACM International Conference on Multimedia, MM 2019, pp. 683–691. Association for Computing Machinery (2019). https://doi.org/10.1145/3343031.3351041 ISBN 978-1-4503-6889-6
28. Kim, H., Jhoo, H.Y., Park, E., Yoo, S.: Tag2Pix: line art colorization using text tag with SECat and changing loss. In: 2019 IEEE/CVF International Conference on Computer Vision (ICCV), pp. 9055–9064 (2019). https://arxiv.org/abs/1908.05840
29. Thasarathan, H., Nazeri, K., Ebrahimi, M.: Automatic temporally coherent video colorization. arXiv:1904.09527 (2019)
30. Shi, M., Zhang, J.-Q., Chen, S.-Y., Gao, L., Lai, Y., Zhang, F.-L.: Reference-based deep line art video colorization. IEEE Trans. Vis. Comput. Graph. 29(6), 2965–2979 (2022)

31. Christophe, S., Mermet, S., Laurent, M., Touya, G.: Neural map style transfer exploration with GANs. Int. J. Cartography **8**(1), 18–36 (2022). https://doi.org/10.1080/23729333.2022.2031554

32. Beaulieu, M., Foucher, S., Haberman, D., Stewart, C.,: Deep image- to-image transfer applied to resolution enhancement of sentinel-2 images. In: IGARSS 2018–2018 IEEE International Geoscience and Remote Sensing Symposium, pp. 2611–2614 (2018). https://doi.org/10.1109/IGARSS.2018.8517655 ISSN: 2153-7003

33. Suraj, K.A., Swamy, S.H., Shetty, S.S., Jayashree, R.: A deep learning technique for image inpainting with GANs. In: Gunjan, V.K., Zurada, J.M. (eds.) Modern Approaches in Machine Learning and Cognitive Science: A Walkthrough. SCI, vol. 956, pp. 33–42. Springer, Cham (2021). https://doi.org/10.1007/978-3-030-68291-0_4

34. Zhang, H., Sindagi, V., Patel, V.M.: Image de-raining using a conditional generative adversarial network. IEEE Trans. Circ. Syst. Video Technol. **30**(11), 3943–3956 (2020). https://doi.org/10.1109/TCSVT.2019.2920407. ISSN 1558–2205

35. Liu, B., Song, K., Elgammal, A.: Sketch-to-art: synthesizing stylized art images from sketches. arXiv:2002.12888 (2020)

36. Wang, C., Xu, C., Wang, C., Tao, D.: Perceptual adversarial networks for image-to-image transformation. IEEE Trans. Image Process. **27**(8), 4066–4079 (2018). https://doi.org/10.1109/TIP.2018.2836316. ISSN 1941–0042

37. AlBahar, B., Huang, J.-B.: Guided image-to-image translation with bi-directional feature transformation. In: Proceedings of the IEEE/CVF International Conference on Computer Vision, pp. 9016–9025 (2019)

38. Aizawa, K., et al.: Building a manga dataset "manga109" with annotations for multimedia applications. IEEE Multimedia **27**(2), 8–18 (2020). https://doi.org/10.1109/mmul.2020.2987895

39. Morishita, Y.: Why are Manga not colored?. https://thejapaneseway.com/why-are-manga-not-colored/

40. Isola, P., Zhu, J.-Y., Zhou, T., Efros, A.A.: Image-to-image translation with conditional adversarial networks. arXiv:1611.07004 (2016)

41. Kim, T.: Anime Sketch Colorization Pair (2021). https://www.kaggle.com/datasets/ktaebum/anime-sketch-colorization-pair

42. Nazeri, K., Ng, E., Ebrahimi, M.: Image colorization using generative adversarial networks. In: Proceedings of Tenth International Conference on Articulated Motion and Deformable Objects (AMDO), pp. 85–94 (2018). https://doi.org/10.1007/978-3-319-94544-6_9. ISBN 978-3-319-94543-9

43. He, K., Zhang, X., Ren, S., Sun, J.: Deep residual learning for image recognition. arXiv:1512.03385 (2015)

44. Cosine Similarity Pytorch. https://pytorch.org/docs/stable/generated/torch.nn.CosineSimilarity.html

45. Ronneberger, O., Fischer, P., Brox, T.: U-Net: convolutional networks for biomedical image segmentation. arXiv:1505.04597 (2015)

46. Falcon, W., Cho, K.: A framework for contrastive self-supervised learning and designing a new approach. arXiv preprint arXiv:2009.00104 (2020)

47. Buslaev, A., Iglovikov, V.I., Khvedchenya, E., Parinov, A., Druzhinin, M., Kalinin, A.A.: Albumentations: fast and flexible image augmentations. Information **11**(2), 125 (2020). https://doi.org/10.3390/info11020125. ISSN 2078–2489

48. Falcon, W., et al.: Pytorch lightning. GitHub (2019). https://github.com/PyTorchLightning/pytorch-lightning

49. Kaggle (2010). https://www.kaggle.com/

50. Mudhalwadkar, N.P.: Hugging Face Demo. https://huggingface.co/spaces/nmud19/Sketch2ColourDemo
51. Borji, A.: Pros and Cons of GAN evaluation measures: new developments. arXiv:2103.09396 2021
52. Krizhevsky, A., Nair, V., Hinton, G.: Cifar-10 (canadian institute for advanced research). https://www.cs.toronto.edu/~kriz/cifar.html
53. Mudhalwadkar, N.: CIFAR10 FID score statistics npz. https://www.kaggle.com/code/nmud19/cifar10-fid-score-statistics-npz/notebook
54. Yeongseop, L., Lee, S.: Automatic colorization of anime style illustrations using a two-stage generator. Appl. Sci. **10**, 8699 (2020). https://doi.org/10.3390/app10238699

Portrait Matting via Semantic and Detail Guidance

Deming Wang, Changxin Gao, and Nong Sang[✉]

Key Laboratory of Image Processing and Intelligent Control, School of Artificial
Intelligence and Automation, Huazhong University of Science and Technology,
Wuhan, China
{dmwang,cgao,nsang}@hust.edu.cn

Abstract. Portrait matting is a challenging computer vision task that
aims to estimate the per-pixel opacity of the foreground human regions.
To produce high-quality alpha mattes, the majority of available methods
employ a user-supplied trimap as an auxiliary input. However, obtaining trimap is difficult, which restricts the application of these methods.
Recently, trimap-free approaches have been developed, but the alpha quality is significantly lower than that of trimap-based methods due to the lack
of guidance. In this paper, we propose a portrait matting framework via
semantic and detail guidance. We use the mask obtained from portrait
segmentation as semantic guidance to improve semantic understanding of
portrait matting, and we present a detail encoder block to capture the low-
level feature around the subject as detail guidance, which helps to refine
alpha details, such as hair. The proposed approach achieves remarkable
results on both composition and real-world benchmarks.

Keywords: Deep image matting · Portrait matting · Portrait
segmentation

1 Introduction

Image matting aims to distinguish background and foreground to obtain the
high-quality alpha matte of the foreground object as accurately as possible.
Portrait matting is a subtask of image matting task, which focuses more on the
prediction of the boundary around the human body and the hair. Formally, an
image $I \in \mathbb{R}^{H \times W \times 3}$ is a composite of a foreground image $F \in \mathbb{R}^{H \times W \times 3}$, a
background image $B \in \mathbb{R}^{H \times W \times 3}$ and alpha matte $\alpha \in \mathbb{R}^{H \times W}$ with a linear
mixing assumption. The matting problem can be formulated as follows:

$$I_i = \alpha_i F_i + (1 - \alpha_i)B_i, \ \alpha_i \in [0, 1] \tag{1}$$

where $i = (x, y)$ denotes the pixel position in the image I, α_i is the opacity at
pixel i, F_i and B_i are the foreground and background color at pixel i, respectively.
It can be seen that image matting is an ill-posed problem given 3 known values
but 7 values need to be solved for each pixel.

H. Lu et al. (Eds.): ACPR 2023, LNCS 14406, pp. 165–178, 2023.
https://doi.org/10.1007/978-3-031-47634-1_13

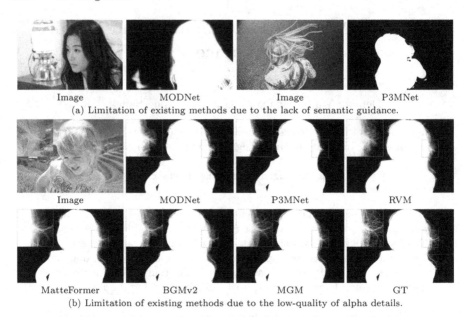

(a) Limitation of existing methods due to the lack of semantic guidance.

(b) Limitation of existing methods due to the low-quality of alpha details.

Fig. 1. Limitation of existing method. (a) Bad cases from recent works [11,14] due to semantic understanding fails. Parts of the background are wrongly predicted as foreground or parts of human are not completely segmented. (b) Existing methods [11, 14,19,20,22,29] are still inadequate in alpha details prediction.

To decrease the difficulty of this ill-posed problem, previous matting approaches usually require a well-annotated trimap which represents the foreground, background and unknown areas in the image. The basic idea is enhancing the unknown areas to get a more accurate alpha matte. Although such annotation has been proven powerful in image matting task, it is not feasible to provide the trimap because most users have difficulty in creating a trimap, which is very restricted in practice.

Recently, many researchers focused on developing methods on trimap-free portrait matting. Some early works [6,23] generated pseudo trimap first and then predicted alpha matte from the trimap. MGM [29] proposed mask guided matting and designed a progressive refinement module(PRM). MODNet [11] proposed a light-weight portrait matting method without auxiliary input. P3MNet [14] proposed a portrait matting method with good generation capability when following the Privacy-Preserving Training setting. These methods, however, produce subpar segmentation when dealing with complex real-world images since they only employ limited, largely synthetic matting datasets for end-to-end training.

We explore at the failure cases of the existing trimap-free approaches and find that they frequently result from poor semantic understanding and subpar alpha details. Figure 1 (a) demonstrates how some background elements are incorrectly segmented as foreground or human parts, demonstrating the poor semantic comprehension of current approaches. Current approaches perform significantly worse in detail prediction than those that incorporate additional information, as demonstrated in Fig. 1 (b). To address the above problems, we propose a portrait matting framework via semantic and detail guidance. On the one hand, we employ human mask as semantic guidance for matting, following MGM [29], and the mask is generated by an off-the-shelf human segmenter in order to increase the capacity of semantic comprehension. On the other hand, we present a detail encoder to capture multi-scale low-level features around the subject, and a detail fusion module in the decoder to fuse the deep feature and the low-level feature, which is useful to recover alpha details.

Our contributions can be summarized as follows:

- We propose a portrait matting method via semantic and detail guidance. We use the mask acquired via human segmentation as input to guide alpha prediction, and we also design the implicit detail guidance on the network structure.
- We introduce a detail encoder to capture the low-level features surrounding the subject under the detail guidance and a detail fusion module in the matting decoder to fuse them, which helps to recover alpha details, such as hair.
- We conduct extensive experiments to analyze the effectiveness of our approach. The proposed approach achieves remarkable results on both composition and real-world benchmarks.

2 Related Work

2.1 Traditional Image Matting

Traditional image matting methods are mainly divided into sampling-based and propagation-based, according to the way of using the color features. Sampling-based methods [8,25] estimate foreground and background color statics through sampling pixels in the definite foreground/background areas to infer the alpha values of the unknown areas. Propagation-based methods [2,9,12,13] assume neighboring pixels are correlated, and estimate alpha matte by propagating the alpha value of the foreground and background pixels to the unknown areas.

2.2 Deep Image Matting

With the great progress of deep learning and the rise of computer vision technology, many methods based on convolution neural networks(CNN) have been proved successful in many areas, including detection , classification [17,18], and segmentation [3,4,27]. It also have achieved great success in image matting. Deep learning image matting algorithms can be divided into trimap-based and trimap-free methods, among which trimap-based methods account for the majority.

For the trimap-based methods, [26] is the first representative method to apply CNN in image matting and releases the Composition-1K dataset, which are followed by a series of valuable works advancing the state-of-the-art matting performance. [5,21] propose a novel index-guided upsampling and unpooling operations in the encoder-decoder structure to better keep details in the predictions. [28] proposes a patch-based method for high resolution inputs with a module addressing cross-patch dependency and consistency issues between patches. [22] uses prior-tokens which represent the context of global regions and a modified Swin Transformer block to achieve good performance.

For the trimap-free methods, [23] integrates high-level semantics and appearance cues. High-level semantics can provide features of foreground and background as well as contour, while appearance cues provide texture and boundary details. In this method, channel attention mechanism is used for semantic features and temporal attention mechanism is used for appearance cues. Alpha Matte is predicted by fusing the learned features with different degrees. [6] uses a semantic network to predict trimap and then concatenates it with RGB images as input to the matting network. [15,16] only use RGB images as input, predict both trimap and alpha matte, and then fuse them to get the final alpha matte.

2.3   Portrait Matting

Portrait matting is a class-specific image matting task, where the semantic information of the foreground object, namely, human is known. Known human semantics effectively guides portrait matting methods and they usually do not require auxiliary input. [14] focuses on the privacy-preserving portrait matting problem and releases the P3M dataset. [20] proposes a video portrait matting framework, which uses a recurrent decoder to improve the robustness in complex real-world scenes. [11] proposes a matting objective decomposition network and a novel strategy to adjust to the real-world scenario. [30] proposes a cascade matting network with deformable graph refinement to predict the alpha matte from low resolution to high resolution. [1] proposes a high-resolution detail branch to extract fine-grained details of the foreground and a semantic context branch to improve the detail prediction because of better semantic correctness.

3   Method

As seen in Fig. 2, our framework includes an off-the-shelf human segmenter and a matting network for mask-to-alpha refinement. Our mating network consists of a context encoder, a detail encoder and a matting decoder.

3.1   Context Encoder

Effective feature extraction is a typical and crucial component of any deep learning approach. As previously noted, we suggest applying a segmentation mask to enhance matting predictions. We adopt ResNet-50-D [10] as feature extraction

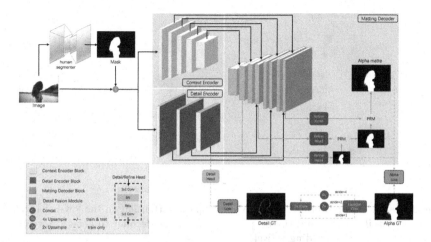

Fig. 2. Proposed network. Given an RGB image, human segmenter obtains an initial mask for matting, the context encoder extracts the deep features, the detail encoder captures the low-level features, the matting decoder fuses the deep features and low-level features to refine the unknown area of human margin and predict the alpha matte.

backbone followed by an ASPP module for context encoder. The input, the concatenation of image and segmentation mask, is 32× downsampled in the context encoder. The context encoder can only get the foreground's feature representation because of its low capacity, which is insufficient to get the fine-grained detail. In order to retrieve the detail information, another encoder must be added.

3.2 Detail Encoder

Parallel to the context encoder is the detail encoder. The detail encoder is responsible for extracting alpha details, which is a kind of low-level information. We specified a large number of channels for the detail encoder in order to allow it to encode rich detail information. Following [7], we model the detail prediction as a binary segmentation mask in the training stage. First of all, we generate the ground-truth detail map from the ground-truth alpha matte by Laplacian operator. As illustrated in Fig. 2, we insert a detail head (Conv-BN-ReLU-Conv) in stage 3 of the detail encoder. After that, we use the ground-truth detail map as the guidance to supervise the low-level layers in the detail encoder to generate the feature of alpha details.

In order to obtain the ground-truth detail map, we use the Laplacian operator on the ground-truth alpha matte to generate the ground-truth binary detail. First of all, we produce soft thin detail feature maps by the Laplacian operator with different strides to obtain detail information. After that, we upsample the detail feature map to the input image size and fuse them with a trainable 1 × 1 convolution. Eventually, we transform them into the ground-truth final binary detail by a threshold 0.1, which has rich boundary and detail information.

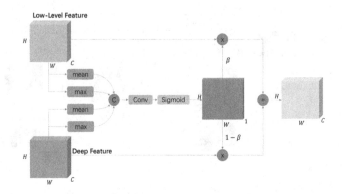

Fig. 3. Detail Fusion Module(DFM). We use spatial attention on the low-level feature from the detail encoder and the deep feature from the decoder to generate weight β, then they are fused according to weight β.

As shown in Fig. 2, we guide the detail encoder to encode alpha details by using detail heads to produce the detail map, which is proved to be effective to enhance the detail feature representation.

3.3 Matting Decoder

Our matting decoder inputs the segmentation feature from the context encoder and the low-level feature from the detail encoder, outputs matting results at 1/8, 1/4, and 1/1 scale. During the decoding progress, we use Detail Fusion Module(DFM) to combine the low-level feature from the detail encoder and the deep feature gradually. Finally, we adopt PRM module to refine the alpha matte based on the matting results at three scales.

Detail Fusion Module. We propose DFM to enrich the representation of fused features by spatial attention. As shown in the Fig. 3, the module uses spatial attention to generate weight β, and the low-level feature from the detail encoder and the deep feature from the matting decoder are fused according to weight β. In detail, the input features are denoted as F_{deep} and F_{low}, we first apply max and mean operations to the input features in the channel axis to generate four features, of which the dimension is $\mathbb{R}^{H \times W}$. After that, we concatenate these four features and apply 1×1 Conv and sigmoid operation to them. Finally, the final output feature F_{out} is obtained by adding the context encoder feature and decoder feature according to the weight β. We can formulate the above procedure as follows:

$$
\begin{aligned}
\beta =& Sigmoid(Conv(concat(\\
& Mean(F_{low}), Max(F_{low}), \\
& Mean(F_{deep}), Max(F_{deep}))))
\end{aligned}
$$

$$
F_{out} = \beta F_{low} + (1 - \beta)F_{deep}
$$

(2)

Progressive Refinement Module. During the decoding progress, we use Progressive Refinement Module(PRM) [29] to refine the alpha matte. First, we predict matting result at 1/8, 1/4, and 1/1 scale and then resized to input resolution. After that, these matting result are progressively refined, and transparent regions shrink gradually through the PRM. Specifically, for the current scale l, we obtain a self-guidance mask g_l from the alpha matte of previous scale α_{l-1}. We generate the refined alpha matte $\alpha_l \in \mathbb{R}^{H \times W}$ and self-guidance mask $g_l \in \mathbb{R}^{H \times W}$ using the following function:

$$\alpha_l = \alpha_l' g_l + \alpha_{l-1}(1 - g_l) \tag{3}$$

$$g_l(x,y) = \begin{cases} 1, & \text{if } 0 < \alpha_{l-1}(x,y) < 1, \\ 0, & \text{otherwise.} \end{cases} \tag{4}$$

where α_l' denotes the matting result at the current scale l. The self-guidance mask g_l defines the transparent region($0 < \alpha < 1$) in the alpha matte of previous scale α_{l-1} as non-confident region. The refined alpha matte is generated from the matting result α_l', pixels in the non-confident region are preserved and other pixels are replaced with pixels in the alpha matte of previous scale α_{l-1}. In this way, the current level only needs to focus on the unknown region.

4 Training

In order to train our network, we use the combination of Adobe Image Matting(AIM) and Distinction-646(D646) datasets. Since we focus on the portrait matting task, we select all human images for the training. In the end, there are 201 foreground images in the AIM dataset and 363 foreground images in the D646 dataset. The total foreground images are 564, and we use BG-20K dataset as background images.

For the matting decoder, following [29], We apply ℓ_1 regression loss, composition loss and laplacian loss. We denote the ground-truth alpha with $\hat{\alpha}$ and the predicted alpha with α. The overall loss function is the summation of them:

$$\mathcal{L}(\hat{\alpha}, \alpha) = \mathcal{L}_{\ell_1}(\hat{\alpha}, \alpha) + \mathcal{L}_{comp}(\hat{\alpha}, \alpha) + \mathcal{L}_{lap}(\hat{\alpha}, \alpha) \tag{5}$$

The loss is applied to all output matting alphas at $\frac{1}{8}, \frac{1}{4}, 1$ scale with adaptive self-guidance mask g_l calculated in Eq. (4) to focus on refining the uncertain region at each scale. We set different weights for different scales and the alpha loss function can be formulated as:

$$\mathcal{L}_{alpha} = \sum_l w_l \mathcal{L}(\hat{\alpha}_l \cdot g_l, \alpha_l \cdot g_l) \tag{6}$$

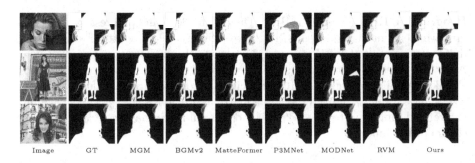

Image   GT   MGM   BGMv2   MatteFormer   P3MNet   MODNet   RVM   Ours

Fig. 4. A visual comparison of our method and other matting methods on composition benchmarks.

where w_l is the loss weight assigning to the output of different scales , We use $w_{\frac{1}{8}} : w_{\frac{1}{4}} : w_1 = 1 : 2 : 3$ in our experiments.

For the detail encoder, following [7], we apply binary cross-entropy and dice loss to jointly optimize the detail learning. We denote the ground-truth detail-map with $\hat{d}$ and the predicted detail-map with d. The detail loss function can be formulated as:

$$\mathcal{L}_{detail} = \mathcal{L}_{dice}(\hat{d}, d) + \mathcal{L}_{bce}(\hat{d}, d) \tag{7}$$

where $\mathcal{L}_{bce}$ denotes the binary cross-entropy loss and $\mathcal{L}_{dice}$ denotes the dice loss, which is formulated as follows:

$$\mathcal{L}_{dice} = 1 - \frac{2 \sum_i^{H \times W} \hat{d}^i d^i + \epsilon}{\sum_i^{H \times W} (\hat{d}^i)^2 + \sum_i^{H \times W} (d^i)^2 + \epsilon} \tag{8}$$

where H and W denote the height and width of the predicted detail map, i denotes the i-th pixel and ϵ is a Laplace smoothing item to avoid zero division. We set $\epsilon = 1$ in our experiments.

The final weighted loss is a combination of the alpha loss and the detail loss:

$$\mathcal{L}_{final} = \lambda_1 \mathcal{L}_{alpha} + \lambda_2 \mathcal{L}_{detail} \tag{9}$$

The training lasts for 100,000 iterations on 4 GPUs with warm-up at the first 5000 iterations and cosine learning rate decay. We use crop size 512, batch size of 6 for each GPUs, Adam optimizer with $\beta_1 = 0.5$ and $\beta_2 = 0.999$, and the learning rate is initialized to 1×10^{-3}.

5   Experiments

In this section, we show our experimental settings and compare our evaluation results with other methods on the following five benchmarks, including two composition datasets and three real-world datasets. We also conduct further ablation experiments to evaluate the performance of our method.

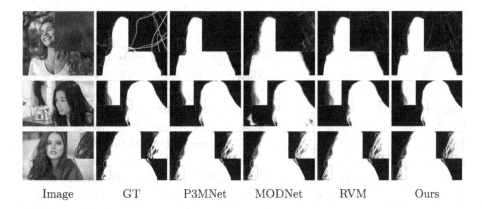

| Image | GT | P3MNet | MODNet | RVM | Ours |

Fig. 5. A visual comparison of our method and other matting methods on real-world benchmarks.

5.1 Benchmarks and Evaluation Metrics

AIM. We select 11 images that contain persons from AIM dataset for testing. We follow the same strategy in the portrait matting literature and combine each person with 20 different background images which are selected from top-220 of BG-20K test set.

D646. Similar to AIM, we select 11 human images and combine them with the last 220 background images from BG-20K test set.

PPM-100. Photographic Portrait Matting benchmark (PPM-100) contains 100 finely annotated portrait images with various backgrounds. The samples in PPM-100 are more natural and have richer postures than composition images.

P3M-500-NP. Privacy-Preserving dataset is a large-scale privacy-preserving portrait matting benchmark, which has a great diversity of postures. In order to avoid the unknown influence of face blur on evaluation, we only use the images without face obfuscation from P3M-10k dataset.

RWP. This dataset is a real-world image matting dataset consisting of 637 diverse and high-resolution images. Moreover, since the dataset mainly contains solid objects where the body can be easily predicted, and also labeled detail masks covering the hair region and other soft tissues, which tells where the most important details of the image are located.

Evaluation Metrics. We use five common quantitative metrics to evaluate the alpha mattes, including the sum of absolute differences (SAD), mean squared error (MSE), mean absolute difference (MAD), connectivity error (Conn) and gradient error (Grad). The lower value of the metric, the better the prediction quality. Note that MSE and MAD values are scaled by 10^3.

Table 1. Quantitative results on composition benchmarks. '↓': lower values are better.

Method	Input	Dataset	SAD↓	MSE↓	MAD↓	Conn↓	Grad↓
MGM [29]	Image,Mask	AIM	22.10	2.85	10.51	17.11	9.65
BGMv2 [19]	Image,Background	AIM	15.81	1.52	6.07	14.03	13.25
MatteFormer [22]	Image,Trimap	AIM	**11.77**	**1.08**	**5.58**	**9.62**	**8.43**
P3MNet [14]	Image	AIM	93.91	33.28	40.86	93.12	38.59
MODNet [11]	Image	AIM	80.67	23.58	33.18	74.47	29.08
RVM [20]	Image	AIM	67.11	17.54	27.07	60.73	28.84
Ours	Image	AIM	**50.23**	**12.67**	**21.63**	**31.36**	**16.93**
MGM [29]	Image,Mask	D646	18.94	1.56	6.78	14.40	6.50
BGMv2 [19]	Image,Background	D646	12.55	0.63	3.44	10.22	11.02
MatteFormer [22]	Image,Trimap	D646	**6.01**	**0.21**	**2.06**	**3.92**	**2.88**
P3MNet [14]	Image	D646	59.83	14.48	19.31	58.93	35.86
MODNet [11]	Image	D646	30.91	3.54	10.52	25.65	32.86
RVM [20]	Image	D646	27.81	4.94	10.50	28.60	35.24
Ours	Image	D646	**17.83**	**2.73**	**6.41**	**10.61**	**7.64**

Table 2. Quantitative results on real-world benchmarks. '↓': lower values are better.

Method	Input	Dataset	Whole Image					Details		
			SAD↓	MSE↓	MAD↓	Conn↓	Grad↓	SAD↓	MSE↓	MAD↓
P3MNet [14]	Image	PPM-100	130.84	12.86	15.61	130.42	56.37	-	-	-
MODNet [11]	Image	PPM-100	95.10	4.47	8.60	80.82	64.26	-	-	-
RVM [20]	Image	PPM-100	108.17	6.53	10.95	105.19	63.13	-	-	-
Ours	Image	PPM-100	**81.77**	**3.58**	**6.01**	**52.19**	**46.33**	-	-	-
P3MNet [14]	Image	P3M-500-NP	**11.23**	**3.50**	**6.50**	12.51	**10.35**	-	-	-
MODNet [11]	Image	P3M-500-NP	23.83	7.39	13.80	20.16	16.79	-	-	-
RVM [20]	Image	P3M-500-NP	20.97	7.06	11.10	19.17	15.30	-	-	-
Ours	Image	P3M-500-NP	14.89	4.60	8.89	**12.32**	12.41	-	-	-
P3MNet [14]	Image	RWP	36.47	18.62	27.26	36.36	61.36	**19.34**	80.71	146.59
MODNet [11]	Image	RWP	46.29	20.88	33.49	42.35	60.81	21.88	77.07	159.85
RVM [20]	Image	RWP	42.63	22.70	33.81	39.63	66.26	24.84	80.30	161.23
Ours	Image	RWP	**35.93**	**14.55**	**26.53**	**32.75**	**57.51**	19.64	**67.67**	**145.72**

5.2   Quantitative Evaluation

In this section, we present the experimental results and compare our approach with the SOTA works, including MGM [29], BGMv2 [19], MatteFormer [22], P3MNet [14], MODNet [11] and video matting method RVM [20]. Note that we generate 10 frames video by repeating 10 times for every image and evaluate the last frame result for RVM.

Results on Composition Datasets. Experimental results on composition datasets are shown in Table 1. It show that our method outperforms other automatic image matting methods in all metrics. On the AIM dataset, our method is found superior to the P3MNet, MODNet and RVM in all metrics. Conversely, MGM, BGMv2 and MatteFormer get much better results than other automatic image matting method due to the benefit from additional input such as the coarse mask, the background of the input image and a trimap. These additional inputs make the task easier and more accurate. On the D646 dataset, we again outperform the P3MNet, MODNet and RVM. We even get better result than MGM on SAD, MAD and Conn. In Fig. 4, we present our results, input image, ground truth and the outputs of other methods. Our method predicts much fewer semantic errors and more hair details than other automatic image matting methods.

Table 3. Ablation study for the architecture. We individually investigated the effect of the detail encoder and the detail fusion module. The experiments are performed on the D646 dataset.

Case	SAD↓	MSE↓
Base model	24.17	3.92
Base model + Detail Encoder	21.89	3.78
Base model + Detail Encoder + DFM	20.75	3.52

Results on Real-World Datasets. Table 2 show the results of different automatic image matting methods evaluated on real-world benchmarks. For these datasets, since the images are real-world images, there are no mask, background images and trimap. Therefore, we could not test MGM, BGMv2 and Matte-Former on these datasets. For complex scene data PPM-100 and RWP which contain diversity of background, rich postures and hair details, our method outperforms other methods in most of metrics. However, on the P3M-500-NP benchmark, our method is only better than RVM and MODNet, but not as good as P3MNet. Through the analysis of dataset, the proportion of images containing hair details on the P3M-500-NP dataset is smaller than that on other datasets. Our method tends to capture details and has no advantage on this dataset. Figure 5 shows visual comparison results on real-world datasets among different methods demonstrating the effectiveness of our method.

5.3   Ablation Study

This section introduces the ablation study to validate the effects of different parameters on the performance.

Modules. We firstly perform the ablation study to evaluate the effects of the detail encoder and the detail fusion module. According to the Table 3, both the detail encoder and the detail fusion module are significantly useful to improve the performance of the proposed method. Because, the detail encoder capture the low-level features which helps to recover alpha details, while the detail fusion module enhances the alpha matte generation performance.

Detail Guidance. We further examine the effect of detail guidance on the performance. We propose the detail encoder to capture the low-level feature and insert detail head to improve the representation of the detail area. Table 4 shows the effect of different positions to insert detail head. As we can see, detail guidance can obviously improve matting performance. We choose to insert the detail head only at the third stage of the detail encoder, which further improves SAD($20.75 \rightarrow 17.83$) and MSE($3.52 \rightarrow 2.73$). Figure 6 illustrates the gradual attention on the alpha details of the detail encoder. With the help of detail guidance, our method can better recover the alpha detail. As shown in Table 3 and Table 4, adding detail encoder to encode detail information and inserting detail head to guide detail feature extraction can improve the performance on accuracy.

Table 4. Ablation study for detail guidance. We add the auxiliary detail head to different positions of detail encoder. Here, $stage_i$ represents the auxiliary detail head added after s stage. The experiments are performed on the D646 dataset.

$stage_1$	$stage_2$	$stage_3$	SAD↓	MSE↓
			20.75	3.52
✓	✓	✓	18.01	2.98
✓	✓		20.59	3.27
	✓	✓	17.91	2.86
✓		✓	18.02	2.90
✓			20.31	3.49
	✓		20.66	3.18
		✓	**17.83**	**2.73**

6   Conclusion

In this work, we propose a portrait matting framework via semantic and detail guidance. On the one hand, we employ human mask as semantic guidance for matting and the mask is generated by an off-the-shelf human segmenter in order to increase the capacity of semantic comprehension. On the other hand, we present a detail encoder to capture multi-scale low-level features around the subject, and a detail fusion module in the decoder to fuse the deep feature and the low-level feature, which is useful to recover alpha details. By this design, our framework can handle many challenging cases successfully. Experiments demonstrate that our proposed framework achieves remarkable results on both composition and real-world benchmarks. Comprehensive ablation studies also validate our contributions.

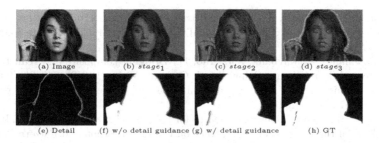

(a) Image   (b) $stage_1$ (c) $stage_2$ (d) $stage_3$

(e) Detail   (f) w/o detail guidance (g) w/ detail guidance   (h) GT

Fig. 6. Examples showing visual explanations for features in the different stages of the Detail Encoder. Following the Grad-CAM [24], we visualize the Grad-CAMs of Detail Encoder. The visualization shows that Detail Encoder can encode the spatial detail, e.g., hair and human boundary, gradually.

References

1. Chen, G., et al.: PP-matting: high-accuracy natural image matting. arXiv preprint arXiv:2204.09433 (2022)
2. Chen, Q., Li, D., Tang, C.K.: KNN matting. IEEE Trans. Pattern Anal. Mach. Intell. **35**(9), 2175–2188 (2013)
3. Cheng, B., Misra, I., Schwing, A.G., Kirillov, A., Girdhar, R.: Masked-attention mask transformer for universal image segmentation. In: Proceedings of the IEEE/CVF Conference on Computer Vision and Pattern Recognition, pp. 1290–1299 (2022)
4. Cheng, B., Schwing, A., Kirillov, A.: Per-pixel classification is not all you need for semantic segmentation. Adv. Neural. Inf. Process. Syst. **34**, 17864–17875 (2021)
5. Dai, Y., Lu, H., Shen, C.: Learning affinity-aware upsampling for deep image matting. In: Proceedings of the IEEE/CVF Conference on Computer Vision and Pattern Recognition, pp. 6841–6850 (2021)
6. Deora, R., Sharma, R., Raj, D.S.S.: Salient image matting. arXiv preprint arXiv:2103.12337 (2021)
7. Fan, M., et al.: Rethinking BiseNet for real-time semantic segmentation. In: Proceedings of the IEEE/CVF Conference on Computer Vision and Pattern Recognition, pp. 9716–9725 (2021)
8. He, K., Rhemann, C., Rother, C., Tang, X., Sun, J.: A global sampling method for alpha matting. In: CVPR 2011, pp. 2049–2056. IEEE (2011)
9. He, K., Sun, J., Tang, X.: Fast matting using large kernel matting Laplacian matrices. In: 2010 IEEE Computer Society Conference on Computer Vision and Pattern Recognition, pp. 2165–2172. IEEE (2010)
10. He, T., Zhang, Z., Zhang, H., Zhang, Z., Xie, J., Li, M.: Bag of tricks for image classification with convolutional neural networks. In: Proceedings of the IEEE/CVF Conference on Computer Vision And Pattern Recognition, pp. 558–567 (2019)
11. Ke, Z., Sun, J., Li, K., Yan, Q., Lau, R.W.: ModNet: real-time Trimap-free portrait matting via objective decomposition. In: Proceedings of the AAAI Conference on Artificial Intelligence, vol. 36, pp. 1140–1147 (2022)
12. Lee, P., Wu, Y.: Nonlocal matting. In: CVPR 2011, pp. 2193–2200. IEEE (2011)
13. Levin, A., Lischinski, D., Weiss, Y.: A closed-form solution to natural image matting. IEEE Trans. Pattern Anal. Mach. Intell. **30**(2), 228–242 (2007)

14. Li, J., Ma, S., Zhang, J., Tao, D.: Privacy-preserving portrait matting. In: Proceedings of the 29th ACM International Conference on Multimedia, pp. 3501–3509 (2021)
15. Li, J., Zhang, J., Maybank, S.J., Tao, D.: Bridging composite and real: towards end-to-end deep image matting. Int. J. Comput. Vision **130**(2), 246–266 (2022)
16. Li, J., Zhang, J., Tao, D.: Deep automatic natural image matting. arXiv preprint arXiv:2107.07235 (2021)
17. Li, Y., et al.: Neural architecture search for lightweight non-local networks. In: Proceedings of the IEEE/CVF Conference on Computer Vision and Pattern Recognition, pp. 10297–10306 (2020)
18. Li, Y., et al.: Shape-texture debiased neural network training. arXiv preprint arXiv:2010.05981 (2020)
19. Lin, S., Ryabtsev, A., Sengupta, S., Curless, B.L., Seitz, S.M., Kemelmacher-Shlizerman, I.: Real-time high-resolution background matting. In: Proceedings of the IEEE/CVF Conference on Computer Vision and Pattern Recognition, pp. 8762–8771 (2021)
20. Lin, S., Yang, L., Saleemi, I., Sengupta, S.: Robust high-resolution video matting with temporal guidance. In: Proceedings of the IEEE/CVF Winter Conference on Applications of Computer Vision, pp. 238–247 (2022)
21. Lu, H., Dai, Y., Shen, C., Xu, S.: Indices matter: learning to index for deep image matting. In: Proceedings of the IEEE/CVF International Conference on Computer Vision, pp. 3266–3275 (2019)
22. Park, G., Son, S., Yoo, J., Kim, S., Kwak, N.: MatteFormer: transformer-based image matting via prior-tokens. In: Proceedings of the IEEE/CVF Conference on Computer Vision and Pattern Recognition, pp. 11696–11706 (2022)
23. Qiao, Y., et al.: Attention-guided hierarchical structure aggregation for image matting. In: Proceedings of the IEEE/CVF Conference on Computer Vision and Pattern Recognition, pp. 13676–13685 (2020)
24. Selvaraju, R.R., Cogswell, M., Das, A., Vedantam, R., Parikh, D., Batra, D.: Grad-CAM: visual explanations from deep networks via gradient-based localization. In: Proceedings of the IEEE International Conference on Computer Vision, pp. 618–626 (2017)
25. Shahrian, E., Rajan, D., Price, B., Cohen, S.: Improving image matting using comprehensive sampling sets. In: Proceedings of the IEEE Conference on Computer Vision and Pattern Recognition, pp. 636–643 (2013)
26. Xu, N., Price, B., Cohen, S., Huang, T.: Deep image matting. In: Proceedings of the IEEE Conference on Computer Vision and Pattern Recognition, pp. 2970–2979 (2017)
27. Yu, C., Wang, J., Peng, C., Gao, C., Yu, G., Sang, N.: Bisenet: bilateral segmentation network for real-time semantic segmentation. In: Proceedings of the European Conference on Computer Vision (ECCV), pp. 325–341 (2018)
28. Yu, H., Xu, N., Huang, Z., Zhou, Y., Shi, H.: High-resolution deep image matting. In: Proceedings of the AAAI Conference on Artificial Intelligence, vol. 35, pp. 3217–3224 (2021)
29. Yu, Q., et al.: Mask guided matting via progressive refinement network. In: Proceedings of the IEEE/CVF Conference on Computer Vision and Pattern Recognition, pp. 1154–1163 (2021)
30. Yu, Z., Li, X., Huang, H., Zheng, W., Chen, L.: Cascade image matting with deformable graph refinement. In: Proceedings of the IEEE/CVF International Conference on Computer Vision, pp. 7167–7176 (2021)

Scene Text Detection with Box Supervision and Level Set Evolution

Mengbiao Zhao[1,2], Fei Yin[1,2], and Cheng-Lin Liu[1,2(✉)]

[1] State Key Laboratory of Multimodal Artificial Intelligence Systems,
Institute of Automation of Chinese Academy of Sciences, Beijing 100190, China
`zhaomengbiao2017@ia.ac.cn`, {`fyin,liucl`}`@nlpr.ia.ac.cn`
[2] School of Artificial Intelligence, University of Chinese Academy of Sciences, Beijing
100049, China

Abstract. For arbitrarily-shaped scene text detection, most existing
methods require expensive polygon-level annotations for supervised
training. In order to reduce the cost in data annotation, we propose
a novel bounding box supervised scene text detection method, which
needs training images only labeled in rectangular boxes. The detection
model integrates the classical level set model with deep neural network.
It consists a backbone network, a text proposal network, and a text segmentation network. For weakly-supervised training of the segmentation
network using box supervision, the proposed method iteratively learns
a series of level sets through a Chan-Vese energy based loss function.
The segmentation network is trained by minimizing the fully differentiable level set energy function wherein the text instance boundary is
iteratively updated. Further, both the input image and its deep features
are employed in the level set energy function to improve the convergence. The proposed method can be trained in weakly-supervised or
mixed-supervised manner. Extensive experiments on five benchmarks
(ICDAR2015, C-SVT, CTW1500, Total-Text, and ICDAR-ArT) show
that our mixed-supervised model can achieve competitive detection performance.

Keywords: Scene text detection · Box supervision · Level set
evolution

1 Introduction

Scene text detection, aimed to localize the text instances in scene images, is
a fundamental step for text information extraction in scene understanding,
autonomous driving, human-computer interaction, and so on. In recent years,
deep learning based methods have made great process in horizontal text detection [11,24], multi-oriented text detection [7,36], and arbitrary-shaped text
detection [16,26]. However, these methods suffer from a drawback in that the
detector relies heavily on a large amount of annotated data during training.
Particularly, arbitrarily-shaped scene text detection requires the text instance

H. Lu et al. (Eds.): ACPR 2023, LNCS 14406, pp. 179–193, 2023.
https://doi.org/10.1007/978-3-031-47634-1_14

boundaries in training data to be annotated in polygons. Acquiring such a polygon annotated dataset costs a large amount of human labor and financial resources, and has impeded its application in real problems.

To reduce the cost of data annotation, an alternative is to utilize weak annotations. Bounding boxes provide information about individual objects and their locations. According to the Amazon Mechanical Turk (MTurk), the upright bounding box annotations are about 4× cheaper than polygon annotations [2,14]. Many researchers [20,29,34] have tackled scene text detection using bounding box annotations. They focus on generating pseudo boundary labels by an independent model, which needs to employ extra auxiliary data and post-processing techniques like pseudo label filtering to obtain precise pseudo labels. Due to the involved multiple separate steps, the training pipeline becomes complicated with many hyper-parameters. The reported performance of such weakly-supervised training was also largely inferior to that of training with polygon-level annotations.

To address the above limitations, we propose a novel method for box supervised scene text detection, which integrates the classical level set model [1,19] with deep neural network delicately. Our detection model consists a backbone network, a text proposal network and a text segmentation network. While the text proposal network can be trained using box supervision directly, the segmentation network is trained in weak supervision through level set energy minimization. Unlike the existing box supervised methods [20,29,34], the proposed method iteratively learn a series of level set functions for implicit curve evolution within the annotated bounding box in an end-to-end manner. Inspired by [10], we introduce an energy function based on the classical continuous Chan-Vese energy functional [1]. By minimizing the fully differentiable energy function, the level set for each text instance is iteratively optimized within its corresponding bounding box annotation. Furthermore, to robustly evolve the level set curves towards the boundary of the text instance, we also consider high-level deep features in addition to the input image. The proposed method can also be trained in mix-supervised manner, when adding some strongly-annotated data. Experiments on five public benchmark datasets demonstrate the promise and competitiveness of the proposed method.

The contributions of this work are summarized as follows:

(1) We proposed a novel bounding box supervised scene text detection method based on level-set evolution, which can be trained in weakly supervised or mix-supervised manner.
(2) A differentiable level set energy function based on the Chan-Vese function is introduced for facilitating box-supervised training.
(3) Extensive experiments on five datasets (ICDAR2015 [9], C-SVT [22], CTW1500 [14], Total-Text [2], and ICDAR-ArT [3]) show that using only 10% strongly annotated data combined with 90% weakly annotated data, our mixed supervised model yields performance comparable to fully supervised model.

In the rest of this paper, Sect. 2 reviews related work; Sect. 3 describes the proposed method; Sect. 4 presents experimental results, and Sect. 5 concludes the paper.

2 Related Work

2.1 Scene Text Detection

The existing scene text detection methods can be roughly classified into two categories: regression based and segmentation based. The former is mainly built on generic object detectors [8,13,21] with various text-specific modifications. Gupta et al. [5] improves over the YOLO [21] and Fully Convolutional Networks (FCN) [17] for text prediction densely, while further adopts the filter and regression steps for removing the false positives. TextBoxes [11] adjusted the anchor ratios of SSD [13] to detect large-aspect-ratio scene texts. On basis of the Dense-Box [8], EAST [36] and DDR [7] directly detect the quadrangles of text words in a per-pixel manner without using anchors and proposals. Although these methods make great progress on benchmarks where text boundary is labeled by quadrangles or rectangles, they perform insufficiently on arbitrary shaped texts.

Segmentation based methods take advantage of semantic segmentation, utilizing convolution operations to extract visual features for pixel-level prediction. Among them, TextSnake [15] predicts text regions and various geometry of text to detect oriented and curved texts effectively. Mask TextSpotter [16] detects arbitrary-shape text instances in an instance segmentation manner based on Mask R-CNN [6]. PSENet [26] segments text instance by progressively expanding kernels at different scales. Wang et al. [27] proposed a pixel aggregation network, which is equipped with a low computational-cost segmentation head and a learnable post processor. These methods can detect arbitrarily-shaped texts, but usually require large amount of strongly annotated data (e.g., polygon-level annotations) for training.

2.2 Weakly-Supervised Scene Text Detection

To alleviate the expensive data annotation cost, there have been some attempts of weakly-supervised scene text detection. WeText [23] proposed to use character-level pseudo labels to boost the word detection performance. Wu et al. [30] proposed weakly-supervised framework for scene text detection, which is trained on images annotated with scribble lines. Sun et al. [22] published a large dataset, where each image is only annotated with one dominant text, and proposed an algorithm to combine these partially annotated data and strongly annotated data for joint training. Wu et al. [29] proposed to train arbitrarily-shaped text detector with bounding-box annotated data in dynamic self-training strategy. Qin et al. [20] proposed to train text detector using only a small amount of pixel-level annotated data and a large amount of bounding-box annotated data, and adopted a novel strategy which utilizes ground-truth bounding boxes to generate pseudo mask annotations. These methods focus on the generation of pseudo boundary labels from weak annotations, which often require multiple training stages or modules to achieve promising performance. Unlike the above methods, the proposed level set-based approach is learned in an end-to-end manner, by iteratively aligning the text boundaries.

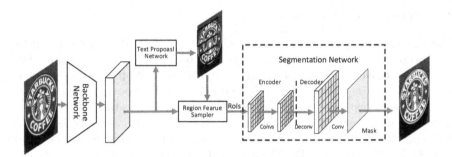

Fig. 1. The architecture of scene text detection based on instance segmentation.

3   Proposed Method

The proposed bounding box supervised scene text detection framework consists of two major parts: a segmentation based scene text detector and a level set energy function, which enables the neural network to learn a series of level set functions evolving to the instance boundaries progressively.

3.1   Segmentation Based Detection Model

The framework of the proposed segmentation based scene text detection is illustrated in Fig. 1. It consists of four modules: backbone network, text proposal network, region feature sampler, and segmentation network. Specifically, the text proposal network generates horizontal text proposals based on features extracted by the backbone network. Given extracted convolution features and text proposals, region features are sampled by the region feature sampler and fed into the segmentation network for predicting text instance masks.

Text Proposal Network. Inspired by CenterNet [35], we reformulate the text detection task as a keypoint detection problem. The head of text proposal network has two branches: (1) The classification branch calculates a heatmap, where the peaks are supposed to be text centers; (2) The regression branch predicts the offsets from each peak to the upper left and lower right corners of the proposal box.

Region Feature Sampler. The features of proposal region are sampled trough ROI-Align [6] from the original image feature map. Region features of spatial size 32×32 are sampled for the segmentation network.

Segmentation Network. As shown in Fig. 1, the segmentation network can be viewed as an encoder-decoder structure: an encoder with four convolution layers and a deconvolution layer as decoder for mask prediction.

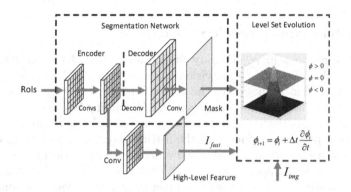

Fig. 2. Text instance segmentation based on level-set evolution.

3.2 Level Set Model in Image Segmentation

Before describing our box-supervised scene text detection model which incorporates level set evolution, we herein introduce the basic level set model. Level set based methods [1,18,19] formulate image segmentation as a consecutive energy minimization problem. For instance, the Mumford-Shah level set model [18] segments an image I by finding a parametric contour C, which partitions the image plane $\Omega \in \mathbb{R}^2$ into n disjoint regions $\Omega_1, ..., \Omega_n$. The Mumford-Shah energy function $F^{MS}(u, C)$ can be defined as:

$$F^{MS}(u_1, ..., u_n, \Omega_1, ..., \Omega_n) = \sum_{i=1}^{n} \left[\int_{\Omega_i} (I - u_i)^2 dx dy + \mu \int_{\Omega_i} |\nabla u_i|^2 dx dy + \gamma |C_i| \right],$$
(1)

where u_i is a piecewise smooth function approximating the input I, which ensures the smoothness inside each region Ω_i. μ and γ are weighted parameters.

On the basis of Mumford-Shah model, Chan and Vese [1] further introduced variational level set and proposed an energy function as:

$$F^{CV}(\phi, c_1, c_2) = \int_{\Omega} |I(x, y) - c_1|^2 \mathrm{H}(\phi(x, y)) dx dy$$

$$+ \int_{\Omega} |I(x, y) - c_2|^2 (1 - \mathrm{H}(\phi(x, y))) dx dy$$
(2)

$$+ \gamma \int_{\Omega} |\nabla \mathrm{H}(\phi(x, y))| dx dy,$$

where H is the Heaviside function and $\phi(x,y)$ is the level set function, whose zero crossing contour $C = \{(x,y) : \phi(x,y) = 0\}$ divides the image space Ω into two disjoint regions: inside contour $\Omega_1 = \{(x,y) : \phi(x,y) > 0\}$ and outside contour $\Omega_2 = \{(x,y) : \phi(x,y) < 0\}$. Specifically, the first two terms of Eq. (2) intend to fit the data, and the third term regularizes the zero level contour with a non-negative parameter γ. Image segmentation is achieved by finding a level set function $\phi(x,y) = 0$ with c_1 and c_2 that minimize the energy F^{CV}.

3.3   Box-Supervised Scene Text Detection

This work aims to achieve arbitrary-shaped scene text detection with model trained with bounding box supervision. As shown in Fig. 1, the detector first extracts text region proposals in the image through a text proposal network, which can be trained under the supervision of bounding box annotations. After proposal generation, the region feature sampler module is used to extract features from the text proposal regions, and the features are fed into the segmentation network, which consists an encoder and a decoder for generating the final text instance masks. For images annotated with bounding boxes, it is not feasible to train the segmentation branch using a pixel classification loss function. Therefore, we propose a weakly supervised loss function based on the level set energy function to supervise the training of this branch.

Given an input image $I(x,y)$, we tend to predict the text boundary curve by evolving a level set implicitly within the region of annotated bounding box $\mathcal{B}$. Specifically, we treat each positive mask map within box $\mathcal{B}$ as the level set $\phi(x,y)$, and its corresponding pixel space of input image $I(x,y)$ is denoted as Ω. The text boundary is zero level, denoted as $C = \{(x,y) : \phi(x,y) = 0\}$, which partitions the box region into two disjoint regions, corresponding to text and non-text (background), respectively.

In order to get accurate text boundary, we learn a series of level sets $\phi(x,y)$ by minimizing the following energy function:

$$F(\phi, I, c_1, c_2, \mathcal{B}) = \int_{\Omega \in \mathcal{B}} |I^*(x,y) - c_1|^2 \sigma(\phi(x,y)dxdy$$
$$+ \int_{\Omega \in \mathcal{B}} |I^*(x,y) - c_2|^2 (1 - \sigma(\phi(x,y)))dxdy \qquad (3)$$
$$+ \gamma \int_{\Omega \in \mathcal{B}} |\nabla \sigma(\phi(x,y)|dxdy,$$

where $I^*(x,y)$ denotes the normalized input image, and γ is a non-negative parameter. Here, we modify the Chan-Vese model by replacing the Heaviside function with the Sigmoid function $\sigma()$, which is smooth for facilitating gradient-based energy minimization. The first two parts of Eq. (3) drive the level set function $\phi(x,y)$ to separate the box region into text regions Ω and background regions $\bar{\Omega}$. c_1 and c_2 denote the mean values of the text and background regions, respectively, which can be calculated by:

$$c_1(\phi) = \frac{\int_{\Omega \in \mathcal{B}} I^*(x,y)\sigma(\phi(x,y))dxdy}{\int_{\Omega \in \mathcal{B}} \sigma(\phi(x,y))dxdy},$$

$$c_2(\phi) = \frac{\int_{\Omega \in \mathcal{B}} I^*(x,y)(1 - \sigma(\phi(x,y)))dxdy}{\int_{\Omega \in \mathcal{B}}(1 - \sigma(\phi(x,y)))dxdy}. \tag{4}$$

During training, the energy function F can be optimized using stochastic gradient descent. At time step $t \geq 0$, the derivative of energy function F upon ϕ is:

$$\frac{\partial \phi}{\partial t} = -\frac{\partial F}{\partial \phi} = -\nabla\sigma(\phi)\left[(I^*(x,y) - c_1)^2 - (I^*(x,y) - c_1)^2 + \gamma div\left(\frac{\nabla\phi}{|\nabla\phi|}\right)\right], \tag{5}$$

where ∇ and $div(\cdot)$ denote spatial derivative and divergence operator, respectively. Therefore, ϕ is updated by:

$$\phi_i = \phi_{i-1} + \Delta t \frac{\partial \phi_{i-1}}{\partial t}. \tag{6}$$

The optimal boundary C of the text instance is obtained by minimizing the energy function F via iteratively fitting ϕ:

$$\inf_{\Omega \in \mathcal{B}} \approx 0 \approx F(\phi_i). \tag{7}$$

The above process can be seen as the implicit contour evolution in the direction of the energy function descent, and the final contour prediction results are obtained accordingly.

During training, the level-set energy function encourages the aggregation of the interior and exterior regions of the object within the bounding box. However, if we only aggregate the input image $I(x,y)$, the evolution process may be difficult to converge. This is because $I(x,y)$ only contains low-level features such as object shape and color, which are sensitive to environmental factors such as lighting and camera angles in real scenarios. To obtain more robust evolution performance, we also consider high-level features. As shown in Fig. 2, we make use of the output features of the encoder of the segmentation network, which is further fed into a 1×1 convolution layer to extract high-level features. Therefore, the overall energy function of the level set evolution model based on the input image and high-level features can be formulated as:

$$F(\phi) = \lambda_1 * F(\phi, I_{img}, c_{img_1}, c_{img_2}, \mathcal{B}) + \lambda_2 * F(\phi, I_{feat}, c_{feat_1}, c_{feat_2}, \mathcal{B}), \tag{8}$$

where I_{img} and I_{feat} are the input image and high-level feature map, respectively. c_{img_1}, c_{img_2}, c_{feat_1}, c_{feat_2} are the mean values of the corresponding input items. λ_1 and λ_2 are the balance coefficients.

Denoting the loss functions of the text proposal network and the segmentation network as L_{det} and L_{seg}, respectively, the overall loss function of the detector is:

$$L = L_{det} + L_{seg}, \tag{9}$$

where L_{seg} takes different forms depending on the format of the data annotations: (1) For bounding box annotated data, L_{seg} uses the energy function in Eq. (8); (2) For strongly annotated data (e.g., polygon shape contour annotation), L_{seg} uses Focal Loss [12] for pixel-level classification. Therefore, the instance segmentation-based detector supports both strongly supervised training and weakly supervised training based on the level set energy function, which integrates polygon supervision and bounding box supervision in a unified scene text detection framework. If the training dataset mixes strongly annotated data and weakly annotated data, then mix-supervised learning can be performed on the mixed dataset.

Table 1. Performance of different methods on ICDAR2015 dataset.

Method	Precision	Recall	F-measure	FPS
EAST [36]	83.6	73.5	78.2	13.2
DDR [7]	82.0	80.0	81.0	-
TextSnake [15]	84.9	80.4	82.6	1.1
PSENet [26]	86.9	84.5	85.7	1.6
Mask TextSpotter [16]	91.6	81.0	86.0	4.8
PAN++ [27]	**91.4**	**83.9**	**87.5**	12.6
Fully	87.4	83.5	85.4	**18.6**
Mixed	$85.6_{\pm 0.33}$	$83.0_{\pm 0.24}$	$84.3_{\pm 0.28}$	
Weakly	79.7	78.9	79.3	

Table 2. Performance of different methods on C-SVT dataset.

Method	Precision	Recall	F-measure	FPS
DB+oCLIP [31]	81.5	70.9	75.8	-
EAST [36]	73.4	**79.3**	76.2	-
PSENet+oCLIP [31]	**90.7**	67.0	77.1	-
Sun et al.-Train [22]	80.4	74.6	77.4	-
Sun et al.-Train+400K Weak [22]	81.7	75.2	78.3	-
Fully	84.4	74.4	**79.1**	20.9
Mixed	$82.3_{\pm 0.23}$	$75.0_{\pm 0.37}$	$78.4_{\pm 0.29}$	
Weakly	82.2	68.9	75.0	

4   Experiments

4.1   Datasets

To demonstrate the effectiveness of the proposed method, we conduct experiments on five public benchmark datasets.

ICDAR2015 dataset [9] contains 1,000 training images and 500 test images. This dataset contains incidental scene texts, and each instance is labeled as a quadrangle with 4 vertexes in word-level.

C-SVT dataset [22] contains 430,000 training images, of which 30,000 are fully annotated (in polygons of adaptive number of vertices) and the remaining are weakly annotated in bounding boxes. In our experiment, we only use the fully annotated images for the convenience of evaluation.

CTW1500 dataset [14] contains 1,000 training images and 500 test images. Besides horizontal and multi-oriented texts, at least one curved text is contained in each image. Each text is labeled as a polygon with 14 vertexes in line-level.

Total-Text dataset [2] has 1,255 training images and 300 test images, including curved texts, as well as horizontal and multi-oriented texts. Each text is labeled as a polygon with 10 vertexes in word-level.

ICDAR-ArT dataset [3] consists of 5,603 training images and 4,563 test images, containing multilingual arbitrary-shaped texts. Each text is labeled with polygons of adaptive number of vertices.

Table 3. Performance of different methods on CTW1500 dataset.

Method	Precision	Recall	F-measure	FPS
PSENet-1 s [26]	84.8	79.7	82.2	3.9
ContourNet [28]	83.7	84.1	83.9	4.5
PAN++ [27]	87.1	81.1	84.0	**36.0**
Zhang *et al.* [33]	**87.8**	81.5	84.5	12.2
Dai *et al.* [4]	82.3	**87.2**	**84.7**	11.8
Fully	86.5	80.8	83.6	28.5
Mixed	$87.2_{\pm 0.37}$	$79.5_{\pm 0.26}$	$83.2_{\pm 0.28}$	
Weakly	78.9	77.3	78.1	

Table 4. Performance of different methods on Total-Text dataset.

Method	Precision	Recall	F-measure	FPS
Wu *et al.*-TAS [30]	78.5	76.7	77.6	11.2
SelfText [29]	82.5	77.6	80.1	-
TextRay [25]	83.5	77.9	80.6	-
Dai *et al.* [4]	82.0	**88.5**	85.2	11.8
PAN++ [27]	89.9	81.0	85.3	**38.3**
Zhang *et al.* [33]	**90.3**	84.7	**87.4**	10.3
Fully	87.2	83.0	85.0	21.2
Mixed	$88.3_{\pm 0.43}$	$80.7_{\pm 0.27}$	$84.3_{\pm 0.30}$	
Weakly	82.3	75.8	78.9	

4.2   Implementation Details

We implemented the model with Pytorch 1.1 on a workstation with 2.9 GHz 12-core CPU, GTX Titan X and Ubuntu 64-bit OS. We adopt the DLA-34 [32] as the backbone network. The detection model is pre-trained with SynthText [5] dataset, and then fine-tuned on the training set of each real dataset separately for 200 epochs with batchsize 36. The initial learning rate is set as 1×10^{-4} and is divided by 2 at 80th, 120th, 150th, and 170th epoch. The data is augmented by: (1) rescaling images with ratio from 0.5 to 2.0 randomly, (2) flipping horizontally and rotating in range $[-10°, 10°]$ randomly, (3) cropping 640×640 random samples from the transformed image. In the inference stage, the short side of input image is scaled to a fixed length (720 for ICDAR2015, 460 for CTW1500, 640 for Total-Text and C-SVT, and 960 for ICDAR-ArT), with aspect ratio kept.

4.3   Experimental Results

The proposed level-set evolution based text detection framework can work in modes of fully-supervised training, weakly-supervised training, and mixed-supervised training. For ease of analyzing the experimental results, we first provide definitions for different models.

(1) **Fully**: Model trained with all strongly annotated training images, which are annotated with polygons.
(2) **Weakly**: Model trained with all training images, which are annotated with bounding boxes.
(3) **Mixed**: Model trained with all training images, of which 10% are annotated with polygons, and 90% are annotated with bounding boxes. Considering the impact of data split, we split the data five times randomly, and report the average results and standard deviations.

As shown in Tables 1-5, our fully-supervised model achieves 85.4%, 79.1%, 83.6%, 85.0%, 74.2% of F-measure on five datasets, respectively. Although there

Fig. 3. Example of detection results of our fully supervised model.

Table 5. Performance of different methods on ICDAR-ArT dataset.

Method	Precision	Recall	F-measure	FPS
TextRay [25]	76.0	58.6	66.2	-
Dai et al. [4]	66.1	**84.0**	74.0	11.8
Fully	**84.5**	66.2	**74.2**	**22.0**
Mixed	$80.6_{\pm 0.43}$	$68.5_{\pm 0.27}$	$74.0_{\pm 0.30}$	
Weakly	80.4	60.8	69.2	

is a small gap between our method and the state-of-the-art methods in terms of detection performance, our method performs superior in terms of speed. Some examples of text detection results are shown in Fig. 3, where the detection model can accurately locate horizontal, multi-oriented and curved texts.

When training with only bounding box supervision, our weakly-supervised model achieves 79.3%, 75.0%, 78.1%, 78.9% and 69.2% of F-measure on five datasets, respectively. The performance gap between the weakly-supervised model and the fully-supervised model is significant. However, considering that the weakly-supervised models only use the more cost-effective box annotations, these results are acceptable and promising.

When 10% strongly annotated data is mixed with 90% weakly annotated during training, our mixed-supervised model achieves 84.3%, 78.4%, 83.2%, 84.3% and 74.0% of F-measure on five datasets, respectively. Compared with the weakly-supervised models, the performance gains are 5.0%, 7.4%, 5.1%, 5.4%, and 4.8% respectively. In addition, the performance gaps between our mixed-supervised models and the fully-supervised models are around 1% on five datasets. Using only 10% strongly annotated data, we can achieve the performance close to the fully-supervised models. This demonstrates the effectiveness of our mixed-supervised framework.

Table 6. The influence of feature size of RoIs on the performance of scene text detector.

Feature size	Precision	Recall	F-measure
7×7	86.2	80.1	83.0
14×14	87.9	82.6	85.2
32×32	87.4	**83.5**	**85.4**
48×48	**89.4**	80.9	84.9

Table 7. The effect of level-set energy on the performance of mixed-supervised models.

Dataset	F_{img}	F_{feat}	Precision	Recall	F-measure
CTW1500	-	-	83.4	**80.6**	82.0
	✓	-	84.4	80.1	82.6
	✓	✓	**87.2**	79.5	**83.2**
Total-Text	-	-	85.3	80.6	82.9
	✓	-	84.5	**82.3**	83.4
	✓	✓	**88.3**	80.7	**84.3**

4.4 Ablation Studies

The Influence of the Size of the Region Features. The proposed instance segmentation based scene text detector adopts a region feature sampler to sample features from region of interest. To analyze the impact of the size of region features on detection performance, we conduct comparative experiments on the ICDAR2015 dataset. Table 6 shows the results of four different region feature sizes. As the size increases, the detection performance also improves, indicating that larger map of region features favors segmentation tasks. Considering the tradeoff between the performance and efficiency, the size 32×32 is taken in other experiments.

The Effectiveness of the Level-Set Energy. To validate the effectiveness of the level-set energy function, we compare the performance of mixed supervised models under different settings on CTW1500 and Total-Text datasets. Firstly, a mixed supervised experiment is conducted using a baseline model trained without the level set energy function, i.e., the bounding box annotated data is only used to train the text localization network, while the segmentation network is trained with the polygon annotated data only. As shown in Table 7, the baseline model yields F-measure of 82.0% and 82.9% on the two datasets, respectively. Subsequently, the weakly supervised loss function based on the level set energy is added to the baseline model, which only contained image inputs. This mixed supervised model improves the performance by 0.6% and 0.5% on the two datasets, respectively. Finally, high-level features are introduced into the weakly supervised loss function, and the performance of the mixed supervised models are further improved, indicating that the introduction of high-level features benefits level set evolution.

The influence of the number of high-level feature channels. As mentioned before, we add a high-level feature extraction branch (1×1 convolution layer) in the segmentation network for calculating the weakly supervised loss function based on the level-set energy. To verify the influence of the number of channels in the high-level feature on the performance of the mixed supervised models, we conducted a comparative experiment on the ICDAR2015 dataset. As shown in Table 8, four different channel numbers are attempted, and it can

Table 8. The influence of high-level feature channels on ICDAR2015 dataset.

Number of channels	Precision	Recall	F-measure
5	84.9	82.2	83.5
7	**87.6**	80.9	84.2
9	85.6	**83.0**	**84.3**
11	84.0	84.1	84.1

be observed that the performance of the mixed supervised model continuously improves with the increase of channel numbers. However, too large number of channels may deteriorate the performance due to model overfitting. The channel number 9 is chosen in our final experiments.

5   Conclusion

We propose a level-set evolution based box supervised scene text detection framework, which adopts a segmentation based scene text detection model to predict the instance-aware mask as the level set for each text instance. By minimizing the Chan-Vese energy function based level-set energy function, the level set for each text instance is iteratively optimized within its corresponding bounding box annotation. The proposed method can be trained in weakly-supervised or mixed-supervised manner, largely reducing the cost of training data annotation. Extensive experiments on five datasets show that using only 10% strongly annotated data combined with 90% weakly annotated data, our mixed supervised model yields performance comparable to fully-supervised model. In the future, weakly and mixed supervised learning methods are to be tested and improved on larger image datasets.

Acknowledgements. This work was supported in part by the National Key Research and Development Program under Grant 2020AAA0108003 and the National Natural Science Foundation of China (NSFC) under Grant 61721004.

References

1. Chan, T.F., Vese, L.A.: Active contours without edges. IEEE Trans. Image Process. **10**(2), 266–277 (2001)
2. Ch'ng, C.K., Chan, C.S.: Total-text: a comprehensive dataset for scene text detection and recognition. In: Proceedings of the International Conference on Document Analysis and Recognition, vol. 1, pp. 935–942 (2017)
3. Chng, C.K., et al.: ICDAR2019 robust reading challenge on arbitrary-shaped text-RRC-art. In: Proceedings of the International Conference on Document Analysis and Recognition, pp. 1571–1576 (2019)
4. Dai, P., Zhang, S., Zhang, H., Cao, X.: Progressive contour regression for arbitrary-shape scene text detection. In: Proceedings of the IEEE Conference on Computer Vision and Pattern Recognition, pp. 7393–7402 (2021)

5. Gupta, A., Vedaldi, A., Zisserman, A.: Synthetic data for text localisation in natural images. In: Proceedings of the IEEE Conference on Computer Vision and Pattern Recognition, pp. 2315–2324 (2016)
6. He, K., Gkioxari, G., Dollár, P., Girshick, R.: Mask R-CNN. In: Proceedings of the IEEE International Conference on Computer Vision, pp. 2961–2969 (2017)
7. He, W., Zhang, X.Y., Yin, F., Liu, C.L.: Deep direct regression for multi-oriented scene text detection. In: Proceedings of the IEEE International Conference on Computer Vision, pp. 745–753 (2017)
8. Huang, L., Yang, Y., Deng, Y., Yu, Y.: DenseBox: unifying landmark localization with end to end object detection. arXiv preprint arXiv:1509.04874 (2015)
9. Karatzas, D., et al.: ICDAR2015 competition on robust reading. In: Proceedings of the International Conference on Document Analysis and Recognition, pp. 1156–1160 (2015)
10. Li, W., Liu, W., Zhu, J., Cui, M., Hua, X.S., Zhang, L.: Box-supervised instance segmentation with level set evolution. In: Avidan, S., Brostow, G., Cissé, M., Farinella, G.M., Hassner, T. (eds.) Computer Vision. ECCV 2022. LNCS, vol. 13689, pp. 1–18. Springer, Cham (2022). https://doi.org/10.1007/978-3-031-19818-2_1
11. Liao, M., Shi, B., Bai, X., Wang, X., Liu, W.: TextBoxes: a fast text detector with a single deep neural network. In: Proceedings of the AAAI Conference on Artificial Intelligence, vol. 31 (2017)
12. Lin, T.Y., Goyal, P., Girshick, R., He, K., Dollár, P.: Focal loss for dense object detection. In: Proceedings of the IEEE International Conference on Computer Vision, pp. 2980–2988 (2017)
13. Liu, W., Anguelov, D., Erhan, D., Szegedy, C., Reed, S., Fu, C.-Y., Berg, A.C.: SSD: single shot multibox detector. In: Leibe, B., Matas, J., Sebe, N., Welling, M. (eds.) ECCV 2016. LNCS, vol. 9905, pp. 21–37. Springer, Cham (2016). https://doi.org/10.1007/978-3-319-46448-0_2
14. Liu, Y., Jin, L., Zhang, S., Zhang, S.: Detecting curve text in the wild: new dataset and new solution. arXiv preprint arXiv:1712.02170 (2017)
15. Long, S., Ruan, J., Zhang, W., He, X., Wu, W., Yao, C.: TextSnake: a flexible representation for detecting text of arbitrary shapes. In: Ferrari, V., Hebert, M., Sminchisescu, C., Weiss, Y. (eds.) ECCV 2018. LNCS, vol. 11206, pp. 19–35. Springer, Cham (2018). https://doi.org/10.1007/978-3-030-01216-8_2
16. Lyu, P., Liao, M., Yao, C., Wu, W., Bai, X.: Mask TextSpotter: an end-to-end trainable neural network for spotting text with arbitrary shapes. In: Ferrari, V., Hebert, M., Sminchisescu, C., Weiss, Y. (eds.) Computer Vision – ECCV 2018. LNCS, vol. 11218, pp. 71–88. Springer, Cham (2018). https://doi.org/10.1007/978-3-030-01264-9_5
17. Milletari, F., Navab, N., Ahmadi, S.A.: V-Net: fully convolutional neural networks for volumetric medical image segmentation. In: Proceedings of the International Conference on 3D Vision, pp. 565–571 (2016)
18. Mumford, D.B., Shah, J.: Optimal approximations by piecewise smooth functions and associated variational problems. Communications on Pure and Applied Mathematics (1989)
19. Osher, S., Sethian, J.A.: Fronts propagating with curvature-dependent speed: algorithms based on Hamilton-Jacobi formulations. J. Comput. Phys. **79**(1), 12–49 (1988)
20. Qin, X., Zhou, Y., Yang, D., Wang, W.: Curved text detection in natural scene images with semi-and weakly-supervised learning. In: Proceedings of the International Conference on Document Analysis and Recognition, pp. 559–564 (2019)

21. Redmon, J., Divvala, S., Girshick, R., Farhadi, A.: You only look once: unified, real-time object detection. In: Proceedings of the IEEE Conference on Computer Vision and Pattern Recognition, pp. 779–788 (2016)
22. Sun, Y., Liu, J., Liu, W., Han, J., Ding, E., Liu, J.: Chinese street view text: large-scale Chinese text reading with partially supervised learning. In: Proceedings of the IEEE International Conference on Computer Vision, pp. 9086–9095 (2019)
23. Tian, S., Lu, S., Li, C.: WeText: scene text detection under weak supervision. In: Proceedings of the IEEE International Conference on Computer Vision, pp. 1492–1500 (2017)
24. Tian, Z., Huang, W., He, T., He, P., Qiao, Yu.: Detecting text in natural image with connectionist text proposal network. In: Leibe, B., Matas, J., Sebe, N., Welling, M. (eds.) ECCV 2016. LNCS, vol. 9912, pp. 56–72. Springer, Cham (2016). https://doi.org/10.1007/978-3-319-46484-8_4
25. Wang, F., Chen, Y., Wu, F., Li, X.: TextRay: contour-based geometric modeling for arbitrary-shaped scene text detection. In: Proceedings of the ACM International Conference on Multimedia, pp. 111–119 (2020)
26. Wang, W., E., Li, X., Hou, W., Lu, T., Yu, G., Shao, S.: Shape robust text detection with progressive scale expansion network. In: Proceedings of the IEEE Conference on Computer Vision and Pattern Recognition, pp. 9336–9345 (2019)
27. Wang, W., et al.: PAN++: towards efficient and accurate end-to-end spotting of arbitrarily-shaped text. IEEE Trans. Pattern Anal. Mach. Intell. **44**(9), 5349–5367 (2021)
28. Wang, Y., Xie, H., Zha, Z.J., Xing, M., Fu, Z., Zhang, Y.: ContourNet: taking a further step toward accurate arbitrary-shaped scene text detection. In: Proceedings of the IEEE Conference on Computer Vision and Pattern Recognition, pp. 11753–11762 (2020)
29. Wu, W., et al.: SelfText Beyond Polygon: Unconstrained text detection with box supervision and dynamic self-training. arXiv preprint arXiv:2011.13307 (2020)
30. Wu, W., Xing, J., Yang, C., Wang, Y., Zhou, H.: Texts as lines: text detection with weak supervision. Math. Probl. Eng. **2020**, 1–12 (2020)
31. Xue, C., Zhang, W., Hao, Y., Lu, S., Torr, P.H., Bai, S.: Language Matters: A weakly supervised vision-language pre-training approach for scene text detection and spotting. In: In: Avidan, S., Brostow, G., Cissé, M., Farinella, G.M., Hassner, T. (eds.) Computer Vision. ECCV 2022. LNCS, vol. 13688, pp. 284–302 . Springer, Cham (2022). https://doi.org/10.1007/978-3-031-19815-1_17
32. Yu, F., Wang, D., Shelhamer, E., Darrell, T.: Deep layer aggregation. In: Proceedings of the IEEE Conference on Computer Vision and Pattern Recognition, pp. 2403–2412 (2018)
33. Zhang, S.X., Zhu, X., Yang, C., Wang, H., Yin, X.C.: Adaptive boundary proposal network for arbitrary shape text detection. In: Proceedings of the IEEE International Conference on Computer Vision, pp. 1305–1314 (2021)
34. Zhao, M., Feng, W., Yin, F., Zhang, X.Y., Liu, C.L.: Mixed-supervised scene text detection with expectation-maximization algorithm. IEEE Trans. Image Process. **31**, 5513–5528 (2022)
35. Zhou, X., Wang, D., Krähenbühl, P.: Objects as points. arXiv preprint arXiv:1904.07850 (2019)
36. Zhou, X., et al.: EAST: an efficient and accurate scene text detector. In: Proceedings of the IEEE Conference on Computer Vision and Pattern Recognition, pp. 5551–5560 (2017)

Sarcasm Detection in News Headlines Using Evidential Deep Learning-Based LSTM and GRU

Md. Shamsul Rayhan Chy$^{(\boxtimes)}$, Md. Shamsul Rahat Chy,
Mohammad Rakibul Hasan Mahin, Mohammad Muhibur Rahman,
Md Sabbir Hossain, and Annajiat Alim Rasel

School of Data and Sciences, Brac University, Dhaka, Bangladesh
{md.shamsul.rayhan.chy,shamsul.rahat.chy,
mohammad.rakibul.hasan.mahin,mohammad.muhibur.rahman,
md.sabbir.hossain1}@g.bracu.ac.bd

Abstract. Sarcasm has become quite inter-related with the day to day life of all. In news robust sarcasm is often used to grab the attention of the viewers. This research aims to detect sarcasm using Evidential deep learning. This technique uses uncertainty estimations for identifying the sentiments from news headlines dataset. Also, LSTM and GRU have been used with Evidential deep learning approach. The purpose of using LSTM is that it can classify texts from headlines in order to analysis the sentiments. Moreover, we have used GRU which is an recurrent neural networks (RNN) and it effectively models sequential data. The architecture of the GRU network is ideally suited for identifying dependencies and extended contextual relationships within news headings. Overall, our proposed model uses Evidential deep learning based LSTM and GRU to identify the sentiments of robust sarcasms from news headlines.

Keywords: evidential deep learning · lstm · gru · sarcasm detection · nlp

1 Introduction

Sarcasm is used to express feeling in a humouric way where positive words are generally used to make a statement but it contains a negative meaning in the written text. Using sarcasm is a technique to grab attention of others as this type of statements are often very facetious. Sarcasm is also used to express an opinion on a particular viewpoint. Its recognition has becoming more crucial in many applications of natural language processing. In this study, we discuss methods, problems, difficulties, and potential future applications of sarcasm detection [1]. In this research, we have used Evidential deep learning technique to analize the sentiment of news headlines. Evidential deep learning entails the incorporation of uncertainty estimation into deep learning models through the utilisation of Bayesian inference procedures. The model can identify circumstances when it lacks adequate data or runs across unclear inputs thanks to uncertainty estimations. Uncertainty estimation also supports with the assessment of model confidence. It is crucial to have a grasp of the dependability and trustworthiness of the model's predictions in order to be able to use it in key applications such as medical diagnosis and legal analysis. We have also integrated LSTM with Evidential deep learning and the purpose of it is to identify the sentiment of the news headlines. LSTM can process each word in news headlines in sequence and the final output of it is used to classify the sentiment of the respective headline.

2 Related Works

Robust sarcasm detection from news headlines is a challenging with the use of Evidential deep learning. There are some related works with sarcasm detection. Various kind of techniques has been used to detect the sentiment analysis of sarcasms.

In the paper [2], the authors have experimented with an algorithm of STSM which is sentiment topic sarcasm mixture. A lot of features has been used for the development of the model such as pragmatic features and lexicon based. The main concept of this model is that the influence of some topics in detecting sarcasm is more than others.

Paper [3] provides an ensemble model to detect sarcasm on the internet. The used dataset is prepared on previously trained various word-embedding models. Here weighted average obtained the highest accuracy in case of both the datasets. Authors of paper [4] proposed a model named C-Net. It extracts contextual knowledge from texts in a serial fashion way. Then it categorises the texts into sarcastic or non-sarcastic.

Authors of [5] built a transformer based method where recurrent CNN-RoBERTA model is used to find the sarcasm in given statements. In paper [6], authors have proposed a new behavioral model for detecting sarcasm. They have used a lexicon-based technique. Their SCUBA model can detect whether a person is sarcastic or not using past data. This model uses various approach and among them SCUBA++ achieves the highest accuracy 92.94%.

The authors of [7] used a set of features. The features are derived in a manner that utilises various components of the tweet and encompasses various forms of sarcasm. Their proposed approach achieves higher accuracy of 83.1% compared to some baseline approaches like n-grams. In [8], authors have used supervised machine learning methods for detecting sarcasm on Czech and English Twitter datasets. The paper focuses on the document level sarcasm detection. They have used various n-grams with frequency greater than three and a set of language independent features. SVM classifier with the feature set achieves best result on Czech dataset with F-measure 0.582.

From [9], there are two different groups of machine learning algorithms AMLA and CMLA. In AMLA group the most prevalent method was discovered to be SVM (22.58%), followed by Logistic Regression Method (19.35%), Nave Bayes (9.67%), and Random Forest. For recognising the sarcastic tweets, algorithms in the CMLA group were found to be utilised less often (3.22%). So, here the AMLA group algorithms are the ones that are most frequently used to detect sarcasm. Authors of [10] used Hybrid Ensemble Model with Fuzzy Logic to detect sarcasm over social media platforms. Here they used the Reddit dataset, twitter dataset and the headlines dataset. Their model makes use of BERT-base, Word2Vec, and GloVe. The stated portion from the three previously discussed strategies is used by the fuzzy logic layer to assess the categorization probability of all three processes. This model achieves the best accuracy in all three datasets which are respectively 85.38%, 86.8% and 90.81%.

Islam et al. [11] investigate the reliability of text categorization systems, specifically focusing on the uncertainty associated with Transformer-based models like BERT and XLNet in comparison to RNN versions such as Long Short-Term Memory and Gated Recurrent Unit. In order to determine the level of uncertainty associated with these models, the technique of employing dropouts during the inference phase, commonly referred to as Monte Carlo dropout, is utilised. An alternative study presents a fresh methodology for estimating both aleatoric and epistemic uncertainties in stereo matching through an end-to-end process. The authors present a statistical distribution called the Normal Inverse-Gamma (NIG) distribution, which can be utilised to measure the level of uncertainty. Instead of employing straight regression from aggregated features, the approach involves predicting uncertainty parameters for each conceivable disparity. These parameters are then averaged using the advice provided by the matching probability distribution [12]. Evidential deep learning is also very popular in uncertainty estimation and reliabilty analyzing [13–15].

From our literature study we see that reliability measurements are not considered when detecting sarcastic news. Our study focuses on this particular problem with Evidential Deep Learning.

3   Dataset

In our research, we have used the news headlines dataset [16]. The purpose of using this dataset is to avoid label and language noise. This dataset contains sarcastic News headlines from the news website named TheOnion. On the other hand, this dataset also contains non-sarcastic and real parts which has been collected from the HuffPost news website. In this dataset there are 28,619 headlines which contains both sarcastic and non-sarcastic. The language used in the headlines of this dataset is formal as all the writings have been done by professional writers. That is why there is very little chance of spelling mistake in the headlines. Also, as one of the news website that provided only the sarcastic texts, that is why there is high chance that the quality of label is controlled in the respective dataset.

4   Methodology

4.1   Evidential Deep Learning

Evidential deep learning is used in natural language processing (NLP) to resolve the limitations of conventional deep learning models. This technique used uncertainty estimations. The weights and biases in this model are treated as random variables with prior distributions by Bayesian neural networks (BNNs), which were used in its construction. We use variational inference, a method that improves the Evidence Lower Bound (ELBO) by repeatedly changing the variational distribution to closely resemble the real posterior distribution, to approximate the posterior distribution over the model parameters. The fluctuation seen in these forecasts offers insightful information about the level of uncertainty around the model's results. Also, confidence intervals are derived from uncertainty estimations. Instances where the model lacks assurance or runs across inputs that are intrinsically unclear are indicated by higher uncertainty levels. The model's confidence is shown by variables like predictive variance, entropy, or quantiles of the predictive distribution.

Theory of Evidence. Neural Networks can have K outputs and the equality of it can be written as

$$u + \sum_{k=1}^{K} b_k = 1 \tag{1}$$

Here b_k is interpreted as the belief mass of the kth class and the uncertainty mass of the particular outputs is u and b_k is defined as follows

$$b_k = \frac{e_k}{S} \tag{2}$$

Now the e_k is k^{th} class evidence and S is strength of Dirichlet and is defined as follows

$$S = \sum_{k=1}^{K} (e_k + 1) \tag{3}$$

which leaves u the following portion

$$u = \frac{K}{S} \tag{4}$$

Replacing $e_k + 1$ with a_k

$$\alpha_k = e_k + 1 \tag{5}$$

Here resultant sinplex vector a is used as the density in a Dirichlet

$$D(\boldsymbol{p} \mid \boldsymbol{\alpha}) = \begin{cases} \frac{1}{B(\boldsymbol{\alpha})} \prod_{i=1}^{K} p_i^{\alpha_i - 1} & \text{for } \boldsymbol{p} \in \mathcal{S}_K \\ 0 & \text{otherwise} \end{cases} \tag{6}$$

$\mathcal{S}_K$ can be defined as

$$\mathcal{S}_K = \left\{ p \mid \sum_{i=1}^{K} p_i = 1 \text{ and } 0 \le p_1, \ldots, p_K \le 1 \right\} \tag{7}$$

Finally, the probability of kth is calculated as

$$\hat{p}_k = \frac{\alpha_k}{S} \tag{8}$$

Reliability Evaluation of the Classification Algorithm. Classification Algorithm Reliability Evaluation (Stable Operational Profile) According to the literature, we presume that the chance of not failing on a randomly selected input $d_r \in D$ [17] is how the black-box dependability is stated. The priors $f_i(x)$ are set to Beta $(\alpha_i = 1, \beta_i = 1)$ with the assumption that each class represents an operational profile of traffic sign recognition and that no prior information regarding the incidence of failures within partitions is known. Let's assume that N_i represents the quantity of test photos sent to the algorithm as input and r_i represents the quantity of errors.

The Dirichlet distribution $D(\alpha_1, \ldots, \alpha_n)$, which modelled the OPP prior to the new observation, will be transformed by the new information $N_1, \ldots, N_n$ into:

$$D(\alpha_1 + N_1, \ldots, \alpha_n + N_n)$$

The revised distribution of the operational profile's or partition S_i's conditional probability of failing to recognise class i will be:

$$f_{F_i} = B(\alpha_i + r_i, \beta_i + N_i - r_i) \tag{9}$$

The expected value of f_{F_i} can be calculated as:

$$E[F_i] = \frac{\alpha_i + r_i}{\beta_i + \alpha_i + N_i} \tag{10}$$

Finally the reliability is calculated as taking each OPP_i as $1/10$

$$E[R] = 1 - \sum_{i=1}^{43} OPP_i \times E[F_i] = 1 - 0.1 \times \sum_{i=1}^{43} \frac{\alpha_i + r_i}{\beta_i + \alpha_i + N_i} \tag{11}$$

4.2   LSTM

LSTM is known as Long Short Term Memory. The idea to use LSTM is that is can use to classify texts and to analysis sentiment of texts. LSTM use the mechanism of memory cell where it has three gates connected to each of the cell. Input gate, forget gate and output gate. With the use of these LSTM is capable to retain any information or to forget it. A sigmoid activation function is used to decide which data to keep or discard from input or previous cell. This technique make predictions based on the relavant data. Along with the capability to use memory cell it can make effective predictions in order to analysis the sentiment of any written text. For analyzing sentiment it also uses an embedding layer. This layer helps to map each word of a sentence and each word here gets a vector representation and after training it can learn the most informative vector representation for each word. The model then processes sequence of word vectors and a sentiment based on the prediction is achieved. It also uses backpropagation strategy for training the data. The model contains one bidirectional LSTM layer then we add a dense layer with 20 nodes and finally we add a dropout layer with 50% dropout rate. We add global max pooling for decreasing the computational cost.

4.3 GRU

GRU is a form of architecture for recurrent neural networks (RNN) that effectively models sequential data. GRU incorporates gating mechanisms that allow the network to capture and retain pertinent data over extended sequences. This gating mechanism, which consists of reset and update gates, permits the model to selectively update and retain pertinent information while discarding irrelevant or redundant data. The GRU's gating mechanism regulates the passage of information through the network, allowing it to capture textual dependencies and contextual information. Backpropagation through time (BPTT), which extends the concept of backpropagation to sequential data, is used to train the GRU model. This method allows for the efficient updating of the model's weights and biases by propagating error gradients over time. GRU is utilised to assess a model's ability to generalise to unobserved data by evaluating its performance on the validation and test sets. GRU permits the network to selectively update and retain pertinent data while discarding irrelevant or redundant data. This mechanism facilitates comprehension of the subtleties of sarcasm and tone in headlines. The model contains one bidirectional GRU layer then we add a dense layer with 20 nodes and finally we add a dropout layer with 50% dropout rate. We add global max pooling for decreasing the computational cost.

5 Results and Analysis

In this section, we analyze the performance of our proposed models. We assess the models using a variety of performance criteria, such as test accuracy, test AUC score, and Reliability (Table 1) .

Here, the table above shows the raw and uncertain-aware performances of LSTM and GRU. The LSTM model was trained with weight parameters of 1,499,309. During the evaluation, it attained an accuracy of 82% and an AUC-score of 0.81. The reliability score is 0.49. The GRU model, on the other hand, performed slightly worse having slightly less weight parameters of 1,447,149. It did not outperform the LSTM model in terms of accuracy and AUC-score,

Table 1. Result Comparison

Model	LSTM	GRU
Number of Parameters	1,499,309	1,447,449
Test Accuracy	82%	78%
Test AUC	0.81	0.77
Reliability Score	0.49	0.43

attaining 78% and 0.77 respectively. Moreover, the model achieves an reliability score of 0.43.

The training vs validation curves are shown in Fig. 1 and in Fig. 2. The epochs are the same and requires only 4. The fitting is considerably more stable in GRU but the performance of LSTM is better.

Considering the reliability score and other evaluation measures, we can say that LSTM is a better model to go forward with. The small difference of weight parameters is negligible since the performance is noticeably better.

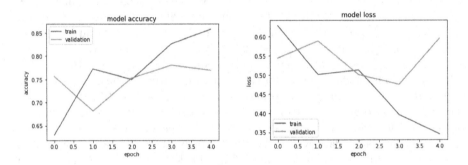

Fig. 1. Accuracy and Loss curve of LSTM Model

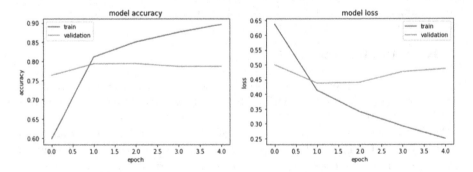

Fig. 2. Accuracy and Loss curve of GRU Model

6   Conclusion & Future Works

In this study, we have conducted research on news headlines dataset using LSTM and GRU. The LSTM-based model, when compared to the GRU model, achieves a higher level of accuracy with 82% while GRU has an accuracy of 78%. Additionally, its AUC score is higher than that of the GRU model. In addition, we take into account the readability score, and the LSTM algorithm once again demonstrates superior performance in this category. In our future works, we would like to expand the scope of our study to include additional approaches to assessing uncertainty, such as monte carlo dropout and active learning, for example. Due to the fact that recognizing sarcasm is a challenging endeavor and that there is a great deal of room for ambiguity, it is recommended that several uncertainty and reliability metrics be employed.

References

1. Chaudhari, P., Chandankhede, C.: Literature survey of sarcasm detection. In: 2017 International Conference on Wireless Communications, Signal Processing and Networking (WiSPNET), pp. 2041–2046 (2017)
2. Krishnan, N., Rethnaraj, J., Saravanan, M.: Sentiment topic sarcasm mixture model to distinguish sarcasm prevalent topics based on the sentiment bearing words in the tweets. J. Amb. Intell. Human. Comput. **12**, 6801–6810 (2021)
3. Goel, P., Jain, R., Nayyar, A., Singhal, S., Srivastava, M.: Sarcasm detection using deep learning and ensemble learning. Multimed. Tools App. **81**, 43229–43252 (2022)
4. Jena, A., Sinha, A., Agarwal, R.: C-Net: contextual network for sarcasm detection (2020)
5. Potamias, R., Siolas, G., Stafylopatis, A.: A Transformer-based approach to Irony and Sarcasm detection (2019)
6. Rajadesingan, A., Zafarani, R., Liu, H.: Sarcasm detection on twitter: a behavioral modeling approach. In: WSDM 2015 - Proceedings Of The 8th ACM International Conference on Web Search and Data Mining, pp. 97–106 (2015)
7. Bouazizi, M., Ohtsuki, T.: A pattern-based approach for sarcasm detection on twitter. IEEE Access **4**, 5477–5488 (2016)
8. Ptácek, T., Habernal, I., Hong, J.: Sarcasm Detection on Czech and English Twitter. In: International Conference on Computational Linguistics (2014)
9. Sarsam, S., Al-Samarraie, H., Alzahrani, A., Wright, B.: Sarcasm detection using machine learning algorithms in Twitter: a systematic review. Int. J. Mark. Res. **62**, 578–598 (2020)
10. Sharma, D., Singh, B., Agarwal, S., Pachauri, N., Alhussan, A., Abdallah, H.: Sarcasm detection over social media platforms using hybrid ensemble model with fuzzy logic. Electronics **12**, 937 (2023)
11. Islam, M., et al.: RNN variants vs transformer variants: uncertainty in text classification with monte Carlo dropout. In: 2022 25th International Conference On Computer And Information Technology (ICCIT), pp. 7–12 (2022)
12. Wang, C., et al.: Uncertainty estimation for stereo matching based on evidential deep learning. Pattern Recogn. **124**, 108498 (2022)

13. Bao, W., Yu, Q., Kong, Y.: Evidential deep learning for open set action recognition. In: Proceedings Of The IEEE/CVF International Conference on Computer Vision (ICCV), pp. 13349–13358 (2021)
14. Capellier, E., Davoine, F., Cherfaoui, V., Li, Y.: Evidential deep learning for arbitrary LIDAR object classification in the context of autonomous driving. In: 2019 IEEE Intelligent Vehicles Symposium (IV), pp. 1304–1311 (2019)
15. Ulmer, D., Hardmeier, C., Frellsen, J.: A Survey on Evidential Deep Learning Methods For Uncertainty Estimation, Prior and Posterior Networks (2023)
16. Misra, R., Arora, P.: Sarcasm detection using news headlines dataset. AI Open. 4, 13–18 (2023)
17. Pietrantuono, R., Popov, P., Russo, S.: Reliability assessment of service-based software under operational profile uncertainty. Reliab. Eng. Syst. Saf. **204**, 107193 (2020)

Style Recognition of Calligraphic Chinese Characters Based on Morphological Convolutional Neural Network

Qing Jiao[✉], Zhenyu Wang, Huan Sun, Junhui Zhu, and Junping Wang

Xidian University, Xi'an, China
1914847383@qq.com

Abstract. As an indispensable part of the excellent traditional Chinese culture, calligraphic Chinese characters have gradually evolved into different style types in the development process, which has raised the threshold for users to learn and appreciate calligraphy. With the development of deep learning technology, deep feature extraction technology based on convolutional neural network has made important breakthroughs in the task of calligraphy Chinese character style recognition. However, there are still problems such as lack of suitable datasets and easy loss of detailed feature information when extracting features, which lead to low accuracy of style recognition of calligraphy Chinese character. Therefore, this paper proposes a dilation pool subset based on morphological operators, and combines with residual block structure to build morphological convolutional neural network (MCNN) for calligraphy style recognition. The experimental results on 5 kinds of calligraphy Chinese character style datasets show that the recognition accuracy of the proposed method is 99.17%, and the recognition accuracy of cursive and running style is significantly improved by 4%–6% compared with other methods, which verifies the effectiveness of the proposed method for the style recognition of calligraphy Chinese characters. This study provides an effective solution for recognizing the style of Chinese characters in real scenes, and also has important research significance for broadening the application range of mathematical morphology.

Keywords: Morphological Convolutional Neural Network · Dilation Pool Subnetwork · Style Recognition

1 Introduction

Chinese calligraphy has a long history. As an important part of this long-standing traditional culture, Chinese characters have a long history of development, gradually evolving from the original oracle bone script, big seal etc. to modern representative regular, seal, cursive, running and official [1]. However, each Chinese character has its own style and is very different, which increases the difficulty of recognizing the style of calligraphy Chinese characters. It is difficult for the general public to learn and appreciate the calligraphy. Therefore, it is of great research significance to study the recognition of calligraphy Chinese character style.

H. Lu et al. (Eds.): ACPR 2023, LNCS 14406, pp. 203–215, 2023.
https://doi.org/10.1007/978-3-031-47634-1_16

In the past ten years, computer-aided calligraphy has made great progress in the research of Chinese characters, and the digitization of Chinese historical calligraphy works will also become an inevitable trend in the development of traditional Chinese calligraphy art. Traditional feature extraction methods include three processes: image preprocessing, feature extraction and classification to achieve style recognition. With the fast development of deep learning, the calligraphy Chinese character style recognition network model based on deep learning has become the mainstream, and the deep features extracted by it improve the accuracy and overall recognition rate of calligraphic Chinese style recognition. Classical convolutional neural network (CNN) models such as AlexNet, VGGNet, and ResNet are used to identify calligraphy Chinese character styles [2]. The CNN contains a convolutional structure, which first extracts deep features from calligraphy Chinese character images through the operation of convolutional layer, and then selects features and filters information through the pooling layer. Finally, after the training and learning of the neural network, the calligraphy Chinese character style recognition task is completed.

However, the existing recognition methods are difficult to select accurate calligraphy Chinese character features, and the deep features extracted based on CNN are still affected by image noise and other factors, and the filtering of small feature-sensitive images through the max-pooling layer will cause information detail loss [3], especially for similar styles of line writing and cursive writing style is difficult to accurately recognize. Therefore, we build a dilation pool subnetwork based on morphological operators to replace the max-pooling layer in CNN, and combined with residual block structure to build a morphologic convolutional neural network (MCNN) to recognize five calligraphic Chinese character styles: regular, seal, cursive, running and official.

The rest of this paper is organized as follows: the related works is introduced in Sect. 2. Section 3 introduces a classic CNN network. Section 4 gives a detailed explanation of the new method we proposed. Section 5 shows experiments and analysis of the new method. Section 6 summarizes this paper and points out the future research directions.

2 Related Works

With the development of artificial intelligence technology, deep feature extraction technology based on deep learning is becoming more and more mature, and many researchers have made breakthroughs in calligraphy Chinese character style recognition. Li et al. [4] used the existing China Academic Digital Associative Library(CADAL) to build eight models with different numbers of convolutional layers and filters based on the VGGNet network for style identification. Jiulong et al. [5] can also be used for other image style recognition problems by using the stack autoencoder of the deep neural network to extract features, distinguish the correct character style and foreign character style with the trained single-classification SVM, and pick out the outliers. Pengcheng et al. [6] extracted three features representing calligraphy Chinese character features, two were global feature GIST and local feature SIFT, and the other was the depth feature extracted by CNN. By evaluating the effectiveness of three feature methods on three classifiers through experiments, it was found that deep features achieved better recognition rates than using the other two feature methods Wen[7] proposes a method for automatically identifying the calligraphy style of full-page documents, using self-built datasets to compare the accuracy on different CNN models, but the recognition accuracy on the line book is only 89%. Chen [8] uses AlexNet network to perform calligraphy style recognition on CADAL, compared with traditional feature extraction methods such as PCA, and experiments show that the proposed calligraphy style recognition is more efficient, and the interface construction of Chinese character scoring system is realized.

In recent years, the strong theoretical foundation of mathematical morphology has made it widely used in various fields, such as image denoising, image classification, edge detection [9, 10] and so on. The main idea of mathematical morphology is to use "structural element" as a sliding window to perform morphological dilation, erosion, opening, closing operations and other operations on the image. Due to the structural similarity between morphological nonlinear operations and convolutional operations, some researchers have developed an interest in using morphological operators when using neural networks to process various image tasks. Since 2018, Mondal et al. [11] have proposed a dense morphological network, which uses nonlinear operations instead of basic linear combination operations, thus eliminating the additional nonlinear activation function. The experiment shows that the network with morphological operation can approximate any smooth function, and the parameters required are less than those required by the normal neural network, but the network is limited to one-dimensional feature vectors as input. Franchi et al. [12] proposed a new method using morphological operators in an end-to-end deep learning framework and verified it in edge detection. The deep morphological network proposed by Nogueira et al. [13] can not only optimize the four basic morphological operations and top hat operations, but also learn features according to the input data, and achieve certain results in grayscale image classification tasks. Aouad et al. [14] introduced a binary morphological neural network based on convolutional neural network, which can learn the basic operators of morphology and have certain results in medical imaging applications, but its input and output are binary images.

3   A Typical CNN Network – ResNet

Convolutional neural network (CNN) is a class of deep neural networks that are mainly used to extract features and classify decisions. ResNet is a typical CNN network structure, a new residual network created by He Kaiming et al. [15] in 2015 and won the ImageNet competition that year.

The key to the ResNet lies in its basic building block: the residual block. The two residual block structures commonly used in ResNet are shown in Fig. 1. Figure 1 (a) is BasicBlock, and Fig. 1 (b) is Bottleneck. If the input of the residual block is set to x, it represents the residual path $F(x)$, which is an identity map, also known as "shortcut", then two different paths $F(x)$ and x form a single residual block. The residual path of BasicBlock consists of 2 convolutional layers of size. Bottleneck is composed of convolutional layers with dimensions of 1×1, 3×3, and 1×1 connected in turn, of which two 1×1 convolutional layers are the input first dimensionality reduction and then dimensionality upgrading operation, so as to reduce the network computing

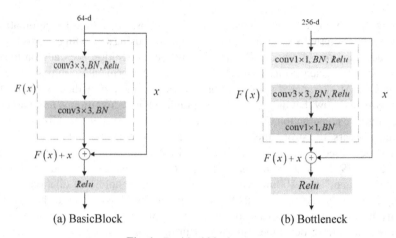

Fig. 1. Residual block structure

complexity, generally used in residual networks with a network depth greater than 50 layers.

The ResNet network framework composed of multiple similar residual block cascades is shown in Fig. 2, artificially using compartments to connect to weaken the strong connection between each layer, and changing the number of residual blocks can obtain networks with different learning capabilities. In addition, ResNet also uses a batch normalization(BN) layers to preprocess the data to compensate for gradient vanishing or gradient explosion. Therefore, ResNet is the most groundbreaking work in the development of deep learning, and it is also one of the most widely used convolutional neural networks to date.

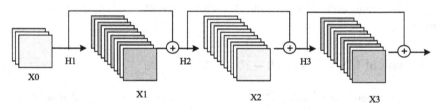

Fig. 2. ResNet Network Framework

4 Proposed Method MCNN

For calligraphy Chinese character images dominated by black, gray and white, If the max-pooling layer is used in CNN, all non-maximum pixels in the window will be automatically lost when the feature filtering is carried out. When the pixel values adjacent to the image differ greatly, only the pixel values of the light area are retained to a large extent, while the pixel values of the dark areas are ignored, resulting in the loss of detailed feature information in the dark areas, which will seriously affect the recognition effect. In this section, we build a dilation pool subnetwork based on morphological operators to replace the max-pooling layer, and propose a calligraphy Chinese character style recognition method based on morphological convolutional neural network.

4.1 MCNN Network Architecture

Morphological convolutional neural network (MCNN) consists of input layer, convolutional layer, dilation pool subnet, four convolutional blocks layer, a fully connected layer, and output layer, as shown in Fig. 3.

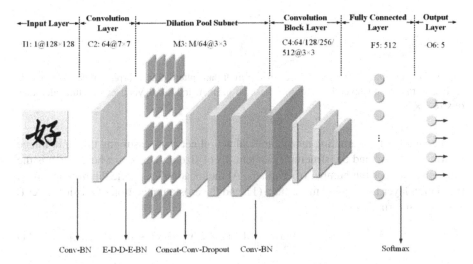

Fig. 3. MCNN Network Structure

As can be seen from Fig. 3, the input layer inputs a grayscale image of size 128 × 128. Next, preliminary feature extraction is completed in the convolutional layer and BN processing is performed. Extracting morphological features and preserving detailed information from the dilation pool subnet. Then, the deep feature is extracted through four convolution blocks. The BasicBlock residual block shown in Fig. 1(a) is used in each convolution block, the Relu function is selected as the activation function, and BN processing is performed after each convolution layer. The fully connected layer integrates features, and finally classifies them in the output layer using Softmax.

The dilation pool subnet structure is shown in Fig. 4, consisting of sequentially connected multipath alternating morphological neural networks, merging layers, convolutional layers, and Dropout layers. The multipath alternating morphological neural network includes five parallels and alternating E-D structures and D-E structures, which indirectly implement open and close operations, extract image features, and construct filters to achieve filtering functions. The merging layer linearly connects the number of output channels of multiple alternating morphological neural networks. Then, the convolutional layer is used to reduce or increase the dimensionality of the number of channels to adapt to the network output. Finally, the Dropout layer is used for optimization, and a certain number of neurons are randomly activated to prevent overfitting.

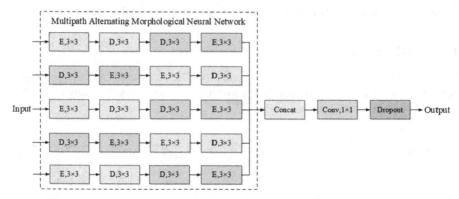

Fig. 4. Dilation pool subnet structure. In the multipath alternating morphological network, E represents the erosion layer, D represents the dilation layer, and each layer uses structural elements of size 3 × 3

In a multipath alternating morphological neural network, assuming the input image of size a × b × c and the structural element SE of size m × n × c, where a × b is the input size and c is the number of channels. At the location (x, y), the dilation operation of dilation layer D is shown in formula (1), and the erosion operation of erosion layer E is shown in formula (2).

$$\delta(F, W_D^M)_{(x,y)} = \max_{i \in W_1, j \in W_2, k \in W_3} \left(F(x + i, y + j, k) + W_D^M(i, j, k) \right) \tag{1}$$

$$\delta(F, W_D^M)_{(x,y)} = \max_{i \in W_1, j \in W_2, k \in W_3} \left(F(x + i, y + j, k) + W_D^M(i, j, k) \right) \tag{2}$$

where $W_D(i, j, k)$, $W_E(i, j, k)$ represents the structural elements of the dilation layer and the erosion layer respectively, and (i, j, k) is the index of the corresponding structural elements. The number of structural elements used in each layer is represented as M ($M = 1, 2, 3 \ldots$), $W_1 = \{1, 2, \ldots, m\}$, $W_2 = \{1, 2, \ldots, n\}$, $W_3 = \{1, 2, \ldots, c\}$.

From formula (1), it can be seen that the process of dilation operation and max-pooling operation is similar. Therefore, the process of selecting the maximum value for max-pooling can be seen as a pooling operation performed by dilation operator with rectangular structural element. We learn dilation operators in the dilation pool subnet by constructing E-D and D-E structures to replace the max-pooling layer. In addition, the combination of morphological operators can not only achieve image filtering, but also enhance the ability to extract features.

The parameter settings for the MCNN network are as follows:

1. We use a grayscale image as the input image.
2. Let the convolutional kernel of the convolutional layer after the input layer has size 7 × 7 with stride 2, and use the same filling method to preserve the style features, then, perform BN processing on the features.

3. The dilation pool subnet includes 5 parallel and alternating E-D structures and D-E structures, with 16 structural elements of size 3 × 3 used for dilation layer D and erosion layer E in each path with stride 1. Before merging channels, perform BN processing on the output of each channel, and the output channel of the merging layer is 5 × 16. The convolutional layer uses 64 convolutional kernels of size 1 × 1, with stride 1, filled with same, and nonlinearly activated using the Relu function. The probability of randomly activating neurons in the Dropout layer is set to 0.5 to ensure that half of the probability is randomly activated during training, thus achieving nonlinear processing.

4. Let the four convolutional blocks as Conv1, Conv2, Conv3, and Conv4. Conv1 convolution block is composed of three identical BasicBlock residual blocks. Each residual block contains two 3 × 3 convolution layers. The number of channels in each convolution layer is 64 with stride 1. After that, BN processing is performed. Conv2 convolutional blocks are composed of four residual blocks, with the first residual block consisting of two 3 × 3 convolutional layers and one 1 × 1 convolutional layer in steps of 2, 1, and 2, respectively. The remaining three residual blocks all consist of two 3 × 3 convolutional layers in steps of 1, with all residual block channels having 128 channels. Conv3 convolutional blocks are composed of six residual blocks, with the first residual block consisting of two 3x3 convolutional layers and one convolutional layer in steps of 2, 1, and 2, respectively. The remaining five residual blocks all consist of two 3 × 3 convolutional layers in steps of 1, with all residual block channels having 256 channels. The Conv4 convolutional block is composed of three residual blocks, with the first residual block consisting of two 3 × 3 convolutional layers and one convolutional layer, with steps of 2, 1, and 2, respectively. The other two residual blocks all include two 3 × 3 convolutional layers with steps of 1, and all residual block channels have 512 channels.

5. The fully connected layer integrates features, retaining 512 neurons.

6. The output layer uses the Softmax function for classification and recognition, with 5 calligraphy styles assigned as 5 classification tasks. Therefore, setting the number of neurons to 5 can complete the recognition of calligraphy Chinese character styles by building a network.

4.2 Network Training

We use the CrossEntropy Loss as the loss function of the network. For the minimization of loss, Adam optimizer with parameter settings ($lr = 0.001$, $\beta1 = 0.9$, $\beta2 = 0.999$) is employed. Back-propagation algorithm is used to update the SEs and the weights in the convolution layers and fully connected layer of MCNN. The network is trained up to 50 epochs on extended dataset with batch size of 32. For all the experiments, we have initialized the structuring elements randomly using standard glorot uniform initializer.

5 Experiment and Analysis

In order to verify the effectiveness of our proposed method, we conducted extensive experiments on datasets of 5 calligraphy Chinese character styles.

5.1 Experimental Setup and Dataset

In terms of hardware, the CPU is i7–9700 K, with a CPU clock speed of 3.60 GHz and a GPU of NVIDIA GeForce RTX 2080. In terms of software, we use Window 10, configure TensorFlow 2.1.0 as the programming framework, use PyCharm programming software, and the programming environment is Python 3.7.

At present, many calligraphy and Chinese character recognition studies use a limited number of calligraphy character library datasets, which are difficult to meet the recognition needs in real scenarios. Therefore, we bulid datasets based on Chinese character font and morphological transformations. Firstly, collect 800 commonly used Chinese characters from 5 calligraphy styles through the internet, each with 6–10 different forms. By using Python image processing tools to convert individual character images into "jpg" files and categorize them by category, an original dataset of 27821 images containing 5 calligraphy Chinese characters was bulit. In the actual acquisition process of calligraphy images, affected by the shooting angle, shooting environment and other external conditions, the calligraphy Chinese characters will have a certain degree of deformation. We also combine the Chinese characters (affine transformation, noise transform and inverse transform) and morphological transform (dilation, erosion, open and close) to expand the image of the collected original dataset, Finally, an extended dataset with 390,922 images is built to form diverse forms and support the training of deep learning networks.

In order to meet training needs, we divides the extended dataset into training, validation, and testing sets in a 7:1:2 ratio. The specific division is shown in Table 1.

Table 1. Statistics on Division of Extended Dataset

	Regular	Seal	Cursive	Running	Official	Total
Train	74054	51141	52167	48568	47720	273650
Validation	10578	7305	7452	6938	6817	39090
Test	21157	14611	14904	13876	13634	78182
Total	105789	73057	74523	69382	68171	390922

5.2 Reults of Style Recognition

This section shows the effect of MCNN network trained on the test set to recognize five styles of calligraphy Chinese characters, and uses confusion matrix, accuracy (Acc), precision (Pre), recall (Rec) and F1 score to evaluate the recognition performance. And compare it with the use of maximum pooling layer and other recognition methods in the network.

Test the proposed method on the test set, and the confusion matrix is shown in Table 2.

Table 2. Statistical Results of MCNN on the Recognition of 5 Calligraphic Chinese Character Styles

True	Predictive value					Total
	Regular	Seal	Cursive	Running	Official	
Regular	**21070**	0	5	74	8	21157
Seal	4	**14561**	9	3	34	14611
Cursive	18	6	**14716**	160	4	14904
Running	152	1	116	**13597**	10	13876
Official	8	27	3	5	**13591**	13634
Total	21252	14595	14849	13839	13647	78182

The accuracy, recall, and F1 scores calculated from Table 2 are shown in Table 3.

Table 3. Recognition Results of MCNN for 5 Calligraphic Chinese Character Styles (%)

	Regular	Seal	Cursive	Running	Official	Average
Acc	99.14	99.77	99.10	98.25	99.59	**99.17**
Rec	99.58	99.66	98.74	97.99	99.68	**99.13**
F1 Score	99.36	99.71	98.92	98.12	99.63	**99.15**

From Tables 2 and 3, it can be seen that MCNN has achieved very high recognition rates in all five calligraphy Chinese character styles, with average Acc, Rec and F1 score of 99.17%, 99.13%, and 99.15%, respectively, meeting practical application requirements. Due to the clear and simple structural features of seal and official script, the Acc of these two styles are 99.77% and 99.59%, respectively, slightly higher than other styles, and other indicators also show the same results. Due to the style of running script being between regular script and cursive script, the recognition rate of running script is relatively low, with Rec of 97.99%, and even some images are mistakenly recognized as regular or cursive script.

In order to further verify the recognition performance of the MCNN method proposed in this paper, calligraphy Chinese character images were randomly selected from the test set for testing, and the results obtained are shown in Fig. 5.

From Fig. 5, it can be seen that the majority of calligraphy Chinese character styles can be correctly recognized, with only a few style recognition errors, such as "cursive script" being recognized as "running script". Therefore, the MCNN method proposed in this paper can effectively complete the task of calligraphy Chinese character style recognition and achieve the expected results.

Fig. 5. Random test results of calligraphy Chinese character style recognition network

In order to verify the effectiveness of using the proposed dilation pool subnet in MCNN network in improving recognition accuracy, recognition tests were conducted on ResNet network and MCNN network respectively, and the comparison results are shown in Table 4.

Table 4. Comparison results of max-pooling layer and dilation pool subnet (%)

	Original Dataset	Extended Dataset
ResNet (Max-Pooling Layer)	92.84	96.33
MCNN (Dilation Pool Subnet)	94.35	99.17

From Table 4, it can be seen that compared to the max-pooling layer, the recognition accuracy of using dilation pool subnet in MCNN is significantly improved on both the original and extended dataset. On the original dataset, the recognition accuracy using dilation pool subnet is 1.51% higher than using the max-pooling layer. On the extended dataset, the recognition accuracy is 2.84% higher. Therefore, the dilation pool subnet proposed in this paper not only reduces the loss of information details, but also is effective in improving the accuracy of calligraphy Chinese character style recognition.

In order to better demonstrate the effectiveness of the MCNN method proposed in this paper in calligraphy Chinese character style recognition tasks, a comparison was made between this method and other methods, and the results are shown in Table 5.

Table 5. Comparison of Recognition Results of Different Recognition Methods (%)

Methods	Recognition rate of calligraphy Chinese character style					Average
	Regular	Seal	Cursive	Running	Official	
Inception v4	99.0	99.0	96.0	99.0	99.0	98.40
MNOPP	95.6	96.9	96.7	96.8	97.1	96.61
AlexNet	95.7	99.1	93.6	93.4	98.3	96.02
Ours	**99.14**	**99.77**	**99.10**	**98.25**	**99.59**	**99.17**

Pang [16] achieved a recognition rate of 98.9% on the running script using the Inception V4 network, because the proportion of running script in the dataset reached 34%, while the proportion of running script in this paper was only 17.7%, achieving a recognition rate of 98.25%. Compared to Xiaoyan Ji 's use of DenseNet network for style recognition [17], the MCNN method proposed in this paper has an improvement of 2.07% in recognition of cursive style and 2.08% in recognition of running style. Chen [8] used a fine-tuned AlexNet network for style recognition on the existing CADAL standard character library dataset, and the average recognition rate for the five calligraphy styles was the lowest. The experimental results show that the proposed method effectively improves the recognition accuracy of calligraphy Chinese character styles, especially in the difficult to recognize cursive and running script styles, reaching 99.10% and 98.25% respectively, which is 4%–6% higher than other methods, and the recognition accuracy is significantly higher than other algorithms.

6 Conclusion

In this paper, we propose a calligraphy Chinese character style recognition method based on morphological convolutional neural network (MCNN). In MCNN, a dilation pool subnet with E-D and D-E structures is built based on morphological operators to replace the max-pooling layer. By adjusting the number of parallel paths and structural elements in the dilation pool subnet, the optimal dilation pool subnet structure is obtained. Combined with residual block structure, we built the MCNN, and the recognition accuracy of MCNN is up to 99.17%. After verification, our method helps to improve style recognition performance, achieving better results compared to using the max-pooling layer, especially in similar style running and cursive scripts, with higher recognition accuracy than other methods. In this paper, morphological operators and CNN are fused to solve the problem of feature loss caused by the max-pooling layer to a certain extent, and broaden the use of mathematical morphology. In the future, morphological operators can be directly used to extract features, or combined with neural networks for image edge detection, image denoising, etc.

Acknowledgement. This work was supported by the National Natural Science Foundation of China under Grant 61872433.

References

1. Wang, C.: The recognition system of Chinese calligraphy style based on deep learning. In: International Conference on Multi-modal Information Analytics, pp. 728–735. Springer, Cham (2022). Doi: https://doi.org/10.1007/978-3-031-05237-8_90
2. Dai, F., Tang, C., Lv J.: Classification of calligraphy style based on convolutional neural network. In: Neural Information Processing: 25th International Conference, ICONIP 2018, Siem Reap, Cambodia, December 13-16, 2018, Proceedings, Part IV 25, pp. 359–370. Springer (2018)
3. Saeedan, F., Weber, N., Goesele, M., et al.: Detail-preserving pooling in deep networks. In: Proceedings of the IEEE Conference on Computer Vision and Pattern Recognition, pp. 9108–9116 (2018)
4. Cd Li, B.: Convolution neural network for traditional Chinese calligraphy recognition. CS231N final project (2016)
5. Jiulong, Z., Luming, G., Su, Y., et al.: Detecting chinese calligraphy style consistency by deep learning and one-class SVM. In: 2017 2nd International Conference on Image, Vision and Computing (ICIVC). IEEE, pp. 83–86 (2017)
6. Pengcheng, G., Gang, G., Jiangqin, W., et al.: Chinese calligraphic style representation for recognition. Int. J. Document Anal. Recogn. (IJDAR) **20**, 59–68 (2017)
7. Wen, Y., Sigüenza, J.A.: Chinese calligraphy: character style recognition based on full-page document. In: Proceedings of the 2019 8th International Conference on Computing and Pattern Recognition, pp. 390–394 (2019)
8. Chen, L.: Research and application of chinese calligraphy character recognition algorithm based on image analysis. In: 2021 IEEE International Conference on Advances in Electrical Engineering and Computer Applications (AEECA), pp. 405–410. IEEE (2021)
9. Wang, C., Deng, C., Yue, X., et al.: Detection algorithm based on wavelet threshold denoising and mathematical morphology. Int. J. Performability Eng. **16**(3), 470 (2020)

10. Franchi, G., Angulo, J., Moreaud, M., et al.: Enhanced EDX images by fusion of multimodal SEM images using pansharpening techniques. J. Microsc.Microsc. **269**(1), 94–112 (2018)
11. Mondal, R., Santra, S., Chanda, B.: Dense morphological network: an Universal Function Approximator. CoRR, abs/1901.00109 (2019)
12. Franchi, G., Fehri, A., Yao, A.: Deep morphological networks. Pattern Recogn. Recogn. **102**, 107246 (2020)
13. Nogueira, K., Chanussot, J., Dalla Mura, M., et al.: An introduction to deep morphological networks. IEEE Access **9**, 114308–114324 (2021)
14. Aouad, T., Talbot, H.: Binary multi channel morphological neural network. arXiv preprint arXiv (2022)
15. He, K., Zhang, X., Ren, S., et al.: Deep residual learning for image recognition. In: Proceedings of the IEEE conference on computer vision and pattern recognition, pp. 770–778 (2016)
16. Pang, B., Wu, J.: Chinese calligraphy character image recognition and it's applications in web and wechat applet platform. In: Proceedings of the ACM/IEEE Joint Conference on Digital Libraries in 2020, pp. 253–260 (2020)
17. Ji, X.: Research on content and style recognition of calligraphy characters based on deep learning. Xidian University, Xi' an (2022)

Active Semantic Localization with Graph Neural Embedding

Mitsuki Yoshida, Kanji Tanaka$^{(\boxtimes)}$, Ryogo Yamamoto, and Daiki Iwata

University of Fukui, Bunkyo, Fukui 3-9-1, Japan
tnkknj@u-fukui.ac.jp

Abstract. Semantic localization, i.e., robot self-localization with semantic image modality, is critical in recently emerging embodied AI applications such as point-goal navigation, object-goal navigation and vision-language navigation. However, most existing works on semantic localization have focused on passive vision tasks without viewpoint planning, or rely on additional rich modalities such as depth measurements. Thus, this problem largely remains unsolved. In this work, we explore a lightweight, entirely CPU-based, domain-adaptive semantic localization framework called Graph Neural Localizer. Our approach is inspired by two recently emerging technologies, including (1) scene graphs, which combine the viewpoint- and appearance-invariance of local and global features, and (2) graph neural networks, which enable direct learning and recognition of graph data (i.e., non-vector data). Specifically, a graph convolutional neural network is first trained as a scene graph classifier for passive vision, and then its knowledge is transferred to a reinforcement-learning planner for active vision. The results of experiments with self supervised learning and unsupervised domain adaptation scenarios with a photo-realistic Habitat simulator validate the effectiveness of the proposed method.

Keywords: Graph neural embedding · Active semantic localization · Knowledge transfer · Domain adaptation

1 Introduction

Semantic localization, i.e., robot self-localization with semantic image modality, is critical in recently emerging embodied AI applications such as point-goal navigation [45], object-goal navigation [4] and vision language navigation [38] (e.g., Habitat Challenge [9]). Studies have shown that the performance of semantic localization is the key bottleneck in these navigation applications [8].

Most existing works on semantic localization have focused on passive vision tasks without considering viewpoint planning [29], or rely on additional rich modalities such as depth measurements [36]. Thus, this problem remains largely unsolved. Furthermore, current methods rely on expensive GPU hardware to

Supported by JSPS KAKENHI Grant Numbers 23K11270, 20K12008.

H. Lu et al. (Eds.): ACPR 2023, LNCS 14406, pp. 216–230, 2023.
https://doi.org/10.1007/978-3-031-47634-1_17

train deep learning models for state recognition [5] and action planning [23]. This limits their application domains and for example, makes them inapplicable to lightweight robotics applications such as household personal robots [16].

Motivated by these challenges, in this study, we present a lightweight, entirely CPU-based, domain-adaptive semantic localization framework called Graph Neural Localizer. Our approach is inspired by two recently emerging technologies, including (1) scene graphs [44], which combine the viewpoint- and appearance-invariance of local and global features, and (2) graph neural networks [42], which can directly learn or recognize graph data (i.e., non-vector data). Specifically, a graph convolutional neural network is first trained as a scene graph classifier for passive vision, and then its knowledge is transferred to a next-best-view planner for active vision. Although such knowledge transfer tasks from passive to active self-localization have been recently explored for conventional models [18], they have not been sufficiently considered for graph neural network models, given that they have only recently been developed. To address this limitation, we consider scene parsing [49], unsupervised knowledge transfer [6], and efficient reinforcement-learning [30] in this work. We implemented, evaluated, and discuss a method to perform these tasks. The results of experiments on two scenarios, including self-supervised learning [21] and unsupervised domain adaptation [43] using a photo-realistic Habitat simulator [35] validate the effectiveness of the proposed method.

The contributions of this study are summarized as follows. (1) We propose an entirely CPU-based lightweight framework for solving semantic localization in both active and passive vision tasks. (2) We also combine a scene graph and a graph neural network to perform semantic localization, presenting a new framework called Graph Neural Localizer. To the best of our knowledge, the proposed approach is the first such method explored in the relevant literature. (3) The results of an experimental evaluation show that the proposed method outperformed a baseline method in terms of self-localization performance, computational efficiency, and domain adaptation (Fig. 1).

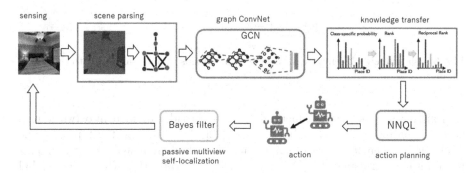

Fig. 1. Our framework generates a scene-graph, embeds it, and transfers it to the action planner.

2 Related Work

Visual robot self-localization has been extensively studied in various formulations [24] such as image retrieval [7], multi-hypothesis tracking [1], geometric matching [29], place classification [41], and viewpoint regression [25]. It is also closely related to the task of loop closure detection [37], an essential component of visual robot mapping. In this study, we focus on the task of place classification formulation, in which supervised and self-supervised learning of image classifier are directly applicable and have become a predominant approach [15] (Fig. 2).

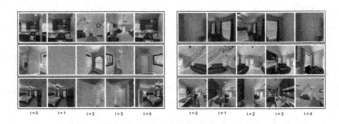

Fig. 2. Examples of view sequences. Left and right panels show successful and unsuccessful cases of self-localization, respectively.

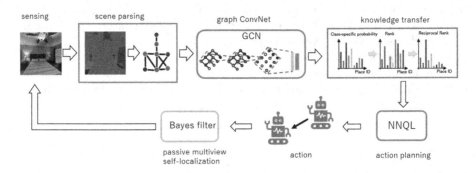

Fig. 3. Our framework generates a scene-graph, embeds it, and transfers it to the action planner.

Existing self-localization methods may be broadly divided into two approaches, including local and global features [22], depending on the type of scene model used. The local feature approach describes an image in a viewpoint-invariant manner using a "bag" of keypoint-level features [10], whereas the global feature approach describes an image in an appearance-invariant manner using a single image-level feature [2]. There is also a hybrid approach called a part feature [33], in which scenes are described in a viewpoint-invariant and appearance-invariant manner using subimage-level features. The scene graph model [44] used in this research can be considered as an extension of the part feature, in that it can describe not only part features by graph nodes, but also the relationships between parts by graph edges.

Appearance features, manually designed or deeply learned, are a predominant approach for in-domain self-localization [37]. In contrast, the semantic feature used in this study has proven to be advantageous in cross-domain setups (e.g., cross-modality [32], cross-view [48], cross-dataset [39]) as in [29], which have been enabled by recent advances in deep semantic imaging technology [39].

Most existing works on semantic localization have focused on passive self-localization tasks without viewpoint planning [29], or have relied on additional rich modalities such as 3D point clouds [36]. In contrast, in our framework, both passive and active self-localization tasks are addressed, and both training and deployment stages do not rely on other modalities. Note that semantic localization can be ill-posed for a passive observer, as many viewpoints may not provide any discriminative semantic feature. Active self-localization aims to adapt an observer's viewpoint trajectory, avoiding non-salient scenes that do not provide a landmark view or moving efficiently toward places that are likely to be most informative with the aim of reducing sensing and computation costs. Most existing works on active localization focus on rich modalities such as RGB imaging [11] and 3D point clouds [5]. In contrast, the issue of active semantic localization has not been sufficiently explored.

Active self-localization is also related to other active vision tasks, including first-person-view semantic navigation (e.g., point-goal [45], vision-language [38], and object-goal navigation [4]), which have recently emerged in studies on robotics and computer vision. However, most existing works assume the availability of ground-truth viewpoint information during training episodes. In contrast, the availability of such rich ground-truth information is not assumed in this work. Rather, only a sparse reward given upon successful localization is assumed as supervision. As described above, the issues of visual place classification, scene graph, graph neural networks, and active vision have been researched independently. To the best of our knowledge, this work is the first to bring together these approaches to address the emerging issue of semantic localization (Fig. 4).

3   Problem

The problem of active self-localization is formulated as an instance of a discrete-time discounted Markov decision process (MDP) in which agents (i.e., robots) interact with probabilistic environments [34]. A time discounted MDP is a general formulation comprising a set of states S, a set of actions A, a state transition distribution P, a reward function R, and a discount rate γ. In our specific scenario, S is a set of embeddings of first-person-view images, A is a set of possible rotating r or forward f motions, and R is the reward given upon successful localization.

The application domain of active self-localization covers various sensor modalities (e.g., monocular cameras, LRF, sonar), operating environments

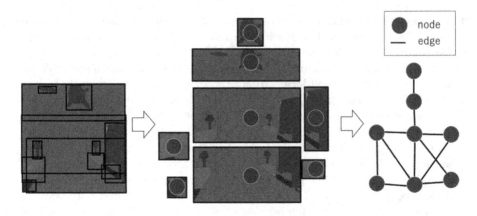

Fig. 4. Semantic scene graph.

(e.g., university campuses, offices, underwater, and airborne) and various types of domains (e.g., object placement, viewpoint trajectories, and variations in weather and lighting conditions). Nevertheless, rich training environments are provided only for very limited application scenarios. The Habitat simulator [35], which provides photo-realistic RGB images, is one such valuable training environment for embodied AI. Therefore, we adopted this platform in this work.

In our proposed approach, semantic images are generated from the RGB images by using an independent off-the-shelf model for semantic segmentation as detailed in Sect. 4.1. Although ideal low-noise semantic images could be provided by the Habitat simulator, we did not rely on them to focus on the more realistic setting.

The performance of an active vision system should be measured in terms of its generalization ability [27]. To do so, maintaining a domain gap between the training and testing domains is important. In this work, we consider a specific type of cross-domain scenario called "cross-view localization" in which a domain gap is defined as the difference in the distribution of starting viewpoints between the training and deployment domains. Specifically, the amount of domain gap is controlled by two preset parameters, called location difference T_{xy} and bearing difference T_θ. Given T_{xy} and T_θ, the training and testing sets of the starting viewpoints are sampled in the following procedure. First, the testing set $\{(x^i_{test}, y^i_{test}, \theta^i_{test})\}$ is uniformly sampled from the robot's workspace. Then, the training samples $\{(x, y, \theta)\}$ are sampled by iteratively sampling a location (x, y) that satisfies the condition $((x^i_{test} - x)^2 + (y^i_{test} - y)^2)^{1/2} > T_{xy}$, and then checking the bearing condition $|\angle(\theta^i_{test} - \theta)| > T_\theta$ between it and its nearest-neighbor testing sample.

In the experimental evaluation, we considered 25 different settings of location and bearing difference (T_{xy}, T_θ), comprising combinations of 5 different settings of location difference T_{xy} ($\in \{0.2, 0.4, 0.6, 0.8, 1.0\}$), and 5 different settings of bearing difference T_θ ($\in \{10, 30, 50, 70, 90\}$).

4   Approach

Figure 3 shows the semantic localization framework. It consists of three main modules, including (1) a scene parser module that parses an image into a semantic scene graph, (2) a graph embedding module that embeds a semantic scene graph into a state vector, and (3) an action planner module that maps the state vector to an action plan. Each module is detailed in the subsequent subsections.

4.1   Semantic Scene Graph

Similarity-preserving image-to-graph mapping is one of most essential requirements for scene graph embedding in active vision systems. It is particularly necessary for an agent's behavior to be reproduced similarly in different domains. Most existing models such as deep learning-based scene graph generation methods [49] are not designed for localization applications and thus typically do not preserve similarity well.

As an alternative, we employ a conservative two-step heuristics [49], which consists of (1) detecting part regions (i.e., nodes), and (2) inferring inter-part relationships (i.e., edges). For the node generation step, an image of size 512×512 is segmented into part regions using a semantic segmentation model [47], which consists of a ResNet model [12] and a Pyramid Pooling Module [46] trained on the ADE20K dataset. Each semantic region is represented by a semantic label and a bounding box.

To enhance the reproducibility, the semantic labels are re-categorized into 10 coarser meta-classes, including "wall," "floor," "ceiling," "bed," "door," "table," "sofa," "refrigerator," "TV," and "Other." Regions with an area of less than 5000 pixels were considered as dummy objects and removed. For the second edge connection step, we consider two types of conditions under which a part node pair is connected by an edge. The first is that the pair of bounding boxes of those parts overlap, and the second is that Euclidean distance between the bounding box pair (i.e., minimum point-to-region distance) is within 20 pixels. In preliminary experiments, we found that this heuristics often worked effectively.

To enhance the discriminativity of the model, a spatial attribute of the part region called "size/location" word [3] is used as additional attributes of the node feature. Regarding the "size" word, we classify the part into one of three size-words according to the area of the bounding box, including "small (0)" $S < S_o$, "medium (1)" $S_o \leq S < 6S_o$, and "large (2)" $6S_o \leq S$, where S_o is a constant corresponding to the 1/16 of the image area. Regarding the "location" word, we discretize the center location of the bounding box using a grid of 3 x 3 = 9 cells and define the cell ID ($\in[0,8]$) as the location word.

Note that all the attributes above are interpretable semantic words, and complex appearance or spatial attributes such as real-valued descriptors are not introduced. Finally, the node feature is defined in the joint space of semantic, size, and location words as a 10 x 3 x 9 = 270 dimensional one-hot vector.

4.2 State Recognizer

A graph convolutional neural network (GCN) model is used to embed a scene graph into the state vector. The architecture of the GCN is identical to that used in our recent publication [26], in which implementation of the GCN used the deep graph library from [40].

In the above paper [26], the 2D location (x, y) was used as the state representation for a passive self-localization application, ignoring the bearing attribute θ. In contrast, in the active self-localization scenario considered in this work, the bearing attribute θ plays a much more important role. That is, the robot should change its behavior depending on the bearing angle even when the location (x, y) is unchanged. Therefore, the robot's workspace is modeled as a 3D region in the location-bearing space (x, y, θ), and it is partitioned into a regular grid of place classes using a location and bearing resolution of 2 m and 30 deg, respectively.

Another key difference is the necessity of knowledge transfer from passive to active vision. The class-specific probability map output by the GCN (i.e., passive vision) is often uncalibrated as the knowledge to be transferred. In fact, in most existing works, convolutional neural networks are used as a ranking function or classifier [17,31,41], rather than a probability map regressor [28]. The class-specific rank value vector could be naively used as a feature to be transferred. However, such a rank vector is often inappropriate as a feature vector because the most confident classes with the highest probabilities are assigned the lowest values. Instead, a reciprocal rank vector [6] is used as a feature vector and as the state vector for the reinforcement learning for active vision. Note that reciprocal rank vector is an additive feature, and has been shown to exhibit several desirable properties in studies on multimodal information fusion [19].

4.3 Multi- Hypothesis Tracking

The results of active multi-view classification need to be aggregated incrementally in real-time and a particle filter is employed for the incremental estimation of pose (location/bearing) [1].

The spatial resolution required to track particles in the particle filter framework typically needs to be much higher than that of the place classes [11]. Therefore, a simple max pooling operation is used to convert the particles' location attributes to class-specific rank values regardless of their bearing attributes. The particle set must be initialized at the beginning of a training or testing episode. It could be naively initialized by uniformly sampling the location and bearing attributes of the particles. However, this often results in a large number of useless particles, which are lossy in terms of both space and time. Instead, we used a guided sampling strategy [13], in which $M = 5000$ initial particles were sampled from only $k = 3$ place classes that received the highest initial observation likelihood based on the first observation at the first viewpoint ($t = 0$) in each episode. Empirically, such a guided sampling strategy tended to contribute to a significant reduction in the number of particles and computational cost with no or little loss of localization accuracy.

4.4   Action Planner

Most reinforcement learning-based action planners suffer from sparse rewards as well as high-dimensionality of the state-action spaces. This issue of the "curse of dimensionality" is addressed by introducing an efficient nearest neighbor-based approximation of Q-learning (NNQL) as in [30].

The training procedure for this approximation is an iterative process of indexing state-action pairs associated with the latest Q-values to the database. Importantly, it stores the Q-values for only those points that are experienced in the training stage, rather than every possible point in the high-dimensional state-action space, which is intractable. Note that the number of Q-values to be stored is significantly reduced by this strategy and becomes independent of the dimensionality.

The action planning procedure is a process of searching for similar samples over the database using the queried state and averaging the k Q-values that are linked to $k = 4$ nearest-neighbor state-action pairs $N(s, a)$ of the state-action pair (s, a), as given below.

$$Q(s, a) = |N(s, a)|^{-1} \sum_{(s', a') \subset N(s,a)} Q(s', a') \tag{1}$$

Exceptionally, if there exists a state-action pair equivalent to (s, a) within the range of quantization error, it is considered as a revisited state-action pair and, the Q-value associated with that state-action pair is returned directly.

According to the theory of Q-learning [34], the Q-function is updated as

$$Q(s_t, a_t) \leftarrow Q(s_t, a_t) + \alpha[r_{t+1} + \gamma \max Q(s_{t+1}, a) - Q(s_t, a_t)] \tag{2}$$

where s_{t+1} is the state to which it is transited from the state s_t by executing the action a_t, α is the learning rate, and γ is the discount factor.

It should be noted that this database allows the Q-function at any past checkpoint to be recovered at low cost. Let S_t and $Q_t(s, a)$ denote the state-action pairs stored in the database and the Q-value linked to (s, a) at the t-th episode. For any past checkpoint $t'(< t)$, $S_{t'}$ is a subset of S_t (i.e., $S_{t'} \in S_t$). Therefore, the Q-function at checkpoint t' can be recovered from $Q_{t'}(s, a)$, which consumes a negligible amount of storage compared to the high-dimensional state-action pairs S_t. Note that a novel type of $Q_{t'}(s, a)$ "not-available (N/A)" needs to be introduced for this purpose with little storage overhead. This allows us to store many different versions of the Q-function $Q_{t'_1}, \cdots, Q_{t'_T}$ in memory at each checkpoint $t'_1, \cdots, t'_T$. Such stored parameters have been shown to be beneficial for avoiding catastrophic forgetting [14] and for improved learning [20].

5   Experiments

5.1   Dataset

The 3D photo-realistic simulator Habitat-Sim and the dataset HM3D were used as training and deployment (testing) environments, as detailed in Sect. 3. Three

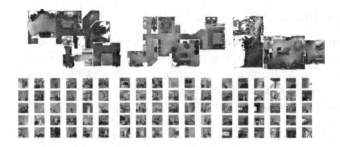

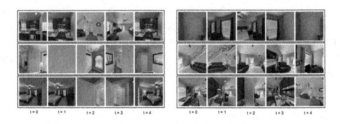

Fig. 5. The robot workspaces and examples images for "00800-TEEsavR23oF," "00801-HaxA7YrQdEC," and "00809-Qpor2mEya8F" datasets.

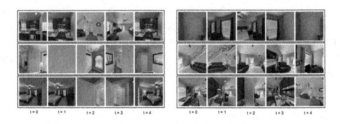

Fig. 6. Examples of view sequences. Left and right panels show successful and unsuccessful cases of self-localization, respectively.

datasets called "00800-TEEsavR23oF," "00801-HaxA7YrQdEC," and "00809-Qpor2mEya8F" from the Habitat-Matterport3D Research Dataset (HM3D) were considered and imported to the Habitat simulator. A bird's-eye-view of the scene and a first-person-view image in the environment are shown in Fig. 5.

5.2 Implementation Details

For the GCN, the number of training iterations was set as 100, with a batch size of 32 and a learning rate of 0.001. For each dataset, a GCN classifier was trained using 10,000 training scenes with class labels as supervision.

In both training and deployment stages, the robot started from a random location in the environment, performed an initial sensing, and then executed an episode consisting of a sequence of length $L = 4$ of plan-action-sense cycles.

The state for NNQL training and deployment at each viewpoint was represented by the latest class-specific reciprocal rank feature. The reward function returned the value of +1 if the Top-1 predicted place class is correct or −1 if it is incorrect. For NNQL training, the number of iterations was set as 10,000, the learning rate α of the Q-function was 0.1, and the discount factor γ was 0.9. An ϵ-greedy algorithm with $\epsilon = (0.1(n + 1) + 1)^{-1}$ was used for the n-th episode. A checkpoint was set every $(1000i)$-th episode, at which the trainable parameters were saved at each checkpoint in a compact form as explained in Sect. 4.4. The number of test episodes for each experiment was 100.

Table 1. Performance results.

Domain-gap		Dataset x Method											
T_{xy}	T_θ	00800-TEEsavR23oF				00801-HaxA7YrQdEC				00809-Qpor2mEya8F			
		SV	MV	Ours	DA	SV	MV	Ours	DA	SV	MV	Ours	DA
1.0	90	38	52	61	54	47	49	52	53	43	41	52	49
	70	38	53	62	52	36	52	55	50	43	48	52	52
	50	45	52	58	57	43	51	57	60	37	54	54	54
	30	46	54	57	58	48	54	60	60	43	51	53	57
	10	43	55	54	51	45	54	58	67	42	52	59	58
0.8	90	52	62	66	70	46	52	56	52	44	54	55	56
	70	46	57	55	57	39	53	49	57	50	48	53	53
	50	38	50	56	56	49	53	54	53	40	49	54	49
	30	40	54	54	53	43	50	58	62	33	44	47	44
	10	47	59	66	68	42	57	53	53	36	49	46	48
0.6	90	39	46	43	42	41	56	58	62	37	45	45	47
	70	42	56	53	49	49	53	62	61	37	40	44	48
	50	42	51	56	57	46	51	51	56	46	59	51	50
	30	48	53	55	59	46	49	52	53	35	46	52	52
	10	33	47	49	41	34	51	55	61	50	56	55	53
0.4	90	33	49	51	52	43	49	55	54	47	48	53	56
	70	42	55	56	52	43	47	60	59	44	48	49	47
	50	48	57	60	57	42	55	59	60	40	50	48	53
	30	46	57	54	53	40	46	48	51	38	50	60	58
	10	40	49	54	50	47	53	54	52	34	54	57	53
0.2	90	36	54	56	57	46	60	60	60	41	48	50	51
	70	50	60	63	60	41	51	52	52	48	53	49	47
	50	51	59	60	62	50	54	54	56	34	46	51	48
	30	38	47	57	55	46	59	55	55	40	50	45	48
	10	49	55	57	53	43	53	56	51	33	53	56	54

We also conducted experiments on unsupervised domain adaptation (UDA). The domain adaptation task considered evaluated the models at all checkpoints against a small validation set (size 10) from the testing domain, and we adopted the best-performing model.

The robot workspace was represented by a 3D region in the location-bearing (i.e., x-y-θ) space and was partitioned into place classes by a grid-based partitioning with the location resolution of 2 m and a bearing resolution of $\pi/6$ rad.

The proposed active multi-view method was compared against baseline single-view and passive multi-view methods. The single-view method differs from the multi-view methods in terms of its problem setting, in that no action planning is considered, but the robot performs the initial sensing and localization at the initial viewpoint (i.e., $t = 0$) and then immediately terminates the algorithm and outputs the self-localization result. The passive multi-view method differs from the active method only in that the next action at each viewpoint is randomly sampled from the action space. Note that this passive multi-view framework is a standard method for passive self-localization and can be viewed as a strong baseline. In particular, as the episode length (number of observed actions per episode) increases, the performance of passive multi-view self-localization using this random action planner is guaranteed to asymptotically approach the performance of the best-performing NBV planner.

5.3   Results

For each of the three datasets, we evaluated self-localization for the above three different methods and for 25 different settings of T_{xy} and T_θ as described in Sect. 3 (Fig. 7).

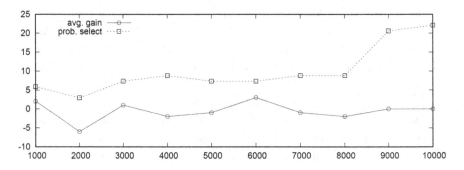

Fig. 7. Results in unsupervised domain adaptation (UDA) applications.

Top-1 accuracy was used as the primary index of performance. Table 1 shows the performance results after 10,000 NNQL training cycles. "SV" and "MV" are single-view and multi-view passive localizations. "Ours" is multi-view active localization, our way. "DA" is an addition of unsupervised domain adaptations to "Ours".

Figure 7 shows the results on the testing set for the experiments on unsupervised domain adaptation. "avg. gain" shows the increase in performance with UDA compared to the performance without UDA (horizontal axis: checkpoint, vertical axis: increase in top-1 accuracy performance). As can be seen, the model at the checkpoint that performed well on the validation set does not necessarily perform well on the test. Therefore, improving the generalization performance of UDA is left for future study. "prob. select" indicates the rate at which each checkpoint model was selected (horizontal axis: checkpoint, vertical axis: selection ratio). Note that adding the selection ratios on the vertical axis for all checkpoints adds up to 100 percent. As expected, models with later checkpoints had a higher proportion of cases with better validation performance and were selected more frequently.

Regarding the domain adaptation results, early checkpoint models were also often selected as the best models in some test episodes. However, these models did not perform well, because the models acquired in the training domain often already had sufficient generalization ability in this experiment. Unfortunately, the conditions under which a domain-adaptive model might outperform a pre-trained model are unclear; this issue remains as a topic for further research. Nevertheless, we believe that the proposed method is versatile and effective in any domain adaptation application because it is lightweight enough to store different versions of the learning parameters at all checkpoints in memory.

Figure 6 illustrates examples of actions and view-images in the testing stage. The variable t indicates the ID of plan-action-sense cycle ID, where $t = 0$ corresponds to the initial sense at the starting viewpoint by the robot.

The computational times required for scene graph generation, GCN, and viewpoint planning were 18, 0.10, 10 [ms] (Intel Core i7, 3.60 GHz), respectively which was faster than real time.

In most datasets, the passive multi-view method and the proposed method showed higher performance than the single-view method. The results of the experiments showed that the proposed approach significantly improved accuracy for a wide variety of datasets.

Figure 6 shows some examples of success and failure. As may be observed from the figure, the behavior of robots moving to locations with dense natural landmark objects often improved visual place recognition performance. For example, at the initial viewpoint, the robot was facing the wall and could not observe any effective landmarks at all, but it was able to detect the door by changing its heading direction at the next viewpoint, and the self-localization accuracy was improved using this landmark object. A typical failure case is also shown in Fig. 6, in which majority of the viewpoints in the episode were facing featureless objects such as walls and windows. Another notable trend is that the recognition success rate decreased when the viewpoint was too close to the object, which resulted in narrow field-of-view.

6   Concluding Remarks

In this work, we have proposed an entirely CPU-based lightweight framework for solving semantic localization in both active and passive self-localization tasks. To the best of our knowledge, the present work is the first to combine a scene graph and a graph neural network to perform semantic localization, presenting a new framework called Graph Neural Localizer. Experiments show that the proposed method outperformed a baseline method in terms of self-localization performance, computational efficiency, and domain adaptation.

References

1. Boniardi, F., Valada, A., Mohan, R., Caselitz, T., Burgard, W.: Robot localization in floor plans using a room layout edge extraction network. In: 2019 IEEE/RSJ International Conference on Intelligent Robots and Systems (IROS), pp. 5291–5297. IEEE (2019)
2. Bonin-Font, F., Burguera, A.: Nethaloc: a learned global image descriptor for loop closing in underwater visual slam. Expert. Syst. **38**(2), e12635 (2021)
3. Cao, Y., Wang, C., Li, Z., Zhang, L., Zhang, L.: Spatial-bag-of-features. In: 2010 IEEE Computer Society Conference on Computer Vision and Pattern Recognition, pp. 3352–3359. IEEE (2010)
4. Chaplot, D.S., Gandhi, D.P., Gupta, A., Salakhutdinov, R.R.: Object goal navigation using goal-oriented semantic exploration. Adv. Neural. Inf. Process. Syst. **33**, 4247–4258 (2020)
5. Chaplot, D.S., Parisotto, E., Salakhutdinov, R.: Active neural localization. arXiv preprint arXiv:1801.08214 (2018)
6. Cormack, G.V., Clarke, C.L., Buettcher, S.: Reciprocal rank fusion outperforms condorcet and individual rank learning methods. In: Proceedings of the 32nd International ACM SIGIR Conference on Research and Development in Information Retrieval, pp. 758–759 (2009)
7. Cummins, M., Newman, P.: Appearance-only slam at large scale with fab-map 2.0. Int. J. Robot. Res. **30**(9), 1100–1123 (2011)
8. Datta, S., Maksymets, O., Hoffman, J., Lee, S., Batra, D., Parikh, D.: Integrating egocentric localization for more realistic point-goal navigation agents. In: Conference on Robot Learning, pp. 313–328. PMLR (2021)
9. Desai, S.S., Lee, S.: Auxiliary tasks for efficient learning of point-goal navigation. In: Proceedings of the IEEE/CVF Winter Conference on Applications of Computer Vision, pp. 717–725 (2021)
10. Garcia-Fidalgo, E., Ortiz, A.: iBoW-LCD: an appearance-based loop-closure detection approach using incremental bags of binary words. IEEE Robot. Autom. Lett. **3**(4), 3051–3057 (2018)
11. Gottipati, S.K., Seo, K., Bhatt, D., Mai, V., Murthy, K., Paull, L.: Deep active localization. IEEE Robot. Autom. Lett. **4**(4), 4394–4401 (2019). https://doi.org/10.1109/LRA.2019.2932575
12. He, K., Zhang, X., Ren, S., Sun, J.: Deep residual learning for image recognition. In: Proceedings of the IEEE Conference on Computer Vision and Pattern Recognition, pp. 770–778 (2016)
13. Huang, G.: Particle filtering with analytically guided sampling. Adv. Robot. **31**(17), 932–945 (2017)
14. Kemker, R., McClure, M., Abitino, A., Hayes, T., Kanan, C.: Measuring catastrophic forgetting in neural networks. In: Proceedings of the AAAI Conference on Artificial Intelligence, vol. 32 (2018)
15. Kim, G., Park, B., Kim, A.: 1-day learning, 1-year localization: long-term lidar localization using scan context image. IEEE Robot. Autom. Lett. **4**(2), 1948–1955 (2019)
16. Kim, K., et al.: Development of docking system for mobile robots using cheap infrared sensors. In: Proceedings of the 1st International Conference on Sensing Technology, pp. 287–291. Citeseer (2005)
17. Krizhevsky, A., Sutskever, I., Hinton, G.E.: ImageNet classification with deep convolutional neural networks. Commun. ACM **60**(6), 84–90 (2017)

18. Kurauchi, K., Tanaka, K., Yamamoto, R., Yoshida, M.: Active domain-invariant self-localization using ego-centric and world-centric maps. In: Tistarelli, M., Dubey, S.R., Singh, S.K., Jiang, X. (eds.) Computer Vision and Machine Intelligence, pp. 475–487. Springer Nature Singapore, Singapore (2023). https://doi.org/10.1007/978-981-19-7867-8_38
19. Kurland, O., Culpepper, J.S.: Fusion in information retrieval: Sigir 2018 half-day tutorial. In: The 41st International ACM SIGIR Conference on Research & Development in Information Retrieval, pp. 1383–1386 (2018)
20. Laine, S., Aila, T.: Temporal ensembling for semi-supervised learning. arXiv preprint arXiv:1610.02242 (2016)
21. Liu, X., Zhang, F., Hou, Z., Mian, L., Wang, Z., Zhang, J., Tang, J.: Self-supervised learning: generative or contrastive. IEEE Trans. Knowl. Data Eng. **35**(1), 857–876 (2021)
22. Lowry, S., et al.: Visual place recognition: a survey. IEEE Trans. Robot. **32**(1), 1–19 (2015)
23. Mancini, M., Bulo, S.R., Ricci, E., Caputo, B.: Learning deep NBNN representations for robust place categorization. IEEE Robot. Autom. Lett. **2**(3), 1794–1801 (2017)
24. Masone, C., Caputo, B.: A survey on deep visual place recognition. IEEE Access **9**, 19516–19547 (2021)
25. Mo, N., Gan, W., Yokoya, N., Chen, S.: Es6d: a computation efficient and symmetry-aware 6d pose regression framework. In: Proceedings of the IEEE/CVF Conference on Computer Vision and Pattern Recognition, pp. 6718–6727 (2022)
26. Ohta, T., Tanaka, K., Yamamoto, R.: Scene graph descriptors for visual place classification from noisy scene data. In: ICT Express (2023)
27. Ragab, M., et al.: ADATIME: a benchmarking suite for domain adaptation on time series data. arXiv preprint arXiv:2203.08321 (2022)
28. Roy, A., Todorovic, S.: Monocular depth estimation using neural regression forest. In: Proceedings of the IEEE Conference on Computer Vision and Pattern Recognition, pp. 5506–5514 (2016)
29. Schönberger, J.L., Pollefeys, M., Geiger, A., Sattler, T.: Semantic visual localization. In: Proceedings of the IEEE Conference on Computer Vision and Pattern Recognition, pp. 6896–6906 (2018)
30. Shah, D., Xie, Q.: Q-learning with nearest neighbors. In: Advances in Neural Information Processing Systems, vol. 31 (2018)
31. Simonyan, K., Zisserman, A.: Two-stream convolutional networks for action recognition in videos. In: Advances in Neural Information Processing Systems, vol. 27 (2014)
32. Song, Y., Soleymani, M.: Polysemous visual-semantic embedding for cross-modal retrieval. In: Proceedings of the IEEE/CVF Conference on Computer Vision and Pattern Recognition, pp. 1979–1988 (2019)
33. Sünderhauf, N., Shirazi, S., Dayoub, F., Upcroft, B., Milford, M.: On the performance of convnet features for place recognition. In: 2015 IEEE/RSJ International Conference on Intelligent Robots and Systems (IROS), pp. 4297–4304. IEEE (2015)
34. Sutton, R.S., Barto, A.G.: Reinforcement Learning: An introduction. MIT Press, Cambridge (2018)
35. Szot, A., et al.: Habitat 2.0: training home assistants to rearrange their habitat. In: Advances in Neural Information Processing Systems (NeurIPS) (2021)
36. Toft, C., Olsson, C., Kahl, F.: Long-term 3d localization and pose from semantic labellings. In: Proceedings of the IEEE International Conference on Computer Vision Workshops, pp. 650–659 (2017)

37. Tsintotas, K.A., Bampis, L., Gasteratos, A.: The revisiting problem in simultaneous localization and mapping: a survey on visual loop closure detection. IEEE Trans. Intell. Transp. Syst. **23**(11), 19929–19953 (2022)
38. Wang, H., Wang, W., Liang, W., Xiong, C., Shen, J.: Structured scene memory for vision-language navigation. In: Proceedings of the IEEE/CVF Conference on Computer Vision and Pattern Recognition, pp. 8455–8464 (2021)
39. Wang, L., Li, D., Liu, H., Peng, J., Tian, L., Shan, Y.: Cross-dataset collaborative learning for semantic segmentation in autonomous driving. In: Proceedings of the AAAI Conference on Artificial Intelligence, vol. 36, pp. 2487–2494 (2022)
40. Wang, M., et al.: Deep graph library: towards efficient and scalable deep learning on graphs. CoRR abs/1909.01315 (2019). http://arxiv.org/abs/1909.01315
41. Weyand, T., Kostrikov, I., Philbin, J.: PlaNet - photo geolocation with convolutional neural networks. In: Leibe, B., Matas, J., Sebe, N., Welling, M. (eds.) ECCV 2016. LNCS, vol. 9912, pp. 37–55. Springer, Cham (2016). https://doi.org/10.1007/978-3-319-46484-8_3
42. Wu, Z., Pan, S., Chen, F., Long, G., Zhang, C., Philip, S.Y.: A comprehensive survey on graph neural networks. IEEE Trans. Neural Netw. Learn. Syst. **32**(1), 4–24 (2020)
43. Xu, B., Zeng, Z., Lian, C., Ding, Z.: Few-shot domain adaptation via mixup optimal transport. IEEE Trans. Image Process. **31**, 2518–2528 (2022)
44. Xu, P., Chang, X., Guo, L., Huang, P.Y., Chen, X., Hauptmann, A.G.: A survey of scene graph: generation and application. IEEE Trans. Neural Netw. Learn. Syst **1** (2020)
45. Ye, J., Batra, D., Wijmans, E., Das, A.: Auxiliary tasks speed up learning point goal navigation. In: Conference on Robot Learning, pp. 498–516. PMLR (2021)
46. Zhao, H., Shi, J., Qi, X., Wang, X., Jia, J.: Pyramid scene parsing network. In: Proceedings of the IEEE Conference on Computer Vision and Pattern Recognition, pp. 2881–2890 (2017)
47. Zhou, B., Zhao, H., Puig, X., Fidler, S., Barriuso, A., Torralba, A.: Scene parsing through ade20k dataset. In: Proceedings of the IEEE Conference on Computer Vision and Pattern Recognition, pp. 633–641 (2017)
48. Zhou, B., Krähenbühl, P.: Cross-view transformers for real-time map-view semantic segmentation. In: Proceedings of the IEEE/CVF Conference on Computer Vision and Pattern Recognition, pp. 13760–13769 (2022)
49. Zhu, G., et al.: Scene graph generation: a comprehensive survey. arXiv preprint arXiv:2201.00443 (2022)

A Multimodal Approach to Single-Modal Visual Place Classification

Tomoya Iwasaki, Kanji Tanaka$^{(\boxtimes)}$, and Kenta Tsukahara

University of Fukui, 3-9-1 Bunkyo, Fukui, Japan
tnkknj@u-fukui.ac.jp

Abstract. Visual place classification from a first-person-view monocular RGB image is a fundamental problem in long-term robot navigation. A difficulty arises from the fact that RGB image classifiers are often vulnerable to spatial and appearance changes and degrade due to domain shifts, such as seasonal, weather, and lighting differences. To address this issue, multi-sensor fusion approaches combining RGB and depth (D) (e.g., LIDAR, radar, stereo) have gained popularity in recent years. Inspired by these efforts, we revisit the single-modal RGB visual place classification without requiring additional sensing devices, by exploring the use of pseudo-depth measurements from recently-developed techniques of "domain-invariant" monocular estimation as an additional pseudo depth modality. To this end, we develop a novel multimodal neural network for fully self-supervised training/classifying RGB and pseudo-D data. The results of experiments on challenging cross-domain scenarios with public NCLT datasets are presented to demonstrate effectiveness of the proposed approach.

Keywords: Visual place classification · Self-supervised learning · Multimodal RGB-D fusion · Monocular depth estimation

1 Introduction

Self-localization from first-person-view monocular RGB images is a fundamental problem in visual navigation and robotics. This problem has important applications such as first-person-view point-goal [26], vision-language [22], and object-goal navigation [3], which have recently emerged as important topics of study in robotics and computer vision. These problems are typically formulated as tasks of visual place classification [24], in which the goal is to classify a first-person-view image into one of several predefined place classes. This is a problem domain where supervised or self-supervised learning is directly applicable and has become a predominant approach [11].

A difficulty arises owing to the fact that self-localization models are often trained and tested on data from different domains. Domain shifts due to such as seasonal factors and varying weather and lighting conditions often degrade

Supported by JSPS KAKENHI Grant Numbers 23K11270, 20K12008.

H. Lu et al. (Eds.): ACPR 2023, LNCS 14406, pp. 231–244, 2023.
https://doi.org/10.1007/978-3-031-47634-1_18

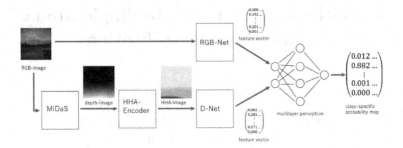

Fig. 1. Pseudo RGB-D multimodal framework.

the performance of self-localization models that are overfitted to a given training domain and thus sensitive to changes in viewpoint and appearance. Hence, domain-invariant and domain-adaptive models are preferable. In machine learning, this is most relevant to the issue of "domain adaptation" [23], which aims to address the shortage of large amounts of labeled data by using various types of transfer learning techniques ranging from feature distribution alignment to modifications to model pipelines.

The present work is inspired by recent research efforts to solve this problem by fusing information from RGB and depth (D) sensors. The key idea is to combine the RGB image modality with other depth sensors (e.g., LIDAR, radar, and stereo), to address the ill-posed-ness of monocular vision. Studies have shown that these additional depth measurements provide effective invariant cues for self-localization, such as information on the viewpoint-invariant 3D structure of landmark objects. However, these methods rely on additional sensing devices, which limits their versatility and affordability. Nevertheless, the domain-invariance property of depth measurements makes this approach very attractive for cross-domain self-localization.

In this work, we propose to exploit the recently-developed techniques of "domain-invariant" monocular depth (D) estimation as an additional pseudo depth modality, and to reformulate the single-modal RGB visual place classification as a pseudo-multimodal classification problem (Fig. 1). Unlike most existing monocular depth estimation techniques, the domain-invariant depth modality (e.g., [17]) requires neither retraining nor supervision, and it is obviously valuable for our fully self-supervised scenarios. Specifically, a CNN-based place classifier is trained for each of these two modalities, RGB and D, and the two CNNs are integrated into a multilayer perceptron model. The two CNNs can be supervised, diagnosed, and retrained independently, which allows flexible and versatile design for domain adaptation scheme. We conducted an experimental evaluation on challenging cross-domain self-localization scenarios using the public NCLT (University of Michigan North Campus Long-Term Vision and Lidar) dataset [2], and the results validate effectiveness of the proposed framework.

The contributions of this research are summarized as follows. (1) We address the underexplored ill-posed-ness of the long-term single-modal visual place classification problem from a novel perspective of multimodal RGB-D fusion. (2) We present a novel multimodal CNN architecture for fusing RGB- and pseudo-D images from domain-invariant monocular depth estimation. (3) The results of experiments using the public NCLT dataset show that the proposed method frequently contributed to improved performance.

The remainder of this study is organized as follows. In Section 2, we provide a short overview of the relevant literature. In Section 3, we formulate the problem of single-modal visual place classification in the context of long-term robot navigation. Section 4 describes the proposed framework to extend a single-modal classifier for multimodal operation. In Section 5, we present and discuss the experimental results. Finally, Section 6 briefly summarizes our findings with some concluding remarks.

2   Related Work

The problem of self-localization has been studied extensively for many different indoor and outdoor applications such as image retrieval [4], geometric matching [19], loop closure detection [6], place classification [24], and viewpoint regression [14]. In this study, we focus on the classification formulation, in which the goal is to classify a first-person-view image as an instance of one of several predefined classes representing different places. This is a problem domain where supervised or self-supervised learning is directly applicable and has become a predominant approach [11].

Multimodal RGB-D sensor fusion is among the most active topics of research on cross-domain self-localization. In [1], LIDAR, and radar were thoroughly compared in terms of their cross-season self-localization performance. In [21], a highly robust scheme for long-term self-localization was explored in which a semantic geometric model was reconstructed from RGB-D and semantic (RGB-D-S) images with a prior map. In [16], a highly versatile self-localization framework for autonomous driving with LIDAR sensors was constructed. The authors of [13] explored the simultaneous training and deployment of an online self-localization task called loop closure detection using LIDAR and imagery in a long-term map maintenance scenario. The results of these studies clearly show that RGB-D fusion is effective for achieving a good trade-off between robustness and accuracy in cross-domain scenarios.

In existing studies of cross-domain multimodal ("RGB-X") self-localization, thus far, monocular depth estimation has not been fully explored as an additional modality ("X"), mainly because technology for monocular depth estimation with domain-invariance has only recently become available [17]. Furthermore, many existing studies on cross-domain self-localization focus on image retrieval and matching rather than classification, which has become more practical owing to recent advances in deep learning technology. Of note, other types of additional modalities have also become more popular. In particular, in the era of deeplearning, semantic imagery from deep semantic models has become a key focus in some recent studies. In parallel with this work, we are also conducting research along these lines [15]. However, in contrast to our approach, many studies have relied on depth measurements derived from prior or 3D reconstructions such as 3D point-cloud maps. In addition, the use of semantic features could be considered orthogonal and complimentary to our approach based on pseudo-depth.

Finally, monocular depth estimation has attracted a great deal of attention in recent years in studies on machine learning and computer vision. Early work on monocular depth estimation used simple geometric assumptions, nonparametric methods, or MRF-based formulations [18]. More recently, the advent of powerful convolutional networks has enabled the development of models that can directly regress D images from RGB images [5]. However, most existing methods assume the availability of additional sensor modalities in the training stage as a means of self-supervised domain adaptation [7], which is not available in our case. The present work is most relevant to and developed based on the recently developed technique of "domain-invariant" monocular depth estimation described in [17], which allows us to regress a depth (D) image from an RGB image in both indoor and outdoor environments without relying on an additional sensor modality and an adaptation stage.

To summarize, our problem and the proposed method are most relevant to two independent fields, including single-modal cross-domain visual place classification and multimodal sensor integration. However, the intersection of these two fields of research has not yet been sufficiently explored. In this study, we consider this issue by using "domain-invariant" monocular depth estimation as intermediate approach. To the best of our knowledge, no previous study has investigated the topic in this context.

Fig. 2. Pseudo depth images.

3   Self-Supervised Long-Term Visual Place Classification

In long-term robot navigation, training or retraining of a visual place classifier should be conducted in a completely self-supervised manner, without relying on external sensing devices such as GPS or 3D environment models. In this study, we consider a wheeled mobile robot with three degrees of freedom (DoF), although the proposed framework is sufficiently general to be extended to applications with vehicles with six DoF such as drones. Nonetheless, the robot's operating environment usually contains unmodeled three-dimensional undulations and elevation changes, such as small hills, which may affect the performance of visual recognition systems.

We focus on a simplified setup, with single-session supervised training and single-view classification. That is, we assume that a visual sequence collected by a survey robot navigating the entire workspace in a single session is used as the sole supervision, and that the visual place classifier takes a single-view monocular image as the sole query input. Nevertheless, this approach could be easily extended to multi-session supervision and multi-view self-localization setups, as in [25].

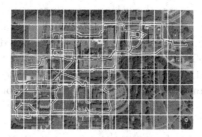

Fig. 3. A top-down view of the robot workspace with a grid of predefined place classes.

The training stage starts with the robot navigating a target environment and collecting view sequences along the viewpoint-trajectory in the training domain. We assume that the viewpoint-trajectory has a sufficiently long travel distance and many loop closures, which allows sufficiently accurate viewpoint reconstruction via structure-from-motion, SLAM, or visual odometry. Next, viewpoints are divided into place classes by spatially coarse partitioning of the robot's workspace (Fig. 3). Note that the ground-truth viewpoint-to-class mapping is defined with respect to the reconstructed training viewpoint-trajectory, without assuming the availability of any GPS measurements.

We now formulate the classification task. Let x_i be the view image at the i-th viewpoint, and let y_i be the place class to which the viewpoint belongs, and the training data is expressed in the form $S^{train} = \{(x_i, y_i)\}$. Then, the training objective is to optimize the parameters of the classifier

$$y = f(x) \tag{1}$$

using the training data S^{train} such that the prediction performance for the test sample $x \in S^{test}$ in the unknown domain is maximized.

The robot's workspace is partitioned into a regular grid of $10 \times 10 = 100$ place classes (Fig. 3), for the following four reasons. (1) The grid-based place definition provides a flexible place definition for cross-domain self-localization scenarios. This is in contrast to in-domain scenarios such as the planet-scale place classification in [24], where the spatial distribution of viewpoints is known in advance, which allows a more spatially efficient adaptive place partitioning. (2) The grid can be extended to unseen place classes found in new domains. For example, in [11], an entropy-based discovery of unseen place classes is considered for a cross-domain place classification from an on-board Velodyne 3D scanner. (3) The grid-based place definition is often used for local and global path planning in visual robot navigation. For example, in [12], the place-specific knowledge of a visual place classifier is transferred to a reinforcement learning-based next-best-view path planner. (4) The number of place classes, a key hyperparameter, should be consistent with practical applications in the domain of the NCLT dataset. A setting of 100, is consistent with the "coarser" grid cells in [11], long-term knowledge distillation in [10], and active self-localization in [12].

We observe that compared to other image classification tasks such as object recognition, the visual place classification task involves several unique and noteworthy properties. (1) Even when the robot follows the same route, the viewpoint-trajectories are not exactly the same between the training and deployment domains. In fact, comparing the two extreme cases of navigating along the right and left edges of the route, the viewpoint positions may often be more than 1 m apart. (2) Differences in bearing often have a greater impact on prediction results than differences in place class, especially in typical outdoor workspaces where scenes with wide-open spaces dominate and many objects are far from the robot vehicle's turning center. (3) Due to differences in robot navigation tasks and changes in the local traversability of the workspace, the routes used in the training and testing phases may not overlap completely. This yields unseen place classes, which significantly complicates the problem.

4   Multimodal Extension of Single-Modal Classifier

Our experimental setup, a multimodal extension of a single-modal classifier, was specifically tailored to evaluate the proposed extension of RGB to RGB-D. To this end, we considered a conventional setup of training a CNN as a single-modal RGB monocular image classifier and used this as our baseline model, as described in Sect. 4.1. Such a monocular image classification tasks are known to be significantly ill-posed due to the complex nonlinear mapping of the 3D world to 2D images, as well as to domain shifts. To regularize the ill-posed problem, we introduce a monocular depth estimator as explained in Sect. 4.2 and further transform the depth image into a regularized HHA image as described in Sect. 4.3. Then, we train another single-modal HHA-image classifier CNN designed to take synthetic HHA images as input. Finally, the outputs of the two CNNs, "RGB-Net" and "HHA-Net", were fused by an integration network with a multilayer perceptron, which is then finetuned using the entire dataset for supervision as detailed in Sect. 4.4.

4.1   Visual Classifier and Embedding

For the baseline classifier, we fine-tune a pretrained CNN, VGG-16, to our datasets. VGG-16 is a CNN model proposed by the Visual Geometry Group of University of Oxford and was the winner of the 2014 ILSVRC object identification challenge [20]. It consists of 13 convolutional layers and 3 fully connected layers for a total of 16 layers. We trained a CNN model

$$y = f^{CNN}(x) \tag{2}$$

to perform place classification by fine-tuning the fully connected layers with the convolutional layers frozen.

In the proposed framework, the same CNN is also used as a means of image embedding as given below.

$$f^{RGB}(x) = g^{RGB} \circ h^{RGB}(x), \tag{3}$$

where h^{RGB} is the embedding function. It is well known that the signals of the fully-connected layer (FCL) of such a CNN can be considered as an embedding of an input image to a discriminative feature vector. We performed a grid search with an independent validation set to find an optimal FCL that best suited our application. As a result, a second fully connected layer was found to be optimal, and we therefore decided to use this configuration for the image embedding throughout all the experiments.

4.2   Monocular Depth Estimation

We used MiDaS as a means of monocular depth estimation. MiDaS was originally presented by Ranftl et al. [17], to address the performance degradation of conventional monocular depth estimation models trained from insufficient datasets that therefore cannot generalize well to diverse environments, and to address the difficulty of large-scale capture of diverse depth datasets. In [17], a strategy for combining complementary sources of data was introduced, and improved performance was demonstrated using a flexible loss function and a new strategy for principle-based data set mixing. Furthermore, the no-retraining property is obviously valuable for our cross-domain scenarios. Specifically, the MiDaS takes an RGB scene image x as input and returns a pseudo depth image y^{MiDaS}:

$$y^{MiDaS} = f^{MiDaS}(x). \tag{4}$$

Fig. 2 shows examples of the estimated depth image.

4.3   Depth Image Encoding

We further propose to encode the single-channel depth image provided by the monocular depth estimation into a much more informative 3-channel HHA image. HHA is an image encoding method proposed by [9] that encodes each pixel of a given image using three channels representing "Height above ground", "Horizontal disparity" and "Angle with gravity". The angle with the direction of gravity is estimated and then used to compute the height from the ground. The horizontal parallax for each pixel is obtained from the inversely proportional relationship with the original depth value.

The overall algorithm is an iterative process of updating the gravity vector. Let us consider the t-th iteration, that is, $t \geq 1$:

1. The input point cloud is split into a set $N_{\parallel}$ of points parallel to the gravity vector and a set $N_{\perp}$ of points perpendicular to the gravity vector and the remainder, where

$$N_{\parallel} = \{n : \angle(n, g_{i-1}) < d \vee \angle(n, g_{i-1}) > \pi - d\}$$

$$N_{\perp} = \{n : \pi/2 - d < \angle(n, g_{i-1}) < \pi/2 + d\}$$

   The initial estimate for the gravity vector g is the y-axis. For the variable d, we used the setting of $d = \pi/4$ for $t \leq 5$ and $d = \pi/12$ for $t > 5$.
2. The gravity vector g_i is updated by

$$\min_{g:\|g\|_2=1} \sum_{n \in N_{\perp}} \cos^2(\angle(n, g)) + \sum_{n \in N_{\parallel}} \sin^2(\angle(n, g)).$$

As a result, a given depth image is transformed into a 3-channel HHA image. In an ablation study, we compared the original 1-channel depth image with the 3-channel HHA encoded image in terms of the performance of the CNN classifier and found a considerable decrease in performance in the former case.

Given the HHA modality:

$$y^{DIE} = f^{DIE}(x), \tag{5}$$

the same CNN and embedding architectures as (3) are used for the HHA modality.

$$f^{HHA}(x) = g^{HHA} \circ h^{HHA}(x). \tag{6}$$

4.4   Multimodal Network

Two independent CNN models called RGB-Net and HHA-Net are respectively trained using the RGB and HHA images as the input modalities, and then a pair of image embeddings from the CNN pair is integrated by an additional integration network. At first glance, one might expect this integration network to play two different roles. The first is that of switching to diagnose inputs from RGB-Net and HHA-Net to filter out invalid inputs. This diagnostic problem is nontrivial because we only have two inputs; even if inconsistencies are detected between them, we cannot distinguish which is invalid. Another role is that of a weighted average of inputs. This mixing problem is relatively easy to solve, at least naively. For example, a naive approach would be to average RGB-Net and HHA-Net outputs. However, we observed that this approach was often useless, and yielded worse performance than either RGB or HHA-Net.

Our proposed method is to implement this mixing with a trainable multi-layer-perceptron (MLP). This strategy worked well, as shown in the experimental section. Note that this use of an MLP as a mixing function has also been successfully adopted in many contexts such as that of multi-supervisor knowledge transfer [8]. The MLP consists of three layers, each respectively including 8192, 1024, and 100 neurons. The number of neurons for the input layer, 8192, corresponds to the concatenation of the pair of 4096-dimensional embeddings from the two networks (i.e., $4096 \times 2 = 8192$). The number of neurons for the output layer, 100, corresponds to the number of place classes.

4.5   Training

Our framework employs several learnable parameters: f^{RGB}, f^{MiDaS}, f^{HHA}, f^{DIE}, and f^{MLP}. We assume the parameters of f^{MiDaS} and f^{DIE} are domain invariant, whereas those of f^{RGB}, f^{HHA}, and f^{MLP} must be fine-tuned to the target domain. Note that the model is trained efficiently by the following procedure.

1. The CNN model f^{RGB} is trained using the RGB images $X^{RGB} = S^{train}$ and the given ground-truth class labels.
2. All the RGB images X^{RGB} are transformed to HHA images X^{HHA} by using the models f^{MiDaS} and f^{DIE}.
3. The CNN model f^{HHA} is trained using the HHA images X^{HHA} and the given ground-truth class labels.
4. All the RGB images X^{RGB} are fed to the trained embedding model h^{RGB} to obtain embeddings Y^{RGB}.
5. All the HHA images S^{HHA} are fed to the trained embedding model h^{HHA} to obtain embeddings Y^{HHA}.
6. All the corresponding pairs from Y^{RGB} and Y^{HHA} are concatenated to obtain a training set Y^{MLP} for f^{MLP}.
7. f^{MLP} is finally trained using the set Y^{MLP} as supervision.

Fig. 4. Image samples from datasets "WI," "SP," "SU," and "AU".

5   Experiments

5.1   Dataset

The NCLT, one of the most popular datasets for cross-season visual robot navigation, was used for performance evaluation. The NCLT dataset is a collection of outdoor images collected by a Segway vehicle every other week from January 8, 2012 to April 5, 2013 at the University of Michigan North Campus. For each dataset, the robot travels indoor and outdoor routes on the university campus, while encountering various types of static and dynamic objects, such as desks, chairs, pedestrians and bicycles, and also experiences long-term cross-dataset changes such as snow cover, weather changes, and building renovations. In this work, the on-board front-facing camera of the vehicle was used as the main modality. Also, the associated GPS data was used only as the ground-truth for the self-localization task. Figure 3 shows the bird's eye view of the robot workspace and viewpoint-trajectories.

Four datasets with IDs, 2012/03/31 (SP), 2012/08/04 (SU), 2012/11/17 (AU), and 2012/01/22 (WI) are used for the current experiments. The number of images in these $N = 4$ datasets is 26,364, 24,138, 26,923 and 26,208, respectively. The image was resized from the original size of 1,232 × 1,616 pixels to 256 × 256 pixels. Example images in each dataset are shown in Fig. 4. Different experiments were conducted by using each of all the $N(N-1) = 12$ pairings of the four datasets as the training-test dataset pair.

The robot workspace is defined by the bounding box of all viewpoints and partitioned into a 10×10 grid of place classes, before the training and test stages.

5.2   Results

As mentioned in Sect. 4.1, a VGG-16 model was used as a conventional method for comparison. This model was exactly the same as the VGG-16 used in the proposed method as a feature extractor, with exactly the same training procedure, conditions and hyperparameters.

The performance was evaluated in terms of top-1 accuracy, which is defined as the ratio of successful test samples over the entire testing set. A given testing sample was considered as successful if and only if its maximum likelihood class was consistent with the ground-truth class.

As an ablation study, we also trained an alternative baseline single-modal CNN model called "HHA-Net", which used the HHA-images instead of the RGB-images as input to the CNN model, with the same procedure as the abovementioned baseline model.

Table 1 shows the results in terms of performance. It may be observed that the proposed method outperformed the methods compared, RGB-Net and HHA-Net, in all the 12 combinations of training and testing datasets, and its recognition performance improved by from 3.9pt to 13.5pt.

Several examples of the input image, the ground-truth class image, and the predicted class image for successful and failed examples are respectively shown in Figs. 5 and 6. In both figures, the columns from left to right indicate the (RGB, HHA) image pair of the test sample, the place class that received the highest likelihood visualized by a training sample image pair, and a ground-truth image. It may be observed that the proposed method intelligently identified the shapes of mountains and roads, the presence or absence of buildings, and so forth, and used this information for classification. In contrast, classification often failed in confusing scenes where even a human could get lost. We also encountered errors in mistaking buildings for trees, which could be compensated for in future research by introducing semantic features.

These results show that the proposed approach of multimodal formulation of single-modal visual place classification led to significant improvements in performance and robustness.

Table 1. Top-1 accuracy [%].

training	test	Ours	RGB-Net	(gain)	HHA-Net	(gain)
1/22	3/31	62.4	58.5	+3.9	56.3	+6.1
	8/4	49.1	40.2	+8.9	43.4	+5.7
	11/17	40.6	31.7	+8.9	37.8	+2.8
3/31	1/22	60.4	48.7	+11.7	55.3	+5.1
	8/4	59.3	47.1	+12.2	52.9	+6.4
	11/17	40.6	27.1	+13.5	38.3	+2.3
8/4	1/22	42.4	32.6	+9.8	40.0	+2.4
	3/31	57.8	49.2	+8.6	49.9	+7.9
	11/17	37.2	26.3	+10.9	31.3	+5.9
11/17	1/22	41.3	29.3	+12	39.1	+2.2
	3/31	48.8	38.2	+10.6	41.5	+7.3
	8/4	38.8	29.2	+9.6	32.1	+6.7

Fig. 5. Success examples.

Fig. 6. Failure examples.

6 Concluding Remarks

In this work, we have revisited the challenging problem of single-modal cross-domain visual place classification from a new perspective of pseudo multimodal RGB-D fusion. The proposed approach is based on two domain-invariant schemes. The first performs pseudo-multimodal fusion to inherit the domain-invariance of multimodal sensor integration without requiring additional sensing devices. The second is the introduction of domain-invariant pseudo-depth measurement, referred to as domain-invariant monocular depth estimation. We have presented an effective framework for information processing and information fusion of these multimodal data and validated the effectiveness of our approach in a practical long-term robot navigation scenario. The results confirmed that the proposed method clearly contributed to an improvement in observed performance on all the datasets considered.

References

1. Burnett, K., Wu, Y., Yoon, D.J., Schoellig, A.P., Barfoot, T.D.: Are we ready for radar to replace lidar in all-weather mapping and localization? IEEE Robot. Autom. Lett. **7**(4), 10328–10335 (2022)
2. Carlevaris-Bianco, N., Ushani, A.K., Eustice, R.M.: University of michigan north campus long-term vision and lidar dataset. Int. J. Robot. Res. **35**(9), 1023–1035 (2016)
3. Chaplot, D.S., Gandhi, D.P., Gupta, A., Salakhutdinov, R.R.: Object goal navigation using goal-oriented semantic exploration. Adv. Neural. Inf. Process. Syst. **33**, 4247–4258 (2020)
4. Cummins, M., Newman, P.: Appearance-only slam at large scale with fab-map 2.0. Int. J. Robot. Res. **30**(9), 1100–1123 (2011)
5. Eigen, D., Puhrsch, C., Fergus, R.: Depth map prediction from a single image using a multi-scale deep network. In: Advances in Neural Information Processing Systems, vol. 27 (2014)
6. Garcia-Fidalgo, E., Ortiz, A.: iBoW-LCD: an appearance-based loop-closure detection approach using incremental bags of binary words. IEEE Robot. Autom. Lett. **3**(4), 3051–3057 (2018)
7. Garg, R., B.G., V.K., Carneiro, G., Reid, I.: Unsupervised CNN for single view depth estimation: geometry to the rescue. In: Leibe, B., Matas, J., Sebe, N., Welling, M. (eds.) ECCV 2016. LNCS, vol. 9912, pp. 740–756. Springer, Cham (2016). https://doi.org/10.1007/978-3-319-46484-8_45
8. Gou, J., Yu, B., Maybank, S.J., Tao, D.: Knowledge distillation: a survey. Int. J. Comput. Vision **129**, 1789–1819 (2021)
9. Gupta, S., Girshick, R., Arbeláez, P., Malik, J.: Learning rich features from RGB-D images for object detection and segmentation. In: Fleet, D., Pajdla, T., Schiele, B., Tuytelaars, T. (eds.) ECCV 2014. LNCS, vol. 8695, pp. 345–360. Springer, Cham (2014). https://doi.org/10.1007/978-3-319-10584-0_23
10. Hiroki, T., Tanaka, K.: Long-term knowledge distillation of visual place classifiers. In: 2019 IEEE Intelligent Transportation Systems Conference (ITSC), pp. 541–546. IEEE (2019)
11. Kim, G., Park, B., Kim, A.: 1-day learning, 1-year localization: long-term lidar localization using scan context image. IEEE Robot. Autom. Lett. **4**(2), 1948–1955 (2019)
12. Kurauchi, K., Tanaka, K., Yamamoto, R., Yoshida, M.: Active domain-invariant self-localization using ego-centric and world-centric maps. In: Tistarelli, M., Dubey,

S.R., Singh, S.K., Jiang, X. (eds.) Computer Vision and Machine Intelligence, pp. 475–487. Springer Nature Singapore, Singapore (2023)

13. Lázaro, M.T., Capobianco, R., Grisetti, G.: Efficient long-term mapping in dynamic environments. In: 2018 IEEE/RSJ International Conference on Intelligent Robots and Systems (IROS), pp. 153–160. IEEE (2018)

14. Mo, N., Gan, W., Yokoya, N., Chen, S.: Es6d: a computation efficient and symmetry-aware 6d pose regression framework. In: Proceedings of the IEEE/CVF Conference on Computer Vision and Pattern Recognition, pp. 6718–6727 (2022)

15. Ohta, T., Tanaka, K., Yamamoto, R.: Scene graph descriptors for visual place classification from noisy scene data. In: ICT Express (2023)

16. Pham, Q.H., et al.: A 3d dataset: towards autonomous driving in challenging environments. In: 2020 IEEE International Conference on Robotics and Automation (ICRA), pp. 2267–2273. IEEE (2020)

17. Ranftl, R., Lasinger, K., Hafner, D., Schindler, K., Koltun, V.: Towards robust monocular depth estimation: mixing datasets for zero-shot cross-dataset transfer. IEEE Trans. Pattern Anal. Mach. Intell. **44**(3), 1623–1637 (2020)

18. Saxena, A., Sun, M., Ng, A.Y.: Make3d: learning 3d scene structure from a single still image. IEEE Trans. Pattern Anal. Mach. Intell. **31**(5), 824–840 (2008)

19. Schönberger, J.L., Pollefeys, M., Geiger, A., Sattler, T.: Semantic visual localization. In: Proceedings of the IEEE Conference on Computer Vision and Pattern Recognition, pp. 6896–6906 (2018)

20. Simonyan, K., Zisserman, A.: Very deep convolutional networks for large-scale image recognition. arXiv preprint arXiv:1409.1556 (2014)

21. Toft, C., Olsson, C., Kahl, F.: Long-term 3d localization and pose from semantic labellings. In: Proceedings of the IEEE International Conference on Computer Vision Workshops, pp. 650–659 (2017)

22. Wang, H., Wang, W., Liang, W., Xiong, C., Shen, J.: Structured scene memory for vision-language navigation. In: Proceedings of the IEEE/CVF conference on Computer Vision and Pattern Recognition, pp. 8455–8464 (2021)

23. Wang, M., Deng, W.: Deep visual domain adaptation: a survey. Neurocomputing **312**, 135–153 (2018)

24. Weyand, T., Kostrikov, I., Philbin, J.: PlaNet - photo geolocation with convolutional neural networks. In: Leibe, B., Matas, J., Sebe, N., Welling, M. (eds.) ECCV 2016. LNCS, vol. 9912, pp. 37–55. Springer, Cham (2016). https://doi.org/10.1007/978-3-319-46484-8_3

25. Yang, N., Tanaka, K., Fang, Y., Fei, X., Inagami, K., Ishikawa, Y.: Long-term vehicle localization using compressed visual experiences. In: 2018 21st International Conference on Intelligent Transportation Systems (ITSC), pp. 2203–2208. IEEE (2018)

26. Ye, J., Batra, D., Wijmans, E., Das, A.: Auxiliary tasks speed up learning point goal navigation. In: Conference on Robot Learning, pp. 498–516. PMLR (2021)

A Simplified Student Network with Multi-teacher Feature Fusion for Industrial Defect Detection

Mingjing Pei[1,2,3,4] and Ningzhong Liu[1,3,4](✉)

[1] College of Computer Science and Technology, Nanjing University of Aeronautics and Astronautics, Nanjing, China
lnz_nuaa@163.com
[2] School of Electronics and Information Engineering, West Anhui University, Lu'an, China
[3] MIIT Key Laboratory of Pattern Analysis and Machine Intelligence, Nanjing, China
[4] Collaborative Innovation Center of Novel Software Technology and Industrialization, Nanjing, China

Abstract. Improved industrial defect detection is deemed critical for ensuring high-quality manufacturing processes. Despite the effectiveness of knowledge distillation in detecting defects, there are still challenges in extracting useful features and designing a better student network. In this study, a new framework based on knowledge distillation is proposed to address these issues. To avoid overfitting and balance anomaly detection between image and pixel levels, a simplified student decoding network is designed. To extract more diverse features, a multi-teacher network is used in the teacher network. Simple addition and concatenation operations for feature maps were not sufficient, the method fuses features iteratively using attention mechanisms utilized for the multi-teacher networks. The approach is evaluated on two benchmark datasets for industrial defect detection, Mvtec and BTAD, and significantly improved performance is achieved compared to the other methods. An average accuracy of 99.22% and 97.46% for image-level and pixel-level ROC-AUC, respectively, is achieved on the Mvtec dataset, and 93.47% and 96.3% on the BTAD dataset. The proposed framework shows effectiveness in detecting defects in industrial settings, as demonstrated by the results.

Keywords: Industrial defect detection · Reverse knowledge distillation · Multi-teacher model

1 Introduction

Industrial defect detection is a technology that aims to identify defects in various industrial products to ensure their quality and maintain production stability. It has a wide range of applications, including unmanned quality inspection [1], intelligent inspection [2], and video surveillance [3]. However, industrial defect detection faces several challenges. One major challenge is related to data. Industrial defect detection requires large amounts of high-quality data to train and improve their accuracy. However, obtaining such data can be challenging, as defects may be rare or unpredictable, and collecting and labeling data can be time-consuming and expensive. Another challenge is related to the complexity of industrial environments. Industrial defect detection must be able to identify defects in images with complex backgrounds, such as those with reflections or shadows, and in images with multiple types of defects. Finally, industrial defect detection must be highly accurate to detect subtle defects that may be difficult to identify with the human eye.

These challenges have led to the development of different approaches. It is usually divided into three categories. The first category is the synthesis of abnormal samples [4, 5]. These methods utilize neural networks for the binary classification of normal and synthetic abnormal samples. However, It requires pre-processing operations in the image, thereby increasing model complexity, and may not be able to effectively capture the complexity of real-world anomalies. The second category relies on pixel-level image comparison by reconstructing a normal image. Self-encoding and generative models, such as AE [6] and GAN [7], are commonly used in these methods. However, this approach may not align the reconstructed pixels with the input image and may alter the style of the image, leading to detection errors and performance degradation. The third category focuses on feature similarity, where the features extracted by convolutional neural networks, and anomalous regions have distinguishable feature embeddings [8]. These methods are more tolerant to noise interference and have better robustness in detection. Frameworks of teacher-student networks have been proposed on the basis of feature similarity [9], but they suffer from limitations such as insufficient feature extraction and the risk of overfitting due to using the same architecture.

To address these issues, a new network architecture has been designed. First, the insufficiency of extracting sufficiently diverse or representative features by using a single teacher network may be encountered. To tackle this problem, a multi-teacher network has been proposed to extract features with more diversity. Second, simple addition and concatenation operations may prove insufficient to achieve optimal performance when combining the learned features from multiple teacher networks. To overcome this problem, an iterative attention-based feature fusion method has been employed. Additionally, if the teacher and student network structures are identical, overfitting may occur. In such cases, the student network may overlearn to reconstruct abnormal regions, resulting in poor generalization performance during testing. To avoid this situation, a simplified student network has been designed with a different structure from the teacher network.

The key contributions of this work can be summarized as follows:

1. A network architecture consisting of multiple teachers and a student is utilized. The architecture extracts image features from multiple models.
2. Simple addition and concatenation operations for feature maps not be sufficient. To combine the features extracted from the multi-teacher networks, the iterative attention feature fusion method is employed. In order to prevent overfitting, the student and teacher networks use distinct architectures that are not consistent with each other.
3. To demonstrate the efficacy of our approach, numerous experiments were performed on industrial datasets.

2 Related Work

2.1 Reconstruction-Based Methods

Reconstruction-based methods are commonly used to detect anomalies by calculating pixel-level or image-level anomaly scores based on the reconstruction error, which is measured by models such as Auto-Encoders and Generative Adversarial Networks (GANs). However, these models can reconstruct abnormal samples well due to the generalization capability of neural networks, making it challenging to distinguish normal and abnormal samples accurately. To address this issue, researchers have modified the network architecture by incorporating memory mechanisms [10], generating pseudo-anomaly samples [11], and using image masking strategies [12]. These modifications aim to improve the ability to discriminate between normal and abnormal samples. However, current methods still have limited discrimination ability in real-world anomaly detection scenarios. To overcome these limitations, some researchers have proposed preprocessing techniques, such as Omni-frequency Channel-selection [13], to compress and restore individual images, and incorporate Position and Neighborhood Information to achieve better reconstruction results. While the reconstruction-based method is intuitive and has strong interpretability, existing methods can suffer from biases that result in detection errors and limit detection performance. For instance, the reconstructed image may have misaligned pixels or change the style of the original image. Additionally, the pixel-level comparison can be sensitive to noise, resulting in poor detection robustness.

2.2 Embedding-Based Methods

Embedding-based methods aim to detect anomalies by comparing the embedding vectors of normal and abnormal samples using a trained network. Commonly used approaches include defining embedding similarity, one-class classification [14, 16], and Gaussian distributions [15]. The literature [14] and [16] are popular methods that define a compact one-class distribution using normal sample vectors. To handle high-dimensional data, Deep SVDD has been adopted to estimate feature representations using deep networks. However, using the entire image embedding can only determine whether an image is normal or not, but cannot locate the abnormal regions. To address this issue, some researchers [17, 18] have used patch-level embeddings to produce an anomaly map, where each patch represents a point in the feature space. This approach allows for the localization of abnormal regions in the image. The literature [19] has proposed methods to obtain a better feature space representation by adapting the target dataset's features. Additionally, some researchers have used a decoupled hypersphere to further improve detection performance. Recently, a flow-based idea has been proposed to perform density estimation and calculate anomaly scores [20]. The goal of these methods is to find distinguishable embeddings, making them more robust to noise and other sources of interference.

2.3 Knowledge Distillation

Knowledge distillation networks typically consist of two networks. The student network imitates the output of the teacher network in order to simplify the model and reduce its resource requirements. In the field of anomaly detection, during the training phase, only normal samples are used, and through training, the feature vectors extracted by the teacher and student networks are very similar. During the testing phase, if an abnormal sample is encountered, the similarity of the feature vectors extracted by the two networks is very low. Using this idea, we can detect anomalies. Currently, based on this idea, there have been many works. For example, the framework proposed by the US method [21] includes a teacher network and multiple student networks. Through distillation of the last layer, multiple students imitate the output of the teacher network for anomaly detection. However, considering that the distillation of the last layer is insufficient, MKD [22] uses multiple feature layers for distillation, achieving good results. In order to further improve detection performance, reference [8] attempted to propose a reverse distillation architecture, compressing the extracted features through the teacher network and then decoding them through the student network, achieving good results. In addition, DeSTSeg [23] introduced the segmentation concept into the knowledge distillation architecture. This study is based on the reverse distillation framework to perform anomaly detection.

3 Method

The objective is to use a reverse distillation framework to detect anomalies in an input image by training a student network to imitate the behavior of multiple teachers' networks. By leveraging this approach, the student network can accurately identify anomalies in new images. In Fig. 1, in the training phase, firstly, there are three pre-trained teacher networks to extract the features of normal images, and then the features of different layers are fused by the multi-scale feature fusion module(MFF). Secondly, the output of the MFF module is fused using the iterative attention feature fusion module(iAFF), and then the obtained feature maps are compressed using the one-class embedding(OCE) module to obtain low-dimensional vectors. Finally, the low-dimensional vectors are decoded using the simplified student network to obtain the feature maps of each layer. The loss function is calculated by the feature layer corresponding to the teacher network. In the testing phase, the test images are modeled to obtain each feature layer of the simplified student network, and then the feature maps are fused to obtain the final anomaly results.

3.1 Multi-teacher Models

Most distillation network architectures are designed to distill knowledge from a one-teacher to one student. However, in the process of human learning, students often learn from multiple teachers. By incorporating multiple teacher models, a student model can benefit from multiple interpretations of the task. Ensemble learning with multiple teacher network predictions has been shown to outperform one teacher network. Therefore, we propose a distillation network architecture that utilizes multiple teachers to enhance the student model's performance.

Rich features are extracted from images using ResNet18, ResNet34, and Wide_ResNet50, which have been pre-trained on ImageNet. The model based on the resnet network family has a total of four convolutional blocks. We only used the previous

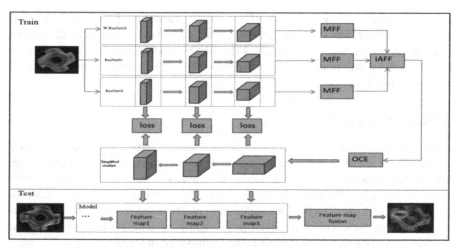

Fig. 1. An overview can be provided for the framework that has been proposed for the detection and localization of anomalies. The figure contains a training phase and a testing phase. In the training phase, there are three pre-trained teacher networks, feature fusion (MFF, iAFF), feature compression (OCE), and a simplified student network. In the testing phase, the feature maps of each feature layer of the student network are output by the model, and the visualization results can be obtained by the feature map fusion module.

three convolutional blocks to obtain the feature maps, removing the last convolutional block. To facilitate the use of a single decoding network in calculating the loss, the feature channels from the multiple teacher's networks need to be fused. This can be achieved through a simple concatenation operation. Once the feature channels have been fused, cosine similarity is used as the loss function for knowledge transfer.

During training, the input image is resized to 224 * 224 * 3. By fusion of the corresponding feature layers of the three networks, the first layer generates a feature map with dimensions of 64 * 64 * 384, the second layer generates a feature map with dimensions of 32 * 32 * 768, and the third layer generates a feature map of size 16 * 16 * 1536.

3.2 Feature Fusion and Dimensional Compression

Since each layer of each teacher network has different feature map sizes, feature map fusion needs to be done in order to get a uniform size. In addition, to effectively combine the learned features of a multi-teacher network, simple addition, and concatenation operations may not yield optimal results. As a solution, iterative attention feature fusion is adopted.

The MFF module is a type of module that facilitates multi-scale fusion by combining feature maps of varying sizes into a uniform size. This process results in a final feature map that is 16 * 16 in size and has a channel count of 3072. The IAFF module addresses short and long skip connections and the fusion of features caused within the Inception layer. Meanwhile, it is shown that the initial integration of feature maps can be a bottleneck and can be mitigated by adding another attention level. Specific details about IAFF can be found in the references [24]. After the iAFF module is applied, the feature map is resized to a size of 16 * 16 * 3072. The dimensionality of the feature vector is reduced by the OCE block, which employs ResNet's residual connection block. Further details about this module can be found in [9]. Ultimately, a feature map is 8 * 8 * 2048 is obtained as the output of the OCE block. Eventually, 3072 dimensions are compressed into 2048 dimensions.

3.3 Student Network

Some previous studies on knowledge distillation architectures for anomaly detection have employed identical architectures. However, this approach may lead to overfitting, as the student network can easily reconstruct the features of the anomaly region, thereby negatively impacting the detection performance. Therefore, a more suitable network architecture needs to be devised. Additionally, to ensure compatibility between the feature channels of the intermediate layers in the multiple teacher networks, a simplified decoding network is designed. The structure is illustrated in Fig. 2.

Figure 2 is a simplified student decoding network. The right side of the figure shows the student decoding network and the left side shows the basic blocks. There are a total of three layers in the student decoding network, and each layer contains the basic blocks.

The Residual Connection Block from ResNet [25] serves as the inspiration for the basic blocks, which use to combine feature maps of different scales. The first branch includes a deconvolution layer and a BatchNorm layer, it can keep original features. The second branch consists of two 1 * 1 convolutions and a 3 * 3 convolution. In this procedure, the 1 * 1 operation is first performed on the image, then the 1 * 1 convolution and 3 * 3 convolution are passed respectively, and finally, the concat operation is performed. The purpose is to reduce the amount of computation. To match the feature map size of the teacher network, a 4 * 4 deconvolution layer is applied in one branch of the Basic Block. The output of the two branches is combined through summation and then passed through a ReLU layer.

To match the structure of the teacher network, the student decoder module has the same three-layer structure, but in an inverted order. The D3 module is constructed with a Basic Block and a convolutional layer. The 1 * 1 convolutional layer is responsible for adjusting the number of input channels to match that of the corresponding teacher network's output channels. On the other hand, the D2 and D1 modules both consist of a Basic Block, which is used to maintain the original features and fuse feature maps of different scales.

3.4 Loss Function

Minimizing this loss function is the main objective of the training process. In out model, the formula for calculating a two-dimensional anomaly map [27] is as follows.

$$M^k(h, w) = 1 - \frac{f_T^k(h, w) f_S^k(h, w)}{\left\| f_T^k(h, w) \right\| \cdot \left\| f_S^k(h, w) \right\|} \tag{1}$$

The height and width of the feature map are denoted by h and w, respectively, while the number of feature layers is represented by k. The variables $f_T^k(h, w)$ and $f_S^k(h, w)$

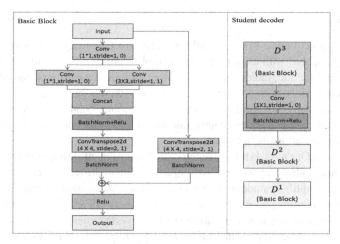

Fig. 2. A simplified student decoding network.

denote the feature vectors. The loss function is defined as shown in (2).

$$L = \sum_{k=1}^{3} \left\{ \frac{1}{H_k W_k} \sum_{h=1}^{H_k} \sum_{w=1}^{W_k} M^k(h, w) \right\} \tag{2}$$

4 Experiments

4.1 Datasets

The MVTec AD dataset [27] has been developed with a focus on industrial inspection, and it serves as a means of comparing different methods for anomaly detection. The dataset comprises 15 categories of objects and textures, with each class being further divided into a training set and a testing set. The training set consists of 3629 images of typical objects, while the test set includes 1725 images.

As for the BTAD dataset [28], it contains 2830 images showcasing actual industrial anomalies in 3 different products. The dataset contains 3 categories, including 2 for objects and 1 for texture, with 1800 images for training and 741 images for testing.

4.2 Implementation Details

The experiments were carried out on an Ubuntu 18.04 operating system using an NVIDIA GTX Geforce 2070s GPU. In these experiments, we employed pre-trained ResNet18, ResNet34, and Wide_ResNet50 as the backbone. All images in the MVTec and BTAD datasets were resized to 256 * 256 pixels. To optimize our model, we used the Adam optimizer. The learning rate was scheduled using the cosine annealing strategy. We trained our model for 200 epochs, using a batch size of 4.

4.3 Results

To assess the effectiveness of our model for image-level anomaly detection, the performance was compared with existing methods. Table 1 presents the results of our image-level anomaly detection, indicating that our model achieved superior performance compared to other models, with a score of 99.22. Moreover, our method also demonstrated better results in terms of texture and object class, reaching 99.54 and 99.9, respectively, when compared to other models. These findings suggest that our model is an effective approach to image anomaly detection.

Furthermore, Our model showed remarkable improvement compared to other models in performance, indicating the positive impact of our multi-teacher networks, feature fusion, and a simplified student decoding network. Our method differs from the US method in that we utilize an inverse teacher-student network architecture, while the US does not. We hypothesize that in the absence of an inverse structure, the student network may not effectively identify anomalous regions. Notably, some categories such as Grid, Pill, and Zipper demonstrated better results than our method, although our performance was comparable to theirs.

For pixel-level anomaly detection, we compared our method with several baselines including SPADE, Cutpaste, Draem, UniAD, NSA, and ADRD. However, it should be noted that our comparison did not encompass all the methods presented in the image-level anomaly detection evaluation, and there were instances where some data were not disclosed in the publication.

Based on the results presented in Table 2, it is evident that our method achieved a good performance in pixel-level anomaly detection, with a ROC-AUC score of 97.46, indicating its effectiveness. Our method achieves optimal results in some categories, e.g. Transistor, and Zipper. The Draem method achieves good results in some categories where it is based on pixel-level segmentation. This provides a good idea for pixel-level localization.

Table 1. Results of image-level anomaly detection on the MVTec dataset.

Category		RIAD	US	PaDiM	Cutpaste	NSA	Draem	UniAD	ADRD	Ours
Texture	Carpet	84.2	91.6	99.8	93.9	95.6	97	99.9	98.9	**100**
	Grid	99.6	81	96.7	**100**	99.9	99.9	98.5	**100**	99.8
	Leather	100	88.2	**100**	**100**	99.9	**100**	**100**	**100**	**100**
	Tile	98.7	99.1	98.1	94.6	100	**99.6**	99	99.3	98.2
	Wood	93	97.7	99.2	99.1	97.5	99.1	97.9	99.2	99.7
	Average	95.1	91.5	98.8	97.5	98.6	99.12	99.06	99.48	**99.54**
Object	Bottle	99.9	99.0	99.9	98.2	97.7	99.2	**100**	**100**	**100**
	Cable	81.9	86.2	92.7	81.2	94.5	91.8	97.6	95	**98.6**

(continued)

Table 1. (*continued*)

Category		RIAD	US	PaDiM	Cutpaste	NSA	Draem	UniAD	ADRD	Ours
	Capsule	88.4	86.1	91.3	98.2	95.2	**98.5**	85.3	96.3	97.6
	Hazelnut	83.3	93.1	92	98.3	94.7	**100**	99.9	99.9	**100**
	Metal nut	88.5	82.0	98.7	99.9	98.7	98.7	99	**100**	**100**
	Pill	83.8	87.9	93.3	94.9	99.2	**98.9**	88.3	96.6	97
	Screw	84.5	54.9	85.8	88.7	90.2	93.9	91.9	97	**97.8**
	Toothbrush	100	95.3	96.1	99.4	100	**100**	95	99.5	**100**
	Transistor	90.9	81.8	97.4	96.1	95.1	93.1	**100**	96.7	98.3
	Zipper	98.1	91.9	90.3	99.9	99.8	**100**	96.7	98.5	99.7
	Average	89.9	85.8	93.8	95.5	96.5	97.41	95.37	97.95	**98.9**
Average		91.7	87.7	95.5	96.1	97.2	98.27	96.6	98.72	**99.22**

The VT-ADL and autoencoder method were also compared with our model on the BTAD dataset. It can be observed from Table 3 that other models were outperformed by our method. Since pixel-level anomaly detection scores were not provided by other methods, they could not be compared. In categories 1 and 2, better results than our method were achieved by the other method.

Figure 3 shows the visualization results of our models. The red area indicates the area considered by the model to be the higher anomaly region. We show the original image, the mask image, and the visualization result separately. From the results, we can see that our model can accurately detect the defective regions, which indicates that our model has good detection performance.

Table 2. ROC-AUC results for pixel-level anomaly detection on the MVTec AD dataset are present-ed. The best-performing method for each category is highlighted in bold.

Category		SPADE	Cutpaste	Draem	NSA	UniAD	ADRD	Ours
Texture	Carpet	97.5	98.3	96.2	95.5	98	98.9	**99.3**
	Grid	93.7	97.5	**99.5**	99.2	94.6	99.3	99.2
	Leather	97.6	99.5	98.9	99.5	98.3	99.4	99.4
	Tile	87.4	90.5	**99.5**	99.3	91.8	95.6	94.5
	Wood	88.5	95.5	**97**	90.7	93.4	95.3	94
	Average	92.9	96.3	**98.2**	96.8	97.8	97.7	97.28
Object	Bottle	98.4	97.6	**99.3**	98.3	98.1	98.7	98.4
	Cable	97.2	90	95.4	96	96.8	**97.4**	97.3

(*continued*)

Table 2. (*continued*)

Category		SPADE	Cutpaste	Draem	NSA	UniAD	ADRD	Ours
	Capsule	99.0	97.4	94.1	97.6	97.9	98.7	98.4
	Hazelnut	99.1	97.3	**99.5**	97.6	98.8	98.9	99
	Metal nut	98.1	93.1	**98.7**	98.4	95.7	97.3	96.6
	Pill	96.5	95.7	97.6	98.5	95.1	98.2	96.1
	Screw	98.9	96.7	**99.7**	96.5	97.4	99.6	99.3
	Toothbrush	97.9	98.1	98.1	94.9	97.8	**99.1**	99
	Transistor	94.1	93.0	90.0	88	98.7	92.5	**93.5**
	Zipper	96.5	99.3	98.6	94.2	96.0	98.2	**98.7**
	Average	97.6	95.7	97.1	96	97	**97.86**	97.63
Average		96.5	96	97.5	96.3	97.4	**97.78**	97.46

Table 3. Results of image-level and pixel-level anomaly detection for the BTAD dataset. The symbol "-" indicates that the method does not provide a pixel-level anomaly score.

BTAD	AE + MSE	AE + MSE + SSIM	VT-ADL	Ours
0	49/-	53/-	99/-	**100**/99.6
1	92/-	**96**/-	94/-	94.6/92.3
2	95/-	**89**/-	77/-	85.8/97
Mean	78/-	79/-	90/-	**93.47**/96.3

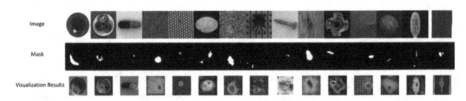

Fig. 3. Visualization results of image anomaly detection.

In Fig. 4, statistics of the abnormal scores were presented. The results indicate that the model could effectively distinguish between normal and abnormal samples. However, there were some categories where the distinction was not clear, indicating the need for an improved model.

4.4 Ablation Study

Table 4 shows the impact of pretraining and non-pretraining networks on image-level and pixel-level anomaly detection results, demonstrating the significance of pretraining

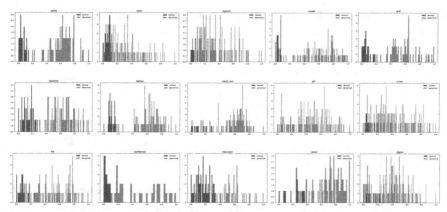

Fig. 4. The abnormal scores were statistically analyzed, and the distinction between normal and abnormal samples was displayed in the histogram. Normal samples were represented by blue bars, while abnormal samples were represented by yellow bars.

in image feature extraction. Results reveal that utilizing pretraining can enhance the accuracy by approximately 25 points, suggesting that pretraining is effective in capturing image features.

Table 4. Results of anomaly detection using our model, comparing the performance of models trained with and without pretraining.

Three Teachers Network	Unpretrained	Pretrained
Texture	77.42/70.12	99.7/97.28
Object	68.94/78.17	98.9/97.63
Average	73.18/74.15	99.22/97.46

Table 5 presents the results of different modifications made to the original network for image-level and pixel-level anomaly detection. The baseline represents the original network. The simplified student network corresponds to our own designed student network, which replaces the original one. The multi-teachers network involves using three teacher networks instead of one. For the feature fusion of multiple teachers, the attention iteration module was introduced.

Employing different architectures for the teacher and student networks can lead to improved results. This highlights the potential risk of overfitting when using a high-performing student network, which may inadvertently recover anomalies.

The adoption of multi-teacher networks can enhance the extraction of feature representations, as evidenced in Table 5, where the image-level anomaly detection results improve significantly, while the pixel-level anomaly detection results remain relatively unchanged.

Table 5. Evaluating the effectiveness of the proposed networks and modules in detecting anomalies.

Baseline	Simplified Student	Three Teachers	iAFF	Value
√				98.72/97.78
√	√			98.77/97.93
√	√	√		98.91/97.56
√	√	√	√	99.22/97.46

Adopting iterative attention feature fusion can further enhance the quality of feature extraction. Table 5 demonstrates that the employment of these modules leads to improved results in image-level anomaly detection tasks.

5 Conclusion

A new framework for industrial defect detection is proposed, which involves the use of reverse knowledge distillation with three teachers. To prevent overfitting and balance image and pixel detection, a simplified student decoding network was created. To extract more features, a multi-teacher network was used for the teacher network. However, simple addition and concatenation of feature maps were found to be inadequate, and therefore an iterative attention feature fusion method was employed to effectively combine the features of the multi-teacher networks. Extensive experiments are conducted on two datasets, Mvtec and BTAD, and it is demonstrated that the anomaly detection scores of image-level tasks are improved by our approach. However, the improvement in pixel-level performance has decreased, and further investigation is needed to enhance it in the future.

Acknowledgements. This research is supported in part by the Natural Science Foundation of Jiangsu Province of China (BK20222012), Guangxi Science and Technology Project (AB22080026/2021AB22167), National Natural Science Foundation of China (No. 61375021) and the Natural Science Key Project of Anhui Provincial Education Department (No. KJ2020A0636, No. KJ2021A0937, No. 2022AH051683, No. 2022AH051670, No. 2022AH051669).

References

1. Lee, J.H., et al.: A new image-quality evaluating and enhancing methodology for bridge inspection using an unmanned aerial vehicle. Smart Struct. Syst. **27**(2), 209–226 (2021)
2. Ullah, W., et al.: Artificial intelligence of things-assisted two-stream neural network for anomaly detection in surveillance big video data. Futur. Gener. Comput. Syst.. Gener. Comput. Syst. **129**, 286–297 (2022)
3. Patrikar, D.R., Parate, M.R.: Anomaly detection using edge computing in video surveillance system. Int. J. Multimedia Inf. Retrieval **11**(2), 85–110 (2022)

4. Li, C.-L., Sohn, K., Yoon, J., Pfister, T.: Cutpaste: self-supervised learning for anomaly detection and localization. In: Proceedings of the IEEE/CVF Conference on Computer Vision and Pattern Recognition, pp. 9664–9674 (2021)
5. Schlüter, H.M., Tan, J., Hou, B., Kainz, B.: Natural synthetic anomalies for self-supervised anomaly detection and localization. In: Avidan, S., Brostow, G., Cissé, M., Farinella, G.M., Hassner, T. (eds.) ECCV 2022. LNCS, vol. 13691, pp. 474–489. Springer, Cham (2022). https://doi.org/10.1007/978-3-031-19821-2_27
6. Wang, S., et al.: Auto-AD: autonomous hyperspectral anomaly detection network based on fully convolutional autoencoder. IEEE Trans. Geosci. Remote Sens.Geosci. Remote Sens. 60, 1–14 (2021)
7. Lu, H., Du, M., Qian, K., He, X., Wang, K.: GAN-based data augmentation strategy for sensor anomaly detection in industrial robots. IEEE Sens. J. 22(18), 17464–17474 (2021)
8. Pei, M., Liu, N., Gao, P., Sun, H.: Reverse knowledge distillation with two teachers for industrial defect detection. Appl. Sci. 13(6), 3838 (2023)
9. Deng, H., Li, X.: Anomaly detection via reverse distillation from one-class embedding. In: Proceedings of the IEEE/CVF Conference on Computer Vision and Pattern Recognition, pp. 9737–9746 (2022)
10. Roth, K., Pemula, L., Zepeda, J., Schölkopf, B., Brox, T., Gehler, P.: Towards total recall in industrial anomaly detection. In: Proceedings of the IEEE/CVF Conference on Computer Vision and Pattern Recognition, pp. 14318–14328 (2022)
11. Ding, C., Pang, G., Shen, C.: Catching both gray and black swans: open-set supervised anomaly detection. In: Proceedings of the IEEE/CVF Conference on Computer Vision and Pattern Recognition, pp. 7388–7398 (2022)
12. Ristea, N.-C., et al.: Self-supervised predictive convolutional attentive block for anomaly detection. In: Proceedings of the IEEE/CVF Conference on Computer Vision and Pattern Recognition, pp. 13576–13586 (2022)
13. Liang, Y., Zhang, J., Zhao, S., Wu, R., Liu, Y., Pan, S.: Omni-frequency channel-selection representations for unsupervised anomaly detection. arXiv preprint arXiv:2203.00259 (2022)
14. Chen, Y., Tian, Y., Pang, G., Carneiro, G.: Deep one-class classification via interpolated gaussian descriptor. In: Proceedings of the AAAI Conference on Artificial Intelligence, vol. 36, no. 1, pp. 383–392 (2022)
15. Sun, X., Yang, Z., Zhang, C., Ling, K.-V., Peng, G.: Conditional Gaussian distribution learning for open set recognition. In: Proceedings of the IEEE/CVF Conference on Computer Vision and Pattern Recognition, pp. 13480–13489 (2020)
16. Zhang, F., Fan, H., Wang, R., Li, Z., Liang, T.: Deep dual support vector data description for anomaly detection on attributed networks. Int. J. Intell. Syst. 37(2), 1509–1528 (2022)
17. Defard, T., Setkov, A., Loesch, A., Audigier, R.: Padim: a patch distribution modeling framework for anomaly detection and localization. In: Del Bimbo, A., et al. (eds.) ICPR 2021. LNCS, vol. 12664, pp. 475–489. Springer, Cham (2022). https://doi.org/10.1007/978-3-030-68799-1_35
18. Wang, S., Wu, L., Cui, L., Shen, Y.: Glancing at the patch: anomaly localization with global and local feature comparison. In: Proceedings of the IEEE/CVF Conference on Computer Vision and Pattern Recognition, pp. 254–263 (2022)
19. Lee, S., Lee, S., Song, B.C.: CFA: coupled-hypersphere-based feature adaptation for target-oriented anomaly localization. IEEE Access 10, 78446–78454 (2022)
20. Yu, J., et al.: Fastflow: unsupervised anomaly detection and localization via 2D normalizing flows. arXiv preprint arXiv:2111.07677 (2021)
21. Wang, G., Han, S., Ding, E., Huang, D.: Student-teacher feature pyramid matching for anomaly detection. arXiv preprint arXiv:2103.04257 (2021)

22. Salehi, M., Sadjadi, N., Baselizadeh, S., Rohban, M.H., Rabiee, H.R.: Multiresolution knowledge distillation for anomaly detection. In: Proceedings of the IEEE/CVF Conference on Computer Vision and Pattern Recognition, pp. 14902–14912 (2021)
23. Zhang, X., Li, S., Li, X., Huang, P., Shan, J., Chen, T.: DeSTSeg: segmentation guided denoising student-teacher for anomaly detection. arXiv preprint arXiv:2211.11317 (2022)
24. Dai, Y., Gieseke, F., Oehmcke, S., Wu, Y., Barnard, K.: Attentional feature fusion. In: Proceedings of the IEEE/CVF Winter Conference on Applications of Computer Vision, pp. 3560–3569 (2021)
25. He, K., Zhang, X., Ren, S., Sun, J.: Deep residual learning for image recognition. In: IEEE Conference on Computer Vision and Pattern Recognition (CVPR) (2016)
26. Yu, J., Liu, J.: Two-dimensional principal component analysis-based convolutional autoencoder for wafer map defect detection. IEEE Trans. Ind. Electron. **68**(9), 8789–8797 (2020)
27. Bergmann, P., Fauser, M., Sattlegger, D., Steger, C.: MVTec AD–a comprehensive real-world dataset for unsupervised anomaly detection. In: Proceedings of the IEEE/CVF Conference on Computer Vision and Pattern Recognition, pp. 9592–9600 (2019)
28. Mishra, P., Verk, R., Fornasier, D., Piciarelli, C., Foresti, G.L.: VT-ADL: a vision transformer network for image anomaly detection and localization. In: 2021 IEEE 30th International Symposium on Industrial Electronics (ISIE), pp. 01–06. IEEE (2021)

A Simple Method to Directly Determine Novel Class Weight of CNN for Generalized Few-Shot Learning

Keiichi Yamada[✉]

Department of Information Engineering, Meijo University, Aichi, Japan
yamadak@meijo-u.ac.jp

Abstract. This paper addresses the problem of machine learning for image classification, where a convolutional neural network (CNN) that has already learned the base classes learns novel classes from a small number of examples. Machine learning from a small number of examples is called few-shot learning (FSL). FSL that focuses on the classification performance of both base and novel classes in the joint space of these two classes is a challenging problem called generalized few-shot learning (GFSL). We propose a simple method for GFSL for image classification that adds the output unit of a novel class to the final layer of a CNN that has already trained on base classes and directly sets the weight vector of the output unit. Compared to existing methods, the proposed method has the advantage that the norms of the weight vectors of the final layer of the CNN need not be normalized during the training process on the base classes. We demonstrate the effectiveness of the proposed method on miniImageNet and tieredImageNet, two representative benchmark datasets for FSL.

Keywords: Image classification · Generalized few-shot learning · Convolutional neural network

1 Introduction

Convolutional neural networks (CNNs) have achieved high performance in image classification tasks. CNN classifiers typically require hundreds or thousands of supervised training data to achieve high performance. The collection, labeling, and computation of such training data are time-consuming and expensive. In contrast, the human vision system can learn and recognize novel concepts from only a few examples. The reason why humans can learn from a small number of examples is that they learn new knowledge based on the knowledge they have already learned. In this paper, we address the problem of learning novel classes from a small number of examples given a CNN that has already learned the base classes.

The problem of machine learning with a small number of examples is called few-shot learning (FSL). Most studies on FSL (e.g., [5,13,19,21]) have focused on

H. Lu et al. (Eds.): ACPR 2023, LNCS 14406, pp. 259–272, 2023.
https://doi.org/10.1007/978-3-031-47634-1_20

the classification performance of novel classes. In contrast, this paper addresses a problem called generalized few-shot learning (GFSL), which focuses on the classification performance of both base and novel classes in the joint space of these two classes. In GFSL, the model is required to learn the novel classes without forgetting the base classes already learned.

In previous research [12], a method was proposed to adopt the embedding vector of a novel training sample as the weight vector of the output unit for the novel class. However, for this method to be effective, the CNN must be trained so that the norms of the weight vectors of the final layer are normalized. Since standard CNNs do not normalize the norms of the final layer weights, retraining is required on the base class data. In other words, it must have access to a large amount of data for the base classes. In contrast, in this paper we propose a method for directly determining the weight of the output unit for the novel class from a small number of examples for standard CNNs, which do not normalize the norms of the final layer weights.

The contributions of this work are as follows: (1) a simple method to add novel classes to an already trained standard CNN, setting the weights of novel class units directly based on the embedding of the training examples, without fine-tuning the CNN; (2) an extensive study to demonstrate the GFSL performance of the proposed method on miniImageNet and tieredImageNet datasets using two different CNN models.

2   Related Work

FSL achieves low performance when using typical supervised learning methods because the model overfits to a small number of training samples. The main approaches to FSL are metric learning [9,11,19–21], meta-learning [5,10,13,16], and data augmentation [1,7,12,15,17,22]. These approaches are sometimes used in combination. Our proposed method is based on metric learning. The output of the last hidden layer of the CNN can be viewed as the output of the embedding function (i.e., embedding vector) for the CNN input.

Early work on GFSL [7] proposed a method for hallucinating additional training examples for novel classes by transferring modes of variation from the base classes. Later, Qi et al. [12] proposed an imprinting method to directly set the final layer weights of a CNN classifier for novel classes from the embeddings of training examples. Gidaris et al. [6] introduced an attention-based few-shot classification weight generator and implemented a classifier as the cosine similarity function between feature representations and classification weight vectors. In addition, Shi et al. [18] proposed a graph-convolutional global prototypical network, which models representative prototypes for all novel and base classes jointly. Furthermore, Kukleva et al. [8] proposed a three-stage framework of balancing between learning novel classes, forgetting base classes, and calibration across them. GFSL is also being studied in the problems of object detection [4] and action recognition [3].

The method proposed in this paper is closest to that outlined in [6]. In [6], the norms of the weight vectors of the final layer are normalized to unit length, and the rectified linear unit (ReLU) activation function of the last hidden layer is removed. In contrast, the method proposed in this paper does not require normalization of the weight vectors or removal of the ReLU function.

3   Method

Let $y(x)$ be the output of the last hidden layer of the CNN for input x and $w^{(i)}$ be the weight vector of the i-th class unit u_i in the final layer. In addition, let the activation function of the last hidden layer be ReLU. The output z_i of unit u_i is the inner product $\langle w, y \rangle$ of w and y. The final output of the CNN is obtained by applying the softmax function to the output from the units of the final layer. Suppose now that x_{novel} is an example of the novel class to learn. The weight vector of the base class is denoted as $w_{\text{base}}^{(i)}$ with a subscript 'base'.

Consider adding the output unit u_{novel} corresponding to the novel class to the final layer of a CNN that has already learned the base classes (see Fig. 1(a)). In previous research, noting that w and y are symmetric in the output unit, it was proposed to adopt the embedding vector $y(x_{\text{novel}})$ as the weight vector w_{novel} of the output unit u_{novel}. However, for this to be effective, the norms of w and y must be normalized to unit length so that they are symmetric. In this study, we propose a method to directly set the weight vector w_{novel} of the output units u_{novel} for standard CNNs where norm normalization is not performed.

Based on the principle of metric learning with CNN, the inner product of $y(x_q)$ and $w_{\text{base}}^{(i)}$ can be seen as the degree to which the test input x_q is the i-th base class. In addition, the inner product of $y(x_q)$ and $y(x_{\text{novel}})$ indicates the degree to which the test input x_q is the novel class for which x_{novel} is given as an example. In other words, to learn a novel class, we only need to add an output unit u_{novel} with $y(x_{\text{novel}})$ as its weight vector w_{novel}. However, to determine whether x_q is the i-th base class or the novel class, the norm of $w_{\text{base}}^{(i)}$ and $y(x_{\text{novel}})$ must be relatively normalized.

Now, let $w_{\text{base}}^{(\nu)}$ be the base class weight vector that is the nearest neighbor of $y(x_{\text{novel}})$ in terms of the inner product distance. Then, we focus on where to set the decision boundary between the novel class and the base class of $w_{\text{base}}^{(\nu)}$. When the norms of $w_{\text{base}}^{(\nu)}$ and w_{novel} are equal, the decision boundary between the base and novel classes is in the middle of $w_{\text{base}}^{(\nu)}$ and w_{novel} because the output of the output unit is the inner product of $y(x_q)$ and the weight vector. If the norm of w_{novel} is larger than that of $w_{\text{base}}^{(\nu)}$, the boundary shifts toward the novel class, whereas if it is smaller, it shifts toward the base class. Previous studies centered the boundary by normalizing the norms of the weight vectors. However, we considered the possibility of approximating this without using normalization. Specifically, we considered that we could adjust the norm of w_{novel}. In other words, this involves $w_{\text{novel}} = \alpha\, y(x_{\text{novel}})$, and adjusting the coefficient α.

A simple way to determine α is to assume that α is the average of the norm of $w_{\text{base}}^{(i)}$ over all base classes i. However, this method is not always effective, as demonstrated in Sect. 4. This is because the norm of $w_{\text{base}}^{(i)}$ varies with class i

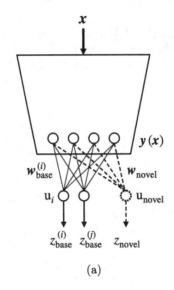

(a)

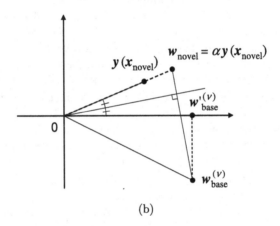

(b)

Fig. 1. Overview of the proposed method. (a) Output unit u_{novel} of the novel class is added to the final layer of the CNN, which has already learned the base class. (b) Method of determining the weight vector $\boldsymbol{w}_{novel}$ of the output unit u_{novel}. $\boldsymbol{w}_{base}^{(v)}$ is the weight vector of the base class output unit that is nearest to $\boldsymbol{y}(\boldsymbol{x}_{novel})$ in terms of the inner product distance. $\boldsymbol{w'}_{base}^{(v)}$ is a vector in which the negative elements of $\boldsymbol{w}_{base}^{(v)}$ are replaced by zero. $\boldsymbol{w}_{novel}$ is determined so that the middle of the angle between $\boldsymbol{w'}_{base}^{(v)}$ and $\boldsymbol{y}(\boldsymbol{x}_{novel})$ is the decision boundary.

(see Fig. 3(a)). Therefore, we consider focusing on the base class weight vector $\boldsymbol{w}_{\text{base}}^{(\nu)}$ that is the nearest neighbor of $\boldsymbol{y}(\boldsymbol{x}_{\text{novel}})$ in terms of the inner product distance, and set α so that the boundary is in the middle of $\boldsymbol{w}_{\text{base}}^{(\nu)}$ and $\boldsymbol{w}_{\text{novel}}$. However, this also fails to learn the novel class, as also demonstrated in Sect. 4.

We observed that good results are obtained when α is determined such that the decision boundary is the middle of the angle between $\boldsymbol{w'}_{\text{base}}^{(\nu)}$ and $\boldsymbol{y}(\boldsymbol{x}_{\text{novel}})$ as illustrated in Fig. 1(b), where $\boldsymbol{w'}_{\text{base}}^{(\nu)}$ is the vector in which the negative elements of $\boldsymbol{w}_{\text{base}}^{(\nu)}$ are replaced by zeros. The proposed method is a heuristic method; however, the reason for its effectiveness can be explained in the case of a two-dimensional space as follows. Since the last hidden layer has an activation function, ReLU, $\boldsymbol{y}$ has no negative elements. Therefore, $\boldsymbol{y}$ never enters a region where the elements of the vector are negative. Therefore, if α is determined so that the decision boundary is the middle of the angle between $\boldsymbol{w}_{\text{base}}^{(\nu)}$ and $\boldsymbol{y}(\boldsymbol{x}_{\text{novel}})$, then in the case illustrated in Fig. 2, $\boldsymbol{y}(\boldsymbol{x}_q)$ will never be assigned to the class on the $\boldsymbol{w}_{\text{base}}^{(\nu)}$ side. In contrast, the proposed method determines α so that the decision boundary is the middle of the possible angle range that $\boldsymbol{y}$ can take between $\boldsymbol{w}_{\text{base}}^{(\nu)}$ and $\boldsymbol{y}(\boldsymbol{x}_{\text{novel}})$, as illustrated in Fig. 1(b), so $\boldsymbol{y}(\boldsymbol{x}_q)$ can be assigned to the class on the $\boldsymbol{w}_{\text{base}}^{(\nu)}$ side.

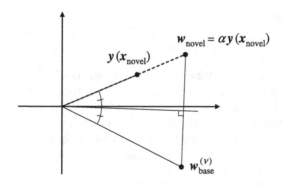

Fig. 2. If the norms of $\boldsymbol{w}_{\text{base}}^{(\nu)}$ and $\boldsymbol{w}_{\text{novel}}$ are equal, the decision boundary between the base class and novel class is the middle of the angle between $\boldsymbol{w}_{\text{base}}^{(\nu)}$ and $\boldsymbol{y}(\boldsymbol{x}_{\text{novel}})$.

Specifically, α is obtained as follows:

$$\alpha = \frac{||\boldsymbol{w}_{\text{base}}^{(\nu)}|| \cos(\theta_a - \theta_b/2)}{||\boldsymbol{y}(\boldsymbol{x}_{\text{novel}})|| \cos(\theta_b/2)}, \tag{1}$$

$$\theta_a = \cos^{-1} \frac{\langle \boldsymbol{w}_{\text{base}}^{(\nu)}, \boldsymbol{y}(\boldsymbol{x}_{\text{novel}}) \rangle}{||\boldsymbol{w}_{\text{base}}^{(\nu)}|| \, ||\boldsymbol{y}(\boldsymbol{x}_{\text{novel}})||}, \tag{2}$$

$$\theta_b = \cos^{-1} \frac{\langle \boldsymbol{w'}_{\text{base}}^{(\nu)}, \boldsymbol{y}(\boldsymbol{x}_{\text{novel}}) \rangle}{||\boldsymbol{w'}_{\text{base}}^{(\nu)}|| \, ||\boldsymbol{y}(\boldsymbol{x}_{\text{novel}})||}. \tag{3}$$

Note that θ_a is the angle between $\boldsymbol{w}_{\mathrm{base}}^{(\nu)}$ and $\boldsymbol{y}(\boldsymbol{x}_{\mathrm{novel}})$, and θ_b is the angle between $\boldsymbol{w'}_{\mathrm{base}}^{(\nu)}$ and $\boldsymbol{y}(\boldsymbol{x}_{\mathrm{novel}})$. (1) is derived from $\alpha\|\boldsymbol{y}(\boldsymbol{x}_{\mathrm{novel}})\|\cos(\theta_b/2) = \|\boldsymbol{w}_{\mathrm{base}}^{(\nu)}\|\cos(\theta_a - \theta_b/2)$.

In summary, the method proposed in this paper is as follows:

1. Determine $\boldsymbol{w}_{\mathrm{base}}^{(\nu)}$ that is the nearest neighbor of $\boldsymbol{y}(\boldsymbol{x}_{\mathrm{novel}})$ in terms of the inner product distance.
2. From $\boldsymbol{w}_{\mathrm{base}}^{(\nu)}$, $\boldsymbol{y}(\boldsymbol{x}_{\mathrm{novel}})$, and $\boldsymbol{w'}_{\mathrm{base}}^{(\nu)}$, calculate α using (1)–(3), where $\boldsymbol{w'}_{\mathrm{base}}^{(\nu)}$ is a vector in which the negative elements of $\boldsymbol{w}_{\mathrm{base}}^{(\nu)}$ are replaced by zero.
3. Add a unit $\mathrm{u}_{\mathrm{novel}}$ to the final layer with $\alpha\,\boldsymbol{y}(\boldsymbol{x}_{\mathrm{novel}})$ as $\boldsymbol{w}_{\mathrm{novel}}$.

Note that when only one $\boldsymbol{w}_{\mathrm{base}}^{(\nu)}$ of the nearest neighbor is used, it is easily affected by the fluctuation of each individual $\boldsymbol{w}_{\mathrm{base}}$. Therefore, it is preferable to use the average of the α calculated for the k nearest neighbors, $\boldsymbol{w}_{\mathrm{base}}^{(\nu_1)}, ..., \boldsymbol{w}_{\mathrm{base}}^{(\nu_k)}$, as the α to be multiplied by $\boldsymbol{y}(\boldsymbol{x}_{\mathrm{novel}})$. This is illustrated in Sect. 4. The explanation thus far assumes 1-shot task (i.e., one training sample per class); in the case of M-shot task (i.e., M training samples, $\boldsymbol{x}_{\mathrm{novel}}^{(1)}, ..., \boldsymbol{x}_{\mathrm{novel}}^{(M)}$, per class), it is preferable to apply the above method with the average of M embedding vectors, $\boldsymbol{y}(\boldsymbol{x}_{\mathrm{novel}}^{(1)}), ..., \boldsymbol{y}(\boldsymbol{x}_{\mathrm{novel}}^{(M)})$, as $\boldsymbol{y}(\boldsymbol{x}_{\mathrm{novel}})$.

4   Experiment

4.1   Datasets

Two common benchmark datasets for FSL, miniImageNet [21] and tieredImageNet [15], were used in the experiments. Both are subsets of ImageNet [2]. For miniImageNet, there were 64 base classes and 20 novel classes. We used the split used in [13]. Following [6], the training (base_train) and testing (base_test) data of the base class were 600 and 300 images per class, respectively, while the training (novel_train) and testing (novel_test) data of the novel class were M and 100 images per class, respectively.

For tieredImageNet, There were 351 base classes and 160 novel classes. The base_train and base_test were 1182 (on average) and 100 images per class, respectively, while the novel_train and novel_test were M and 1277 (on average) images per class, respectively.

In the experiment, we primarily evaluated 5-way 1-shot and 10-way 1-shot learning. In addition, we evaluated 1-way 1-shot learning with incremental learning, that is, one novel class at a time, up to 10-way. We also experimented with 5-way 5-shot. Note that N-way M-shot signifies that the number of novel classes to be learned is N and the number of training samples per class is M.

4.2   CNN Models

Conv4 and ResNet18 were used in the experiments. Conv4 is a CNN with four Conv blocks, each of which consists of a 64-channel 3×3 convolutional layer, batch normalization, ReLU, and 2×2 max-pooling. For the experiments, we used a CNN with a configuration in which two fully-connected layers were connected after the fourth Conv block. The first fully-connected layer (i.e., last hidden layer) had 512 units and the ReLU activation function. A dropout (rate $= 0.5$) was placed between the fully-connected layers.

The architecture of ResNet18 is almost identical to that of the 18-layer residual network in [10]. However, the initial 7×7 convolution is changed to 3×3. After the global average pooling, two fully-connected layers are connected. The first fully-connected layer (last hidden layer) has 512 units and the ReLU activation function.

4.3 Training Method

Both Conv4 and ResNet18 were trained from scratch by base_train with cross-entropy loss using mini-batch stochastic gradient descent with momentum and weight decay. The momentum was set to 0.9, while the weight decay was set to 5×10^{-4}.

The learning rate for Conv4 was 10^{-3} for 60 epochs, then 10^{-4} for 10 epochs, and 10^{-5} for 10 epochs, for both datasets. The learning rate for ResNet18 was 10^{-2} for 60 epochs, then 10^{-3} for 10 epochs, and 10^{-4} for 10 epochs for tieredImageNet. For miniImageNet, the learning rate for ResNet18 was 3×10^{-2} for 60 epochs, 10^{-3} for 10 epochs, and 10^{-4} for 10 epochs. When training these CNNs, we applied the common data augmentation methods of random crop, horizontal flip, rotation, density variation, and jitter to the training data.

4.4 Evaluation Metrics

In GFSL, high accuracy is required for both base and novel classes, and there is generally a trade-off between the two. Therefore, the harmonic mean (hm/J) and arithmetic mean (am/J) of the accuracy of base_test and novel_test in the joint space of the base and novel classes are commonly used as representative evaluation metrics. They are also used in this study, and the results are reported in Sect. 4.5.

4.5 Experimental Results

Tables 1 and 2 present the experimental results for (a) miniImageNet and (b) tieredImageNet. The upper side of each table displays the results for Conv4, while the lower side displays the results for ResNet18. N/N and B/B denote the correct rates for novel_test in the novel class space and base_test in the base class space, respectively. N/J and B/J denote the correct rates of novel_test and base_test in the joint space of base and novel classes, respectively. Furthermore, hm/J and am/J denote the harmonic and arithmetic means of N/J and B/J, respectively. As mentioned above, we focus on hm/J and am/J as measures of accuracy.

Table 1. Experimental results on miniImageNet and tieredImageNet for 5-way 1-shot learning

(a) miniImageNet

		Accuracy (%)					
		N/N (5/5)	B/B (64/64)	N/J (5/69)	B/J (64/69)	hm/J	am/J
Conv4	Ours-1	53.54	64.16	39.61	51.38	**44.73**	**45.49**
	Ours-5	53.69	64.16	39.20	52.06	**44.72**	**45.63**
	ComparisonA	53.69	64.16	28.52	58.77	38.40	43.65
	ComparisonB	53.69	64.16	47.44	40.75	43.84	44.09
	ComparisonC	53.32	64.16	46.57	41.37	43.81	43.97
ResNet18	Ours-1	61.56	78.63	53.03	62.81	57.51	57.92
	Ours-5	62.08	78.63	53.01	63.73	**57.88**	**58.37**
	ComparisonA	61.91	78.63	4.59	78.43	8.66	41.51
	ComparisonB	61.91	78.63	58.62	51.70	54.94	55.16
	ComparisonC	61.50	78.63	58.17	51.56	54.67	54.86

(b) tieredImgNet

		Accuracy (%)					
		N/N (5/5)	B/B (351/351)	N/J (5/356)	B/J (351/356)	hm/J	am/J
Conv4	Ours-1	57.65	40.09	41.77	34.82	**37.98**	38.29
	Ours-5	58.09	40.09	40.98	35.40	**37.99**	38.19
	ComparisonA	58.38	40.09	52.96	26.78	35.57	39.87
	ComparisonB	58.38	40.09	51.94	28.14	36.51	**40.04**
	ComparisonC	57.10	40.09	50.05	28.40	36.24	39.22
ResNet18	Ours-1	65.68	68.11	64.47	41.24	50.30	52.86
	Ours-5	67.49	68.11	66.20	42.64	**51.87**	**54.42**
	ComparisonA	68.25	68.11	67.41	38.93	49.36	53.17
	ComparisonB	68.25	68.11	68.03	28.02	39.70	48.03
	ComparisonC	65.26	68.11	65.02	26.49	37.64	45.75

In Tables 1 and 2, Ours-1 and Ours-5 refer to the results of the proposed method: Ours-1 is the case where α is calculated from one nearest neighbor $w_{\text{base}}^{(\nu)}$, while Ours-5 is the case where instead of one nearest neighbor $w_{\text{base}}^{(\nu)}$, the average of five α is calculated for the neighborhoods $w_{\text{base}}^{(\nu_1)}$ to $w_{\text{base}}^{(\nu_5)}$. Tables 1 and 2 also display the results of three comparison methods. ComparisonA is the case where α is fixed at 1, while ComparisonB is the case where α is the average

Table 2. Experimental results on miniImageNet and tieredImageNet for 10-way 1-shot learning

(a) miniImageNet

		Accuracy (%)					
		N/N (5/5)	B/B (64/64)	N/J (5/69)	B/J (64/69)	hm/J	am/J
Conv4	Ours-1	53.54	64.16	39.61	51.38	**44.73**	**45.49**
	Ours-5	53.69	64.16	39.20	52.06	**44.72**	**45.63**
	ComparisonA	53.69	64.16	28.52	58.77	38.40	43.65
	ComparisonB	53.69	64.16	47.44	40.75	43.84	44.09
	ComparisonC	53.32	64.16	46.57	41.37	43.81	43.97
ResNet18	Ours-1	61.56	78.63	53.03	62.81	57.51	57.92
	Ours-5	62.08	78.63	53.01	63.73	**57.88**	**58.37**
	ComparisonA	61.91	78.63	4.59	78.43	8.66	41.51
	ComparisonB	61.91	78.63	58.62	51.70	54.94	55.16
	ComparisonC	61.50	78.63	58.17	51.56	54.67	54.86

(b) tieredImgNet

		Accuracy (%)					
		N/N (5/5)	B/B (351/351)	N/J (5/356)	B/J (351/356)	hm/J	am/J
Conv4	Ours-1	57.65	40.09	41.77	34.82	**37.98**	38.29
	Ours-5	58.09	40.09	40.98	35.40	**37.99**	38.19
	ComparisonA	58.38	40.09	52.96	26.78	35.57	39.87
	ComparisonB	58.38	40.09	51.94	28.14	36.51	**40.04**
	ComparisonC	57.10	40.09	50.05	28.40	36.24	39.22
ResNet18	Ours-1	65.68	68.11	64.47	41.24	50.30	52.86
	Ours-5	67.49	68.11	66.20	42.64	**51.87**	**54.42**
	ComparisonA	68.25	68.11	67.41	38.93	49.36	53.17
	ComparisonB	68.25	68.11	68.03	28.02	39.70	48.03
	ComparisonC	65.26	68.11	65.02	26.49	37.64	45.75

of the norm of all $w_{\text{base}}^{(i)}$. ComparisonC is the case where the negative elements of $w_{\text{base}}^{(\nu)}$ are not replaced by zero. Note that ComparisonA, ComparisonB, and ComparisonC all use one nearest neighbor $w_{\text{base}}^{(\nu)}$.

Tables 1 and 2 indicate that the accuracy, hm/J and am/J, is higher for Ours-1, and Ours-5 than for the comparison methods in most cases. Moreover, the accuracy of Ours-5 is higher than that of Ours-1. The higher accuracy of

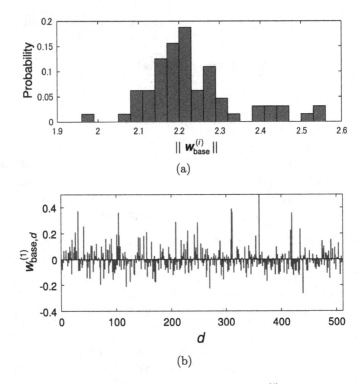

Fig. 3. (a) Distribution of the norm of the weight vector $w_{\text{base}}^{(i)}$ over all i and (b) value of each dimension d of the weight vector $w_{\text{base}}^{(1)}$ as an example of $w_{\text{base}}^{(i)}$, for the case of miniImageNet+ResNet.

Table 3. Comparison with existing studies for 5-way 1-shot learning on miniImageNet

		Accuracy (%)					
		N/N (5/5)	B/B (64/64)	N/J (5/69)	B/J (64/69)	hm/J	am/J
Conv4	Ours-5	53.69	64.16	39.20	52.06	44.72	45.63
	PN [19]†	53.88	54.02	0.02	54.02	0.04	27.02
	DFSL [6]†	55.80	69.93	40.30	58.54	**47.74**	**49.42**
	RGFSL [18]	55.08	65.14	39.86	54.65	46.10	47.25
ResNet	Ours-5	62.08	78.63	53.01	63.73	**57.88**	**58.37**
	IW [12]‡	47.17	61.78	31.25	47.72	37.77	39.49
	DFSL [6]‡	56.83	70.15	41.32	58.04	48.27	49.68
	AAN [14]‡	56.14	77.58	45.61	63.92	53.24	54.76
	LCwoF lim [8]	60.78	79.89	53.78	62.89	57.39	57.84

† Results from [18]. ‡ Results from [8]

Ours-1 than that of ComparisonC indicates that setting the negative element of $w_{\text{base}}^{(\nu)}$ to zero has a positive effect. ComparisonA and ComparisonB have higher am/J than that of Ours-1 in some cases, but are less accurate than Ours-1 in

Table 4. Comparison with existing studies for 5-way 5-shot learning on miniImageNet

		Accuracy (%)					
		N/N (5/5)	B/B (64/64)	N/J (5/69)	B/J (64/69)	hm/J	am/J
ResNet	Ours-5	75.78	78.63	63.05	68.98	**65.88**	**66.01**
	IW [12][‡]	67.56	69.07	46.96	58.92	52.26	52.94
	DFSL [6][‡]	72.82	70.03	59.27	58.68	58.97	58.98
	AAN [14][‡]	69.72	77.58	60.82	64.14	62.43	62.48
	LCwoF lim [8]	77.65	79.96	68.58	64.53	**66.49**	**66.55**

[‡] Results from [8]

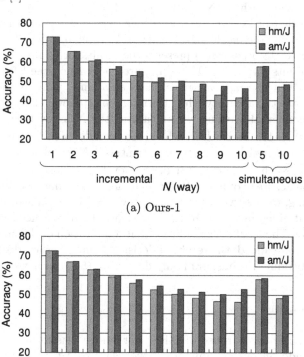

(a) Ours-1

(b) Ours-5

Fig. 4. Results of incremental learning by 1-way 1-shot for the case of miniImageNet+ResNet18.

many other cases and for hm/J; therefore, ComparisonA, and ComparisonB are not always effective.

Figure 3(a) presents the distribution of the norm of $w_{\text{base}}^{(i)}$ over all i for miniImageNet+ResNet as an example. In this case, the mean of the norm of $w_{\text{base}}^{(i)}$

is 2.23. Figure 3(b) presents the values of the elements of each dimension d of $w_{\text{base}}^{(1)}$ as an example of $w_{\text{base}}^{(i)}$ for the case of miniImageNet+ResNet. As the figure illustrates, many elements of $w_{\text{base}}^{(i)}$ take negative values.

Tables 3 and 4 present a comparison with the results of existing studies. Note that 5-way 5-shot uses a method in which the average of the five embedded vectors, $y(x_{\text{novel}}^{(1)})$ to $y(x_{\text{novel}}^{(5)})$, is used as $y(x_{\text{novel}})$. In the case of 5-way 1-shot learning on miniImageNet illustrated in Table 3, the accuracy of Ours-5 is not as high as that of DFSL or RGFSL in the case of Conv4; however, in the case of ResNet, the accuracy of Ours-5 is higher than that of the other methods. In the case of 5-way 5-shot with ResNet displayed in Table 4, the accuracy of Ours-5 is comparable to that of LCwoF lim and higher than that of the other methods.

Figure 4 presents the results of incremental learning by 1-way 1-shot for mini-ImageNet+ResNet18. Figure 4(a) presents the results for Ours-1, while Fig. 4(b) presents the results for Ours-5. In both figures, 1 to 10 on the left side indicate the accuracy when learning one novel class at a time, while 5 and 10 on the right side indicate the accuracy when learning 5 or 10 novel classes at a time. In the case of incremental learning, when learning the Nth novel class, the weight vector of the $N-1$th novel class, which has already been learned, is a $w_{\text{base}}^{(i)}$. In the non-incremental learning case, in contrast, N novel classes are learned simultaneously, so the weight vector of the novel class does not become $w_{\text{base}}^{(i)}$. Comparing the accuracy of 5 and 10 for incremental learning and that for simultaneous learning, we observe that the accuracy of incremental learning is slightly lower than that of learning 5 or 10 classes at once; however, the accuracy is generally the same. The results also indicate that a limitation of this method is that as novel classes are added, the resulting decision boundaries are distributed over very close embedding regions, gradually degrading the accuracy of the network.

5   Conclusion

In this paper, for the purpose of GFSL for image classification, we propose a method to add an output unit of a novel class to a CNN that has already been trained on the base class and directly set the weight vector. The proposed method does not require the norms of the weight vectors of the final layer of the CNN to be normalized. The proposed method is applicable also to simultaneous and incremental learning of multiple novel classes. Experiments on Conv4 and ResNet18 using miniImageNet and tieredImageNet demonstrated the effectiveness of the proposed method.

References

1. Chen, Z., Fu, Y., Wang, Y.X., Ma, L., Liu, W., Hebert, M.: Image deformation meta-networks for one-shot learning. In: 2019 IEEE/CVF Conference on Computer Vision and Pattern Recognition, pp. 8672–8681 (2019)
2. Deng, J., Dong, W., Socher, R., Li, L.J., Li, K., Fei-Fei, L.: Imagenet: a large-scale hierarchical image database. In: 2009 IEEE Conference on Computer Vision and Pattern Recognition, pp. 248–255 (2009)
3. Dwivedi, S.K., Gupta, V., Mitra, R., Ahmed, S., Jain, A.: Protogan: towards few shot learning for action recognition. In: 2019 IEEE/CVF International Conference on Computer Vision Workshop, pp. 1308–1316 (2019)
4. Fan, Z., Ma, Y., Li, Z., Sun, J.: Generalized few-shot object detection without forgetting. In: 2021 IEEE/CVF Conference on Computer Vision and Pattern Recognition, pp. 4525–4534 (2021)
5. Finn, C., Abbeel, P., Levine, S.: Model-agnostic meta-learning for fast adaptation of deep networks. In: Proceedings of the 34th International Conference on Machine Learning. Proceedings of Machine Learning Research, vol. 70, pp. 1126–1135 (2017)
6. Gidaris, S., Komodakis, N.: Dynamic few-shot visual learning without forgetting. In: 2018 IEEE/CVF Conference on Computer Vision and Pattern Recognition, pp. 4367–4375 (2018)
7. Hariharan, B., Girshick, R.: Low-shot visual recognition by shrinking and hallucinating features. In: 2017 IEEE International Conference on Computer Vision, pp. 3037–3046 (2017)
8. Kukleva, A., Kuehne, H., Schiele, B.: Generalized and incremental few-shot learning by explicit learning and calibration without forgetting. In: 2021 IEEE/CVF International Conference on Computer Vision (2021)
9. Li, W., Wang, L., Xu, J., Huo, J., Gao, Y., Luo, J.: Revisiting local descriptor based image-to-class measure for few-shot learning. In: 2019 IEEE/CVF Conference on Computer Vision and Pattern Recognition, pp. 7253–7260 (2019)
10. Li, Z., Zhou, F., Chen, F., Li, H.: Meta-SGD: learning to learn quickly for few-shot learning, arXiv preprint, arXiv:1707.09835 (2017)
11. Oreshkin, B., Rodríguez López, P., Lacoste, A.: Tadam: task dependent adaptive metric for improved few-shot learning. In: Advances in Neural Information Processing Systems, vol. 31, pp. 721–731 (2018)
12. Qi, H., Brown, M., Lowe, D.G.: Low-shot learning with imprinted weights. In: 2018 IEEE/CVF Conference on Computer Vision and Pattern Recognition, pp. 5822–5830 (2018)
13. Ravi, S., Larochelle, H.: Optimization as a model for few-shot learning. In: International Conference on Learning Representations (2017)
14. Ren, M., Liao, R., Fetaya, E., Zemel, R.: Incremental few-shot learning with attention attractor networks. In: Advances in Neural Information Processing Systems, vol. 32 (2019)
15. Ren, M., et al.: Meta-learning for semi-supervised few-shot classification. In: International Conference on Learning Representations (2018)
16. Rusu, A.A., et al.: Meta-learning with latent embedding optimization. In: International Conference on Learning Representations (2019)
17. Schwartz, E., et al.: Delta-encoder: an effective sample synthesis method for few-shot object recognition. In: Advances in Neural Information Processing Systems, vol. 31 (2018)

18. Shi, X., Salewski, L., Schiegg, M., Welling, M.: Relational generalized few-shot learning. In: The 31st British Machine Vision Virtual Conference (2020)
19. Snell, J., Swersky, K., Zemel, R.: Prototypical networks for few-shot learning. In: Advances in Neural Information Processing Systems, vol. 30, pp. 4077–4087 (2017)
20. Sung, F., Yang, Y., Zhang, L., Xiang, T., Torr, P.H., Hospedales, T.M.: Learning to compare: relation network for few-shot learning. In: 2018 IEEE/CVF Conference on Computer Vision and Pattern Recognition, pp. 1199–1208 (2018)
21. Vinyals, O., Blundell, C., Lillicrap, T., kavukcuoglu, k., Wierstra, D.: Matching networks for one shot learning. In: Advances in Neural Information Processing Systems, vol. 29, pp. 3630–3638 (2016)
22. Wang, Y.X., Girshick, R., Hebert, M., Hariharan, B.: Low-shot learning from imaginary data. In: 2018 IEEE/CVF Conference on Computer Vision and Pattern Recognition, pp. 7278–7286 (2018)

ET-HDR: An Efficient Two-Stage Network for Specular Highlight Detection and Removal

Yuyang Lin[1,2], Yan Yang[1,2(✉)], Yongquan Jiang[1,2], Xiaobo Zhang[1,2],
and Pengyun Song[3]

[1] School of Computing and Artificial Intelligence, Southwest Jiaotong University,
Chengdu 611756, People's Republic of China
linyuyang2333@my.swjtu.edu.cn, yyang@swjtu.edu.cn
[2] Engineering Research Center of Sustainable Urban Intelligent Transportation,
Ministry of Education, Chengdu 611756, People's Republic of China
[3] School of Electrical Engineering, Southwest Minzu University, Chengdu 610225,
People's Republic of China

Abstract. The detection and removal of specular highlights is a critical issue in computer vision and image processing tasks. In this paper, we propose an efficient end-to-end deep learning model named ET-HDR for automatically detecting and removing specular highlights in a single image. Specifically, the model consists of two stages. Firstly, the first stage employs a U-shaped network structure composed of efficient transformer modules to learn the context features of different scales in the highlight image. Subsequently, the second stage utilizes a channel attention refinement module that preserves the original image resolution to learn spatial detail information in the image, further extracting and refining highlight features. Simultaneously, an inter-stage feature fusion mechanism is introduced to enrich the feature information. Ultimately, the model extracts an accurate range and color representation of highlight features, which can generate precise and natural highlight-free images through simple convolution operations. Experiments on the publicly available Specular Highlight Detection and Removal Dataset (SHIQ) demonstrate that our approach outperforms current state-of-the-art methods in specular highlight detection and removal tasks.

Keywords: Deep Learning · Highlight Detection · Highlight Removal

1 Introduction

Specular highlighting is a prevalent physical phenomenon in the real world, which often occurs on the surface of objects with highly reflective materials and presents a high-gloss bright spot. However, such highlights usually bring interference and uncertainty to the content of images, which can affect some computer vision and image processing tasks and degrade the performance of the tasks, including object detection, text recognition, and so on. Therefore, how to efficiently detect and remove specular highlights from images has become an important issue in computer vision research.

H. Lu et al. (Eds.): ACPR 2023, LNCS 14406, pp. 273–287, 2023.
https://doi.org/10.1007/978-3-031-47634-1_21

In recent decades, many methods have been proposed to solve the challenging problem of specular highlight detection and removal. For specular detection, most existing methods detect various forms of pixel thresholds to determine whether an area is a specular region [1, 2]. These methods have the assumption that light is white and highlights are made up of the brightest series of pixels. Therefore, these methods cannot eliminate the semantic ambiguity between white (or near-white) materials and highlights in complex real-world scenes, resulting in the inability to accurately locate highlights. For highlight removal, the traditional methods usually remove highlights based on different constraints or assumptions, such as using color space [3, 4] or polarization information [5]. Because these methods are designed for specific scenes or materials, they are difficult to apply to more complex real-world images. Recently, some methods have begun to utilize deep learning-based methods [6–10] to remove specular highlights from a single image. However, most existing methods typically only use single-stage model structures to extract highlight features without further refinement, resulting in some generated highlight-free images that exhibit incomplete highlight removal in highlight regions and the presence of artifacts in non-highlight regions.

In this paper, we propose a novel two-stage network model structure for joint highlight detection and removal, named the Efficient Two-stage Highlight Detection and Removal network (ET-HDR). ET-HDR consists of an efficient transformer U-Net module, an efficient Channel Attention Refinement Network (CARNet), and some convolutional modules. Inspired by [11], to reduce the model complexity, an efficient channel-spatial attention module is designed to learn highlight attention features and an efficient channel attention block (CAB) is designed in CARNet to learn spatial details. Additionally, a feature fusion mechanism is developed that allows the model to fully utilize the feature at each stage. Ultimately, ET-HDR can generate an accurate highlight mask image and a natural highlight-removed image. To address the issue of imbalanced highlight and non-highlight regions in the image, the varifocal loss function [19] is used to calculate the loss, which focuses the model more on the highlight regions during training. The contributions of this paper can be summarized as follows:

- A two-stage highlight detection and removal model that learns and fuses feature information at different stages to obtain a highlight feature that is rich in context and accurate in spatial information.
- An efficient transformer structure and a highlight refinement network that can help the model extract accurate highlight features quickly and effectively.
- Using and demonstrating the effectiveness of the varifocal loss function in improving the model's highlight detection ability, leading to better overall training performance of the model.
- Experimental results on the benchmark dataset SHIQ demonstrate that the model outperforms existing state-of-the-art algorithms in single-image highlight detection and removal tasks.

The remainder of this paper is structured as follows: Sect. 2 briefly overviews related work in highlight detection and removal; Sect. 3 describes the details of the proposed method; Sect. 4 presents the experimental results; Sect. 5 provides the conclusion.

2 Related Works

2.1 Highlight Detection

In early research on highlight detection, some color constancy-based highlight detection methods were proposed by [13]. Zhang et al. [2] defined highlight detection as a non-negative matrix factorization (NMF) problem based on the assumption that the number of specular highlights is small. Li et al. [1] presented an adaptive robust principal component analysis (RPCA) method to robustly detect specular highlights in endoscopic image sequences. While these methods are effective and easy to implement, they mistakenly recognize objects with a white appearance or high-intensity pixels as highlights. Recently, Fu et al. [14] proposed a large-scale dataset for specular highlight detection in real-world images. Based on this dataset, they also proposed a deep neural network that utilizes multi-scale contextual contrast features for highlight detection. And the proposed methods have significantly improved the accuracy of high light detection compared to these methods.

2.2 Highlight Removal

Based on Traditional Methods. Akashi et al. [15] optimized the sparse non-negative matrix factorization (NMF) method and separated the specular reflection component using an improved sparse NMF method. Guo et al. [16] used a sparse and low-rank reflection model to remove highlights and improved the robustness of the model by imposing non-negative constraints on the weighted matrix. However, these methods cannot differentiate white objects from highlight areas at the semantic level, resulting in artifacts or distortions in non-highlight areas in some of the generated results. Subsequently, some researchers began to study the use of polarization information to process highlights. Nayar et al. [17] obtained constraints on the reflection components for each pixel by simultaneously using color and polarization information to separate the diffuse reflection component. However, these methods are only applicable to certain specific scenarios, and in real-world scenarios, some specular highlights cannot be completely removed.

Based on Deep Learning Methods. Recently, deep learning-based methods have been widely used for removing specular highlights in single images. Fu et al. [8] proposed a Joint Specular Highlight Detection and Removal (JSHDR) model, which extracts highlight features at different scales in an image through a dilated spatial contextual feature aggregation (DSCFA) module, and then generates corresponding highlight mask, highlight intensity map, and non-highlight map based on the extracted features. Wu et al. [10] captured global contextual information of channel direction by using a distribution-based channel attention module to remove highlights. Although many methods based on deep learning have been proposed, the existing methods still have problems such as highlight residue and color difference in real-world images. Compared to these methods, the proposed methods can effectively solve these problems.

3 Proposed Method

In this paper, we propose an end-to-end network architecture for joint detection and removal of highlights in real-world images. Given an input image with highlights, the ultimate goal is to detect the location of highlights, recover the highlight regions, and generate corresponding highlight mask images and highlight-removed images. The model consists of two main stages: U-Net and CARNet, as illustrated in Fig. 1. The details of the proposed network architecture and loss functions are presented below.

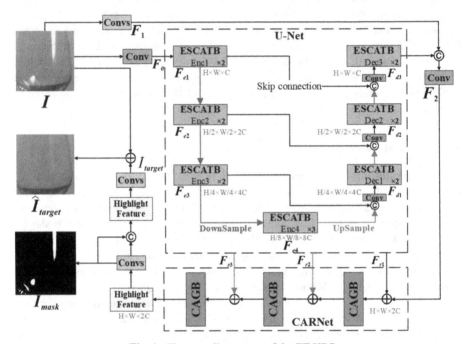

Fig. 1. The overall structure of the ET-HDR.

3.1 Overall Pipeline

Given a highlight image $I \in R^{H \times W \times 3}$, ET-HDR first applies convolution to obtain the low-level feature embedding $F_0 \in R^{H \times W \times C}$, where $H \times W$ represents the spatial dimensions of the image, and C denotes the number of channels. Subsequently, the feature F_0 is processed by the first-stage U-shaped network, generating encoder features $E[F_{e1}, F_{e2}, F_{e3}, F_{e4}]$ and decoder features $D[F_{d1}, F_{d2}, F_{d3}]$ separately. To facilitate the model's learning of contextual features, encoder features E are connected to decoder features D via skip connections. Then, by employing convolution for feature encoding of image I, feature F_1 is obtained, and F_1 is concatenated with F_{d3} to produce feature F_2, which is fed into the second-stage CARNet. Simultaneously, the fused feature $R[F_{r1}, F_{r2}, F_{r3}]$, derived from feature E and feature D through upsampling and convolution operations, is incorporated into the second stage, yielding the final highlight feature $F_{highlight} \in R^{H \times W \times 2C}$. Lastly, a convolution operation is performed on $F_{highlight}$ to generate the corresponding mask image I_{mask} and highlight residual image I_{target}. The final de-highlighted image is denoted as $\hat{I}_{target} = I + I_{target}$.

3.2 U-Net

In the first stage, the U-shaped structure mentioned in [12] is used and the MDTA module in its transformer module was replaced with an efficiency spatial channel attention block (ESCAB). The final first stage of the network consists of ESCATB and GDFN [12], whose module structure is shown in Fig. 2.

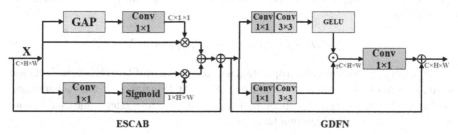

Fig. 2. Efficient Transformer module structure, including Efficiency Space-Channel Attention Block (ESCAB) and Gated-Dconv Feed-Forward Network (GDFN) [12].

Efficiency Space-Channel Attention Block (ESCAB). To reduce computational resources and improve the inference speed of the model, an efficient attention module is designed as shown on the left side of Fig. 2. Given a feature $X \in R^{H \times W \times C}$, this module performs spatial attention and channel attention operations on X separately. Inspired by [11], unnecessary operations such as convolutions and activation functions are removed in generating attention weights, and simple operations are used to obtain effective attention weights. Then, X is multiplied with these two weights separately to obtain the channel attention output $CA(X)$ and spatial attention output $SA(X)$, and finally fuse these two results through an addition operation and obtain the output of the module $Att(X)$ through a residual connection. Overall, the process of ESCAB can be defined as:

$$CA(X) = X * Conv_{1 \times 1}(GAP(X)) \tag{1}$$

$$SA(X) = X * Sigmoid(Conv_{1 \times 1}(X)) \tag{2}$$

$$Att(X) = CA(X) + SA(X) + X \tag{3}$$

where $Conv_{1 \times 1}$ is the convolution operation with a kernel size of 1, $GAP()$ is a global average pooling operation, and $Sigmoid()$ is a Sigmoid activation function.

3.3 CARNet

In the second stage, a channel attention refinement network (CARNet) is designed, which contains a channel attention group block (CAGB) and a feature fusion block (FFB).

Channel Attention Group Block (CAGB). As shown in Fig. 3, a CAGB consists of multiple channel attention blocks (CAB) and a convolution. The structure of a CAB is shown in Fig. 3, and the process of CAB can be defined as:

$$CAB(X) = Conv_{1\times1}(CA(SG(DW_{3\times3}(X)))) + X \tag{4}$$

where $DW_{3\times3}$ is a deep detachable convolution operation with core 3, $SG()$ is a gated operation [11], CA represents the expression in Eq. (1). Then, the process of CAGB can be defined as:

$$CAGB(X) = Conv_{1\times1}(CAB_{1\rightarrow n}(X)) + X \tag{5}$$

where $Conv_{1\times1}$ is the convolution operation with a kernel size of 1 and N is the calculation through several CABs, where n = 4 in this paper. CAGB mainly uses channel attention mechanism to learn spatial details of the feature map that integrates contextual feature information, refining the highlight features.

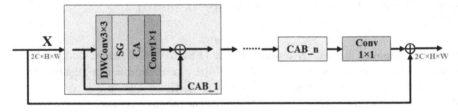

Fig. 3. Channel attention group block (CAGB)

Feature Fusion Block (FFB). As shown in Fig. 4, this module mainly uses upsampling and convolution operations to reshape the encoder and decoder features of each layer in the first stage into $H \times W \times 2C$. In order to avoid increasing too much computational cost, we design to fuse the obtained features through addition operation.

3.4 Loss Function

Loss of Highlight Detection. The specular highlight detection task can be viewed as a binary classification problem. The binary cross-entropy (BCE) loss function is commonly used to solve binary classification problems and is also often used in computer vision tasks such as edge detection and semantic segmentation. However, for specular highlight detection, the highlight region typically only occupies a small portion of the entire image. If using BCE loss, there will be an issue of imbalanced positive samples (highlight region) and negative samples (non-highlight region). Therefore, we consider

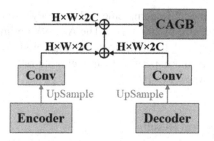

Fig. 4. Feature fusion block (FFB)

using the varifocal loss [19], which can reduce the proportion of negative samples during training, allowing the model to more accurately detect the highlight region. The definition of this loss function is as follows:

$$L_{varifocal}(p, q) = \begin{cases} -log(p)q = 1 \\ -\alpha p^\gamma log(1 - p)q = 0 \end{cases} \tag{6}$$

where p represents the predicted value of the highlight region pixel, q represents the true value of the highlight region pixel, and α and γ are hyperparameters. In this paper, $\alpha = 0.75$ and $\gamma = 2.0$.

Highlight Removal Loss. For specular highlight removal, we use the more stable and robust charbonnier loss [20] to calculate the loss. The definition of this loss function is as follows:

$$L_{char}(y, \bar{y}) = \frac{1}{N} \sum_{i=1}^{N} \rho(y - \bar{y}) \tag{7}$$

$$\rho(x) = \sqrt{x^2 + \varepsilon^2} \tag{8}$$

where y represents the generated non-highlight image, $\bar{y}$ represents the ground truth, ρ represents the penalty function and ε is a constant. In this paper, $\varepsilon = 10^{-4}$.

Overall Loss. The total loss function is defined as:

$$Loss = \lambda_1 L_{varifocal} + \lambda_2 L_{char} \tag{9}$$

where in our experiments, $\lambda_1 = 0.02$ and $\lambda_2 = 1.0$.

4 Experiments

4.1 Implementation Details

Dataset. The model was trained on the SHIQ dataset [8], which consists of 9,825 training instances and 1,000 testing instances. Each instance is accompanied by an input image (highlight image), a target image (non-highlight image), a highlight intensity image, and a highlight mask image. Among them, highlight images and non-highlight images are manually collected from the same perspective. And the dataset contains a large number of reflective materials such as metal, plastic, glass and so on. All images in this dataset have a resolution of 200×200.

Training Settings. The model was implemented using PyTorch on NVIDIA GeForce 3090, with an image input size of 200×200. The AdamW optimizer [21] was used for the network with a batch size of 4, and the total training iterations were 300, which took approximately 20 hours. In our experiments, the learning rate was set to 10^{-4} and the weight decay coefficient was set to 10^{-4}.

4.2 Detection and Removal Results

Figure 5 shows the highlights detection and removal results of some representative images selected from the SHIQ dataset. The examples in the figure include objects with different materials, such as transparent plastic, glass, and metal. From the Fig. 5, it noted that the proposed model can not only accurately locate highlight points, but also effectively remove them from these objects.

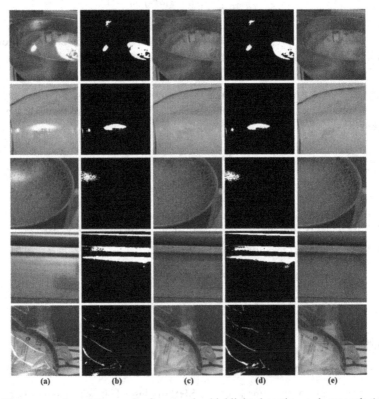

Fig. 5. The proposed model's results for specular highlight detection and removal: (a) input images, (b) ground-truth masks of the specular highlights, (c) ground-truth diffuse images, (d) detection results of the proposed method, and (e) our removal results of the proposed method.

4.3   Comparisons

Highlight Detection
We first compare the highlight detection results of the proposed method with those of previous methods, including traditional methods [1, 2] and most advanced methods based on deep learning [8, 14, 18]. For quantitative evaluation metrics, two commonly used evaluation indicators are used: detection accuracy (Acc) and balanced error rate (BER). They are defined by the following equations:

$$Acc = \frac{TP + TN}{TP + TN + FP + FN} \qquad (10)$$

$$BER = \frac{1}{2}\left(\frac{FP}{TN + FP} + \frac{FN}{TN + TP}\right) \qquad (11)$$

where TP, TN, FP, and FN represent the numbers of true positives, true negatives, false positives, and false negatives, respectively. Higher accuracy and lower BER indicate better detection results. Table 1 reports the quantitative comparison of the proposed method with previous methods on highlight detection results in the SHIQ testing set. The data in the Table 1 shows that the proposed method achieved the best results in terms of accuracy, while the proposed method performed slightly worse in terms of BER.

Table 1. Quantitative comparison of the proposed method with state-of-the-art highlight detection methods on the SHIQ dataset.

Methods	Acc ↑	BER ↓
NMF [1]	0.70	18.8
ATA [2]	0.71	24.4
SHDN [14]	0.91	6.18
JSHDR [8]	0.93	5.92
Wu [18]	0.97	**5.92**
Ours	**0.99**	7.21

Highlight Removal
Quantitative Comparison. We compare the proposed methods with other methods for removing highlights, including traditional methods [15, 16, 22–26] and the recent methods based on deep learning [6–10, 27–29]. For this part of the quantitative evaluation index, PSNR and SSM [30] are used to compare different methods for highlight removal. They are defined by the following equations:

$$PSNR = 10 \cdot log_{10}\left(\frac{MAX^2}{MSE}\right) \qquad (12)$$

$$SSIM\,(x, y) = \frac{\left(2\mu_x\mu_y + c_1\right)\left(2\sigma_{xy} + c_2\right)}{\left(\mu_x^2 + \mu_y^2 + c_1\right)\left(\sigma_x^2 + \sigma_y^2 + c_2\right)} \tag{13}$$

where MAX represents the maximum possible pixel value of the image, and MSE denotes the mean squared error between the generated and target images. x and y are the two images being compared, μ_x and μ_y are their respective means, σ_x and σ_y represent their standard deviations, σ_{xy} is the covariance of x and y, and c_1 and c_2 are constants to prevent division by zero. In general, the larger the PSNR and SSM scores, the better the removal results. Table 2 reports the quantitative results of the proposed method for highlight removal on the SHIQ test set. The results from the table show that the proposed method has better PSNR and SSM scores than all the methods being compared.

Table 2. The proposed method is quantitatively compared with the state-of-the-art highlight removal methods on the SHIQ dataset. The best results are highlighted in bold.

Methods	PSNR ↑	SSIM ↑
Tan [22]	11.04	0.400
Shen [23]	13.90	0.420
Yang [24]	14.31	0.500
Akashi [15]	14.01	0.520
Shi [25]	18.21	0.610
Guo [16]	17.18	0.580
Multi-class GAN [6]	27.63	0.885
Yamamoto [26]	19.54	0.630
SPEC [7]	19.56	0.690
Yi [27]	21.32	0.720
Wu [10]	28.24	0.941
JSHDR [8]	34.13	0.860
Cycle-GAN [9]	30.94	0.970
Huang [28]	35.72	0.910
Bifurcated-CNN [29]	31.68	0.972
Ours	**37.27**	**0.976**

Visual Comparison. Figure 6 shows the results of highlight removal using different methods on the dataset. From the results, it noted that the traditional methods of removing highlights ((c), (d), (e) in the Fig. 6) either do not remove highlights effectively, or produce large areas of color distortion. In contrast, the deep learning-based highlight removal methods ((f), (g), (h) in the Fig. 6) can effectively remove highlights and generate natural non-highlight images. Compared with the other two advanced methods based on deep learning, the proposed method has the following advantages: From the results in the yellow box in the first row, it noted that the proposed method can effectively distinguish the semantic ambiguity between white or light objects and highlights, while (f) and (g) both mistakenly recognize the white cup walls as highlights; From the results in the second line of the green box, it noted that the proposed method can remove the highlight areas completely, and (f) and (g) there are some highlight residues; From the results in the third line of the red box, it noted that the proposed method produces more natural results, while non-highlight images generated by (f) and (g) have some color distortion.

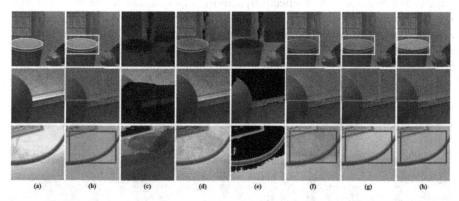

(a)   (b)   (c)   (d)   (e)   (f)   (g)   (h)

Fig. 6. Visual comparison examples of highlight removal methods on the SHIQ dataset: (a) input, (b) ground truth, and (c) Tan [22], (d) Akashi [15], (e) Yamamoto [26], (f) JSHDR [8], (g) Huang [28], (h) proposed method.

Efficiency

In terms of performance efficiency, the proposed method is compared with other deep learning-based highlight removal methods. Parameters (M), GFLOPs, and FPS are used for quantitative evaluation. Table 3 reports a quantitative comparison of the proposed method with other methods in terms of speed. As can be seen from the data in the table, the proposed method can effectively detect and remove bright light.

Table 3. The proposed method is compared in efficiency with other methods, all of which run on the i9-12900K RTX3090.

Method	Param (M)↓	GFLOPs ↓	FPS ↑	PSNR ↑
JSHDR [8]	54.29	416.26	0.4	34.13
Huang [28]	34.29	67.54	7.7	35.72
Ours	**4.75**	**25.6**	**33.3**	**37.27**

4.4 Ablation Studies

To validate the effectiveness of the proposed network architecture and loss functions, we compared the network with its ablated versions. Visual examples of ablation studies are shown in Fig. 7, and the corresponding quantitative results are presented in Table 4. From Fig. 7 and Table 4, it noted that the complete model achieves the best performance. As shown (c), (f), (g) in Fig. 7, although using U-Net (stage one) alone can accurately detect highlight regions, without further refining the spatial details of highlight features, color distortion may occur in the region after highlight removal. In contrast, using CARNet (stage two) alone is unable to effectively remove highlights due to the lack of spatial context information. As the data in Table 4 shows, the absence of either attention module in the spatial-channel attention module leads to a decline in highlight detection and removal quality. As shown in Figure 7(c) and (d), compared to using BCE loss, using the varifocal loss function can not only learn highlight regions more accurately, but also better learn the corresponding diffuse components, resulting in non-highlight images

Fig. 7. Visual examples of model ablation experiments: (a) input, (b) ground truth, and (c) complete method, (d) without using varifocal loss, (e) without fusion module, (f) with only U-Net, (g) with only CARNet, (h) with only the CA module, and (i) with only the SA module.

Table 4. Quantitative comparison of ablation study, corresponding to Fig. 7.

Method	PSNR ↑	SSIM ↑	Acc ↑	BER ↓
(d) without using varifocal loss	36.63	0.975	0.99	9.07
(e) without fusion module	36.74	0.975	0.99	7.54
(f) with only U-Net	36.07	0.973	0.99	9.21
(g) with only CARNet	33.09	0.959	0.98	14.58
(h) with only the CA module	37.15	0.975	0.99	7.379
(i) with only the SA module	36.39	0.974	0.99	7.627
Full method	**37.27**	**0.976**	**0.99**	**7.21**

that are closer to ground truth. As shown in Figure 7(c) and (e), the absence of inter-stage fusion module would prevent the effective transmission of contextual features from stage one to stage two, leading to some errors in the generated images in the highlight region.

5 Conclusions

In this study, we propose a novel end-to-end two-stage network architecture for jointly detecting and removing specular highlights in single images. Furthermore, we design an efficient spatial-channel attention module to effectively extract highlight features in the images and employ a varifocal loss function to enhance the model's performance. These modules and two-stage structures can help the model accurately locate the position of highlights and restore them, while also addressing the issues of residual highlights and color distortion in the restored area. Although the proposed method has achieved good results on the SHIQ dataset, its generalizability to all real-world highlight images or specific image domains remains challenging. In the future, we would like to develop a larger and more diverse dataset for highlight detection and removal, which will further demonstrate the effectiveness of our proposed method and improve the model's universality. In addition, we would like to improve the highlight recovery module (CNN) to further enhance the model's ability to generate accurate highlight region recovery images based on different highlight features.

Acknowledgments. The research work was supported by the National Natural Science Foundation of China (No. 61976247) and the Fundamental Research Funds for the Central Universities (No. 2682021ZTPY110).

References

1. Li, R., Pan, J., Si, Y., Yan, B., Hu, Y., Qin, H.: Specular reflections removal for endoscopic image sequences with adaptive-RPCA decomposition. IEEE Trans. Med. Imaging **39**, 328–340 (2020)
2. Zhang, W., Zhao, X., Morvan, J.-M., Chen, L.: Improving shadow suppression for illumination robust face recognition. IEEE Trans. Pattern Anal. Mach. Intell. **41**(3), 611–624 (2019)
3. Huang, J., Jin, W., Zhao, D., Qin, N., Li, Q.: Double-trapezium cylinder codebook model based on YUV color model for foreground detection with shadow and highlight suppression. J. Signal Process. Syst. **85**, 221–233 (2016)
4. Shafer, S.A.: Using color to separate reflection components. Color. Res. Appl. **10**, 210–218 (1985)
5. Cui, Z., Gu, J., Shi, B., Tan, P., Kautz, J.: Polarimetric multi-view stereo. In: Proceedings of the IEEE Conference on Computer Vision and Pattern Recognition, pp. 1558-1567 (2017)
6. Lin, J., El Amine Seddik, M., Tamaazousti, M., Tamaazousti, Y., Bartoli, A.: Deep multi-class adversarial specularity removal. In: Felsberg, M., Forssén, P.-E., Sintorn, I.-M., Unger, J. (eds.) SCIA 2019. LNCS, vol. 11482, pp. 3–15. Springer, Cham (2019). https://doi.org/10.1007/978-3-030-20205-7_1

7. Muhammad, S., Dailey, M.N., Farooq, M., Majeed, M.F., Ekpanyapong, M.: Spec-Net and Spec-CGAN: deep learning models for specularity removal from faces. Image Vis. Comput. **93**, 103823 (2020)
8. Fu, G., Zhang, Q., Zhu, L., Li, P., Xiao, C.: A multi-task network for joint specular highlight detection and removal. In: Proceedings of the IEEE/CVF Conference on Computer Vision and Pattern Recognition, pp. 7752–7761 (2021)
9. Hu, G., Zheng, Y., Yan, H., Hua, G., Yan, Y.: Mask-guided cycle-GAN for specular highlight removal. Pattern Recogn. Lett. **161**, 108–114 (2022)
10. Wu, Z., et al.: Single-image specular highlight removal via real-world dataset construction. IEEE Trans. Multim. **24**, 3782–3793 (2021)
11. Chen, L., Chu, X., Zhang, X., Sun, J.: Simple baselines for image restoration. In: Computer Vision–ECCV 2022: 17th European Conference, Tel Aviv, Israel, October 23–27, 2022, Proceedings, Part VII, pp. 17–33. Springer, Cham (2022). https://doi.org/10.1007/978-3-031-200 71-7_2
12. Zamir, S.W., Arora, A., Khan, S., Hayat, M., Khan, F.S., Yang, M.-H.: Restormer: efficient transformer for high-resolution image restoration. In: Proceedings of the IEEE/CVF Conference on Computer Vision and Pattern Recognition, pp. 5728–5739 (2022).
13. El Meslouhi, O., Kardouchi, M., Allali, H., Gadi, T., Benkaddour, Y.A.: Automatic detection and inpainting of specular reflections for colposcopic images. Centr. Eur. J. Comput. Sci. **1**, 341–354 (2011)
14. Fu, G., Zhang, Q., Lin, Q., Zhu, L., Xiao, C.: Learning to detect specular highlights from real-world images. In: Proceedings of the 28th ACM International Conference on Multimedia, pp. 1873–1881 (2020).
15. Akashi, Y., Okatani, T.: Separation of reflection components by sparse non-negative matrix factorization. In: Cremers, D., Reid, I., Saito, H., Yang, M.-H. (eds.) ACCV 2014. LNCS, vol. 9007, pp. 611–625. Springer, Cham (2015). https://doi.org/10.1007/978-3-319-16814-2_40
16. Guo, J., Zhou, Z., Wang, L.: Single image highlight removal with a sparse and low-rank reflection model. In: Proceedings of the European Conference on Computer Vision (ECCV), pp. 268–283 (2018)
17. Nayar, S.K., Fang, X.-S., Boult, T.: Separation of reflection components using color and polarization. Int. J. Comput. Vision **21**, 163–186 (1997)
18. Wu, Z., Guo, J., Zhuang, C., Xiao, J., Yan, D.-M., Zhang, X.: Joint specular highlight detection and removal in single images via Unet-transformer. Comput. Vis. Media **9**, 141–154 (2023)
19. Zhang, H., Wang, Y., Dayoub, F., Sunderhauf, N.: Varifocalnet: An iou-aware dense object detector. In: Proceedings of the IEEE/CVF Conference on Computer Vision and Pattern Recognition, pp. 8514–8523 (2021)
20. Lai, W.-S., Huang, J.-B., Ahuja, N., Yang, M.-H.: Fast and accurate image super-resolution with deep Laplacian pyramid networks. IEEE Trans. Pattern Anal. Mach. Intell. **41**, 2599–2613 (2018)
21. Loshchilov, I., Hutter, F.: Decoupled weight decay regularization. arXiv preprint arXiv:1711. 05101 (2017)
22. Tan, R.T., Ikeuchi, K.: Separating reflection components of textured surfaces using a single image. In: Ikeuchi, K., Miyazaki, D. (eds.) Digitally Archiving Cultural Objects, pp. 353–384. Springer, Boston (2008). https://doi.org/10.1007/978-0-387-75807_17
23. Shen, H.-L., Zheng, Z.-H.: Real-time highlight removal using intensity ratio. Appl. Opt. **52**, 4483–4493 (2013)
24. Yang, Q., Tang, J., Ahuja, N.: Efficient and robust specular highlight removal. IEEE Trans. Pattern Anal. Mach. Intell. **37**, 1304–1311 (2014)
25. Shi, J., Dong, Y., Su, H., Yu, S.X.: Learning non-lambertian object intrinsics across shapenet categories. In: Proceedings of the IEEE Conference on Computer Vision and Pattern Recognition, pp. 1685–1694 (2017)

26. Yamamoto, T., Nakazawa, A.: General improvement method of specular component separation using high-emphasis filter and similarity function. ITE Trans. Media Technol. Appl. **7**, 92–102 (2019)

27. Yi, R., Tan, P., Lin, S.: Leveraging multi-view image sets for unsupervised intrinsic image decomposition and highlight separation. In: Proceedings of the AAAI Conference on Artificial Intelligence, pp. 12685–12692 (2020)

28. Huang, Z., Hu, K., Wang, X.: M2-Net: Multi-stages Specular Highlight Detection and Removal in Multi-scenes. arXiv preprint arXiv:2207.09965 (2022)

29. Xu, J., Liu, S., Chen, G., Liu, Q.: Highlight detection and removal method based on bifurcated-CNN. In: Liu, H., et al. (eds.) ICIRA 2022. LNCS, vol. 13458, pp. 307–318. Springer, Cham (2022). https://doi.org/10.1007/978-3-031-13841-6_29

30. Wang, Z., Bovik, A.C., Sheikh, H.R., Simoncelli, E.P.: Image quality assessment: from error visibility to structural similarity. IEEE Trans. Image Process. **13**, 600–612 (2004)

A Class Incremental Learning Algorithm for a Compact-Sized Probabilistic Neural Network and Its Empirical Comparison with Multilayered Perceptron Neural Networks

Shunpei Morita, Hiroto Iguchi, and Tetsuya Hoya[✉]

Department Computer Engineering, CST, Nihon University, 7-24-1, Narashino-dai,
Funabashi-City, Chiba 274-8501, Japan
houya.tetsuya@nihon-u.ac.jp

Abstract. It is well known that class incremental learning using deep learning is difficult to achieve, since deep learning approaches inherently suffer from the catastrophic forgetting in the training mode. In contrast, a probabilistic neural network is capable of performing classification tasks based upon a set of local spaces, each composed of a training pattern, and thereby class incremental learning can be robustly performed. In this paper, we propose a class incremental learning method by exploiting the property of a probabilistic neural network, while reducing effectively the number of the training patterns to be stored within the hidden layer, and compare the performance of the class incremental learning tasks obtained using a multilayered perceptron model with that using a probabilistic neural network. Simulation results using seven publicly available datasets show that both the classification accuracies of an original probabilistic neural network and the proposed incremental learning method are 2.59 to 26.58 times higher than that of the deep learning in class incremental learning. Moreover, we observed that the class incremental learning performed using a probabilistic neural network exhibited a robust performance compared to the deep neural networks with iCaRL. In addition, it was observed that the proposed learning method was able to reduce effectively the number of the units in the hidden layer, while with the decrease in accuracy by only 1.77% to 7.06%, compared to the original one.

Keywords: Probabilistic neural network · Multilayered perceptron · Deep learning · Class incremental learning · Pattern classification

1 Introduction

Deep learning (DL) [1] is one of the most widely used learning methods in the field of machine learning, and it has made significant contributions to the development of pattern recognition technologies. In particular, deep neural networks

(DNNs) [2] are nowadays prevalent in both academic studies and industrial applications, and many image classifier models, including VGG [3], ResNet [4] and AlexNet [5], for instance, have been used across a wide range of fields. In many of the cases, the performance of a classification model is typically evaluated after the training performed in an iterative fashion, using the entire set of the training patterns. In practice, however, it is often the case that the training patterns are not ready to be available for all the classes but given only partially at a time and those of the remaining classes come later. Therefore, it is desirable to perform a continual learning (CL) [6], where the network training continues with the incoming new patterns. Within the CL principle, a number of class incremental learning (CIL) [7] approaches have been proposed to date [8–10]. In CIL, a pattern classifier is augmented with new classes, using only an additional set of the patterns for the new classes. However, it has been increasingly acknowledged, as pointed out in [11–13], that catastrophic forgetting of previously learned classes is a major problem in DL for performing the CIL/CL.

According to the taxonomy proposed in [14], the CIL approaches for DL proposed to date can be classified into the three categories of i) data-centric, ii) model-centric, and iii) algorithm-centric ones. For i), the CIL method in [8] introduces maximum entropy regularization (MER) into the loss function in order to prevent overfitting to the uncertain knowledge, and a confident fitting is given as penalty. In contrast, the method in [9] utilizes the dynamically expandable representation (DER) and can be categorized as a type ii) approach, based upon the classification in [14]. Within the method, the representation previously learned by a DNN is frozen and new additional feature extractors are learned for the additional tasks. For iii) the method in [10], i.e. weight aligning (WA), maintains the fairness between the previously learned and new classes. One of the other model-centric CIL methods is elastic weight consolidation (EWC) [15], and it is claimed in [15] that the old tasks can be memorized by slowing down the learning pace of some selected network parameters. However, the work in [14] reports rather counterfactual simulation results. In addition, replay methods have received much attention in the CIL for DNNs, and iCaRL [11] is particularly widely used among them. The iCaRL attempts to get over the catastrophic forgetting by adding some previously trained data to the newly incoming data. Although several methods have proposed to date, it is said that the catastrophic forgetting inherent to DNNs has still not been fully overcome.

In contrast to the DNN approaches described above, probabilistic neural network (PNN) [16] is another artificial neural network model, originally proposed for pattern classification problems. The original PNN model has only a single hyperparameter to be given a priori, and its training is straightforwardly completed in a one-shot manner; each training pattern is accommodated as the attribute vector of a second layer unit. Moreover, it is also shown in a recent study [17] that the parallel implementation of a PNN using k-means clustering enables its reference (testing) mode to be performed superior to a DNN, by exploiting the independence property of the arithmetic operations for each unit in the hidden layer, as well as those in each output layer unit representing a single class.

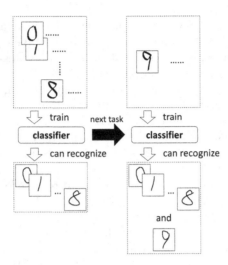

Fig. 1. The flow of the class incremental learning.

In this paper, we propose a novel class incremental learning algorithm for a PNN with a reduced number of the hidden layer units (a.k.a. compact sized PNN; CS-PNN) and empirically verify its effectiveness by comparing a DNN and PNN with the original training scheme. The organization of the paper is as follows: Sect. 2 describes what CIL is, followed by a brief introduction of the PNN, and comparison between the CIL on a PNN and DNN. Section 3 proposes a new CIL algorithm for PNN. Section 4 is devoted to the simulation study, i) comparing a DNN and the original PNN under the CIL situations, each yielding the baseline, and then ii) evaluating the classification performance of the CS-PNN. Section 4 provides the summary of the present work and suggests some future directions.

2 Preliminary Studies

2.1 Class Incremental Learning

In [11], CIL is meant to be the task of learning incrementally some additional classes for an already learned model, so that the newly added classes can be also identified by the model, besides the classes already learned. For instance, provided that a model has been trained for the classification task of handwritten digits and is capable of performing the task only partially, e.g. the digits from zero to eight, an additional learning is performed on the model, so that a new digit nine can also be classified, in addition to the nine digits already learned, as illustrated in Fig. 1.

2.2 Probabilistic Neural Network

A PNN is a feed-forward neural network composed of an input and output layer, with linear-sum activation units for the latter, and a single hidden layer with the

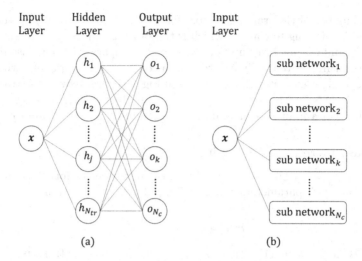

(a)   (b)

Fig. 2. (a) The structure of a PNN with a total number of training patterns and N_c classes, and (b) The PNN represented as a composite structure by a set of the N_c class-independent sub-networks.

nonlinear units. Figure 2 (a) illustrates the structure of a PNN. In Fig. 2, each of the hidden layer units has a radial basis function (RBF) in terms of Gaussian response function as an activation function:

$$h_j(\boldsymbol{x}) = \exp\left(-\frac{\|\boldsymbol{x} - \boldsymbol{c}_j\|_2^2}{\sigma^2}\right) \tag{1}$$

where $\|\cdots\|_2$ denotes $L2$-norm, h_j, $\boldsymbol{x}$, and $\boldsymbol{c}_j$ are respectively the output value of the j-th hidden layer unit, the input vector, and the attribute vector representing one of the training patterns, and where σ is the radius unique to all the RBFs. Each hidden layer unit is connected to an output layer unit corresponding to the class to which the training pattern belongs. In PNN, the weight between a hidden layer and output layer units is set as follows:

$$w_{j,k} = \begin{cases} 1 & \text{if } \boldsymbol{c}_j \text{ belongs to class } k, \\ 0 & \text{otherwise.} \end{cases} \tag{2}$$

In the output layer, each unit yields the activation value:

$$o_k = \frac{1}{U_k} \sum_{j=1}^{U_k} w_{k(j),k} h_{k(j)}(\boldsymbol{x}) \tag{3}$$

$$N_{tr} = \sum_{k=1}^{N_c} U_k \tag{4}$$

where $w_{k(j),k}$ is the weight between the j-th RBF belonging to class k and the k-th output layer unit, U_k is the number of the training vectors for class k, N_{tr} is the total number of the training vectors for all the classes, and $k(j)$ is the ID of the RBFs that belong to class k (which is the same as o_k). In a PNN, since both the hidden and output layer units are completely separated from class to class, the network can be eventually regarded as a composite network consisting of its class-independent subnetworks, as shown in Fig. 2 (b). Moreover, the training of the original PNN is completed in only 2 steps: i) storing each training vector as the attribute of a hidden layer unit and ii) determining σ in (1) appropriately.

2.3   Class Incremental Learning on DNN and PNN

For training a DNN, DL aims to minimize the output error for w, i.e. a certain set of the network parameters, where the input vector x is given:

$$w \leftarrow w - \eta \frac{\partial E(x, w)}{\partial w} \tag{5}$$

where E is the error function, for which a categorical cross entropy is often used in classification problems, and η is the learning rate. Then, in the situation where the network parameters are optimized for a new set of the training patterns, it is quite often the case that the knowledge acquired from new training patterns can easily override the weight and bias parameters optimized using previous patterns. This is the main cause of the catastrophic forgetting occurring in a DNN. Therefore, in the situation where the CIL is performed on a DNN, the problem arises in the pattern classification tasks, as the classification accuracy for a new class is apt to decline dramatically. In other words, this is due to the fact that the model can be optimized *only* for a particular set of the training patterns for a new class.

In contrast to the DNNs, PNN does not suffer from such forgetting, as the network training on a PNN essentially proceeds by only adding each hidden layer unit with storing a training vector as an attribute vector within the RBF, as described earlier. Moreover, in the situation where the dataset given is well-balanced, it is considered that the feature space can be reasonably covered by a set of the local subspaces spanned by the respective attribute vectors, each stored in a hidden layer unit, and thereby it is considered that an additional learning such as the CIL can be effectively and straightforwardly carried out.

3   Class Incremental Learning Algorithm for a Compact-Sized Probabilistic Neural Network

Here, we propose a new method applied for training the PNN, i.e. a compact-sized probabilistic neural network (CS-PNN) for CIL, with reducing the number of units in the hidden layer. In the CS-PNN, each unit in the hidden layer memorizes the location of a selected training vector in the feature space. Also, the number of the hidden layer units can be suppressed by updating the location of some existing vector, if a new training vector is located nearby the existing one, without adding it as a new attribute vector. The training algorithm for the CS-PNN is summarized as follows.

step 1. For the first training pattern belonging to a new class $(k=1,2,\ldots,N_c)$, add $h_{k(j=1)}$ into the hidden layer with $c_{k(i=1)} = x_{tr(k,i=1)}$, and o_k into the output layer.

step 2. For $i = 2,3,\ldots,U_k$, perform the following for all the remaining training patterns:

If $\exists h_k; h_k(x_{tr(k,i)}) > \theta_k$ then update c_j for the unit h_j which yields a maximum output value among the existing units belonging to class k to the average between $x_{tr(k,i)}$ and c_j as follows:

$$c_j \leftarrow \frac{x_{tr(k,i)} + c_j}{2} \qquad (6)$$

Otherwise, add $h_{k(i)}$ into the hidden layer with $c_{k(i)} = x_{tr(k,i)}$, as well as o_k to the output layer, if it does not exist yet, and connect $h_{k(i)}$ to o_k (i.e. with the weight unity in between);

Note that applying the CS-PNN algorithm in the above will automatically generate the units in both the hidden and output layers, where necessary. Also, since the parameters $c_j (j = 1, 2, \ldots, U_k; U_k$ is the number of training patterns belonging to class k) are updated only for the subnet representing a single class, the CIL is performed without affecting to the attribute vectors stored in other subnets (i.e. representing the respective classes). Moreover, during the operation of the CIL algorithm in the above, only the attribute vector of the unit which is the nearest to the training is updated, while the stored vectors in other units remain intact, with only a small and necessary change in the feature space spanned. In addition, since only the attribute vectors of the units with their activations larger than the threshold are updated, a smaller value of θ can lead to a further reduction in the number of the hidden layer units, depending upon the situations. Note, however, that there needs a trade-off between the performance, since, with a small setting of θ, the chance that the attribute located far from the primary feature space for a particular class can be selected for the update increases. For this reason, a care should be taken for the choice of the value θ, besides the unique radius σ in (1).

4 Simulation Study

We conducted a series of the simulations, aimed for comparing the CIL capabilities of the DNN, original PNN, and the proposed CS-PNN.

In the simulation study, we used the seven publicly available datasets: abalone, isolet, letter-recognition, MNIST, optdigits, pendigits, and wdbc; one obtained from the MNIST [18], and the remaining six from the UCI machine learning repository [19]. Then, each pattern vector of a dataset was normalized within the range of $[-1, 1]$:

$$x_i \leftarrow 2\left(\frac{x_i - x_{i\text{MIN}}}{x_{i\text{MAX}} - x_{i\text{MIN}}} - 0.5\right) \qquad (7)$$

Table 1. Summary of the seven datasets used for the simulation study.

Dataset	#Training	#Testing	#Classes	#Features per pattern
abalone	2088	2089	3	7
isolet	2252	1559	26	617
letter-recognition	16000	4000	26	16
MNIST	60000	10000	10	784
optdigits	3823	1797	10	64
pendigits	7494	3498	10	16
wdbc	398	171	2	30

where i is the ID of an attribute vector. The properties of the seven datasets used for the simulations are summarized in Table 1. For the unique hyper-parameter of a PNN, σ was set by the following equation, and the setting was used through all the simulations, which yielded relatively a reasonable performance for each dataset:

$$\sigma = \frac{d_{\text{MAX}}}{N_c} \tag{8}$$

where d_{MAX} is the maximum distance computed using all the pairs of the training patterns across all the classes used for training, and N_c is the number of classes.

In the case of training a DNN, an entire set of the training vectors was divided into those of the respective class, and each set of the vectors was presented to the network as one batch at a time for the training. For the DNN, once an iterative training session using the batch belonging to a certain class was completed, the batch for other class was used for the next iterative training session. This manner of the subsequent training sessions continued till the last class.

4.1   Comparison Between the DNN and Original PNN Under the CIL Situation

In this simulation, we first compared the DNN and PNN for the baseline tasks of the CIL. For the baseline tasks, each batch for the class till the last was subsequently presented to a DNN/PNN and the CIL at each presentation was performed. Then, the classification accuracy after completing the CIL was evaluated for each of the two models, using the testing vectors. In the tasks, therefore, each training pattern vector was stored, as described earlier, as an attribute vector of a unit in the hidden layer of a PNN, while the parameter setting, as well as the training, of the DNN was done based upon the following manner:

- Number of the Hidden Layers: varied from 1 to 3.
- Training Algorithm: Adam [20] (learning rate = 0.01, $\alpha = 0.9$, $\beta = 0.999$).
- Number of Epochs in an Iterative Training Session:
  - Patterns for the first class (i.e. the first CIL task): 20 epochs.

Table 2. Simulation results comparing the classification accuracies, obtained after the completion of the training for all the classes in the CIL situation, and showing the baseline performance of DNN and PNN, under the CIL situation.

Dataset	Acc. of DNN [%]						Acc. of PNN[%]
	1 hidden layer		2 hidden layers		3 hidden layers		
	1 epoch	20 epochs	1 epoch	20 epochs	1 epoch	20 epochs	
abalone	36.05	36.05	36.05	36.05	31.02	36.05	**57.25**
isolet	11.61	7.7	3.85	3.85	3.85	3.85	**86.34**
letter-recognition	3.62	3.95	3.95	3.95	3.95	3.95	**96.23**
MNIST	10.09	10.09	10.09	10.09	10.09	10.09	**96.50**
optdigits	10.52	10.02	10.91	10.02	10.02	10.02	**98.39**
pendigits	18.7	17.64	15.04	9.61	9.61	9.61	**94.25**
wdbc	37.43	37.43	37.43	37.43	37.43	37.43	**97.08**

- Patterns for other classes (i.e. other remaining tasks): once epoch/20 epochs.

In the setting for the DNN above, the three hyper-parameters for the Adam, which is considered as one of the state-of-the-art DL algorithms, were those given as the default values used in PyTorch [21] except for the learning rate, whereas the numbers of the epochs chosen were based upon the preliminary simulations; it was empirically confirmed that 20 epochs were sufficient to reach a convergent state for each run. The simulation results are summarized in Table 2. In this table, we obviously see that a DNN is not able to perform properly the CIL tasks at all, where the number of classes was increased one-by-one. On the other hand, the classification accuracies obtained using a PNN were always higher than those obtained using the DNNs for all the seven datasets used in the simulation study. As shown in Table 2, it was observed that the classification accuracy by a PNN was around 2.5 times as high as those by DNNs for the wdbc case, whereas 26.5 times higher for the letter-recognition case. For the CIL tasks using the MNIST, we then analyzed the classification accuracies in each class obtained by a DNN with three hidden layers, upon the iterative training of 20 epochs in each additional training task. In the analysis, we confirmed that the accuracies for the preciously learned classes were all dropped to zero, except that of 100% for each new class just learned. Therefore, it is said that the catastrophic forgetting did occur in the early stage of learning in each case of the DNNs, since there was no significant difference between the classification accuracies for the one-epoch cases and those of the twenty epochs, as shown in Table 2. From these observations, it can be therefore concluded that a PNN is capable of performing the CIL, without any serious forgetting occurred, as reported in [22], while the DNNs are not.

Table 3. Simulation results comparing the classification accuracy and the number of the RBFs using the original PNN and CS-PNN for each of the seven datasets.

Dataset		Original PNN	CS-PNN			
			$\theta = 0.6$	$\theta = 0.7$	$\theta = 0.8$	$\theta = 0.9$
abalone	Acc. [%]	**57.25**	36.96	44.23	44.71	44.47
	Num. RBFs	2088	**11**	14	23	37
isolet	Acc. [%]	**86.34**	83.64	85.12	86.14	86.14
	Num. RBFs	2252	**2126**	2161	2187	2240
letter-recognition	Acc. [%]	**96.23**	90.68	92.40	94.20	95.60
	Num. RBFs	16000	**9703**	10667	11635	12809
MNIST	Acc. [%]	**96.50**	91.14	95.38	96.12	96.48
	Num. RBFs	60000	**47240**	47476	47778	50177
optdigts	Acc. [%]	98.39	98.11	98.22	**98.44**	98.33
	Num. RBFs	3823	**2819**	2986	3208	3471
pendigits	Acc. [%]	94.25	93.62	94.23	93.42	**95.57**
	Num. RBFs	7494	**1873**	2404	3200	4487
wdbc	Acc. [%]	**97.08**	82.46	82.46	83.63	**97.08**
	Num. RBFs	398	**9**	19	26	65

4.2 Evaluation of Classification Accuracy and Reduction Rate of Hidden Layer Units for the Proposed CS-PNN

We then conducted another set of simulations, in order to validate the classification performance in the case where the CS-PNN was applied. The simulation results are shown in Tables 3 and 4 and Figs. 3 and 4.

Table 3 summarizes both the classification accuracies and number of hidden layer units after performing the incrementally training of a PNN by applying the proposed algorithm (i.e. CS-PNN) in Sect. 3.

In Table 4, a performance comparison of both the relative difference in terms of classification accuracy and reduction rate of RBFs between the original PNN and CS-PNN, calculated using the values in Table 3, is shown. The relative difference and reduction rate were calculated, respectively, as follows:

$$\text{Relative Difference} = \text{Acc. of original PNN} - \text{Acc. of CS-PNN} \tag{9}$$

$$\text{Reduction Rate} = 1 - \frac{\text{Num. RBFs in each CS-PNN}}{\text{Num. RBFs in original PNN}} \tag{10}$$

Here, the relative difference in (9) is introduced for a straightforward comparison of the difference between the classification accuracy of the original PNN and CS-PNN; a minus value shows the accuracy of CS-PNN inferior to that of the original PNN. As shown in the bottom two rows in Table 4, the average

Table 4. Comparison of relative difference in classification accuracy between the original PNN and CS-PNN, and reduction rate of hidden layer units (RBFs).

Dataset		CS-PNN			
		$\theta = 0.6$	$\theta = 0.7$	$\theta = 0.8$	$\theta = 0.9$
abalone	Relative Difference [%]	−20.30	−13.02	**−12.54**	−12.78
	Reduction rate of RBFs [%]	**99.47**	99.33	98.90	98.23
isolet	Relative Difference [%]	−2.69	−1.22	**−0.19**	−0.19
	Reduction rate of RBFs [%]	**5.60**	4.04	2.89	0.53
letter-recognition	Relative Difference [%]	−5.55	−3.82	−2.03	**−0.63**
	Reduction rate of RBFs [%]	**39.36**	33.33	27.28	19.94
MNIST	Relative Difference [%]	−5.36	−1.12	−0.38	**−0.02**
	Reduction rate of RBFs [%]	**21.27**	20.87	20.37	16.37
optdigts	Relative Difference [%]	−0.28	−0.17	**0.06**	−0.06
	Reduction rate of RBFs [%]	**26.26**	21.89	16.09	9.21
pendigits	Relative Difference [%]	−0.63	−0.03	−0.83	**1.32**
	Reduction rate of RBFs [%]	**75.01**	67.92	57.30	40.13
wdbc	Relative Difference [%]	−14.62	−14.62	−13.45	**0.00**
	Reduction rate of RBFs [%]	**97.74**	95.23	93.74	83.67
Avg.	Relative Difference [%]	−7.06	−4.86	−4.19	**−1.77**
	Reduction rate of RBFs [%]	**52.10**	48.95	45.18	38.30
Med	Relative Difference [%]	−5.36	−1.22	−0.83	**−0.06**
	Reduction rate of RBFs [%]	**39.36**	33.33	27.28	19.94

over the relative difference for each value of θ for the CS-PNN was −7.06%, −4.86%, −4.19%, and −1.77%, respectively, whereas the corresponding median, which was computed over these results, was respectively as −5.63%, −1.22%, −0.83%, and −0.06%. Therefore, overall, a dramatic performance degradation as in the DNNs was not observed for the CS-PNN, compared to the original PNN. In Table 4, it is, however, observed that the range of the decrease in terms of the classification accuracy for both the abalone and wdbc datasets is relatively larger than that for other datasets. The possible reason for such a deterioration is ascribed to the relatively higher reduction rate of the hidden layer units, as shown in Table 4, and/or the removal of the units yielding a significant impact on the classification performance. In contrast, the accuracies obtained using the CS-PNN for the other five datasets, i.e. isolet, letter-recognition, MNIST, optdigits, and pendigits, are all shown to remain almost intact, each with a relatively high reduction rate of the RBFs (except the isolet case with $\theta = 0.6$), as shown in Table 4.

On the other hand, the reduction rates for both the abalone and wdbc (except for θ=0.09) were over 90%, while a significant decrease in terms of the classification accuracy of over 10% was also observed. In contrast, the relative difference in

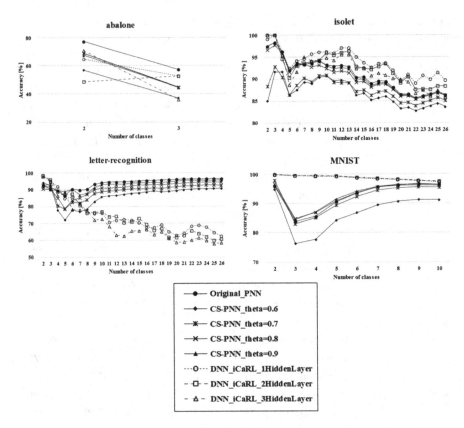

Fig. 3. Classification accuracies obtained using original PNN, CS-PNN (θ=0.6,0.7,0.8,0.9), and iCaRL on DNN ($K = 0.2 \times$ the number of all training data), with the number of classes varied for the abalone, isolet, letter-recognition, and MNIST datasets.

classification accuracy for the five cases of the isolet, letter-recognition, MNIST, optdigits, and pendigits almost always stayed below the corresponding averaged one, while the reduction rates of the RBFs were varied greatly with the setting of θ as shown in the bottom in Table 4. This indicates that an appropriate setting of θ by somehow taking into account the overall distribution of the distances between the input and attribute vectors is necessary, so as to effectively reduce the number of the RBFs. Therefore, it is considered, as a rule of thumb in practice, that the value of the unique radius σ is first tuned to yield a higher classification accuracy, then θ is varied for an effective reduction in the number of the RBFs.

In sum, from these observations, it is said that the CS-PNN can effectively select the training pattern vectors to be accommodated within the hidden units, while maintaining relatively well-separated class boundaries in between, as compared to the original PNN approach.

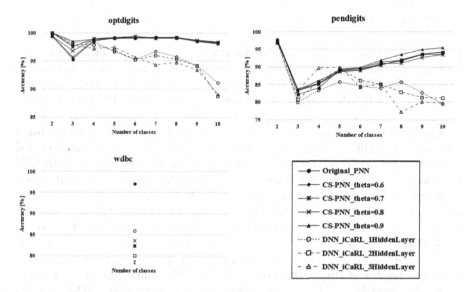

Fig. 4. Classification accuracies obtained using original PNN, CS-PNN (θ=0.6,0.7,0.8,0.9), and iCaRL on DNN ($K = 0.2 \times$ the number of all training data), with the number of classes varied for the optdigits, pendigits, and wdbc datasets.

Figures 3 and 4 show the changes in the classification accuracy of the CIL with an original PNN, CS-PNN, and the DNN with iCaRL. In this simulation, the memory size K for the iCaRL, i.e., the number of stored data for the subsequent additional training task, was set at 0.2 times the number of all training data in each dataset. In Figs. 3 and 4, we observe that for all the datasets except the abalone the classification accuracy almost always stays above 70–80%. Moreover, as shown in Figs. 3 and 4, the accuracy for all the four datasets but the abalone, isolet, and wdbc was improved steadily, albeit sometimes exhibiting a sudden drop at an earlier CIL task, and remained relatively high afterwards, unlike the DNN without applying the iCaRL. In addition, it was confirmed that the accuracy of the iCaRL consistently showed a decrease with each additional training for the letter-recognition, optdigits, and pendigits cases, compared to the CS-PNN. In the isolet case, however, the accuracy of CS-PNN was lower than iCaRL at the early stages, though the classification accuracy of the CS-PNN approached that of the iCaRL as the additional training tasks proceeded. A similar trend was observed for the MNIST case. In contrast, for the abalone and wdbc, the CS-PNN and iCaRL exhibited no significant difference in the accuracy. Therefore, it is said that the CS-PNN performed effectively for all the seven datasets used for the simulation study compared to the CIL of the DNN with iCaRL.

5   Conclusion

In this work, we have firstly shown that a PNN is capable of performing the CIL, through the simulation study using seven publicly available datasets in comparison with the DNNs. We have then proposed the CS-PNN, for the purpose of effectively reducing the number of the hidden layer units in a PNN, while maintaining a reasonably high classification performance. It has also been observed that performing a CIL is virtually not possible by a bare DNN approach using the Adam algorithm for all the cases, due to the catastrophic forgetting occurred during the simulation, while the CS-PNN can cope moderately well with the CIL. Compared to the iCaRL, CS-PNN can also perform robustly in the CIL tasks. Moreover, it is worth mentioning that,unlike DNNs, the training of a PNN is fast, as the training does not require iterative training of the network parameters at all but can be simply done by assigning some selected training data to the hidden layer unit's attributed vectors as described in this work. It is also notable that, beside the hidden layer units, the network obtained via the CS-PNN has a varying number of output units during a CIL task, unlike conventional, fixed-sized DNN models. In addition, it is also reported in [23] that a PNN exhibits the high robustness against an adversarial attack.

Future work is directed to the investigation of the effective choice of the unique radius σ of a PNN, as well as that applicable to the CS-PNN.

References

1. Lecun, Y., Bengio, Y., Hinton, G.: Deep learning. Nature **521**, 436–444 (2015)
2. Schmidhuber, D.E., Hinton, G.E., Williams, R.J.: Deep learning in neural networks: an overview. Neural Netw. **61**, 85–117 (2015)
3. Karen, S., Andrew, Z.: Very deep convolutional networks for large-scale image recognition. The 3rd International Conference on Learning Representations, https://arxiv.org/pdf/1409.1556. Accessed 29 May 2023
4. Kaiming, H., Xiangyu, Z., Shaoqing, R. Jian, S.: Deep residual learning for image recognition. In: 2016 IEEE Conference on Computer Vision and Pattern Recognition, pp. 770–778 (2016)
5. Alex, K., Ilya, S., Geoffrey, E, H.: ImageNet classification with deep convolutional neural networks. In: Advances in Neural Information Processing Systems 25 (2012)
6. Sebastian, T., Tom, M.M.: Lifelong robot learning. Robot. Auton. Syst. **15**(1–2), 25–46 (1995)
7. McClelland, J.L., McNaughton, B.L., O'Reilly, R.C.: Why there are complementary learning systems in the hippocampus and neocortex: insights from the successes and failures of connectionist models of learning and memory. Psychol. Rev. **102**(3), 419–457 (1995)
8. Dahyun, K., Jhwan, B., Yeonsik, J., Jonghyun C.: Incremental learning with maximum entropy regularization: rethinking forgetting and intransigence. https://arxiv.org/abs/1902.00829. Accessed 29 May 2023
9. Shipeng, Y., Jiagwei, X., Xuming, H.: Der: dynamically expandable representation for class incremental learning. In Proceedings of the IEEE Conference on Computer Vision and Pattern Recognition, pp. 3013–3022 (2021)

10. Bowen, Z., Xi, X., Guojun, G., Bin, Z., Shu-Tao, X.: Maintaining discrimination and fairness in class incremental learning. In: Proceedings of the IEEE Conference on Computer Vision and Pattern Recognition, pp. 13205–13224 (2020)
11. Sylvestre-Alivise, R., Alexander, K., Georg, S., Christoph, H. L.: iCaRL: incremental classifier and representation learning. In: Proceedings of the IEEE Conference on Computer Vision and Pattern Recognition, pp. 2001–2010 (2017)
12. McCloskey, M., Cohen, N.J.: Catastrophic interference in connectionist networks: the sequential learning problem. Psychol. Learn. Motiv. **24**, 109–165 (1989)
13. Ratcliff, R.: Connectionist models of recognition memory: constraints imposed by learning and forgetting functions. Psychol. Rev. **97**(2), 285–308 (1990)
14. Da-Wei, Z., Qi-Wei, W., Zhi-Hong, Q., Han-Jia, Y., De-Chuan, Z., Ziwei, L.: Deep class-incremental learning: a survey. https://arxiv.org/pdf/2302.03648.pdf. Accessed 29 May 2023
15. James, K., et al.: Overcoming catastrophic forgetting in neural networks. PANS **114**(13), 3521–3526 (2017)
16. Specht, D.F.: Probabilistic neural networks. Neural Netw. **3**(1), 109–118 (1990)
17. Takahashi, K., Morita, S., Hoya, T.: An analytical comparison between the pattern classifiers based upon a multilayered perceptron and probabilistic neural network in parallel implementation. Int. Conf. Art. Neural Netw. **3**, 544–555 (2022)
18. LeCun, Y., Cortes, C., Burges, C. J. C.: The MNIST database. http://yann.lecun.com/exdb/mnist/. Accessed 19 Aug 2021
19. Dua, D., Graff, C.: UCI machine learning repository. Univ. California Irvine, Irvine, CA. http://archive.ics.uci.edu/ml. Accessed 29 May 2023
20. Diederik, P. K., Jimmy, B.: Adam: a method for stochastic optimization. https://arxiv.org/abs/1412.6980. Accessed 29 May 2023
21. Pytorch, Team.: PyTorch: An imperative style, high-performance deep learning library. https://pytorch.org. Accessed 01 June 2023
22. Hoya, T.: On the capability of accommodating new classes within probabilistic neural networks. IEEE Trans. Neural Netw. **14**(2), 450–453 (2003)
23. Ian J. G., Jonathon, S., Christian, S.: Explaining and harnessing adversarial examples. International Conference on Learning Representations. https://arxiv.org/abs/1412.6572. Accessed 29 May 2023

Smooth Mask Matters: A Stroke Smoothing Text Removal Framework

Chuyu Tu[1], Zhifei Zhang[1], Rui Shu[1], Shuyang Feng[1], Xuekuan Wang[2], Yuping Qiu[1], and Cairong Zhao[1(✉)]

[1] Tongji University, Shanghai, China
{2133055,zhifeizhang,2133056,fengshuyang,ypqiu,zhaocairong}@tongji.edu.cn
[2] Baidu Inc., Beijing, China

Abstract. Most Scene Text Removal (STR) frameworks are based on predicting the text mask. The predicted text mask is either supervised by the text stroke mask label or the text box mask label in training. We find some matters related to the text stroke mask label, including the label being noisy and the inappropriate 0–1 text stroke mask representation (hard mask). We propose that these matters could be handled by the smooth text stroke mask. Specifically, we made considerable synthetic text segmentation data (text image and its smooth text stroke mask label) by a text image synthesis engine and then trained the text stroke segmentation sub-network of our framework only on the above synthetic data. We also discover that most STR frameworks lack an effective receptive field in their text region inpainting network, which limits their perception ability of the global structure. For the receptive field issue, we devise a two-stage coarse-to-refinement text region inpainting sub-network that consists of a coarse-inpainting stage with a global receptive field and a refinement stage with a local receptive field. Experiments on the benchmark datasets demonstrate that our framework outperforms existing state-of-the-art methods in all Image-Eval metrics and Detection-Eval metrics.

Keywords: Scene Text Removal · Text Stroke Mask · Background Inpainting

1 Introduction

Scene Text Removal (STR), which aims to cover text region with visually plausible content in natural images, has gained significant attention due to its important applications in scene text image editing and privacy protection.

Early studies [19,29] sought to directly erase all text in scene images without any prior knowledge, but the produced results tended to be blurry and leaky. Recent STR methods [2,7–9,18] based on text stroke segmentation have made tremendous progress. However, because all STR datasets do not provide the explicit text stroke mask label, the text stroke mask label is obtained by binarizing the difference between the text image and the corresponding ground truth,

© The Author(s), under exclusive license to Springer Nature Switzerland AG 2023
H. Lu et al. (Eds.): ACPR 2023, LNCS 14406, pp. 302–316, 2023.
https://doi.org/10.1007/978-3-031-47634-1_23

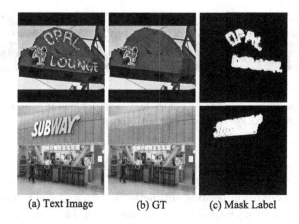

(a) Text Image   (b) GT   (c) Mask Label

Fig. 1. Examples of noisy text stroke mask labels.

which could be noisy and inaccurate (Fig. 1). Another issue about the text stroke mask label is that simply using the hard binary text stroke mask representation, where 0 for the background and 1 for the text stroke, would lead to bias in the text region inpainting generator because some text strokes are indistinguishable from the background (Fig. 2).

The two issues mentioned above demonstrate that scene text removal (STR) requires careful text segmentation. One straight trick to boost the performance of STR is to enhance text segmentation accuracy. [3] revealed that training a text stroke segmentation network focused on a bounding box is significantly easier than using the entire image. Recently, [15] comprehensively analyzed prominent STR models and evaluated the performance of several previous methods [17,24,25,29] after standardized re-implementation with the same input conditions in a fair manner. Specifically, the standard supposed that the ground truth of all text bounding boxes was known, all methods were trained and evaluated on the same datasets, and made the non-text region of the source image is the same as the text-free image label. In succession, our proposed framework, a Stroke Smoothing Text Removal Framework (SSTRF), follows this standard. Figure 3 shows the pipeline of SSTRF. SSTRF is composed of a Text Stroke Segmentation sub-Network (TSSN) and a Text Region Inpainting sub-Network (TRIN).

Inspired by [23], we only use synthetic word level image data generated by a modern text image synthesis engine to train TSSN and then use TSSN to predict on real word level image data. To deal with the hard binary text stroke mask representation issue, we use the text image synthesis engine to generate an alternative text stroke mask label, denoted as the smooth text stroke mask, which not only indicates the position of the text strokes, but also reflects the degree of integration between the text and the background.

Besides, previous image inpainting methods [20,22] indicated the lack of an effective receptive field in both the inpainting network and the loss function is

Word Instance   Mask Label

Fig. 2. In some word instances of real data, text strokes blend in with the background, but the hard binary text stroke mask can not represent this feature.

the critical factor in producing unsatisfactory inpainting results. Therefore, we design the text region inpainting sub-network as a two-stage inpainting network that consists of a coarse-inpainting sub-network with a global receptive field and a refinement sub-network with a local receptive field. The coarse-inpainting sub-network based on fast Fourier convolutions [6] has an image-wide receptive field and is optimized with the use of Focal Frequency Loss [13] which minimizes the loss of important frequency information. The cascaded refinement sub-network with a small receptive field is conducive to rectifying the local structures and textures.

In summary, the main contributions of this paper are listed as follows:

- We propose the smooth text stroke mask generated by a text image synthesis engine, which avoids the defects of the hard binary text stroke mask in the task of scene text removal.
- We propose a two-stage coarse-to-refinement text region inpainting sub-network that consists of a coarse-inpainting stage with a global receptive field to inpaint the text region and a refinement stage with a local receptive field to repair some local defects.
- Extensive experiments on SCUT-EnsText, Oxford and SCUT-Syn demonstrate that SSTRF significantly outperforms previous state-of-the-art methods.

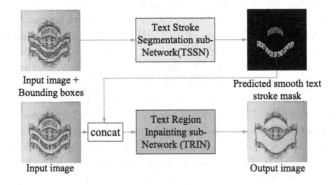

Fig. 3. The pipeline of the proposed stroke smoothing text removal framework.

Text image   Smooth mask   Hard binary mask   Smooth mask heatmap Hard binary mask heatmap

Fig. 4. Examples generated by SynthTIGER. Mask heatmaps are provided for visualization of the mask value.

2 Method

2.1 Smooth Text Stroke Mask Representation

In the synthetic text image rendering process, the text mask represents the transparency of the text region (0 represents complete transparency, 1 represents complete opacity), while the transparency of the text region reflects the degree of integration between the text region and the background. We denote the text mask in the synthetic text image rendering process as the smooth text stroke mask. SynthTIGER [28] is a novel synthetic text image generator for the scene text recognition task. The synthetic data produced by SynthTIGER well approximates the real scene text data. We exploited SynthTIGER [28] to generate one million synthetic text images and corresponding smooth text stroke masks. Figure 4 shows the comparison between the smooth text stroke mask and the hard binary text stroke mask. The hard binary text stroke mask equally handles the border and the interior. The textures of the text boundary, on the other hand, are always similar to the background and more transparent than the interior. Treating them equally will impose burdens on the text region inpainting sub-network due to improper bias. In contrast, the smooth text stroke mask is level and smooth from the inside to the border.

2.2 Architecture Overview

SSTRF is composed of a Text Stroke Segmentation sub-Network (TSSN) and a Text Region Inpainting sub-Network (TRIN), which are trained separately. Figure 5 shows the pipeline of TSSN. First, given the input image and corresponding text bounding boxes, word instance images are cropped from the input image. Next, each word instance image is sent to TSSN to obtain the corresponding predicted smooth word stroke mask. Finally, the complete predicted smooth text stroke mask is derived by placing the predicted smooth word stroke masks on the initial locations.

As illustrated in Fig. 6, TRIN comprises a coarse-inpainting stage and a refinement stage. Specifically, the coarse-inpainting stage takes the source image concatenated with the smooth text stroke mask predicted by TSSN as input and produces a coarse-inpainting image. Subsequently, the refinement sub-network transforms the coarse-inpainting image into the final result.

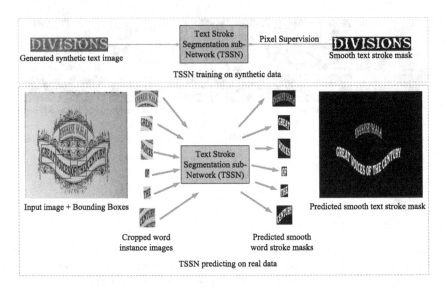

Fig. 5. Scheme of the predicted smooth text stroke mask generation procedure. TSSN is trained on synthetic data at first, in inference, it takes cropped word instance images as inputs and outputs the corresponding predicted smooth word stroke masks. Then the complete predicted smooth text stroke mask is obtained by putting the predicted smooth word stroke masks back in the original positions.

2.3 Text Stroke Segmentation Sub-Network (TSSN)

TexRNet [27] is adopted for extracting the smooth text stroke mask in TSSN. It comprises a backbone, key feature pooling, and an attention module. Key feature pooling and the attention module are intended to refine the backbone output features for the text-domain. The backbone of TexRNet is either ResNet101-DeeplabV3+ [4] or HRNetV2-W48 [26]. We choose HRNetV2-W48 as the backbone of TexRNet.

As shown in Fig. 5, we only train TSSN on synthetic data and directly predict the smooth text stroke mask on real data for TRIN.

2.4 Text Region Inpainting Sub-Network (TRIN)

NAFBlock [5] serves as the fundamental for TRIN. As shown in Fig. 7, we propose FFC-NAFBlock, which is derived from NAFBlock by substituting vanilla convolutions for fast Fourier convolutions, which have an image-wide receptive field. The pipeline of TRIN is depicted in Fig. 6. TRIN is a two-stage U-Net style encoder-decoder sub-network containing a coarse-inpainting stage and a refinement stage. The four-channel input is a source image concatenated with the predicted smooth text stroke mask I_{in}. Two Convs and twelve FFC-NAFBlocks make up the coarse-inpainting stage. The Conv is used to expand or reduce the feature channels while the FFC-NAFBlocks process the main inpainting.

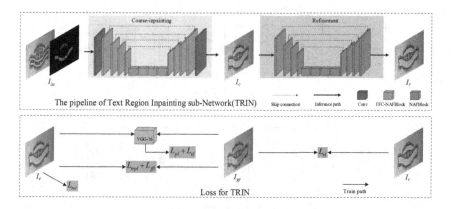

Fig. 6. The overview of TRIN. It consists of a coarse-inpainting sub-network and a refinement sub-network. The coarse-inpainting sub-network generates a rough intermediate result. The refinement sub-network produces the final result.

The coarse-inpainting stage produces a coarse result I_c. The refinement stage is made up of twelve NAFBlocks. I_c is routed to the refine-inpainting stage, where it is transformed into the refined result I_r. Both I_c and I_r are composited, meaning that non-text regions are the same as the source image.

2.5 Loss Functions of Text Region Inpainting Sub-Network (TRIN)

We employ six loss functions to train TRIN, including text region pixel loss, frequency loss, perceptual loss, style loss, total variation loss, and refinement loss. We denote the coarse-inpainting image as I_c, refined image as I_r, ground truth as I_{gt}, and the text box mask as M. Note we use the text box mask instead of the predicted smooth text stroke mask to indicate the text region position.

Text Region Pixel Loss. Text Region Pixel Loss is designed to optimize the pixel-level reconstruction only in the text region of the coarse-inpainting image, which is defined as:

$$L_{trpl}(M, I_c, I_{gt}) = \frac{sum(\|\mathbf{M} \odot (\mathbf{I_c} - \mathbf{I_{gt}})\|_1)}{sum(\mathbf{M})}. \tag{1}$$

Focal Frequency Loss. To reduce gaps between real images and generated images in the frequency domain, [13] proposed Focal Frequency Loss, which enables the network to adaptively pay attention to frequency components that are hard to synthesize by down-weighting the easy ones. We utilize Focal Frequency Loss to optimize the synthesis quality of the coarse-inpainting image

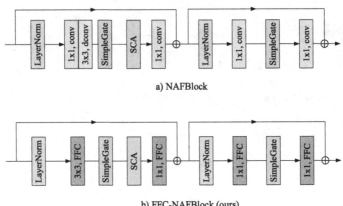

a) NAFBlock

b) FFC-NAFBlock (ours)

Fig. 7. Comparison between FFC-NAFBlock and NAFBlock. LayerNrom, SimpleGate and Simplified Channel Attention (SCA) are explained in [5]. FFC is explained in [6].

further. Focal Frequency Loss is formulated as follows:

$$L_{ffl}(I_c, I_{gt}) = \frac{1}{HW} \sum_{u=0}^{H-1} \sum_{v=0}^{W-1} w(u,v)|F_{I_c}(u,v) - F_{I_{gt}}(u,v)|^2. \quad (2)$$

$$w(u,v) = |F_{I_c}(u,v) - F_{I_{gt}}(u,v)|^\alpha. \quad (3)$$

where H means the image height, W means the image width, α is the scaling factor for flexibility ($\alpha=1$ in our experiments), F is the 2D discrete Fourier transform, and (u,v) represents the coordinate of a spatial frequency on the frequency spectrum.

Perceptual Loss. Perceptual Loss [14] makes generated images high-quality and more realistic with the help of a pre-trained VGG-16 [21] network. Perceptual Loss is defined as:

$$L_{pl}(I_c, I_{gt}) = \sum_{i=1}^{3} \|\phi_i(I_c) - \phi_i(I_{gt})\|_1. \quad (4)$$

where ϕ_i refers to the ith activation layer of the pre-trained VGG-16 network.

Style Loss. Style loss [10] used neural representations to separate and recombine the content and style of arbitrary images. We utilize the proposed Style Loss to measure the difference in style between the coarse-inpainting image and the ground truth. Similar to Perceptual Loss, Style Loss is defined as:

$$L_{sl}(I_c, I_{gt}) = \sum_{i=1}^{3} \frac{\|\varphi(\phi_i(I_c)) - \varphi(\phi_i(I_{gt}))\|_1}{H_i W_i C_i}. \quad (5)$$

Fig. 8. Qualitative results for ablation studies. (a) The input images; (b) Baseline results; (c) Baseline + STSM; (d) Baseline + STSM + FFC; (e) Baseline + STSM + FFC + FFL; (f) Baseline + STSM + FFC + FFL + Refinement;

where ϕ_i refers to the *ith* activation layer of the pre-trained VGG-16 network, $\varphi(x) = x^T x$ is the gram matrix operator, and $H_i W_i C_i$ refers to the shape of *ith* feature map.

Total Variation Loss. Total Variation Loss [14] is employed to preserve spatial continuity and smoothness in the coarse-inpainting image for global denoising.

$$L_{tvl}(I_c) = \sum_{i,j} \|I_c^{i,j+1} - I_c^{i,j}\|_1 + \|I_c^{i+1,j} - I_c^{i,j}\|_1. \tag{6}$$

where i, j is the coordinate of each pixel.

Refine Loss. The refined image is pixel-wise constrained using the Charbonnier term to approximate the ground truth. Refine Loss is written as:

$$L_{rl}(I_r, I_{gt}) = \sum_{i,j} \sqrt{(I_r^{i,j} - I_{gt}^{i,j})^2 + \epsilon^2}. \tag{7}$$

where i, j is the coordinate of each pixel, ϵ equals $1e - 6$.

Final Loss Function. The final loss function is as follows:

$$L_f = \lambda_1 L_{trpl} + \lambda_2 L_{ffl} + \lambda_3 L_{pl} + \lambda_4 L_{sl} + \lambda_5 L_{tvl} + \lambda_6 L_{rl} \tag{8}$$

We set $\lambda_1 = 6$, $\lambda_2 = 1$, $\lambda_3 = 0.05$, $\lambda_4 = 100$, $\lambda_5 = 0.1$ and $\lambda_6 = 1$ empirically.

3 Experiments

3.1 Datasets

To evaluate the the effectiveness of SSTRF, we conduct experiments on the three widely used benchmarks, SCUT-Syn [29], SCUT-EnsText [17], and Oxford dataset [11].

SCUT-Syn. SCUT-Syn is a synthetic dataset generated by SynthText [11]. It contains a training set of 8,000 images and a testing set of 800 images. The background images of this dataset are mainly collected from real scene, and the text instances in the background images are manually rubbed out.

SCUT-EnsText. SCUT-EnsText contains a total of 3,562 images with diverse text characteristics. It is split into a training set of 2,749 images and a testing set of 813 images. The text instances of this dataset are in various shapes, including horizontal text, arbitrary quadrilateral text, and curved text. Each instance is in either English or Chinese, and it is manually erased and filled with a visually plausible background by annotators using Adobe Photoshop.

Oxford. The Oxford dataset contains 0.8 million images generated from 8,000 text-free images. For a fair comparison, we follow the split strategy of GaRNet [15], in which 95% images are selected for training, 10,000 images are selected for testing, and the rest are used for validation. And the background images in the training set and the testing set are not duplicates.

3.2 Evaluation Metrics

To thoroughly examine the performance of our model, we utilize both Image-Eval and Detection-Eval metrics. Specifically, Image-Eval metrics include: 1) Peak Signal to Noise Ratio (PSNR); 2) Structural Similarity Index Measure (SSIM); 3) Mean Square Error (MSE); 4) Average of the Gray-level absolute Error (AGE); 5) Fréchet inception distance (FID) [12]. The higher PSNR, SSIM, and lower MSE, AGE, and FID denote better results. Detection-Eval metrics include Recall (R), Precision (P), and F-measure (F), which are defined as:

$$IoUMat_{i,j} = \frac{area(intersection(G_i, G_j))}{area(union(G_i, G_j))} \tag{9}$$

$$Recall(G, D) = \frac{\sum_i IF(max(IouMat_{i,j}) > t)}{|G|} \tag{10}$$

$$Precision(G, D) = \frac{\sum_j IF(max(IouMat_{i,j}) > t)}{|D|} \tag{11}$$

$$F - measure = \frac{2 \times Recall \times Precision}{Recall + Precision} \tag{12}$$

where G denotes the set of ground truth bounding boxes; D represents the set of detected bounding boxes; t is the threshold, commonly set to 0.5; IF denotes a logical function. The formula 9 calculates the IoU matrix between ground truth and detected bounding boxes. CRAFT [1] is used as an auxiliary scene text detector for evaluation. The lower R, P, and F indicate more text instances are concealed. To comprehensively compare with recent state-of-the-art methods, we evaluate PSNR, SSIM, AGE, R, P, and F metrics on SCUT-EnsNet; PSNR, SSIM, MSE, and FID metrics on SCUT-Syn; and PSNR, SSIM, AGE, R, P, and F metrics on Oxford.

3.3   Implementation Details

To train TSSN, we collected a corpus of 50,000 English and 30,000 Chinese words, over 2,000 English and Chinese fonts, and 14,630 background images without text for generating one million synthetic text images and corresponding smooth text stroke masks. TexRNet is the actual text mask extractor in TSSN. In the training process of TRIN, the input size is fixed at 256×256, and the batch size is set to 12. The Adam solver and cosine annealing schedule are adopted to optimize TRIN with $\beta = (0.9, 0.9)$ and the initial learning rate is set to 0.0001. One NVIDIA 3090 GPU is used in all experiments.

Table 1. Ablation Study on SCUT-EnsText. SSIM is represented by % in the table. The best score is highlighted in bold

	Image Eval		
	PSNR↑	SSIM↑	AGE↓
BaseLine	40.53	97.98	0.85
BaseLine+STSM	42.30	98.14	0.71
BaseLine+STSM+FFC	42.91	98.19	0.69
BaseLine+STSM+FFC+FFL	43.04	98.39	0.65
BaseLine+STSM+FFC+FFL+Refinement	**43.23**	**98.47**	**0.64**

3.4   Ablation Study

We conduct experiments on SCUT-EnsText to verify the validity of the smooth text stroke mask (STSM), fast Fourier convolution (FFC), Focal Frequency Loss (FFL) and the refinement stage (Refinement).

BaseLine. Our baseline also consists of a Text Stroke Segmentation sub-Network (TSSN) and a Text Region Inpainting sub-Network (TRIN). TexRNet is also the text mask extractor in the TSSN of the baseline, but it is supervised by the noisy hard binary text stroke mask obtained by binarizing the difference between the text image and the corresponding ground truth. The TRIN of the baseline is the original NAFNet, which has the the same structure as the coarse-inpainting stage illustrated in Fig. 6, but all FFC-NAFBlocks blocks are original

NAFBlocks. Table 1 shows the effectiveness of each part. "+STSM" indicates that TSSN is trained on synthetic data and predicts the smooth text stroke mask on scene text removal datasets. "+FFC" means that the FFC-NAFBlocks displace NAFBlocks in TRIN. "+FFL" implies that the loss functions of TRIN add Focal Frequency Loss. "+Refinement" denotes that the refinement stage is added to the tail of TRIN. Figure 8 shows the qualitative results.

Smooth Text Stroke Mask: Table 1 shows that the smooth text stroke mask significantly improves the performance of the baseline under weak supervision, with increases of 1.77, 0.16 in PSNR, SSIM and a decrease of 0.14 in AGE. Such a remarkable promotion is due to the fact that the smooth text stroke mask effectively distinguishes text regions with different erasure difficulties in comparison to the hard binary text stroke mask. Meanwhile, the comparison between Fig. 8 (b) and Fig. 8 (c) indicates that the smooth text stroke mask prevents the network from filling the incorrect background textures.

FFC and FFL: The effective receptive field of TRIN is expanded by fast Fourier convolutions (FFCs), which is advantageous for the overall structure perception of an image. As shown in Table 1, the incorporation of FFCs into NAFBlocks significantly improves all metrics, with gains of 0.61, 0.05 in PSNR and SSIM, and a decrease of 0.02 in AGE. The frequency domain gaps between the coarse-inpainting image and the ground truth are minimized using Focal Frequency Loss (FFL). After the training loss function of TRIN adds FFL, the network results in modest gains of 0.13, 0.2 in PSNR and SSIM, and a slight decrease of 0.04 in AGE on average. By comparing Fig. 8 (c) with Fig. 8 (d), FFC makes the network comprehend the whole image structure and fixes some undesired completions. Figure 8 (d) shows that FFL makes the generated results smoother and more level.

Refinement: It is not always optimal to have a large receptive field for inpainting the text region. The refinement stage aims to improve local structures and texture details in a small receptive field. Table 1 demonstrates that the combination of the coarse-inpainting sub-network (with a large receptive field) and a refinement sub-network (with a small receptive field) further achieves a slight improvement in the output image by 0.19 in PSNR, 0.08 in SSIM, and 0.01 in AGE, respectively. As shown in Fig. 8 (e) and Fig. 8 (f), the local defects can be removed more thoroughly.

Table 2. Comparison with state-of-the-art methods on SCUT-EnsText. The results of EnsNet, MTRNet, MTRNet++, and EraseNet were re-implemented and reported by GaRNet [15] under the new standard. The methods with "*" indicate that our reimplementation. SSIM, Precision (P), Recall (R) and F-measure (F) are represented by % in the table. The best score is highlighted in bold.

Method	Image Eval			Detection Eval		
	PSNR↑	SSIM↑	AGE↓	P↓	R↓	F↓
EnsNet	32.99	95.16	1.85	73.1	54.7	62.6
MTRNet	36.89	96.41	0.97	69.8	41.1	51.2
MTRNet++	36.50	96.51	1.35	58.6	20.5	30.4
EraseNet	40.18	97.98	0.69	37.3	6.1	10.3
GaRNet	41.37	98.46	**0.64**	15.5	1.0	1.8
CTRNet*	42.84	98.46	0.72	-	-	-
SSTRF (Ours)	**43.23**	**98.47**	**0.64**	**7.3**	**0.4**	**0.9**

3.5 Comparison with State-of-the-Arts

We compare the performance of SSTRF with recent state-of-the-art methods on the SCUT-EnsText, SCUT-Syn, and Oxford datasets. The quantitative results of the three datasets are given in Table 2, Table 3, and Table 4, respectively. For the SCUT-EnsText and Oxford datasets, the results of EnsNet, MTRNet, MTR-Net++, and EraseNet were re-implemented and reported by [15] under the new standard. We also re-implement CTRNet [16] under the new standard and report the result for SCUT-EnsText. The results for the three datasets demonstrate that SSTRF outperforms existing state-of-the-art methods on all Image-Eval metrics and Detection-Eval metrics, indicating that SSTRF can effectively erase the text on natural images and fill reasonable background textures.

Table 3. Comparison with state-of-the-art methods on SCUT-Syn. SSIM, and MSE are represented by % in the table. The best score is highlighted in bold.

Method	Image Eval			
	PSNR↑	SSIM↑	MSE↓	FID↓
Pix2pix	26.76	91.08	0.27	47.84
STE	25.40	90.12	0.65	46.39
EnsNet	36.23	96.76	0.04	19.96
EraseNet	38.32	97.67	0.02	9.53
MTRNet++	34.55	98.45	0.04	-
Weak supervision	37.46	93.64	-	-
PERT	39.40	97.87	0.02	-
Stroke-Based	38.60	97.55	0.02	-
CTRNet	41.28	98.50	0.02	3.84
SSTRF (Ours)	**44.31**	**98.79**	**0.01**	**3.66**

Table 4. Comparison with state-of-the-art methods on Oxford. SSIM, Precision (P), Recall (R) and F-measure (F) are represented by % in the table. The best score is highlighted in bold.

Method	Image Eval			Detection Eval		
	PSNR↑	SSIM↑	AGE↓	P↓	R↓	F↓
EnsNet	39.74	97.94	0.77	55.1	14.0	22.3
MTRNet	40.03	97.69	0.80	58.6	13.7	22.2
MTRNet++	40.64	97.94	0.73	64.0	15.9	25.4
EraseNet	42.98	98.75	0.56	31.4	**0.0**	1.4
GaRNet	43.64	98.64	0.55	18.9	0.1	0.3
SSTRF (Ours)	**43.93**	**99.13**	**0.42**	**6.3**	**0.0**	**0.1**

4 Conclusion

In this paper, we propose a new scene text removal framework (SSTRF) that utilizes the smooth text stroke mask and introduces a two-stage coarse-to-refinement text region inpainting sub-network that consists of a coarse-inpainting stage with a global receptive field and a refinement stage with a local receptive field to relieve the effective receptive field problem. We analyze the advantages of the smooth text stroke mask and predict the smooth text stroke mask on real data in a weakly supervised manner. The ablation study based on NAFNet shows the effectiveness of our proposed smooth text stroke mask and text region inpainting sub-network. SSTRF also significantly outperforms all existing state-of-the-art methods on three benchmark datasets in terms of all Image-Eval metrics and Detection-Eval metrics.

References

1. Baek, Y., Lee, B., Han, D., Yun, S., Lee, H.: Character region awareness for text detection. In: 2019 IEEE/CVF Conference on Computer Vision and Pattern Recognition (CVPR), pp. 9357–9366 (2019)
2. Bian, X., Wang, C., Quan, W., Ye, J., Zhang, X., Yan, D.M.: Scene text removal via cascaded text stroke detection and erasing. Comput. Visual Media 8(2), 273–287 (2022)
3. Bonechi, S., Bianchini, M., Scarselli, F., Andreini, P.: Weak supervision for generating pixel-level annotations in scene text segmentation. Pattern Recogn. Lett. **138**, 1–7 (2020)
4. Chen, L.-C., Zhu, Y., Papandreou, G., Schroff, F., Adam, H.: Encoder-Decoder with Atrous Separable Convolution for Semantic Image Segmentation. In: Ferrari, V., Hebert, M., Sminchisescu, C., Weiss, Y. (eds.) ECCV 2018. LNCS, vol. 11211, pp. 833–851. Springer, Cham (2018). https://doi.org/10.1007/978-3-030-01234-2_49
5. Chen, L., Chu, X., Zhang, X., Sun, J.: Simple baselines for image restoration. In: Avidan, S., Brostow, G., Cissé, M., Farinella, G.M., Hassner, T. (eds.) Computer Vision - ECCV 2022, pp. 17–33. Springer, Cham (2022). https://doi.org/10.1007/978-3-031-20071-7_2

6. Chi, L., Jiang, B., Mu, Y.: Fast fourier convolution. In: Larochelle, H., Ranzato, M., Hadsell, R., Balcan, M., Lin, H. (eds.) Advances in Neural Information Processing Systems, vol. 33, pp. 4479–4488. Curran Associates, Inc. (2020)

7. Cho, J., Yun, S., Han, D., Heo, B., Choi, J.Y.: Detecting and removing text in the wild. IEEE Access **9**, 123313–123323 (2021)

8. Conrad, B., Chen, P.I.: Two-stage seamless text erasing on real-world scene images. In: 2021 IEEE International Conference on Image Processing (ICIP), pp. 1309–1313 (2021)

9. Du, X., Zhou, Z., Zheng, Y., Wu, X., Ma, T., Jin, C.: Progressive scene text erasing with self-supervision (2022)

10. Gatys, L., Ecker, A., Bethge, M.: A neural algorithm of artistic style. J. Vis. **16**(12), 326–326 (2016)

11. Gupta, A., Vedaldi, A., Zisserman, A.: Synthetic data for text localisation in natural images. In: 2016 IEEE Conference on Computer Vision and Pattern Recognition (CVPR), pp. 2315–2324 (2016)

12. Heusel, M., Ramsauer, H., Unterthiner, T., Nessler, B., Hochreiter, S.: GANs trained by a two time-scale update rule converge to a local nash equilibrium. In: Guyon, I., et al. (eds.) Advances in Neural Information Processing Systems, vol. 30. Curran Associates, Inc. (2017)

13. Jiang, L., Dai, B., Wu, W., Loy, C.C.: Focal frequency loss for image reconstruction and synthesis. In: 2021 IEEE/CVF International Conference on Computer Vision (ICCV), pp. 13899–13909 (2021)

14. Johnson, J., Alahi, A., Fei-Fei, L.: Perceptual Losses for Real-Time Style Transfer and Super-Resolution. In: Leibe, B., Matas, J., Sebe, N., Welling, M. (eds.) ECCV 2016. LNCS, vol. 9906, pp. 694–711. Springer, Cham (2016). https://doi.org/10.1007/978-3-319-46475-6_43

15. Lee, H., Choi, C.: The surprisingly straightforward scene text removal method with gated attention and region of interest generation: a comprehensive prominent model analysis. In: Avidan, S., Brostow, G., Cissé, M., Farinella, G.M., Hassner, T. (eds.) Computer Vision - ECCV 2022, pp. 457–472. Springer, Cham (2022). https://doi.org/10.1007/978-3-031-19787-1_26

16. Liu, C., et al.: Don't forget me: accurate background recovery for text removal via modeling local-global context. In: Avidan, S., Brostow, G., Cissé, M., Farinella, G.M., Hassner, T. (eds.) Computer Vision - ECCV 2022, pp. 409–426. Springer, Cham (2022). https://doi.org/10.1007/978-3-031-19815-1_24

17. Liu, C., Liu, Y., Jin, L., Zhang, S., Luo, C., Wang, Y.: EraseNet: end-to-end text removal in the wild. IEEE Trans. Image Process. **29**, 8760–8775 (2020)

18. Lyu, G., Zhu, A.: PSSTRNET: progressive segmentation-guided scene text removal network. In: 2022 IEEE International Conference on Multimedia and Expo (ICME), pp. 1–6 (2022)

19. Nakamura, T., Zhu, A., Yanai, K., Uchida, S.: Scene text eraser. In: 2017 14th IAPR International Conference on Document Analysis and Recognition (ICDAR), vol. 01, pp. 832–837 (2017)

20. Quan, W., Zhang, R., Zhang, Y., Li, Z., Wang, J., Yan, D.M.: Image inpainting with local and global refinement. IEEE Trans. Image Process. **31**, 2405–2420 (2022)

21. Simonyan, K., Zisserman, A.: Very deep convolutional networks for large-scale image recognition. In: International Conference on Learning Representations (2015)

22. Suvorov, R., et al.: Resolution-robust large mask inpainting with fourier convolutions. In: 2022 IEEE/CVF Winter Conference on Applications of Computer Vision (WACV), pp. 3172–3182 (2022)

23. Tang, Z., Miyazaki, T., Sugaya, Y., Omachi, S.: Stroke-based scene text erasing using synthetic data for training. IEEE Trans. Image Process. **30**, 9306–9320 (2021)

24. Tursun, O., Denman, S., Zeng, R., Sivapalan, S., Sridharan, S., Fookes, C.: MTR-Net++: one-stage mask-based scene text eraser. Comput. Vis. Image Underst. **201**, 103066 (2020)

25. Tursun, O., Zeng, R., Denman, S., Sivapalan, S., Sridharan, S., Fookes, C.: MTR-Net: a generic scene text eraser. In: 2019 International Conference on Document Analysis and Recognition (ICDAR), pp. 39–44 (2019)

26. Wang, J., et al.: Deep high-resolution representation learning for visual recognition. IEEE Trans. Pattern Anal. Mach. Intell. **43**(10), 3349–3364 (2021)

27. Xu, X., Zhang, Z., Wang, Z., Price, B., Wang, Z., Shi, H.: Rethinking text segmentation: a novel dataset and a text-specific refinement approach. In: 2021 IEEE/CVF Conference on Computer Vision and Pattern Recognition (CVPR), pp. 12040–12050 (2021)

28. Yim, M., Kim, Y., Cho, H.-C., Park, S.: SynthTIGER: synthetic text image generator towards better text recognition models. In: Lladós, J., Lopresti, D., Uchida, S. (eds.) ICDAR 2021. LNCS, vol. 12824, pp. 109–124. Springer, Cham (2021). https://doi.org/10.1007/978-3-030-86337-1_8

29. Zhang, S., Liu, Y., Jin, L., Huang, Y., Lai, S.: EnsNet: ensconce text in the wild. Proceedings of the AAAI Conference on Artificial Intelligence **33**(01), 801–808 (2019)

Guided U-Net Aided Efficient Image Data Storing with Shape Preservation

Nirwan Banerjee$^{(\boxtimes)}$, Samir Malakar, Deepak Kumar Gupta, Alexander Horsch, and Dilip K. Prasad

Bio-AI Lab, Department of Computer Science, UiT The Arctic University of Norway, 9037 Tromsø, Norway
nirwan.banerjee@uit.no

Abstract. The proliferation of high-content microscopes (∼32 GB for a single image) and the increasing amount of image data generated daily have created a pressing need for compact storage solutions. Not only is the storage of such massive image data cumbersome, but it also requires a significant amount of storage and data bandwidth for transmission. To address this issue, we present a novel deep learning technique called Guided U-Net (GU-Net) that compresses images by training a U-Net architecture with a loss function that incorporates shape, budget, and skeleton losses. The trained model learns to selects key points in the image that need to be stored, rather than the entire image. Compact image representation is different from image compression because the former focuses on assigning importance to each pixel in an image and selecting the most important ones for storage whereas the latter encodes information of the entire image for more efficient storage. Experimental results on four datasets (CMATER, UiTMito, MNIST, and HeLA) show that GU-Net selects only a small percentage of pixels as key points (3%, 3%, 5%, and 22% on average, respectively), significantly reducing storage requirements while preserving essential image features. Thus, this approach offers a more efficient method of storing image data, with potential applications in a range of fields where large-scale imaging is a vital component of research and development.

Keywords: Compact Image Representation · Guided U-Net · Budget Loss · Shape Loss · Skeleton Loss · Storage Efficient

1 Introduction

Rapid advancement in digital technology has led to an exponential increase in the data generated daily. With the availability of the internet, social media, and smartphones, people are generating a considerable amount of digital content like texts, images, audio, and video. The sheer volume of data generated is quite large, with estimates suggesting that humans create and consume around 328.77 million terabytes of data daily and 120 zettabytes of data every year, with videos accounting for over half of internet traffic[1]. Even a single image from the domains

---

[1] https://explodingtopics.com/blog/data-generated-per-day.

H. Lu et al. (Eds.): ACPR 2023, LNCS 14406, pp. 317–330, 2023.
https://doi.org/10.1007/978-3-031-47634-1_24

like microscopy, nanoscopy, telescope, and satellite can generate a very large amount of data, similar in the orders of magnitude to the amount of data used by humans in a year. Specifically, the latest advancements in microscopy, like the CNI v2.0 microscope [15], can generate a single image of up to 32 gigabytes (Table 1). In contrast, multiple images in a z-stack or a time-series video can exceed a terabyte. Table 1 cites more such cases.

Table 1. Illustration of storage requirements for different microscopic data.

Type of cell organelle	Microscope	Image dimension	Size of image
Mitochondria	Deconvolutional	2048 × 2048	8.38 MB
	OMX	1024 × 1024	2.09 MB
	Confocal	512 × 512	0.52 MB
	RCM scan	2048 × 2048	8.38 MB
Vesicles, Lysosomes	Deconvolutional	2048 × 2048	8.38 MB
	Confocal	100 × 100	0.02 MB
Membrane/Cytoskeleton for Actin or Microtubule	Deconvolutional	2048 × 2048	8.38 MB
	Epiflourescent	2048 × 2048	8.38 MB
Liver Tissue	CNI v2.0	10240 × 10240	∼32000 MB

Storing and analyzing such large-sized data pose significant challenges to the scientific community, particularly in the field of biological sciences, where high-quality microscopy provides crucial information for potential breakthroughs in medical science. As we continue generating such voluminous data, a few of the concerns, but not limited to, that may arise in the future are as follows.

- **Storage issue:** One of the primary reasons for the inefficient storing of increased amounts of data is the requirement of expensive storage space. Traditional data storage methods, such as on-premise devices, can quickly become cost-prohibitive as data volumes increase. Thus, organizations may require to invest in buying storage from options like cloud storage, which can pose an extra cost to AI-driven products. Moreover, these increased numbers of data centers, in turn, convert these solutions into less sustainable and environmentally unfriendly ones.
- **Energy consumption:** Another issue with storing large amounts of data is the energy required. Data centers, which store massive amounts of data, are some of the largest energy consumers in the world. More data means more use of energy to store.
- **Data transmission cost:** The increased volume of data means an increased number of bits to transmit while sending data from one device to another. This scenario will consume more time and hence cost.

Overall, storing data in its original form is resource-intensive and ill impacts the environment. Thus, developing strategies for storing data using their compressed representation is vital to retrieve essential information only when required. By the term compressed representation of a datum (say, $\mathbb{D}$), we mean here storing it with less memory (say, $\mathbb{D}'$), i.e., $memoryUsage(\mathbb{D}') \ll memoryUsage(\mathbb{D})$. However, in the present work, we try to tackle this imminent problem in the premise of images. The work aims to represent images with fewer pixels while preserving their shape after kernel-based image reconstruction. Intuitively, to achieve the goal, we have tried to represent an input image (say, I with dimension $H \times W$) by selecting its key points. Let the method select m ($\ll H * W$) number of key points. The key points can be stored as x and y coordinates, costing $2 * m$. We can construct a new image (say, O with dimension $H \times W$) by setting the key points, and then by employing kernel-based convolution, the I can be reconstructed. Lowering the value of m, we can achieve more storage efficiency.

In this paper, we propose a deep learning-based method for the compressed representation of an image. Please note that we have restricted ourselves to grayscale images. Our method involves training a deep neural network (U-Net architecture [11]) to learn a compressed representation of images aiming to preserve the overall shape of the image. During model training, we apply point spread function (PSF) kernel-based image reconstruction from the set of selected points that are required to remember. The model is guided by three different losses, viz., budget, shape, and skeleton, and thus we call this model Guided U-Net (GU-Net). GU-Net can effectively reduce the storage requirement for an image to store.

2   Related Studies

The current work deals with representing image data in a compressed way while aiming to preserve their shapes. Some similar approaches are boundary-based representation, skeletonization, edge-based representation, and the like. Skeletonization is a popular approach for compact representation since it uses the least number of pixels. Hence, we discuss some state-of-the-art skeletonization approaches ranging from classical to deep learning.

2.1   Classical Approaches

Several conventional approaches exist for generating the skeleton of an image. Here, for simplicity, we discuss four well-known classical approaches. The thinning algorithms are one of the most popular approaches for skeletonization. Thinning refers to removing pixels from a component's boundary in an image until obtaining single pixel width. Some popular thinning methods proposed by Zhang et al. [17], Guo et al. [7], and Rosenfeld [12] relied on a set of rules to remove pixels to form the skeleton iteratively. However, thinning algorithms are sensitive to noise, and they may produce multiple skeletons or break the connectivity of the object in the image. The Medial Axis Transform (MAT) [6] is another popular approach for skeletonization. The MAT is a mathematical representation of the central axis of an object. It is obtained by estimating the

Voronoi diagram of the object boundary. The MAT has the advantage of preserving the connectivity of the object in the image and can handle noise well. However, generating the Voronoi diagram can be computationally expensive, especially for large-sized microscopy and nanoscopy images/videos. Morphological operations, such as erosion and dilation, are primarily used in morphological skeletonization. The morphological skeletonization algorithm involves iterating a set of morphological operations until a skeleton is obtained. Methods following this approach have the advantage of being implementation friendly and can handle noise to some extent. However, the resulting skeleton may be thicker than the skeleton obtained by other methods. Distance transform that computes the distance of each pixel in an object from the object boundary is also used to obtain the skeleton of an object by finding the points where the distance function is maximized. Distance transform-based skeletonization has the advantage of being fast and efficient. However, it may not preserve the connectivity of the object in the image and is susceptible to noise.

2.2   Deep Learning Approaches

Recently researchers have been focusing on designing deep-learning methods to extract the skeleton from an image. It treats the problem as either a pixel-to-pixel classification or an image-to-image translation. In both cases, a deep learning-aided segmentation protocol is used. A few deep learning-based methods dealing mentioned problem are discussed here. DeepSkeleton [14] proposes a multi-task learning framework that simultaneously learns the object skeleton and the object's scale at each pixel. The method is based on holistic edge detection that produces a set of side outputs used to refine the object skeleton at different scales. This framework consists of two key components: a Scale-associated Deep Side Output (SDSO) and a multi-task loss function. The SDSO module uses a series of convolutional layers to extract features at different scales from the input image. The multi-task loss function combines a skeletonization loss and a scale estimation loss, which jointly optimize the network to produce high-quality skeletons at multiple scales. It can be used on natural images. PSPU-SkelNet [2] uses three U-Net architectures for extracting point clouds from a given shape point cloud. The authors also introduce a novel loss function called the Symmetric Chamfer Distance (SCD) loss, which considers the extracted skeleton's accuracy and completeness. The SCD loss is defined as the average distance between each point on the Ground Truth (GT) skeleton and its nearest point on the predicted skeleton, and vice versa. SkelGAN [9] tries font skeletonization using a modified U-Net structure and a PatchGAN discriminator. The authors also proposed a novel loss function called the skeleton consistency loss, which encourages the generator to produce skeletons that match the structure of the input font image and have consistent topology and connectivity. In work [1], the authors used MAT to generate the skeleton from a binary image. This algorithm first computes the MAT of the object, and then the skeleton is obtained by pruning the MAT based on a set of criteria, such as the degree of curvature and the distance of points from the boundary of the object.

The aforementioned approaches focus primarily on skeleton generation from natural or binary images. It is noteworthy to mention that our focus is not on generating the skeleton of an image but on obtaining a compact representation of an image from where we can regenerate the image using some simple but effective convolutional operator. Thus, our representation might differ visually from the actual skeleton but the regenerated images look similar to the actual image. This discussion is clear from the images shown in Fig. 1. In this figure, we showcase the problem associated with skeleton-based (see Fig. 1) or edge-based (see Fig. 1) reconstruction when employed on an epifluorescent mitochondria images. This figure also contains output from the current method (see Fig. 1).

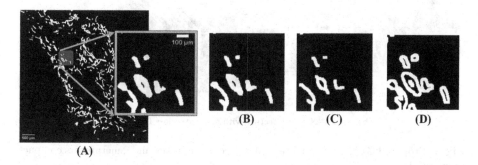

Fig. 1. Visual comparison of (A) original image taken from UiTMito [13] against reconstructed images obtained by employing PSF-based reconstruction from the compact representations generated using (B) our method (SSIM score= 0.9766) (C) skeletonization [7] (SSIM score = 0.9516) (D) edge detection [5] (SSIM score = 0.9040).

3 GU-Net: Detailed Description

In this section, we introduce GU-Net, a semi-supervised deep learning model used for shape-preserving compact representation of 2D data. We consider 2D data as a set of points in Euclidean space, and GU-Net suppresses data points while trying to maintain the original shape. A crucial aspect of our method is the ability to reconstruct the original data from its compact version. We employ our reconstruction technique (see Sect. 3.3). We use the U-Net architecture as a base segmentation network to segment an image into a set of points. However, we incorporate three loss functions to constrain the segmentation process: the skeleton loss encourages the model to select points near the skeleton of an input object; the shape loss guides the model to generate images with persistent shapes; and the budget loss controls the number of selected points, which the user specifies. Figure 2b shows the overall architecture of the proposed method.

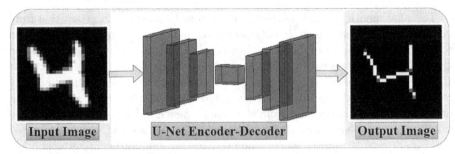

(a) Overall working procedure of the proposed method

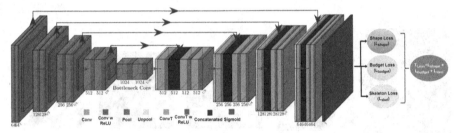

(b) Used U-Net architecture with associated loss functions

Fig. 2. Proposed GU-Net architecture that accepts an image and generates its compact representation.

3.1   Base Segmentation Network

The segmentation network used in GU-Net shares many similarities with the U-Net architecture [11]. Specifically, the up and down sampling components remain unchanged, while modifications have been made to the input feeding mechanism and the loss function. The selection of the U-Net model for this problem is based on its resilience in diverse applications that require accurate segmentation of images, such as biomedical image analysis. The strength of this architecture lies in its ability to generate high-resolution output images while maintaining the spatial information of the input image. This feature makes it particularly useful in object detection and recognition tasks, where preserving object boundaries is crucial. Moreover, the U-Net architecture can handle various input sizes and is computationally efficient, making it suitable for real-time applications.

During model design, instead of providing binary masks as labels to the U-Net architecture, we provide the skeleton of the input images generated by the method proposed by Zang et al. [17] as segmentation GT for the network. Such a setting encourages the network to select key points near the skeleton of the input image. One can feed the edges to the network as GT images, but such a setting will lead to selecting more key points. In addition to this, three loss functions (discussed in Subsect. 3.2) have been designed here to guide the network to select better key points.

3.2 Loss Functions

It has already been mentioned that GU-Net is guided by three different loss functions: skeleton loss, budget loss, and shape loss. Here, we discuss these loss functions (Fig. 3).

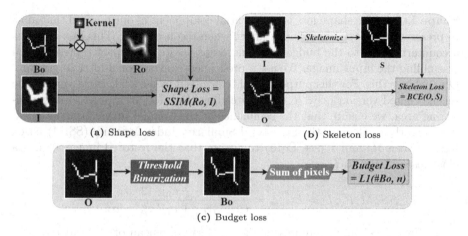

(a) Shape loss   (b) Skeleton loss

(c) Budget loss

Fig. 3. Computation of different loss functions used in this work.

Given an image I, output image O is generated by a segmentation network M (here GU-Net) and is represented by Eq. 1.

$$M(I) = O(\sim I) \tag{1}$$

Skeleton Loss: The skeleton loss guides the GU-Net to choose key points from the neighbour of the skeleton. The skeleton of the training images is provided to the GU-Net as a segmentation GT. Given an input image I, the skeleton S is calculated using Zhang's algorithm. The BCE loss is then calculated between O and S (see Eq. 2).

$$L_{skel}(O, S) = -W * [S \cdot log(O) + (1 - S) \cdot log(1 - O)] \tag{2}$$

Budget Loss: The budget loss works towards minimizing the number of selected key points from I. The number of selected pixels in O is calculated by binarizing O using a global threshold value. Given threshold t, binarized version B_o of O is calculated using Eq. 3.

$$B_o(x, y) = \begin{cases} 0, & \text{if } O(x, y) \leq t \\ 1, & \text{otherwise} \end{cases} \tag{3}$$

During model training, $t = 0.3$ is set. Thus, $n = \sum \sum B_o(x, y)$ is the number of selected key points in O. Next, we calculate the $L1$ norm (see Eq. 4) between n and a small integer n', user input representing the selected key points.

$$\sum B_o = L_{budget} = |n - n'| \tag{4}$$

Shape Loss: The shape loss is an essential component of our method that aims to preserve the shape of the input image when reconstructed. This loss serves as a counterbalance to the budget loss and helps create a compact representation resembling the input image. We use a predefined convolutional filter to generate O to achieve this. For this purpose, B_o is convolved by a 5×5 kernel to create the reconstructed version (say, R_o). By spreading the effect of a pixel to its neighboring area, we ensure that the semblance of the original image is maintained. Next, we then calculate the Structural Similarity Index Measure (SSIM) based loss between R_o and I (see Eq. 5) to ensure that the restored image attains a close resemblance to I.

$$SSIM(R_o, I) = L_{shape} = \frac{(2 \cdot \mu_{R_o} \mu_I + c_1) \cdot (2 \cdot \sigma_{R_o I} + c_2)}{(\mu_{R_o}^2 + \mu_I^2 + c_1)(\sigma_{R_o}^2 + \sigma_I^2 + c_2)} \tag{5}$$

In Eq. 5, μ_{R_o}, and μ_I represent the pixel sample mean of R_o, and I respectively while standard deviations of all pixel intensities present in R_o, and I are represented by σ_{R_o}, and σ_I respectively. Also, $\sigma_{R_o I}$ is the covariance between R_o and I. $c_1 = k_1 L^2, c_2 = k_2 L^2$ are two variables to stabilize the division with a weak denominator where L is the dynamic range of pixel values while $k_1 = 0.01, k_2 = 0.03$ are two constant values.

3.3   Method of Reconstruction

To reconstruct the actual image from compact representations generated by GU-Net, we use a simple but efficient PSF kernel. We convolve this kernel with B_o to generate the R_o. However, we use two more kernels: the Gaussian kernel, and the Mean kernel to test the effectiveness of our choice i.e., the PSF kernel. A comparative result is shown in Fig. 4, which visually ensures the effectiveness of the use of the PSF kernel in the reconstruction process.

4   Result and Discussion

In this work, we have designed GU-Net, which tries to generate the compressed representation of an input image. We have evaluated its performance on four diversified datasets to test its effectiveness. Notably, GU-Net is trained only on one dataset, and the trained module generates the compressed representation on other datasets. We have provided qualitative as well as quantitative performance. Additionally, we have performed some classification tasks to test how the reconstructed images behave.

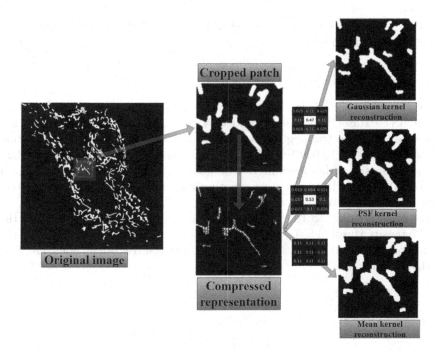

Fig. 4. Illustration of reconstruction process with varying kernels applied on a sample image taken from the UiTMito [13] dataset.

4.1 Database Description

The datasets in use are described here. Two handwritten (digit and word images) and two fluorescence microscopy datasets are considered for testing GU-Net's applicability almost on contrasting domains. **MNIST** [16] is a well-known dataset of handwritten digits widely used to benchmark different classification problems. The dataset consists of 70,000 images of handwritten digits, each of which is grayscale and has a resolution of 28×28 pixels. The images are labeled with their corresponding digit. **CMATERdb2.1.2** [3] (CMATER) is a handwritten Bangla word recognition dataset. It contains handwritten words representing 120 popular city names of the state of West Bengal, India. Each city name has 150 different handwritten samples. In short, this database is used for 120 class classification problems, primarily used for holistic word recognition purposes [10]. The **UitMito** dataset [13] is a collection of fluorescence microscopy images of live cells stained with a mitochondrial-specific fluorescent dye. The dataset contains 1000 2D grayscale images, each with a resolution of 1024×1024 pixels, and was captured over 1000 s. The dataset is split into a training set of 800 images and a test set of 200 images. The **2D HeLa** [4] (HeLa)dataset consists of fluorescence microscopy images of HeLa cells that have been stained with organelle-specific fluorescent dyes. The dataset includes images of 10 organelles, including DNA (nuclei), endoplasmic reticulum (ER), cis/medial Golgi (Giantin), cis Golgi

326   N. Banerjee et al.

(GPP130), lysosomes (Lamp2), mitochondria, nucleoli (Nucleolin), actin, endosomes (TfR), and tubulin.

4.2   Model Training

For training the model, we use the MNIST dataset. The model is trained on the MNIST dataset. The training dataset was divided into the training and the validation set. The training set consists of 50,000 images, and the validation dataset consists of 10,000 images. The images are of size 28 × 28. The Adam optimizer is used with a learning rate of 0.001. A batch size of 512 is used for a total of 10 epochs. Here we present experimental results for the hyperparameters used in the model training as shown in Fig. 5. We plot the RMSE and SSIM scores corresponding to the hyperparametric setup: the pixel budget and the pixel intensity threshold. As evident from Fig. 5a, we get the least RMSE at the setup point (10, 0.3), and we also get the highest SSIM score at point (10, 0.3) as shown in Fig. 5b.

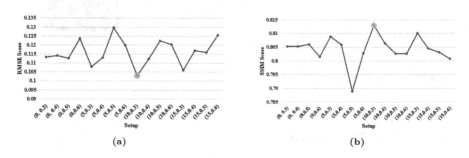

(a)   (b)

Fig. 5. Performance of the GU-Net in terms of (a) RMSE, and (b) SSIM scores with varying hyperparameters marked as (pixel budget, pixel intensity threshold)

4.3   Results

We assess the performance of GU-Net both qualitatively and quantitatively. We show some reconstructed images in Fig. 6. The figure shows that the proposed model can generate very close to the actual image while having less number of key points that are needed to store the images for future use (see Fig. 4).

For quantitative analysis, we use two different evaluation strategies. We perform image-to-image comparisons and classification performance on reconstructed images. We use root mean squared error (RMSE) and SSIM metrics for image-to-image comparison. The results are shown in Table 2b. This table shows the GU-Net's performance with varying kernels used during the reconstruction process on the top of selected key points. The threshold values are chosen experimentally (results shown in Fig. 5). Using these threshold values, significant compression is achieved as shown in Fig. 7a while still maintaining

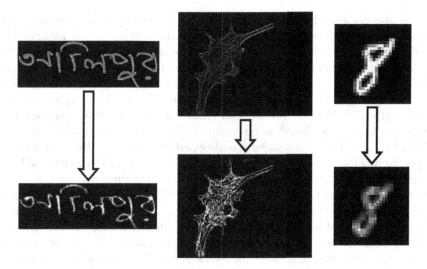

Fig. 6. Original (top) and reconstructed (bottom) images of the CMATER, HeLA, and MNIST datasets (left to right).

high reconstruction similarity scores (see Table 2a). The total number of pixels in the photos, expressed in bytes, was used to compute the storage needed for the original photographs. The total number of pixels for the entire dataset was then determined. We only record the key points' coordinates in bytes for the compressed picture representations. The full dataset is gone through this process again. The dataset's photos' dimensions are stored in an additional 2 bytes. These results ensure that the reconstructed images retain the crucial features of the original images and the overall quality of the reconstructed images is closely maintained.

Table 2. Quantitative comparisons of different compact representation methods.

(a) GU-Net with varying kernels. Here GU-Net selects keypoints and the mentioned kernels are used in the reconstruction process. $Th.$ represents the threshold value used for selecting keypoints in GU-Net. $\uparrow$, and $\downarrow$ represent larger, and smaller values mean better result respectively.

Dataset	Th.	Kernel	SSIM ($\uparrow$)	RMSE ($\downarrow$)
MNIST [16]	0.5	PSF	0.7943	0.0628
		Gaussian	**0.8397**	**0.0621**
		Mean	0.8041	0.0742
UiTMito [13]	0.005	PSF	**0.9526**	**0.0256**
		Gaussian	0.9431	0.0392
		Mean	0.9448	0.0364
CMATER [3]	0.5	PSF	**0.8344**	**0.0328**
		Gaussian	0.8267	0.0384
		Mean	0.8139	0.0455
HeLA [4]	0.05	PSF	**0.8885**	**0.0654**
		Gaussian	0.8592	0.0704
		Mean	0.8517	0.0744

(b) GU-Net with other compact representation techniques

Dataset	Method	SSIM ($\uparrow$)	RMSE ($\downarrow$)
MNIST	GU-Net	**0.8397**	**0.0621**
	Skeletonization	0.7926	0.1063
	PSPU-SkelNet	0.7470	0.1501
	Canny Edge	0.7922	0.1104
UiTMito	GU-Net	**0.9526**	**0.0256**
	Skeletonization	0.9393	0.0710
	PSPU-SkelNet	0.9407	0.0705
	Canny Edge	0.9388	0.0710
CMATER	GU-Net	**0.8344**	**0.0328**
	Skeletonization	0.7918	0.0648
	PSPU-SkelNet	0.7974	0.0775
	Canny Edge	0.7916	0.0783
HeLA	GU-Net	**0.8885**	**0.0654**
	Skeletonization	0.8337	0.1287
	PSPU-SkelNet	0.8873	0.0916
	Canny Edge	0.8034	0.1499

We also use classification accuracy to test the quality of the reconstructed images. Our goal does not involve generating the best scores for any particular dataset. Instead we test how the classification performance is affected by the proposed compressed representation of the images. We use a pre-trained EfficientNet B0 [8] model for the classification tasks. The classification task is performed using both original and reconstructed images. This experiment was conducted on MNIST, CMATER, and HeLa datasets, and the results are presented in Fig. 7b. The classification accuracy obtained on reconstructed MNIST, CMATER, and UiTMito images has dropped by 1.66%, 2.41%, and 13.16%, respectively. From Figs. 7a and 7b, it can be observed that in the case of HeLa dataset, the model demonstrated relatively poorer performance compared to the other datasets. The reason is that this dataset's biological structures contain many scattered points, leaving little room for ample reduction. Further, there is much bleeding of labeling fluid around the cell organelles, leading to a less efficient compact representation. Overall, our approach demonstrates promising results across all four datasets, showcasing the effectiveness of our discussed method for data compression, visualization, and preservation tasks.

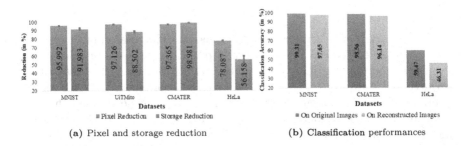

(a) Pixel and storage reduction   (b) Classification performances

Fig. 7. The comparison between compact representation and classification performances. The UiTMito dataset is not applicable for classification tasks.

4.4   Comparison with Other Compact Image Representation

To test the effectiveness of GU-Net aided image compact representation concerning some existing image representation techniques, namely Skeletonization [7], PSPU-SkelNet [2], and Canny edge [5], we choose the reconstruction kernel that performs the best (see Table 2a) during the reconstruction process. The performances of other existing methods and GU-Net are shown in Table 2b. Our method provides better SSIM and RMSE scores than traditional (i.e., Skeletonization and Canny Edge) and deep-learning-based (i.e., PSPU-SkelNet) methods. Moreover, when considering the visual quality of the reconstructed images (see Fig. 1), a noticeable distinction further supports our approach's efficacy.

5 Conclusion

In the present work, we develop GU-Net that selects key points to compactly store an image. GU-Net uses budget, shape, and skeleton losses while using U-Net architecture in the backbone. The effectiveness of the compact representation of images using GU-Net has been evaluated on four datasets: MNIST, CMATER, UiTMito, and HeLa. The visual and quantitative findings are promising. Despite the success of GU-Net, there is still room for improvement. It has already been observed that GU-Net fails to achieve similar results compared to others due to the presence of scattered points. Therefore, fruitful techniques, at least an effective reconstruction process, need to be devised for images with ample scattered points like HeLa in the future. GU-Net could be applied to more data to test its generalization capabilities. Finally, the work can be extended to 3-channel images in the future.

Acknowledgment. This work was supported by the nanoAI Research Council of Norway Project No. 325741, H2020 Project (OrganVision) 964800, and VirtualStain (UiT) Cristin Project ID: 2061348.

References

1. Abu-Ain, W., Abdullah, S.N.H.S., Bataineh, B., Abu-Ain, T., Omar, K.: Skeletonization algorithm for binary images. Procedia Technol. **11**, 704–709 (2013)
2. Atienza, R.: Pyramid U-network for skeleton extraction from shape points. In: Proceedings of the IEEE/CVF Conference on Computer Vision and Pattern Recognition Workshops (2019)
3. Bhowmik, S., Malakar, S., Sarkar, R., Basu, S., Kundu, M., Nasipuri, M.: Off-line Bangla handwritten word recognition: a holistic approach. Neural Comput. Appl. **31**, 5783–5798 (2019)
4. Boland, M.V., Murphy, R.F.: A neural network classifier capable of recognizing the patterns of all major subcellular structures in fluorescence microscope images of hela cells. Bioinformatics **17**(12), 1213–1223 (2001)
5. Canny, J.: A computational approach to edge detection. IEEE Trans. Pattern Anal. Mach. Intell. **6**, 679–698 (1986)
6. Castleman, K.R.: Digital Image Processing. Prentice Hall Press, Hoboken (1996)
7. Guo, Z., Hall, R.W.: Fast fully parallel thinning algorithms. CVGIP Image Understanding **55**(3), 317–328 (1992)
8. He, K., Zhang, X., Ren, S., Sun, J.: Deep residual learning for image recognition. In: Proceedings of the IEEE Conference on Computer Vision and Pattern Recognition, pp. 770–778 (2016)
9. Ko, D.H., Hassan, A.U., Majeed, S., Choi, J.: SkelGAN: a font image skeletonization method. J. Inf. Process. Syst. **17**(1), 1–13 (2021)
10. Malakar, S., Sharma, P., Singh, P.K., Das, M., Sarkar, R., Nasipuri, M.: A holistic approach for handwritten Hindi word recognition. Int. J. Comput. Vision Image Process. (IJCVIP) **7**(1), 59–78 (2017)
11. Ronneberger, O., Fischer, P., Brox, T.: U-Net: convolutional networks for biomedical image segmentation. In: Navab, N., Hornegger, J., Wells, W.M., Frangi, A.F. (eds.) MICCAI 2015. LNCS, vol. 9351, pp. 234–241. Springer, Cham (2015). https://doi.org/10.1007/978-3-319-24574-4_28

12. Rosenfeld, A.: A characterization of parallel thinning algorithms. Inf. Control **29**(3), 286–291 (1975)

13. Sekh, A.A., et al.: Physics-based machine learning for subcellular segmentation in living cells. Nat. Mach. Intell. **3**(12), 1071–1080 (2021)

14. Shen, W., Zhao, K., Jiang, Y., Wang, Y., Bai, X., Yuille, A.: Deepskeleton: learning multi-task scale-associated deep side outputs for object skeleton extraction in natural images. IEEE Trans. Image Process. **26**(11), 5298–5311 (2017)

15. Villegas-Hernández, L.E., et al.: Chip-based multimodal super-resolution microscopy for histological investigations of cryopreserved tissue sections. Light Sci. Appl. **11**(1), 43 (2022)

16. Yan, L., Corinna, C., Burges, C.: The MNIST dataset of handwritten digits (1998)

17. Zhang, T.Y., Suen, C.Y.: A fast parallel algorithm for thinning digital patterns. Commun. ACM **27**(3), 236–239 (1984)

HO3-SLAM: Human-Object Occlusion Ordering SLAM Framework for Traversability Prediction

Jonathan Tay Yu Liang and Kanji Tanaka[✉]

University of Fukui, Fukui, Japan
tnkknj@u-fukui.ac.jp

Abstract. Detecting traversable areas from monocular vision is a fundamental problem for safe and efficient indoor robot navigation. Recent advances in deep learning have made it possible to detect floor regions stably and robustly. However, most existing methods rely on the direct visibility of the floor, which is often violated in crowded scenes like office environments, limiting their effectiveness. To address this limitation, we explore a novel approach that leverages pedestrian observation. By observing pedestrian behavior and assuming the floor region they occupy as traversable, we complement existing solutions. Recent advancements in computer vision techniques, including dynamic object detection (e.g., YOLO object detector), absolute localization of stationary objects (e.g., SLAM), and relative localization between dynamic and stationary objects (e.g., Occlusion ordering), enable the implementation of this approach. We developed a prototype system by extending state-of-the-art techniques in dynamic SLAM and object detection and conducted real-world experiments to demonstrate its basic performance. Our approach has significant potential for applications in challenging domains such as human-robot collaboration and long-horizon action planning.

Keywords: SLAM · Occlusion Ordering · Traversability Prediction

1 Introduction

Detecting traversable areas using monocular cameras is crucial for safe and efficient robot navigation. This problem has been extensively studied in computer vision, with various approaches such as obstacle detection [1], free space detection [2], and 3D reconstruction [3–5]. Many researchers have used deep learning models to predict pixel-level depth values from images [1], while others have developed vision-based algorithms that gradually expand into free space from the robot's feet [2]. Additionally, some studies have focused on reconstructing 3D geometric models using the robot's onboard camera view sequence [3–5]. However, most of the existing studies assume that the floor area is directly visible, which is not always the case in crowded scenarios. For instance, in crowded scenes like an office where humans and robots collaborate [6], obstacles (e.g., desks) often occlude the floor areas humans are standing on. In such situations, floor detection methods become ineffective, and neither obstacle detection nor 3D reconstruction methods can provide floor information.

H. Lu et al. (Eds.): ACPR 2023, LNCS 14406, pp. 331–343, 2023.
https://doi.org/10.1007/978-3-031-47634-1_25

To address this issue, we propose an innovative approach to learning traversable areas by tracking pedestrians, i.e., observing the behaviour of pedestrians assuming that the floor region they are standing on is traversable. From our observation, it is recently becoming possible to implement this new approach by combining state-of-the-art of computer vision techniques, including (1) detection of dynamic objects (e.g., YOLO [7] object detector), (2) absolute localization of stationary objects (e.g., DynaSLAM [8]), and (3) relative localization between dynamic and stationary objects (e.g., Occlusion ordering). Moreover, typical objects in human environments like desks are not tall enough to occlude a pedestrian's entire body. Finally, we infer the occlusion order of stationary objects and pedestrians in the same image coordinate system to localize the pedestrians in terms of their position relative to the stationary objects, whose absolute coordinates are reconstructed. We will be using Detectron2 instance segmentation mask method [9] and bounding box method for occlusion order reasoning. After that, we make an ablation study on the combination of the methods to achieve more desirable results. We conducted preliminary experiments that showed how deep learning based YOLOv7 [7] detectors could easily detect regions in human images. Although the lower body and floor contact areas of humans are often occluded, the head and upper body are detectable and not occluded.

This research is closely related to the large-body research area of pedestrian observation. However, most of them are not intended for traversable region analysis. Furthermore, many of them assumed a fixed-point camera. To the best of our knowledge, the current work is the first to explore traversable area analysis from moving cameras [10].

In summary, our approach to learning traversable areas by tracking pedestrians represents a significant improvement over existing methods that rely on the assumption that the floor area is directly visible. By leveraging the maturity of human detection technology and the occlusion patterns of stationary objects and pedestrians, our approach can effectively detect traversable areas in crowded scenes, making robot navigation safer and more efficient.

2 Related Works

This section presents most relevant approaches and draws a relation to these previous works of the proposed method. Furthermore, we clearly state the application domain to which the proposed method contributes. In particular, we will focus on work that assumes monocular vision rather than other sensor modalities such as 3D point cloud scanners or stereo cameras. We extensively took advantage of the easy accessibility of monocular cameras for the usage of SLAM system and further explored the achievability of such system.

Traversable region detection problem is closely related to visual reconstruction problems such as structure-from-motion (SfM) [4], simultaneous localization and mapping (SLAM) [3, 11, 12] and visual odometry (VO) [5]. These approaches aim to reconstruct the robot's ego-motion and geometric environment models from the robot's view sequence. Among them, SLAM, a problem setup that sequentially updates environmental geometric models or maps from live view sequences, is most relevant to this work. Existing solutions of SLAM can be divided into filtering-based [13] and optimization-based methods [14], with the latter dominating the current state of the art. While most of existing optimization-based methods assume stationary or semi-stationary environments, new types of SLAM techniques have emerged in recent years that addresses a dynamic environment [12], as we focus on in this study. In particular, our implementation is inspired by one of the state-of-the-art technologies, DynaSLAM [8], which will be detailed in the subsections described later. However, all of the existing reconstruction techniques only targeted specific traversable regions that are directly visible from the robot. In contrast, our approach aims to predict traversable regions that are not directly visible by using the indirect means of pedestrian observation.

Traversable region detection technology contributes to several important applications of visual navigation such as point goal navigation [15], object goal navigation [16] and coverage path planning [17]. In these applications, representations based on traversable regions are often used for state recognition and action planning. Compared with existing traversable region detection techniques that aim to reconstruct directly visible regions, our approach extends the scope of the reconstruction target from visual regions to even invisible regions which pedestrians are standing on. This brings a number of benefits. First, from the perspective of human-robot collaboration [6], the area where the pedestrian is standing often contains more contextual and semantic information that is important for the task compared to other areas. Second, from the perspective of state recognition and action planning, considering not only the visible area but also the invisible areas enable rich state representation and long-horizon exploration planning [18]. It should be noted that there are other approaches to traversable region detection [19], such as obstacle detection and floor detection [2] and monocular depth regression [1]. These approaches again aim to recognize obstacle-free regions or traversable floor regions that are directly visible to the robot. Therefore, they and our approach are in a complementary relationship.

2.1 DynaSLAM

DynaSLAM is a state-of-the-art visual simultaneous localization and mapping (SLAM) algorithm that builds on the foundation of ORB-SLAM2 [20]. One of the primary challenges in dynamic SLAM is distinguishing between camera motion and object motion within the scene. DynaSLAM overcomes this by using a probabilistic model to estimate the likelihood of an object's motion. If an object's motion is inconsistent with the predicted motion based on the camera's motion, it is identified as a dynamic object and removed from the map.

Our approach shares the design philosophy with DynaSLAM in two respects. First, our approach is also modular, with several modules such as static object modeling and dynamic object detection, each of which is connected to the ever-growing cutting-edge research field, including object detection [7], tracking [21], scene parsing [22], reconstruction [3], inpainting [23], occlusion reasoning, and action planning [17]. Second, the module group for stationary object recognition and the module group for dynamic object recognition are clearly separated, which allows us to focus on research and development of the latter module group without modifying the former module group.

However, our approach is different from DynaSLAM in many aspects. In particular, it introduces a new type of observation that is independent of the observations used by DynaSLAM. That is, relative observations of interactions between stationary and dynamic objects are used by our new observation model, in contrast to the absolute metric observations from stationary and dynamic objects used by DynaSLAM.

3 Approach

Our approach leverages the strengths of ORB-SLAM3 [24] and YoloV7 [7] human detection model to address the challenge of reasoning the occlusion order of humans and objects in crowded environments. ORB-SLAM3 is a leading visual SLAM algorithm that provides real-time tracking of the camera pose and map features. Meanwhile, YoloV7 is a highly accurate and efficient deep learning-based object detection model, which has superior performance in human detection.

Our framework has three sub-modules: static object modeling, moving object detection, and occlusion order inference. Given these modules, the system localizes the pedestrian region on the floor by sequentially performing static object modeling, moving object detection, and occlusion order inference. The subsections below provide details on each module used.

3.1 Static Object Modelling

The generation of 3D point clouds using ORB-SLAM3 [24] is a major advancement in vision and robotics. SLAM involves navigating and mapping unknown environments, and existing approaches can be categorized as filter-based (e.g., EKF [25]) or optimization-based (e.g., Graph-SLAM [26]). Filter-based methods provide real-time estimation updates, while optimization-based methods offer accurate and consistent maps. ORB-SLAM3, the latest version of the ORB-SLAM algorithms [27], is a powerful tool that can be used with various camera types and incorporates new features, including the robust DBoW3 feature descriptor [28]. Its output is a highly accurate point cloud representing the robot's environment, bringing significant progress to SLAM and applications in robotics and computer vision.

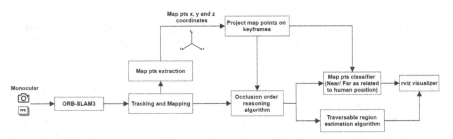

Fig. 1. Block diagram of our proposed framework. A segmented video stream in rosbag format is pass into ORB-SLAM3 [24]. The feature points coordinates are extracted and projected onto the keyframes for visualization. By comparing the map pts 3D location/distance to the camera and the location of the human to the camera, we classify the map pts to two simple classes (Near and Far). We can obtain the human estimated location in the 3D map and hence estimate the traversable region. The final outcome can be visualized using rviz visualizer [30].

3.2 Dynamic Object Detection

In our study, we utilized two different approaches for pedestrian detection: YOLO V7 [7], a representative object detector and the state-of-the-art model at the time of this writing, and Detectron2, which we used to treat pedestrian detection as a semantic segmentation problem. While YOLO V7 represents the human region as a bounding box, Detectron2 [9], represents it as a free-form region, allowing for a more accurate approximation of the human domain. Conversely, YOLO V7's bounding box representation offers a high frame rate, making it an attractive option in scenarios where speed is critical.

To compare the performance of these two methods, we conducted experiments to evaluate their accuracy and computational speed in the common field of real-time processing. Our results, which are reported in the experimental section, shed light on the relative strengths and weaknesses of the two approaches. Ultimately, our study provides valuable insights for researchers and practitioners seeking to optimize pedestrian detection performance for real-time applications.

3.3 Occlusion Order Inference

Pedestrian tracking is a fundamental task in computer vision that aims to locate and follow people's movement in visual scenes. However, occlusions caused by other humans or objects can pose significant challenges to accurate pedestrian localization. To address this issue, we have developed a technique called occlusion-ordering-based relative-depth estimation which aims to analyze depth values to determine the occlusion order of humans and objects. By leveraging occlusion-ordering information, it becomes possible to discern which person or object appears to be in front of another. Specifically, when one person's occlusion order is consistently greater than that of another person or object, it suggests that the latter is occluded by the former. This method is particularly useful in crowded environments where people and objects are likely to overlap, making it difficult to accurately track individual pedestrians.

The implementation of occlusion-ordering-based relative-depth estimation has practical applications for various fields, including indoor robot navigation, where accurate pedestrian localization is necessary for detecting traversable regions. By improving the accuracy of pedestrian tracking, this approach can enhance the ability of robots to navigate in crowded indoor environments and operate safely and efficiently in these settings.

3.4 Implementation Details

We developed a prototype of the proposed system by adding some changes to the public code of ORB-SLAM3 [24]. In particular, we modified some of the original code by adding some functionalities with some built-in ORB-SLAM3 APIs. We make use of ROS nodes to achieve concurrent process of ORB-SLAM3, extraction and projection of feature points and keyframes, occlusion ordering algorithm, and finally visualization on rviz visualizer. The framework is capable of processing data from a moving camera, perform human occlusion ordering algorithm and finally output the result on rviz visualizer concurrently. The traversable region will be clearly shown on the rviz visualizer as well. From Fig. 1, we can see the flowchart block diagram of the framework. The entire framework consists of two main components: ORB-SLAM3 and occlusion mapping.

3.5 ORB-SLAM3 Components

1. Feature points and keyframes extraction.

The initial stage of this framework includes the ORB-SLAM3 process. We obtain feature points generated by ORB-SLAM3, which are shown as green feature points on the map in this context. In ORB-SLAM3, the feature points are obtained using the Oriented FAST and Rotated BRIEF (ORB) feature detector and descriptor. The ORB feature detector identifies key points in the image based on their high intensity gradients and corner-like structures. Once the key points are detected, the ORB descriptor is computed for each key point. These key points serve as potential feature points, each consisting of coordinate information that can be extracted for our purposes. In the original framework, ORB-SLAM3 also outputs the keyframes information.

To achieve this, we modified the original ros_mono.cc, System.cc and System.h files. In ros_mono.cc, a new function is added to save the keyframe trajectory and feature points coordinates. A logic is added to check if a new keyframe is added and save it as images in the image grabber function. Two functions are added to System.cc and System.h: GetLastKeyFrameID(), SaveMapAndTracjectory().

Modifications have been made to the image grabber class in ros_mono.cc to publish 3D points and 2D projections into a custom ROS topic. The 2D projection features the projection of feature points onto the keyframes.

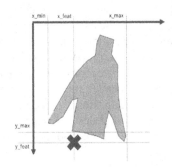

Fig. 2. Projected feature points in rviz visualizer.   **Fig. 3.** Occlusion ordering algorithm.

2. Projection of feature points onto keyframes.

While the coordinate information of the feature points is being extracted, the green feature points are projected onto the keyframes concurrently [10]. A Python code has been developed for this process. Initially, the keyframe pose is represented as a quaternion, so we need to convert it into a 3x3 matrix before passing it to OpenCV [29] which calculates it. We can visualize the projection with rviz [30] visualizer as shown in Fig. 2. The trajectory and feature points are clearly visible in this visualizer. The green points represent the feature points that are being projected onto the current keyframe, while the red points represent the feature points generated by ORB-SLAM3. The green trajectory represents the camera position trajectory.

3.6 Occlusion Mapping Components

In this component, a custom message type called TrackedFrame.msg has been created. It will be used by ORB-SLAM3 to publish the required information.

1. Occlusion ordering algorithm.

A Python code detect.py which is modified from the original detectron2 code was used to provide human detection model, Detectron2 human masking and occlusion ordering algorithm. In this code, TrackedFrame.msg was read and near/ far points was calculated. The outcome was published to rviz visualizer for visualization purposes. The occlusion ordering algorithm makes use exclusively of the human area range and the feature points coordinates in 2D space. This is simply a 2-class classification problem where we classify the feature points as in front of or behind the human with higher probability.

As shown in Fig. 3, the 'X' represents the feature points with coordinates (x_feat, y_feat). (x_min, x_max, y_min, y_max) represents the human area range. A simple if-else statement loop can determine and estimate the position of the feature points with higher probability. It could efficiently be integrated into SLAM systems and be used in environments with greatly degraded visual information. We label the feature points in our output video for a better visualization of the algorithm. The cases for the feature points labels are as follows:

Fig. 4. Feature points occlusion reasoning value annotations

Fig. 5. Feature points annotations with occlusion ordering algorithm.

d = '-1' when the feature points are in front of the human.
d = '1' when the feature points are behind of the human.
d = '0' when the feature points are not available/ not in range of the human area.

As shown in Fig. 4, the feature points which are in range of the human area are correctly classified as '-1' which means that the feature points are in front of the human. On the other hand, the feature points that are in the x range and out of y range can be classified as '1' which means the feature points are behind the human with a higher probability. In a '0' case, it means that the feature points are out of the human area range and are not available to be classified. We execute the occlusion ordering algorithm

338   J. Tay Yu Liang and K. Tanaka

and then projects the feature points onto keyframes to find the estimated location of the human in 3D space. Once again, the outcome can be visualized with rviz visualizer with colored feature points. As shown in Fig. 5, the board that is behind the human has a lot of feature points built by ORB-SLAM3 [24]. The feature points 3D coordinates are used to be compared with the human location and hence are classified as '1' which means that is behind the human. We can ultimately visualize this with rviz [30] visualizer. For the scene in Fig. 5, as shown in Fig. 6, we can observe that there are points that are colored as Orange and Purple.

Fig. 6. Feature points colored for visualization purpose.

The orange cluster is the feature points which are behind the human in this scene. All the points that are labeled as '1' and observed at the current frame are colored as orange and classified as behind the human. On the other hand, feature points that are classified as purple are the points that are in front of the human. On the other hand, if the human is standing behind the board, as shown in Fig. 7 and Fig. 8, the purple cluster would simply represent the feature points of the board, which is in front of the human. The visualized results are as shown in Fig. 10. By observation, we can conclude that the human is standing right in between the orange and purple cluster.

Fig. 7. Human standing behind the board.   **Fig. 8.** Human standing behind the board visualized.

2. Occupancy Grid Map.

We can concurrently display the map points using a 2D occupancy grid map using rviz visualizer as well as shown in Fig. 9. The map shows a red box indicating the possible human position, and a map of obstacles being marked. The red arrow indicates the current camera point-of-view. The traversable region in the map is marked with grey contour in the visualizer. The grid map is obtained by using the built in OccupancyGrid message type in ROS. The occupancy grid map can hold values from 0 to 100. Close to 0 is considered to be free space and close to 100 is considered to be occupied. Every time an obstacle is marked the value will increase by 10. The concurrent process is achievable with the usage of ROS nodes, and we can continuously update the frames to the visualizer with a moving camera video.

Fig. 9. Occupancy Grid map as shown in rviz.

4 Experimental Results

4.1 Experimental Environment Setup

We first set up the test environment in a wide area to build a map with ORB-SLAM3 [24] as shown in Fig. 10. A large object, such as a board, is positioned somewhere in the middle to serve as the occlusion object.

Fig. 10. Example Scene.   **Fig. 11.** Human occluded scenario.

The video stream is utilized to track and map the environment, aiming to generate a map with a sufficient number of sparse feature points using ORB-SLAM3. Consequently, the environment needs to be spacious enough to ensure the acquisition of a high-quality map with sparse feature points.

4.2 Preparing Input Video

As the framework is capable of executing ORB-SLAM3 mapping and the occlusion ordering algorithm at the same time, a video stream featuring a human subject who for the occlusion ordering algorithm is present, as shown in Fig. 11. The pedestrian performed a natural walking motion without understanding the intention of the experiment. We scan and map the environment as much as possible with the human moving in the scene. The video is then converted to rosbag format, <video>.bag.

4.3 Running with Data Obtained

Once we have the rosbag file ready, we simply start up an ORB-SLAM3 process with the occlusion algorithm and rviz visualizer running concurrently. All the process runs concurrently at once as shown in Fig. 12.

Fig. 12. Processes running concurrently.   **Fig. 13.** An instance of ground-truth annotation.

4.4 Studying with Annotated Ground Truth

We randomly sampled 50 feature points and manually annotated their correct classifications (Behind or in front). By comparing the ground truth with our system's runs, we investigated the algorithm's performance. We randomly selected 5 frames and calculated the average percentage of correctly labeled feature points. All the feature points are annotated relative to the human position, as shown in Fig. 13. Observation by eyes and manual annotation is carried out to obtain an accurate ground truth. The framework classifies the feature points with different colors in rviz [30] for visualization purposes. As shown in Table 1, an outstanding correctness rate of 96.71% has been achieved.

The results are recorded in the Table 1:

Table 1. Ground truth vs Actual run performance (Abbreviations: GT – Ground Truth, R – Run)

No	Annotated feature points				
	GT_Front	*GT_Behind*	*R_Front*	*R_Behind*	*%*
1	2	48	2	48	100.00
2	4	46	4	46	100.00

(continued)

Table 1. (*continued*)

No	Annotated feature points				
	GT_Front	*GT_Behind*	*R_Front*	*R_Behind*	*%*
3	7	43	7	43	100.00
4	35	15	32	18	91.43
5	38	12	35	15	92.11
Average = 96.71					

For ground truth assessment, we randomly selected 5 frames and manually annotated the green feature points. We compared the accuracy of our framework with the ground truth annotations to evaluate its performance. Based on our experiments, the algorithm demonstrates exceptional performance when the human is positioned in front of the occlusion. Our proposed framework exhibits robustness and is deemed to perform well.

4.5 Ablation Study

Table 2 presents the results of a series of ablation studies that combine the modules in the proposed framework. These studies utilize human-object occlusion ordering datasets to evaluate the performance of the methods employed. The occlusion ordering algorithm is executed using the YOLO v7 [7] human detection model. Traditionally, bounding boxes are applied around the detected objects when using such human detection models. In our case, we can directly use the bounding box edges (x_min, x_max, y_min, y_max) to determine the position of the feature points using the algorithm. A detailed explanation is provided in Fig. 3. Alternatively, we can incorporate the Detectron2 instance segmentation mask for this purpose. It is worth noting that during the ORB-SLAM3 [24] process, unwanted map can occasionally be generated on dynamic objects, which in our case, is the human. To address this issue, we can apply a filter using the same Detectron2 mask on the human area. This filtering method is essentially what we have employed in our proposed framework. We processed 3 different datasets and evaluated their performances using different methods. The correctness ratio represents the percentage of correctly labeled feature points compared to manually annotated ground truths. The method used is the same as shown in Table 1. We randomly sampled 50 feature points from random frames and annotated them through observation. The limitations of the bounding box method in obtaining an accurate contour of the human pose present an obvious flaw in this study. For example, when the human is positioned behind an object, the bounding box may include points that are located at the side of the human contour, leading to a larger inaccuracy in the estimation. On the other hand, utilizing Detectron2 to acquire the contour of the human shape offers a significantly more reliable and accurate method. This approach allows us to filter out unwanted feature points associated with the human and obtain a precise boundary that corresponds to the actual human pose.

Table 2. Ablation studies with different module.

	1st	2nd	3rd
Mask with Mask filter (Proposed)	1.0	0.96	0.98
B.Box with Mask filter	0.87	0.79	0.78
B.Box	0.75	0.71	0.73

5 Conclusions

In conclusion, our research introduces a simple yet robust human-object occlusion ordering framework for estimating traversable regions in crowded environments using SLAM systems. By leveraging the position of pedestrians, we can accurately predict traversable areas based on the occlusion order between humans and objects. The framework's simplicity makes it easy to implement and integrate into existing SLAM systems, while still demonstrating remarkable robustness in handling occlusions in complex and dense environments. This has significant implications for various applications, such as robot navigation and autonomous vehicles, where accurately predicting traversable areas is crucial for safe and efficient movement.

References

1. A. Bhoi, "Monocular Depth Estimation: A Survey," arXiv:1901.09402, p. 8 (2019)
2. Xu, Y., Ghamisi, P.: Consistency-regularized region-growing network for semantic segmentation of urban scenes with point-level annotations. IEEE Trans. Image Process. 31, 5038–5051 (2022)
3. Cadena, C., et al.: Past, Present, and Future of simultaneous localization and mapping: towards the robust-perception age. IEEE Trans. Rob. 32(6), 1309–1332 (2017)
4. Moran, D., Koslowky, H., Kasten, Y., Maron, H., Galun, M., Basri, R.: Deep permutation equivariant structure from motion. In: IEEE/CVF International Conference on Computer Vision (ICCV), pp. 5976–5986 (2021)
5. Wang, S., Clark, R., Wen, H., Trigoni, N.: DeepVO: towards end-to-end visual odometry with deep recurrent convolutional neural networks. In: 2017 IEEE International Conference on Robotics and Automation (ICRA), pp. 2043–2050 (2017)
6. Selvaggio, M., Cognetti, M., Nikolaidis, S., Ivaldi, S., Siciliano, B.: Autonomy in physical human-robot interaction: a brief survey. IEEE Robot. Autom. Lett. 6(4), 7989–7996 (2021)
7. Bochkovskiy, A., Liao, H.-Y.M., Wang, C.-Y.: YOLOv7: trainable bag-of-freebies sets new state-of-the-art for real-time object detectors. arXiv (2022)
8. Bescos, B., Fácil, J.M., Civera, J., Neira, J.: DynaSLAM: tracking, mapping, and inpainting in dynamic scenes. IEEE Robot. Autom. Lett. 3(4), 4076–4083 (2018)
9. Wu, Y., Kirillov, A., Massa, F., Lo, W.-Y., Girshick, R.: Detectron2, Facebook (2019). https://github.com/facebookresearch/detectron2. Accessed 19 Mar 2023
10. Jonathan Tay, T.K.: HO3-SLAM: human-object occlusion ordering as add-on for enhancing traversability prediction in dynamic SLAM. In: IEEE ICPRS2023, Guayaquil, Ecuador (2023)
11. Davison, A.J., Reid, I.D., Molton, N.D., Stasse, O.: MonoSLAM: real-time single camera SLAM. IEEE Trans. Pattern Anal. Mach. Intell. 29(6), 1052–1067 (2007)

12. Zhao, L., Wei, B., Li, L., Li, X.: A review of visual SLAM for dynamic objects. In: 2022 IEEE 17th Conference on Industrial Electronics and Applications (ICIEA), pp. 1080–1085 (2022)
13. Lin, M., Yang, C., Li, D.: An improved transformed unscented FastSLAM with adaptive genetic resampling. IEEE Trans. Industr. Electron. 66(5), 3583–3594 (2019)
14. Zhou, H., Hu, Z., Liu, S., Khan, S.: Efficient 2D graph slam for sparse sensing, iros, pp. 6404–6411 (2022)
15. Zhao, X., Agrawal, H., Batra, D., Schwing, A.G.: The surprising effectiveness of visual odometry techniques for embodied pointgoal navigation. In: Proceedings of the IEEE/CVF International Conference on Computer Vision (ICCV), pp. 16127–16136 (2021)
16. Zhu, Y., Mottaghi, R., Kolve, E., Lim, J.J., Gupta, A., Fei-Fei, L., Farhadi, A.: Target-driven visual navigation in indoor scenes using deep reinforcement learning. In: 2017 IEEE International Conference on Robotics and Automation (ICRA), pp. 3357–3364 (2017)
17. Chaplot, D.S., Gandhi, D., Gupta, S., Gupta, A., Salakhutdinov, R.: Learning to explore using active neural slam (2020)
18. Hoang, C., Sohn, S., Choi, J., Carvalho, W., Lee, H.: Successor feature landmarks for long-horizon goal-conditioned reinforcement learning. Adv. Neural. Inf. Process. Syst. 34, 269633–326975 (2021)
19. Stadler, D., Beyerer, J.: Improving multiple pedestrian tracking by track management and occlusion handling. In: Proceedings of the IEEE/CVF Conference on Computer Vision and Pattern Recognition (CVPR), pp. 10958–10967 (2021)
20. Mur-Artal, R., Tardos, J.D.: ORB-SLAM2: an open-source slam system for monocular, stereo, and RGB-D cameras. IEEE Trans. Rob. 33(5), 1255–1262 (2017)
21. Li, X., Ma, C., Wu, B., He, Z., Yang, M.-H.: Target-aware deep tracking. In Proceedings of the IEEE/CVF Conference on Computer Vision and Pattern Recognition (CVPR) (2019)
22. Singh, R., Gupta, P., Shenoy, P., Sarvadevabhatla, R.: Float: factorized learning of object attributes for improved multi-object multi-part scene parsing. In: Proceedings of the IEEE/CVF Conference on Computer Vision and Pattern Recognition (CVPR), pp. 1445–1455 (2022)
23. Kim, D., Woo, S., Lee, J.-Y., Kweon, I.S.: Deep video inpainting. In: Proceedings of the IEEE/CVF Conference on Computer Vision and Pattern Recognition (CVPR) (2019)
24. Campos, C., Elvira, R., Rodriguez, J.J.G., Montiel, J.M.M., Tardos, J.D.: ORB-SLAM3: an accurate open-source library for visual, visual-inertial and multi-map SLAM. IEEE Trans. Rob. 37(6), 1874–1890 (2021)
25. Agramonte, R., Urrea, C.: Kalman Filter: historical overview and review of its use in robotics 60 years after its creation (2021)
26. Thrun, S., Montemerlo, M.: The GraphSLAM algorithm with applications to large-scale mapping of urban structures (2006)
27. Mur-Artal, R., Montiel, J.M.M., Tardos, J.D.: ORB-SLAM: a versatile and accurate monocular SLAM system. IEEE Trans. Rob. 31(5), 1147–1163 (2015)
28. Muñoz-Salinas, R.: DBoW3, 17 02 2017. https://github.com/rmsalinas/DBow3. Accessed 19 Mar 2023
29. Culjak, I., Abram, D., Dzapo, H., Pribanic, T., Cifrek, M.: A brief introduction to OpenCV. In: 2012 Proceedings of the 35th International Convention MIPRO, Opatija, Croatia, pp. 1725–1730 (2012)
30. Woodal, W.: rviz, ROS, 16 05 2018. http://wiki.ros.org/rviz. Accessed 19 Mar 2023

Fingerprint Indexing with Minutiae-Aided Fingerprint Multiscale Representation

Song Wu, Zheng Wang, Zexi Jia, Chuanwei Huang, Hongyan Fei,
and Jufu Feng[✉]

Key Laboratory of Machine Perception (MOE), School of Intelligence Science and
Technology, Peking University, Beijing 100871, People's Republic of China
{wusong,fengjf}@pku.edu.cn

Abstract. The huge fingerprint database limits the speed of large-scale
fingerprint identification, which can be alleviated by fingerprint indexing.
The previous fixed-length representation used for fingerprint indexing
achieves unsatisfactory performance due to no good use of fingerprint
domain knowledge. Inspired by some attempts to introduce minutiae
information, in this paper, we propose a tailored framework to extract
the minutiae-aided fingerprint multiscale representation for fingerprint
indexing. We design Minutiae Distribution and Directions Map (MDDM)
to encode the information contained in minutiae. Inputting into the
network along with the fingerprint images, the MDDM guide the network to pay more attention to the minutiae information. Considering
the deep features with high resolution contain more small object information, i.e., the minutiae, we introduce the tailored Multiscale Feature
Fusion (MFF) module to better use the semantic information in different layers. Extensive experiments show that the proposed fixed-length
representation achieves better indexing performance on all benchmarks.

Keywords: Fingerprint Indexing · Minutiae-aided Representation ·
Multiscale Feature Fusion

1 Introduction

In large-scale fingerprint identification, the efficiency and accuracy of Automatic
Fingerprint Identification Systems (AFIS) are equally important [23]. Fingerprint indexing plays a key role in keeping the accuracy and improving the efficiency of fingerprint identification. Its goal is to filter dissimilar fingerprints and
retain several candidates with the tailored fingerprint representation and indexing strategy from the huge database for subsequent matching. The difficulty is
how to get the compact and discriminative fingerprint representation by using
the rich information contained in the fingerprints.

Previous works focus on the hand-crafted fingerprint representation [1,2,6,
13–15,21,22,25], which require the complex design process and specific domain

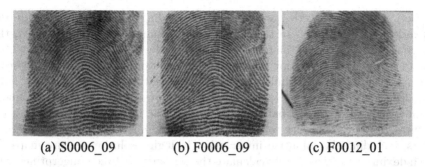

(a) S0006_09   (b) F0006_09   (c) F0012_01

Fig. 1. The motivation of our proposed model. The above three fingerprints are from NIST SD4 [33]. The minutiae extracted by FingerNet [31] are marked in blue in each fingerprint. (a) and (b) are matched fingerprints, and (c) is the non-matched fingerprint with (a) and (b). Although the three fingerprints have similar patterns, the distribution and types of minutiae between non-matched fingerprints are different, which can be used to enhance the indexing performance of the global feature.

knowledge. With the development of deep learning, deep features from Convolution Neural Networks (CNNs) make some achievements in fingerprint identification. These deep features can be divided into local features and global features. The local features, mostly based on the minutiae, often rely on the complex similarity calculation strategies [4,5], which limits the efficiency of fingerprint identification. In contrast, the global features, i.e., the fixed-length fingerprint representation, represent each fingerprint as a fixed-length vector [3,16,27], and the similarity between two vectors can be efficiently calculated by inner product. However, the performance of the fixed-length representation proposed in these methods is limited due to the lack of domain knowledge in the fingerprint. Minutiae, as the key points in fingerprints, contain more unique information, such as their distribution, quantity and directions. As shown in Fig. 1, non-matched fingerprints with similar global patterns have different distributions of minutiae, which helps to enhance the indexing performance of the fingerprint representation. Follow-up works [7,28–30,34] introduce the minutiae information into the fixed-length representation. Song et al. [28] extract the representation of minutiae and aggregate them as fixed-length features. Some works [7,29,30] learn the fixed-length representation from the intermediate feature maps guided by the auxiliary minutiae extraction task. The auxiliary task may have a negative effect on the main task, i.e., the extraction of fingerprint representation, in the multi-task learning setting. Wu et al. [34] guide the fixed-length representation to focus on both the global and local minutia regions with the constraint on the matching relations of minutiae. Their work does not use the information contained in the minutiae, such as distributions and directions.

In this paper, we propose a tailored framework to extract the minutiae-aided fingerprint multiscale representation for fingerprint indexing, which takes the distributions and directions of minutiae into account. Specifically, we input the proposed Minutiae Distribution and Direction Map (MDDM) into the feature extraction network together with the corresponding fingerprints, to guide the network to pay attention to the information of minutiae. On the MDDM, the corresponding position of the minutiae uses the values of the trigonometric function to represent the direction information. In addition, we design the Multiscale Feature Fusion (MFF) module, inspired by the feature pyramid networks [17]. The deep features in the deeper layers with low resolution are likely to ignore the information of these small-scale minutiae. The introduction of multi-scale features guides the network to pay attention to more information from different layers, including the minutiae information in high-resolution feature maps. In the indexing stage, we directly calculate the similarity between fingerprints with the inner product of the proposed fixed-length fingerprint representation. Based on the similarities, we retain a certain proportion of candidates, so as to achieve the purpose of fingerprint indexing.

The main contributions of our paper are as follows: (i) We introduce the domain knowledge in fingerprint to extract the fixed-length representation for indexing. The information of minutiae is taken into account in our proposed Minutiae Distribution and Direction Map (MDDM) to improve the performance of fingerprint representation. (ii) We tailor a network with a Multiscale Feature Fusion (MFF) module, which use the feature map from different layers to better integrate the complementary semantic information of the network, especially for the information of minutiae contained in high-resolution feature maps. (iii) Extensive experimental results show our proposed fixed-length fingerprint representation has better indexing performance compared to the previous methods.

There are five chapters in our paper. In Sect. 1, we give an introduction to our paper, including a brief comment on the fingerprint indexing, motivations and contributions. In Sect. 2, we carefully summarize the related works in fingerprint indexing. In Sect. 3, we give specific discussions on our proposed modules and our fingerprint indexing pipeline. In Sect. 4, we make fair and extensive comparisons with previous methods and design several ablation studies. In Sect. 5, we make a conclusion of the paper.

2   Related Work

Fingerprint indexing plays an important role in large-scale fingerprint identification, which can remove the most of dissimilar fingerprints from the huge database and improve efficiency and speed. A compact and discriminative fingerprint representation can realize fast fingerprint indexing with a simple indexing strategy. The early works focus on designing the hand-crafted fingerprint representation [1,2,6,13–15,21,22,25]. These hand-crafted features often require extensive expert knowledge and complex design process with limited representation ability.

Recently, deep features from the Convolution Neural Networks (CNNs) show amazing representation ability in various computer vision tasks [10,20,31]. In the field of fingerprint indexing, fingerprint representations can be broadly categorized into variable-length features [4,5,9] and fixed-length features [3,7,16,27–30,34]. The variable-length representation often relies on the complex similarity calculation strategies, which limits the efficiency and speed of fingerprint indexing. Instead, the fixed-length representation relies on simple similarity calculation strategies with high efficiency and speed. Two methods [3,27] represent each fingerprint as a fixed-length vector with CNNs. Li *et al.* [16] use paired minutia-centered patches to alleviate the insufficient training due to the lack of paired fingerprints. However, these methods have limited performance due to the lack of domain knowledge specific to fingerprints. To address this, follow-up works [7,28–30,34] introduce the minutiae information into the fixed-length representation. Song *et al.* [28] extract the minutiae representation and aggregate them as the fixed-length features. Some works [7,29,30] learn the fixed-length representation from the intermediate feature maps guided by the auxiliary minutiae extraction task. However, the presence of the auxiliary task in multi-task learning scenarios may have a negative impact on the primary task of fingerprint representation. Wu *et al.* [34] incorporate constraints on the matching relations of minutiae to guide the fixed-length representation to focus on both the global patterns and local minutiae regions. Their approach does not use the information contained in the minutiae, such as distribution and directions.

3   Methods

In this section, we discuss our proposed framework for the extraction of fixed-length fingerprint representation. Firstly, we discuss the details of the Minutiae Distribution and Directions Map (MDDM) to show how to introduce the minutiae information into the proposed representation. Then, we describe the tailored Multiscale Feature Fusion (MFF) module for better incorporating the rich semantic information from the different layers, especially for the minutiae. At last, we introduce the total pipeline for offline training and online indexing. The overview of our proposed method is shown in Fig. 2.

3.1   Minutiae Distribution and Directions Map (MDDM)

Given a fingerprint image x with the spatial size $H \times W$ and corresponding N_m minutiae $M = \{m^i = (m_x^i, m_y^i, m_\theta^i) | i = 1, 2, \cdots, N_m\}$, how to extract the fixed-length fingerprint representation from both image and minutiae? (m_x^i, m_y^i) denotes the coordinate of the minutia m^i, and m_θ^i denotes its direction. Unlike the image, the minutiae are data in non-euclidean form, which cannot be directly input into the CNNs. It is crucial to convert the original minutiae set M into the Euclidean form and retain as much information contained in the minutiae as possible.

   As the key domain knowledge in fingerprint, minutiae are stable and robust to fingerprint impression conditions [23]. For each fingerprint, the distribution of minutiae is not the same. At the same time, the direction of each minutia also has rich biometric information. Inspired by this, we design the Minutiae Distribution and Directions Map (MDDM) to retain more information in minutiae when

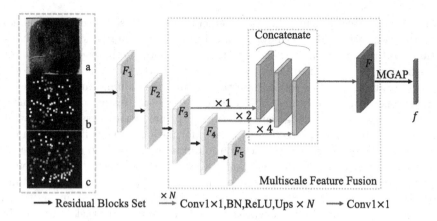

Fig. 2. The pipeline of our proposed model. (a) Fingerprint images. (b–c) The first and second channels of the proposed Minutiae Distribution and Direction Map (MDDM). MGAP denotes the Mask Global Average Pooling operation. Ups×N denotes upsampling N times operation. With the aid of MDDM, our network obtains the fixed-length minutiae-aid fingerprint representation. In order to better use the semantic information of different layers in the deep network, especially the minutiae information in the high-resolution feature map, we introduce the Multiscale Feature Fusion (MFF) module.

converting the original minutiae into the Euclidean form. We define the Minutiae Distribution and Directions Map $\mathcal{M} \in R^{H \times W \times 2}$ as

$$\mathcal{M}(i,j,k) = \begin{cases} k\sin(m_\theta) + (1-k)\cos(m_\theta), & \text{dist}_1(i,j,m_x,m_y) \leq T \\ 0, & \text{otherwise} \end{cases}, \quad (1)$$

where $\text{dist}_1(i,j,m_x,m_y)$ denote the L_1 distance between pixels (i,j) on MDDM $\mathcal{M}$ and the minutia $m = (m_x, m_y, m_\theta)$, and $k \in \{0,1\}$ denotes the channel index of MDDM $\mathcal{M}$. The first channel ($k = 0$) encodes x coordinate information, and the second channel ($k = 1$) encodes y coordinate information. In Eq. (1), T denotes the size of minutia mask in $\mathcal{M}$. For the MDDM $\mathcal{M}$, the adjacent regions of each minutiae reflect their direction information.

After obtaining the fingerprint-related knowledge, people can identify the minutiae from the fingerprint image x. As for the CNNs, they can pay attention to minutiae information under the appropriate guidance. A common attempt is to introduce the minutiae extraction as an auxiliary task to learn a fixed-length representation from the intermediate features [7,29,30]. However, in this multi-task learning framework, there may be conflicts between tasks, which has negative effects on the main tasks, i.e., the extraction of representation. Given the corresponding minutiae M, we can use it directly as an input to let the network focus on the minutiae and related regions. In this paper, as shown in Fig. 2, we directly concatenate the fingerprint image x and corresponding $\mathcal{M}$ and input them into our tailored network, which will be discussed in the next section.

The existence of $\mathcal{M}$, as a priori of minutiae, indicates the fingerprint x where and what the minutiae are. The motivation behind this operation is similar to that of the indicator mask in the inpainting task [19, 35], which guide the network to pay more attention to the specific area.

3.2 Multiscale Feature Fusion (MFF) Module

Previous methods [4, 5, 27] introduce the input of different sizes or positions to learn the corresponding representation with more information. In fact, for the same input, the CNNs will learn different semantic information at different layers, which can improve the performance of the final task [17, 18]. Besides, as the key points in fingerprint, the spatial size of minutiae is very small. The feature maps in the deeper layers may lose the minutiae information due to the low resolution. To better use the information of minutiae, we hope to be able to take advantage of the shallow features of the network.

Our backbone for the representation extraction is based on the ResNet [11]. Considering the insufficient training data and the prevention of overfitting, we use 30 residual block modules following our tailored Multiscale Feature Fusion (MFF) module as our base model. As shown in Fig. 2, each of the six modules forms a set. After each input passes through a set of residual modules, the size of the output feature map is reduced by half. The output feature maps of 5 sets of residual modules are F_1, F_2, F_3, F_4 and F_5. The resolution of F_1 and F_2 is too high, which will cause a large computational burden. Thus, we only use the intermediate feature maps F_3, F_4 and F_5. Due to the inconsistency of these three feature maps, we use a convolution layer, following a batch normalization layer [12], a ReLU layer [8] and a nearest upsampling layer, to process them. After obtaining the feature maps with the same spatial size, we concatenate and input them into a 1×1 convolution layer to alleviate the square effect caused by the upsampling to get the final feature map F. The spatial size of F is $\frac{H}{8} \times \frac{W}{8}$, which is common used resolution for the minutiae extraction [4, 5, 7, 31]. With the tailored MFF module, we use multiscale feature maps with rich semantic information from different layers.

Inspired by the weighted averaged operation [34], we introduce the segmentation to obtain the fixed-length representation f from the Mask Global Average Pooling (MGAP) of the final feature map F. The fixed-length representation f can be calculated:

$$f = \mathrm{MGAP}(F, S) = \frac{1}{N} \sum_{i,j} s(i,j) F(i,j), \tag{2}$$

where N denotes the number of non-zeros elements in the segmentation $S \in \{0, 1\}^{\frac{H}{8} \times \frac{W}{8}}$. In this way, more information related to the foreground of the fingerprint is taken into account. We do not increase the weight of minutia-centered regions like [34] because we hope the network can learn the importance under the guidance of the proposed MDDM. In order to facilitate the training and the calculation of the similarity, we normalize the f in advance.

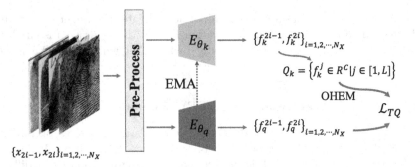

Fig. 3. The offline training stage of our proposed model. The feature generated by the key network E_{θ_k} fills the historical queue Q_k. The latest generated features will gradually replace the earlier ones. We select the most difficult negative examples (non-matched fingerprints) from the Q_k for each anchor-positive pair (matched paired fingerprints) to get the triples under the Online Hard Example Mining (OHEM) strategy. We use the $\mathcal{L}_{TQ}$ to constrain these triples from each batch. In the online indexing, only the query network E_{θ_q} is kept.

3.3 Offline Training

Each fingerprint and its corresponding MDDM are represented as a fixed-length fingerprint representation as shown in Fig. 2. The goal of offline training is to obtain such fingerprint representation, and its similarity with another fingerprint can reflect the similarity between them. We can achieve this problem in the metric learning framework. In our problem, we hope that the similarity of representation between matched fingerprints is as large as possible, and the similarity of unmatched fingerprints is as small as possible. Li *et al.* [16] introduce the triplet loss [26] into the extraction of fixed-length representation for indexing. Wu *et al.* [34] introduce the momentum strategy [10] to increase the batch size and improve the performance of their proposed representation.

In the offline training stage, as shown in Fig. 3, we introduce the triplet loss with momentum strategy to learn a robust and compact fixed-length representation. We select the more informative triples for the triplet loss with the Online Hard Example Mining (OHEM) strategy to accelerate the convergence of the network.

Following the previous works [10,34], we have two encoders with the same structures: the query network $E_{\theta_q}(\cdot)$ and the key network $E_{\theta_k}(\cdot)$. The parameters of $E_{\theta_q}(\cdot)$ are updated with the gradient propagation while these of $E_{\theta_k}(\cdot)$ are updated with the Exponential Moving Average (EMA) strategy. The features of the historical batches, generated by E_{θ_k}, are retained in a historical feature queue $Q_k \in R^{L \times C}$ to enlarge the triples search space. L and C denote the length of the queue and the dimensions of each feature. The latest generated features will gradually replace the earlier ones.

From the whole training set, we random samples N_X fingers and 2 impressions of each finger to get a mini-batch $X = \{x_1, x_2, \cdots, x_{2N_X-1}, x_{2N_X}\}$. In

X, for $i \in N_X$, x_{2i-1} and x_{2i} are 2 different impressions of the same finger. We get the two sets of features $\mathcal{F}_q = \{f_q^1, f_q^2, \cdots, f_q^{2N_X-1}, f_q^{2N_X}\}$ and $\mathcal{F}_k = \{f_k^1, f_k^2, \cdots, f_k^{2N_X-1}, f_k^{2N_X}\}$ through two encoders. The earliest $2N_X$ features retained in the historical queue are replaced by $\mathcal{F}_k$. The triplet loss with the historical queue for each triple can be calculated as:

$$\mathcal{L}_{TQ}^1(2i-1, j) = \max(0, \mathrm{dist}_2(f_q^{2i-1}, f_k^{2i}) - \mathrm{dist}_2(f_q^{2i-1}, f_k^j) - m_t) \qquad (3)$$

and

$$\mathcal{L}_{TQ}^2(2i, j) = \max(0, \mathrm{dist}_2(f_q^{2i}, f_k^{2i-1}) - \mathrm{dist}_2(f_q^{2i}, f_k^j) - m_t), \qquad (4)$$

where m_t denotes the hyper-parameters of the margin and dist_2 denotes the L_2 distance of two vectors. The total triplet loss with the historical queue are

$$\mathcal{L}_{TQ} = \frac{1}{2N_X} \sum_i [\mathcal{L}_{TQ}^1(2i-1, j) + \mathcal{L}_{TQ}^2(2i, j)]. \qquad (5)$$

Note that each feature is normalized before calculating the loss according to the Eq. (5). Only the query network $E_{\theta_q}(\cdot)$ is kept for the online indexing.

3.4 Online Indexing

In the online fingerprint indexing stage, a fingerprint and its corresponding minutiae are represented as a fixed-length vector through our proposed method. Each vector is normalized. The similarity between fingerprints x_1 and x_2 can be calculated as the cosine similarity:

$$sim(x_1, x_2) = <f_{x_1}, f_{x_2}> . \qquad (6)$$

In Eq. (6), $< \cdot, \cdot >$ denotes the inner product of two representations, which is equal to the cosine similarity due to the normalization of each representation.

When obtaining the fixed-length representation of a query fingerprint, we compare it with the fingerprints in the database and retain several candidates based on the similarity of representation for subsequent fingerprint matching.

3.5 Data Processing

Apart from the fingerprint image, we require the minutiae to generate the Minutiae Distribution and Directions Map as shown in Fig. 2. We also require the segmentation to aggregate the feature maps and get the fixed-length fingerprint representation. It is time-consuming to manually annotate the minutiae and segmentation. With the development of deep learning, FingerNet [31] can replace traditional fingerprint processing, including enhancement, segmentation and minutiae extraction. In this paper, we use FingerNet to get the enhancement, segmentation and minutiae of an original fingerprint in advance.

4   Experiments

4.1   Datasets and Metrics

Datasets. In this paper, we have four datasets as shown in Table 1. Rolled Fingerprint Dataset (RFD) and Extended Rolled Fingerprint Dataset (ERFD) are two rolled fingerprint databases with no overlap, provided by a forensic agency. There are $87,613$ fingers with 2 impressions from $8,800$ different subjects in RFD. The split strategy of RFD for training and validation is shown in Table 1. Each fingerprint image in RFD has the spatial size 640×640 with 500 dpi. NIST SD4 [33] and NIST SD14 [32] are two common benchmarks in fingerprint indexing. There are $2,000$ and $27,000$ pairs of rolled fingerprints in NIST SD4 and NIST SD14 respectively. Each fingerprint image in NIST SD4 has the spatial size 512×512 with 500 dpi. Each fingerprint image in NIST SD14 has the spatial size 832×768 with 500 dpi. To better simulate the fingerprint indexing on the large fingerprint database, we introduce the ERFD to enlarge the search space. Note that these four datasets have similar characteristics.

Table 1. The details of related datasets in our paper.

Name	Partition	Subject	Finger	Impressions	Fingerprint
RFD	-	8,800	87,613	2	175,226
	Train	*8,500*	*85,000*	*2*	*170,000*
	Validation	*300*	*2,613*	*2*	*5,226*
ERFD	Test	10,000	99,704	1	99,704
NIST SD4 [33]	Test	2,000	2,000	2	4,000
NIST SD14 [32][a]	Test	27,000	27,000	2	54,000

[a] Only the last 2,700 pairs are used for test following the previous works.

Metrics. The common indicator for fingerprint indexing is the error rate under a given penetration rate. Since previous methods report the results on a limited gallery, this indicator cannot reflect the performance well. Thus, following the previous work [34], we report the top-k accuracy of fingerprint identification, which is more precise. Besides, we also report the computational time of our proposed methods.

4.2   Experimental Details

Our model is trained from scratch on GeForce GTX 1080Ti for 40 epochs in an end-to-end manner. We implement our framework in Pytorch [24]. The batch size is 50. We use the SGD optimizer with the default setting. We use the cosine decay strategy to update the learning rate with the initial learning rate $1e-3$.

We use random rotation and translation as our data augmentation. The range of rotation is from $-20°$ to $20°$ and the range of translation is from -20 to 20 pixels.

Table 2. The indexing performance on NIST SD4 [33] and NIST SD14 [32]. The best results are highlighted in **bold font**. The indexing results with extended rolled fingerprint database (ERFD) are underlined.

Methods[a]	Types	NIST SD4			NIST SD14		
		k = 1	k = 5	k = 20	k = 1	k = 5	k = 27
Song and Feng [27]	Fixed-length	-	-	93.30	-	-	-
Cao and Jain [3]	Fixed-length	-	-	98.65	-	-	98.93
Li et al. [16]	Fixed-length	99.27	99.65	99.82	99.04	99.70	99.89
Song et al. [28]	Fixed-length	-	-	99.20	-	-	99.60
Enngelsma et al. [7]	Fixed-length	98.70	-	99.75	99.22	-	99.93
Wu et al. [34]	Fixed-length	**99.65**	99.70	99.75	99.93	**100.00**	**100.00**
Ours	Fixed-length	99.60	**99.80**	**99.90**	**99.96**	100.00	100.00
COTS A[b] [7]	Variable-length	99.55	-	-	99.92	-	-
Ours with ERFD	Fixed-length	<u>99.45</u>	<u>99.70</u>	<u>99.80</u>	<u>99.78</u>	<u>99.85</u>	<u>99.93</u>

[a] Due to unreleased codes and unreported results, we use the '-' to fill the table.
[b] COTS A denotes the reported version of a minutiae-based matching algorithm in [7].

4.3   Indexing Performance

We make a fair comparison on the indexing performance with previous methods [3,7,16,27,28,34] on two benchmarks, NIST SD4 [33] and NIST SD14 [32]. Due to the unreleased models and codes, we directly repeat the results in their papers. Based on the error rate under the 1% penetration rate, as shown in Table 2, we report the top-20 accuracy and top-27 accuracy in NIST SD4 [33] and NIST SD14 [32] respectively. Our proposed method achieves 99.60% and 99.96% top-1 accuracy which is better than the previous methods. The matched fingerprint can be ranked in the top-2 for the NIST SD14 from the whole database. 99.80% the matched fingerprint can be ranked in the top-5 for the NIST SD4. In order to simulate the situation of large-scale indexing, we introduce the ERFD. The performance of our proposed model degrades slightly. However, there are still 99.70% and 99.85% target fingerprints of the query fingerprints in the top 5. The experimental results show that our proposed fixed-length representation can be used to measure the similarity between two fingerprints with the simple inner product operation. Thus, the proposed fixed-length representation can be used to filter the dissimilar fingerprints in advance to reduce the search space for the subsequent fine-matching process.

4.4   Matching Time

The computational requirement for indexing is also crucial to evaluate the performance of fingerprint indexing. Our experiment platform is a server with Intel(R) Xeon(R) CPU E5-26380 v4 @ 2.40GHz with TITAN RTX GPU. The average cost time for feature extraction is about 30ms per fingerprint. Following the previous works [7,34], we evaluate the search time for a query against the 1.1 million simulated gallery. The average search time is about 3.4ms on GPU. The template size of the proposed fingerprint representation is 256 bytes per fingerprint.

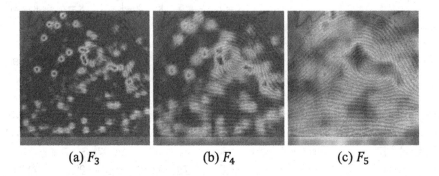

(a) F_3 (b) F_4 (c) F_5

Fig. 4. The visualization of the intermediate feature maps.

4.5   Ablation Studies

Table 3. Ablation studies on feature maps from different layers on NIST SD4 with ERFD.

Model	k = 1	k = 5	k = 20
w/o F_3	98.35	99.00	99.50
w/o F_4	98.90	99.35	99.65
w/o F_3&F_4	97.85	98.65	99.05
Ours	**99.45**	**99.70**	**99.80**

Table 4. Ablation studies on each proposed module on NIST SD4 with ERFD.

Model	k = 1	k = 5	k = 20
w/o MDDM	96.40	98.15	99.15
w/o MFF	97.85	98.65	99.05
Ours	**99.45**	**99.70**	**99.80**

Impact of Multiscale Feature Fusion Module. In our proposed method, we introduce Multiscale Feature Fusion (MFF) module to better use the semantic information on the feature map from different layers. As shown in Table 3, we remove the intermediate feature maps F_3 and F_4. The indexing performance drops a lot. The reason is that these feature maps do provide complementary information to F_5.

In Fig. 4, we give an example of the visualization of the intermediate feature maps F_3, F_4 and F_5 following [36] to show which regions of the input are focused on the various features used by our MFF. As shown in Fig. 4(a–b), F_3 and F_4 mainly focus on the minutiae and their adjacent regions, which shows the use of these features is indeed conducive to the fusion of the corresponding information of minutiae. As shown in Fig. 4(c), F_5 mainly focuses on the global pattern of the fingerprint, which is complementary to the former F_3 and F_4. Therefore, our MFF module effectively uses the complementary information and integrates domain knowledge to improve the final representation performance.

Impact of Minutiae-Aided Information. We convert the original minutiae into the proposed MDDM and input them into the network with the corresponding images to guide the network to pay attention to more domain knowledge in the fingerprint. We drop the MDDM (Model *w/o MDDM*) and make a fair comparison with our proposed model. As shown in Table 4, the performance of indexing becomes worse. After removing the proposed MDDM, the obtained fixed-length representation lacks the domain knowledge of fingerprint. Similar to the problem in contrastive learning, a single vector describes the whole input image, which will make the vector only focus on the limited region, thus affecting performance.

5 Conclusions

In this paper, we take the minutiae into account and design a framework to extract fixed-length fingerprint representation for fingerprint indexing. In order to introduce the information of minutiae, we design the Minutiae Distribution and Directions Map (MDDM). The MDDM, as the prior domain knowledge, is input into the proposed network along with the corresponding fingerprint images. Due to the small size of minutiae in each fingerprint, we tailor the network with the Multiscale Feature Fusion (MFF) module to use deep features from different layers, especially the feature map with high resolution, which is proved to be crucial for small object detection. Extensive experiments show that the proposed representation achieves better indexing performance on all benchmarks without or with an extended large-scale fingerprint database. The fingerprint domain knowledge can help to enhance the discrimination of fingerprint fixed-length representation and improve the performance of fingerprint indexing.

References

1. Bhanu, B., Tan, X.: A triplet based approach for indexing of fingerprint database for identification. In: Bigun, J., Smeraldi, F. (eds.) AVBPA 2001. LNCS, vol. 2091, pp. 205–210. Springer, Heidelberg (2001). https://doi.org/10.1007/3-540-45344-X_29
2. Bhanu, B., Tan, X.: Fingerprint indexing based on novel features of minutiae triplets. IEEE Trans. Pattern Anal. Mach. Intell. **25**(5), 616–622 (2003). https://doi.org/10.1109/TPAMI.2003.1195995

3. Cao, K., Jain, A.K.: Fingerprint indexing and matching: an integrated approach. In: 2017 IEEE International Joint Conference on Biometrics, pp. 437–445 (2017). https://doi.org/10.1109/BTAS.2017.8272728

4. Cao, K., Jain, A.K.: Automated latent fingerprint recognition. IEEE Trans. Pattern Anal. Mach. Intell. **41**(4), 788–800 (2019). https://doi.org/10.1109/TPAMI.2018.2818162

5. Cao, K., Nguyen, D., Tymoszek, C., Jain, A.K.: End-to-end latent fingerprint search. IEEE Trans. Inf. Forensics Secur. **15**, 880–894 (2020). https://doi.org/10.1109/TIFS.2019.2930487

6. Cappelli, R., Ferrara, M., Maltoni, D.: Minutia cylinder-code: a new representation and matching technique for fingerprint recognition. IEEE Trans. Pattern Anal. Mach. Intell. **32**(12), 2128–2141 (2010). https://doi.org/10.1109/TPAMI.2010.52

7. Engelsma, J.J., Cao, K., Jain, A.K.: Learning a fixed-length fingerprint representation. IEEE Trans. Pattern Anal. Mach. Intell. **43**(6), 1981–1997 (2021). https://doi.org/10.1109/TPAMI.2019.2961349

8. Glorot, X., Bordes, A., Bengio, Y.: Deep sparse rectifier neural networks. In: Proceedings of the Fourteenth International Conference on Artificial Intelligence and Statistics, vol. 15, pp. 315–323 (2011). https://doi.org/10.1109/IWAENC.2016.7602891

9. Gu, S., Feng, J., Lu, J., Zhou, J.: Latent fingerprint registration via matching densely sampled points. IEEE Trans. Inf. Forensics Secur. **16**, 1231–1244 (2021). https://doi.org/10.1109/TIFS.2020.3032041

10. He, K., Fan, H., Wu, Y., Xie, S., Girshick, R.B.: Momentum contrast for unsupervised visual representation learning. In: IEEE/CVF Conference on Computer Vision and Pattern Recognition, pp. 9726–9735 (2020). https://doi.org/10.1109/CVPR42600.2020.00975

11. He, K., Zhang, X., Ren, S., Sun, J.: Identity mappings in deep residual networks. In: Leibe, B., Matas, J., Sebe, N., Welling, M. (eds.) ECCV 2016. LNCS, vol. 9908, pp. 630–645. Springer, Cham (2016). https://doi.org/10.1007/978-3-319-46493-0_38

12. Ioffe, S., Szegedy, C.: Batch normalization: accelerating deep network training by reducing internal covariate shift. In: Proceedings of the 32nd International Conference on Machine Learning, vol. 37, pp. 448–456 (2015)

13. Jain, A.K., Prabhakar, S., Hong, L., Pankanti, S.: Fingercode: a filterbank for fingerprint representation and matching. In: IEEE Conference on Computer Vision and Pattern Recognition, p. 2187 (1999). https://doi.org/10.1109/CVPR.1999.784628

14. Jiang, X., Yau, W.: Fingerprint minutiae matching based on the local and global structures. In: 15th International Conference on Pattern Recognition, pp. 6038–6041 (2000). https://doi.org/10.1109/ICPR.2000.906252

15. Leung, K., Leung, C.H.: Improvement of fingerprint retrieval by a statistical classifier. IEEE Trans. Inf. Forensics Secur. **6**(1), 59–69 (2011). https://doi.org/10.1109/TIFS.2010.2100382

16. Li, R., Song, D., Liu, Y., Feng, J.: Learning global fingerprint features by training a fully convolutional network with local patches. In: 2019 International Conference on Biometrics, pp. 1–8 (2019). https://doi.org/10.1109/ICB45273.2019.8987387

17. Lin, T., Dollár, P., Girshick, R.B., He, K., Hariharan, B., Belongie, S.J.: Feature pyramid networks for object detection. In: 2017 IEEE Conference on Computer Vision and Pattern Recognition, pp. 936–944 (2017). https://doi.org/10.1109/CVPR.2017.106

18. Lin, T., Dollár, P., Girshick, R.B., He, K., Hariharan, B., Belongie, S.J.: Feature pyramid networks for object detection. In: IEEE Conference on Computer Vision and Pattern Recognition, pp. 936–944 (2017). https://doi.org/10.1109/CVPR.2017.106

19. Liu, B., Feng, J.: Palmprint orientation field recovery via attention-based generative adversarial network. Neurocomputing **438**, 1–13 (2021). https://doi.org/10.1016/j.neucom.2021.01.049

20. Liu, B., Wang, Z., Feng, J.: Palmnet: a robust palmprint minutiae extraction network. In: Pattern Recognition - 6th Asian Conference, ACPR, vol. 13188, pp. 459–473 (2021). https://doi.org/10.1007/978-3-031-02375-0_34

21. Liu, M., Yap, P.: Invariant representation of orientation fields for fingerprint indexing. Pattern Recognit. **45**(7), 2532–2542 (2012). https://doi.org/10.1016/j.patcog.2012.01.014

22. Lumini, A., Maio, D., Maltoni, D.: Continuous versus exclusive classification for fingerprint retrieval. Pattern Recognit. Lett. **18**(10), 1027–1034 (1997). https://doi.org/10.1016/S0167-8655(97)00127-X

23. Maltoni, D., Maio, D., Jain, A.K., Prabhakar, S.: Handbook of Fingerprint Recognition, 2nd edn (2009). https://doi.org/10.1007/978-1-84882-254-2

24. Paszke, A., et al.: Pytorch: an imperative style, high-performance deep learning library. CoRR abs/1912.01703 (2019)

25. Ratha, N.K., Bolle, R.M., Pandit, V.D., Vaish, V.: Robust fingerprint authentication using local structural similarity. In: Proceedings Fifth IEEE Workshop on Applications of Computer Vision, pp. 29–34 (2000). https://doi.org/10.1109/WACV.2000.895399

26. Schroff, F., Kalenichenko, D., Philbin, J.: Facenet: a unified embedding for face recognition and clustering. In: IEEE Conference on Computer Vision and Pattern Recognition, pp. 815–823 (2015). https://doi.org/10.1109/CVPR.2015.7298682

27. Song, D., Feng, J.: Fingerprint indexing based on pyramid deep convolutional feature. In: 2017 IEEE International Joint Conference on Biometrics, pp. 200–207 (2017). https://doi.org/10.1109/BTAS.2017.8272699

28. Song, D., Tang, Y., Feng, J.: Aggregating minutia-centred deep convolutional features for fingerprint indexing. Pattern Recognit. **88**, 397–408 (2019). https://doi.org/10.1016/j.patcog.2018.11.018

29. Takahashi, A., Koda, Y., Ito, K., Aoki, T.: Fingerprint feature extraction by combining texture, minutiae, and frequency spectrum using multi-task CNN. In: IEEE International Joint Conference on Biometrics, pp. 1–8 (2020). https://doi.org/10.1109/IJCB48548.2020.9304861

30. Tandon, S., Namboodiri, A.M.: Transformer based fingerprint feature extraction. In: 26th International Conference on Pattern Recognition, pp. 870–876 (2022). https://doi.org/10.1109/ICPR56361.2022.9956435

31. Tang, Y., Gao, F., Feng, J., Liu, Y.: Fingernet: an unified deep network for fingerprint minutiae extraction. In: 2017 IEEE International Joint Conference on Biometrics, pp. 108–116 (2017). https://doi.org/10.1109/BTAS.2017.8272688

32. Watson, C.: NIST special database 14. NIST mated fingerprint card pairs 2 (MFCP2) (1970)

33. Watson, C.: NIST special database 4. NIST 8-bit gray scale images of fingerprint image groups (1970)

34. Wu, S., Liu, B., Wang, Z., Jia, Z., Feng, J.: Minutiae-awarely learning fingerprint representation for fingerprint indexing. In: IEEE International Joint Conference on Biometrics, pp. 1–8 (2022). https://doi.org/10.1109/IJCB54206.2022.10007996

35. Yu, J., Lin, Z., Yang, J., Shen, X., Lu, X., Huang, T.S.: Free-form image inpainting with gated convolution. In: IEEE/CVF International Conference on Computer Vision, pp. 4470–4479 (2019). https://doi.org/10.1109/ICCV.2019.00457
36. Zhang, F., Xin, S., Feng, J.: Deep dense multi-level feature for partial high-resolution fingerprint matching. In: 2017 IEEE International Joint Conference on Biometrics, pp. 397–405 (2017). https://doi.org/10.1109/BTAS.2017.8272723

Increasing Diversity of Omni-Directional Images Generated from Single Image Using cGAN Based on MLPMixer

Atsuya Nakata[✉], Ryuto Miyazaki, and Takao Yamanaka

Sophia University, Tokyo, Japan
{a-nakata-7r0,r-miyazaki-7m7}@eagle.sophia.ac.jp, takao-y@sophia.ac.jp

Abstract. This paper proposes a novel approach to generating omni-directional images from a single snapshot picture. The previous method has relied on the generative adversarial networks based on convolutional neural networks (CNN). Although this method has successfully generated omni-directional images, CNN has two drawbacks for this task. First, since a convolutional layer only processes a local area, it is difficult to propagate the information of an input snapshot picture embedded in the center of the omni-directional image to the edges of the image. Thus, the omni-directional images created by the CNN-based generator tend to have less diversity at the edges of the generated images, creating similar scene images. Second, the CNN-based model requires large video memory in graphics processing units due to the nature of the deep structure in CNN since shallow-layer networks only receives signals from a limited range of the receptive field. To solve these problems, MLPMixer-based method was proposed in this paper. The MLPMixer has been proposed as an alternative to the self-attention in the transformer, which captures long-range dependencies and contextual information. This enables to propagate information efficiently in the omni-directional image generation task. As a result, competitive performance has been achieved with reduced memory consumption and computational cost, in addition to increasing diversity of the generated omni-directional images.

Keywords: GAN (Generative Adversarial Networks) · MLPMixer · 360 image · Image Synthesis

1 Introduction

An omni-directional image, or a 360-degree image, is usually captured by a camera which has a field of view covering approximately the entire sphere, and is represented in the equi-rectangular projection. A wide range of applications are considered such as virtual reality, driving recorders, robotics, and social networking services. However, the availability of these images is still limited compared with ordinary snapshot pictures, because they cannot be taken without a specialized omni-directional camera. To solve this problem, a method of generating the

© The Author(s), under exclusive license to Springer Nature Switzerland AG 2023
H. Lu et al. (Eds.): ACPR 2023, LNCS 14406, pp. 359–373, 2023.
https://doi.org/10.1007/978-3-031-47634-1_27

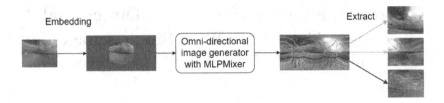

Fig. 1. Outline of omni-directional image generation from single snapshot picture

omni-directional images from a snapshot picture with the generative adversarial networks (GAN) [3] has been proposed [15]. In this method, the generator was composed of the encoder-decoder structure with convolutional layers, which was trained with the adversarial loss by inputting an embedded snapshot picture in the equi-rectangular projection as a conditional input (conditional GAN [7,13]).

Since a convolutional filter only receives the small range of local signals (small receptive field), the previous method [15] has two drawbacks for the omni-directional image generation task. First, it has been difficult to propagate the information of the input snapshot picture embedded in the center of an omni-directional image as shown in Fig. 1 to the edges of the omni-directional image. Since the scene information is input to the CNN-based omni-directional image generator in the previous method [15] as a conditional input, the edges of the omni-directional images for different input pictures for a scene might be similar scene images at the edges. Second, the CNN-based model requires large video memory in graphics processing units (GPU) due to the nature of the deep structure in CNN since shallow-layer networks only receives signals from a limited range of the receptive field.

Although the self attention technique [19] proposed for the natural language processing can represent long-distance dependencies and was successfully applied to the image recognition tasks [2], it is prone to overfit and is not suitable for small datasets. An alternative architecture, MLPMixer [18], can also represent the long distance dependencies, but can easily adjust the network size. With this architecture, high resolution images can be created with shallow layers by efficiently propagating the information from the center of an image to the edges. Therefore, this architecture was adopted in the proposed method for generating omni-directional images from a single snapshot picture. This property of MLPMixer also contributes to generating diversified omni-directional images conditioned on the input snapshot picture in a scene class, since the information of the input picture is efficiently propagated to the edges, generating different omni-directional images for a scene class depending on the input picture. The outline of the proposed method is shown in Fig. 1.

The contributions of this paper include:

(1) To construct a novel architecture to generate omni-directional images from a single snapshot picture with lower memory consumption and computational cost.
(2) To design novel loss functions to appropriately train the MLPMixer-based omni-directional generator.
(3) To generate qualitatively more natural and diversified omni-directional images depending on an input snapshot picture by propagating information efficiently from the center of the image to the edges.

2 Related Works

2.1 Omni-Directional Image Generation

A method to generate omni-directional images from a snapshot picture has been proposed in [15]. This method synthesizes natural landscape omni-directional images from a snapshot picture embedded in the equi-rectangular projection, by extrapolating the surrounding region using conditional GAN (cGAN) [7,13], where the conditional input is the snapshot picture. This cGAN is an image-to-image translation method to generate images corresponding to an input picture. In the previous method of generating omni-directional images, the generator has been constructed with the U-Net structure [16] composed of convolutional neural networks, which require a large memory to save a number of feature maps in the deep structure. This method has also proposed convolutional layers conditioned on a scene class label to train a network for all scene classes depending on the scene labels. In addition to this work, several researchers have also been working on the omni-directional image generation [5,22]. In [5], omni-directional images have been generated using GAN and Variational AutoEncoder (VAE) by considering scene symmetry, which use a lot of convolutional layers so that it requires a large memory. The other work [22] has proposed a method based on a latent diffusion model, which generates high quality omni-directional images from a variety of masked images. However, the diffusion model requires longer inference time than GAN since it requires iterative inference.

The purpose of our paper is to improve the methods to generate omni-directional images by efficiently propagating the information of an input snapshot picture to the edges with lower computational cost and memory consumption.

2.2 Generative Adversarial Networks

A number of models have been developed to improve the quality of the generated images [21], since the generative adversarial networks (GAN) [3] were proposed. Among them, cGAN [7,13] has been adopted in the previous work of generating omni-directional images [15], and was also used in our proposed method. In order to improve the stability of the training in GAN, a method to regularize the gradients of the discriminator outputs to the discriminator inputs (discriminator gradients) has been proposed [4], by adding a term for the L2 norm of the discriminator gradients to the loss function (Gradient Penalty). In addition, R1 gradient penalty has been also proposed by limiting the regularization of the discriminator gradients only on the true distribution (real images) [12], in contrast to R2 gradient penalty which regularizes the discriminator gradients only on the generated images. In our proposed method, the R1 gradient penalty was adopted to make the training stable.

Although most of the GAN models have been based on CNN similar to the models for other tasks in the computer vision, the recent advances in the image classification task have proved that the self-attention model called transformer proposed in natural language processing (NLP) [19] is also useful for visual image processing. The model called vision transformer has applied the transformer model in NLP to the image classification task by dividing the input image to patches and treating them as visual words [2]. The advantage of the self attention in the transformer over the convolutional layer in CNN is the ability of modeling the long-distance dependencies. While the convolutional filters in CNN only receive the signals from the small local receptive field, the self attention can receive signals from every position in an image to incorporate the global information. Thus, the vision transformer has achieved state-of-the-art accuracy in the imagenet classification task when a large-scale training database is available [2].

However, one of the problems of the transformer model has been tendency to overfit [10] and the high computational cost, which make it difficult to be applied to the image generation in the high resolution. An alternative model to the self attention in the transformer has been proposed as MLPMixer [18]. This model first divides the input image to local patches in the similar way to the transformer, but then these signals are processed by a multi-layer perceptron (MLP) instead of the self attention. This enables the model to receive global information with lower computational cost than the self attention. These vision transformer and MLPMixer have been also applied to GAN as TransGAN [8] and MixerGAN [1]. In our proposed method, MLPMixer was incorporated into the omni-directional image generator and discriminator.

3   Proposed Method

3.1   Generator

The architecture of the proposed model for the omni-directional image generator and discriminator is shown in Fig. 2. This model generates multi-scale images using the hierarchical structure, and they are integrated into an omni-directional image as the output of the generator. The inputs of the generator are a snapshot picture embedded in the equi-rectangular projection and a random vector sampled from a multi-modal Gaussian distribution. These inputs are first processed by MLPMixerBlock to produce both an output image in the low resolution and a feature map for the next block. Then, the feature map

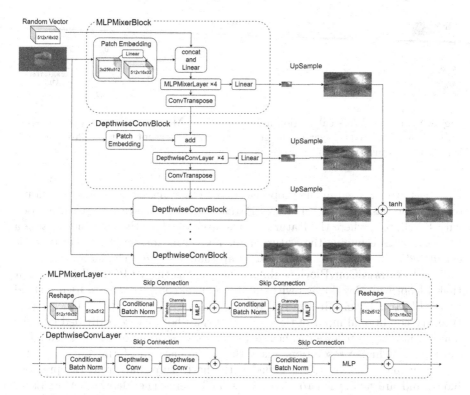

Fig. 2. Proposed architecture of omni-directional image generator using MLPMixer

from the previous block and the embedded snapshot picture are processed by the DepthwiseConvBlock. Since the information of the snapshot picture at the center of the input image is propagated to the edges in the low resolution using MLPMixer, the following blocks do not have to use MLPMixer, and instead use the depth-wise convolutions. The feature maps from the MLPMixerBlock and the DepthwiseConvBlock are hierarchically processed in the following blocks to produce the omni-directional images in multi resolutions, and then are summed into an omni-directional image as the output of the generator.

In the MLPMixerBlock, the input snapshot picture embedded in the equirectangular projection is processed by Patch Embedding, where the non-overlapping patches of the input image with the size of $2^{(N-1)} \times 2^{(N-1)}$ (16×16 in the 5-block structure) are transformed into encoded vectors using a fully connected (FC) layer (linear). After the channel compression in the concatenated feature map of the encoded vectors and the input random vectors, the feature map is processed with 4 MLPMixerLayers to produce the output image and a feature map for the next layer. The MLPMixerLayer is composed of 2 MLPs for channel-wise processing and patch-wise processing with conditional batch normalizations [20]. Although the original MLPMixer [18] uses the layer normalization, the conditional batch normalization conditioned on the scene class

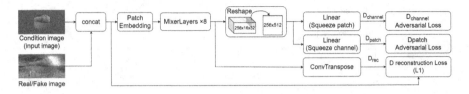

Fig. 3. Structure of loss calculation in discriminator. MixerLayers are the same structure as the MLPMixer Layer in the generator (Fig. 2), except that the layer normalization is used instead of the conditional batch normalization

label was instead used in the proposed method to train the networks depending on the scene class label. After the MLPMixerLayers, the feature map is processed with PatchSplit, where the feature map is upsampled for the next block using a FC layer with reshaping the feature map. The output of the MLPMixerBlock is calculated by compressing the feature-map channels into 3 channels.

The DepthwiseConvBlock is almost the same as the MLPMixerBlock except that 4 DepthwiseConvLayers without the channel compression are used instead of 4 MLPMixerLayers. In the i-th block ($i = 2, ..., N$) with the N-block structure, the conditional input of the embedded snapshot picture is divided into the non-overlapping patches with the size of $2^{N-i} \times 2^{N-i}$ to represent detailed information in the higher resolution. Then, the patches are transformed into encoded vectors using a FC layer, are added with the feature map from the previous block, and are forwarded to DepthwiseConvLayers. The DepthwiseConvLayer is also similar to MLPMixerLayer except for replacing the channel-wise MLP processing with the 2 depth-wise convolution layers, where a different convolution kernel is applied to each channel. In higher resolution blocks, the number of patches increases to represent the detailed information, leading to the high computational cost in the channel-wise processing with MLP. Therefore, this channel-wise processing with MLP is replaced by the depth-wise convolutions. In the depth-wise convolutions, the circular padding is used in the left and right edges to represent the continuity in the omni-directional image.

In the experiments, the five hierarchical blocks were used to realize the omni-directional generator. The network structure of integrating the generated images in the multi-scale resolutions by summation was based on the structure in Style-GAN2 [9]. The mechanism of training a network with conditional scene class labels using the conditional batch normalization was the mechanism similar to the previous work of generating omni-directional images using the conditional convolution layers [15]. During the training of the proposed network, the true scene class labels from the database were used for the conditional inputs. For the inference, the scene class labels were estimated from the input snapshot pictures using the ResNet-based scene recognition network [26] fine-tuned to the omni-directional image database.

3.2   Discriminator

In the generative adversarial networks, a discriminator is trained to distinguish real images and the images generated by a generator, and is used for training the generator to make the generated images as real as possible. The structure of the loss calculation in the discriminator is shown in Fig. 3. The MLPMixer is also used in the discriminator by removing the global average pooling layer from the original MLPMixer networks [16] to calculate the local patch loss similar to the loss in PatchGAN [7]. This patch loss, D_{patch} in Fig. 3, is calculated by compressing the feature map from the mixer layers in MLPMixer to the single channel. Similar to this patch loss, the channel loss $D_{channel}$ in Fig. 3 is also calculated for each channel by compressing the feature map along the spatial dimension to the single patch. The adversarial loss in the proposed method is calculated from both the patch loss and the channel loss. It is noted that the layer normalizations in MLPMixer of the discriminator are not replaced by the conditional batch normalization unlike the generator. In addition to the adversarial loss, the reconstruction loss is also used for training the discriminator as a self-supervised regularization [11]. The output of the mixer layers in MLPMixer is upsampled using Transposed Convolution, and then is used to calculate the reconstruction loss with the real image or the generated image, as shown in Fig. 3 (D_{rec}). This reconstruction loss in the discriminator is based on the method in Lightweight GAN [11], although the reconstruction loss is calculated only for real images in the Lightweight GAN. This reconstruction loss in the discriminator is also added to the loss for training the generator. The details of each loss in both the generator and the discriminator are explained in the next section.

3.3   Loss Functions

In the generative adversarial networks, the generator and the discriminator are trained alternately. The loss function for training the generator is composed of three components: the adversarial loss (L_{adv}), the reconstruction loss of the generator in the range where the input snapshot picture is embedded (L_{rec}), and the reconstruction loss of the discriminator for the regularization ($L_{dis\,rec}$). On the other hand, the loss function for training the discriminator is composed of two components: the adversarial loss (L_{adv}), and the reconstruction loss of the discriminator ($L_{dis\,rec}$).

$$\min_{G} L_{adv} + L_{rec} + L_{dis\,rec} \tag{1}$$

$$\min_{D} L_{adv} + L_{dis\,rec} \tag{2}$$

The non-saturating loss [3] is used for the adversarial losses in the generator. The loss for the discriminator is defined by the following equation.
Adversarial loss for training the discriminator:

$$
\begin{aligned}
L_{adv\,m} = & - E_{x,y}\left[\log D_m(x,y)\right] \\
& - E_{x,z}\left[\log\left(1 - D_m\left(x, G(x,z)\right)\right)\right]
\end{aligned}
\tag{3}
$$

For training the generator, the adversarial loss is usually explained by maximization of Eq. 3. Instead of maximizing Eq. 3, the following loss is minimized in non-saturating loss, where $D_m(x, G(x, z))$ is maximized as in the original representation but the gradient is steeper in the non-saturating loss [3]. Adversarial loss for training the generator:

$$L_{adv\ m} = -E_{x,z}\left[\log\left(D_m\left(x, G(x, z)\right)\right)\right] \tag{4}$$

G and D represent the generator and the discriminator, respectively. x, y, and z are the input snapshot picture as the conditional input, the actual omni-directional image, and a random vector. m represents channel or patch, so that $L_{adv\ channel}$ and $L_{adv\ patch}$ are calculated from $D_{channel}$ and D_{patch} in Fig. 2, respectively. The overall adversarial loss (L_{adv}) is represented by Eq. 5.

$$L_{adv} = L_{adv\ patch} + \lambda_{ch} L_{adv\ channel} \tag{5}$$

λ_{ch} is a hyper-parameter to adjust the balance between the two terms.

The reconstruction loss of the generator is calculated as the L1 norm only in the range where the input snapshot picture is embedded, given by Eq. 6 using the mask y_{mask} representing the calculating range and the Hadamard product ($\otimes$).

$$L_{rec} = |\ y_{mask} \otimes (\ G(x, z) - y\ )\ | \tag{6}$$

The reconstruction loss of the discriminator is also calculated as the L1 norm, but for the whole image area.

$$L_{dis\ rec} = |\ D_{in} - D_{rec}(D_{in})\ | \tag{7}$$

D_{in} represents the 6-channel feature map consisting of the conditional input (the embedded snapshot picture) and the actual omni-directional image y or the output of the generator $G(x, z)$. This loss is used for the self-supervised regularization in the discriminator [11].

3.4   Stabilization of Training

For the stabilization of the training, the differential data augmentation [25] was adopted, where the data augmentation methods were applied to the inputs of the discriminator to suppress the over-fitting. Since the proposed method generates omni-directional images which have the property of the continuity between the left and right edges, 'roll' was applied for the shift augmentation in the horizontal direction. In addition to the data augmentation in the discriminator inputs, this 'roll' function was also used on the omni-directional images in the database before extracting the input snapshot pictures from the omni-directional images to increase the training data. In order to make the training more stable, the R1 gradient penalty [12] was also used during the training of the discriminator by adding the penalty term to the loss function in Eq. 2.

4   Experimental Setup

The omni-directional images in 24 outdoor scenes from the SUN360 dataset [23] were used in the experiments. The other outdoor-scene classes in SUN360 were excluded because there were less than 10 images in each class. As described in Sect. 3.4, the data augmentation of the omni-directional images using 'roll' was applied before extracting the snapshot pictures. A snapshot picture was extracted from an omni-directional image after the augmentation, and was embedded in the equi-rectangular projection to create the databases for the training. After the snapshot picture was normalized in the range between -1 and 1, the surrounding region of the embedded snapshot picture was padded with 0. The λ_{ch} in Eq. 5 was set to 0.1 and 0.01 in the training of the generator and the discriminator, respectively.

The CNN-based omni-directional image generator in the previous work [15] was used as a baseline method for the comparison in the experiments. In this method, the generator was composed of U-Net based on CNN, while the discriminator also consisted of CNN based on PatchGAN [7]. Non-saturating adversarial loss and reconstruction loss for the generator were used for the training.

The proposed method was trained for 200,000 iterations with the batch size of 16, while the baseline method was trained for 170,000 iterations with the batch size of 3. Since the performance was deteriorated after the 170,000 iterations in the baseline method, the baseline model was evaluated with the performance at the 170,000 iterations. The batch sizes were set to the maximum sizes with GPU of GTX1080Ti.

5   Results

After training the generator, omni-directional images were generated from the snapshot pictures extracted from the 861 test omni-directional images in the database. For this inference, the scene class labels were estimated using the scene recognition networks, ResNet18 [26], fine-tuned with the images extracted from the SUN360 dataset, and then were input to the generator as the conditional information for the conditional batch normalization. For the evaluation, 10 snapshot pictures were extracted from a generated omni-directional image in different horizontal directions for each elevation angle of 90, 45, 0, -45, -90 degrees. Quantitative evaluation was conducted on Frechet Inception Distance (FID) [6], Inception Score (IS) [17], recognition rate of the scene label, and Learned Perceptual Image Patch Similarity(LPIPS) [24]. FID is a metric that measures the similarity between feature distributions of real images and generated images. IS represents diversity and perceptual recognizability. LPIPS is a perceptual similarity metrics between two images, and is included for the evaluation to measure diversity of the generated images within a scene class, where the larger value means more diversified images. Furthermore, Multiply-ACcumulate (MAC), the memory consumption, and the inference speed were also evaluated during the inference only using the generator with the batch size 1 on CPU (Core i9-10850K) and on GPU (GeForce RTX3090). MAC represents the number of sum-of-product operations. In addition, the sample images generated using the proposed method were qualitatively compared with the generated images using the baseline method [15].

Table 1. Quantitative evaluation of proposed method compared with baseline. Each metric was calculated for the plane images extracted from the generated omnidirectional images at the elevation angles (90, 45, 0, −45, −90) degrees.

	Metrics	Elevation angle [degree]					Avg
		90	45	0	−45	−90	
Baseline [15]	FID(↓)	54.84	30.56	21.26	44.58	59.52	42.15
	IS(↑)	3.48	3.07	3.53	3.78	3.69	3.51
	Accuracy(↑)	24.36	**36.41**	**50.70**	**45.77**	**32.37**	**37.92**
	LPIPS(↑)	0.626	0.591	0.597	0.627	0.674	0.623
Proposed	FID(↓)	**32.65**	**20.66**	**16.23**	**37.24**	**53.55**	**32.07**
	IS(↑)	**3.92**	**3.50**	**3.77**	**4.28**	**4.61**	**4.02**
	Accuracy(↑)	**26.64**	32.97	49.08	43.23	26.82	35.75
	LPIPS(↑)	**0.648**	**0.605**	**0.622**	**0.657**	**0.724**	**0.651**

Table 2. Comparison of inference speed and model size

	Inference speed [ms]		Parameters	MAC	Forward/backward pass size	Total size
	CPU	GPU	[M]	[G]	[MB]	[MB]
Baseline [15]	792.31	28.78	217.63	567.42	897.65	1769.73
Proposed	**62.19**	**11.03**	**14.40**	**2.14**	**306.27**	**365.42**

5.1   Quantitative Evaluation

For the quantitative evaluation, the results on FID, IS, recognition rate, and LPIPS are shown in Table 1. For FID, IS, and LPIPS, the proposed method significantly outperformed the baseline method. Thus, the quality (FID, IS) and diversity (LPIPS) of the generated images were improved by the proposed method. However, the recognition rate in the proposed method was comparative or slightly lower than the baseline in many elevation angles. This may be due to the fact that the generated images in the baseline method tend to depend more on the scene class label because of the lack of information from an input picture near the edges than the proposed method. Thus, the baseline method generated similar textures at the edges of the images depending only on the scene label for various conditional input pictures.

The results on MAC, the memory consumption, and the inference speed are shown in Table 2. The inference speed in the proposed method was 12.7 times

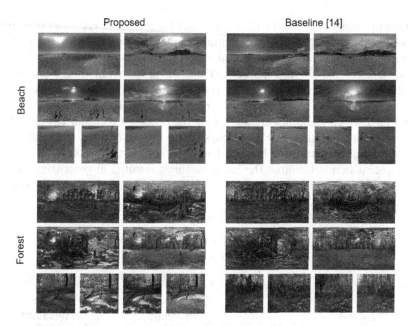

Fig. 4. Sample images generated by proposed method and baseline method [15]. For each class of 'Beach' and 'Forest', 4 sample images were generated for different input pictures in the same scene embedded at the center of the equirectangular projection. To see the diversity within the class, enlarged images of the red-frame regions are shown below the 4 sample images.

Fig. 5. Limitations of proposed method. The information of the input pictures at the center of the images was not appropriately propagated to edges.

faster on CPU and 2.6 times faster on GPU than the baseline method. The total number of parameters and MAC were significantly reduced to less than $1/15$ and $1/265$ of the baseline, respectively. The amount of memory used during the inference was greatly reduced from the baseline, which would enable inference even on devices with low GPU memories.

5.2 Qualitative Evaluation

The sample images generated by both the proposed and baseline methods [15] are show in Fig. 4 for the scene classes of Beach and Forest. For each class, 4 sample images were generated for different input pictures in the same scene embedded at the center of the equiretangular projection. To see the diversity within the class, enlarged images of the red-frame regions of the sample images are shown below the 4 sample images. For both the scenes, similar textures were generated in the enlarged regions among 4 different input samples in the baseline method. On the other hand, the proposed method successfully generated different textures with various color tones and shadings. Thus, the proposed method increased the diversity of the generated images by propagating the information of the input pictures embedded at the center of the omni-directional image.

In Fig. 5, failed examples are shown for the proposed method. It was difficult to generate natural images for the scenes with artificial objects, probably due to the small number of training images. For these scenes, the textures for different scenes were generated around the input pictures, resulted in generating unnatural images for these scenes. A possible solution would be to increase the training data for these scenes.

Table 3. Results of ablation studies. Metrics for $0°$ of evaluation angle and Avg over elevation angles (90, 45, 0, -45, -90) were compared.

settings		FID($\downarrow$)		IS($\uparrow$)		Accuracy[%]($\uparrow$)	
		$0°$	Avg	$0°$	Avg	$0°$	Avg
	Proposed	**16.23**	**32.07**	3.77	4.02	**49.08**	**35.75**
(1)	BN instead of Conditional BN	73.84	91.43	3.64	3.83	30.47	19.74
(2)	w/o L_{disrec}	50.14	68.97	**3.93**	4.02	33.72	25.71
(3)	w/o Channel Loss	77.13	98.84	3.87	4.05	37.15	26.69
(4)	w/o Multiple Inputs	82.60	101.47	3.56	3.81	37.28	24.96
(5)	w/o MLPMixerLayer	204.11	294.94	2.76	2.06	8.73	5.39
(6)	Transformer instead of MLPMixer	19.46	36.29	3.76	4.06	44.44	32.59

5.3   Ablation Study

Since the proposed method introduces several components to construct the model, an ablation study was conducted to investigate the influence of each component on the generated image quality. The hyper-parameters such as batch size were set to the same value as the proposed method without the optimization to each settings in the ablation study. The following settings were tested.

(1) Batch Norm (BN) instead of Conditional Batch Norm: The conditional batch normalization was replaced by the batch normalization.
(2) w/o L_{disrec}: The networks were trained without the reconstruction loss for the discriminator, introduced to the proposed model for self-supervised regularization.
(3) w/o Channel Loss: The networks were trained using adversarial loss only with patch loss, but without the channel loss.
(4) w/o Multiple Inputs: The input snapshot picture was only input to the first MLPMixer block.

(5) w/o MLPMixerLayer: The first block in the proposed method was replaced by DepthwiseConvLayer from MLPMixerLayer, resulted in the model without MLPMixer.

(6) Transformer instead of MLPMixer: The MLPMixer was replaced by the Transformer with positional encoding and conditional batch normalization.

The results in the ablation study are shown in Table 3. It can be seen from the results that FID and accuracy (recognition rate) were best in the proposed method, and significantly decreased without any components, although IS in some settings was comparable with the proposed method. This means that all the components are indispensable to achieve the performance as high as the proposed method. The high IS with low accuracy in the settings (2) and (3) means that a lot of omni-directional images with wrong scene classes were generated with good image quality (high IS), so that this would indicate that the model was sensitive to the miss-classification of the scene recognition of the input snapshot pictures in the settings (2) and (3). Thus, the reconstruction loss for the discriminator and the channel loss would be beneficial to achieve robustness against the miss-classification. Among the settings, the performance was most significantly decreased in the settings (5) without MLPMixerLayer. This means that the propagation of the information from the center to the edges is the key property to obtain the high quality omni-directional images. The performance was also lower with Transformer (6) than with MLPMixerLayer (Proposed). This may be due to the fact that self-attention tends to overfit and is not suitable for small data sets.

6   Conclusions

In this paper, a novel architecture for generating omni-directional images from a snapshot picture was proposed. In order to propagate the information efficiently from the center to the edges, MLPMixer was adopted with the depthwise convolutions in the hierarchical structure. By introducing regularization terms in the loss function to make the training stable, the proposed model was successfully trained, and generated high quality and diverse omni-directional images with lower memory consumption and computational costs than the CNN-based model. It was confirmed that the generated omni-directional images were quantitatively and qualitatively competitive or even better than the CNN-based model.

The proposed model would be useful not only for the omni-directional image generation, but also for out-painting tasks in general. One of the problems in the proposed model was the training speed due to the gradient penalty, which was calculated separately from the gradients in back-propagation. This would be improved by calculating the gradients both for the gradient penalty and the back-propagation at the same time, or by introducing other regularization methods to make the training stable, such as spectral normalization [14]. Furthermore, large-scale datasets of omni-directional images should be constructed to improve the deep-learning models in the omni-directional image processing.

This work was supported by JSPS KAKENHI Grant Number JP21K11943.

References

1. Cazenavette, G., De Guevara, M.L.: MixerGAN: An MLP-based architecture for unpaired image-to-image translation. ArXiv (2021)
2. Dosovitskiy, A., et al.: An image is worth 16 × 16 words: transformers for image recognition at scale. In: ICLR (2021)
3. Goodfellow, I., et al.: Generative adversarial nets. In: NeurIPS (2014)
4. Gulrajani, I., Ahmed, F., Arjovsky, M., Dumoulin, V., Courville, A.: Improved training of Wasserstein GANs. ArXiv (2017)
5. Hara, T., Mukuta, Y., Harada, T.: Spherical image generation from a single image by considering scene symmetry. AAAI **35**(2), 1513–1521 (2021)
6. Heusel, M., Ramsauer, H., Unterthiner, T., Nessler, B., Hochreiter, S.: GANs trained by a two time-scale update rule converge to a local Nash equilibrium. In: NeurIPS (2017)
7. Isola, P., Zhu, J.Y., Zhou, T., Efros, A.A.: Image-to-image translation with conditional adversarial networks. In: CVPR (2017)
8. Jiang, Y., Chang, S., Wang, Z.: Transgan: Two pure transformers can make one strong GAN, and that can scale up. In: NeurIPS (2021)
9. Karras, T., Laine, S., Aittala, M., Hellsten, J., Lehtinen, J., Aila, T.: Analyzing and improving the image quality of StyleGAN. In: CVPR (2020)
10. Lee, S.H., Lee, S., Song, B.C.: Vision transformer for small-size datasets. ArXiv (2021)
11. Liu, B., Zhu, Y., Song, K., Elgammal, A.: Towards faster and stabilized GAN training for high-fidelity few-shot image synthesis. In: ICLR (2021)
12. Mescheder, L., Geiger, A., Nowozin, S.: Which training methods for GANs do actually converge? In: ICML (2018)
13. Mirza, M., Osindero, S.: Conditional generative adversarial nets. ArXiv (2014)
14. Miyato, T., Kataoka, T., Koyama, M., Yoshida, Y.: Spectral normalization for generative adversarial networks. In: ICLR (2018)
15. Okubo, K., Yamanaka, T.: Omni-directional image generation from single snapshot image. In: SMC (2020)
16. Ronneberger, Olaf, Fischer, Philipp, Brox, Thomas: U-net: convolutional networks for biomedical image segmentation. In: Navab, Nassir, Hornegger, Joachim, Wells, William M.., Frangi, Alejandro F.. (eds.) MICCAI 2015. LNCS, vol. 9351, pp. 234–241. Springer, Cham (2015). https://doi.org/10.1007/978-3-319-24574-4_28
17. Salimans, T., et al.: Improved techniques for training GANs. In: NeurIPS (2016)
18. Tolstikhin, I., et al.: MLP-mixer: An all-MLP architecture for vision. In: NeurIPS (2021)
19. Vaswani, A., et al.: Attention is all you need. In: NeurIPS (2017)
20. de Vries, H., Strub, F., Mary, J., Larochelle, H., Pietquin, O., Courville, A.C.: Modulating early visual processing by language. In: NeurIPS (2017)
21. Wang, Z., She, Q., Ward, T.E.: Generative adversarial networks: a survey and taxonomy. ArXiv (2019)
22. Wu, T., Zheng, C., Cham, T.J.: IPO-LDM: depth-aided 360-degree indoor RGB panorama outpainting via latent diffusion model. ArXiv (2023)
23. Xiao, J., Ehinger, K.A., Oliva, A., Torralba, A.: Recognizing scene viewpoint using panoramic place representation. In: CVPR (2012)
24. Zhang, R., Isola, P., Efros, A.A., Shechtman, E., Wang, O.: The unreasonable effectiveness of deep features as a perceptual metric. In: CVPR (2018)

25. Zhao, S., Liu, Z., Lin, J., Zhu, J.Y., Han, S.: Differentiable augmentation for data-efficient GAN training. In: NeurIPS (2020)
26. Zhou, B., Lapedriza, A., Khosla, A., Oliva, A., Torralba, A.: Places: a 10 million image database for scene recognition. IEEE Trans. PAMI **40**(6), 1452–1464 (2018)

An Automated Framework for Accurately Classifying Financial Tables in Enterprise Analysis Reports

Ho-Jung Kim[1], Yeong-Eun Jeon[1], Won-Seok Jung[2], Dae-Hyun Bae[2], Yung-Il Park[2], and Dong-Ok Won[1(✉)]

[1] Department of Artificial Intelligence Convergence, Hallym University, Chuncheon, Gangwon 24252, Republic of Korea
dongok.won@hallym.ac.kr
[2] Yonhap Infomax Inc., Jong-lo Seoul 03143, Republic of Korea

Abstract. Despite significant advancements in artificial intelligence technology, image processing (classification) has not made as much progress as other fields, especially natural language processing. Slowly, technologies such as Transformers are being implemented in the field of image processing, but due to disparities in data format, they are not widely utilized. Moreover, the size of image data is typically quite large, limiting the amount of data that can be used for training. Therefore, we wish to optimize existing models and proposes a framework for the automatic detection, extraction, and classification of report table images from financial analysis. The framework is designed to address the difficulties encountered by the financial industry, where table data shapes can vary, making it difficult to extract and utilize the data and necessitating extensive manual labor. Detected tables with 99.9% accuracy using Cascade-TabNet and filtered out unnecessary data with 97.93% accuracy using DenseNet. For classification of tables, we developed a mix model that combines various features to achieve 95.2% precision. The overall framework achieved an average precision of 97.37%, making it suitable for automated environments requiring minimal human intervention.

Keywords: Finance · Table · Classification · Commercial system · Enterprise analysis report

1 Introduction

Artificial Intelligence (A.I.) is an extremely intriguing technology in the 21st century. Although research on A.I. began a while ago, the performance of the hardware and design at the time did not meet researchers' expectations, rendering the performance meaningless and limiting it to the level of early research. A.I. research has exploded and rapidly evolved from simple shape classification

© The Author(s), under exclusive license to Springer Nature Switzerland AG 2023
H. Lu et al. (Eds.): ACPR 2023, LNCS 14406, pp. 374–384, 2023.
https://doi.org/10.1007/978-3-031-47634-1_28

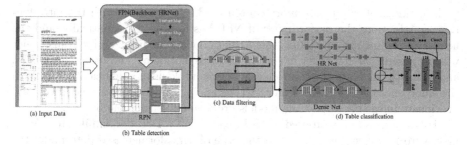

Fig. 1. Overview of the proposed framework: (a) The input data consists of each page of an enterprise analysis report published by a securities company. (b) Table detection is performed using cascade-tablenet. The structure of cascade-tablenet is briefly explained in (b). (c) Unnecessary table images are filtered out from the tables detected in the input report image. One of the key components of the proposed framework is shown in (d), which explains how HRNet and DenseNet are mixed and decoded using Up Convolution to enhance the necessary features for classification and improve performance.

(circles, triangles, squares, etc.) to the realm of creation, such as the generation of images, music, and text, as hardware has reached unmatched performance levels in recent years. This technology's development potential, yet is limitless. As a consequence, an A.I. model that performs classification tasks cannot generate images, despite the fact that it is capable of performing a variety of tasks. However, expanding the range within similar or identical tasks is possible (for instance, by adding classes to classification tasks). Moreover, the level of difficulty in problem-solving can vary significantly depending on the field in which the technology is applied and the data used for learning. In the case of classification tasks, for instance, it is evident that the level of difficulty in solving the classification problem for clear images (e.g., images with clear morphological features, such as cars and airplanes) and handwritten sentences (e.g., optical character recognition) is notably different. This standard is based on whether the problem can be easily solved by humans. Still, classification technology has predominantly evolved into a field that classifies clear images, and its performance is based on the ImageNet dataset [1]. But classification is not limited to images; it is the most fundamental task required in numerous fields. As stated previously, the employed technology differs depending on the field and the data employed. In the case of images, a Convolutional Neural Network (CNN) is utilized to extract and classify data features. Recurrent Neural Networks (RNNs) are typically employed in fields with continuous data, as opposed to images. While research in the field of computer vision stagnated as a consequence of the ImageNet dataset attending to the classification problem, Natural Language Processing (NLP) has made tremendous strides, beginning with Attention [2], which was developed to find meaning in continuous data fragments. Sentence data in NLP are converted into word tokens for use in RNN. However, unlike general signal data, each word token has a distinct meaning and additional tokens attached to the front and back, making interpretation more complicated. Nonetheless, with the introduction of Attention, the performance of NLP has improved dramatically, and the field is expanding rapidly. Later, this Attention was enhanced, and a Transformer was proposed that stored each word in a Vocab dictionary and used Key, Query, and Value to calculate the connectivity between tokens more efficiently [3]. With the emergence of this Transformer, A.I. technology underwent a revolution, and previously infeasible large-scale models are now appearing one by one.

Transformers are composed of an Encoder and a Decoder, similar to a Variable Auto Encoder (Decoder), and the type of Transformer used determines the appropriate function. In classification and prediction tasks, the Encoder structure is typically used to construct the model, such as the Bidirectional Encoder Representations from Transformers (BERT) model [4] serving as an example. The BERT model can perform multiple tasks, such as predicting the next sentence, filling in blanks, and classifying sentences, and its performance is exemplary. As transformers revolutionized performance in NLP, attempts were made to apply them to computer vision, with the Vision Transformer [5] being proposed for vision classification, where there had been little advancement in CNN. However, Transformers are powerful but come with significant challenges, such as the large memory consumption required for calculating Multi-head Attention and the need for a large amount of training data. Therefore, while it is not a problem to use relatively small images for training, the inability to use large images poses a challenge in the field of computer vision for easily employing transformers. To address this issue, the Squeeze and Excitation Network (SENet) [6] method was developed to mimic the characteristics of transformers and is easily implementable in CNN-based models. This network proposes to extract attention features from images and pass them to CNN for simple computation of attention. Beginning with this network, it was expanded to Efficient Net [7], which extracts image features efficiently, and then further developed into Global Context Network (GCNet) [8], which calculates global attention for the entire image as opposed to local attention. However, GCNet requires a significant amount of memory to compute global attention, which is addressed by the Spatial Attention [9] technique.

In this paper, on the basis of previous research, we propose a framework for automatically detecting, extracting, and classifying table images within financial analysis reports. The majority of previous research on table images has focused on table detection and document structure recognition [10,11]. However, classification of table images has not been a major focus, primarily because the majority of tables used in public institutions or pre-determined formats are relatively straightforward to classify. In the financial industry, table data shapes can vary depending on the analyst who created the report, making it difficult to extract and utilize the data. This has resulted in considerable inconvenience and the use of 99 percent manual labor in processing related tasks. Our proposed framework is intended to address these issues.

2 Automated Classification Framework

2.1 Detecting and Extracting Table in Documents

Detecting and extracting table areas from documents has been the subject of extensive research, and the performance of existing models is highly satisfactory. In the majority of prior studies, CNN-based models were employed, but Transformer-based models have recently gained traction. In contrast, this paper makes use of Cascade-TableNet (TabNet) [10], a table detection model based on Cascade-fRCNN. In the Transformer-based model, MASTER-Table [11] demonstrates superior performance and data distortion resistance when evaluated solely on the basis of its performance. This model is an adaptation of the MASTER base OCR model [12]. However, Transformer-based models require a large amount of training data by their very nature, and the MASTER model calculates multi-head global contexts as features from the input image. Even necessitates a large amount of memory for the calculation of single global context, which adding multiple heads increases memory consumption even further. MASTER-Table, which is based on the aforementioned model, is therefore also challenging to implement in our proposed automated framework due to its costly nature.

TabNet was selected as the most appropriate model for our environment, despite the fact that it may not be the most cutting-edge methodology. This model is based on Cascade-fRCNN, so its model size is larger than typical CNN-based models, but its performance is guaranteed to be superior. In fact, this model's performance has been evaluated on multiple datasets, and on the ICDAR13 dataset [13], it demonstrated remarkable accuracy of 100 percent. It also performed admirably in diverse Table detection challenges. This model employs High-Resolution Network (HRNet) [14] as a backbone to extract features from the input Document image, and detects Table regions using the Feature Pyramid Network (FPN) and Region Proposal Network (RPN) structures of fRCNN. In the proposed framework, the detected regions are cropped and utilized for subsequent filtering and classification steps.

2.2 Filtering the Data Between Informative and Useless Content

There are numerous tables in enterprise analysis reports that do not contain actual data, such as analyst information and report publishing information. In order to reach a high level of accuracy when learning TabNet in the proposed framework, all table contents are used for training to be detected, so unnecessary data should be filtered. Given that the required data may vary depending on the system's operating environment, it may be utilized selectively of this part. We developed a distinct 2-class classification model in order to obtain only the required data. The classification model used was the Densely Connected Convolutional Network (DenseNet) [15].

Compared to other commonly used CNN-based models, DenseNet was found to be more suitable for our task because the table data itself does not easily exhibit local or global features that can be easily detected by a model additional techniques. This problem is not due to the data itself, but rather the criteria we use to classify the data. We will briefly introduce the criteria for classifying the data in relation to data collection later on.

2.3 Classification Model for Financial Table Data

One important aspect of our proposed solution is the mixed model depicted in Fig. 1. We combined two models because the performance of a single model alone was insufficient to solve the problem. Details can be found in the section titled "Results" We began by attempting to confirm the possibility of solving the problem with a basic CNN model, and then moved on to increasingly complex models. In the classification model developed for our proposed framework, HRNet and DenseNet were combined. One of the key components of HRNet, the exchange unit, is implemented as repeated multi-scale fusion, which takes in s response maps as input and outputs $s + 1$ response maps. The output is composed of an aggregation of the input maps, and the function $a(X_i, k)$ is a function that upsamples or downsamples X_i from resolution i to resolution k. So, the input response maps: $\{X_1, X_2, \ldots, X_s\}$ and results output response map:$\{Y_1, Y_2, \ldots, Y_s\}$. Each resolution outputs are an aggregation of the input maps.

$$Y_k = \sum_{i=1}^{s} a(X_i, k) \tag{1}$$

In final form, the exchange unit between stages has an additional output map.

$$Y_{s+1} = a(Y_{s,s+1}) \tag{2}$$

Through this method, HRNet is able to divide the resolution into n subnetworks and transition each feature, resulting in maps with greater detail. On the other side, define the tensor for DenseNet inputs: $X = (x_1, \ldots, x_N), x_n \in \mathbb{R}^{(C \times H \times W)}$ the output tensor Y, which is the result of passing X through a series of dense blocks, transition layers, and a final classification layer: $Y = f_L(T_L)$ where f_L is final classification layer and T_L is the output of the last transition layer. Each dense block is composed of a series of convolutional layers that are connected to each other in a dense fashion. Let's denote the output of the i_{th} convolutional layer in the j_{th} dense block as H_{ij}:

$$H_{ij} = f(\mathrm{Conv}_{jk}(H_{ij} - 1)), k \in \{1, \ldots, K\} \tag{3}$$

where Conv_{jk} is the k_{th} convolutional layer in the j_{th} dense block, f is the activation function (e.g. ReLU), and K is the number of convolutional layers in each dense block. The output of the entire dense block is given by:

$$H_j = \mathrm{Concatenate}(H_0, H_1, \ldots, H_{i-1}, H_i) \tag{4}$$

where Concatenate is the operation that concatenates the feature maps from all previous layers. Therefore, in the case of DenseNet, it is possible to obtain layer-specific features by aggregating all features from the entire image. Based on this fact, we decided to mix the direction of the model by combining two models. Specifically, we added the values obtained from each model, and we slightly twisted this process by using concat and sum for each output as a single output. Let's define a new tensor X_{mix} by combining the two output tensors, Y_1 and Y_2 where both outputs are the tensors before going through the classification layer on each model.

$$X_{mix} = \text{Concatenate}(Y_1, Y_2, Y_1 + Y_2) \tag{5}$$

Using the result X_{mix}, we achieved a significantly high accuracy in classification. However, in order to further improve the performance, we conducted classification using features decoded by Transpose Convolution in the classification part like Fully Convolutional Network [16].

3 Dataset

The dataset used in our study is self-collected. We did not use other commonly available datasets such as ICDAR, TableBank [17], and FinTabNet [18] because the classification criteria used in actual problem-solving are completely different. Therefore, we obtained data that meets the criteria and conducted training and testing. The total number of data is shown in Table 1.

3.1 Method for Collecting Data

We obtained data from actual reports used in the field, as opposed to virtual data or easily accessible web-based information. Analysts from Korean securities firms such as "Kiwoom", "Samsung", and "Dong-bu" published and authored the reports are used. From these reports, we extracted data for three tasks: "table detection", "data filtering", and "classification". More than 1,400 reports were gathered, and tables were found in 11,872 pages. 34,202 tables were extracted from these pages, of which 8,329 were necessary for filtering training not classification. The remaining 25,873 table data were utilized for training classification.

Table 1. Number of classes and data on Our dataset

Class	1	2	3	4	5	6
Quarter	3617	370	358	542	1753	1067
Year	13328	1179	969	168	245	

Class	7	8	9	10	11
Quarter	235	228	121	263	121

3.2   Data Classification Criteria

Classification criteria for table data differ significantly from those used for other types of general datasets. Based on their form and content, they are divided into two categories, and there are also classes that combine these two categories. Here are some examples.

- The first classification is determined by the column header content. If the table's header contains the letter "Q", it is categorized as a "Quarter" table. In contrast, if the table does not contain "Q" and only contains the year value "Y" or "20xx", it is categorized as a "Year" table.
- The classification of classes is determined by the composition of row and column headers. Classes are distinguished in accordance with whether the row header is divided into one column, two columns, or more. Similarly, this rule can be applied to column headers.
- If the row headers are only divided into one column, but their contents are differentiated by indentation or alignment, they are classified as belonging to different classes despite their similar appearance.
- If the column header contains "Q" it is classified as a Quarter table, but if it contains content other than quarter values, such as "YoY", it is classified as a different class, even if the overall shape is similar.

The mentioned conditions are only a small portion of the criteria that differentiate the data classes in our dataset and are one of the reasons why the problem is challenging. The proposed framework was trained on a dataset that was compiled by the author. The ratio of training data to validation data was 7:3, and newly published reports that were not included in the training data were used to evaluate the system.

4   Results

We measured the accuracy of each stage to evaluate the proposed framework as a whole, and used the average accuracy as an evaluation metric by aggregating them. And the system we used was equipped with an RTX 3090 TI GPU model, and the hardware level, including the CPU, was run on a commonplace PC environment.

4.1   Table Detection

In addition to fine-tuning a pre-trained model on our own data for table detection using transfer learning, we evaluated its overall performance on the pre-trained data to determine how well it performed on the existing pre-trained data.

In the Table 2 we can see that the original model performed well on the test dataset and also demonstrated very high accuracy on our own dataset. In addition, additional evaluation metrics demonstrate an adequate level of performance. The model utilized 1–2 GB of GPU memory in its running environment

Table 2. Result of Cascade TabNet using variable dataset

Dataset		Accuracy	Precision	Recall	F1
ICDAR13		1.0	1.0	1.0	1.0
Table	Both	0.934	0.9299	0.9571	0.9433
Bank	Word	0.955	0.9592	0.9728	0.966
	Latex	0.941	0.9435	0.9549	0.9492
Our		**0.99**	**0.9872**	**0.9635**	**0.9748**

Table 3. Evaluation results of each model for filtering task.

Model	Accuracy	Precision	Recall	F1
Simple-CNN	0.951	0.951	0.9307	0.9367
HR-Net	0.945	0.9442	0.9432	0.9419
SE-Net	0.957	0.953	0.9425	0.9491
EfficientNet-b2	0.969	0.966	0.961	0.9593
Dense Net	**0.9793**	**0.979**	**0.979**	**0.979**

and could support up to eight concurrent workers. It took approximately 2–3 seconds to process a full-size document image and 25–40 s to process a 15-17-page report. Due to these factors, we incorporated Cascade TabNet into our framework for table detection, excluding transformer and other excessively large models.

4.2 Filtering Useless Table Data

As justification for selecting and employing DenseNet, we evaluated a number of models for the filtering task, and the results are displayed in Table 3. As the name suggests, Simple-CNN is an extremely basic model consisting only of simple CNN layers. As shown in the table, all models in the list demonstrated excellent performance, which is likely due to the relative simplicity of the filtering task, which involves only two classes. The performance of the Simple-CNN model was maximized through hyperparameter tuning. However, the model's accuracy remained between 93 and 95%, and other models demonstrated comparable levels. All models utilized in this test were optimized to the greatest extent possible via hyperparameter tuning. Nonetheless, only EfficientNet and DenseNet surpassed this threshold. Although the model size of DenseNet is larger than that of EfficientNet, the difference in system performance is not statistically significant, and DenseNet performed better at the same level. We consequently adopted DenseNet.

Table 4. Evaluation results of each model for classification task.

Model	Accuracy	Precision	Recall	F1
Simple-CNN	0.816	0.825	0.802	0.795
HR-Net	0.843	0.851	0.828	0.839
SE-Net	0.855	0.859	0.831	0.826
EfficientNet-b2	0.872	0.877	0.857	0.8505
Dense Net	0.89	0.882	0.866	0.865
Model mix - basic (our)	**0.935**	**0.9324**	**0.9305**	**0.9314**
Model mix - FCN (our)	**0.952**	**0.9516**	**0.9514**	**0.9511**

4.3 Classification of Table Data

Looking at Table 4 we also evaluated the models used in the filtering task for table classification; however, the overall performance was not as good as we had hoped. As with the filtering task, DenseNet demonstrated the best performance, with average accuracy remaining above 89%. After undergoing hyperparameter tuning, all models were obviously in their optimal state. However, it can be seen that the model that combined DenseNet and HRNet performed significantly better than other models. The features obtained from each HRNet resolution and the overall features of DenseNet appear to have assisted in the classification of tables, as anticipated. In addition, the mix model with the decoding portion supplemented by a transpose convolution layer like FCN demonstrated superior performance. As there is a classification criterion related to the table's content, it would appear possible to obtain additional character features in the restored resolution through decoding.

5 Conclusion

We proposed an automated framework for extracting table data from securities analysts' enterprise analysis reports. Through training and evaluation with real data, we elucidated the models used for each framework component and the rationale behind their selection. The three models we chose demonstrated extremely high accuracy for each task they performed: the table detection task demonstrated nearly 99% accuracy, the 2-class classification task demonstrated 97.93% accuracy for filtering unnecessary data, and the performance for classifying actual table data for each purpose was 95.2%. Although the accuracy of the last classification task is relatively low, it can be considered to have an acceptable level of accuracy as a general classification criterion was not applied. Moreover, when evaluating the performance of the entire framework as opposed to each individual component, it demonstrated a very high level of accuracy with an average accuracy of 97.37%, which is adequate for building an automated system with some human intervention in real-world environments. We intend to develop and improve the models used for each task based on this framework in order to create a framework with a higher level of performance, as there is room for improvement in the current models.

Acknowledgements. This work was supported by Institute of Information and Communications Technology Planning and Evaluation (IITP) grant funded by the Korea government (MSIT) (No. 2021-0-02068, Artificial Intelligence Innovation Hub).

References

1. Deng, J., Dong, W., Socher, R., Li, L.J., Li, K., Fei-Fei, L.: ImageNet: a large-scale hierarchical image database. In: IEEE Conference on Computer Vision and Pattern Recognition, pp. 248–255 (2009)
2. Luong, M.T., Pham, H., Manning, C.D.: Effective approaches to attention-based neural machine translation. In: Conference on Empirical Methods in Natural Language Processing, pp. 1412–1421 (2015)
3. Vaswani, A., et al.: Attention is all you need. In: Advances in Neural Information Processing Systems, pp. 5998–6008 (2017)
4. Devlin, J., Chang, M.W., Lee, K., Toutanova, K.: BERT: pre-training of deep bidirectional transformers for language understanding. In: Conference of the North American Chapter of the Association for Computational Linguistics, pp. 4171–4186 (2019)
5. Dosovitskiy, A., et al.: An image is worth 16x16 words: transformers for image recognition at scale. In: 9th International Conference on Learning Representations (2021)
6. Hu, J., Shen, L., Sun, G.: Squeeze-and-excitation networks. In: IEEE/CVF Conference on Computer Vision and Pattern Recognition, pp. 7132–7141 (2018)
7. Tan, M., Le, Q.: EfficientNet: rethinking model scaling for convolutional neural networks. In: Proceedings of the 36th International Conference on Machine Learning, vol. 97, pp. 6105–6114 (2019)
8. Cao, Y., Xu, J., Lin, S., Wei, F., Hu, H.: GCNet: non-local networks meet squeeze-excitation networks and beyond. In: Proceedings of the IEEE/CVF International Conference on Computer Vision, Workshops (2019)
9. Woo, S., Park, J., Lee, J.Y., Kweon, I.S.: CBAM: convolutional block attention module. In: Proceedings of the European Conference on Computer Vision, pp. 3–19 (2018)
10. Prasad, D., Gadpal, A., Kapadni, K., Visave, M., Sultanpure, K.: Cascadetabnet: an approach for end to end table detection and structure recognition from image-based documents. In: Proceedings of the IEEE/CVF Conference on Computer Vision and Pattern Recognition Workshops, pp. 572–573 (2020)
11. Ye, J., et al.: PingAn-VCGroup's Solution for ICDAR 2021 Competition on Scientific Literature Parsing Task B: Table Recognition to HTML arXiv:2105.01848 (2021)
12. Lu, N., et al.: MASTER: multi-aspect non-local network for scene text recognition. Pattern Recognit. **117**, 107980 (2021)
13. Göbel, M.C., Hassan, T., Oro, E., Orsi, G.: ICDAR 2013 table competition. IEEE Computer Society, pp. 1449–1453 (2013)

14. Sun, K., Xiao, B., Liu, D., Wang, J.: Deep high-resolution representation learning for human pose estimation. In: Proceedings of the IEEE/CVF Conference on Computer Vision and Pattern Recognition, pp. 5693–5703 (2019)
15. Huang, G., Liu, Z., Weinberger, K.Q., Maaten, L.: Densely connected convolutional networks. In: Proceedings of the IEEE Conference on Computer Vision and Pattern Recognition, pp. 4700–4708 (2017)
16. Long, J., Shelhamer, E., Darrell, T.: Fully convolutional networks for semantic segmentation. In: Proceedings of the IEEE Conference on Computer Vision and Pattern Recognition, pp. 3431–3440 (2015)
17. Li, M., Cui, L., Huang, S., Wei, F., Zhou, M., Li, Z.: TableBank: table benchmark for image-based table detection and recognition. In: Proceedings of the Twelfth Language Resources and Evaluation Conference, pp. 1918–1925 (2020)
18. Zheng, X., Burdick, D., Popa, L., Zhong, X., Wang, N.X.R.: Global table extractor (GTE): a framework for joint table identification and cell structure recognition using visual context. In: Proceedings of the IEEE Winter Conference on Applications of Computer Vision, pp. 697–706 (2021)

NeCa: Network Calibration for Class Incremental Learning

Zhenyao Zhang and Lijun Zhang[✉]

National Key Laboratory for Novel Software Technology, Nanjing University, Nanjing 210023, China
{zhangzhenyao,zhanglj}@lamda.nju.edu.cn

Abstract. Class incremental learning (CIL) aims to continually learn unseen classes in new tasks without forgetting the previous ones. However, deep neural networks are prone to make a biased prediction towards classes in the most recently learned task, dubbed task-recency bias. Most recent studies make a post-training adjustment on the last fully connected layer to alleviate this problem but ignore the feature extractor. This work proposes a novel training framework termed network calibration (NeCa) that simultaneously adjusts the last fully connected layer and the feature extractor. Specifically, we combine the post-training adjustment process with the training process into a balanced learning module, whose loss function is corrected based on the prior probabilities of classes. In this module, the parameters of the whole network are well-calibrated via backpropagation. Additional knowledge transmission and decaying regularization modules further mitigate catastrophic forgetting in CIL. Experiment results manifest that NeCa outperforms the state-of-the-art methods on three mainstream datasets, including MNIST, CIFAR-100, and ImageNet-100, which validates the effectiveness of our framework. Furthermore, we conduct experiments with the prevalent vision transformer backbone, and the consistently excellent performance demonstrates that NeCa is also competently suited for attention-based models.

Keywords: Class incremental learning · Catastrophic forgetting · Class imbalance · Classification · Deep learning

1 Introduction

In recent years, deep neural networks (DNNs) have achieved excellent performance on various visual tasks [9, 10]. However, their success is generally limited to a single task. Compared with humans, DNNs seem to be tremendously forgetful. Specifically, when a new task arrives, DNNs are prone to forget the knowledge gained on the old task, which is known academically as catastrophic forgetting [4, 22]. Nowadays, the increasing volume of data and privacy issues create an urgent need for a learning paradigm to continually adapt to new tasks while maintaining performance on old ones.

To delve into catastrophic forgetting, researchers have proposed three incremental learning scenarios: task-incremental learning, domain-incremental learning, and class-incremental learning (CIL) [27]. They differ in whether the task identities are provided at inference and whether the task identities must be inferred. CIL is the most difficult of the three because it has to predict unknown task identities. Researchers widely adopt a size-limited exemplar memory [25] and knowledge distillation technique [19] for CIL. With their help, the overall accuracy does improve, but predictions are still extremely biased towards the classes in the most recently learned task. The limitation is termed task-recency bias (TRB) [20], illustrated in Fig. 1.

Recently, several works aim to correct TRB, most of which argue that an imbalanced training set is the main reason and the last fully connected layer suffers the most. So they perform a post-training adjustment on the last fully connected layer, which does improve the performance to some extent [25,30,34]. However, their methods leave the feature extractor, which is also trained on the same imbalanced dataset, untouched. To improve this, we present a simple and effective training framework named network calibration (NeCa) that miti-

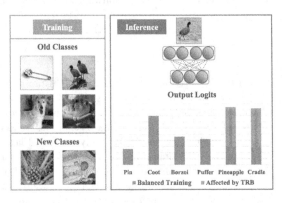

Fig. 1. Compared to the model trained in the balanced dataset, the TRB-affected model produced extremely high output logits for the new classes, leading to inference errors.

gates TRB by simultaneously tuning the last fully connected layer and the feature extractor in a one-stage training.

In total, NeCa is composed of three parts. **Balanced Learning**: We confront an imbalanced training set in each task because of the size limitation of exemplar memory. To address this issue, we calibrate the traditional classification loss via the prior probability of each class and propose the calibrated cross-entropy (CCE) loss. Through minimizing CCE loss, we calibrate the whole network (including the feature extractor ignored by previous work) to obtain a more balanced classification boundary. **Knowledge Transmission**: To transfer the knowledge along with the task, we apply knowledge distillation (KD) [12] between the models of two adjacent tasks. We restrict the output logits of the models to be as consistent as possible. This module can pass on the performance gains from other modules. **Decaying Regularization**: As the training set starts from a small part of the whole dataset, we heuristically adopt a stronger regularization at the beginning to prevent overfitting and weaken it as the task progresses to combat forgetting.

To sum up, our contribution is threefold: (i) Taking the information of prior probability into account, we propose CCE loss to confront the imbalanced training set in CIL. Optimizing CCE loss will calibrate the whole network especially the feature extractor neglected in previous works. (ii) We propose a novel training framework called NeCa consisting of three parts. They can promote each other very well and make the model's prediction more balanced throughout the task continuum. (iii) Extensive experiment results manifest that, compared with the current state-of-the-art methods, our framework achieves the best performance on three mainstream datasets, including MNIST, CIFAR-100, and ImageNet-100. Furthermore, experiments on vision transformers demonstrate that NeCa is equally applicable to attention-based models.

2   Related Work

Class incremental learning (CIL) approaches are roughly classified into the following four categories: (i) Structure-based methods fix the parameters related to previous tasks and assign more to new tasks [1,24,31]. (ii) Regularization-based methods try to minimize the impact of learning a new task imposing on the old ones [2,3,15,19]. (iii) Rehearsal methods provide training samples of previous tasks by storing a small number of exemplars or generating synthetic images or features [5,25,26,30]. (iv) Bias-correction methods aim to alleviate task-recency bias (TRB) [5,13,25,30,34]. Our framework network calibration (NeCa) belongs to (ii), (iii), and (iv) at the same time, and the following is a brief overview of these three categories.

Knowledge Distillation. Knowledge distillation (KD) [12] belongs to the broad category of regularization-based methods. Li and Hoiem [19] first utilize KD in incremental learning to keep the model's response for old tasks. After this, KD became a popular technique used to retain the knowledge of old tasks in CIL. Rebuffi *et al.* [25] store a limited number of previous exemplars for training and expand the KD loss for them. Wu *et al.* [30] introduce a scalar to adjust the weight between KD loss for remembering the previous knowledge and classification loss for learning the new ones. Ahn *et al.* [2] impose KD independently on the output logits associated with each task and propose a novel separated softmax layer to implement it.

Rehearsal. CIL can proceed without preserving any examples from the previous task [3,14,19,33]. In contrast, rehearsal-based methods use a limited amount of previously seen exemplars or learn to generate them [26]. As far as we know, Rebuffi *et al.* [25] first introduce the exemplar rehearsal method into CIL with a nearest-means-of-exemplars classification strategy at inference. Due to its performance improvement and ease of deployment, rehearsal is prevalent in recent works [2,13,18,30,31,34]. Prabhu *et al.* [23] keep a balanced exemplar memory by greedily collecting samples over the previous tasks, and they train a model from scratch in the next task using samples only in the memory. Verwimp *et al.* [28] provide both conceptual and strong empirical evidence to interpret the benefits and harms of the rehearsal-based method in the CIL scenario.

Bias Correction. The bias in the bias correction refers to the TRB. Despite resorting to sorts of techniques to prevent forgetting, the model tends to make a biased prediction towards the newest classes. To correct TRB, Rebuffi *et al.* [25] observe the last fully connected layer of a model manifests higher bias than the modules before it, *i.e.*, the feature extractor. So they abandon the fully connected layer and utilize only the feature extractor at inference. Castro *et al.* [5] take advantage of data augmentation and propose a second-stage training phase called balanced fine-tuning. Wu *et al.* [30] add a bias correction layer following the last fully connected layer and train it on a balanced dataset obtained by down-sampling while freezing the feature extractor. Hou *et al.* [13] utilize the hard negative classes of a new class to rectify the imbalanced class embeddings. Furthermore, they note that the weight and bias of the last fully connected layer are distorting between old and new classes. Inspired by this finding, Zhao *et al.* [34] propose a simple and effective method to adjust the weight of the last fully connected layer via its norms. Unlike previous approaches, our framework NeCa adjusts the parameters of the feature extractor and merges the bias correction stage into the training phase.

3   Method

In this section, we first give a formal formulation of class incremental learning (CIL) and then detail our proposed framework, namely network calibration (NeCa), which consists of three main components: balanced learning, knowledge transmission, and decaying regularization (illustrated in Fig. 2).

3.1   Problem Formulation

CIL is composed of T tasks coming in a row. In each task $t = 1, 2, \cdots, T$, we get a new training set $\mathcal{D}^t$ that consists of C^t classes we have never seen before, which implies that $\mathcal{L}^i \cap \mathcal{L}^j = \varnothing, \forall i \neq j$, where $\mathcal{L}^i$ denotes the label space of $\mathcal{D}^i$. Note that we need to expand the model parameters for the new classes on the last fully connected layer. It is easy to get a model that performs well on task t by simply adopting a traditional cross-entropy (CE) loss on $\mathcal{D}^t$:

$$L_{CE}(\mathcal{D}^t) = \frac{1}{|\mathcal{D}^t|} \sum_{(X,y) \in \mathcal{D}^t} \mathcal{L}_{CE}^t(X, y). \tag{1}$$

Let $C_{old}^t = \sum_{i=1}^{t-1} C^i$ and $C_{all}^t = \sum_{i=1}^{t} C^i$, we can express CE loss for a single item as

$$\mathcal{L}_{CE}^t(X, y) = \sum_{c=1}^{C_{all}^t} -\mathbb{1}_{\{c=y\}} \log u_c(X), \tag{2}$$

in which $\mathbb{1}_{\{c=y\}}$ is the indicator function and $u_c(\cdot)$ denotes the prediction probability for the c-th class.

Note that before task t, our model has seen C_{old}^t classes from the previous datasets $\mathcal{D}^1, \mathcal{D}^2, \cdots, \mathcal{D}^{t-1}$. Only optimizing (1) will tremendously deteriorate the performance of the model on the previous tasks, which is termed catastrophic forgetting. To alleviate this phenomenon, we typically apply a size-limited exemplar memory $\mathcal{M}$ (size is limited to $|\mathcal{M}| < m$ and $m \ll \sum_{i=1}^{t} |\mathcal{D}^i|$) to randomly preserve $\lfloor m/C_{all}^t \rfloor$ items in each class after a task in a balanced manner and recall them at the next task. Thus, the CE loss at task t is adopted on both $\mathcal{D}^t$ and $\mathcal{M}$, *i.e.*, $L_{CE}(\mathcal{D}^t \cup \mathcal{M})$. However, the prior probability of each class in $\mathcal{D}^t \cup \mathcal{M}$ is extremely biased, and the CE loss does not apply to the situation anymore.

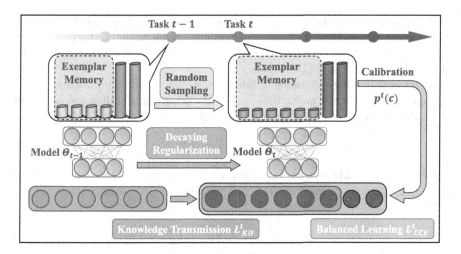

Fig. 2. An overview of our framework NeCa, containing balanced learning (the yellow part), knowledge transmission (the green part), and decaying regularization (the orange part) (Color figure online)

3.2 Balanced Learning

Biased prior probability leads to biased prediction, which is exactly the cause of task-recency bias (TRB). However, the distribution information of prior probability depicts the degree of imbalance of each class, which we can utilize to correct the imbalanced output logits for each class. We intend to construct a more balanced learning process by using prior probabilities.

Considering a general situation, at task t, our training set contains C_{all}^t different classes. Suppose the number of samples from c-th class is $n(c)$, the prior probability of c-th class can be estimated by

$$p^t(c) = \frac{n(c)}{\sum_{i=1}^{C_{all}^t} n(i)}. \tag{3}$$

Then we demonstrate how this information corrects the imbalanced prediction probability. As the main reason for TRB, while training with an imbalanced dataset, the prediction probabilities $u(\cdot)$ of the dominant classes (*i.e.*, the new classes in class incremental learning) are prone to be unexpectedly high. Inspired by recent approaches to class imbalance [21,32], we address this problem by correcting the prediction probability of c-th class $u_c(\cdot)$ with the prior probability of c-th class $p^t(c)$ at inference:

$$v_c(\cdot) = \frac{u_c(\cdot)}{p^t(c)}, \tag{4}$$

applying normalization on $v_c(\cdot)$, we get the calibrated prediction probability as

$$\hat{u}_c(\cdot) = \frac{v_c(\cdot)}{\sum_{i=1}^{C_{all}^t} v_i(\cdot)}. \tag{5}$$

Through the above post-training calibration, the prediction probabilities $\hat{u}_c(\cdot)$ become more balanced and result in a considerable overall accuracy. But post-training adjustment optimizes no parameter of the model. To complement this, we introduce the calibration into the CE loss (2).

As for post-training calibration at inference, we turn it into a pre-training scaling imposed on the prediction probabilities $u_c(\cdot)$. The pre-training scaling can be considered as the inverse process of the post-training calibration (4):

$$v_c'(\cdot) = p^t(c) \cdot u_c(\cdot), \tag{6}$$

after the same normalization in (5), we get $\hat{u}_c'(\cdot)$. The calibrated cross-entropy (CCE) loss can be obtained by replacing prediction probabilities $u_c(\cdot)$ in the CE loss (2) with $\hat{u}_c'(\cdot)$:

$$\mathcal{L}_{CCE}^t(X, y) = \sum_{c=1}^{C_{all}^t} -\mathbb{1}_{\{c=y\}} \log \hat{u}_c'(X). \tag{7}$$

Combining the above Eqs. (5), (6), and (7), we obtain the complete formulation of CCE loss:

$$\mathcal{L}_{CCE}^t(X, y) = \sum_{c=1}^{C_{all}^t} -\mathbb{1}_{\{c=y\}} \log \frac{e^{o_c(X) + \mu \log p^t(c)}}{\sum_{i=1}^{C_{all}^t} e^{o_i(X) + \mu \log p^t(i)}}, \tag{8}$$

where $o_i(\cdot)$ denotes the i-th class output of the current model and μ, like temperature in the knowledge distillation (KD) technique, is an additional hyperparameter controlling the smoothness magnitude. When $\mu = 0$, it degenerates as the traditional CE loss, and the neural network will not put additional attention on the old classes. When $\mu = 1$, (8) is equivalent to (7). As μ increases, the model begins to focus more on the old classes.

At inference, we use the prediction probabilities $u_c(\cdot)$ without additional operation. As shown in Table 1, the pre-training scaling in (6) shares the same effect as the post-training calibration in (4), $i.e.$, it produces a balanced classification boundary. However, unlike the post-training calibration leaves all the parameters untouched, optimizing CCE loss will influence each parameter positively (including the last fully connected layer and the feature extractor). When the model becomes a teacher model of the knowledge transmission module in Sect. 3.3, its output logits will be more balanced and teach more useful knowledge than a sub-balanced one.

Table 1. The relation between the post-training calibration and the pre-training scaling

Method	Training w/	Inference w/
Post-training calibration	$u_c(\cdot)$	$u_c(\cdot)/p^t(c)$
Pre-training scaling	$p^t(c) \cdot u_c(\cdot)$	$u_c(\cdot)$

3.3 Knowledge Transmission

To transmit the knowledge, we preserve the teacher model Θ_{t-1} at the end of task $(t-1)$, then utilize KD to train the model Θ_t at task t. Specifically, the KD loss can be formulated as

$$L_{KD}(\mathcal{D}^t \cup \mathcal{M}) = \frac{1}{|\mathcal{D}^t \cup \mathcal{M}|} \sum_{(X,y)\in\mathcal{D}^t\cup\mathcal{M}} \mathcal{L}_{KD}(X), \tag{9}$$

in which KD loss for a single item $\mathcal{L}_{KD}(\cdot)$ is defined as

$$\mathcal{L}_{KD}(X) = \sum_{c=1}^{C_{old}^t} -\hat{q}_c(X) \log q_c(X), \tag{10}$$

$$\hat{q}_c(X) = \frac{e^{\frac{\hat{o}_c(X)}{\tau}}}{\sum_{i=1}^{C_{old}^t} e^{\frac{\hat{o}_i(X)}{\tau}}}, \quad q_c(X) = \frac{e^{\frac{o_c(X)}{\tau}}}{\sum_{i=1}^{C_{old}^t} e^{\frac{o_i(X)}{\tau}}},$$

where $\hat{o}_i(\cdot)$ denote the i-th class output of the previous model Θ_{t-1}, and τ is the temperature controlling the smoothness magnitude of the target distribution during KD.

Finally, we combine (8) with (10) as Wu *et al.* [30] did, and the overall loss on task t becomes

$$L^t = (1 - \lambda^t)L_{CCE}(\mathcal{D}^t \cup \mathcal{M}) + \lambda^t L_{KD}(\mathcal{D}^t \cup \mathcal{M}), \tag{11}$$

in which $\lambda^t = C_{old}^t/C_{all}^t$ is a hyperparameter of the trade-off between the balanced learning loss and the knowledge transmission loss.

Note that every parameter in our teacher model Θ_{t-1} has been calibrated by optimizing CCE loss at the previous task, thus the student Θ_t will learn a more balanced classification boundary, which will also promote a more balanced training in the current task.

3.4 Decaying Regularization

At the practical training phase, we often add a regularization term $\gamma^t \|\Theta_t\|_2$ ($\|\Theta_t\|_2$ denotes the 2-norm sum of each weight and bias in the model Θ_t) outside the overall loss (11). This term drives all model parameters toward zero to prevent overfitting.

As we should impose a stronger regularization on the parameters when trained on a smaller dataset, we replace the fixed regularization in previous works with a decaying way. At the beginning of a class incremental learning problem, we always fit the model on a tiny dataset, which is a small part of the complete dataset. A stronger regularization helps prevent overfitting. After that, overly strong regularization tends to make the parameters vanish, thus we weaken the regularization to protect the parameters fitted in previous tasks. Specifically, we formulate the decaying regularization parameter as

$$\gamma^t = \frac{1}{t} \cdot \gamma^1, \tag{12}$$

in which γ^1 is the regularization parameter of the first task, relying on the dataset and the total number of tasks T. In addition, we have tried linear decaying regularization

$$\gamma^t = \left(1 - \frac{t-1}{T}\right) \cdot \gamma^1, \tag{13}$$

but it is not as good as the reciprocal decaying in (12).

Algorithm 1.. Network Calibration

Input: Datasets $\mathcal{D}^1, \mathcal{D}^2, \cdots, \mathcal{D}^T$
Output: Classification models $\Theta_1, \Theta_2, \cdots, \Theta_T$
Initialize: Exemplar memory $\mathcal{M} = \varnothing$, decaying regularization factor γ^1
Parameter: Random initialized model Θ_0

1: **for** $t = 1, \cdots, T$ **do**
2:    Input the dataset $\mathcal{D}^t$ for task t
3:    **if** $t = 1$ **then**
4:       $\Theta_t \leftarrow$ Optimize Θ_{t-1} with $L_{CE}(\mathcal{D}^1) + \gamma^1 \|\Theta_{t-1}\|_2$
5:    **else**
6:       Update decay regularization factor γ^t by (12)
7:       Calculate λ^t and estimate prior probabilities $p^t(\cdot)$ by (3)
8:       $\Theta_t \leftarrow$ Optimize Θ_{t-1} with $(1-\lambda^t)L_{CCE}(\mathcal{D}^t \cup \mathcal{M}) + \lambda^t L_{KD}(\mathcal{D}^t \cup \mathcal{M}) + \gamma^t \|\Theta_{t-1}\|_2$
9:    **end if**
10:   $\mathcal{M} \leftarrow$ Sample averagely and randomly from $\mathcal{D}^t \cup \mathcal{M}$
11:   Output a classification model Θ_t for task t
12: **end for**

Finally, summarizing the above three parts yields Algorithm 1. As can be seen, NeCa is easy to deploy because no additional training phase and complex data sampling method (*e.g.*, herding in iCaRL [25]) are needed.

4 Experiments

In this section, we evaluate our proposed framework network calibration (NeCa) in the class incremental learning (CIL) scenario and compare NeCa with some state-of-the-art methods. Moreover, we apply NeCa to both ResNet [10, 11] and vision transformer (ViT) [8], to demonstrate its model-independent attribute.

4.1 Datasets, Baselines and Experimental Details

Our experiments involve three datasets with significantly diverse data volumes, including MNIST [17], CIFAR-100 [16], and a subset of ImageNet ILSVRC 2012 [7], *i.e.*, ImageNet-100. MNIST contains 60,000 bi-level images of handwritten digits 0 to 9 for training and 10,000 for testing. CIFAR-100 contains 50,000 RGB images at 32×32 resolution from 100 classes for training and 10,000 images for testing. ImageNet

ILSVRC 2012 is a larger dataset containing about 1.2 million images at different resolutions from 1,000 classes for training and 50,000 for evaluation. As for ImageNet-100, we randomly select 100 classes from the former.

We choose the following typical or state-of-the-art methods (also mentioned in Sect. 2) for comparison:

- **LwF** [19]: Retain the previous knowledge via knowledge distillation only.
- **iCaRL** [25]: Use an exemplar memory and predict using the outputs of the feature extractor in a nearest-means-of-exemplars way.
- **EEIL** [5]: Introduce an additional balanced training phase and impose stronger data augmentation.
- **BiC** [30]: Add additional modules, which require an independent training phase, to correct the task-recency bias (TRB) in the last fully connected layer.
- **WA** [34]: Make post-training adjustments, utilizing the information of the magnitude of its norms, only to the parameters of the last fully connected layer.
- **SS-IL** [2]: Propose a novel separate softmax module, which calculates loss independently for the output logits of each task, especially suitable for large-scale datasets.

For CIFAR-100, we only adopt random cropping, horizontal flipping, and normalization for data augmentation in all experiments. For all methods, we use a 32-layer ResNet [10, 11] and an SGD optimizer with a momentum of 0.9. We vary the total number of tasks as $T = \{2, 5, 10, 20\}$ with correspondence to batch size $= 32$, $m = 2000$, $\tau = 4$, $\gamma^1 = 0.00005 \cdot T$, and $\mu = 1.5$. The learning rate starts from 0.1 and reduces to 1/10 of the previous after 100, 150, and 200 epochs (250 epochs in total).

For MNIST, we only adopt normalization for data augmentation. All details are the same as in CIFAR-100 except $\gamma^1 = 0.00004 \cdot T$ and $\mu = 1$. The learning rate starts from 0.01 and reduces to 0.001 after the 5-th epoch (10 epochs in total).

For ImageNet-100, we use an 18-layer ResNet. Except for $\gamma^1 = 0.00001 \cdot T$, all other details are the same as in CIFAR-100. The learning rate starts from 0.1 and reduces to 1/10 of the previous after 30, 60, 80, and 90 epochs (100 epochs in total).

4.2 Results

On MNIST, we take the average of 5 experiments and report the accuracy of the last task A_T in Table 2 and the average accuracy across all tasks $\overline{A}$ in Table 3. The performance gaps among these methods are not very significant because the task is quite simple, but our method NeCa still achieves a slight lead. Note that, in Table 3 we use Joint to denote the method of saving all previous data for joint training, which is generally regarded as the upper bound indicator of performance that can be obtained in class incremental learning tasks.

On CIFAR-100, we take the average of 5 experiments and report the top-1 accuracy at each task in Fig. 3, the accuracy of the last task A_T in Table 2, and the average accuracy across all tasks $\overline{A}$ in Table 3. We denote the performance of jointly training all data as the upper bound. Among the methods of comparison, WA is the strongest baseline method. Compared with it, NeCa exceeds its accuracy at each task, and the

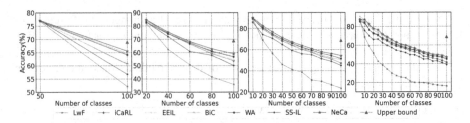

Fig. 3. CIL results on CIFAR-100 with a total number of 2, 5, 10, and 20 tasks respectively

average accuracy of all tasks increases by about 0.82, 1.71, 1.76, and 2.93 for 2-, 5-, 10-, and 20-step CIL scenarios, respectively. The improvement achieved by NeCa is more pronounced when the total number of tasks increases.

On ImageNet-100, we take the average of 3 experiments and report the top-1 and top-5 accuracy (denoted by 10 and 10* respectively in the T attribute) in Table 2 and Table 3. The results further indicate that NeCa still performs well on a larger dataset. As a method designed for large-scale datasets, SS-IL becomes the strongest baseline method. Compared with it, NeCa still surpasses about 4.12 and 0.96 on the average top-1 and top-5 accuracy of all tasks, respectively. Our framework especially improves a large margin on the top-1 accuracy.

Table 2. Last accuracy A_T (%) at different CIL settings

Model	ResNet-32						ResNet-18		ViT-M	ViT-B
Dataset	MNIST		CIFAR-100				ImageNet-100		CIFAR-100	
T	2	5	2	5	10	20	10	10*	10	
LwF	98.13	92.17	52.13	35.75	23.48	16.03	21.25	37.22	12.34	70.78
iCaRL	98.26	93.18	60.69	53.62	47.09	41.37	49.88	78.42	27.91	86.93
EEIL	98.37	96.61	60.47	54.42	50.02	44.28	52.74	80.02	41.80	84.89
BiC	98.62	96.89	64.71	56.69	50.75	46.96	58.88	81.96	45.40	86.37
WA	98.86	97.22	64.15	56.70	51.44	44.97	56.78	79.20	47.49	73.32
SS-IL	97.83	87.96	56.74	50.03	44.87	38.77	59.24	85.70	44.72	87.28
NeCa	**99.21**	**98.10**	**65.55**	**59.01**	**54.10**	**47.15**	**64.22**	**86.56**	**49.72**	**87.87**
Joint	99.67		68.93				82.34	95.21	67.52	96.46

4.3 Experiments on Vision Transformer

ViT [8] is attention-based, which separates the input image into several parts and calculates the potential correlation between them. ViT has the same prediction head (*i.e.*, the fully connected layer behind the [class] token) as ResNet does, thus can be rationally calibrated via NeCa. In this section, we transfer NeCa into the ViT model. Table 4 presents the details of our ViT models.

Table 3. Average accuracy $\overline{A}$ (%) at different CIL settings

Model	ResNet-32						ResNet-18		ViT-M	ViT-B
Dataset	MNIST		CIFAR-100				ImageNet-100		CIFAR-100	
T	2	5	2	5	10	20	10	10*	10	
LwF	98.98	96.05	64.49	54.47	45.19	32.84	49.26	64.75	36.47	83.40
iCaRL	99.08	97.65	68.83	67.62	64.46	59.21	69.78	90.10	46.79	91.89
EEIL	99.11	98.15	68.77	67.92	64.94	62.23	69.69	89.92	55.96	90.71
BiC	99.26	98.39	70.88	68.91	65.87	62.22	71.60	90.27	57.46	91.61
WA	99.39	98.79	70.50	68.31	66.40	60.58	71.16	89.72	59.85	87.32
SS-IL	98.88	92.52	66.94	64.72	61.12	55.16	71.04	91.96	56.58	91.94
NeCa	**99.57**	**99.21**	**71.32**	**70.02**	**68.16**	**63.51**	**75.16**	**92.92**	**60.83**	**93.12**

Table 4. Specific information about ViT-M and ViT-B

	Input size	Patch size	Depth	Head	Feature dimension	Pre-training status
ViT-M	32×32	2×2	6	8	512	From scratch
ViT-B	224×224	16×16	12	12	768	Pretrained on ImageNet-1000

On CIFAR-100, ViT-M is prone to overfit because it contains no convolutional operation. To alleviate this situation, we additionally apply RandAugment [6] in data augmentation. We train around 20000 steps for every task with an SGD optimizer and utilize the cosine annealing learning rate with the warmup technique. Besides, due to the prevalence of big data, it is urgent to investigate a continual learning method for strongly pre-trained models [29]. The ViT-B is a stronger model that has been pre-trained on ImageNet-1000 with a top-1 accuracy of around 0.81. On CIFAR-100, we apply ViT-B in the CIL setting. We train around 4000 steps for every task with an SGD optimizer and utilize the cosine annealing learning rate. We report their top-1 accuracy results in the two rightmost columns of Table 2 and Table 3. The results show that on the pre-trained ViT-B, the WA method has a very drastic performance degradation due to the hard modification of the classifier parameters, while NeCa achieves the best performance through adaptively calibrating the whole network, showing its generalizability and effectiveness.

4.4 Ablation Studies

To further analyze the role of each factor in NeCa, we consider some variants of our method. After evaluating them in a 10-step CIL scenario on CIFAR-100, we report the accuracy of the last task A_T, the average accuracy of all tasks $\overline{A}$, and forgetting rate $A_1 - A_T$ (the accuracy gap between the first and last task) in the three rightmost columns of Table 5, where KT and DR denote knowledge transmission and decaying regularization modules respectively. In V_3, CCE* indicates using post-training calibration mentioned in Sect. 3.2 rather than optimizing CCE loss. This method has poor performance because, like the comparison method in Sect. 4.1, it does not calibrate the relevant parameters of the model. Ablation studies show that every part of NeCa plays an active role and is indispensable. When used in combination, they can outperform state-of-the-art methods.

4.5 Analysis on Hyperparameter

In this section, we analyze the hyperparameter μ in the CCE loss (8). As discussed in Sect. 3.2, the CCE loss imposes greater emphasis on older classes when μ increases. However, an overhigh μ causes the model to ignore the new classes. It is a trade-off between the level of concern for the old and new classes, and we can set an optimal value for μ. Our experiment finds that the optimal μ is always in the range from 1 to 2 for every dataset. As shown in Table 6, we report the average accuracy across all tasks $\overline{A}$ when μ varies in [1,2]. Results demonstrate that our method is not very sensitive to the value of μ, which implies that our approach is easy to deploy across datasets without excessive hyperparameter tuning.

Table 5. Accuracy results of the variants

Variant	Loss	KT	DR	A_T (%)	$\overline{A}$ (%)	$A_1 - A_T$ (%)
V_1	CE	✓	✗	$34.75_{\pm1.25}$	$56.66_{\pm1.08}$	51.35
V_2	CE	✓	✓	$34.04_{\pm0.56}$	$58.43_{\pm0.45}$	55.40
V_3	CCE*	✓	✓	$40.67_{\pm0.66}$	$62.75_{\pm0.36}$	50.03
V_4	CCE	✗	✓	$43.83_{\pm1.07}$	$62.52_{\pm1.15}$	46.60
V_5	CCE	✓	✗	$52.96_{\pm0.41}$	$67.17_{\pm0.75}$	36.58
NeCa	CCE	✓	✓	$\mathbf{54.10_{\pm0.54}}$	$\mathbf{68.16_{\pm0.43}}$	**36.00**

Table 6. Influence of μ in CCE loss

μ	1.0	1.2	1.4	**1.5**	1.6	1.8	2.0
$\overline{A}$	66.88	66.48	67.15	**68.16**	65.67	66.34	66.43

4.6 Balanced Classification Boundaries

In this section, we demonstrate the effect of the NeCa training framework on the classification boundaries between the old and new classes of the classification model.

As shown in Fig. 4, when optimizing the CE loss (2), due to the inconsistent data distribution between the training and testing sets, the classification boundary that performs well on the training set may lead to many misjudgments when stepping into the test phase. The optimization of the CCE loss (8) will shift the original classification boundary by a distance toward the center of the new class, allowing the model to make more balanced inferences about the old and new classes, thus solving the TRB problem.

Experimentally, we record the accuracy of each CIL method on Cifar-100 for multiple tasks on both old and new classes and then calculate their average gap. The results in Table 7 demonstrate that NeCa allows the final classification boundary to reach the most balanced state thanks to the calibration of the whole network parameters, thus resulting in the minimal accuracy gap between the old and new classes and the highest overall accuracy.

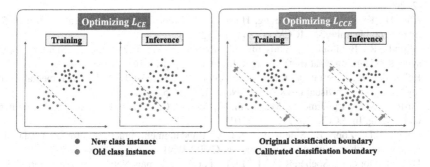

Fig. 4. Impact of optimizing CCE loss on the classification boundary between old and new classes

Table 7. The accuracy gap between the old and new classes of various CIL methods

Method	Classes	Task 2	Task 4	Task 6	Task 8	Task 10	Accuracy gap
iCaRL	old	83.4	66.6	59.1	51.2	45.5	12.34
	new	74.0	70.6	69.5	66.0	68.6	
EEIL	old	78.0	69.3	60.6	52.1	49.0	9.11
	new	84.3	72.2	69.7	68.9	59.4	
BiC	old	75.8	67.8	61.2	53.8	50.1	8.13
	new	87.8	75.9	68.4	60.7	56.7	
WA	old	79.3	67.5	62.0	56.2	51.5	7.64
	new	85.5	80.2	69.2	62.3	57.5	
NeCa	old	85.0	70.9	63.5	58.4	53.7	**6.50**
	new	81.1	77.1	72.4	62.1	63.5	

5   Conclusion

In this work, we combat the task-recency bias problem in the class incremental learning scenario. We propose a novel framework network calibration (NeCa) to calibrate the whole network via the prior probability and pass the ability of balanced prediction through knowledge distillation. Finally, the decaying regularization further improves the performance. Extensive experiments confirm the effectiveness and generalizability of NeCa. However, the bottleneck of having to preserve some of the samples remains unresolved. In the future, we will try to extend NeCa into the memory-free scenario.

Acknowledgements. This work was partially supported by NSFC (61976112), and Fundamental Research Funds for the Central Universities (2023300246).

References

1. Abati, D., Tomczak, J., Blankevoort, T., Calderara, S., Cucchiara, R., Bejnordi, B.E.: Conditional channel gated networks for task-aware continual learning. In: CVPR, pp. 3930–3939 (2020)
2. Ahn, H., Kwak, J., Lim, S., Bang, H., Kim, H., Moon, T.: SS-IL: separated softmax for incremental learning. In: ICCV, pp. 844–853 (2021)
3. Aljundi, R., Babiloni, F., Elhoseiny, M., Rohrbach, M., Tuytelaars, T.: Memory aware synapses: learning what (not) to forget. In: ECCV, pp. 144–161 (2018)
4. Belouadah, E., Popescu, A., Kanellos, I.: A comprehensive study of class incremental learning algorithms for visual tasks. Neural Netw. **135**, 38–54 (2021)
5. Castro, F.M., Marín-Jiménez, M.J., Guil, N., Schmid, C., Alahari, K.: End-to-end incremental learning. In: ECCV, pp. 241–257 (2018)
6. Cubuk, E.D., Zoph, B., Shlens, J., Le, Q.V.: Randaugment: practical automated data augmentation with a reduced search space. In: CVPR Workshops, pp. 3008–3017 (2020)
7. Deng, J., Dong, W., Socher, R., Li, L., Li, K., Fei-Fei, L.: ImageNet: a large-scale hierarchical image database. In: CVPR, pp. 248–255 (2009)
8. Dosovitskiy, A., et al.: An image is worth 16x16 words: transformers for image recognition at scale. In: ICLR (2021)
9. He, K., Gkioxari, G., Dollár, P., Girshick, R.B.: Mask R-CNN. In: ICCV, pp. 2980–2988 (2017)
10. He, K., Zhang, X., Ren, S., Sun, J.: Deep residual learning for image recognition. In: CVPR, pp. 770–778 (2016)
11. He, K., Zhang, X., Ren, S., Sun, J.: Identity mappings in deep residual networks. In: Leibe, B., Matas, J., Sebe, N., Welling, M. (eds.) ECCV 2016. LNCS, vol. 9908, pp. 630–645. Springer, Cham (2016). https://doi.org/10.1007/978-3-319-46493-0_38
12. Hinton, G.E., Vinyals, O., Dean, J.: Distilling the knowledge in a neural network. arXiv preprint arXiv:1503.02531 (2015)
13. Hou, S., Pan, X., Loy, C.C., Wang, Z., Lin, D.: Learning a unified classifier incrementally via rebalancing. In: CVPR, pp. 831–839 (2019)
14. Jian, Y., Yi, J., Zhang, L.: Adaptive feature generation for online continual learning from imbalanced data. In: PAKDD, vol. 13280, pp. 276–289 (2022)
15. Kirkpatrick, J., et al.: Overcoming catastrophic forgetting in neural networks. PNAS **114**(13), 3521–3526 (2017)
16. Krizhevsky, A.: Learning multiple layers of features from tiny images. Technical report (2012)
17. LeCun, Y., Cortes, C.: MNIST handwritten digit database. Public (2010)
18. Lee, K., Lee, K., Shin, J., Lee, H.: Overcoming catastrophic forgetting with unlabeled data in the wild. In: ICCV, pp. 312–321 (2019)
19. Li, Z., Hoiem, D.: Learning without forgetting. In: ECCV, pp. 614–629 (2016)
20. Masana, M., Liu, X., Twardowski, B., Menta, M., Bagdanov, A.D., van de Weijer, J.: Class-incremental learning: survey and performance evaluation. arXiv preprint arXiv:2010.15277 (2020)
21. Menon, A.K., Jayasumana, S., Rawat, A.S., Jain, H., Veit, A., Kumar, S.: Long-tail learning via logit adjustment. In: ICLR (2021)
22. Parisi, G.I., Kemker, R., Part, J.L., Kanan, C., Wermter, S.: Continual lifelong learning with neural networks: a review. Neural Netw. **113**, 54–71 (2019)

23. Prabhu, A., Torr, P.H.S., Dokania, P.K.: GDumb: a simple approach that questions our progress in continual learning. In: Vedaldi, A., Bischof, H., Brox, T., Frahm, J.-M. (eds.) ECCV 2020. LNCS, vol. 12347, pp. 524–540. Springer, Cham (2020). https://doi.org/10.1007/978-3-030-58536-5_31

24. Rajasegaran, J., Hayat, M., Khan, S.H., Khan, F.S., Shao, L.: Random path selection for continual learning. In: NeurIPS, pp. 12648–12658 (2019)

25. Rebuffi, S., Kolesnikov, A., Sperl, G., Lampert, C.H.: iCaRL: incremental classifier and representation learning. In: CVPR, pp. 5533–5542 (2017)

26. Shin, H., Lee, J.K., Kim, J., Kim, J.: Continual learning with deep generative replay. In: NeurIPS, pp. 2990–2999 (2017)

27. van de Ven, G.M., Tolias, A.S.: Three scenarios for continual learning. arXiv preprint arXiv:1904.07734 (2019)

28. Verwimp, E., Lange, M.D., Tuytelaars, T.: Rehearsal revealed: the limits and merits of revisiting samples in continual learning. In: ECCV, pp. 9385–9394 (2021)

29. Wu, T., et al.: Class-incremental learning with strong pre-trained models. In: CVPR, pp. 9591–9600 (2022)

30. Wu, Y., et al.: Large scale incremental learning. In: CVPR, pp. 374–382 (2019)

31. Yan, S., Xie, J., He, X.: DER: dynamically expandable representation for class incremental learning. In: CVPR, pp. 3014–3023 (2021)

32. Ye, H., Chen, H., Zhan, D., Chao, W.: Identifying and compensating for feature deviation in imbalanced deep learning. arXiv preprint arXiv:2001.01385 (2020)

33. Yu, L., et al.: Semantic drift compensation for class-incremental learning. In: CVPR, pp. 6980–6989 (2020)

34. Zhao, B., Xiao, X., Gan, G., Zhang, B., Xia, S.: Maintaining discrimination and fairness in class incremental learning. In: CVPR, pp. 13205–13214 (2020)

Object Detection Algorithm Based on Bimodal Feature Alignment

Ying Sun[1,2(✉)], Zhiqiang Hou[1,2], Chen Yang[1,2], Sugang Ma[3], and Jiulun Fan[1]

[1] School of Computer Science and Technology, Xi'an University of Posts and Telecommunications, Xi'an 710121, China
Aurorasuny@163.com
[2] Key Laboratory of Network Data Analysis and Intelligent Processing of Shaanxi Province, Xi'an 710121, China
[3] School of Communications and Information Engineering, Xi'an University of Posts and Telecommunications, Xi'an 710121, China

Abstract. A dual-modal feature alignment based object detection algorithm is proposed for the full fusion of visible and infrared image features. First, we propose a two stream detection model. The algorithm supports simultaneous input of visible and infrared image pairs. Secondly, a gated fusion network is designed, consisting of a dual-modal feature alignment module and a feature fusion module. Medium-term fusion is used, which will be used as the middle layer of the dual-stream backbone network. In particular, the dual-mode feature alignment module extracts detailed information of the dual-mode aligned features by computing a multi-scale dual-mode aligned feature vector. The feature fusion module recalibrates the bimodal fused features and then multiplies them with the bimodal aligned features to achieve cross-modal fusion with joint enhancement of the lower and higher level features. We validate the performance of the proposed algorithm using both the publicly available KAIST pedestrian dataset and a self-built GIR dataset. On the KAIST dataset, the algorithm achieves an accuracy of 77.1%, which is 17.3% and 5.6% better than the accuracy of the benchmark algorithm YOLOv5-s for detecting visible and infrared images alone; on the self-built GIR dataset, the detection accuracy is 91%, which is 1.2% and 14.2% better than the benchmark algorithm for detecting visible and infrared images alone respectively. And the speed meets the real time requirements.

Keywords: Object detection · Gated networks · Early Fusion · Dual-modal · Feature alignment

1 Introduction

Object detection is one of the fundamental tasks in the field of computer vision. There are important applications in security surveillance, autonomous driving

Supported in part by the National Natural Science Foundation of China under Grant 62072370 and in part by the Natural Science Foundation of Shaanxi Province under Grant No. 2023-JC-YB-598.

and military fields [1, 2]. However, the commonly used detectors are usually single-mode detectors. Detection using only single-mode images does not perform well at night or in unfavourable environments such as fog, rain or dust. Therefore, many efforts consider the use of dual-mode images, such as visible and infra-red images. Combining both images for detection can improve the results. At present, there are still some challenges in multimodal detection. One is the lack of publicly available datasets for multimodal image alignment. The large number of publicly available datasets and pre-trained models are usually for visible images, and there are fewer publicly available annotated datasets for infrared images, and even fewer annotated datasets aligned in pairs. The second is the central issue, namely how to fuse feature information from different modalities. There are usually three types of fusion for multimodal image feature fusion: early fusion, mid-fusion and late fusion. Early fusion refers to fusion before feature extraction, constructing a dual stream input of visible and infrared images, and then extracting features by CNN after fusion, such as the MM DistilleNet framework proposed by Valverde et al. [3], which consists of multiple teacher modules including multiple modalities of visible, depth and infrared images, while extracting complementary features after early fusion by each modality into the student network. Mid-term fusion refers to the extraction of features by different input streams for visible and IR, and the features are fused in the middle convolution layer of the model. For example, Liu et al. [4] designed four ConvNet fusion architectures, and the experimental results showed that the mid-term fusion model with feature fusion at the middle convolution layer had the most effective detection; Konig et al. [5] proposed a multispectral RPN, and the experimental results were analysed to The best convolution layer for fusing visible and infrared image features in RPN is the third layer, which belongs to mid-term fusion. The biggest advantage of mid-term fusion is that the fusion position can be chosen flexibly. Late fusion means that each modal image is trained separately to obtain the prediction result, and the decision is made to fuse the final result, as in Pfeuffer et al. [6], where the visible image and the depth feature map are extracted by different encoders, and then the final prediction result is obtained by decision. After the above analysis, this chapter proposes a target detection algorithm based on bimodal feature alignment with mid-term fusion. The main contributions of are summarized as follows:

- A dual-stream object detection algorithm is proposed, which can input both visible and infrared image pairs.
- We proposed a gated fusion network. It is used in layers 3, 4 and 5 of the dual-stream backbone network. The module facilitates bi-modal fusion and feature interaction, allowing the model to take full advantage of the complementary nature of the two features.
- Specifically, the gated fusion network comprises a bimodal feature alignment module and a feature fusion module. The bimodal feature alignment module extracts the edge information of the aligned features. The feature fusion module obtains the bimodal fused features by calibrating them twice.

The performance of the proposed algorithm is validated on the publicly available KAIST pedestrian dataset and on a self-built GIR dataset.

2 Related Work

2.1 Single-Modal Object Detection Algorithm

Object detection algorithms based on deep learning can be divided into two categories: two-stage object detectors and one-stage detectors. The two-stage object detection algorithm is region-based. The detector first extracts a set of object proposals from images. Region proposals are then revised to obtain detection results. The main representative algorithms are R-CNN [7], Fast R-CNN [8], and Faster R-CNN [9]. One-stage object detection algorithms generate detection results directly from images. Detectors have faster detection speed but lower accuracy, such as SSD [10] and YOLO series [11–15]. In the subsequent version of YOLO, YOLOv5 [15] is a simple and efficient detection model. The algorithm divided the image into multiple grids. When the center of the target fell into a grid, the grid was responsible for predicting the target. And introduced multi-scale feature map prediction to obtain richer feature information. Based on the above, three detection heads are used to simultaneously predict the results of feature maps of different scales. In addition, Anchor-free object detection algorithms are gradually emerging, such as CornerNet [16], CenterNet [17], and FCOS [18]. These algorithms do away with the use of anchor boxes, transforming the object detection problem into a combination of keypoint localization.

2.2 Bi-modal Object Detection Algorithm

Bimodal target detection is one of the research areas in computer vision. In recent years, images of two different modalities have also been gradually applied to detection tasks. Devaguptapu et al. [19] used CycleGAN to create a strategy for synthesizing IR images and fused visible and IR images using an illumination-aware fusion framework to improve the performance of object detection in IR images; Yang et al. [20] used illumination sub-networks to assign weights to combine visible and IR images to detect pedestrians; Wang et al. [21] designed a redundant information suppression network that suppresses cross-modal redundant information and helps to fuse complementary information from visible and IR; Geng et al. [22] implemented cross-modal person re-identification and dual camera tracking using visible IR through channel information exchange; Zhang et al. [23] proposed an end-to-end network for RGB-T multimodal saliency target detection, which converts the RGB-T saliency detection challenging task into a CNN feature fusion problem; Fang et al. [24] proposed a simple and efficient cross-modal feature fusion method under the guidance of Transformer's scheme, making full use of different modalities to improve detection accuracy.

3 Proposed Approach

3.1 Overview

The benchmark algorithm for this chapter is YOLOv5-s. The overall framework of the proposed bimodal feature alignment-based target detection algorithm is shown in Fig. 1, which mainly consists of a dual-stream backbone network, a Gated Fusion Network (GFN) and the Neck and detection head parts of the benchmark algorithm.

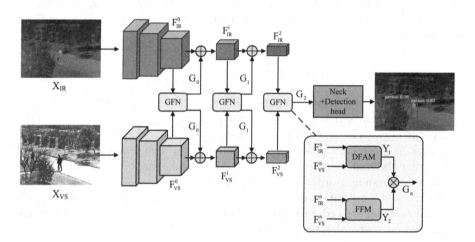

Fig. 1. Overall structure of the dual modal object detection network.

Infrared images X_{IR} and visible images X_{VS} are used as input to a dual-stream backbone network, in which a total of three gated fusion networks are used. Three fusions are performed at layers 3, 4 and 5. The infrared features extracted in the third layer are noted as F_{IR}^0 and the visible features are noted as F_{VS}^0. Both F_{IR}^0 and F_{VS}^0 are fed into the gated fusion network at the same time to obtain feature G_0 after the first fusion. Add G_0 to F_{IR}^0 and F_{VS}^0 respectively pixel by pixel to obtain the fourth layer of the network features F_{IR}^1 and F_{VS}^1, which are used as input to the second gated fusion network. Similarly, repeat the above operation in turn until the third fused feature G_2 is output through the third gated fusion network, which is fed to the Neck and detection head of the benchmark algorithm for target classification and localisation. The gated fusion network consists of a Dual-modal Feature Aligned Module (DFAM) and a Feature Fusion Module (FFM), where both DFAM and FFM have inputs of F_{IR}^n and F_{VS}^n, $n \in [0, 2]$. The DFAM module is used to extract the detail information of the two modal aligned features and the output is obtained by successive pooling operations. The DFAM module extracts the detail information of the two modal aligned features and splices them by successive pooling operations to obtain output Y_1. The FFM fully fuses the bimodal features to obtain output

Y_2. Multiplying and gives the gated convolutional network output G_n, $n \in [0,2]$. Thus, in each fusion, the low-level features and the high-level features are used to jointly control the bimodal fusion, thus improving the detection performance.

3.2 Dual Mode Feature Alignment Module

The structure of the bimodal feature alignment module DFAM is shown in Fig. 2, with inputs F_{IR}^n and F_{VS}^n. First, after integrating the feature channels by 1×1 convolution, the visible feature F_{VS} and the infrared feature F_{IR} are subjected to a low-level feature alignment operation to obtain the feature alignment vector V_{BAi}, as shown by the red arrow in the figure, and the calculation process can be expressed in:

$$V_{BAi} = \frac{GAP\,(F_{VS} \times F_{IR})}{GAP\,(F_{VS} + F_{IR})} \tag{1}$$

where i indicates the number of times this operation was performed, $i \in [1,4]$, and GAP represents global average pooling.

Specifically, a global average pooling operation is performed by multiplying F_{VS} and F_{IR} pixel by pixel, and then adding the two features together and performing a global average pooling operation, using the former divided by the latter, to obtain a first-order feature alignment vector V_{BA1}. V_{BA1} contains much of the detailed information of the bimodal feature. To obtain the rich semantic information of higher-order features, successive maximum pooling operations are performed on first-order bimodal features F_{VS} and F_{IR}, respectively, in steps of 2, to obtain visible and infrared features at three scales. A per-order feature alignment vector is calculated for each order feature, andV_{BA1}, V_{BA2}, V_{BA3} and V_{BA4} are stitched together by channel dimension to obtain a multi-scale feature alignment vector, and the process can be expressed as:

$$V_{BA} = Concat\,(V_{BA1}, V_{BA2}, V_{BA3}, V_{BA4}) \tag{2}$$

A scale reshape is applied to V_{BA}, and then the output feature Y_1, which is the same size as the first-order bimodal feature, is obtained by an upsampling operation.

The output features contain aligned features from the visible and infrared low-level features, as well as high-level features with rich semantic information, so that DFAM controls and enhances cross-modal fusion by combining low-level and high-level features.

3.3 Feature Fusion Module

Inspired by the literature [25], the FFM achieves visible and infrared feature interaction through two calibration fusions, the specific structure of which is shown in Fig. 3. First, the inputs are F_{VS}^n and F_{IR}^n, which are convolved 1×1 to integrate the feature channels to obtain visible feature F_{VS} and infrared feature

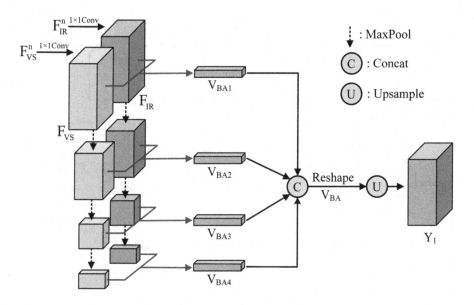

Fig. 2. The structure of Dual mode feature alignment module.

F_{IR}. Multiplying F_{VS} and F_{IR} pixel by pixel, the output interaction feature is noted as F_{fuse}.

During the fusion phase, a total of two feature recalibrations are performed and the entire recalibration process is represented by:

$$F_{re}\left(f\right) = Up_{\times 2}\left(Conv_{3\times 3}\left(Down_{\times 2}\left(f + F_{fuse}\right)\right)\right) \qquad (3)$$

where, Up denotes upsampling, Down denotes downsampling, ×2 denotes 2x, F_{re} denotes calibration feature function, and f denotes input features.

The visible image is rich in feature information, so the fusion makes full use of the visible feature 1, and before the first feature calibration, F_{VS} is added to F_{fuse} as the input to the Re-Calibration Module (RCM). The specific operation of the RCM is: the input features are bilinearly interpolated with a 2-fold downsample operation to increase the perceptual field, and then convolved by 3×3 convolution, so that the subsequent convolution can extract the global information, and the features are passed through BN and ReLU activation function layers to accelerate the convergence speed during training. Finally, a bilinear interpolation 2x upsampling is performed to obtain the first recalibration feature f' of the same size as the input feature map, as described in:

$$f' = F_{re}\left(F_{VS}\right) \qquad (4)$$

The first recalibration feature f' is input to the RCM and a second feature calibration is performed to obtain the second recalibration feature f''. This process can be expressed as:

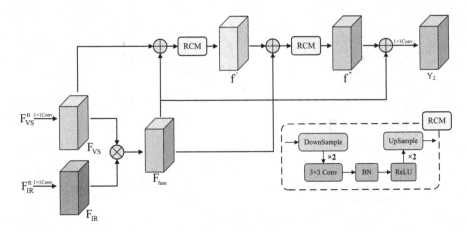

Fig. 3. The structure of Feature fusion module.

$$f'' = F_{re}\left(f'\right) \tag{5}$$

The calibrated feature f'' extracts the detail information of the feature, adds it with the interactive feature F_{fuse} to enhance the expression of visible and infrared features, and finally, the output feature Y_2 is obtained by integrating the feature channels through 1×1 convolution.

After obtaining fused features through multiple fusions, FFM is multiplied pixel by pixel with the output 1 of DFM to obtain the output of the gated convolutional network by using DFM and FFM, GFN achieves weighting of low-level features and high-level features to obtain bimodal fused features containing rich detail information and semantic information, and uses them as the input of the next layer of the network to enhance the complementarity of bimodal features, thus enhancing detection performance.

4   Experiments

4.1   Experimental Settings

The experiments were conducted with Ubuntu 16.04, i5-8400 CPU, NVIDIA GeForce GTX 1080Ti GPU (11 GB video memory), CUDA and CUDNN versions 10.0 and CUDNN 7.4.2. Python and PyTorch platforms were used. The SGD optimizer was used to iteratively update the network parameters during training, with the momentum parameter set to 0.937 and the BatchSize set to 8. A total of 150 Epochs were trained, and the resolution of all images was uniformly adjusted to 640×640 when loading the data, before the overall network was trained end-to-end.

4.2 Datasets and Evaluation Indicators

In this paper, the algorithm is evaluated using two datasets, the first being the publicly available KAIST pedestrian dataset [26] and the second being a self-built GIR dataset. Both datasets contain image pairs corresponding to Visible (VS) and Infrared (IR), and the experiments in this paper train and test the visible images, the IR images and the image pairs composed of both separately. In this paper, all types of images share a set of labels.

(1) KAIST pedestrian dataset

The KAIST pedestrian datase has a total of 95,328 images, each of which contains both visible and infrared image versions. The dataset captures regular traffic scenes including schoolyards, streets and countryside during daytime and nighttime respectively. As the original dataset was poorly annotated and the dataset was taken from successive frames of video with little difference between adjacent images, some degree of dataset cleaning was performed. The cleaning rules are as follows: the training set is taken every 2 images and all images that do not contain any pedestrians are removed. After this operation 7601 images from the training set [27] are obtained, 4755 from daytime and 2846 from nighttime. The test set is taken every 19 images, keeping the negative samples. This resulted in 2252 test set [5] images, 1455 daytime and 797 nighttime images. The labels of the original dataset contain three categories: person, people and cyclist, which are difficult to distinguish when the lighting conditions are poor or the resolution is low. Therefore, in this paper, the label category is only labeled as person.

(2) GIR dataset

The GIR dataset is a generic target dataset created by this paper. The images come from the RGBT210 dataset established by Cheng-Long Li's team [28], and each image contains two versions of RGB colour images and infrared images. 5105 images were selected from this dataset and divided into 4084 training images and 1021 test images. The images were annotated and 10 classes of targets were identified as person, dog, car, bicycle, plant, motorcycle, umbrella, kite, toy, and ball.

The algorithm evaluation metrics used in the experiments were Average Precision (AP), Frames Per Second (FPS), Precision (P), and Recall (R). The AP represents the average detection precision, 0.50:0.95 refers to the average of AP for all categories calculated at 0.05 intervals from IoU 0.5 to 0.95. FPS represents the number of images detected per second, which can effectively reflect the detection speed of the algorithm.

4.3 Ablation Studies

The algorithm in this chapter performs ablation experiments on both the publicly available KAIST dataset and the self-built GIR dataset. And the performance of the algorithm in this chapter is evaluated in comparison with the benchmark algorithm.

(1) KAIST dataset

To better validate the effectiveness of the proposed module, ablation experiments were conducted on the KAIST dataset for the bimodal feature alignment module DFAM and the feature fusion module FFM respectively, and the results are recorded in Table 1.

Table 1. Ablation experiments on the KAIST dataset.

Method	GFN		Input	$AP_{0.5:0.95}$	$AP_{0.5}$	FPS
	DFAM	FFM				
YOLOv5-s			VS	26.7	59.8	112
YOLOv5-s			IR	32	71.5	112
YOLOv5-s-DFAM	✓		VS+IR	32.6	73.1	100
YOLOv5-s-FFM		✓	VS+IR	34.2	74.6	92
Ours	✓	✓	VS+IR	36.3	77.1	80

As can be seen from the table, on the YOLOv5-s model, the detection accuracy is 59.8% when the input is a single-mode image and only the visible image (VS) is input. When the input is infrared (IR) only, the detection accuracy is 71.5%. When the input is a dual-mode image, the detection accuracy is 73.1% when only DFAM is added. When only FFM was added, the detection accuracy was 74.6%; using a GFN consisting of DFM and FFM, the detection accuracy improved to 77.1%. Clearly, there is a substantial improvement in detection accuracy by using dual-mode image features to complement each other. Although the proposed algorithm is slightly slower than the benchmark algorithm, there is a significant improvement in detection accuracy. And it extends the application scenarios of traditional detection algorithms.

To show the detection results more intuitively, some of the visualisation results are shown in Fig. 4. (a) shows the GT on the visible image, (b) shows the GT on the IR image, (c) shows the detection results of the benchmark algorithm on the visible image, (d) shows the results on the IR image, and (e) shows the visualised detection results of the algorithm in this chapter. In the first row, the target is smaller, the person is not visible in the visible image and the target is not detected. In contrast, in the infrared image the person is more visible and the target is detected. However, the algorithm in this chapter not only detects the target but also has a higher confidence score than the infrared image. The second line is a false detection on the visible image. The IR image improves the error detection, but there are missed detections. The algorithm in this chapter detects all targets and has a higher confidence score. In the third row, poorly lit targets are not detected in the visible images and there are false detections in the IR images. The algorithm in this chapter improves the false and missed detections to some extent. Thus, both images have advantages and disadvantages, and full integration of the dual-mode image features can improve the performance of the detection algorithm.

(2) GIR dataset

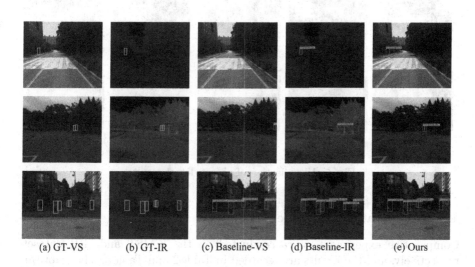

(a) GT-VS   (b) GT-IR   (c) Baseline-VS   (d) Baseline-IR   (e) Ours

Fig. 4. Visualisation of object detect results.

To show the detection results more visually, some of the visualisation results are shown in Fig. 5. In the first row, the visible image misses detection. In contrast, the infrared image is detected accurately and the algorithm in this chapter also detects the target accurately and with a higher confidence score than the infrared image. In the second row, the visible image misses and the infrared image incorrectly detects the tree as a person. The algorithm in this chapter is able to improve the problem of false and missed detections by fully fusing visible and infrared features. The third row is the night scene, the visible image misses the car with too much light and there is a wrong detection, the infrared image also does not detect the car and there is a missed detection. In contrast, the algorithm in this chapter is able to detect all targets accurately.

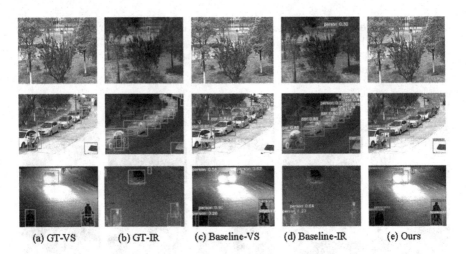

(a) GT-VS   (b) GT-IR   (c) Baseline-VS   (d) Baseline-IR   (e) Ours

Fig. 5. Visualisation of object detect results.

4.4   Comparative Experiments

Comparative experiments were conducted on the KAIST and GIR datasets respectively, and the results are recorded in Table 2 and Table 3. The algorithm was divided into three ways of training: input visible images only, input infrared images only, and input visible and infrared image pairs. To ensure fairness, no pre-training weights were loaded. Compared to single-stage algorithms, such as YOLOX [29], the accuracy of the algorithm in this chapter is improved over YOLOX. Compared to the benchmark algorithm, there is a significant improvement in accuracy, although the speed is reduced. Compared with some classical bimodal detection algorithms, such as MMTOD [19], CMDet [30] and RIS-Net [31], the algorithm in this chapter has higher accuracy and faster speed.

Table 2. Results of comparison experiments on the KAIST dataset.

Input	Method	$AP_{0.5:0.95}$	$AP_{0.5}$	FPS
VS	Faster R-CNN (2015)	24.2	58.3	15
	SSD (2016)	18.1	48.2	38
	RetinaNet (2017)	22.5	57.7	17
	YOLOv3 (2018)	18.3	46.7	56
	FCOS (2019)	22.7	56.7	18
	ATSS (2020)	24.3	57.8	17
	YOLOv4 (2020)	23.7	57.4	55
	YOLOv5-s (2020)	26.4	59.8	112
	YOLOX-s (2021)	27	61.1	49
	YOLOX-m (2021)	27.7	61.8	40
	YOLOF (2021)	22.2	54.1	26
	YOLOv7 (2022)	21.1	52	102
IR	Faster R-CNN (2015)	28.8	68.6	12
	SSD (2016)	23.2	60.9	34
	RetinaNet (2017)	27.8	68.2	14
	YOLOv3 (2018)	25.3	63.6	37
	FCOS (2019)	29.6	69.4	14
	ATSS (2020)	29	69	14
	YOLOv4 (2020)	27.4	68.5	53
	YOLOv5-s (2020)	32	71.5	112
	YOLOX-s (2021)	32.8	72.1	45
	YOLOX-m (2021)	33.5	73.1	40
	YOLOF (2021)	27.3	65.6	25
	YOLOv7 (2022)	30.6	70.9	111
VS+IR	MMTOD (2019)	31.1	70.7	13.2
	CMDet (2021)	28.3	68.4	25.3
	CFT (2021)	29.3	71.2	88
	RISNet (2022)	33.1	72.7	23
	Ours	36.3	77.1	80

5 Conclusion

We propose a dual-mode target detection algorithm based on feature alignment. The algorithm is capable of inputting both visible and infrared image pairs, taking full advantage of the complementary visible and infrared image features. Mid-term fusion is used for more flexible use of gated fusion networks. Used for layers three, four and five of the dual-stream backbone network to facilitate feature cross-modal fusion. In particular, the gated fusion network includes a

Table 3. Results of comparison experiments on the GIR dataset.

Input	Method	$AP_{0.5:0.95}$	$AP_{0.5}$	FPS
VS	YOLOv3 (2018)	41.2	85.7	50
	FCOS (2019)	40.4	84	16
	ATSS (2020)	47.1	87.1	14
	YOLOv4 (2020)	44.5	87.9	53
	YOLOv5-s (2020)	51.4	89.8	111.1
	YOLOX-s (2021)	51.7	90.3	52
	YOLOF (2021)	42.8	76.1	21.3
	YOLOv7 (2022)	50.1	88.2	98.2
IR	YOLOv3 (2018)	35.6	74.2	48.4
	FCOS (2019)	34.5	72.3	12
	ATSS (2020)	35.2	73.4	11.7
	YOLOv4 (2020)	35.8	74.7	49
	YOLOv5-s (2020)	36.6	76.8	111.1
	YOLOX-s (2021)	36.9	76.3	53
	YOLOF (2021)	30.7	68.3	22
	YOLOv7 (2022)	30.6	72.9	110.7
VS+IR	MMTOD (2019)	40.7	84.3	11.2
	CMDet (2021)	48.6	88.9	22.7
	CFT (2021)	54.4	82.1	70.9
	RISNet (2022)	60.5	88	41.6
	Ours	51.9	91	83

dual-mode feature alignment module DFAM and a feature fusion module FFM. The dual-mode feature alignment module extracts detailed information about the dual-mode aligned features through a continuous maximum pooling operation. The feature fusion module recalibrates the fused features twice. This is then multiplied with the bimodal aligned features to improve the detection performance and the speed to meet the real-time requirements. It is found that the heatless target in the infrared image does not complement the visible image well, but rather affects the detection result, and this issue will be investigated in future work.

Acknowledgements. This work is supported by the National Natural Science Foundation of China under grant No. 62072370 and the Natural Science Foundation of Shaanxi Province under grant No. 2023-JC-YB-598.

References

1. Zhou, Y., Tuzel, O.: Voxelnet: end-to-end learning for point cloud based 3D object detection. In: 2018 IEEE Conference on Computer Vision and Pattern Recognition, Salt Lake City, USA, pp. 4490–4499 (2018)
2. Kim, S., Song, W.J., Kim, S.H.: Infrared variation optimized deep convolutional neural network for robust automatic ground target recognition. In: 2017 IEEE Conference on Computer Vision and Pattern Recognition Workshops, Honolulu, USA, pp. 1–8 (2017)
3. Girshick, R., Donahue, J., Darrell, T.: Rich feature hierarchies for accurate object detection and semantic segmentation. In: 2014 IEEE Conference on Computer Vision and Pattern Recognition, pp. 580–587 (2014)
4. Valverde, F.R., Hurtado, J.V., Valada, A.: There is more than meets the eye: self-supervised multi-object detection and tracking with sound by distilling multimodal knowledge. In: 2021 IEEE Conference on Computer Vision and Pattern Recognition, pp. 11612–11621 (2021)
5. Liu, J., Zhang, S., Wang, S.: Multispectral deep neural networks for pedestrian detection. arXiv preprint arXiv:1611.02644 (2016)
6. Konig, D., Adam, M., Jarvers, C., Layher, G.: Fully convolutional region proposal networks for multispectral person detection. In: 2017 IEEE Conference on Computer Vision and Pattern Recognition, Honolulu, USA, pp. 49–56 (2017)
7. Pfeuffer, A., Dietmayer, K.: Optimal sensor data fusion architecture for object detection in adverse weather conditions. In: International Conference on Information Fusion, England, UK, pp. 1–8 (2018)
8. Girshick, R.: Fast R-CNN. In: 2015 IEEE International Conference on Computer Vision, pp. 1440–1448 (2015)
9. Ren, S., He, K., Girshick, R.: Faster R-CNN: towards real-time object detection with region proposal networks. In: Advances in Neural Information Processing Systems, vol. 28, pp. 91–99 (2015)
10. Liu, W., et al.: SSD: single shot MultiBox detector. In: Leibe, B., Matas, J., Sebe, N., Welling, M. (eds.) ECCV 2016. LNCS, vol. 9905, pp. 21–37. Springer, Cham (2016). https://doi.org/10.1007/978-3-319-46448-0_2
11. Redmon, J., Divvala, S., Girshick, R.: You only look once: unified, real-time object detection. In: 2016 IEEE Conference on Computer Vision and Pattern Recognition, pp. 779–788 (2016)
12. Redmon, J., Farhadi, A.: YOLO9000: better, faster, stronger. In: 2017 IEEE Conference on Computer Vision and Pattern Recognition, pp. 7263–7271 (2017)
13. Redmon, J., Farhadi, A.: Yolov3: an incremental improvement. arXiv preprint arXiv:1804.02767 (2018)
14. Bochkovskiy, A., Wang, C.Y., Liao, H.Y.M.: Yolov4: optimal speed and accuracy of object detection. arXiv pre4print arXiv:2004.10934 (2020)
15. YOLOv5. https://github.com/ultralytics/yolov5. Accessed 4 Oct 2022
16. Law, H., Deng, J.: Cornernet: detecting objects as paired keypoints. In: 2018 European Conference on Computer Vision, pp. 734–750 (2018)
17. Zhou, X., Wang, D., Krähenbühl, P.: Objects as points. arXiv preprint arXiv:1904.07850 (2019)
18. Tian, Z., Shen, C., Chen, H.: FCOS: fully convolutional one-stage object detection. In: 2019 IEEE/CVF International Conference on Computer Vision, pp. 9627–9636 (2019)

19. Devaguptapu, C., Akolekar, N., Sharma, M.: Borrow from anywhere: pseudo multi-modal object detection in thermal imagery. In: 2019 IEEE Conference on Computer Vision and Pattern Recognition, Long Beach, USA, pp. 1029–1038 (2019)
20. Yang, L., Ma, R., Zakhor, A.: Drone object detection using RGB/IR fusion. arXiv preprint arXiv:2201.03786 (2022)
21. Wang, Q., Chi, Y., Shen, T., Song, J.: Improving RGB-infrared object detection by reducing cross-modality redundancy. Remote Sens. **14**(9), 2020–2035 (2022)
22. Geng, X., Li, M., Liu, W., Zhu, S.: Person tracking by detection using dual visible-infrared cameras. IEEE Internet Things J. **9**(22), 23241–23251 (2022)
23. Zhang, Q., Huang, N., Yao, L., Zhang, D.: RGB-T salient object detection via fusing multi-level CNN features. IEEE Trans. Image Process. **29**, 3321–3335 (2019)
24. Fang, Q., Han, D., Wang, Z.: Cross-modality fusion transformer for multispectral object detection. arXiv preprint arXiv:2111.00273 (2021)
25. Zhang, W., Ji, G.P., Wang, Z., Fu, K.: Depth quality-inspired feature manipulation for efficient RGB-D salient object detection. In: The 29th ACM International Conference on Multimedia, Chengdu, China, pp. 731–740 (2021)
26. Hwang, S., Park, J., Kim, N.: Multispectral pedestrian detection: benchmark dataset and baseline. In: 2015 IEEE Conference on Computer Vision and Pattern Recognition, pp. 1037–1045 (2015)
27. Li, C., Song, D., Tong, R.: Multispectral pedestrian detection via simultaneous detection and segmentation. arXiv preprint arXiv:1808.04818 (2018)
28. Li, C., Zhao, N., Lu, Y.: Weighted sparse representation regularized graph learning for RGB-T object tracking. In: 2017 Proceedings of the 25th ACM International Conference on Multimedia, pp. 1856–1864 (2017)
29. Ge, Z., Liu, S., Wang, F., Li, Z.: Yolox: exceeding yolo series in 2021. arXiv preprint arXiv:2107.08430 (2021)
30. Sun, Y., Cao, B., Zhu, P., Hu, Q.: Drone-based RGB-infrared cross-modality vehicle detection via uncertainty-aware learning. IEEE Trans. Circuits Syst. Video Technol. **32**(10), 6700–6713 (2019)
31. Wang, Q., Chi, Y., Shen, T., Song, J.: Improving RGB-infrared object detection by reducing cross-modality redundancy. Remote Sens. **14**(9) (2020)

PauseSpeech: Natural Speech Synthesis via Pre-trained Language Model and Pause-Based Prosody Modeling

Ji-Sang Hwang, Sang-Hoon Lee, and Seong-Whan Lee[✉]

Department of Artificial Intelligence, Korea University, Seoul, Korea
{js_hwang,sh_lee,sw.lee}@korea.ac.kr

Abstract. Although text-to-speech (TTS) systems have significantly improved, most TTS systems still have limitations in synthesizing speech with appropriate phrasing. For natural speech synthesis, it is important to synthesize the speech with a phrasing structure that groups words into phrases based on semantic information. In this paper, we propose PuaseSpeech, a speech synthesis system with a pre-trained language model and pause-based prosody modeling. First, we introduce a phrasing structure encoder that utilizes a context representation from the pre-trained language model. In the phrasing structure encoder, we extract a speaker-dependent syntactic representation from the context representation and then predict a pause sequence that separates the input text into phrases. Furthermore, we introduce a pause-based word encoder to model word-level prosody based on pause sequence. Experimental results show PuaseSpeech outperforms previous models in terms of naturalness. Furthermore, in terms of objective evaluations, we can observe that our proposed methods help the model decrease the distance between ground-truth and synthesized speech. Audio samples are available at https://jisang93.github.io/pausespeech-demo/.

Keywords: Text-to-speech · Pre-trained language model · Pause-based prosody modeling

1 Introduction

Text-to-speech (TTS) systems aim to generate high-quality and natural speech from a text. Recently, advancements in generative models [9,35] have led to rapid progress in TTS systems to model both linguistic features and variations (e.g., speaker information, prosody, and background noise). Although TTS systems have significantly improved, most TTS systems face limitations in synthesizing

This work was supported by Institute of Information & communications Technology Planning & Evaluation (IITP) grant funded by the Korea government (MSIT) (No. 2019-0-00079, Artificial Intelligence Graduate School Program (Korea University) and No. 2021-0-02068, Artificial Intelligence Innovation Hub).

H. Lu et al. (Eds.): ACPR 2023, LNCS 14406, pp. 415–427, 2023.
https://doi.org/10.1007/978-3-031-47634-1_31

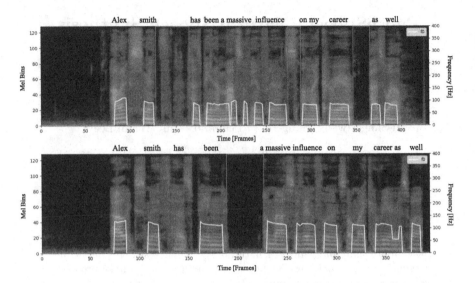

Fig. 1. Comparison between the Mel-spectrogram of two different speakers and the same text. The corresponding text is "Alex Smith has been a massive influence on my career as well". Red boxes represent respiratory pause positions. White lines denote the F0 contour of each utterance. (Color figure online)

speech with proper phrasing structure that groups word into phrases and separates the input text with intentional pauses [17]. These limitations usually lead to a disfluent speech when the TTS systems generate an utterance comprising multiple sentences or a long sentence. The disfluent speech conveys too much information at once due to the wrong phrasing structure, resulting in difficult understanding and perceiving it as unnatural by human listeners. Therefore, it is important to synthesize speech with appropriate phrasing based on semantic and syntactic information to enhance comprehensibility [3] and recall [6,17].

Previous studies [10,12,27,45] have considered using context information from a pre-trained language model (PLM) [4,23] to enhance the naturalness of generated speech. They have leveraged PLM to improve prosody (e.g., pitch, accent, and prominence) that is related to context information. Additionally, [1,7,46] have predicted pauses (also known as phrase breaks) based on extracted semantic meanings to enhance the naturalness and comprehensibility of synthesized speech. However, these systems have some limitations: 1) They do not consider that pauses vary according to the speaker. As illustrated in Fig. 1, the position and duration of each pause vary from person to person even if it is the same text information. 2) They do not reflect the prosody of surrounding pauses. As patterns of intonation surrounding pauses are slightly different, the systems have to consider the variations surrounding pauses.

To address the aforementioned problems, we propose PauseSpeech, a speech synthesis system utilizing the PLM and pause-based prosody modeling. First, we introduce a phrasing structure encoder using a context representation from the

PLM. The phrasing structure encoder encodes the context representation into a speaker-dependent syntactic representation. In the phrasing structure encoder, we predict speaker-dependent pauses using both the syntactic representation and speaker information. Moreover, we propose pause-based prosody modeling to consider the prosody of surrounding pauses in a pause-based word encoder. The pause-based word encoder takes the syntactic representation, a segment-level representation, and word position embedding to extract the pause-based prosody. Experimental results show that PauseSpeech outperforms previous models in terms of naturalness. Furthermore, we can observe in the objective evaluations that our proposed methods help the model decrease the distance between the ground-truth and synthesized speech audio.

2   Related Works

2.1   Text-to-Speech

Recently, neural TTS systems have significantly improved, resulting in high performance. For speech audio generation, TTS systems predict a pre-defined acoustic feature (e.g., Mel-spectrogram) using an acoustic model [33,43], which is converted into a waveform by a vocoder [15,18], or directly generate a waveform [5,14,21]. To predict the pre-defined acoustic features, there are two types of acoustic models: autoregressive (AR) and non-autoregressive (NAR)-TTS systems. AR-TTS systems [39,43] generate each frame of the Mel-spectrogram conditioned on previous frames to model long-term dependency. However, they suffer from slow inference speed and robustness errors, such as word skipping and repetition. NAR-TTS systems [13,20,33] have been proposed to handle these problems. They map the text sequence into the Mel-spectrogram using alignment between the text and Mel-frames sequence. These systems can generate speech faster and more robustly than AR-TTS systems.

For diverse and expressive speech, TTS systems have adopted auxiliary variation modeling. They use explicit features (e.g., pitch, energy) [19,22,30,37] or implicit features [29,31,32] to model prosody. Although these prosody modeling can improve diversity and expressiveness, they still have limitations in synthesizing speech with appropriate phrasing structure considering both semantic and syntactic information. In this paper, we use the contextual information from PLM to learn the proper phrasing structure from the input text sequence.

2.2   Phrase Break Prediction

Recent advancements in deep-learning have been utilized in various fields [16, 41] including TTS to predict explicit features. Previous TTS systems [1,7,17, 40,46] have considered predicting phrase breaks that can be defined as pauses inserted between phrases to learn proper phrasing structure. Generally, there are two types of pauses: a punctuation-based pause and respiratory pause. The punctuation-based pause is usually generated at a punctuation mark in the text

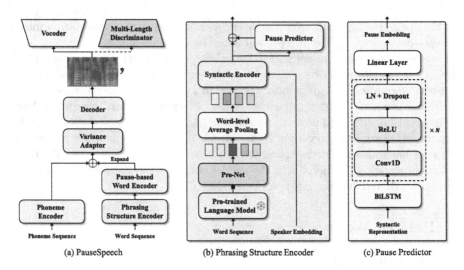

Fig. 2. (a) Overall architecture of PauseSpeech. The dashed line represents that the operation only utilizes during training. (b) In a phrasing structure encoder, we convert subword-level context representation from PLM into word-level context representation with word-level average pooling. A syntactic encoder takes both the word-level context representation and speaker embedding to extract a speaker-dependent syntactic representation. (c) A pause predictor takes the syntactic representation to predict speaker-dependent pauses.

sequence. However, the respiratory pause does not have instructions such as the punctuation mark. Therefore, several TTS systems [7,17] have predicted the respiratory pause and inserted it into space between words. However, generated pauses are still inappropriate due to retrieving the average style in the training dataset.

Several pauses prediction-based TTS systems [1,7,46] have used contextual representation from PLM. Since the contextual representation contains semantic and syntactic information, the extracted contextual representation helps the systems predict the proper positions of the respiratory pause. Inspired by the previous studies, we adopt the PLM to predict the respiratory pause and utilize it to predict speaker-dependent pauses. Furthermore, we classify the respiratory pauses into four categories following [6,46].

3   PauseSpeech

In this paper, we propose a TTS system that uses a pre-trained language model (PLM) and pause-based prosody modeling for natural and expressive speech. We propose a phrasing structure encoder using contextual representation from the PLM to extract syntactic representation and predict pauses. Moreover, we introduce pause-based prosody modeling in a pause-based word encoder to consider explicit variations surrounding pauses. Furthermore, we adopt adversarial learning to enhance the quality of the generated Mel-spectrogram. We describe the details of PauseSpeech in the following subsection.

3.1 Phrasing Structure Encoder

We introduce the phrasing structure encoder that encodes the context representation and speaker information into speaker-dependent syntactic representation. The phrasing structure encoder comprises a pre-net, syntactic encoder, and pause predictor as illustrated in Fig. 2(b).

Syntactic Encoder. We use BERT [4] as the PLM to extract context representation. It is well known that the context representation from BERT contains syntactic information and knowledge of semantic roles [25,36]. In particular, previous studies [11,24] demonstrated that the context representation from the middle layer of BERT contained more prominent syntactic and semantic information than other layers. Therefore, we utilize the syntactic and semantic information by extracting the self-supervised context representation from the input text sequence.

The syntactic encoder is designed to extract the speaker-dependent syntactic representation. We supposed that the human speaker's text cognition varies from person to person, resulting in varying the position and duration of the respiratory pause in human speech. Therefore, the syntactic encoder takes both the context representation and speaker embedding to obtain the syntactic representation that contains syntactic information based on the target speaker's cognition. As BERT extracts the input text sequence into subword-level contextual representation, we process the context representation with word-level average pooling [32,47] to convert the representation into a word-level sequence.

Pause Predictor. We define categories of the respiratory pause according to the pause duration to classify the pause as an intentional/unintentional pause. We use the Montreal forced aligner [28] to obtain the pause duration. Following previous studies [6,46], we categorize the pause into four-class: no pause (0–100 ms), short pause (100–300 ms), medium pause (300–700 ms), and long pause (>700 ms). Moreover, we label each pause class as follows: "0" denotes the no pause, and "1", "2", and "3" represents the short, medium, and long pause, respectively. In this paper, we also define the short pause as the unintentional pause and the medium and long pauses as the intentional pause.

The pause predictor takes the syntactic representation to predict the speaker-dependent pause sequence. The pause predictor comprises two Bi-LSTM layers and 1D-convolutional networks with ReLU activation, layer normalization, and dropout as shown in Fig. 2(c). The final linear layer projects hidden representation into a word-level pause sequence. We encode the pause sequence into trainable pause embedding ad add it to the output of the syntactic encoder. Furthermore, we optimize the pause predictor with a cross-entropy loss between a probability distribution with a softmax function and a target pause label sequence.

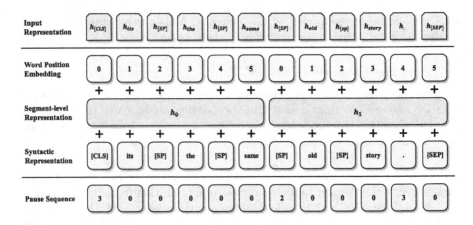

Fig. 3. Input representation for pause-based word encoder. The input representations are the sum of the word-level syntactic representation, segment-level representation, and segment-word position embedding.

3.2   Pause-Based Word Encoder

We introduce a pause-based word encoder to model a pause-based prosody that considers the prosody of word sequence surrounding pauses. For pause-based prosody modeling, inputs to the pause-based word encoder comprise three components as illustrated in Fig. 3: an output of the phrasing structure encoder, a segment-level representation, and word position embedding. The first component is the summation of the output of the syntactic encoder and pause embedding in the phrasing structure encoder. For the second component, we process the output of the phrasing structure encoder with segment-level average pooling. For segmentation, we divide the word sequence into segments with the intentional pause (medium and long pause), which is defined in Subsect. 3.1. Additionally, we design that the punctuation-based pause would be assigned to a previous segment. For the third component, we provide position information within each segment. We implement the same sinusoidal function for the word position embedding, which is used in BERT.

3.3   Adeversarial Learning

The generated Mel-spectrogram from TTS systems generally suffered blurry and over-smoothing problems due to using simple optimization functions such as mean absolute error (MAE), and mean square error (MSE) [34,47]. Following [44,47], we adopt a multi-length discriminator to improve the quality of the generated Mel-spectrogram. The multi-length discriminator distinguishes between the generated and ground-truth Mel-spectrogram,which are randomly sliced by windows of multi-lengths. Moreover, for robust training, we solely train the generator until 50K steps, and then jointly train with the multi-length discriminator after 50K steps.

4   Experiment and Results

4.1   Experimental Setup

Datasets. We trained PauseSpeech on VCTK[1] [42] to synthesize speech. The VCTK dataset contains approximately 46 h of audio for 108 English speakers. We divided the VCTK dataset into three subsets: 40,857 samples for training, 1,500 samples for validation, and 1,500 samples for testing.

In addition, we downsampled the audio at 24,000 Hz for training. We transform the raw waveform into the Mel-spectrogram with 128 bins. For the input of the phoneme encoder, we converted the text sequence into the phoneme sequence using the open-source grapheme-to-phoneme tool[2].

Model Configuration. PauseSpeech consists of a phoneme encoder, phrasing structure encoder, pause-based word encoder, variance adaptor, decoder, and multi-length discriminator as illustrated in Fig. 2(a). The phoneme and pause-based word encoders and the decoder comprise four feed-forward Transformer (FFT) blocks [33] with relative-position encoding [38] following Glow-TTS [13]. For the variance adaptor, we adopt the same architecture in FastSpeech 2 [30]. For adversarial learning, we adopt the multi-length discriminator of SyntaSpeech [47], which comprises stacked convolutional layers with batch normalization.

In the phrasing structure encoder, we use BERT-base model[3] for the PLM. We utilized the 9th layer of BERT to extract the self-supervised contextual representation. As shown in Fig. 2(b), the phrasing structure encoder consists of a pre-net, syntactic encoder, and pause predictor. The pre-net comprises two BiLSTM layers and multiple stacked convolutional layers with ReLU activation, layer normalization, and dropout. The syntactic encoder has the same architecture as the other encoder, which consists of four FFT blocks with relative-position encoding.

Training. We trained PauseSpeech using the Adam optimizer [26] with a learning rate of 2×10^{-4}, $\beta_1 = 0.8$, $\beta_2 = 0.99$, and weight deacy of $\lambda = 0.01$. PauseSpeech has been trained on two NVIDIA RTX A6000 GPUs with 32 sentences per GPU. It takes 400K steps for training until convergence. In addition, we use pre-trained HiFi-GAN [18] as the vocoder to convert the synthesized Mel-spectrogram into raw waveform.

---

[1] https://datashare.ed.ac.uk/handle/10283/3443.
[2] https://github.com/Kyubyong/g2p.
[3] https://huggingface.co/bert-base-uncased.

Table 1. Performance comparison with different methods. Recon. represents reconstruction.

Method	MOS (↑)	PER (↓)	WER (↓)	MCD (↓)	RMSE$_{F0}$ (↓)	DDUR (↓)
GT	3.91 ± 0.03	1.41	3.73	–	–	–
HiFi-GAN (recon.) [18]	3.90 ± 0.03	2.01	4.78	0.94	21.96	–
FastSpeech 2 [30]	3.81 ± 0.03	2.43	5.17	3.60	32.18	0.16
PortaSpeech [32]	3.83 ± 0.03	2.06	4.43	3.55	33.72	**0.13**
PauseSpeech	**3.88 ± 0.03**	**1.32**	**3.44**	**3.42**	**27.66**	**0.13**

4.2   Evaluation Metrics

Subjective Metrics. We conducted the mean opinion score (MOS) evaluation on the test dataset to evaluate the naturalness of the audio via Amazon Mechanical Turk. The MOS test was rated by at minimum of 30 listeners on a scale of 1-5. The MOS evaluation is reported with 95% confidence intervals.

Objective Metrics. We calculated various types of distance between the ground-truth and synthesized audio. We used five objective metrics to evaluate the quality of synthesized speech: 1) Phoneme error rate (PER); 2) Word error rate (WER); 3) Mel-cepstral distortion (MCD); 4) F0 root mean square error (RMSE$_{F0}$); 5) Average absolute difference of the utterance duration (DDUR) [48]. For PER and WER evaluations, we used the open-source automatic speech recognition (ASR) model[4], which is trained over wav2vec 2.0 [2]. We calculated PER and WER between the ASR prediction and target text. For MCD and RMSE$_{F0}$ evaluations, we applied dynamic time warping between the ground-truth and synthesized audio.

4.3   Performance

We compared the audio generated by PauseSpeech with the outputs of the following systems: 1) GT, the ground-truth audio; 2) HiFi-GAN [18], where we reconstructed the audio from the ground-truth Mel-spectrogram using the pre-trained vocoder; 3) FastSpeech 2 [30], 4) PortaSpeech [32]. We converted the synthesized Mel-spectrogram from the acoustic models into a raw waveform using the pre-trained HiFi-GAN.

The results are shown in Table 1. We observed that PauseSpeech outperformed the previous systems in terms of naturalness. Moreover, our proposed model significantly reduced the PER and WER. This indicates that PauseSpeech generates speech with accurate pronunciation. Furthermore, our model achieved better performance in terms of MCD and RMSE$_{F0}$. These observations suggest that PauseSpeech can reduce the distance between the ground-truth and synthesized audio.

---

[4] https://huggingface.co/facebook/wav2vec2-large-960h-lv60-self.

Fig. 4. Visualization of the Mel-spectrogram with varying systems: (a) GT, (b) Fast-Speech 2, (c) PortaSpeech, and (d) PauseSpeech. The corresponding text is "But I am in practice".

We also visualized the Mel-spectrograms of synthesized audio from the varying systems to compare the systems in Fig. 4. In the low-frequency bands of the Mel-spectrogram, we can observe that PauseSpeech generates a similar pitch contour, resulting in expressive prosody. Moreover, PauseSpeech generates more details in the high-frequency bands of the Mel-spectrogram, resulting in natural sounds. These results demonstrate that PauseSpeech can generate high-quality and natural speech audio with accurate pronunciation.

Table 2. Experimental results on the context representations from each different layer of BERT.

Layer	MOS (↑)	PER (↓)	WER (↓)	MCD (↓)	RMSE$_{F0}$ (↓)	DDUR (↓)
Lower layer (1st)	3.91 ± 0.03	1.43	3.56	**3.42**	26.66	0.14
Middle layer (9th)	**3.98 ± 0.03**	1.32	**3.44**	**3.42**	27.66	**0.13**
Higher layer (12th)	3.93 ± 0.03	1.35	3.59	3.44	**26.59**	**0.13**

4.4 Analysis of Self-supervised Representations

Previous studies [11,24] have shown that the middle layer of BERT contains the most prominent syntactic information. In addition, [8] demonstrated that the 8th and 9th layers of pre-trained BERT showed the best subject-verb agreement. Therefore, we divided the layers of BERT into three parts to verify the effectiveness of each part in TTS tasks and selected one layer of each part: the 1st layer of the lower layer, the 9th layer of the middle layer, and the 12th layer of the higher layer. Then, we extracted the self-supervised representation from each layer as an input of the phrasing structure encoder to compare the performance.

As shown in Table 2, the representation of the 9th layer of BERT has better performance than the others in terms of naturalness. Moreover, the representation of the 9th layer of BERT showed the lowest error distance in the most of objective evaluations. In particular, the representation of the 9th layer of BERT significantly decreased PER and WER. These results demonstrate that the middle layer of BERT contains rich information, resulting in improvement in the performance of the TTS system. Additionally, the higher subject-verb agreement may help the TTS model synthesize speech with accurate pronunciation. Hence, we used the representation from the 9th layer of BERT for the phrasing structure encoder.

Table 3. Ablation study of PauseSpeech. PW and PS encoder denotes the pause-based word encoder and the phrasing structure encoder, respectively. Adv. learning represents adversarial learning.

Layer	MOS ($\uparrow$)	MCD ($\downarrow$)	RMSE$_{F0}$ ($\downarrow$)	DDUR ($\downarrow$)
PauseSpeech	**3.98 ± 0.03**	**3.42**	27.66	**0.13**
w/o PW encoder	3.94 ± 0.03	3.46	**27.64**	**0.13**
w/o PS encoder	3.93 ± 0.03	3.50	28.94	0.14
w/o adv. learning	3.92 ± 0.03	3.48	33.48	0.14

4.5   Ablation Study

We conducted an ablation study to demonstrate the effectiveness of each module in PauseSpeech. We compared PauseSpeech with that without the pause-based word encoder and that without the phrasing structure encoder. The results are presented in Table 3. We observed that removing encoders degraded the naturalness of synthesized audio. Moreover, PauseSpeech without the pause-based word and phrasing structure encoders significantly degraded the objective evaluations. These results indicate that our proposed modules are necessary to synthesize natural speech. Furthermore, we trained PauseSpeech without adversarial learning. We observed that removing the adversarial learning significantly degraded the performance. These results indicate that adversarial learning enhances the performance of the system, resulting in synthesizing high-quality and natural speech.

5   Conclusions

In this study, we presented a TTS model, PauseSpeech, which can learn and synthesize speech with a proper phrasing structure using a pre-trained language model and pause-based prosody modeling. We used the contextual representation from the pre-trained BERT and then modeled pause-based prosody based on predicted pauses. Furthermore, we improved the Mel-spectrogram prediction by adopting a multi-length discriminator for adversarial learning. Our experimental results show that PauseSpeech outperforms previous TTS models in terms of naturalness and significantly enhances the pronunciation of synthesized speech. We also conducted ablation studies to verify the effectiveness of each component in PauseSpeech. We see that our method could be applied to various speech datasets to generalize the pause-based prosody modeling and improve the naturalness and pronunciation of synthesized speech. Hence, for future work, we will utilize various speech datasets to verify the effectiveness of PuaseSpeech in multi-lingual scenarios and attempt to control more diverse variations of speech.

References

1. Abbas, A., et al.: Expressive, Variable, and Controllable Duration Modelling in TTS. arXiv preprint arXiv:2206.14165 (2022)
2. Baevski, A., Zhou, Y., Mohamed, A., Auli, M.: wav2vec 2.0: a framework for self-supervised learning of speech representations. In: Advances in Neural Information Processing Systems, vol. 33, pp. 12449–12460 (2020)
3. Braunschweiler, N., Chen, L.: Automatic detection of inhalation breath pauses for improved pause modelling in HMM-TTS. In: SSW, vol. 8, pp. 1–6 (2013)
4. Devlin, J., Chang, M.W., Lee, K., Toutanova, K.: BERT: Pre-Training of Deep Bidirectional Transformers for Language Understanding. arXiv preprint arXiv:1810.04805 (2018)
5. Donahue, J., Dieleman, S., Bińkowski, M., Elsen, E., Simonyan, K.: End-to-End Adversarial Text-to-Speech. arXiv preprint arXiv:2006.03575 (2020)
6. Elmers, M., Werner, R., Muhlack, B., Möbius, B., Trouvain, J.: Take a breath: respiratory sounds improve recollection in synthetic speech. In: Interspeech, pp. 3196–3200 (2021)
7. Futamata, K., Park, B., Yamamoto, R., Tachibana, K.: Phrase Break Prediction with Bidirectional Encoder Representations in Japanese Text-to-Speech Synthesis. arXiv preprint arXiv:2104.12395 (2021)
8. Goldberg, Y.: Assessing BERT's Syntactic Abilities. arXiv preprint arXiv:1901.05287 (2019)
9. Goodfellow, I., et al.: Generative adversarial networks. Commun. ACM **63**(11), 139–144 (2020)
10. Hayashi, T., Watanabe, S., Toda, T., Takeda, K., Toshniwal, S., Livescu, K.: Pre-trained text embeddings for enhanced text-to-speech synthesis. In: Interspeech, pp. 4430–4434 (2019)
11. Hewitt, J., Manning, C.D.: A structural probe for finding syntax in word representations. In: Proceedings of the 2019 Conference of the North American Chapter of the Association for Computational Linguistics: Human Language Technologies, Volume 1 (Long and Short Papers), pp. 4129–4138 (2019)
12. Hida, R., Hamada, M., Kamada, C., Tsunoo, E., Sekiya, T., Kumakura, T.: Polyphone disambiguation and accent prediction using pre-trained language models in Japanese TTS front-end. In: ICASSP 2022-2022 IEEE International Conference on Acoustics, Speech and Signal Processing (ICASSP), pp. 7132–7136. IEEE (2022)
13. Kim, J., Kim, S., Kong, J., Yoon, S.: Glow-TTS: a generative flow for text-to-speech via monotonic alignment search. Adv. Neural. Inf. Process. Syst. **33**, 8067–8077 (2020)
14. Kim, J., Kong, J., Son, J.: Conditional variational autoencoder with adversarial learning for end-to-end text-to-speech. In: International Conference on Machine Learning, pp. 5530–5540. PMLR (2021)
15. Kim, J.H., Lee, S.H., Lee, J.H., Lee, S.W.: Fre-GAN: adversarial frequency-consistent audio synthesis. In: 22nd Annual Conference of the International Speech Communication Association, INTERSPEECH 2021, pp. 3246–3250. International Speech Communication Association (2021)

16. Kim, K.T., Guan, C., Lee, S.W.: A subject-transfer framework based on single-trial EMG analysis using convolutional neural networks. IEEE Trans. Neural Syst. Rehabil. Eng. **28**(1), 94–103 (2019)
17. Klimkov, V., et al.: Phrase break prediction for long-form reading TTS: exploiting text structure information. In: Proceedings of Interspeech 2017, pp. 1064–1068 (2017)
18. Kong, J., Kim, J., Bae, J.: HiFi-GAN: generative adversarial networks for efficient and high fidelity speech synthesis. Adv. Neural. Inf. Process. Syst. **33**, 17022–17033 (2020)
19. Lańcucki, A.: FastPitch: parallel text-to-speech with pitch prediction. In: ICASSP 2021-2021 IEEE International Conference on Acoustics, Speech and Signal Processing (ICASSP), pp. 6588–6592. IEEE (2021)
20. Lee, J.H., Lee, S.H., Kim, J.H., Lee, S.W.: PVAE-TTS: adaptive text-to-speech via progressive style adaptation. In: ICASSP 2022–2022 IEEE International Conference on Acoustics, Speech and Signal Processing (ICASSP), pp. 6312–6316. IEEE (2022)
21. Lee, S.H., Kim, S.B., Lee, J.H., Song, E., Hwang, M.J., Lee, S.W.: HierSpeech: bridging the gap between text and speech by hierarchical variational inference using self-supervised representations for speech synthesis. Adv. Neural. Inf. Process. Syst. **35**, 16624–16636 (2022)
22. Lee, S.H., Yoon, H.W., Noh, H.R., Kim, J.H., Lee, S.W.: Multi-SpectroGAN: high-diversity and high-fidelity spectrogram generation with adversarial style combination for speech synthesis. In: Proceedings of the AAAI Conference on Artificial Intelligence, vol. 35, pp. 13198–13206 (2021)
23. Lewis, M., et al.: BART: Denoising Sequence-to-Sequence Pre-Training for Natural Language Generation, Translation, and Comprehension. arXiv preprint arXiv:1910.13461 (2019)
24. Liu, N.F., Gardner, M., Belinkov, Y., Peters, M.E., Smith, N.A.: Linguistic knowledge and transferability of contextual representations. In: Proceedings of the 2019 Conference of the North American Chapter of the Association for Computational Linguistics: Human Language Technologies, Volume 1 (Long and Short Papers), pp. 1073–1094 (2019)
25. Liu, Y., et al.: RoBERTa: A Robustly Optimized BERT Pretraining Approach. arXiv preprint arXiv:1907.11692 (2019)
26. Loshchilov, I., Hutter, F.: Decoupled Weight Decay Regularization. arXiv preprint arXiv:1711.05101 (2017)
27. Makarov, P., et al.: Simple and Effective Multi-Sentence TTS with Expressive and Coherent Prosody. arXiv preprint arXiv:2206.14643 (2022)
28. McAuliffe, M., Socolof, M., Mihuc, S., Wagner, M., Sonderegger, M.: Montreal forced aligner: trainable text-speech alignment using kaldi. In: Interspeech, vol. 2017, pp. 498–502 (2017)
29. Oh, H.S., Lee, S.H., Lee, S.W.: DiffProsody: Diffusion-based Latent Prosody Generation for Expressive Speech Synthesis with Prosody Conditional Adversarial Training. arXiv preprint arXiv:2307.16549 (2023)
30. Ren, Y., et al.: FastSpeech 2: fast and high-quality end-to-end text to speech. In: International Conference on Learning Representations (2021)
31. Ren, Y., et al.: ProsoSpeech: enhancing prosody with quantized vector pre-training in text-to-speech. In: ICASSP 2022-2022 IEEE International Conference on Acoustics, Speech and Signal Processing (ICASSP), pp. 7577–7581. IEEE (2022)
32. Ren, Y., Liu, J., Zhao, Z.: PortaSpeech: portable and high-quality generative text-to-speech. Adv. Neural. Inf. Process. Syst. **34**, 13963–13974 (2021)

33. Ren, Y., et al.: FastSpeech: fast, robust and controllable text to speech. In: Proceedings of the 33rd International Conference on Neural Information Processing Systems, pp. 3171–3180 (2019)
34. Ren, Y., Tan, X., Qin, T., Zhao, Z., Liu, T.Y.: Revisiting over-smoothness in text to speech. In: Proceedings of the 60th Annual Meeting of the Association for Computational Linguistics (Volume 1: Long Papers), pp. 8197–8213 (2022)
35. Rezende, D., Mohamed, S.: Variational inference with normalizing flows. In: International Conference on Machine Learning, pp. 1530–1538. PMLR (2015)
36. Rogers, A., Kovaleva, O., Rumshisky, A.: A primer in BERTology: what we know about how BERT works. Trans. Assoc. Comput. Linguist. **8**, 842–866 (2021)
37. Seshadri, S., Raitio, T., Castellani, D., Li, J.: Emphasis Control for Parallel Neural TTS. arXiv preprint arXiv:2110.03012 (2021)
38. Shaw, P., Uszkoreit, J., Vaswani, A.: Self-attention with Relative Position Representations. arXiv preprint arXiv:1803.02155 (2018)
39. Shen, J., et al.: Natural TTS synthesis by conditioning wavenet on mel spectrogram predictions. In: 2018 IEEE International Conference on Acoustics, Speech and Signal Processing (ICASSP), pp. 4779–4783. IEEE (2018)
40. Székely, É., Henter, G.E., Beskow, J., Gustafson, J.: Breathing and speech planning in spontaneous speech synthesis. In: ICASSP 2020-2020 IEEE International Conference on Acoustics, Speech and Signal Processing (ICASSP), pp. 7649–7653. IEEE (2020)
41. Thung, K.H., Yap, P.T., Adeli, E., Lee, S.W., Shen, D., Initiative, A.D.N., et al.: Conversion and time-to-conversion predictions of mild cognitive impairment using low-rank affinity pursuit denoising and matrix completion. Med. Image Anal. **45**, 68–82 (2018)
42. Veaux, C., Yamagishi, J., MacDonald, K., et al.: Superseded-CSTR VCTK Corpus: English Multi-Speaker Corpus for CSTR Voice Cloning Toolkit (2016)
43. Wang, Y., et al.: Tacotron: towards end-to-end speech synthesis. In: Proceedings of Interspeech 2017, pp. 4006–4010 (2017)
44. Wu, J., Luan, J.: Adversarially Trained Multi-Singer Sequence-to-Sequence Singing Synthesizer. arXiv preprint arXiv:2006.10317 (2020)
45. Xu, G., Song, W., Zhang, Z., Zhang, C., He, X., Zhou, B.: Improving prosody modelling with cross-utterance BERT embeddings for end-to-end speech synthesis. In: ICASSP 2021–2021 IEEE International Conference on Acoustics, Speech and Signal Processing (ICASSP), pp. 6079–6083. IEEE (2021)
46. Yang, D., Koriyama, T., Saito, Y., Saeki, T., Xin, D., Saruwatari, H.: Duration-Aware Pause Insertion Using Pre-Trained Language Model for Multi-Speaker Text-to-Speech. arXiv preprint arXiv:2302.13652 (2023)
47. Ye, Z., Zhao, Z., Ren, Y., Wu, F.: SyntaSpeech: Syntax-Aware Generative Adversarial Text-to-Speech. arXiv preprint arXiv:2204.11792 (2022)
48. Zhang, J.X., Ling, Z.H., Liu, L.J., Jiang, Y., Dai, L.R.: Sequence-to-sequence acoustic modeling for voice conversion. IEEE/ACM Trans. Audio Speech Lang. Process. **27**(3), 631–644 (2019)

Author Index

H. Lu et al. (Eds.): ACPR 2023, LNCS 14406, pp. 429–433, 2023.
https://doi.org/10.1007/978-3-031-47634-1

Printed in the United States
by Baker & Taylor Publisher Services